RHETORICAL CONSIDERATIONS

SECOND EDITION

RHETORICAL CONSIDERATIONS

Essays for Analysis

Harry Brent
Rutgers University
William Lutz
Rutgers University

Winthrop Publishers, Inc.
Cambridge, Massachusetts

Library of Congress Cataloging in Publication Data

Brent, Harry, comp.
  Rhetorical considerations.

  1. College readers. 2. English language—
Rhetoric. I. Lutz, William. II. Title.
PE1417.B69 1977   808.4   76-23324
ISBN 0-87626-760-6

Acknowledgments begin on page xvii.

10 9 8 7 6 5 4 3 2

For our parents

Harold F. Brent & Anna M. Brent
William E. Lutz & Cora J. Lutz

CONTENTS

CONTENTS ACCORDING TO RHETORICAL TYPES

1 NARRATION

2 DESCRIPTION

3 EXAMPLE

4 PROCESS ANALYSIS

5 DEFINITION

6 CLASSIFICATION AND DIVISION

7 COMPARISON AND CONTRAST

8 CAUSE AND EFFECT

9 INDUCTIVE AND DEDUCTIVE ANALYSIS

10 ANALOGY

11 ARGUMENTATION

12 PERSUASION

PREFACE

The second edition of *Rhetorical Considerations* comes at a time when there is much public concern about the general writing ability of college students. As recently as five years ago, many colleges had dropped required writing courses. Now those courses are back—a response to the realization that a large number of entering students, both in four-year colleges and universities and in community colleges, have great difficulty in expressing their ideas in written form.

To meet the needs of these students, we have revised this book to include a large number of short selections as models for student essays. Most of the eighty selections are very brief, two to five pages in length, and have been chosen, apart from their general interest, for the elementary rhetorical principles they illustrate.

We have also included a goodly number of longer essays illustrating some of the more complex principles of rhetoric and dealing with the kinds of thematic concerns students are likely to encounter in other college courses. Instructors using the book can thus organize a sequence of selections to meet the differing needs of different students.

Again we have included a table of contents according to rhetorical types. As in the first edition, we have sometimes listed a given essay under more than one heading, this again for the purpose of promoting a flexible approach for teacher and student.

We have retained the thematic organization of the book for students and teachers who believe that good writing develops out of a combination of rhetorical analysis and sustained discussion of some single problem of interest. The thematic introductions to each section are designed to be used together with each section's *Rhetorical Analysis* for this purpose. Each selection in the book is followed by both thematic and rhetorical questions as well as a list of vocabulary words.

One of the most important features of this book, in our opinion, is the *Rhetorical Analysis* included in each section. Each *Rhetorical Analysis* is an essay by the editors dealing with the most important rhetorical aspects of one essay appearing in the same section with the *Rhetorical Analysis*. We have incorporated the *Rhetorical Analysis* because it is our experience that students who may learn little from an abstract exposition of rhetorical principles often learn much more if guided by extensive example. Since students must write essays which observe several principles of good rhetoric simultaneously, it makes sense to show them explicitly how skilled writers manage this complex task.

To provide a guide to general rhetorical principles, we begin the book with three essays on rhetoric, two of which deal with the most elementary concerns of the student writer and one, George Orwell's, which addresses more complex concerns.

As in the first edition, we have included a wide-ranging set of selections dealing both with topics of general, contemporary concern and with large questions of humanistic import. Many selections of both kinds are by women and minority-group writers.

Again we would like to thank the many friends and colleagues who generously gave their advice and criticism. The strengths of the book are theirs, the weaknesses ours. In particular we would like to thank Paul O'Connell, Forrest D. Burt, Maurice Baudin, Darrell Hatfield Nicholson, Rosemarie Arbur, Patrick W. Shaw, Jewell A. Friend, Ronald S. Freeman, Sylvia Levy, Nancy Rutyna, Barbara Sonnenschein, Robin Block, and Christine Sarnoski.

ACKNOWLEDGMENTS

Shana Alexander, "Kid's Country." From *Newsweek* Magazine December 11, 1972. Reprinted by permission of the author.

Anonymous, "Death in the First Person." Copyright © February, 1970, The American Journal of Nursing Company. Reproduced with permission from The American Journal of Nursing.

Ronald Arias, "Children of the Barrio." From "The Barrio, Part I and II," © 1966 by IUD Agenda. Reprinted by permission.

Russell Baker, "A Solution to the Population Boom" and "The Great Whale's Mistake." © 1974 by the New York Times Company. Reprinted by permission.

Pierre Bertaux, "The Future of Man." From *Environment and Change* by William Ewald. Reprinted by permission of the Indiana University Press.

Bruno Bettelheim, "Business as Usual." Reprinted with permission of Macmillan Publishing Co., Inc., from *The Informed Heart* by Bruno Bettelheim. Copyright 1960 by The Free Press, a Corporation.

Caroline Bird, "Where College Fails Us." Reprinted courtesy of *Signature* Magazine. Copyright © 1975 Diner's Club Incorporated. Ms. Bird is the author of *The Case Against College* published by Bantam Books.

Myra Bluebond-Langner, "How I Came to Study Dying Children." Copyright © 1975 Myra Bluebond-Langner.

Jacob Bronowski, "The Reach of Imagination." From *The Reach of Imagination*. Reprinted by permission from the *Proceedings* of the American Academy of Arts and Letters, Second Series #17, 1967.

Brigid Brophy, "Monogamy." From *Don't Never Forget* by Brigid Brophy. Copyright © 1966 by Brigid Brophy. Reprinted by permission of Holt, Rinehart and Winston, Publishers.

Susan Brownmiller, "Women Discourage Other Women's Ambitions." From "The Enemy Within" by Susan Brownmiller, *Mademoiselle,* February 1970. © 1970 by Susan Brownmiller. Reprinted by permission of the author.

Jorge Luis Borges, "The Library of Babel." From *Labyrinths,* Jorge Luis Borges. Copyright © 1962 by New Directions Publishing Corporation. Reprinted by permission of New Directions Publishing Corporation.

Martin Buber, "God and the Spirit of Man." From *Eclipse of God* by Martin Buber. Copyright © 1952 by Harper & Row, Publishers, Inc. By permission of Harper & Row, Publishers, Inc.

Joseph Campbell, "The Lesson of the Mask." From *The Masks of God: Primitive Mythology* by Joseph Campbell. Copyright © 1959 by Joseph Campbell. Reprinted by permission of The Viking Press, Inc.

Albert Camus, "The Myth of Sisyphus." From *The Myth of Sisyphus and Other Essays* by Albert Camus, translated by Justin O'Brien. Copyright © 1955 by Alfred A. Knopf, Inc. Reprinted by permission of the publisher.

Robert Claiborne, "The Average American Househusband." © 1974 by The New York Times Company. Reprinted by permission.

Sam Claiborne, "The Househusband's Son Replies." © 1974 by The New York Times Company. Reprinted by permission.

Vine Deloria, Jr., "Custer Died for Your Sins." Reprinted with permission of Macmillan Publishing Co., Inc., from *Custer Died for Your Sins.* Copyright © 1969 by Vine Deloria, Jr.

Paul R. Ehrlich, "Looking Backward from 2000 A.D." From *Global Ecology,* edited by John P. Holdren and Paul R. Ehrlich. Copyright 1971 by Harcourt Brace Jovanovich, Inc., and reprinted with their permission.

Loren Eisley, "The Cosmic Prison." From *The Invisible Pyramid.* Reprinted by permission of Charles Scribner's Sons. Copyright © 1970 Loren Eisley.

Harlan Ellison, " 'Repent, Harlequin!' Said the Ticktockman." Copyright © 1966 by Harlan Ellison. Reprinted by permission of the Author and the Author's Agent, Robert P. Mills, Ltd., New York.

William Faulkner, "Man Will Prevail." Reprinted from *The Faulkner Reader,* copyright 1954 by William Faulkner (Random House, Inc.).

Judy Fayard, "How I Won Bruce, Ruth, and Acapulco." *LIFE* Magazine. Copyright © 1972 Time Inc. Reprinted with permission.

Bruce Jay Friedman, "Lessons of the Street." *Harper's,* September, 1971. © 1971 by Bruce Jay Friedman. Reprinted by permission of Robert Lantz-Candida Donadio Literary Agency, Inc.

Paul Friedman, "Never Lose Your Cool." Copyright 1971 by Paul Friedman.

Nathan Glazer, "The Issue of Cultural Pluralism in America Today." From Joseph Ryan, *White Ethnics: Their Life in Working Class America.* © 1973, pp. 168–175. Reprinted by permission of Prentice-Hall, Inc., Englewood Cliffs, New Jersey.

Günter Grass, "The New Barbarism." Translated from "Diezeit," Hamburg in Atlas World Press Review, July 1975 ©.

Stephanie Harrington, "To Tell the Truth, The Price Is Right." © 1975 by The New York Times Company. Reprinted by permission.

Sydney J. Harris, "Good English Ain't What We Thought." From "Good English Ain't Good Enough." *Strictly Personal* by Sydney J. Harris, courtesy of Field Newspaper Syndicate.

Bessie Head, "The Woman From America." From *Classic Magazine: The Johannesburg Literary Magazine,* Vol. 3, no. 1. Copyright © 1968 by Classic Magazine.

Jane Jacobs, "Cities Need Old Buildings." From *The Death and Life of Great American Cities* by Jane Jacobs. Copyright © 1961 by Jane Jacobs. Reprinted by permission of Random House, Inc.

Susan Jacoby, "The Campus Revisited." Copyright © 1972 by Saturday Review Co. First appeared in *Saturday Review,* November 1972. Used with permission.

Carl Jung, "The Concept of the Collective Unconscious." From *The Collected Works of C. G. Jung,* ed. by Gerhard Adler, Michael Fordham, William McGuire, and Herbert Read, trans. by R. F. C. Hull, Bollingen Series XX, vol. 9i, *The Archetypes and The Collective Unconscious.* (Copyright © 1959 and © 1969 by Bollingen Foundation), pp. 42–50. Reprinted by permission of Princeton University Press.

Stefan Kanfer, "The Full Circle: In Praise of the Bicycle." Reprinted by permission from *TIME,* The Weekly News Magazine; Copyright © Time Inc.

Damon Knight, "The Handler." From *Rogue,* August 1960. Copyright © 1960 by Greenleaf Publishing Co. Reprinted by permission of the author.

Michael Korda, "Time is Power, Money, and Sex." Reprinted by permission of the author.

Charlton Laird, "Folk Roots of Civilization—And Thereby Hangs a Tale." Copyright © 1974 by Charlton Laird. Reprinted by permission of the author.

Ignace Lepp, "The Experience of Death." Reprinted with permission of Macmillan Publishing Co., Inc., from *Death and Its Mysteries* by Ignace Lepp. Copyright © 1968 by Macmillan Publishing Co., Inc.

Oscar Lewis, "A Study of *La Vida.*" From *A Study of Slum Culture: Backgrounds for La Vida* by Oscar Lewis. Copyright © 1968 by Oscar Lewis. Reprinted by permission of Random House, Inc.

Walter Lippmann, "The Decline of the West." Copyright © 1954, The Atlantic Monthly Company, Boston, Mass. Reprinted with permission.

Clare Boothe Luce, "The 21st-Century Woman—Free at Last?" From *SR/World, Incorporated.* August 24, 1974. Reprinted by permission of *Saturday Review* and the author.

Marya Mannes, "Who Am I?" Reprinted by permission of Harold Ober Associates Incorporated. Copyright © 1968 by Marya Mannes.

Rollo May, "The Experience of Becoming a Person." Reprinted from *Man's Search for Himself* by Rollo May, Ph.D. By permission of W. W. Norton & Company, Inc., copyright © 1953 by W. W. Norton & Company, Inc.

Joyce Maynard, "An 18-Year-Old Looks Back on Life." First appeared in *The New York Times Magazine,* April 23, 1972. Copyright © 1972 by Joyce Maynard.

Judith Merril, "Survival Ship." Copyright © 1950, 1976 by Judith Merril. From *Transformations: Understanding World History Through Science Fiction.* Ed. by Daniel Rossell. Reprinted by the permission of Judith Merril, and her agent, Virginia Kidd.

Jessica Mitford, "The Criminal Type." From *Kind and Usual Punishment: The Prison Business* by Jessica Mitford. Copyright © 1973 by Jessica Mitford. Reprinted by permission of Alfred A. Knopf, Inc.

Caroline Moorehead, "A Talk With Simone de Beauvoir." © 1974 by The New York Times Company. Reprinted by permission.

Robert Nisbet, "Knowledge Dethroned." © 1975 by The New York Times Company. Reprinted by permission.

Larry Niven, "The Jigsaw Man." From the book *Dangerous Visions* edited by Harlan Ellison. Copyright © 1967 by Harlan Ellison. Reprinted by permission of Doubleday & Company, Inc.

J. K. Obatala, "Where Did Their Revolution Go?" From *The Nation,* October 2, 1972. Copyright © 1972 *The Nation.* Reprinted by permission.

George Orwell, "Politics and the English Language." From *Shooting an Elephant and Other Essays,* copyright © 1945, 1946, 1949, 1950, by Sonia Brownell Orwell. Reprinted by permission of Harcourt Brace Jovanovich, Inc.

Joseph C. Pattison, "How to Write an 'F' Paper." From *College English.* Copyright © 1963 by the National Council of Teachers of English. Reprinted by permission of the publisher and the author.

Deborah L. Perry, "Because I am Black." Reprinted from *Barnard Alumnae,* Spring 1969. Copyright © 1969, Associate Alumnae of Barnard College. Reprinted by permission.

Marjorie Proops, "In Defense of 'Mere' Women" from "A Year of Propaganda that will do nothing for 'Mere' Women." From *The Times,* March 19, 1975. Reproduced from *The Times* by permission.

Paul Roberts, "How to Say Nothing in Five Hundred Words." From *Understanding English* by Paul Roberts. Copyright © 1958 by Paul Roberts. Reprinted by permission of Harper & Row, Publishers, Inc.

Anne Roiphe, "Confessions of a Female Chauvinist Sow." From: *New York* magazine. Copyright © 1972 by Anne Roiphe. Reprinted by permission of Brandt & Brandt.

Waverly Root, "On Enjoying Food While Millions Starve." © 1975 by The New York Times Company. Reprinted by permission.

Sam Rosenberg, "The Truth About Cinderella." *Cosmopolitan* June 1971. Reprinted by permission of the author.

Bertrand Russell, "What I Have Lived For." From *The Autobiography of Bertrand Russell: 1872–1914* by permission of Little, Brown and Co., in association with the Atlantic Monthly Press. Copyright © 1951, 1952, 1953, 1956 by Bertrand Russell. Copyright © 1961 by Allen and Unwin Ltd. Copyright © 1964 by George Allen and Unwin Ltd.

Carolyn See, "Roxanne of Watts, California." From "Three Family Dropouts in Watts," reprinted from *West* January 29, 1967, by permission of the author.

Harlow Shapley, "Man's Fourth Adjustment." As appearing in *Towards Liberal Education,* 6th, copyright © 1965 by *American Scholar.* Reprinted by permission.

C. P. Snow, "The Moral Un-Neutrality of Science." (Copyright © 1960 C. P. Snow.) Reprinted by permission of Charles Scribner's Sons from *Public Affairs* by C. P. Snow. Copyright © 1971 by C. P. Snow.

Peter Steinfels, "History Is Bunk." Copyright 1973 Commonweal Publishing Co., Inc. Reprinted by permission.

Alvin Toffler, "The Paper Wedding Gown." From *Future Shock,* by Alvin Toffler. Copyright © 1970 by Alvin Toffler. Reprinted by permission of Random House, Inc.

Ruth Whitney, "Needed—A Myth For Our Time." Copyright © 1969 by Condé Nast Publishers, Inc. Reprinted by permission.

RHETORICAL
CONSIDERATIONS

How to Say Nothing in Five Hundred Words

Paul Roberts

*Paul Roberts is widely recognized as one of the leaders of the 1950s
"revolution" in the teaching of English grammar. His books* English
Syntax *(1954) and* Patterns of English *(1956) brought the insights of
descriptive linguistics to problems of composition.*

Nothing About Something

It's Friday afternoon, and you have almost survived another
week of classes. You are just looking forward dreamily to the week end
when the English instructor says: "For Monday you will turn in a
five-hundred-word composition on college football."

Well, that puts a good big hole in the week end. You don't have
any strong views on college football one way or the other. You get
rather excited during the season and go to all the home games and find
it rather more fun than not. On the other hand, the class has been
reading Robert Hutchins in the anthology and perhaps Shaw's
"Eighty-Yard Run," and from the class discussion you have got the
idea that the instructor thinks college football is for the birds. You are
no fool, you. You can figure out what side to take.

After dinner you get out the portable typewriter that you got for
high school graduation. You might as well get it over with and enjoy
Saturday and Sunday. Five hundred words is about two double-spaced
pages with normal margins. You put in a sheet of paper, think up a title,
and you're off:

WHY COLLEGE FOOTBALL SHOULD BE ABOLISHED

College football should be abolished because it's bad for the school and
also bad for the players. The players are so busy practicing that they
don't have any time for their studies.

This, you feel, is a mighty good start. The only trouble is that it's only
thirty-two words. You still have four hundred and sixty-eight to go,
and you've pretty well exhausted the subject. It comes to you that you
do your best thinking in the morning, so you put away the typewriter
and go to the movies. But the next morning you have to do your

1

washing and some math problems, and in the afternoon you go to the game. The English instructor turns up too, and you wonder if you've taken the right side after all. Saturday night you have a date, and Sunday morning you have to go to church. (You shouldn't let English assignments interfere with your religion.) What with one thing and another, it's ten o'clock Sunday night before you get out the typewriter again. You make a pot of coffee and start to fill out your views on college football. Put a little meat on the bones.

WHY COLLEGE FOOTBALL SHOULD BE ABOLISHED

In my opinion, it seems to me that college football should be abolished. The reason why I think this to be true is because I feel that football is bad for the colleges in nearly every respect. As Robert Hutchins says in his article in our anthology in which he discusses college football, it would be better if the colleges had race horses and had races with one another, because then the horses would not have to attend classes. I firmly agree with Mr. Hutchins on this point, and I am sure that many other students would agree too.

One reason why it seems to me that college football is bad is that it has become too commercial. In the olden times when people played football just for the fun of it, maybe college football was all right, but they do not play football just for the fun of it now as they used to in the old days. Nowadays college football is what you might call a big business. Maybe this is not true at all schools, and I don't think it is especially true here at State, but certainly this is the case at most colleges and universities in America nowadays, as Mr. Hutchins points out in his very interesting article. Actually the coaches and alumni go around to the high schools and offer the high school stars large salaries to come to their colleges and play football for them. There was one case where a high school star was offered a convertible if he would play football for a certain college.

Another reason for abolishing college football is that it is bad for the players. They do not have time to get a college education, because they are so busy playing football. A football player has to practice every afternoon from three to six, and then he is so tired that he can't concentrate on his studies. He just feels like dropping off to sleep after dinner, and then the next day he goes to his classes without having studied and maybe he fails the test.

(Good ripe stuff so far, but you're still a hundred and fifty-one words from home. One more push.)

Also I think college football is bad for the colleges and the universities because not very many students get to participate in it. Out of a college of ten thousand students only seventy-five or a hundred play football, if that many. Football is what you might call a spectator sport. That means that most people go to watch it but do not play it themselves.

(Four hundred and fifteen. Well, you still have the conclusion, and when you retype it, you can make the margins a little wider.)

These are the reasons why I agree with Mr. Hutchins that college football should be abolished in American colleges and universities.

On Monday you turn it in, moderately hopeful, and on Friday it comes back marked "weak in content" and sporting a big "D."

This essay is exaggerated a little, not much. The English instructor will recognize it as reasonably typical of what an assignment on college football will bring in. He knows that nearly half of the class will contrive in five hundred words to say that college football is too commercial and bad for the players. Most of the other half will inform him that college football builds character and prepares one for life and brings prestige to the school. As he reads paper after paper all saying the same thing in almost the same words, all bloodless, five hundred words dripping out of nothing, he wonders how he allowed himself to get trapped into teaching English when he might have had a happy and interesting life as an electrician or a confidence man.

Well, you may ask, what can you do about it? The subject is one on which you have few convictions and little information. Can you be expected to make a dull subject interesting? As a matter of fact, this is precisely what you are expected to do. This is the writer's essential task. All subjects, except sex, are dull until somebody makes them interesting. The writer's job is to find the argument, the approach, the angle, the wording that will take the reader with him. This is seldom easy, and it is particularly hard in subjects that have been much discussed: College Football, Fraternities, Popular Music, Is Chivalry Dead?, and the like. You will feel that there is nothing you can do with such subjects except repeat the old bromides. But there are some things you can do which will make your papers, if not throbbingly alive, at least less insufferably tedious than they might otherwise be.

Avoid the Obvious Content

Say the assignment is college football. Say that you've decided to be against it. Begin by putting down the arguments that come to your mind: it is too commercial, it takes the students' minds off their studies, it is hard on the players, it makes the university a kind of circus instead of an intellectual center, for most schools it is financially ruinous. Can you think of any more arguments just off hand? All right. Now when you write your paper, *make sure that you don't use any of the material on this list.* If these are the points that leap to your mind, they will leap to everyone else's too, and whether you get a "C" or a "D" may depend on whether the instructor reads your paper early when he is fresh and tolerant or late, when the sentence "In my opinion, college football has become too commercial," inexorably repeated, has brought him to the brink of lunacy.

Be against college football for some reason or reasons of your own. If they are keen and perceptive ones, that's splendid. But even if they are trivial or foolish or indefensible, you are still ahead so long as they are not everybody else's reasons too. Be against it because the colleges don't spend enough money on it to make it worth while, because it is bad for the characters of the spectators, because the players are forced to attend classes, because the football stars hog all the beautiful women, because it competes with baseball and is therefore un-American and possibly Communist inspired. There are lots of more or less unused reasons for being against college football.

Sometimes it is a good idea to sum up and dispose of the trite and conventional points before going on to your own. This has the advantage of indicating to the reader that you are going to be neither trite nor conventional. Something like this:

> We are often told that college football should be abolished because it has become too commercial or because it is bad for the players. These arguments are no doubt very cogent, but they don't really go to the heart of the matter.

Then you go to the heart of the matter.

Take the Less Usual Side

One rather simple way of getting interest into your paper is to take the side of the argument that most of the citizens will want to avoid. If the assignment is an essay on dogs, you can, if you choose, explain that dogs are faithful and lovable companions, intelligent, useful as guardians of the house and protectors of children, indispensable in police work—in short, when all is said and done, man's best friends. Or you can suggest that those big brown eyes conceal, more often than not, a vacuity of mind and an inconstancy of purpose; that the dogs you have known most intimately have been mangy, ill-tempered brutes, incapable of instruction; and that only your nobility of mind and fear of arrest prevent you from kicking the flea-ridden animals when you pass them on the street.

Naturally, personal convictions will sometimes dictate your approach. If the assigned subject is "Is Methodism Rewarding to the Individual?" and you are a pious Methodist, you have really no choice. But few assigned subjects, if any, will fall in this category. Most of them will lie in broad areas of discussion with much to be said on both sides. They are intellectual exercises, and it is legitimate to argue now one way and now another, as debaters do in similar circumstances. Always take the side that looks to you hardest, least defensible. It will almost always turn out to be easier to write interestingly on that side.

This general advice applies where you have a choice of subjects. If you are to choose among "The Value of Fraternities" and "My Favorite High School Teacher" and "What I Think About Beetles," by all means plump for the beetles. By the time the instructor gets to your paper, he will be up to his ears in tedious tales about the French teacher at Bloombury High and assertions about how fraternities build character and prepare one for life. Your views on beetles, whatever they are, are bound to be a refreshing change.

Don't worry too much about figuring out what the instructor thinks about the subject so that you can cuddle up with him. Chances are his views are no stronger than yours. If he does have convictions and you oppose them, his problem is to keep from grading you higher than you deserve in order to show he is not biased. This doesn't mean that you should always cantankerously dissent from what the instructor says; that gets tiresome too. And if the subject assigned is "My Pet Peeve," do not begin, "My pet peeve is the English instructor who assigns papers on 'my pet peeve.'" This was still funny during the War of 1812, but it has sort of lost its edge since then. It is in general good manners to avoid personalities.

Slip Out of Abstraction

If you will study the essay on college football, you will perceive that one reason for its appalling dullness is that it never gets down to particulars. It is just a series of not very glittering generalities: "football is bad for the colleges," "it has become too commercial," "football is a big business," "it is bad for the players," and so on. Such round phrases thudding against the reader's brain are unlikely to convince him, though they may well render him unconscious.

If you want the reader to believe that college football is bad for the players, you have to do more than say so. You have to display the evil. Take your roommate, Alfred Simkins, the second-string center. Picture poor old Alfy coming home from football practice every evening, bruised and aching, agonizingly tired, scarcely able to shovel the mashed potatoes into his mouth. Let us see him staggering up to the room, getting out his econ textbook, peering desperately at it with his good eye, falling asleep and failing the test in the morning. Let us share his unbearable tension as Saturday draws near. Will he fail, be demoted, lose his monthly allowance, be forced to return to the coal mines? And if he succeeds, what will be his reward? Perhaps a slight ripple of applause when the third-string center replaces him, a moment of elation in the locker room if the team wins, of despair if it loses. What will he look back on when he graduates from college? Toil and torn ligaments. And what will be his future? He is not good enough for pro football, and he is too obscure and weak in econ to succeed in stocks and bonds. College football is tearing the heart from Alfy Simkins and, when it finishes him, will callously toss aside the shattered hulk.

This is no doubt a weak enough argument for the abolition of college football, but it is a sight better than saying, in three or four variations, that college football (in your opinion) is bad for the players.

Look at the work of any professional writer and notice how constantly he is moving from the generality, the abstract statement, to the concrete example, the facts and figures, the illustration. If he is writing on juvenile delinquency, he does not just tell you that juveniles are (it seems to him) delinquent and that (in his opinion) something should be done about it. He shows you juveniles being delinquent, tearing up movie theatres in Buffalo, stabbing high school principals in Dallas, smoking marijuana in Palo Alto. And more than likely he is moving toward some specific remedy, not just a general wringing of the hands.

It is no doubt possible to be *too* concrete, too illustrative or anecdotal, but few inexperienced writers err this way. For most the soundest advice is to be seeking always for the picture, to be always turning general remarks into seeable examples. Don't say, "Sororities teach girls the social graces." Say, "Sorority life teaches a girl how to carry on a conversation while pouring tea, without sloshing the tea into the saucer." Don't say, "I like certain kinds of popular music very much." Say, "Whenever I hear Gerber Spinklittle play 'Mississippi Man' on the trombone, my socks creep up my ankles."

Get Rid of Obvious Padding

The student toiling away at his weekly English theme is too often tormented by a figure: five hundred words. How, he asks himself, is he to achieve this staggering total? Obviously by never using one word when he can somehow work in ten.

He is therefore seldom content with a plain statement like "Fast driving is dangerous." This has only four words in it. He takes thought, and the sentence becomes:

> In my opinion, fast driving is dangerous.

Better, but he can do better still:

> In my opinion, fast driving would seem to be rather dangerous.

If he is really adept, it may come out:

> In my humble opinion, though I do not claim to be an expert on this complicated subject, fast driving, in most circumstances, would seem to be rather dangerous in many respects, or at least so it would seem to me.

Thus four words have been turned into forty, and not an iota of content has been added.

Now this is a way to go about reaching five hundred words, and if you are content with a "D" grade, it is as good a way as any. But if you aim higher, you must work differently. Instead of stuffing your sentences with straw, you must try steadily to get rid of the padding, to make your sentences lean and tough. If you are really working at it, your first draft will greatly exceed the required total, and then you will work it down, thus:

> It is thought in some quarters that fraternities do not contribute as much as might be expected to campus life.
> Some people think that fraternities contribute little to campus life.

> The average doctor who practices in small towns or in the country must toil night and day to heal the sick.
> Most country doctors work long hours.

> When I was a little girl, I suffered from shyness and embarrassment in the presence of others.
> I was a shy little girl.

> It is absolutely necessary for the person employed as a marine fireman to give the matter of steam pressure his undivided attention at all times.
> The fireman has to keep his eye on the steam gauge.

You may ask how you can arrive at five hundred words at this rate. Simply. You dig up more real content. Instead of taking a couple of obvious points off the surface of the topic and then circling warily around them for six paragraphs, you work in and explore, figure out the details. You illustrate. You say that fast driving is dangerous, and then you prove it. How long does it take to stop a car at forty and at eighty? How far can you see at night? Wat happens when a tire blows? What happens in a head-on collision at fifty miles an hour? Pretty soon your paper will be full of broken glass and blood and headless torsos, and reaching five hundred words will not really be a problem.

Call a Fool a Fool

Some of the padding in freshman themes is to be blamed not on anxiety about the word minimum but on excessive timidity. The student writes, "In my opinion, the principal of my high school acted in ways that I believe every unbiased person would have to call foolish." This isn't exactly what he means. What he means is, "My high school principal was a fool." If he was a fool, call him a fool. Hedging the thing about with "in my-opinion's" and "it seems-to-me's" and "as I-see-it's" and "at-least-from-my-point-of-view's" gains you nothing. Delete these phrases whenever they creep into your paper.

The student's tendency to hedge stems from a modesty that in other circumstances would be commendable. He is, he realizes, young and inexperienced, and he half suspects that he is dopey and fuzzy-minded beyond the average. Probably only too true. But it doesn't help to announce your incompetence six times in every paragraph. Decide what you want to say and say it as vigorously as possible, without apology and in plain words.

Linguistic diffidence can take various forms. One is what we call *euphemism*. This is the tendency to call a spade "a certain garden implement" or women's underwear "unmentionables." It is stronger in some eras than others and in some people than others but it always operates more or less in subjects that are touchy or taboo: death, sex, madness, and so on. Thus we shrink from saying "He died last night" but say instead "passed away," "left us," "joined his Maker," "went to his reward." Or we try to take off the tension with a lighter cliché: "kicked the bucket," "cashed in his chips," "handed in his dinner pail." We have found all sorts of ways to avoid saying *mad;* "mentally ill," "touched," "not quite right upstairs," "feeble-minded," "inno-cent," "simple," "off his trolley," "not in his right mind." Even such a now plain word as *insane* began as a euphemism with the meaning "not healthy."

Modern science, particularly psychology, contributes many polysyllables in which we can wrap our thoughts and blunt their force. To many writers there is no such thing as a bad schoolboy. Schoolboys are maladjusted or unoriented or misunderstood or in need of guidance or lacking in continued success toward satisfactory integration of the personality as a social unit, but they are never bad. Psychology no doubt makes us better men or women, more sympathetic and tolerant, but it doesn't make writing any easier. Had Shakespeare been confronted with psychology, "To be or not to be" might have come out, "To continue as a social unit or not to do so. That is the personality problem. Whether 'tis a better sign of integration at the conscious level to display a psychic tolerance toward the maladjustments and repressions induced by one's lack of orientation in one's environment or—" But Hamlet would never have finished the soliloquy.

Writing in the modern world, you cannot altogether avoid modern jargon. Nor, in an effort to get away from euphemism, should you salt your paper with four-letter words. But you can do much if you will mount guard against those roundabout phrases, those echoing polysyllables that tend to slip into your writing to rob it of its crispness and force.

Beware of the Pat Expression

Other things being equal, avoid phrases like "other things being equal." Those sentences that come to you whole, or in two or three doughy lumps, are sure to be bad sentences. They are no creation of yours but pieces of common thought floating in the community soup.

Pat expressions are hard, often impossible, to avoid, because they come too easily to be noticed and seem too necessary to be dispensed with. No writer avoids them altogether, but good writers avoid them more often than poor writers.

By "pat expressions" we mean such tags as "to all practical intents and purposes," "the pure and simple truth," "from where I sit," "the time of his life," "to the ends of the earth," "in the twinkling of an eye," "as sure as you're born," "over my dead body," "under cover of darkness," "took the easy way out," "when all is said and done," "told him time and time again," "parted the best of friends," "stand up and be counted," "gave him the best years of her life," "worked her fingers to the bone." Like other clichés, these expressions were once forceful. Now we should use them only when we can't possibly think of anything else.

Some pat expressions stand like a wall between the writer and thought. Such a one is "the American way of life." Many student writers feel that when they have said that something accords with the American way of life or does not they have exhausted the subject. Actually, they have stopped at the highest level of abstraction. The American way of life is the complicated set of bonds between a hundred and eighty million ways. All of us know this when we think about it, but the tag phrase too often keeps us from thinking about it.

So with many another phrase dear to the politician: "this great land of ours," "the man in the street," "our national heritage." These may prove our patriotism or give a clue to our political beliefs, but otherwise they add nothing to the paper except words.

Colorful Words

The writer builds with words, and no builder uses a raw material more slippery and elusive and treacherous. A writer's work is a constant struggle to get the right word in the right place, to find that particular word that will convey his meaning exactly, that will persuade the reader or soothe him or startle or amuse him. He never succeeds altogether—sometimes he feels that he scarcely succeeds at all—but such successes as he has are what make the thing worth doing.

There is no book of rules for this game. One progresses through everlasting experiment on the basis of ever-widening experience. There are few useful generalizations that one can make about words as words, but there are perhaps a few.

Some words are what we call "colorful." By this we mean that they are calculated to produce a picture or induce an emotion. They are dressy instead of plain, specific instead of general, loud instead of soft. Thus, in place of "Her heart beat," we may write "Her heart *pounded, throbbed, fluttered, danced.*" Instead of "He sat in his chair," we may say, "He *lounged, sprawled, coiled.*" Instead of "It was hot," we may say, "It was *blistering, sultry, muggy, suffocating, steamy, wilting.*"

However, it should not be supposed that the fancy word is always better. Often it is as well to write "Her heart beat" or "It was hot" if that is all it did or all it was. Ages differ in how they like their prose. The nineteenth century liked it rich and smoky. The twentieth has usually preferred it lean and cool. The twentieth century writer, like all writers, is forever seeking the exact word but he is wary of sounding feverish. He tends to pitch it low, to understate it, to throw it away. He knows that if he gets too colorful, the audience is likely to giggle.

See how this strikes you: "As the rich, golden glow of the sunset died away along the eternal western hills, Angela's limpid blue eyes looked softly and trustingly into Montague's flashing brown ones, and her heart pounded like a drum in time with the joyous song surging in her soul." Some people like that sort of thing, but most modern readers would say, "Good grief," and turn on the television.

Colored Words

Some words we would call not so much colorful as colored—that is, loaded with associations, good or bad. All words—except perhaps structure words—have associations of some sort. . . . The meaning of a word is the sum of the contexts in which it occurs. When we hear a word, we hear with it an echo of all the situations in which we have heard it before.

In some words, these echoes are obvious and discussable. The word *mother,* for example, has, for most people, agreeable associations. When you hear *mother* you probably think of home, safety, love, food, and various other pleasant things. If one writes, "She was like a mother to me," he will get an effect which he would not get in "She was like an aunt to me." The advertiser makes use of the associations of *mother* by working it in when he talks about his product. The politician works it in when he talks about himself.

So also with such words as *home, liberty, fireside, contentment, patriot, tenderness, sacrifice, childlike, manly, bluff, limpid.* All of these words are loaded with favorable associations that would be rather hard to indicate in a straightforward definition. There is more than a literal difference between "They sat around the fireside" and "They sat around the stove." They might have been equally warm and happy around the stove, but *fireside* suggests leisure, grace, quiet tradition, congenial company, and *stove* does not.

Conversely, some words have bad associations. *Mother* suggests pleasant things, but *mother-in-law* does not. Many mothers-in-law are heroically lovable and some mothers drink gin all day and beat their children insensible, but these facts of life are beside the point. The thing is that *mother* sounds good and *mother-in-law* does not.

Or consider the word *intellectual.* This would seem to be a complimentary term, but in point of fact it is not, for it has picked up associations of impracticality and ineffectuality and general dopiness. So also with such words as *liberal, reactionary, Communist, socialist, capitalist, radical, schoolteacher, truck driver, undertaker, operator, salesman, huckster, speculator.* These convey meanings on the literal level, but beyond that—sometimes, in some places—they convey contempt on the part of the speaker.

The question of whether to use loaded words or not depends on what is being written. The scientist, the scholar, try to avoid them; for the poet, the advertising writer, the public speaker, they are standard equipment. But every writer should take care that they do not substitute for thought. If you write, "Anyone who thinks that is nothing but a Socialist (or Communist or capitalist)" you have said nothing except that you don't like people who think that, and such remarks are effective only with the most naïve readers. It is always a bad mistake to think your readers more naïve than they really are.

Colorless Words

But probably most student writers come to grief not with words that are colorful or those that are colored but with those that have no color at all. A pet example is *nice*, a word we would find it hard to dispense with in casual conversation but which is no longer capable of adding much to a description. Colorless words are those of such general meaning that in a particular sentence they mean nothing. Slang adjectives, like *cool* ("That's real cool"), tend to explode all over the language. They are applied to everything, lose their orginal force, and quickly die.

Beware also of nouns of very general meaning, like *circumstances, cases, instances, aspects, factors, relationships, attitudes, eventualities,* etc. In most circumstances you will find that those cases of writing which contain too many instances of words like these will in this and other aspects have factors leading to unsatisfactory relationships with the reader resulting in unfavorable attitudes on his part and perhaps other eventualities, like a grade of "D." Notice also what "etc." means. It means "I'd like to make this list longer, but I can't think of any more examples."

How to Write an "F" Paper: Fresh Advice for Students of Freshman English

Joseph C. Pattison

Joseph Pattison teaches freshman English and American Literature at Sacramento State University and has published in various scholarly journals.

Writing an "F" paper is admittedly not an easy task, but one can learn to do it by grasp of the principles to use. The thirteen below, if practiced at all diligently, should lead any student to that fortune in his writing.

Obscure the ideas:

1. Select a topic that is big enough to let you wander around the main idea without ever being forced to state it precisely. If an assigned topic has been limited for you, take a detour that will allow you to amble away from it for a while.
2. Pad! Pad! Pad! Do not develop your ideas. Simply restate them in safe, spongy generalizations to avoid the need to find evidence to support what you say. Always point out repetition with the phrase, "As previously noted. . . ." Better yet, repeat word-for-word at least one or two of your statements.
3. Disorganize your discussion. For example, if you are using the time order to present your material, keep the reader alert by making a jump from the past to the present only to spring back into the past preparatory to a leap into the future preceding a return hop into the present just before the finish of the point about the past. Devise comparable stratagems to use with such other principles for organizing a discussion as space, contrast, cause-effect, and climax.
4. Begin a new paragraph every sentence or two.

By generous use of white space, make the reader aware that he is looking at a page blank of sustained thought.

Like this.

13

Mangle the sentences:

5. Fill all the areas of your sentences with deadwood. Incidentally, "the area of" will deaden almost any sentence, and it is particularly flat when displayed prominently at the beginning of a sentence.

6. Using fragments and run-on or comma-spliced sentences. Do not use a main subject and a main verb, for the reader will get the complete thought too easily. Just toss him part of the idea at a time, as in "Using fragments. . . ." To gain sentence variety, throw in an occasional run-on sentence thus the reader will have to read slowly and carefully to get the idea.

7. Your sentence order invert for statement of the least important matters. That will force the reader to be attentive to understand even the simplest points you make.

8. You, in the introduction, body, and conclusion of your paper, to show that you can contrive ornate, graceful sentences, should use involution. Frequent separation of subjects from verbs by insertion of involved phrases and clauses will prove that you know what can be done to a sentence.

Slovenize the diction:

9. Add the popular "-wise" and "-ize" endings to words. Say, "Timewise, it is fastest to go by U.S. 40," rather than simply, "It is fastest to go by U.S. 40." Choose "circularize" in preference to "circulate." Practice will smartenize your style.

10. Use vague words in place of precise ones. From the start, establish vagueness of tone by saying, "The thing is . . ." instead of, "The issue is. . . ." Make the reader be imaginative throughout his reading of your paper.

11. Employ lengthy Latinate locutions wherever possible. Shun the simplicity of style that comes from apt use of short, old, familiar words, especially those of Anglo-Saxon origin. Show that you can get the *maximum* (L.), not merely the *most* (AS.), from every word choice you make.

12. Inject humor into your writing by using the wrong word occasionally. Write "then" when you mean "than" or "to" when you mean "too." Every reader likes a laugh.

13. Find a "tried and true" phrase to use to clinch a point. It will have a comfortingly folksy sound for the reader. Best of all, since you want to end in a conversational and friendly way, sprinkle your conclusion with clichés. "Put a little frosting on the cake," as the saying goes.

Well, too ensconce this whole business in a nutshell, you, above all, an erudite discourse on nothing in the field of your topic should pen. Thereby gaining the reader's credence in what you say.

Suggestion-wise, one last thing: file-ize this list for handy reference the next time you a paper write.

Politics and the English Language

George Orwell

George Orwell (1903–1950) is chiefly known for his sociological novels 1984 *and* Animal Farm. *In 1949 he received the first award given by* Partisan Review *for general distinction as a writer, the review characterizing his work as "marked by a singular directness and honesty." His pronouncements on both politics and language have frequently exhibited those same characteristics.*

Most people who bother with the matter at all would admit that the English language is in a bad way, but it is generally assumed that we cannot by conscious action do anything about it. Our civilization is decadent and our language—so the argument runs—must inevitably share in the general collapse. It follows that any struggle against the abuse of language is a sentimental archaism, like preferring candles to electric light or hansom cabs to aeroplanes. Underneath this lies the half-conscious belief that language is a natural growth and not an instrument which we shape for our own purposes.

Now, it is clear that the decline of a language must ultimately have political and economic causes: it is not due simply to the bad influence of this or that individual writer. But an effect can become a cause, reinforcing the original cause and producing the same effect in an intensified form, and so on indefinitely. A man may take to drink because he feels himself to be a failure, and then fail all the more completely because he drinks. It is rather the same thing that is happening to the English language. It becomes ugly and inaccurate because our thoughts are foolish, but the slovenliness of our language makes it easier for us to have foolish thoughts. The point is that the process is reversible. Modern English, especially written English, is full of bad habits which spread by imitation and which can be avoided if one is willing to take the necessary trouble. If one gets rid of these habits one can think more clearly, and to think clearly is a necessary first step towards political regeneration so that the fight against bad English is not frivolous and is not the exclusive concern of professional writers. I will come back to this presently, and I hope that by that time the meaning of what I have said here will have become clearer. Meanwhile, here are five specimens of the English language as it is now habitually written.

These five passages have not been picked out because they are especially bad—I could have quoted far worse if I had chosen—but because they illustrate various of the mental vices from which we now suffer. They are a little below the average, but are fairly representative samples. I number them so that I can refer back to them when necessary:

(1) I am not, indeed, sure whether it is not true to say that the Milton who once seemed not unlike a seventeenth-century Shelley had not become, out of an experience ever more bitter in each year, more alien [*sic*] to the founder of that Jesuit sect which nothing could induce him to tolerate.

Professor Harold Laski
(Essay in *Freedom of Expression*).

(2) Above all, we cannot play ducks and drakes with a native battery of idioms which prescribes such egregious collocations of vocables as the basic *put up with* for *tolerate* or *put at a loss* for *bewilder*.

Professor Lancelot Hogben (*Interglossa*).

(3) On the one side we have the free personality: by definition it is not neurotic, for it has neither conflict nor dream. Its desires, such as they are, are transparent, for they are just what institutional approval keeps in the forefront of consciousness; another institutional pattern would alter their number and intensity; there is little in them that is natural, irreducible, or culturally dangerous. But *on the other side*, the social bond itself is nothing but the mutual reflection of these self-secure integrities. Recall the definition of love. Is not this the very picture of a small academic? Where is there a place in this hall of mirrors for either personality or fraternity?

Essay on Psychology in *Politics* (New York)

(4) All the "best people" from the gentlemen's clubs, and all the frantic fascist captains, united in common hatred of Socialism and bestial horror of the rising tide of the mass revolutionary movement, have turned to acts of provocation, to foul incendiarism, to medieval legends of poisoned wells, to legalize their own destruction of proletarian organizations, and rouse the agitated petty-bourgeoisie to chauvinistic fervor on behalf of the fight against the revolutionary way out of the crisis.

Communist Pamphlet.

(5) If a new spirit *is* to be infused into this old country, there is one thorny and contentious reform which must be tackled, and that is the humanization and galvanization of the B.B.C. Timidity here will bespeak canker and atrophy of the soul. The heart of Britain may be sound and of strong beat, for instance, but the British lion's roar at present is like that of Bottom in Shakespeare's *Midsummer Night's Dream*—as gentle as any sucking dove. A virile new Britain cannot continue indefinitely to be traduced in the eyes or rather ears, of the world by the effete languors of Langham Place, brazenly masquerading as "standard English." When the voice of Britain is heard at nine o'clock, better far and infinitely less ludicrous to hear aitches honestly dropped than the present priggish, inflated, inhibited, school-ma'amish arch braying of blameless bashful mewing maidens!

Letter in Tribune.

Each of these passages has faults of its own, but, quite apart from avoidable ugliness, two qualities are common to all of them. The first is staleness of imagery: the other is lack of precision. The writer either has a meaning and cannot express it, or he inadvertently says something else, or he is almost indifferent as to whether his words mean anything or not. This mixture of vagueness and sheer incompetence is the most marked characteristic of modern English prose, and especially of any kind of political writing. As soon as certain topics are raised, the concrete melts into the abstract and no one seems able to think of turns of speech that are not hackneyed: prose consists less and less of *words* chosen for the sake of their meaning, and more and more of *phrases* tacked together like the sections of a prefabricated henhouse. I list below, with notes and examples, various of the tricks by means of which the work of prose-construction is habitually dodged:

Dying metaphors. A newly invented metaphor assists thought by evoking a visual image, while on the other hand a metaphor which is technically "dead" (e.g. *iron resolution*) has in effect reverted to being an ordinary word and can generally be used without loss of vividness. But in between these two classes there is a huge dump of worn-out metaphors which have lost all evocative power and are merely used because they save people the trouble of investing phrases for themselves. Examples are: *Ring the changes on, take up the cudgels for, toe the line, ride roughshod over, stand shoulder to shoulder with, play into the hands of, no axe to grind, grist to the mill, fishing in troubled waters, on the order of the day, Achilles' heel, swan song, hotbed.* Many of these are used without knowledge of their meaning (what is a "rift," for instance?), and incompatible metaphors are frequently mixed, a sure sign that the writer is not interested in what he is saying. Some metaphors now current have been twisted out of their original meaning without those who use them even being aware of the fact. For example, *toe the line* is sometimes written *tow the line*. Another example is *the hammer and the anvil*, now always used with the implication that the anvil gets the worst of it. In real life it is always the anvil that breaks the hammer, never the other way about; a writer who stopped to think what he was saying would be aware of this, and would avoid perverting the original phrase.

Operators or *verbal false limbs*. These save the trouble of picking out appropriate verbs and nouns, and at the same time pad each sentence with extra syllables which give it an appearance of symmetry. Characteristic phrases are *render inoperative, militate against, make contact with, be subjected to, give rise to, give grounds for, have the effect of, play a leading part (role) in, make itself felt, take effect, exhibit a tendency to, serve the purpose of, etc., etc.* The keynote is the elimination of simple verbs. Instead of being a single word, such as *break, stop, spoil, mend, kill,* a verb becomes a *phrase,* made up of a noun or adjective tacked on to some general-purpose verb such as *prove, serve, form, play, render.* In addition, the passive voice is wherever possible used in preference to the active, and noun constructions are used instead of gerunds (*by examination of* instead of *by examining*). The range of verbs is further cut down by means of the *-ize* and *de-* formations, and the banal statements are given an appearance of profundity by means of the *not un-* formation. Simple conjunctions and prepositions are replaced by such phrases as *with respect to, having regard to, the fact that, by dint of, in view of, in the interests of, on the hypothesis that;* and the ends of sentences are saved from anticlimax by such resounding common-places as *greatly to be desired, cannot be left out of account, a development to be expected in the near future, deserving of serious consideration, brought to a satisfactory conclusion,* and so on and so forth.

Pretentious diction. Words like *phenomenon, element, individual* (as noun), *objective, categorical, effective, virtual, basic, primary, promote, constitute, exhibit, exploit, utilize, eliminate, liquidate,* are used to dress up simple statements and give an air of scientific impartiality to biased judgments. Adjectives like *epoch-making, epic, historic, unforgettable, triumphant, age-old, inevitable, inexorable, veritable,* are used to dignify the sordid processes of international politics, while writing that aims at glorifying war usually takes on an archaic color, its characteristic words being: *realm, throne, chariot, mailed fist, trident, sword, shield, buckler, banner, jackboot, clarion.* Foreign words and expressions such as *cul de sac, ancien régime, deus ex machina, mutatis mutandis, status quo, gleichschaltung, weltanschauung,* are used to give an air of culture and elegance. Except for the useful abbreviations *i.e., e.g.,* and *etc.,* there is no real need for any of the hundreds of foreign phrases now current in English. Bad writers, and especially scientific, political and sociological writers, are nearly always haunted by the notion that Latin or Greek words are grander than Saxon ones, and unnecessary words like *expedite, ameliorate, predict, extraneous, deracinated, clandestine, subaqueous* and hundreds of others constantly gain ground from their Anglo-Saxon opposite numbers.[1] The jargon peculiar to Marxist writing (*hyena, hangman, cannibal, petty bourgeois, these gentry, lacquey, flunkey, mad dog, White Guard,* etc.) consists largely of words and phrases translated from Russian, German or French; but the normal way of coining a new word is to use a Latin or Greek root with the appropriate affix and, where necessary, the *-ize* formation. It is often easier to make up words of this kind (*deregionalize, impermissible, extramarital, non-fragmentary* and so forth) than to think up the English words that will cover one's meaning. The result, in general, is an increase in slovenliness and vagueness.

Meaningless words. In certain kinds of writing, particularly in art criticism and literary criticism, it is normal to come across long passages which are almost completely lacking in meaning.[2] Words like *romantic, plastic, values, human, dead, sentimental, natural, vitality,* as used in art criticism, are strictly meaningless, in the sense that they not only do not point to any discoverable object, but are hardly ever expected to do so by the reader. When one critic writes, "The outstanding feature of Mr. X's work is its living quality," while another writes, "The immediately striking thing about Mr. X's work is its peculiar deadness," the reader accepts this as a simple difference of opinion. If words like *black* and *white* were involved, instead of the jargon words *dead* and *living,* he would see at once that language was being used in an improper way. Many political words are similarly

---

[1] An interesting illustration of this is the way in which the English flower names which were in use till very recently are being ousted by Greek ones, *snapdragon* becoming *antirrhinum, forget-me-not* becoming *myosotis,* etc. It is hard to see any practical reason for this change of fashion: it is probably due to an instinctive turning-away from the more homely word and a vague feeling that the Greek word is scientific.

[2] Example: "Comfort's catholicity of perception and image, strangely Whitmanesque in range, almost the exact opposite in aesthetic compulsion, continues to evoke that trembling atmospheric accumulative hinting at a cruel, an inexorably serene timelessness. . . . Wrey Gardiner scores by aiming at simple bull's-eyes with precision. Only they are not so simple, and through this contented sadness runs more than the surface bittersweet of resignation." (*Poetry Quarterly.*)

abused. The word *Fascism* has now no meaning except in so far as it signifies "something not desirable." The words *democracy, socialism, freedom, patriotic, realistic, justice,* have each of them several different meanings which cannot be reconciled with one another. In the case of a word like *democracy,* not only is there no agreed definition, but the attempt to make one is resisted from all sides. It is almost universally felt that when we call a country democratic we are praising it: consequently the defenders of every kind of régime claim that it is a democracy, and fear that they might have to stop using the word if it were tied down to any one meaning. Words of this kind are often used in a consciously dishonest way. That is, the person who uses them has his own private definition, but allows his hearer to think he means something quite different. Statements like *Marshal Pétain was a true patriot, The Soviet Press is the freest in the world, The Catholic Church is opposed to persecution,* are almost always made with intent to deceive. Other words used in variable meanings, in most cases more or less dishonestly, are: *class, totalitarian, science, progressive, reactionary, bourgeois, equality.*

Now that I have made this catalogue of swindles and perversions, let me give another example of the kind of writing that they lead to. This time it must of its nature be an imaginary one. I am going to translate a passage of good English into modern English of the worst sort. Here is a well-known verse from *Ecclesiastes*:

"I returned and saw under the sun, that the race is not to the swift, nor the battle to the strong, neither yet bread to the wise, nor yet riches to men of understanding, nor yet favour to men of skill; but time and chance happeneth to them all."

Here it is in modern English:

"Objective consideration of contemporary phenomena compels the conclusion that success or failure in competitive activities exhibits no tendency to be commensurate with innate capacity, but that a considerable element of the unpredictable must invariably be taken into account."

This is a parody, but not a very gross one. Exhibit (3), above, for instance, contains several patches of the same kind of English. It will be seen that I have not made full translation. The beginning and ending of the sentence follow the original meaning fairly closely, but in the middle the concrete illustrations—race, battle, bread—dissolve into the vague phrase "success or failure in competitive activities." This had to be so, because no modern writer of the kind I am discussing—no one capable of using phrases like "objective consideration of contemporary phenomena"—would ever tabulate his thoughts in that precise and detailed way. The whole tendency of modern prose is away from concreteness. Now analyse these two sentences a little more closely. The first contains forty-nine words but only sixty syllables, and all its words are those of everyday life. The second contains thirty-eight words of ninety syllables: eighteen of its words are from Latin roots, and one from Greek. The first sentence contains six vivid images, and only one phrase (''time and chance'') that could be called vague. The second contains not a single fresh, arresting phrase, and in spite of its ninety syllables it gives only a shortened version of the meaning contained in the first. Yet without a doubt it is the second kind of sentence that is gaining ground in modern English. I do not want to exaggerate. This kind of writing is not yet universal, and outcrops of simplicity will occur here and there in the worst-written page. Still, if you or I were told to write a few lines on the uncertainty of human fortunes, we should probably come much nearer to my imaginary sentence than to the one from *Ecclesiastes*.

As I have tried to show, modern writing at its worst does not consist in picking out words for the sake of their meaning and inventing images in order to make the meaning clearer. It consists in gumming together long strips of words which have already been set in order by someone else, and making the results presentable by sheer humbug. The attraction of this way of writing is that it is easy. It is easier—even quicker, once you have the habit—to say *In my opinion it is not an unjustifiable assumption that* than to say *I think*. If you use ready-made phrases, you not only don't have to hunt about for words; you also don't have to bother with the rhythms of your sentences, since these phrases are generally so arranged as to be more or less euphonious. When you are composing in a hurry—when you are dictating to a stenographer, for instance, or making a public speech—it is natural to fall into a pretentious, Latinized style. Tags like *a consideration which we should do well to bear in mind* or *a conclusion to which all of us would readily assent* will save many a sentence from coming down with a bump. By using stale metaphors, similes and idioms, you save much mental effort, at the cost of leaving your meaning vague, not only for your reader but for yourself. This is the significance of mixed metaphors. The sole aim of a metaphor is to call up a visual image. When these images clash—as in *The Fascist octopus has sung its swan song, the jackboot is thrown into the melting pot*—it can be taken as certain that the writer is not seeing a mental image of the objects he is naming; in other words he is not really thinking. Look again at the examples I gave at the beginning of this essay. Professor Laski (1) uses five negatives in fifty-three words. One of these is superfluous, making nonsense of the whole passage, and in addition these is the slip *alien* for akin, making further nonsense, and several avoidable pieces of clumsiness which increase the general vagueness. Professor Hogben (2) plays ducks and drakes with a battery which is able to write prescriptions, and, while disapproving of the everyday phrase *put up with*, is unwilling to look *egregious* up in the dictionary and see what it means; (3), if one takes an uncharitable attitude towards it, is simply meaningless: probably one could work out its intended meaning by reading the whole of the article in which it occurs. In (4), the writer knows more or less what he wants to say, but an accumulation of stale phrases chokes him like tea leaves blocking a sink. In (5), words and meaning have almost parted company. People who write in this manner usually have a general emotional meaning—they dislike one thing and want to express solidarity with another—but they are not interested in the detail of what they are saying. A scrupulous writer, in every sentence that he writes, will ask himself at least four questions, thus: What am I trying to say? What words will express it? What image or idiom will make it clearer? Is this image fresh enough to have an effect? And he will probably ask himself two more: Could I put it more shortly? Have I said anything that is avoidably ugly? But you are not obliged to go to all this trouble. You can shirk it by simply throwing your mind open and letting the ready-made phrases come crowding in. They will construct your sentences for you—even think your thoughts for you, to a certain extent—and at need they will perform the important service of partially concealing your meaning even from yourself. It is at this point that the special connection between politics and the debasement of language becomes clear.

In our time it is broadly true that political writing is bad writing. Where it is not true, it will generally be found that the writer is some kind of rebel, expressing his private opinions and not a "party line." Orthodoxy, of whatever color, seems to demand a lifeless, imitative style. The political dialects to be found in pamphlets, leading articles, manifestos, White Papers and the speeches of under-secretaries do, of course, vary from party to party, but they are all alike in that one almost never finds in them a fresh, vivid, home-made turn of speech. When one watches some tired hack on the platform mechanically repeating the familiar phrases—*bestial atrocities, iron heel, blood-stained tyranny, free peoples of the world, stand shoulder to shoulder*—one often has a curious feeling that one is not watching a live human being but some kind of dummy: a feeling which suddenly becomes stronger at moments when the light catches the speaker's spectacles and turns them into black discs which seem to have no eyes behind them. And this is not altogether fanciful. A speaker who uses that kind of phraseology has gone some distance towards turning himself into a machine. The appropriate noises are coming out of his larynx, but his brain is not involved as it would be if he were choosing his words for himself. If the speech he is making is one that he is accustomed to make over and over again, he may be almost unconscious of what he is saying, as one is when one utters the responses in church. And this reduced state of consciousness, if not indispensable, is at any rate favorable to political conformity.

In our time, political speech and writing are largely the defence of the indefensible. Things like the continuance of British rule in India, the Russian purges and deportations, the dropping of the atom bombs on Japan, can indeed be defended, but only by arguments which are too brutal for most people to face, and which do not square with the professed aims of political parties. Thus political language has to consist largely of euphemism, question-begging and sheer cloudy vagueness. Defenceless villages are bombarded from the air, the inhabitants driven out into the countryside, the cattle machine-gunned, the huts set on fire with incendiary bullets: this is called *pacification*. Millions of peasants are robbed of their farms and sent trudging along the roads with no more than they can carry: this is called *transfer of population* or *rectification of frontiers*. People are imprisoned for years without trial, or shot in the back of the neck or sent to die of scurvy in Arctic lumber camps: this is called *elimination of unreliable elements*. Such phraseology is needed if one wants to name things without calling up mental pictures of them. Consider for instance some comfortable English professor defending Russian totalitarianism. He cannot say outright, "I believe in killing off your opponents when you can get good results by doing so." Probably, therefore, he will say something like this:

"While freely conceding that the Soviet régime exhibits certain features which the humanitarian may be inclined to deplore, we must, I think, agree that a certain curtailment of the right to political opposition is an unavoidable concomitant of transitional periods, and that the rigors which the Russian people have been called upon to undergo have been amply justified in the sphere of concrete achievement."

The inflated style is itself a kind of euphemism. A mass of Latin words falls upon the facts like soft snow, blurring the outlines and covering up all the details. The great enemy of clear language is insincerity. When there is a gap between one's real and one's declared aims, one turns as it were instinctively to long words and exhausted idioms, like a cuttlefish squirting out ink. In our age there is no such thing as "keeping out of politics." All issues are political issues, and politics itself is a mass of lies, evasions, folly, hatred and schizophrenia. When the general atmosphere is bad, language must suffer. I should expect to find—this is a guess which I have not sufficient knowledge to verify—that the German, Russian and Italian languages have all deteriorated in the last ten or fifteen years, as a result of dictatorship.

But if thought corrupts language, language can also corrupt thought. A bad usage can spread by tradition and imitation, even among people who should and do know better. The debased language that I have been discussing is in some ways very convenient. Phrases like *a not unjustifiable assumption, leaves much to be desired, would serve no good purpose, a consideration which we should do well to bear in mind,* are a continuous temptation, a packet of aspirins always at one's elbow. Look back through this essay, and for certain you will find that I have again and again committed the very faults I am protesting against. By this morning's post I have received a pamphlet dealing with conditions in Germany. The author tells me that he "felt impelled" to write it. I open it at random, and here is almost the first sentence that I see: "[The Allies] have an opportunity not only of achieving a radical transformation of Germany's social and political structure in such a way as to avoid a nationalistic reaction in Germany itself, but at the same time of laying the foundations of a cooperative and unified Europe." You see, he "feels impelled" to write—feels, presumably, that he has something new to say—and yet his words, like cavalry horses answering the bugle, group themselves automatically into the familiar dreary pattern. This invasion of one's mind by ready-made phrases (*lay the foundations, achieve a radical transformation*) can only be prevented if one is constantly on guard against them, and every such phrase anesthetizes a portion of one's brain.

I said earlier that the decadence of our language is probably curable. Those who deny this would argue, if they produced an argument at all, that language merely reflects existing social conditions, and that we cannot influence its development by any direct tinkering with words and constructions. So far as the general tone or spirit of a language goes, this may be true, but it is not true in detail. Silly words and expressions have often disappeared, not through any evolutionary process but owing to the conscious action of a minority. Two recent examples were *explore every avenue* and *leave no stone unturned,* which were killed by the jeers of a few journalists. There is a long list of flyblown metaphors which could similarly be got rid of if enough people would interest themselves in the job; and it should also be possible to laugh the *not un-* formation out of existence,[3] to reduce the amount of Latin and Greek in the average sentence, to drive out foreign phrases and strayed scientific words, and, in general, to make

---

[3] One can cure oneself of the *not un-* formation by memorizing this sentence: A not unblack dog was chasing a not unsmall rabbit across a not ungreen field.

pretentiousness unfashionable. But all these are minor points. The defence of the English language implies more than this, and perhaps it is best to start by saying what it does *not* imply.

To begin with it has nothing to do with archaism, with the salvaging of obsolete words and turns of speech, or with the setting up of a "standard English" which must never be departed from. On the contrary, it is especially concerned with the scrapping of every word or idiom which has outworn its usefulness. It has nothing to do with correct grammar and syntax, which are of no importance so long as one makes one's meaning clear, or with the avoidance of Americanisms, or with having what is called a "good prose style." On the other hand it is not concerned with fake simplicity and the attempt to make written English colloquial. Nor does it even imply in every case preferring the Saxon word to the Latin one, though it does imply using the fewest and shortest words that will cover one's meaning. What is above all needed is to let the meaning choose the word, and not the other way about. In prose, the worst thing one can do with words is to surrender to them. When you think of a concrete object, you think wordlessly, and then, if you want to describe the thing you have been visualizing you probably hunt about till you find the exact words that seem to fit it. When you think of something abstract you are more inclined to use words from the start, and unless you make a conscious effort to prevent it, the existing dialect will come rushing in and do the job for you, at the expense of blurring or even changing your meaning. Probably it is better to put off using words as long as possible and get one's meaning as clear as one can through pictures or sensations. Afterwards one can choose—not simply *accept*—the phrases that will best cover the meaning, and then switch round and decide what impression one's words are likely to make on another person. This last effort of the mind cuts out all stale or mixed images, all prefabricated phrases, needless repetitions, and humbug and vagueness generally. But one can often be in doubt about the effect of a word or a phrase, and one needs rules that one can rely on when instinct fails. I think the following rules will cover most cases:

(i)   Never use a metaphor, simile or other figure of speech which you are used to seeing in print.

(ii) Never use a long word where a short one will do.

(iii) If it is possible to cut a word out, always cut it out.

(iv) Never use the passive where you can use the active.

(v)   Never use a foreign phrase, a scientific word or a jargon word if you can think of an everyday English equivalent.

(iv) Break any of these rules sooner than say anything outright barbarous.

These rules sound elementary, and so they are, but they demand a deep change of attitude in anyone who has grown used to writing in the style now fashionable. One could keep all of them and still write bad English, but one could not write the kind of stuff that I quoted in those five specimens at the beginning of this article.

I have not here been considering the literary use of language, but merely language as an instrument for expressing and not for concealing or preventing thought. Stuart Chase and others have come near to claiming that all abstract words are meaningless, and have used this as a pretext for advocating a kind of political quietism. Since you don't know what Fascism is, how can you struggle against Fascism? One need not swallow such absurdities as this, but one ought to recognize that the present political chaos is connected with the decay of language, and that one can probably bring about some improvement by starting at the verbal end. If you simplify your English, you are freed from the worst follies of orthodoxy. You cannot speak any of the necessary dialects, and when you make a stupid remark its stupidity will be obvious, even to yourself. Political language—and with variations this is true of all political parties, from Conservatives to Anarchists—is designed to make lies sound truthful and murder respectable, and to give an appearance of solidity to pure wind. One cannot change this all in a moment, but one can at least change one's own habits, and from time to time one can even, if one jeers loudly enough, send some worn-out and useless phrase—some *jackboot, Achilles' heel, hotbed, melting pot, acid test, veritable inferno* or other lump of verbal refuse—into the dustbin where it belongs.

What a piece of work is man! How noble in reason!
How infinite in faculty! In form and moving how express
and admirable! In action how like an angel!
In apprehension how like a god! The beauty of the world!
The paragon of animals! And yet, to me,
what is this quintessence of dust?

Hamlet, II, ii.

1

THE INNER PERSON

If a tree falls in the forest and nobody hears it, does it make a sound? College students in philosophy courses have debated this question for the better part of a century trying to answer a fundamental question about human life—does the world exist without humanity? Most people take for granted that it does, but some philosophers, artists, and students think that it would not exist, or at least would not matter, unless they themselves existed. From this point of view, people are the focal point of the world, and it is only through an understanding of our own consciousness that we can understand anything else.

Another, different, philosophical viewpoint holds that humanity is a product of the evolution of nature that began long before any single individual alive today. To understand humanity, therefore, we should study science and history. A third position says that people are not simply and mechanically products of a preexisting natural and social environment, but always interact with that environment to change it and thus to change the consciousness of other human beings.

You may wonder what this brief excursion into philosophy has to do with rhetoric, the art of expressing yourself well. Perhaps you will wonder less if you visualize these different positions in more concrete terms. On your way to physics class you meet a friend who has just decided to drop out of college. You ask him why. He answers, "Why not?" and explains that with all the uncertainties in the modern world, ranging from the threat of nuclear or ecological disaster to the possibility of being killed in an auto accident, it is senseless for people to study physics—as if they thought they could discover or change anything to make life better. "Why study sociology or history?" he continues. "Humanity is incapable of learning from its past and unable to change its future." How do you answer him? Perhaps you agree. Like him, you've perhaps read or heard about Hermann Hesse or Kurt Vonnegut, or listened to the music of Bob Dylan. You feel, at least at frequent intervals, isolated and alone in the world, and *feeling*, you sincerely believe, is what ought to govern peoples' actions. Yes, why study physics when it doesn't seem to matter, at least not for *your* life? If that tree falls in the forest and you're not around to hear it, it does not, in a very real sense, make any noise.

But perhaps you disagree with him. You ask your friend whether he would rather have lived in the twelfth century, as a serf on a feudal estate, without the advantages of modern medicine and technology. You agree that human history is a series of ups and downs, but you argue that over the long run it seems that there is at least the possibility for us to increase our control over nature, to do so in a rational, unexploiting way, and to improve our social organizations. You did not hear the trees fall before the settler's ax, but the chopping made this campus and the local fire station and hospital possible, and these institutions have very real, practical effects on both of you. The study of physics may or may not in your lifetime affect you greatly for the better, though chances are that the application of that study to technology and medicine will make your life easier and healthier than your grandparents'. Even if you see no major benefits in your lifetime, you believe that all human beings have a responsibility to provide a better basis of life for others, even for those unborn.

The argument could easily continue, if you were not late for class, to include discussion relating to music, politics, sex, psychology, literature, religion *ad infinitum*, and the argument would probably become very abstract, much like our philosophical excursion. The possibility, the very likely probability, of your having to engage in very abstract discussions not only in a philosophy course, but in everyday life—simply as a means of talking about very personal questions—leads to a consideration of rhetoric. If such discussions are to be productive,

DOONESBURY   by Garry Trudeau

or even understandable, the people involved must have some facility for dealing with very abstract ideas. Have you ever been confronted with a situation in which you had ideas or feelings to express which you could not turn into words? Have you been forced to describe an important experience by waving your arms around and exclaiming, "Oh! Wow! It was just too much . . . mmm . . . really . . . outasight . . . yeah"? Your exclamation communicates a sense of the special, a sense of wonder which is probably going to prompt your listener to say, "Tell me more about it." If you can do nothing but repeat yourself, neither you nor anybody who talks with you is likely to gain very much information or insight from your subsequent conversation. The essays in this section all deal with personal experience, and all speak of that experience in a combination of concrete and abstract terms. It is hoped you will enjoy reading some of them simply to add to the general perspective of your life. Perhaps a close examination of how they are put together and the creation on your part of essays which deal with questions raised by these selections will help you to speak and write about yourself better.

Each section of this book contains an essay called a "Rhetorical Analysis." The purpose of these analyses is to give you some very specific information about strategies and tactics for writing as they are exemplified in one of the selections you will read. The Rhetorical Analysis in Section 1 deals with Bertrand Russell's essay *What I Have Lived For*. Be sure to read Russell's essay before reading the Rhetorical Analysis.

An 18-Year-Old Looks Back On Life

Joyce Maynard

Joyce Maynard (b. 1953) was raised in Durham, New Hampshire. Her book, Looking Back: A Chronicle of Growing Up Old in the Sixties, *was published in 1973 while she was a sophomore at Yale. She has also published in* Mademoiselle, McCall's, *and other popular magazines.*

1   Every generation thinks it's special—my grandparents because they remember horses and buggies, my parents because of the Depression. The over-30's are special because they knew the Red Scare of Korea, Chuck Berry and beatniks. My older sister is special because she belonged to the first generation of teen-agers (before that, people in their teens were *adolescents*), when being a teen-ager was still fun. And I—I am 18, caught in the middle. Mine is the generation of unfulfilled expectations. "When you're older," my mother promised, "you can wear lipstick." But when the time came, of course, lipstick wasn't being worn. "When we're big, we'll dance like that," my friends and I whispered, watching Chubby Checker twist on "American Bandstand." But we inherited no dance steps, ours was a limp, formless shrug to watered-down music that rarely made the feet tap. "Just wait till we can vote," I said, bursting with 10-year-old fervor, ready to fast, freeze, march and die for peace and freedom as Joan Baez, barefoot, sang "We Shall Overcome." Well, now we can vote, and we're old enough to attend rallies and knock on doors and wave placards, and suddenly it doesn't seem to matter any more.

2   My generation is special because of what we missed rather than what we got, because in a certain sense we are the first and the last. The first to take technology for granted. (What was a space shot to us, except an hour cut from Social Studies to gather before a TV in the gym as Cape Canaveral counted down?) The first to grow up with TV. My sister was 8 when we got our set, so to her it seemed magic and always somewhat foreign. She had known books already and would never really replace them. But for me, the TV set was, like the kitchen sink and the telephone, a fact of life.

3   We inherited a previous generation's hand-me-downs and took in the seams, turned up the hems, to make our new fashions. We took drugs from the college kids and made them a high-school

commonplace. We got the Beatles, but not those lovable look-alikes in matching suits with barber cuts and songs that made you want to cry. They came to us like a bad joke—aged, bearded, discordant. And we inherited the Vietnam war just after the crest of the wave— too late to burn draft cards and too early not to be drafted. The boys of 1953—my year—will be the last to go.

4   So where are we now? Generalizing is dangerous. Call us the apathetic generation and we will become that. Say times are chang-ing, nobody cares about prom queens and getting into the college of his choice any more—say that (because it sounds good, it indicates a trend, gives a symmetry to history) and you make a movement and a unit out of a generation unified only in its common fragmentation. If there is a reason why we are where we are, it comes from where we have been.

5   Like overanxious patients in analysis, we treasure the traumas of our childhood. Ours was more traumatic than most. The Ken-nedy assassination has become our myth: Talk to us for an evening or two—about movies or summer jobs or Nixon's trip to China or the weather—and the subject will come up ("Where were *you* when you heard?"), as if having lived through Jackie and the red roses, John-John's salute and Oswald's on-camera murder justifies our disenchantment.

6   We haven't all emerged the same, of course, because our lives were lived in high-school corridors and drive-in hamburger joints as well as in the pages of Time and Life, and the images on the TV screen. National events and personal memory blur so that, for me, Nov. 22, 1963, was a birthday party that had to be called off and Armstrong's moonwalk was my first full can of beer. If you want to know who we are now; if you wonder how we'll vote, or whether we will, or whether, 10 years from now, we'll end up just like all those other generations that thought they were special—with 2.2 kids and a house in Connecticut—if that's what you're wondering, look to the past because, whether we should blame it or not, we do.

7   I didn't know till years later that they called it the Cuban Missile Crisis. But I remember Castro. (We called him Castor Oil and were awed by his beard—beards were rare in those days.) We might not have worried so much (what would the Communists want with our small New Hampshire town?) except that we lived 10 miles from an air base. Planes buzzed around us like mosquitoes that summer. People talked about fallout shelters in their basements and one family on our street packed their car to go to the mountains. I couldn't understand that. If everybody was going to die, I certainly didn't want to stick around, with my hair falling out and—later—a

plague of thalidomide-type babies. I wanted to go quickly, with my family.

8   Dying didn't bother me so much—I'd never known anyone who died, and death was unreal, fascinating. (I wanted Doctor Kildare to have more terminal cancer patients and fewer love affairs.) What bothered me was the business of immortality. Sometimes, the growing-up sort of concepts germinate slowly, but the full impact of death hit me like a bomb, in the night. Not only would my body be gone—that I could take—but I would cease to think. That I would no longer be a participant I had realized before; now I saw that I wouldn't even be an observer. What especially alarmed me about The Bomb (always singular like, a few years later, The Pill) was the possibility of total obliteration. All traces of me would be destroyed. There would be no grave and, if there were, no one left to visit it.

9   Newly philosophical, I pondered the universe. If the earth was in the solar system and the solar system was in the galaxy and the galaxy was in the universe, what was the universe in? And if the sun was just a dot—the head of a pin—what was I? We visited a planetarium that year, in third grade, and saw a dramatization of the sun exploding. Somehow the image of that orange ball zooming toward us merged with my image of The Bomb. The effect was devastating, and for the first time in my life—except for Easter Sundays, when I wished I went to church so I could have a fancy new dress like my Catholic and Protestant friends—I longed for religion.

10   I was 8 when Joan Baez entered our lives, with long, black, beatnik hair and a dress made out of a burlap bag. When we got her first record (we called her Joan *Baze* then—soon she was simply Joan) we listened all day, to "All My Trials" and "Silver Dagger" and "Wildwood Flower." My sister grew her hair and started wearing sandals, making pilgrimages to Harvard Square. I took up the guitar. We loved her voice and her songs but, even more, we loved the idea of Joan, like the 15th-century Girl of Orleans, burning at society's stake, marching along or singing, solitary, in a prison cell to protest segregation. She was the champion of nonconformity and so—like thousands of others—we joined the masses of her fans.

11   I knew she must but somehow I could never imagine Jackie Kennedy going to the bathroom. She was too cool and poised and perfect. We had a book about her, filled with color pictures of Jackie painting, in a spotless yellow linen dress, Jackie on the beach with Caroline and John-John, Jackie riding elephants in India and Jackie, in a long white gown, greeting Khrushchev like Snow White wel-

coming one of the seven dwarfs. (No, I wasn't betraying Joan in my adoration. Joan was beautiful but human, like us; Jackie was magic.) When, years later, she married Rumpelstiltskin, I felt like a child discovering, in his father's drawer, the Santa Claus suit. And, later still, reading some Ladies' Home Journal exposé ("Jacqueline Onassis's secretary tells all . . .") I felt almost sick. After the first few pages I put the magazine down. I wasn't interested in the fragments, only in the fact that the glass had broken.

12   If I had spent at the piano the hours I gave to television, on all those afternoons when I came home from school, I would be an accomplished pianist now. Or if I'd danced, or read, or painted. . . . But I turned on the set instead, every day, almost, every year, and sank into an old green easy chair, smothered in quilts, with a bag of Fritos beside me and a glass of milk to wash them down, facing life and death with Dr. Kildare, laughing at Danny Thomas, whispering the answers—out loud sometimes—with "Password" and "To Tell the Truth." Looking back over all those afternoons, I try to convince myself they weren't wasted. I must have learned something; I must, at least, have changed.

13   What I learned was certainly not what TV tried to teach me. From the reams of trivia collected over years of quiz shows, I remember only the questions, never the answers. I loved "Leave It to Beaver" for the messes Beaver got into, not for the inevitable lecture from Dad at the end of each show. I saw every episode two or three times, witnessed Beaver's aging, his legs getting longer and his voice lower, only to start all over again with young Beaver every fall. (Someone told me recently that the boy who played Beaver Cleaver died in Vietnam. The news was a shock—I kept coming back to it for days until another distressed Beaver fan wrote to tell me that it wasn't true after all.)

14   I got so I could predict punch lines and endings, not really knowing whether I'd seen the episode before or only watched one like it. There was the bowling-ball routine, for instance: Lucy, Dobie Gillis, Pete and Gladys—they all used it. Somebody would get his finger stuck in a bowling ball (Lucy later updated the gimmick using Liz Taylor's ring) and then they'd have to go to a wedding or give a speech at the P.T.A. or have the boss to dinner, concealing one hand all the while. We weren't supposed to ask questions like "Why don't they just tell the truth?" These shows were built on deviousness, on the longest distance between two points, and on a kind of symmetry which decrees that no loose ends shall be left untied, no lingering doubts allowed. (The Surgeon General is off the track in worrying about TV violence, I think. I grew up in the days

before lawmen became peacemakers. What carries over is not the gunfights but the memory that everything always turned out all right.) Optimism shone through all those half hours I spent in the dark shadows of the TV room—out of evil shall come good.

15   Most of all, the situation comedies steeped me in American culture. I emerged from years of TV viewing indifferent to the museums of France, the architecture of Italy, the literature of England. A perversely homebound American, I pick up paperbacks in bookstores, checking before I buy to see if the characters have foreign names, whether the action takes place in London or New York. Vulgarity and banality fascinate me. More intellectual friends (who watch no TV) can't understand what I see in "My Three Sons." "Nothing happens," they say. "The characters are dull, plastic, faceless. Every show is the same." I guess that's why I watch them—boring repetition is, itself, a rhythm—a steady pulse of flashing Coca-Cola signs, McDonald's Golden Arches and Howard Johnson roofs.

16   I don't watch TV as an anthropologist, rising loftily above my subject to analyze. Neither do I watch, as some kids now tune in to reruns of "The Lone Ranger" and "Superman" (in the same spirit they enjoy comic books and pop art) for their camp. I watch in earnest. How can I do anything else? Five thousand hours of my life have gone into this box.

17   There were almost no blacks in our school. They were Negroes then; the word *black* was hard to say at first. *Negro* got hard to say for a while too, so I said nothing at all and was embarrassed. If you had asked me, at 9, to describe Cassius Clay, I would have taken great, liberal pains to be color-blind, mentioning height, build, eye color and shoe size, disregarding skin. I knew black people only from newspapers and the TV screen—picket lines, National Guardsmen at the doors of schools. (There were few black actors on TV then, except for Jack Benny's Rochester.) It was easy, in 1963, to embrace the Negro cause. Later, faced with cold stares from an all-black table in the cafeteria or heckled by a Panther selling newspapers, I first became aware of the fact that maybe the little old lady didn't want to be helped across the street. My visions of black-and-white-together look at me now like shots from "To Sir With Love." If a black is friendly to me, I wonder, as other blacks might, if he's a sellout.

18   I had no desire to scream or cry or throw jelly beans when I first saw the Beatles on the Ed Sullivan Show. An eighth-grader would have been old enough to revert to childhood, but I was too young to act anything but old. So mostly we laughed at them. We

were in fifth grade, the year of rationality, the calm before the storm. We still screamed when the boys came near us (which they rarely did) and said they had cooties. Barbie dolls tempted us. That was the year when I got my first Barbie. Perhaps they were produced earlier, but they didn't reach New Hampshire till late that fall, and the stores were always sold out. So at the close of our doll-playing careers there was a sudden dramatic switch from lumpy, round-bellied Betsy Wetsys and stiff-legged little-girl dolls to slim, curvy Barbie, just 11 inches tall, with a huge, expensive wardrobe that included a filmy black negligee and a mouth that made her look as if she'd just swallowed a lemon.

19   Barbie wasn't just a toy, but a way of living that moved us suddenly from tea parties to dates with Ken at the Soda Shoppe. Our short careers with Barbie, before junior high sent her to the attic, built up our expectations for teen-age life before we had developed the sophistication to go along with them. Children today are accustomed to having a tantalizing youth culture all around them. (They play with Barbie in the nursery school.) For us, it broke like a cloudburst, without preparation. Caught in the deluge, we were torn—wanting to run for shelter but tempted, also, to sing in the rain.

20   Marijuana and the class of '71 moved through high school together. When we came in, as freshmen, drugs were still strange and new; marijuana was smoked only by a few marginal figures while those in the mainstream guzzled beer. It was called pot then—the words grass and dope came later; hash and acid and pills were almost unheard of. By my sophomore year, lots of the seniors and even a few younger kids were trying it. By the time I was a junior—in 1969—grass was no longer reserved for the hippies; basketball players and cheerleaders and boys with crew-cuts and boys in black-leather jackets all smoked. And with senior year—maybe because of the nostalgia craze—there was an odd liquor revival. In my last month of school, a major bust led to the suspension of half a dozen boys. They were high on beer.

21   Now people are saying that the drug era is winding down. (It's those statisticians with their graphs again, charting social phenomena like the rise and fall of hemlines.) I doubt if it's real, this abandonment of marijuana. But the frenzy is gone, certainly, the excitement and the fear of getting caught and the worry of where to get good stuff. What's happened to dope is what happens to a new record: you play it constantly, full volume, at first. Then, as you get to know the songs, you play them less often, not because you're tired of them exactly, but just because you know them. They're with you always, but quietly, in your head.

22   My position was a difficult one, all through those four years when grass took root in Oyster River High. I was on the side of all those things that went along with smoking dope—the clothes, the music, the books, the candidates. More and more of my friends smoked, and many people weren't completely my friends, I think, because I didn't. Drugs took on a disproportionate importance. Why was it I could spend half a dozen evenings with someone without his ever asking me what I thought of Beethoven or Picasso but always, in the first half hour, he'd ask whether I smoked?

23   It became—like hair length and record collection—a symbol of who you were, and you couldn't be all the other things—progressive and creative and free-thinking—without taking that crumpled roll of dry, brown vegetation and holding it to your lips. You are what you eat—or what you smoke, or what you don't smoke. And when you say "like—you know," you're speaking the code, and suddenly the music of the Grateful Dead and the poetry of Bob Dylan and the general brilliance of Ken Kesey all belong to you as if, in those three fuzzy, mumbled words, you'd created art yourself and uttered the wisdom of the universe.

24   The freshman women's dorm at Yale has no house mother. We have no check-in hours or drinking rules or punishments for having boys in our rooms past midnight. A guard sits by the door to offer, as they assured us at the beginning of the year, physical—not moral—protection. All of which makes it easy for many girls who feel, after high-school curfews and dating regulations, suddenly liberated. (The first week of school last fall, many girls stayed out all night, every night, displaying next morning the circles under their eyes the way some girls show off engagement rings.)

25   We all received the "Sex at Yale" book, a thick, black pamphlet filled with charts and diagrams and a lengthy discussion of contraceptive methods. And at the first women's assembly, the discussion moved quickly from course-signing-up procedures to gynecology, where it stayed for much of the evening. Somebody raised her hand to ask where she could fill her pill prescription, someone else wanted to know about abortions. There was no standing in the middle any more—you had to either take out a pen and paper and write down the phone numbers they gave out or stare stonily ahead, implying that those were numbers *you* certainly wouldn't be needing. From then on it seemed the line had been drawn.

26   But of course the problem is that no lines, no barriers, exist. Where, five years ago a girl's decisions were made for her (she had to be in at 12 and, if she was found—in—with her boyfriend . . .); today the decision rests with her alone. She is surrounded by knowl-

edgeable, sexually experienced girls and if *she* isn't willing to sleep with her boyfriend, somebody else will. It's peer-group pressure, 1972 style—the embarrassment of virginity.

27   Everyone is raised on nursery rhymes and nonsense stories. But it used to be that when you grew up, the nonsense disappeared. Not for us—it is at the core of our music and literature and art and, in fact, of our lives. Like characters in an Ionesco play, we take absurdity unblinking. In a world where military officials tell us "We had to destroy the village in order to save it," Dylan lyrics make an odd kind of sense. They aren't meant to be understood; they don't jar our sensibilities because we're used to *non sequiturs*. We don't take anything too seriously these days. (Was it a thousand earthquake victims or a million? Does it matter?) The casual butcher's-operation in the film "M*A*S*H" and the comedy in Vonnegut and the album cover showing John and Yoko, bareback, are all part of the new absurdity. The days of the Little Moron joke and the elephant joke and the knock-knock joke are gone. It sounds melodramatic, but the joke these days is life.

28   You're not supposed to care too much any more. Reactions have been scaled down from screaming and jelly-bean-throwing to nodding your head and maybe—if the music really gets to you (and music's the only thing that does any more)—tapping a finger. We need a passion transfusion, a shot of energy in the veins. It's what I'm most impatient with, in my generation—this languid, I-don't-give-a-s——ism that stems in part, at least, from a culture of put-ons in which any serious expression of emotion is branded sentimental and old-fashioned. The fact that we set such a premium on being cool reveals a lot about my generation; the idea is not to care. You can hear it in the speech of college students today: cultivated monotones, low volume, punctuated with four-letter words that come off sounding only bland. I feel it most of all on Saturday morning, when the sun is shining and the crocuses are about to bloom and, walking through the corridors of my dorm, I see there isn't anyone awake.

29   I'm basically an optimist. Somehow, no matter what the latest population figures say, I feel everything will work out—just like on TV. I may doubt man's fundamental goodness, but I believe in his power to survive. I say, sometimes, that I wonder if we'll be around in 30 years, but then I forget myself and speak of "when I'm 50. . . ." Death has touched me now—from Vietnam and Biafra and a car accident that makes me buckle my seat belt—but like negative numbers and the sound of a dog whistle (too high-pitched for human ears), it's not a concept I can comprehend. I feel immortal while all the signs around me proclaim that I'm not.

30   We feel cheated, many of us—the crop of 1953—which is why we complain about inheriting problems we didn't cause. (Childhood notions of justice, reinforced by Perry Mason, linger on. Why should I clean up someone else's mess? Who can I blame?) We're excited also, of course: I can't wait to see how things turn out. But I wish I weren't quite so involved, I wish it weren't my life that's being turned into a suspense thriller.

31   When my friends and I were little, we had big plans. I would be a famous actress and singer, dancing on the side. I would paint my own sets and compose my own music, writing the script and the lyrics and reviewing the performance for the New York Times. I would marry and have three children (they don't allow us dreams like that any more) and we would live, rich and famous (donating lots to charity, of course, and periodically adopting orphans), in a house we designed ourselves. When I was older I had visions of good works. I saw myself in South American rain forests and African deserts, feeding the hungry and healing the sick with an obsessive selflessness, I see now, as selfish, in the end, as my original plans for stardom.

32   Now my goal is simpler. I want to be happy. And I want comfort—nice clothes, a nice house, good music and good food, and the feeling that I'm doing some little thing that matters. I'll vote and I'll give to charity, but I won't give myself. I feel a sudden desire to buy land—not a lot, not as a business investment, but just a small plot of earth so that whatever they do to the country I'll have a place where I can go—a kind of fallout shelter, I guess. As some people prepare for their old age, so I prepare for my 20's. A little house, a comfortable chair, peace and quiet—retirement sounds tempting.

Vocabulary

apathetic	symmetry	trauma
germinate	inevitable	perverse
banality	revert	sophistication
tantalize	gynecology	*non sequitur*

Topics for Discussion

1. Is 18 years old too young to look back on life? Have you ever stopped to look back on your life?

2. Do you agree with Maynard that hers "is the generation of unfulfilled expectations"? What expectations are unfulfilled?

3. "We don't take anything too seriously these days." Do you agree with this? What do you take seriously?

4. How much of this essay can you identify with? Were your high school years anything like those described by Maynard?

5. Maynard says she feels cheated. Why?

6. In the last paragraph Maynard outlines her goals. Are these goals similar to yours? How do yours differ? What do Maynard's goals reveal about her?

Rhetorical Considerations

1. This is a very personal essay. What characteristics of the personal essay can you find here? Can one write a personal essay without overusing the pronoun "I"? Does Maynard overuse this pronoun?

2. Maynard says that "generalizing is dangerous." How much does she substantiate her own generalizations? How much of this essay is fact and how much is opinion?

3. Does Maynard make any allusions to out-of-date people or things? How topical is the essay?

4. Does this essay have a thesis? Can you state it in one sentence?

5. How does Maynard use repetition to provide coherence? See, for example, paragraphs 1–3.

What I Have Lived For

Bertrand Russell

Bertrand Russell (1872–1970) received the Nobel Prize for literature in 1950. However, he is perhaps most famous for his work in theoretical mathematics and for his social activism. Together with Alfred North Whitehead he published Principia Mathematica *(1910–1913). Throughout his long life, Russell campaigned against war, most recently against American atrocities in Vietnam.*

1   Three passions, simple but overwhelmingly strong, have governed my life: the longing for love, the search for knowledge, and unbearable pity for the suffering of mankind. These passions, like

great winds, have blown me hither and thither, in a wayward course, over a deep ocean of anguish, reaching to the very verge of despair.

2   I have sought love, first, because it brings ecstasy—ecstasy so great that I would often have sacrificed all the rest of life for a few hours of this joy. I have sought it, next, because it relieves loneliness—that terrible loneliness in which one shivering consciousness looks over the rim of the world into the cold unfathomable lifeless abyss. I have sought it, finally, because in the union of love I have seen, in a mystic miniature, the prefiguring vision of the heaven that saints and poets have imagined. This is what I sought, and though it might seem too good for human life, this is what—at last—I have found.

3   With equal passion I have sought knowledge. I have wished to understand the hearts of men. I have wished to know why the stars shine. And I have tried to apprehend the Pythagorean power by which number holds sway above the flux. A little of this, but not much, I have achieved.

4   Love and knowledge, so far as they were possible, led upward toward the heavens. But always pity brought me back to earth. Echoes of cries of pain reverberate in my heart. Children in famine, victims tortured by oppressors, helpless old people a hated burden to their sons, and the whole world of loneliness, poverty, and pain make a mockery of what human life should be. I long to alleviate the evil, but I cannot, and I too suffer.

5   This has been my life. I have found it worth living, and would gladly live it again if the chance were offered me.

Vocabulary

anguish	ecstasy	unfathomable
abyss	mystic	Pythagorean

Topics for Discussion

1. What, if any, are the passions which govern your life? Reflect on Russell's essay, then on your own existence, and try to write a similar essay. If you find this extremely difficult, it may be that you cannot capture the tone of a ninety-year-old man, close to death, who is reflecting on his past achievements, joys, and sorrows. Perhaps a different kind of essay is more appropriate for you, one which picks

some point in your recent past or near future as a major transition from one kind of life to another—from youth to maturity, for example. In this context, reflect on what your life has been for you and compare those reflections with what you would like your life to be. Write an essay, longer than Russell's, suggested by the comparison.

2. It has been said that twentieth-century nonreligious humanity is humanity without enduring values to live by, humanity without a center for the universe. Using words other than those found in this essay, state what values put order and permanence into existence for Russell. Are these values sufficient, do you think, for living a fulfilling and responsible life?

3. What do love and knowledge have to do with each other? Russell, who was a famous mathematician and scientist, asks the same question as little children—"Why do the stars shine?"—a question which, in its asking, evokes an emotional response. What other scientific questions evoke a similar response? How does one go about answering such questions?

4. What kind of love is Russell talking about in paragraph 2? Is this love spiritual, sexual, or both? Have you experienced similar ecstasy in love? If so, what would you give up in your future to experience similar ecstasy again? Do you think it is necessary to give up anything to have that experience?

5. What is your reaction to Russell's mention of *pity* in paragraph 4? Is pity a noble emotion? Does it do any good for the person pitied? Do you like to be pitied? Could Russell have chosen a better word or phrase? Make a list of some of the differences between pity and love, and, after discussion or some serious thought, write an essay from whatever ideas the list produces.

Rhetorical Considerations

1. See the Rhetorical Analysis at the end of this chapter for an explanation of the devices Russell uses in this forceful and moving short essay.

2. Russell manages to say as much or more in these short paragraphs about the highly abstract concepts of love, knowledge, and pity than any dictionary definition or encyclopedia article could. He does this by creating an intensely personal bond with his reader. What devices does he use to create this bond?

3. Russell's life, like everyone's, must have been governed by hate, anger, ambivalence, and many other emotions and attitudes. Why does he center only on three—those he calls "passions"—for

discussion in his essay? Could his essay be extended to deal with other emotions and still retain its impact?

4. Russell mentions other feelings he has had in life—anguish and joy, for example. Make a list of some of your emotions and use this list as an organizing vehicle for a short personal essay.

Who Am I?

Marya Mannes

Marya Mannes is a nationally syndicated columnist in major United States newspapers and the author of two books: Message from a Stranger *(1948) and* But Will It Sell? *(1964).*

1   Who are you? You singly, not you together. When did it start—that long day's journey into self? When do you really begin to know what you believe and where you're going? When do you know that you are unique—separate—alone?

2   The time of discovery is different for everybody. Some people find themselves in early childhood, some in middle-age, some—the tragic ones—never.

3   I suggest that the first recognition comes when others try to tell you what you are. And although what happened in my generation is supposed to have no relevance to what happens in yours, I know when it happened to me.

4   I may have been six years old when aunts and uncles and cousins used to say: "You look just like your mother!" or "You're the image of your brother!"

5   Now, for reasons that have nothing to do with duty or discipline in that distant day, I loved my family. I loved them because they were interesting, handsome, talented, and loving people. I was lucky. But in spite of that, I felt an immediate, instinctive resistance to any suggestion that I was like them or like anybody else. I didn't want to be like anybody else. I was Me. Myself. Separate. Alone.

6   This is probably as good a time as any to say that if I use the first-person pronoun—if I refer from time to time to my own long, arduous, bumbling journey into self—it is not because of narcissism, but because I have always believed that the particular is more illuminating than the general. Perhaps my dependence as a writer on

direct observation rather than on scholarly research, on living example rather than on sociological method, is the natural result of illiteracy. I never went to college and therefore know much less than you people do. About books, I mean. Or the sciences.

7   But since the laboratory for the study of man is clearly life itself, then I have studied hard in the act of living, of looking, of feeling; involvement rather than detachment; doing as well as being.

8   We were talking of the first discoveries of uniqueness—of being oneself and no one else. Not your father, not your mother, not your sister, not your brother. I. Me.

9   It is then—when you begin not only to know it, but act it—that society moves in. Society says it wants people to be different but it doesn't really mean it. Parents like to believe their children are different from other children—smarter, of course, better-looking and so forth—but most parents are secretly disturbed when their children are *really* different—not like others at all. In fact, very early they start to pigeonhole you in certain ways.

10   Take the difference of sex, for instance. Little girls are pink, little boys are blue. Little girls want dolls, little boys want trains.

11   For a long time, for instance, the word "tom-boy" to a girl held undertones of worry and disapproval. All it meant was that the girl liked to play ball, climb trees, and skin her knees instead of wearing frilly dresses and curtseying. The companion word for boys, of course, was "sissy"—meaning the kid liked music and poetry and hated fighting. These ignorant and damaging labels have now been discredited, thanks largely to you and the more enlightened members of our society. But there is still, alas, a large Squareland left where growing girls are told from the age of twelve onward not only by their mothers but by the mass media that marriage is the only valid female goal and that Career is a dirty word.

12   Even now—even when you here know how silly it is (at least, I hope you do), most parents hear wedding bells the minute a girl is born, most parents see an executive office when a boy is born, and the relentless conditioning starts on its merry way. Educate a girl for the marriage market, educate a boy for success. That you, as a human being, as a separate identity, may not want or fit in with either of these goals is considered not a sign of independence but of deviation—pointing to the couch or—in social terms—failure.

13   That is why these same parents—and they are still a majority—are bewildered, depressed, or plain horrified when their adolescents openly refuse to accept these goals or to share any common identity with any past. Who on earth, their parents moan, will marry this stringy girl with her false eyelashes and shuffling

gait? Who will employ this bearded boy with his grunts and records, his pop and pot? On the other end, how gratified are parents when their clean-cut athletic sons get high marks and their clean and pretty daughters marry the clean-cut boys who get good jobs?

14   You know, I pity you. I pity you for reasons you might not suspect. I pity you because your search for self has been made so self-conscious. You are overexposed in and by the mass media, which never for one instant night and day stop telling you what you are and who you are. With us, decades ago, there was no radio and no television. As adolescents we seldom read papers (they never reported on us) or magazines. The word "teenager," thank God, never existed. From twelve to seventeen we were painful to our parents and not very attractive to ourselves. Our skins and bodies did strange things and we felt strange things. The world paid no attention to us. It didn't interview us, quote us, and ask our advice. We didn't expect it to. We had twenty-five to fifty cents a week to spend for allowance (rich kids got a dollar), but who needed it? Books were in the house or you could borrow them, movies were a quarter, and if you were lucky your family took you to occasional plays or concerts. School was sometimes boring, but we expected it to be. Nobody told us learning ought to be fun. When it was—well, great!

15   Nothing much external happened, except for trips with the family and meetings with friends. There was a lot of unfilled, unstructured, unplanned free time—with no messages coming in from anywhere to distract us, no entertainment at arm's length, no guidance counselors or psychiatrists to tell us what was bugging us. We had a vast amount of inner space to fill by ourselves. In this inner space there was room and time for that very tender, very vulnerable thing called "I" to be born—and grow.

16   For there are really two births—the first physical, the second spiritual. Both share something in common: Premature expulsion, premature exposure, can damage both foetus and soul. The prenatal fluid that protects the foetus until it is ready for air has its counterpart in the secret world of the yet unborn identity.

17   Now I want to make it quite clear that this secret world of child and adolescent is not a matter of protection from reality. Just because a child may grow up in the relative security of home and school and neighborhood doesn't mean that the human comedy-tragedy is not a part of daily life. You are not cut off from experience because the world you live in is physically small. On the contrary, you can be put off from real experience because the world has become too large.

18   And that is precisely why I pity you. You stand naked and

exposed in too large a world, and that prenatal sac of your soul has been so repeatedly punctured by external influences, persuasions, and pressures that it must take super-human will to keep yourself intact. Many of you don't. Or at least you find the only answer to a fragmented self in a fragmented life—or a withdrawal from life.

19   How, in any case, are you ever going to know what you are or who you are when these hundreds of voices are doing the job *for* you? How do you know how much of what you think and do is what you *really* think and want to do, or how much is the feedback from what you hear about yourselves—daily, hourly? A lot of it, of course, is true.

20   You *are* the new power, if only in numbers. You *are* rich, if only in dollars. You *are* smarter than your parents, if only in acquired knowledge. A lot of you take drugs and pills or cop out in communal huddles, living on handouts. I question whether you are more interested in sex than we were, or even more active. The difference here is that it's now so easy to come by, in beds as well as in books, that it may mean less. Obstacles are great aphrodisiacs.

21   I would like to think that those of you who hate war are a majority. I would like to think that those of you who believe that sweeping changes must be made in our whole social, legal, political and economic life are a majority and an acting majority at that.

22   Whatever you are, you can't do anything about making a better society and a better world until you are a productive human being. And you can't be a productive human being, sorting the world out, until you sort yourself out.

23   Until you really attain an expansion of consciousness—not of another world, through hallucination, but of this world, through illumination. Not long ago Professor Lettwin, that dynamic, free-wheeling bear of M.I.T., told an audience of high-school students and undergraduates in Boston that in order to do what they wanted to do—to change the disastrous drift of society—they would have to keep their wits about them. You must be conscious, he exhorted, you must at all times keep your sense of judgment intact. Anything that blurs, that weakens your judgmental values will, in time, make you ineffective. Only your judgment, consciously arrived at, only the intellect and senses in the service of human compassion—will take you where you *want* to go—where this new society *must* go.

24   This I would also passionately advocate. As a long-time rebel, a seeker of new adventures, a destroyer of old myths, I have come to believe that this total awareness is the greatest single attribute of identity, and most preciously to be guarded. That it can be chemically achieved I would very much doubt. For moments, maybe. For the long haul, no. It is one thing—and who doesn't need it?—to seek

escape from the pain of total awareness—in drink or pot. It is another to take the quick exit from reality with the distinct possibility that you may not make the reentry back. Or that if you do, you may never be yourself—your real, your useful, your creative self—again. Fly Now—Pay Later.

25   The price of conscious awareness is stiff—but not that stiff. The price is a very hard look at yourself—alone, and not bolstered by a crowd, a tribe—or even—a wife. And here is where I'm going to stick this already battered neck further out—on the institution of matrimony.

26   Your parents, I would imagine, consider your generation incomprehensible, sometimes frightening, and certainly unconventional. Everything you wear, grow on your face or head, think, believe, do, is way out of their norm.

27   Except marriage. In a world of undreamed-of scope and opportunity and choice, most of you do exactly what your parents did in a much more limited world. You rush to the altar to tie the legal tie from the age of eighteen onward to a girl no older. Here you are in full flower of body and mind (and I speak of both sexes) and with the only pure freedom of action you will ever know again, and you tie yourself to one mate and one hearth before you know who you are.

28   If you're lucky, you will find yourselves *through* each other—the ideal nature of love, the true—and rare—blessing of marriage.

29   If you're not lucky—and the evidence would call you a majority—you will be two half-persons, half-grown, prematurely bound, inhibiting each other's growth, choking up the road to your full development as a human being.

30   Many of our laws and institutions, as you well know, have not yet caught up with reality . . . the fact that men and women cannot be codified. So long as we do others no harm, how we choose to live is our own affair, and ours alone. How you choose to live is yours alone. And if you are able to bring about an intelligent society—I avoid the word "great"—one of the most important things you will have to do is remove the senseless stigmas that still prevail against single men or single women, and against whatever kind of love is the product of deep inner need.

31   One of your great influences already is that in your new sense of community—in part forced upon you by isolation from your elders—you have managed to blur already many of the lines of demarcation—between races, between sexes, between thought and feeling, between feeling and action—which have trapped the former generations in patterns of sterility. The best of you have not only discovered your conscience, but are living it.

32   But apart from the terrible issues of the day—to which the best

of you address your conscience—war in Vietnam, the brutal war in the streets—how much are you living it as individuals, how much in group conformity?

33   How brave, how independent are you when you are alone? I ask this chiefly of my own sex, for I wonder whether girls now really know and want the chances and choices that are open to them, or whether they have been so conditioned by history and habit that they slip back into the old patterns of their mothers the minute they graduate. Oddly enough, this supposed choice between marriage and a career never bothered my generation as much as it seems to have bothered the postwar ones. And I lay the blame for it on a mass media—mainly television, advertising, and women's magazines—which maintain the fiction that the only valid goal for women is marriage and children and domesticity (with a little community work thrown in), and that women who demand and seek more than this from life are at best unfulfilled and at worst unfeminine. It is about time that we realized that many women make better teachers than mothers, better actresses than wives, better mistresses than house-keepers, better diplomats than cooks. Just as many men are better rakes than lawnmowers and better dreamers than providers. We have lost a great deal of talent and wasted a great many lives in the perpetuation of these myths that are called "the role of men" or "the role of women." And just as you have managed to dissipate some of them in your dress, I hope you will dissipate others in your lives. The only thing you need to aspire to, the only ultimate identity you must discover, is that of a human being. The sex, believe it or not, is secondary.

34   But in the search for this human identity, I urge you to re-member one thing. I said before that our first recognition of it comes when we know we are not like anybody else, that we are unique. That is so.

35   But we did not spring into this world through galactic explosion—we did not even burst from the head of Zeus.

36   We came from somewhere. Not just the womb of our mothers and the seeds of our fathers but from a long, long procession of identities—whose genes we possess.

37   Whether we like it or not, we bear the past inside us. Good or bad, it cannot be excised, it cannot be rejected, . . . it should not be. Humanity is a continuous process, and without a past there is no future.

38   In your worship of Now, in your fierce insistence that only the present exists, that you are new on the face of the earth, owing nothing to history—you are cheating yourself. You are not only denying evolution but limiting your future.

39   You may say you have nothing in common with the preceding generation, you may lay the blame for the present entirely on their shoulders and on the mistakes of the past. But what of the others who came before? What of the great rebels, the great innovators, the great voices without which no light, no truth would ever have prevailed? Much of what poets and philosophers and artists and scientists said ten centuries ago is as valid now as it was then. Where would you be, where would we be, without them?

40   On a much humbler level, I remember the photograph albums so many families kept when I was a child. There, in our own, were these strange faces and strange clothes of the dead who preceded me: the tall, gaunt old baker in Poland, the opera singer in Germany, the immigrant furniture dealer in New York, the violinist in Breslau, the General near Kiel, the incredible web of cells and genes contained in my own self.

41   It took me more than twenty years to realize that they lived in me, that I was part of them, and that in spite of distance, time, and difference, I was part of them. I was not, in short, alone.

42   And neither are you. I suppose what I am asking for here is that, along with your pride of generation, you somehow maintain compassion for those who preceded you as well as for those who will come after you.

43   If you will, this is a community just as important as any living community of your own age and time, and if you deny your connection with it, you deny evolution, you deny the human race.

44   Don't play it too cool. The ultimate pattern of life is immense, there are other worlds in other galaxies that may have far transcended ours, and if you aren't turned on more by a shower of meteors than by an electric circus, you're half dead already.

45   You won't find yourself in a crowded room. You may find yourself under the crowded sky of night, where—if you attach yourself to a single star—you will discover that you are one of many millions, but still—One.

46   Listen to your own drum and march to it. You may fall on your face—but then, anybody who never does is—Nobody!

Vocabulary

arduous	narcissism	gait
prenatal	aphrodisiac	stigma
demarcation	dissipate	

Topics for Discussion

1. Among primitive tribes it is a belief that a newborn baby comes into the world as a specific replacement for someone in the extended family who has recently died. For example, the possessions and name of a recently deceased grandfather may be given to an infant boy. What analogous practice does Mannes suggest still survives in modern life? Do such practices rob the individual of his/her identity?

2. What of Mannes's discussion of the socialization of children according to sex roles? Objectively evaluate whether what she says is or is not generally true. Do you have an opinion relating to this subject? What is it? What kinds of arguments would you use to defend it? Write an essay systematically employing those arguments.

3. Mannes quickly mentions several topics important to young people: sex, money, drugs, war. Do you think she is in touch with your generation with respect to these matters?

4. Evaluate Mannes's position on "the role of men" and "the role of women."

5. Mannes urges her audience not to divorce itself from history. Do you see a contempt for the past, a refusal to investigate history among people you know? Is this contempt justified, in your opinion, or do you think that, in the words of George Santayana (*who was he?*), "those who cannot remember the past are condemned to repeat it"?

Rhetorical Considerations

1. The first paragraph is composed of four questions which the author cannot answer because they are directed at your personal experience. What rhetorical strategy is Mannes setting up in asking these questions?

2. The second sentence of the second paragraph contains a good example of parallel structure. Why does Mannes include a variation in the last of the three parallel items?

3. Mannes says that "the particular is more illuminating than the general." Does she implement this sound rhetorical principle in her essay? Cite specific paragraphs in which she does not.

4. Do you think Mannes's comments about not having gone to college have a positive effect on her readers? Is she trying to gain a solid rhetorical foothold by using the disguised cliché "I went to the college of hard knocks"?

5. Examine Mannes's recounting of her personal background. What does she indirectly reveal about the audience she is speaking to?

6. Honestly, do you basically view Mannes's essay as inspiring, or as a pasting together of clichés? Is there a third evaluative position?

7. Suggest ways of joining sequences of short paragraphs (e.g., paragraphs 2–5 and 25–29).

Of the Passing
of the First-Born

W. E. B. DuBois

William Edward Burghardt DuBois (1868–1963) was a major black writer and historian. For more than twenty years he edited the NAACP journal, Crisis.

1   "Unto you a child is born," sang the bit of yellow paper that fluttered into my room one brown October morning. Then the fear of fatherhood mingled wildly with the joy of creation; I wondered how it looked and how it felt,—what were its eyes, and how its hair curled and crumpled itself. And I thought in awe of her,—she who had slept with Death to tear a man-child from underneath her heart, while I was unconsciously wandering. I fled to my wife and child, repeating the while to myself half wonderingly, "Wife and child? Wife and child?"—fled fast and faster than boat and steam-car, and yet must ever impatiently await them; away from the hard-voiced city, away from the flickering sea into my own Berkshire Hills that sit all sadly guarding the gates of Massachusetts.

2   Up the stairs I ran to the wan mother and whimpering babe, to the sanctuary on whose altar a life at my bidding had offered itself to win a life, and won. What is this tiny formless thing, this newborn wail from an unknown world,—all head and voice? I handle it curiously, and watch perplexed its winking, breathing, and sneezing. I did not love it then; it seemed a ludicrous thing to love; but her I loved, my girl-mother, she whom now I saw unfolding like the glory of the morning—the transfigured woman. Through her I came to love the wee thing, as it grew strong; as its little soul unfolded

itself in twitter and cry and half-formed word, and as its eyes caught the gleam and flash of life. How beautiful he was, with his olive-tinted flesh and dark gold ringlets, his eyes of mingled blue and brown, his perfect little limbs, and the soft voluptuous roll which the blood of Africa had moulded into his features! I held him in my arms, after we had sped far away to our Southern home,—held him, and glanced at the hot red soil of Georgia and the breathless city of a hundred hills, and felt a vague unrest. Why was his hair tinted with gold? An evil omen was golden hair in my life. Why had not the brown of his eyes crushed out and killed the blue?—for brown were his father's eyes, and his father's father's. And thus in the Land of the Color-line I saw, as it fell across my baby, the shadow of the Veil.

3   Within the Veil was he born, said I; and there within shall he live,—a Negro and a Negro's son. Holding in that little head—ah, bitterly!—the unbowed pride of a hunted race, clinging with that tiny dimpled hand—ah, wearily!—to a hope not hopeless but unhopeful, and seeing with those bright wondering eyes that peer into my soul a land whose freedom is to us a mockery and whose liberty a lie. I saw the shadow of the Veil as it passed over my baby, I saw the cold city towering above the blood-red land. I held my face beside his little cheek, showed him the star-children and the twinkling lights as they began to flash, and stilled with an even-song the unvoiced terror of my life.

4   So sturdy and masterful he grew, so filled with bubbling life, so tremulous with the unspoken wisdom of a life but eighteen months distant from the All-life,—we were not far from worshipping this revelation of the divine, my wife and I. Her own life builded and moulded itself upon the child; he tinged her every dream and idealized her every effort. No hands but hers must touch and garnish those little limbs; no dress or frill must touch them that had not wearied her fingers; no voice but hers could coax him off to Dream-land, and she and he together spoke some soft and unknown tongue and in it held communion. I too mused above this little white bed; saw the strength of my own arm stretched onward through the ages through the newer strength of his; saw the dream of my black fathers stagger a step onward in the wild phantasm of the world; heard in his baby voice the voice of the Prophet that was to rise within the Veil.

5   And so we dreamed and loved and planned by fall and winter, and the full flush of the long Southern spring, till the hot winds rolled from the fetid Gulf, till the roses shivered and the still stern sun quivered its awful light over the hills of Atlanta. And then one night the little feet pattered wearily to the wee white bed, and the tiny

hands trembled; and a warm flushed face tossed on the pillow, and we knew baby was sick. Ten days he lay there,—a swift week and three endless days, wasting, wasting away. Cheerily the mother nursed him the first days, and laughed into the little eyes that smiled again. Tenderly then she hovered round him, till the smile fled away and Fear crouched beside the little bed.

6   Then the day ended not, and night was a dreamless terror, and joy and sleep slipped away. I hear now that Voice at midnight calling me from dull and dreamless trance,—crying, "The Shadow of Death! The Shadow of Death!" Out into the starlight I crept, to rouse the gray physician,—the Shadow of Death, the Shadow of Death. The hours trembled on; the night listened; the ghastly dawn glided like a tired thing across the lamplight. Then we two alone looked upon the child as he turned toward us with great eyes, and stretched his stringlike hands,—the Shadow of Death! And we spoke no word, and turned away.

7   He died at eventide, when the sun lay like a brooding sorrow above the western hills, veiling its face; when the winds spoke not, and the trees, the great green trees he loved, stood motionless. I saw his breath beat quicker and quicker, pause, and then his little soul leapt like a star that travels in the night and left a world of darkness in its train. The day changed not; the same tall trees peeped in at the windows, the same green grass glinted in the setting sun. Only in the chamber of death writhed the world's most piteous thing—a childless mother.

8   I shirk not. I long for work. I pant for a life full of striving. I am no coward, to shrink before the rugged rush of the storm, nor even quail before the awful shadow of the Veil. But hearken, O Death! Is not this my life hard enough,—is not that dull land that stretches its sneering web about me cold enough,—is not all the world beyond these four little walls pitiless enough, but that thou must needs enter here,—thou, O Death? About my head the thundering storm beat like a heartless voice, and the crazy forest pulsed with the curses of the weak; but what cared I, within my home beside my wife and baby boy? Wast thou so jealous of one little coin of happiness that thou must needs enter there,—thou, O Death?

9   A perfect life was his, all joy and love, with tears to make it brighter,—sweet as a summer's day beside the Housatonic. The world loved him; the women kissed his curls, the men looked gravely into his wonderful eyes, and the children hovered and fluttered about him. I can see him now, changing like the sky from sparkling laughter to darkening frowns, and then to wondering thoughtfulness as he watched the world. He knew no color-line,

poor dear,—and the Veil, though it shadowed him, had not yet darkened half his sun. He loved the white matron, he loved his black nurse; and in his little world walked souls alone, uncolored and unclothed. I—yea, all men—are larger and purer by the infinite breadth of that one little life. She who in simple clearness of vision sees beyond the stars said when he had flown, "He will be happy There; he ever loved beautiful things." And I, far more ignorant, and blind by the web of mine own weaving, sit alone winding words and muttering, "If still he be, and he be There, and there be a There, let him be happy, O Fate!"

10   Blithe was the morning of his burial, with bird and song and sweet-smelling flowers. The trees whispered to the grass, but the children sat with hushed faces. And yet it seemed a ghostly unreal day,—the wraith of Life. We seemed to rumble down an unknown street behind a little white bundle of posies, with the shadow of a song in our ears. The busy city dinned about us; they did not say much, those pale-faced hurrying men and women; they did not say much,—they only glanced and said, "Niggers!"

11   We could not lay him in the ground there in Georgia, for the earth there is strangely red; so we bore him away to the northward, with his flowers and his little folded hands. In vain, in vain!—for where, O God! beneath thy broad blue sky shall my dark baby rest in peace,—where Reverence dwells, and Goodness, and a Freedom that is free?

12   All that day and all that night there sat an awful gladness in my heart,—nay, blame me not if I see the world thus darkly through the Veil,—and my soul whispers ever to me, saying, "Not dead, not dead, but escaped; not bond, but free." No bitter meanness now shall sicken his baby heart till it die a living death, no taunt shall madden his happy boyhood. Fool that I was to think or wish that this little soul should grow choked and deformed within the Veil! I might have known that yonder deep unwordly look that ever and anon floated past his eyes was peering far beyond this narrow Now. In the poise of his little curl-crowned head did there not sit all that wild pride of being which his father had hardly crushed in his own heart? For what, forsooth, shall a Negro want with pride amid the studied humiliations of fifty million fellows? Well sped, my boy, before the world had dubbed your ambition insolence, had held your ideals unattainable, and taught you to cringe and bow. Better far this nameless void that stops my life than a sea of sorrow for you.

13   Idle words; he might have borne his burden more bravely than we,—aye, and found it lighter too, some day; for surely, surely this is not the end. Surely there shall yet dawn some mighty morning to

lift the Veil and set the prisoned free. Not for me,—I shall die in my bonds,—but for fresh young souls who have not known the night and waken to the morning; a morning when men ask of the workman, not "Is he white?" but "Can he work?" When men ask artists, not "Are they black?" but "Do they know?" Some morning this may be, long, long years to come. But now there wails, on that dark shore within the Veil, the same deep voice, *Thou shalt forego!* And all have I foregone at that command, and with small complaint,—all save that fair young form that lies so coldly wed with death in the nest I had builded.

14　　If one must have gone, why not I? Why may I not rest me from this restlessness and sleep from this wide waking? Was not the world's alembic, Time, in his young hands, and is not my time waning? Are there so many workers in the vineyard that the fair promise of this little body could lightly be tossed away? The wretched of my race that line the alleys of the nation sit fatherless and unmothered; but Love sat beside his cradle, and in his ear Wisdom waited to speak. Perhaps now he knows the All-love, and needs not to be wise. Sleep, then, child,—sleep till I sleep and waken to a baby voice and the ceaseless patter of little feet—above the Veil.

Vocabulary

wan	sanctuary	ludicrous
transfigured	voluptuous	tremulous
communion	phantasm	coin
blithe	wraith	insolence
alembic		

Topics for Discussion

1. This essay is DuBois's account of the death of his son. What makes this narrative different from other narratives about death? (See the other essays on death in this section.)

2. Why does DuBois fear fatherhood?

3. Why was DuBois's son's golden hair an evil omen?

4. What is the Veil that DuBois speaks of?

5. How old is DuBois's son when he dies? How does the boy's age heighten the sense of loss?

6. Toward the end of his essay DuBois has conflicting emotions over his son's death. What emotions does he feel? What is his resolution of the conflict?

Rhetorical Considerations

1. Examine DuBois's diction in this essay. How carefully has he chosen his words? Look particularly at the descriptions of his son in paragraphs 2 and 4. What kind of words does he use to describe his son and the things his son does? What does this essay teach you about concrete vs. abstract diction, about denotation and connotation?

2. Why does DuBois capitalize some words in the middle of sentences?

3. Why does DuBois use such words as "nay," "forsooth," "thou," and "aye"? What effect does this create?

4. DuBois uses a great variety of sentence structures. Examine some of the variety. Note especially his use of both very long and very short sentences. Note also internal breaks (dashes, commas) in his longer sentences. What effect is achieved through sentence variety in paragraph 8, for example?

5. What is the tone of this essay? How does DuBois achieve it?

Roxanne of Watts, California

Carolyn See

Carolyn See (b. 1934) frequently contributes essays to Atlantic *and to the* Los Angeles Times Magazine. *She is the author of* The Rest is Done with Mirrors *(1970).*

1   When domestic misery hits in Watts, it immediately and inextricably combines with social disaster. Consider Roxanne, who had lived in Watts for about seven years. Her man left her on the day of Kennedy's assassination in 1963, and she remembers not knowing

which she was crying for—her President's death, or her man's absence. She wasn't in enough control to delegate this tear for this, this for that. Roxanne and her sister were raised in Arkansas by strict, prosperous parents. The girls "went bad"—became pregnant—as teenagers, their parents departing from the Negro stereotype by disowning them. Their parents don't write now, or send money, or ask for pictures of their numerous grandchildren.

2   Like thousands of whites and blacks before them, Roxanne and her sister came to Los Angeles and began to live the strange, isolated, present-tense life of people new to Southern California. Roxanne brought two children with her, both illegitimate, from two different casual encounters. It's not that she wanted them to be casual. Roxanne describes herself as the kind of woman no man would stay with. She hasn't a dazzling personality or ready wit. She isn't cut out to be someone's mistress, but someone's wife. She wants to take care of her children and keep a house and wait all day for her husband to come home and tell her his ideas, his experiences. Waiting is Roxanne's most distinctive trait, but she isn't waiting for anyone. She has never lived with a man for over a week, and those weeks are months apart. Roxanne refutes the theory that Negro women are always strong, competent and tough. She is gentle and shy, and these typically "feminine" attributes have almost ruined her life.

3   Hearing about Roxanne, you expect to see someone sadly plain. In fact, she is stunning and doesn't know it, with a perfect young body and hair worn casually in loose curls, reminiscent of Nancy Wilson as much as anyone else. But she's Nancy Wilson in a shiny blue gabardine skirt, a cheap, see-through nylon blouse, scuffed slippers, and one 79-cent touch of bravado—a red lace bra. Roxanne is all alone. She sits alone in her house in back of another house, denied even the company of the street. She has her children for company—four of them now—but no friends.

4   Roxanne's house is built in the Spanish style of the 1920s. The living room has a beamed ceiling stenciled with antiqued cabbage roses. The art work is 40 years old and faded into delightful shades of green and rose and brown. The front door is fake hand-hewn wood with giant hinges. The walls have ornate wrought-iron electric fixtures. It's the kind of house you walk into and think, "Oh for a couple of gallons of white paint!" Then, sitting a while, you see the holes in the plaster, holes in the linoleum, the torn front screen where flies come in. And the darkness of the kitchen—dark because some previous tenant painted the windows to save the expense of buying curtains. A naked wire dangles from one of the fixtures. The

television set is broken. The plumbing smells bad. You see two or three roaches, and Roxanne says she's afraid at night for the children because of the rats. The lawn in front is 7 inches high, and turning brown. Even a visitor is overcome with lassitude, fatigue, domestic despair. All these things could be fixed—but how? How does a woman patch linoleum or plaster? Or bring home a new screen door in a car she hasn't got? Or deal definitively with a naked electric wire? Part of Roxanne's budget goes for insect spray (as much a staple of the urban poor as chicken wings or grits or greens or cheap wine) but the roaches are in the walls and she can't afford an exterminator at $210 a month. If Roxanne were tough or bossy or even calculatingly sexy, she might get someone to help her with these chores, but she is not.

5   Roxanne's dealings with men—she gives herself in a kind of desperate, joyless romanticism—have changed her life from difficult to unbearable. Her two youngest children have the same father, a man Roxanne is wildly in love with but rarely sees. He has a family of his own. Roxanne named these two children after him and asked him through the courts for child support, but hasn't otherwise interfered in his personal life. The courts ruled against her, throwing the case out of court for lack of evidence. When she found out, she didn't cry. She'd had too much trouble getting the two little ones down for their naps. Instead, she bent over in her chair until her face almost touched her knees, she sucked on her lips, she clasped her arms around the calves of her legs and stayed that way for some time. Later on that night, alone, she cried.

Vocabulary

domestic	inextricably	stereotype
lassitude	fatigue	grits
greens		

Topics for Discussion

1. Is it possible to tell anything about a person just by looking? What do you look at first—facial expression, body movement, clothing?

2. What can you tell about Roxanne just by looking?

3. Roxanne's most distinctive trait is waiting. How does this characteristic contribute to her condition in life?

4. What does the essay emphasize about Roxanne and her life?

5. What does the description of Roxanne's house say about Roxanne?

Rhetorical Considerations

1. Is this a formal or informal essay? Cite evidence from the essay to support your choice.

2. What concrete, specific details are used to describe Roxanne and her life? For what purpose and effect are these details? Are some details missing? Are some stressed and others suppressed?

3. There is a tone of hopelessness in this essay. How is this tone communicated?

4. How does See use rhetorical questions and unexpected details to help describe Roxanne? See especially paragraph 4.

5. Examine the final two sentences of the essay. How does See use sentence variety to achieve an effective conclusion?

The Woman from America

Bessie Head

Bessie Head (b. 1937) was formerly a primary school teacher in South Africa and Botswana and is a freelance writer and novelist. She is author of When Rain Clouds Gather *(1969) and* Maru *(1971).*

1   This woman from America married a man of our village and left her country to come and live with him here. She descended on us like an avalanche. People are divided into two camps, those who feel a fascinated love and those who fear a new thing. The terrible thing is that those who fear are always in the majority. This woman and her husband and children have to be sufficient to themselves

because everything they do is not the way people here do it. Most terrible of all is the fact that they really love each other and the husband effortlessly and naturally keeps his eyes on his wife alone. In this achievement he is seventy years ahead of all the men here.

2   We are such a lot of queer people in the Southern part of Africa. We have felt all forms of suppression and are subdued. We lack the vitality, the push, the devil-may-care temperament of the people of the north of Africa. Life has to seep down to us from there and that pattern is already establishing itself. They do things first, then we. We are always going to be confederators and not initiators. We are very materialistically minded, and I think this adds to our fear. People who hoard little bits of things cannot throw out and expand, and, in doing so, keep in circulation a flowing current of wealth. Basically, we are mean, selfish. We eat each other all the time and God help poor Botswana at the bottom.

3   Then, into this narrow, constricted world came the woman from America like an avalanche upon us. Some people keep hoping she will go away one day, but already her big strong stride has worn the pathways of the village flat. She is everywhere about because she is a woman, resolved and unshakeable in herself. To make matters worse or more disturbing she comes from the West side of America, somewhere near California. I gather from her conversation that people from the West are stranger than most people, and California is a place where odd and weird cults spring up every day. For instance, she once told me about the Church-of-the-Headless-Chicken! It seems an old woman bought a chicken but the place where she bought it was very haphazard about killing and plucking fowls. They did not sever the head properly and when the old woman brought the chicken home and placed it on the kitchen table, it sprang up out of the newspaper and began walking about with no head and no feathers—quite naked. It seems then that the old woman saw a vision, grabbed the chicken and ran next door to a neighbour who had been bed-ridden for many years, and, in great excitement, told him the strange happening. The poor old bed-ridden neighbour leapt from the bed healed of his ailment, and a miracle had been performed. The story spread like wild-fire and in a matter of hours money was collected, a congregation formed, and the Church-of-the-Headless-Chicken was born. The chicken was interviewed by many newspapers and kept alive for some months on soluble food mixture dropped into its open gullet!

4   Then, another thing too. People of the West of America must be the most oddly beautiful people in the world; at least this woman from the West is the most oddly beautiful person I have ever seen.

Every cross current of the earth seems to have stopped in her and blended into an amazing harmony. She has a big dash of Africa, a dash of Germany, some Cherokee, and heaven knows what else. Her feet are big and her body is as tall and straight and strong as a mountain tree. Her neck curves up high and her thick black hair cascades down her back like a wild and tormented stream. I cannot understand her eyes though, except that they are big, black and startled like those of a wild free buck racing against the wind. Often they cloud over with a deep, intense brooding look.

5   It took a great deal of courage to become friends with a woman like that. Like everyone here I am timid and subdued. Authority, everything can subdue me; not because I like it that way but because authority carries the weight of an age pressing down on life. It is terrible then to associate with a person who can shout authority down. Her shouting matches with authority are the terror and sensation of the village. It has come down to this. Either the woman is unreasonable or authority is unreasonable, and everyone in his heart would like to admit that authority is unreasonable. In reality, the rule is: If authority does not like you then you are the outcast and humanity associates with you at their peril. So, try always to be on the right side of authority, for the sake of peace, and please avoid the outcast. I do not say it will be like this forever. The whole world is crashing and inter-changing itself and even remote bush villages in Africa are not to be left out!

6   It was inevitable though that this woman and I should be friends. I have an overwhelming curiosity that I cannot keep within bounds. I passed by the house for almost a month, but one cannot crash in on people. Then one day a dog they have had puppies and my small son chased one of the puppies into the yard and I chased after him. Then one of the puppies became his and there had to be discussions about the puppy, the desert heat, and the state of the world, and as a result of curiosity an avalanche of wealth has descended on my life. My small hut-house is full of short notes written in a wide sprawling hand. I have kept them all because they are a statement of human generosity and the wide care-free laugh of a woman who is as busy as women the world over about things women always entangle themselves in—a man, children, a home . . . Like this . . .

7   "Have you an onion to spare? It's very quiet here this morning and I'm all fagged out from sweeping and cleaning the yard, shaking blankets, cooking, fetching water, bathing children, and there's still the floor inside to sweep, and dishes to wash and myself to bathe— it's endless!"

8   Or again . . .

"Have you an extra onion to give me until tomorrow? If so, I'd appreciate it. I'm trying to do something with these awful beans and I've run out of all my seasonings and spices. A neighbour brought us some spinach last night so we're in the green. I've got dirty clothes galore to wash and iron today."

9   Or . . .

"I'm sending the kids over to get 10 minutes' peace in which to restore my equilibrium. It looks as if rain is threatening. Please send them back immediately so they won't get caught out in it. Any fiction at your house? I could use some light diversion."

10   Or . . .

"I am only returning this tin in order to get these young folk out of my hair long enough *pour faire* my *toilette*. I've still cleaning up to do and I'm trying to collect my thoughts in preparation for the day's work. It looks like we face another scorcher today!"

11   And, very typical . . .

"This has been a very hectic morning! First, I was rushing to finish a few letters to send to you to post for me. Then it began to sprinkle slightly and I remembered you have no raincoat, so I decided to dash over there myself with the letters and the post key. At the very moment I was stepping out of the door, in stepped someone and that solved the letter-posting problem, but I still don't know whether there is any mail for me. I've lost my P.O. Box key! Did the children perhaps drop it out of that purse when they were playing with it at your house yesterday?"

12   Or my son keeps getting every kind of chest ailment and I prefer to decide it's the worst . . .

13   "What's this about whooping cough! Who diagnosed it? Didn't you say he had all his shots and vaccinations? The D.P.T. doesn't require a booster until after he's five years old. Diphtheria—Pertussis (Whooping cough)—Tetanus is one of the most reliable vaccinations. This sounds incredible! You know all three of mine and I have had hoarse, dry coughs but certainly it wasn't whooping cough. Here's Dr. Spock to reassure you!"

14   Sometimes too, conversations get all tangled up and the African night creeps all about and the candles are not lit and the conversation gets more entangled, intense; and the children fall asleep on the floor dazed by it all. The next day I get a book flung at me with vigorous exasperation . . .

15   "Here's C. P. Snow. Read him, dammit!! And dispel a bit of that fog in thy cranium. The chapters on Intellectuals and the Scientific Revolution are stimulating. Read it, dammit!!"

16   I am dazed too by Mr. C. P. Snow. Where do I begin to understand the industrial use of electronics, atomic energy, automation in a world of mud huts? What is a machine tool? he asks. What are the Two Cultures and the Scientific Revolution? The argument could be quaint to one who hasn't even one leg of culture to stand on. But it isn't really, because even a bush village in Africa begins to feel the tug and pull of the spider-web of life. Would Mr. Snow or someone please write me an explanation of what a machine tool is? I'd like to know. My address is: Serowe, Botswana, Africa.

17   The trouble with the woman from America is that people would rather hold off, sensing her world to be shockingly apart from theirs. But she is a new kind of American or even maybe will be a new kind of African. There isn't anyone here who does not admire her. To come from a world of chicken, hamburgers, T.V., escalators and what not to a village mud-hut and a life so tough, where the most you can afford to eat is ground millet and boiled meat? Sometimes you cannot afford to eat at all. Always you have to trudge miles for a bucket of water and carry it home on your head. And to do all this with loud, ringing, sprawling laughter?

18   Black people in America care about Africa and she has come here on her own as an expression of that love and concern. Through her too, one is filled with wonder for a country that breeds individuals about whom, without and within, rushes the wind of freedom. I have to make myself clear, though. She is a different person who has taken by force what America will not give black people. We had some here a while ago, sent out by the State Department. They were very jolly and sociable, but for the most innocent questions they kept saying: "We can't talk about the government. That's politics. We can't talk politics." Why did they come here if they were so afraid of what the American government thinks about what they might think or say in Africa? Why were they so afraid? Africa is not alive for them. It seems a waste of the State Department's money. It seems so strange a thing to send people on goodwill projects and at the same time those people are so afraid that they jump at the slightest shadow. Why are they so afraid of the government of America, which is a government of freedom and democracy? Here we are all afraid of authority and we never pretend anything else. Black people who are sent here by the State Department are tied up in some deep and shameful hypocrisy. It is a terrible pity because such things are destructive to them and hurtful to us.

19   The woman from America loves both Africa and America, independently. She can take what she wants from both and say: "Dammit." It is a most strenuous and difficult thing to do.

Vocabulary

subdue	confederator	initiator
soluble	gullet	cascade
toilette	*pour faire*	

Topics for Discussion

1. The author of this essay is an African resident of a village in Botswana. What does she tell you about herself, directly and indirectly, in this essay?

2. What does Head mean when she says, "We are such a lot of queer people in the Southern part of Africa"?

3. What is Head's attitude toward the woman from America? How is this attitude revealed in the essay?

4. Why do you think Head never mentions the name of the woman from America?

5. What does Head mean when she says that for Americans Africa is not alive?

6. Why does Head believe that "black people who are sent here by the State Department are tied up in some deep and shameful hypocrisy"?

Rhetorical Considerations

1. Examine the sentence style in this essay. What kind of sentences dominate the essay? What effect do these sentences achieve?

2. How are the first and last paragraphs in the essay related? How does Head tie them together?

3. What is the tone of the essay? Why (in paragraph 3) does Head tell the story of the headless chicken?

4. Head shifts back and forth between using the pronouns "I" and "we." To whom does she refer with each pronoun? What is significant about her use of each pronoun?

The Experience of Becoming a Person

Rollo May

Rollo May (b. 1909) has been one of the leaders of the existentialist movement in psychology, which is severely critical of established determinist views in that field. In short, he believes that it is possible for people to decide much of their own fate. His most widely known works include Love and Will *(1968) and* Man's Search for Himself *(1952).*

I

1   This consciousness of self, this capacity to see one's self as though from the outside, is the distinctive characteristic of man. A friend of mine has a dog who waits at his studio door all morning and, when anybody comes to the door, he jumps up and barks, wanting to play. My friend holds that the dog is saying in his barking: "Here is a dog who has been waiting all morning for someone to come to play with him. Are you the one?" This is a nice sentiment, and all of us who like dogs enjoy projecting such cozy thoughts into their heads. But actually this is exactly what the dog cannot say. He can show that he wants to play and entice you into throwing his ball for him, but he cannot stand outside himself and see himself as a dog doing these things. He is not blessed with the consciousness of self.

2   Inasmuch as this means the dog is also free from neurotic anxiety and guilt feelings, which are the doubtful blessings of the human being, some people would prefer to say the dog is not *cursed* with the consciousness of self. Walt Whitman, echoing this thought, envies the animals:

> I think I could turn and live with animals. . . .
> They do not sweat and whine about their condition,
> They do not lie awake in the dark and weep for their sins . . .

3   But actually man's consciousness of himself is the source of his highest qualities. It underlies his ability to distinguish between "I" and the world. It gives him the capacity to keep time, which is simply the ability to stand outside the present and to imagine oneself

back in yesterday or ahead in the day after tomorrow. Thus human beings can learn from the past and plan for the future. And thus man is the historical mammal in that he can stand outside and look at his history; and thereby he can influence his own development as a person, and to a minor extent he can influence the march of history in his nation and society as a whole. The capacity for consciousness of self also underlies man's ability to use symbols, which is a way of disengaging something from what it is, such as the two sounds which make up the word "table" and agreeing that these sounds will stand for a whole class of things. Thus man can think in abstractions like "beauty," "reason," and "goodness."

4   This capacity for consciousness of ourselves gives us the ability to see ourselves as others see us and to have empathy with others. It underlies our remarkable capacity to transport ourselves into someone else's parlor where we will be in reality next week, and then in imagination to think and plan how we will act. And it enables us to imagine ourselves in someone else's place, and to ask how we would feel and what we would do if we were this other person. No matter how poorly we use or fail to use or even abuse these capacities, they are the rudiments of our ability to begin to love our neighbor, to have ethical sensitivity, to see truth, to create beauty, to devote ourselves to ideals, and to die for them if need be.

5   To fulfill these potentialities is to be a person. This is what is meant when it is stated in the Hebrew-Christian religious tradition that man is created in the image of God.

6   But these gifts come only at a high price, the price of anxiety and inward crises. The birth of the self is no simple and easy matter. For the child now faces the frightful prospect of being out on his own, alone, and without the full protection of the decisions of his parents. It is no wonder that when he begins to feel himself an identity in his own right, he may feel terribly powerless in comparison with the great and strong adults around him. In the midst of a struggle over her dependency on her mother, one person had this eloquent dream: "I was in a little boat tied to a big boat. We were going through the ocean and big waves came up, piling over the sides of my boat. I wondered whether it was still tied to the big boat."

7   The healthy child, who is loved and supported but not coddled by his parents, will proceed in his development despite this anxiety and the crises that face him. And there may be no particular external signs of trauma or special rebelliousness. But when his parents consciously or unconsciously exploit him for their own ends or pleasure, or hate or reject him, so that he cannot be sure of minimal

support when he tries out his new independence, the child will cling to the parents and will use his capacity for independence only in the forms of negativity and stubbornness. If, when he first begins tentatively to say "No," his parents beat him down rather than love and encourage him, he thereafter will say "No" not as a form of true independent strength but as a mere rebellion.

8   Or if, as in the majority of cases in the present day, the parents themselves are anxious and bewildered in the tumultuous seas of the changing times, unsure of themselves and beset by self-doubts, their anxiety will carry over and lead the child to feel that he lives in a world in which it is dangerous to venture into becoming one's self.

9   This brief sketch is schematic, to be sure, and it is meant to give us as adults a kind of retrospective picture in the light of which we can better understand how one fails to achieve selfhood. Most of the data for these conflicts of childhood come from adults who are struggling, in dreams, memories or in present-day relations, to overcome what in their past lives originally blocked them in becoming fully born as persons. Almost every adult is, in greater or lesser degree, still struggling on the long journey to achieve selfhood on the basis of the patterns which were set in his early experiences in the family.

10   Nor do we for a moment overlook the fact that selfhood is always born in a social context. Genetically, Auden is quite right:

> . . . for the ego is a dream
> Till a neighbor's need by
> name create it.

Or, as we put it above, the self is always born and grows in interpersonal relationships. But no "ego" moves on into responsible selfhood if it remains chiefly the reflection of the social context around it. In our particular world in which conformity is the great destroyer of selfhood—in our society in which fitting the "pattern" tends to be accepted as the norm, and being "well-liked" is the alleged ticket to salvation—what needs to be emphasized is not only the admitted fact that we are to some extent created by each other but also our capacity to experience, and create, ourselves.

II

11   The consciousness of one's identity as a self certainly is not an intellectual idea. The French philosopher Descartes, at the beginning of the modern period three centuries ago, crawled into his

stove, according to legend, to meditate in solitude all one day trying to find the basic principle for human existence. He came out of his stove in the evening with the famous conclusion "I think, therefore I am." That is to say, I exist as a self because I am a thinking creature. But this is not enough. You and I never think of ourselves as an idea. We rather picture ourselves as doing something, like the psychologist writing his paper, and we then experience in imagination the feelings that we will have when we are in actuality doing that thing. That is to say, we experience ourselves as a thinking-intuiting-feeling and acting unity. The self is thus not merely the sum of the various "roles" one plays—it is the capacity by which one *knows* he plays these roles; it is the center from which one sees and is aware of these so-called different "sides" of himself.

12   After these perhaps high-sounding phrases, let us remind ourselves that after all the experience of one's own identity, or becoming a person, is the simplest experience in life even though at the same time the most profound. As everyone knows, a little child will react indignantly and strongly if you, in teasing, call him by the wrong name. It is as though you take away his identity—a most precious thing to him. In the Old Testament the phrase "I will blot out their names"—to erase their identity and it will be as though they never had existed—is a more powerful threat even than physical death.

13   Two little girl twins gave a vivid illustration of how important it is for a child to be a person in her own right. The little girls were good friends, a fact made especially possible because they complemented each other, one being extrovert and always in the center of the crowd if people came to visit in the house, the other being perfectly happy by herself to draw with her crayons and make up little poems. The parents, as parents generally do with twins, had dressed them alike when they went out walking. When they were about three and a half, the little extrovert girl began to want always to wear a different kind of dress from her sister. If she dressed after her sister, she would even, if necessary, wear an older and less pretty dress so that it would not be the same as the twin was wearing. Or if the sister dressed after her before they went out, she would beg her, sometimes weeping, not to put on the matching dress. For days this puzzled the parents, since the child was not anxious in other ways. Finally the parents, on a hunch, asked the little girl, "When you two go out walking, do you like to have the people on the street say, 'Look at these nice twins'?" Immediately the little girl exclaimed, "No, I want them to say, 'Look at these two different people!'"

14   This spontaneous exclamation, obviously revealing something very important to the little girl, cannot be explained by saying that the child wanted attention; for she would have gotten more attention if she had dressed as a twin. It shows, rather, her demand to be a person in her own right, to have personal identity—a need which was more important to her even than attention or prestige.

15   The little girl rightly stated the goal for every human being—to become a person. Every organism has one and only one central need in life, to fulfill its own potentialities. The acorn becomes an oak, the puppy becomes a dog and makes the fond and loyal relations with its human masters which befit the dog; and this is all that is required of the oak tree and the dog. But the human being's task in fulfilling his nature is much more difficult, for he must do it in self-consciousness. That is, his development is never automatic but must be to some extent chosen and affirmed by himself. "Among the works of man," John Stuart Mill has written, "which human life is rightly employed in perfecting and in beautifying, the first importance surely is man himself. . . . Human nature is not a machine to be built after a model and set to do exactly the work prescribed for it, but a tree, which requires to grow and develop itself on all sides, according to the tendency of the inward forces which make it a living thing." In this charmingly expressed thought, John Stuart Mill has unfortunately omitted the most important "tendency of the inward forces" which make man a living thing, namely that man does not grow automatically like a tree, but fulfills his potentialities only as he in his own consciousness plans and chooses.

16   If any organism fails to fulfill its potentialities, it becomes sick, just as your legs would wither if you never walked. But the power of your legs is not all you would lose. The flowing of your blood, your heart action, your whole organism would be the weaker. And in the same way if man does not fulfill his potentialities as a person, he becomes to that extent constricted and ill. This is the essence of neurosis—the person's unused potentialities, blocked by hostile conditions in the environment (past or present) and by his own internalized conflicts, turn inward and cause morbidity. "Energy is Eternal Delight," said William Blake; "He who desires but acts not, breeds pestilence."

17   Kafka was a master at the gruesome task of picturing people who do not use their potentialities and therefore lose their sense of being persons. The chief character in *The Trial* and in *The Castle* has no name—he is identified only by an initial, a mute symbol of one's lack of identity in one's right. In the staggering and frightful parable, *Metamorphosis*, Kafka illustrates what happens when the

human being forfeits his powers. The hero of this story is a typical, empty modern young man, who lives a routine, vacuous life as a salesman, returning regularly to his middle-class home, eating the same menu of roast beef every Sunday while his father goes to sleep at the table. The young man's life was so empty, implies Kafka, that he woke up one morning no longer a human being but a cockroach. Because he had not fulfilled his status as a man, he forfeited his human potentialities. A cockroach, like lice and rats and vermin, lives off others' leavings. It is a parasite, and in most people's minds a symbol for what is unclean and repugnant. Could there be any more powerful symbol of what happens when a human being relinquishes his nature as a person?

18   But to the extent that we do fulfill our potentialities as persons, we experience the profoundest joy to which the human being is heir. When a little child is learning to walk up steps or lift a box, he will try again and again, getting up when he falls down and starting over again. And finally when he does succeed, he laughs with gratification, his expression of joy in the use of his powers. But this is nothing in comparison to the quiet joy when the adolescent can use his newly emerged power for the first time to gain a friend, or the adult's joy when he can love, plan and create. Joy is the affect which comes when we use our powers. Joy, rather than happiness, is the goal of life, for joy is the emotion which accompanies our fulfilling our natures as human beings. It is based on the experience of one's identity as a being of worth and dignity, who is able to affirm his being, if need be, against all other beings and the whole inorganic world. This power in its ideal form is shown in the life of a Socrates, who was so confident in himself and his values that he could take his being condemned to death not as a defeat but as a greater fulfillment than compromising his beliefs. But we do not wish to imply such joy is only for the heroic and the outstanding; it is as present qualitatively in anyone's act, no matter how inconspicuous, which is done as an honest and responsible expression of his own powers.

Vocabulary

entice	neurotic	empathy
rudiment	trauma	tumultuous
schematic	retrospective	extrovert
spontaneous	potentiality	morbidity
vacuous	relinquish	inconspicuous

Topics for Discussion

1. May says that individual personalities develop in response to their early environments. If this is true, then what are the possibilities for changing one's personality later in life? Discuss how you or someone you know has markedly changed some aspect of personal behavior. To what extent is this change simply a shift in surface activity; to what extent a basic change in attitudes toward the self or the world?

2. May illustrates that the need for recognition of one's personal identity is one of the deepest desires of all people. Other psychologists have pointed out that emotional integrity depends on having one's real inner self accepted by others for what it is. In your experience, have you had to disguise what you really feel yourself to be in order to gain acceptance by others? Have you been bothered by having to act this way in some situations and not in others—going for a job interview as opposed to talking about your feelings to a close friend?

3. May quotes Blake's aphorism, "He who desires but acts not, breeds pestilence." Can you write about a situation from your experience, or from literature or films, where you or a fictional character failed to act and thus lost a possibility for enriching personal existence?

4. May's essay is part of a larger work called *Man's Search for Himself*. Which is more valuable an experience, finding an answer in the search, or the search itself? What social and economic causes have led men and women to "lose themselves" in the first place? In answering this question, focus on a particular event or individual.

Rhetorical Considerations

1. As a practicing clinical psychologist, May has the opportunity to encounter the inmost fears and fantasies of his patients. How does he use his clinical experience for purposes of illustration in this essay? What kinds of experiences are people generally afraid to discuss?

2. May quotes widely from literature and from incidents in the history of ideas. Examine (in paragraph 5) his recounting of Descartes's discovery of the enthymeme, "I think, therefore I am." Why do you think readers of this essay will remember Descartes?

3. What is an enthymeme? Do you use enthymemes in your writing to make unsupported assertions?

4. May often makes comparisons between man and animals or between man and inanimate nature. Find these comparisons in his essay. Are they central to the main point of the essay, or do they serve to create a feeling of familiarity in the reader for the various problems May discusses?

God and the Spirit of Man

Martin Buber

Martin Buber (1878–1965) was a Jewish theologian and philosopher who emphasized human interdependence as central to religious experience. His most famous work, from which the following selection is taken, is I and Thou *(1937).*

1   This book discusses the relations between religion and philosophy in the history of the spirit and deals with the part that philosophy has played in its late period in making God and all absoluteness appear unreal.

2   If philosophy is here set in contrast to religion, what is meant by religion is not the massive fullness of statements, concepts, and activities that one customarily describes by this name and that men sometimes long for more than for God. Religion is essentially the act of holding fast to God. And that does not mean holding fast to an image that one has made of God, nor even holding fast to the faith in God that one has conceived. It means holding fast to the existing God. The earth would not hold fast to its conception of the sun (if it had one) nor to its connection with it, but to the sun itself.

3   In contrast to religion so understood, philosophy is here regarded as the process, reaching from the early becoming independent of reflection to its more contemporary crisis, the last stage of which is the intellectual letting go of God.

4   This process begins with man's longer contenting himself, as did the pre-philosophical man, with picturing the living God, to whom one formerly only called—with a call of despair or rapture which occasionally became His first name—as a Something, a thing among things, a being among beings, an It.

5   The beginning of philosophizing means that this Something changes from an object of imagination, wishes, and feelings to one that is conceptually comprehensible, to an object of thought. It does not matter whether this object of thought is called "Speech" (*Logos*), because in all and each one hears it speak, answer, and directly address one, or "the Unlimited" (*Apeiron*), because it has already leapt over every limit that one may try to set for it, or simply "Being," or whatever. If the living quality of the conception of God refuses to enter into this conceptual image, it is tolerated alongside of it, usually in an unprecise form, as in the end identical with it or at least essentially dependent on it. Or it is depreciated as an unsatisfactory surrogate for the help of men incapable of thought.

6   In the progress of its philosophizing the human spirit is ever more inclined to fuse characteristically this conception, of the Absolute as object of an adequate thought, with itself, the human spirit. In the course of this process, the idea which was at first noetically contemplated finally becomes the potentiality of the spirit itself that thinks it, and it attains on the way of the spirit its actuality. The subject, which appeared to be attached to being in order to perform for it the service of contemplation, asserts that it itself produced and produces being. Until, finally, all that is over against us, everything that accosts us and takes possession of us, all partnership of existence, is dissolved in free-floating subjectivity.

7   The next step already takes us to the stage familiar to us, the stage that understands itself as the final one and plays with its finality: the human spirit, which adjudges to itself mastery over its work, annihilates conceptually the absoluteness of the absolute. It may yet imagine that it, the spirit, still remains there as bearer of all things and coiner of all values; in truth, it has also destroyed its own absoluteness along with absoluteness in general. The spirit can now no longer exist as an independent essence. There now exists only a product of human individuals called spirit, a product which they contain and secrete like mucus and urine.

8   In this stage there first takes place the conceptual letting go of God because only now philosophy cuts off its own hands, the hands with which it was able to grasp and hold Him.

9   But an analogous process takes place on the other side, in the development of religion itself (in the usual broad sense of the word).

10   From the earliest times the reality of the relation of faith, man's standing before the face of God, world-happening as dialogue, has been threatened by the impulse to control the power yonder. Instead of understanding events as calls which make demands on one, one wishes oneself to demand without having to hearken. "I

have," says man, "power over the powers I conjure." And that continues, with sundry modifications, wherever one celebrates rites without being turned to the Thou and without really meaning its Presence.

11   The other pseudoreligious counterpart of the relation of faith, not so elementally active as conjuration but acting with the mature power of the intellect, is unveiling. Here one takes the position of raising the veil of the manifest, which divides the revealed from the hidden, and leading forth the divine mysteries. "I am," says man, "acquainted with the unknown, and I make it known." The supposedly divine It that the magician manipulates as the technician his dynamo, the Gnostic lays bare, the whole divine apparatus. His heirs are not "theosophies" and their neighbours alone; in many theologies also, unveiling gestures are to be discovered behind the interpreting ones.

12   We find this replacement of I-Thou by an I-It in manifold forms in that new philosophy of religion which seeks to "save" religion. In it the "I" of this relation steps ever more into the foreground as "subject" of "religious feeling," as profiter from a pragmatist decision to believe, and the like.

13   Much more important than all this, however, is an event penetrating to the innermost depth of the religious life, an event which may be described as the subjectivizing of the act of faith itself. Its essence can be grasped most clearly through the example of prayer.

14   We call prayer in the pregnant sense of the term that speech of man to God, which, whatever else is asked, ultimately asks for the manifestation of the divine Presence, for this Presence's becoming dialogically perceivable. The single presupposition of a genuine state of prayer is thus the readiness of the whole man for this Presence, simple turned-towardness, unreserved spontaneity. This spontaneity, ascending from the roots, succeeds time and again in overcoming all that disturbs and diverts. But in this our stage of subjectivized reflection not only the concentration of the one who prays, but also his spontaneity is assailed. The assailant is consciousness, the over-consciousness of this man here that he is praying, that he is *praying*, that *he* is praying. And the assailant appears to be invincible. The subjective knowledge of the one turning-towards about his turning-towards, this holding back of an I which does not enter into the action with the rest of the person, an I to which the action is an object—all this depossesses the moment, takes away its spontaneity. The specifically modern man who has not yet let go of God knows what that means: he who is not present perceives no Presence.

15   One must understand this correctly: this is not a question of a special case of the known sickness of modern man, who must attend his own actions as spectator. It is the confession of the Absolute into which he brings his unfaithfulness to the Absolute, and it is the relation between the Absolute and him upon which this unfaithfulness works, in the middle of the statement of trust. And now he too who is seemingly holding fast to God becomes aware of the eclipsed Transcendence.

16   What is it that we mean when we speak of an eclipse of God which is even now taking place? Through this metaphor we make the tremendous assumption that we can glance up to God with our "mind's eye," or rather being's eye, as with our bodily eye to the sun, and that something can step between our existence and His as between the earth and the sun. That this glance of the being exists, wholly unillusory, yielding no images yet first making possible all images, no other court in the world attests than that of faith. It is not to be proved; it is only to be experienced; man has experienced it. And that other, that which steps in between, one also experiences, to-day. I have spoken of it since I have recognized it, and as exactly as my perception allowed me.

17   The double nature of man, as the being that is both brought forth from "below" and sent from "above," results in the duality of his basic characteristics. These cannot be understood through the categories of the individual man existing-for-himself, but only through the categories of his existing as man-with-man. As a being who is sent, a man exists over against the existing being before which he is placed. As a being who is brought forth, he finds himself beside all existing beings in the world, beside which he is set. The first of these categories has its living reality in the relation I-Thou, the second has its reality in the relation I-It. The second always brings us only to the aspects of an existing being, not to that being itself. Even the most intimate contact with another remains covered over by an aspect if the other has not become Thou for me. Only the first relation, that which establishes essential immediacy between me and an existing being, brings me just thereby not to an aspect of it but to that being itself. To be sure, it brings me only to the existential meeting with it; it does not somehow put me in a position to view it objectively in its being. As soon as an objective viewing is established, we are given only an aspect and ever again only an aspect. But it is also only the relation I-Thou in which we can meet God at all, because of Him, in absolute contrast to all other existing beings, no objective aspect can be attained. Even a vision yields no objective viewing, and he who strains to hold fast an after-image

after the cessation of the full I-Thou relation has already lost the vision.

18   It is not the case, however, that the I in both relations, I-Thou and I-It, is the same. Rather where and when the beings around one are seen and treated as objects of observation, reflection, use, perhaps also of solicitude or help, there and then another I is spoken, another I manifested, another I exists than where and when one stands with the whole of one's being over against another being and steps into an essential relation with him. Everyone who knows both in himself—and that is the life of man, that one comes to know both in himself and ever again both—knows whereof I speak. Both together build up human existence; it is only a question of which of the two is at any particular time the architect and which is his assistant. Rather, it is a question of whether the I-Thou relation remains the architect, for it is self-evident that it cannot be employed as assistant. If it does not command, then it is already disappearing.

19   In our age the I-It relation, gigantically swollen, has usurped, practically uncontested, the mastery and the rule. The I of this relation, an I that possesses all, makes all, succeeds with all, this I that is unable to say Thou, unable to meet a being essentially, is the lord of the hour. This selfhood that has become omnipotent, with all the It around it, can naturally acknowledge neither God nor any genuine absolute which manifests itself to men as of non-human origin. It steps in between and shuts off from us the light of heaven.

20   Such is the nature of this hour. But what of the next? It is a modern superstition that the character of an age acts as fate for the next. One lets it prescribe what is possible to do and hence what is permitted. One surely cannot swim against the stream, one says. But perhaps one can swim with a new stream whose source is still hidden? In another image, the I-Thou relation has gone into the catacombs—who can say with how much greater power it will step forth! Who can say when the I-It relation will be directed anew to its assisting place and activity!

21   The most important events in the history of that embodied possibility called man are the occasionally occurring beginnings of new epochs, determined by forces previously invisible or unregarded. Each age is, of course, a continuation of the preceding one, but a continuation can be confirmation and it can be refutation.

22   Something is taking place in the depths that as yet needs no name. To-morrow even it may happen that it will be beckoned to from the heights, across the heads of the earthly archons. The eclipse of the light of God is no extinction; even to-morrow that which has stepped in between may give way.

Vocabulary

conceived	conceptually	surrogate
deprecated	noetically	potentiality
contemplation	subjectivity	annihilates
essence	manifest	manipulates
dynamo	manifold	pregnant
diologically	perceivable	presupposition
spontaneity	diverts	subjectivized
assailed	invincible	eclipsed
transcendence	metaphor	assumption
unillusory	attests	perception
duality	essential	existential
objectively	cessation	solicitude
usurped	superstition	prescribe
archons		

Topics for Discussion

1. Buber's formulation of *I-Thou* and *I-It* as descriptions for human relationships remains quite abstract throughout the essay. Can you use this formula to describe a real relationship you have with another person? To what extent do you view the other as a *Thou*, as an *It*? Here are some subjects to start with:

> your best female friend
> your best male friend
> your parents
> your teacher in this class
> the last cabdriver you met
> the last waitress/waiter you met
> your next blind date
> the students you don't know in this class

How do you think these people view you?

2. Can you think of examples to ilustrate what Buber means when he says that "in our age the *I-It* relation . . . has usurped . . . the mastery and the rule"? Try to generalize further than your personal life. You might ask whether government and business actively foster *I-It* relationships. What institutions foster *I-Thou* relationships? If you can think of none, can you conceive of institutions which would? What are possible sources in contemporary politics, culture, and religion for Buber's "new stream" of genuine human interaction? Be specific.

3. The authors of your text have been personal friends for over a decade, yet they have a formal contract providing for equal division of profits and labor with regard to this book. Do you think that sometimes contractual *I-It* relationships can help to reinforce *I-Thou* relationships? Would you consider making a written contract with the person you live with (husband, wife, boyfriend, girlfriend) regarding the division of household tasks (dishwashing, food shopping, babysitting)? Why? Why not?

4. Throughout the essay Buber connects human relationships with religious experience. Do you think that the connection he makes is valid and, even if valid, necessary? Why? Why not?

Rhetorical Considerations

1. Metaphors involving the cosmos are among the most powerful in the great literature of humanity. At the end of the *Inferno*, Dante emerges from Hell and describes his growth in understanding and his aspirations for the human race with the simple words, ". . . we beheld again the stars." In the juxtaposition of this simple phrase with the tremendous bulk of his epic poem, Dante concretizes his belief in humanity's ability to grasp the supposedly unattainable as real. Buber demands that humanity grasp the unattainable God as real, and he lends emotional weight to this demand through the use of a cosmic metaphor. Identify the metaphor. Might Buber have extended the metaphor further in the essay? What does he do instead? Is he successful in relating very complicated, abstract philosophical concepts to the ordinary bodily operations of blowing one's nose and urinating? What does his mention of these things have in common with Dante's sighting of the stars?

2. Buber argues for a spontaneous spiritual life, a life in which prayer demands the immediate showing forth of the divine presence. How is the central metaphor of the essay appropriate to this demand for spontaneity? Would more complex formulations than the simple phrases *I-Thou*, *I-It* better explain Buber's central theme?

3. Buber does not rely on traditional forms of logic to prove his contentions in this essay. He turns away from rational proof and toward experience to make his case. As a general principle, how useful is this kind of argumentation? Using premises of "faith," "transcendence," and other mystical formulations cannot one justify kindness to animals or Hilter's fascism? Would you opt for reason or emotion as the principal governor of your activity?

Man Will Prevail

William Faulkner

*William Faulkner (1897–1962) is universally regarded as one of the great writers of the twentieth century. Most of his great novels (*Light in August, Go Down Moses, *and* Absalom, Absalom, *among others) are set in his native Mississippi, in the fictional Yoknapatawpha County. He received the Nobel Prize for literature in 1949.*

1   I feel that this award was not made to me as a man, but to my work—a life's work in the agony and sweat of the human spirit, not for glory and least of all for profit, but to create out of the materials of the human spirit something which did not exist before. So this award is only mine in trust. It will not be difficult to find a dedication for the money part of it commensurate with the purpose and significance of its origin. But I would like to do the same with the acclaim too, by using this moment as a pinnacle from which I might be listened to by the young men and women already dedicated to the same anguish and travail, among whom is already that one who will some day stand here where I am standing.

2   Our tragedy today is a general and universal physical fear so long sustained by now that we can even bear it. There are no longer problems of the spirit. There is only the question: When will I be blown up? Because of this, the young man or woman writing today has forgotten the problems of the human heart in conflict with itself which alone can make good writing because only that is worth writing about, worth the agony and the sweat.

3   He must learn them again. He must teach himself that the basest of all things is to be afraid; and, teaching himself that, forget it forever, leaving no room in his workshop for anything but the old verities and truths of the heart, the old universal truths lacking which any story is ephemeral and doomed—love and honor and pity and pride and compassion and sacrifice. Until he does so, he labors under a curse. He writes not of love but of lust, of defeats in which nobody loses anything of value, of victories without hope and, worst of all, without pity or compassion. His griefs grieve on no universal bones, leaving no scars. He writes not of the heart but of the glands.

4   Until he relearns these things, he will write as though he stood among and watched the end of man. I decline to accept the end of

man. It is easy enough to say that man is immortal simply because he will endure: that when the last ding-dong of doom has clanged and faded from the last worthless rock hanging tideless in the last red and dying evening, that even then there will still be one more sound: that of his puny inexhaustible voice, still talking. I refuse to accept this. I believe that man will not merely endure: he will prevail. He is immortal, not because he alone among creatures has an inexhaustible voice, but because he has a soul, a spirit capable of compassion and sacrifice and endurance. The poet's, the writer's, duty is to write about these things. It is his privilege to help man endure by lifting his heart, by reminding him of the courage and honor and hope and pride and compassion and pity and sacrifice which have been the glory of his past. The poet's voice need not merely be the record of man, it can be one of the props, the pillars to help him endure and prevail.

Vocabulary

| commensurate | pinnacle | verity |
| ephemeral | puny | inexhaustible |

Topics for Discussion

1. According to Faulkner, what is the central problem facing the young writer today? What has this problem led to?

2. Faulkner's speech is a reaffirmation of "the old verities and truths of the heart." What are these? What have contemporary writers replaced them with? Mention a particular author.

3. Can you think of any contemporary novels, short stories, or movies which portray people as Faulkner says the modern writer portrays them—with lust not love, experiencing meaningless defeats and victories without hope, and having neither pity nor compassion?

4. Faulkner's conclusion is very direct. He states that man "will not merely endure: he will prevail." What proof does he offer for this statement? Do you agree with him?

5. Would you consider Faulkner's values old-fashioned? Do they have a place in contemporary society? Can you think of any recent literature which conforms to Faulkner's view of the function of the writer and the purpose of literature?

Rhetorical Considerations

1. To whom is Faulkner addressing his speech? Is it the audience at the award presentation or someone else?

2. Could Faulkner have communicated the ideas in this speech with any markedly different tone?

3. How would you characterize the rhythm of this speech? Look carefully at Faulkner's use of short, simple, direct sentences ("He must learn them again"). What function do they play in the rhythm of the speech?

4. This a very short speech, especially for such an important occasion. Does the brevity of the speech contribute to its effectiveness, or would it have been better if Faulkner had expanded and developed his speech more?

5. Faulkner's diction is simple, sometimes bordering on the colloquial. Does this detract from the speech? Is this the kind of diction you would expect from a famous writer at such an important ceremony?

Death in the First Person

Anonymous

1   I am a student nurse. I am dying. I write this to you who are, and will become, nurses in the hope that by my sharing my feelings with you, you may someday be better able to help those who share my experience.

2   I'm out of the hospital now—perhaps for a month, for six months, perhaps for a year—but no one likes to talk about such things. In fact, no one likes to talk about much at all. Nursing must be advancing, but I wish it would hurry. We're taught not to be overly cheery now, to omit the "Everything's fine" routine, and we have done pretty well. But now one is left in a lonely silent void. With the protective "fine, fine" gone, the staff is left with only their own vulnerability and fear. The dying patient is not yet seen as a person and thus cannot be communicated with as such. He is a symbol of what every human fears and what we each know, at least academically, that we too must someday face. What did they say in

psychiatric nursing about meeting pathology with pathology to the detriment of both patient and nurse? And there was a lot about knowing one's own feelings before you could help another with his. How true.

3   But for me, fear is today and dying is now. You slip in and out of my room, give me medications and check my blood pressure. Is it because I am a student nurse, myself, or just a human being, that I sense your fright? And your fears enhance mine. Why are you afraid? I am the one who is dying!

4   I know you feel insecure, don't know what to say, don't know what to do. But please believe me, if you care, you can't go wrong. Just admit that you care. That is really for what we search. We may ask for why's and wherefore's, but we don't really expect answers. Don't run away—wait—all I want to know is that there will be someone to hold my hand when I need it. I am afraid. Death may get to be a routine to you, but it is new to me. You may not see me as unique, but I've never died before. To me, once is pretty unique!

5   You whisper about my youth, but when one is dying, is he really so young anymore? I have lots I wish we could talk about. It really would not take much more of your time because you are in here quite a bit anyway.

6   If only we could be honest, both admit of our fears, touch one another. If you really care, would you lose so much of your valuable professionalism if you even cried with me? Just person to person? Then, it might not be so hard to die—in a hospital—with friends close by.

Vocabulary

vulnerability	psychiatric	pathology
detriment	enhance	

Topics for Discussion

1. Death is not a topic most of us want to talk about. Why is this so? If you were reluctant to read this essay, state why.

2. If the author of this essay were your friend, how would you interact with her? Would you talk about death?

3. If you knew you would die soon, would it change the way you are now living? How, precisely?

4. Benedict Spinoza, a philosopher, once said, "A free man thinks of death least of all things; his is not a meditation of death, but of life." Evaluate Spinoza's words in relation to this essay.

Rhetorical Considerations

1. Note the juxtaposition in paragraph 1 of two short, powerful sentences and one longer sentence. Can you think of alternative arrangements for these sentences?

2. Do you feel something missing in this essay—the lack of details, especially the lack of any indication of the cause of death? Would the addition of details strengthen or weaken the essay?

3. Is there understatement, even ironic humor, in paragraph 4? Is it appropriate?

4. Apart from the obvious reason, why is it appropriate that this letter be written to student nurses?

5. Is the looseness of structure in this essay appropriate? Why or why not? Why would it not be appropriate for most essays?

How I Came to Study Dying Children

Myra Bluebond-Langner

Myra Bluebond-Langner (b. 1948) is an assistant professor of anthropology at Rutgers University in Camden, N.J. The following essay is excerpted from her doctoral dissertation, a study of terminally ill children in a leukemia hospital.

1   When I thought about a dissertation topic, nothing could have been further from my mind than dying children. As a matter of fact, I did not even know, or at least chose to ignore, the fact that there was such a thing as a dying child. With millions of other Americans, I shared the belief that in our country children do not die, except perhaps in accidents, sometimes.

2   At the time I undertook the research I was twenty-two years old, and had neither seen nor experienced the death of a close friend or relative. I had never even attended a funeral. My experiences

with death were limited to the theater, movies, television and literature. My father recalls that when I was about fourteen, I was
fascinated by death, and every poem I wrote at Arts Camp concerned death and dying. For awhile he thought that my writing
teacher was a mortician. After all, who else would think about or
deal with death?

3   There is a tacit assumption that to do a study of the terminally
ill is to be constantly concerned and involved with death. On the
contrary, there is something quite paradoxical about studying the
dying. It is not morbid. The difficulties and hard times come not
when the children are dying, but when they are alive and you know
that they will soon be among the dying.

4   Such times included the moment when Lynn, her pigtails
flopping behind her, came down the hall shouting as she jumped into
my arms, "I'm going home today." Involuntarily I thought, "How
long before she is back here again?" Or when Seth, his body riddled
with pain, I.V.'s running in both arms, his nose packed, tried to
move to a rock-and-roll recording, because he knew that both he
and I needed to see him living. Or when Scott, hearing that one of
his friends died over the weekend, came and hugged me, and simply
said, "I hope that doesn't happen to me." Half defensively and half
longingly I replied, "I hope that doesn't happen to you either."

5   I am like the parents and, at times, the doctors too. Perhaps
this child will be different; perhaps a cure will be found in time—I
want to believe it. Mentally, I review the child's case history,
attending only to those aspects that make his history different from
the other leukemic children who have already died. "Well, he never
had a major bleed," or, "Look how well she responds to the
chemotherapy." I ignore all the bad signs. I think of the progress in
cancer research, of the advertisements from research centers showing "cured" children. I push contradictory evidence out of my
mind.

6   But then reality hits, because I know deep down that this child
will not be different. Perhaps he never had a major bleed, but then
there are the times when they have to stop the drugs because of the
side effects. She responds well to chemotherapy, but her liver no
longer functions properly because of long-term drug damage. Yes,
progress has been made. There may even be a cure tomorrow. It
will not be for these children, however, for the toxic effects of the
drugs have marked them. In fact, they say that some children have
already been cured, but of what have they been cured, and for how
long?

7   Anger quickly replaces these thoughts and feelings. Why this
child? What did he do? Why can't something be done? The anger

builds and is often directed at strangers, people out there too busy to know that a child is living with dying. I walk through the toy department of a large department store, crowded with Christmas shoppers, full of Christmas cheer. While two ladies argue about the best style bike for a nine-year-old boy, I try to find a toy for Peter that will not remind him of the bike that he can no longer ride and maybe will never see again. Another woman is pushing her way ahead in line so that she can be home in time to help her grandchildren decorate the tree. And I laugh to myself. I am in a hurry too. I promised Andy an angel for his tree and if I do not make tracks, Andy may be that angel before I can even get there.

8   The anger soars. It wells up into an indictment of this country for its priorities on spending. It is thrown up to a God I am not quite sure exists, but deserves to be blamed just the same. I have to blame someone, something. How else can I explain to myself the death of a child? If I do not blame someone or something, then I must do something, and what can I or anyone else do? Didn't Dr. Abrams say to the residents, "What makes you think that your medicine is any more powerful than that novena?"

9   The feeling of impotence is overwhelming. The rage has passed. No one heard me. You see, I really did not say or do anything. I am tired. I feel a gnawing sense of guilt that always seems to follow the rage and anger. I can walk out of the hospital, I can leave it all behind me. I can intellectualize it all. I can even profit from it. For out of this experience will come a dissertation, perhaps even a Ph.D. I will become an anthropologist. But these children— they will not become.

10   They have done for me in so many ways, but what have I done for them? For them. It was always so hard to do something for them. They were always doing for everyone else. How we all talked about the Marias who right up until the end asked to be taken to the bathroom, about the Jeffreys who shouted us out of their rooms, and about the Seths who would not let us in; all because they knew when we could not take it.

11   They constantly did for me. They were my teachers. Even in death, they are my teachers. For most of their lives, even when they were sick, they were caught up in the business of living. There were people to talk to, games to play, houses to build, pictures to draw. There was so much to do, and so little time to do it in. Then again, there never really is enough time. Life is a terminal illness for all of us. It is just that some know the end before others.

12   I caught the children's sense of urgency, their fear of wasting time, their knowledge of the finitude of things. I felt that I had to get every word down, as if it were the last. At the same time, I realized

that I had entered into a relationship with these children which required that I take my time and not push them.

13   At the end of the day I was always afraid to leave them. I might miss something. They might not be there when I got back. But I had to leave. After all, I was there to learn as much as I could. I had notes to write up, work to analyze; tasks made more difficult by the depression and fatigue that often came at the day's end.

14   I managed to resolve the conflicts, at least momentarily, enough to write up my research for others to read and to learn from. As it all nears completion, I am plagued by the question, "If I had it to do over again, would I?"

15   My feelings vacillate from day to day. I have changed since the time I did the study. I am older, married, and have experienced the deaths of some of my closest friends and relatives. When I did the research, I had not had these experiences; my "innocence" was in many ways essential to my doing the study as I did and to accomplishing what I did. I am also haunted by another question: how many were helped and how many were hurt by my study? When one does such research, contributions to science are not sufficient justification, in my view. I hope that this study contributes to the memory of the children, to those who cared for them, and to children who still must suffer. If it does not, I have failed. But they never failed me.

Vocabulary

mortician	tacit	paradoxical
morbid	leukemic	chemotherapy
contradictory	toxic	priorities
anthropologist	dissertation	terminal
urgency	finitude	

Topics for Discussion

1. How often do you think of death? Do you agree with Bluebond-Langner that only morticians think of death? Why do you think people avoid thinking about death?

2. Bluebond-Langner says that it is not morbid to study the dying. What are her reasons for claiming this? Do you agree with her?

Can you think of any topics or areas that should not be studied? Does humanity have a right or obligation to learn everything possible? If you agree that humanity does, what are some of the implications of humanity's limitless search for knowledge? Before answering this question, you might read the essay by C. P. Snow in the final section of this book.

3. Why is Bluebond-Langner angry in this essay? At whom is she angry? What does her anger turn to? Why? Are you angry after reading this essay? What is your emotional state after reading this essay?

4. In what way were the children Bluebond-Langner's teachers? What did they teach her?

5. What was the purpose of Bluebond-Langner's research? What good can come of it?

Rhetorical Considerations

1. How objective is this essay? Does Bluebond-Langner maintain a scholarly tone throughout the essay? Does her use of emotion weaken the essay's effectiveness? Which paragraphs in the essay have a scholarly, objective tone, and which paragraphs are emotional? What is her purpose in using each tone?

2. After using the pronoun *I* in paragraphs 1 and 2, Bluebond-Langner shifts to impersonal constructions in paragraph 3. Why?

3. How effective are the examples in paragraph 4? What do they contribute to the tone and development of the essay?

4. Examine the sentence structure in paragraphs 7 and 10. How has Bluebond-Langner used short and long sentences to stress her main idea, as well as tone?

5. Several paragraphs begin with short, powerful sentences, interwoven with longer, more complicated sentences. What effect does Bluebond-Langner achieve through this interplay?

The Experience of Death

Ignace Lepp

Ignace Lepp was a priest and psychotherapist in Paris, France. He died in 1966.

1 Strictly speaking, we can have no immediate experience of death, either our own or that of others. The loss of consciousness is one of the signs of individual death even though we do not die each time we lose consciousness. Even those who have experienced prolonged comas during which they seemed to be dead cannot tell us anything about the experience of death for the simple reason that they did not die. The Gospel speaks of Lazarus and two others Christ is reported to have raised from the dead. But none of them said anything about his death. Moreover, modern exegetes are inclined to think that neither the daughter of the centurion nor the son of the widow of Nain were dead in the clinical sense of the word, and that they underwent miraculous cures rather than resurrection. Lazarus, on the other hand, is thought to have been really dead, since he was three days in the tomb. But the evangelists tell us absolutely nothing about his experience of death. The same is true of the many accounts in Christian and other hagiographies according to which the dead were raised by the saints. Even legends, in which human imagination is given the greatest freedom, are extremely discreet about the experience of death.

2 Some authors think that the closest analogy to the experience of death is mystical ecstasy. St. Paul, Theresa of Avila and a number of other mystics have made this comparison. After being taken up into the "third heaven," Paul expressed the desire to die in order to recapture a similar happiness. But, instead of giving us a detailed account of his experience, Paul said that the language of man is incapable of describing the marvels he witnessed. We shall have occasion later to discuss the value of mediums and the authenticity of the "communications" the deceased are said to impart to them.

3 Karl Jung, as is well known, consecrated a considerable part of his work to the study of the mythologies of different races. He considered mythology to be a valuable source of information concerning the collective unconscious, which he supposed to be common to all men. He pointed out that in many mythologies death is

compared to a return to the womb, where the dead are thought to be reborn. On this basis many authors postulate a parallel between death and birth. Like birth, death brings about a radical mutation in the condition of the living being. There is unquestionably much that is valuable in this image and we will examine it in more detail later on. But since we have no direct knowledge of our own birth, and since no one else does either, we must admit that the comparison between death and birth cannot tell us anything specific about the experience of death.

4   Our experience of death can only be indirect. It is in the presence of another's death that man normally becomes aware that all men are mortal and concludes that he too must die. According to Heidegger we are only capable of communicating our more banal experiences. The deep experiences of life are by nature incommunicable. Since death is one of those basic experiences the spectacle of another's death, no matter how close to us he may have been, would not constitute a genuine psychological experience. In seeing others die we become convinced of our own mortality but as long as we are alive it is merely "someone else" who dies, always another with whom we have no possibility of communication in depth. My own experience, both direct and indirect, of interhuman relations prohibits my sharing Heidegger's pessimism concerning the radical incommunicability of basic experiences. But I admit that such communication is difficult. As a rule we can only communicate with those to whom we are bound by deep emotional bonds. The death of strangers is impersonal and tells us nothing essential about our own death. This perhaps explains the frightening indifference of individuals and peoples confronted with the death of others as a result of war, famine or other catastrophes. For the Germans contaminated by Hitler's racism, it was the impersonal "other" who died in the crematory ovens of Dachau. The Americans, however humanitarian and compassionate they may otherwise be, also looked upon the victims of Hiroshima impersonally. This is also true of the attitude of the majority of Frenchmen toward the atrocities committed in Algeria and other colonies but a short time ago. As I write these lines the news media carry reports of the mass murder of noncombatants in Vietnam by American soldiers convinced that they are serving the cause of freedom and democracy. We are also informed by the same media about the ravages of famine in India while the Western nations are concerned about over-eating. If the death of the Vietnamese and Indians scarcely disturbs most of us, and does not afford even an indirect experience of death, it is again because as far as we are concerned it is the anonymous "other" who dies.

5   But those close to us die too, those with whom our communication is not limited to banalities but touches upon the essential. Their death constitutes an authentic experience of death for us; a part of us dies with them. This is illustrated by a famous passage in St. Augustine's *Confessions* where he speaks of the death of his closest friend . . . :

6   "I marvelled that other men should live, because he, whom I had loved as if he would never die, was dead. I marvelled more that I, his second self, could live when he was dead. Well has someone said of his friend that he is half his soul. For I thought that my soul and his soul were but one soul in two bodies. Therefore, my life was a horror to me, because I would not live as but a half. Perhaps because of this I feared to die, lest he whom I had loved so much should wholly die."

7   There is no doubt that St. Augustine had a real experience of death in the death of this friend. By identifying with him, he experienced, as it were, his own death. He also proved himself extremely capable of the kind of communication that Heidegger says is impossible. Similar testimonies can be found in the works of such writers as Goethe, Montaigne and others who knew the painful experience of death through the loss of a dear friend. Perhaps someday, when human solidarity and our capacity to love all men as we love ourselves are more highly developed, we will not be so indifferent to the death of black people in Africa or yellow people in Asia; perhaps then the wars and famines that victimize them will affect us as the death of Augustine's friend affected him. . . .

8   Of all the living species in our universe, only man knows that he is mortal. It seems that self-consciousness emerged almost simultaneously with his consciousness of death. Nor do we have any evidence that he has ever considered death to be a banal event. Only in our time, and in the materially prosperous West, do men see death as a simple biological fact. But it should be noted that they usually consider the death of others in this perspective rather than their own. I know many materialists who are much concerned with dying and being buried in proper style.

9   It is well known that paleontologists can determine that the remains of centuries ago are human on the basis of evidence furnished by funeral rites and honors rendered to the deceased. From the earliest beginnings of time man has been characterized by a minimal sense of individuality, by a certain capacity to project into the future, from the actual to the possible, and to infer his own fate from the fate of others. In this sense we can say that only man's

death is an actual going away, a departure. And it leaves a profound impression upon those who survive.

10   Thus the death of another can be a genuine experience of death for us on condition that we experience it deeply, that is to say, identify to some extent with the other's death. We have already noted that those in whom the universal sense of human solidarity is highly developed experience each death as a harbinger of their own death, indeed *as* their own death. But ordinarily men can achieve this experience only when loved ones die.

Vocabulary

exegetes	hagiography	analogy
mystic	postulate	mutation
banal	solidarity	perspective
paleontologist	harbinger	

Topics for Discussion

1. What is mystical ecstasy? In what ways does it resemble the experience of death?

2. How can you experience death through the death of another?

3. If our experience of death can only be indirect, how much can we really know about death? How much do we really want to know?

4. Does Lepp feel that the death of someone close can be a good experience? Do you agree with him?

5. After reading this essay, can you reconcile Lepp's contention that no one has ever come back from the dead with the accounts of people who died clinically but who were later revived by such medical techniques as heart massage and who then recounted how it felt to be dead? If you have ever read such an account, compare it to this essay.

6. Lepp says that of all species only we know that we are mortal. How conscious are you of your mortality? Do you feel uncomfortable thinking about it? Do you feel uncomfortable reading this essay? Answering these questions? Discussing death? Why?

Rhetorical Considerations

1. Compare the first and last paragraphs in this essay, particularly the first sentences in each paragraph. Has Lepp contradicted himself? Where in the essay does he present the arguments which lead to his conclusion? How valid is his argument?

2. Examine the sentence structure of the essay and note how frequently Lepp begins sentences with impersonal subjects (It seems . . . , There is . . .) and with personal subjects (We shall . . . , He is . . .). What is the rhetorical reason for this variation in sentence structure?

3. What is the tone of this essay? What specific devices are used to achieve the tone? Why is the kind of tone used in this essay important? Is the tone appropriate to the subject?

4. Lepp cites the Bible in paragraph 1, St. Paul and Theresa of Avila in paragraph 2, and Karl Jung in paragraph 3. What is the purpose of these examples? Do they properly and effectively introduce the main idea of the essay in paragraph 4?

5. Paragraph 5 begins with the word "but," which implies a contrast with the preceding paragraph. Examine paragraphs 4 and 5 and state what this contrast is and how it helps develop Lepp's thesis.

The Handler

Damon Knight

Damon Knight (b. 1922) is a noted science fiction writer, editor, and anthologist. He founded and was president of the Science Fiction Writers of America and received the Hugo Award in 1956 for best science fiction criticism.

1   When the big man came in, there was a movement in the room like bird dogs pointing. The piano player quit pounding, the two singing drunks shut up, all the beautiful people with cocktails in their hands stopped talking and laughing.

2   "Pete!" the nearest woman shrilled, and he walked straight into the room, arms around two girls, hugging them tight. "How's my sweetheart? Susy, you look good enough to eat, but I had it for

lunch. George, you pirate—'' he let go both girls, grabbed a bald blushing little man and thumped him on the arm—''you were great, sweetheart, I mean it, really great. Now HEAR THIS!'' he shouted, over all the voices that were clamoring Pete this, Pete that.

3   Somebody put a martini in his hand, and he stood holding it, bronzed and tall in his dinner jacket, teeth gleaming white as his shirt cuffs. ''We had a show!'' he told them.

4   A shriek of agreement went up, a babble of did we have a *show* my God Pete listen a *show*—

5   He held up his hand. ''It was a good show!''

6   Another shriek and babble.

7   ''The sponsor kinda liked it—he just signed for another one in the fall!''

8   A shriek, a roar, people clapping, jumping up and down. The big man tried to say something else, but gave up, grinning, while men and women crowded up to him. They were all trying to shake his hand, talk in his ear, put their arms around him.

9   ''I love ya *all!*'' he shouted. ''Now what do you say, let's live a little!''

10   The murmuring started again as people sorted themselves out. There was a clinking from the bar. ''Jesus, Pete,'' a skinny pop-eyed little guy was saying, crouching in adoration, ''when you dropped that fishbowl I thought I'd pee myself, honest to God—''

11   The big man let out a bark of happy laughter. ''Yeah, I can still see the look on your face. And the fish, flopping all over the stage. So what can I do, I get down there on my knees—'' the big man did so, bending over and staring at imaginary fish on the floor. ''And I say, 'Well, fellows, back to the drawing board!' ''

12   Screams of laughter as the big man stood up. The party was arranging itself around him in arcs of concentric circles, with people in the back standing on sofas and the piano bench so they could see. Somebody yelled, ''Sing the goldfish song, Pete!''

13   Shouts of approval, please-do-Pete, the goldfish song.

14   ''Okay, okay.'' Grinning, the big man sat on the arm of a chair and raised his glass, ''And a vun, and a doo—vere's de moosic?'' A scuffle at the piano bench. Somebody banged out a few chords. The big man made a comic face and sang, ''Ohhh—how I wish . . . I was a little fish . . . and when I want some quail . . . I'd flap my little tail.''

15   Laughter, the girls laughing louder than anybody and their red mouths farther open. One flushed blonde had her hand on the big man's knee, and another was sitting close behind him.

16   ''But seriously—'' the big man shouted. More laughter.

17   ''No seriously,'' he said in a vibrant voice as the room quieted, ''I want to tell you in all seriousness I couldn't have done it alone. And incidentally I see we have some foreigners, litvaks and other members of the press here tonight, so I want to introduce all the important people. First of all, George here, the three-fingered band leader—and there isn't a guy in the world could have done what he did this afternoon—George, I love ya.'' He hugged the blushing little bald man.

18   ''Next my real sweetheart, Ruthie, where are ya? Honey, you were the greatest, really perfect—I mean it, baby—'' He kissed a dark girl in a red dress who cried a little and hid her face on his broad shoulder. ''And Frank—'' he reached down and grabbed the skinny pop-eyed guy by the sleeve, ''What can I tell you? A sweetheart?'' The skinny guy was blinking, all choked up; the big man thumped him on the back. ''Sol and Ernie and Mack, my writers, Shakespeare should have been so lucky—'' One by one, they came up to shake the big man's hand as he called their names; the women kissed him and cried. ''My stand-in,'' the big man was calling out, and ''my caddy,'' and ''Now,'' he said, as the room quieted a little, people flushed and sore-throated with enthusiasm, ''I want you to meet my handler.''

19   The room fell silent. The big man looked thoughtful and startled, as if he had had a sudden pain. Then he stopped moving. He sat without breathing or blinking his eyes. After a moment there was a jerky motion behind him. The girl who was sitting on the arm of the chair got up and moved away. The big man's dinner jacket split open in the back, and a little man climbed out. He had a perspiring brown face under a shock of black hair. He was a very small man, almost a dwarf, stoop-shouldered and round-backed in a sweaty brown singlet and shorts. He climbed out of the cavity in the big man's body, and closed the dinner jacket carefully. The big man sat motionless and his face was doughy.

20   The little man got down, wetting his lips nervously. Hello, Fred, a few people said. ''Hello,'' Fred called, waving his hand. He was about forty, with a big nose and big soft brown eyes. His voice was cracked and uncertain. ''Well, we sure put on a show, didn't we?''

21   Sure did, Fred, they said politely. He wiped his brow with the back of his hand. ''Hot in there,'' he explained, with an apologetic grin. Yes I guess it must be, Fred, they said. People around the outskirts of the crowd were beginning to turn away, form conversational groups; the hum of talk rose higher. ''Say, Tim, I wonder if I could have something to drink,'' the little man said. ''I don't like to leave him—you know—'' He gestured toward the silent big man.

22   "Sure, Fred, what'll it be?"

23   "Oh—you know—a glass of beer?"

24   Tim brought him a beer in a pilsener glass and he drank it thirstily, his brown eyes darting nervously from side to side. A lot of people were sitting down now; one or two were at the door leaving.

25   "Well," the little man said to a passing girl, "Ruthie, that was quite a moment there, when the fishbowl busted, wasn't it?"

26   "Huh? Excuse me, honey, I didn't hear you." She bent nearer.

27   "Oh—well, it don't matter. Nothing."

28   She patted him on the shoulder once, and took her hand away. "Well, excuse me, sweetie, I have to catch Robbins before he leaves." She went on toward the door.

29   The little man put his beer glass down and sat, twisting his knobby hands together. The bald man and the pop-eyed man were the only ones still sitting near him. An anxious smile flickered on his lips; he glanced at one face, then another. "Well," he began, "that's one show under our belts, huh, fellows, but I guess we got to start, you know, thinking about—"

30   "Listen, Fred," said the bald man seriously, leaning forward to touch him on the wrist, "why don't you get back inside?"

31   The little man lookat at him for a moment with sad hound-dog eyes, then ducked his head, embarrassed. He stood up uncertainly, swallowed and said, "Well—" He climbed up on the chair behind the big man, opened the back of the dinner jacket and put his legs in one at a time. A few people were watching him, unsmiling. "Thought I'd take it easy for a while," he said weakly, "but I guess—" He reached in and gripped something with both hands, then swung himself inside. His brown, uncertain face disappeared.

32   The big man blinked suddenly and stood up. "Well *hey* there," he called, "what's the matter with this party anyway? Let's see some life, some action—" Faces were lighting up around him. People began to move in closer. "What I mean, let me hear that beat!"

33   The big man began clapping his hands rhythmically. The piano took it up. Other people began to clap. "What I mean, are we alive here or just waiting for the wagon to pick us up? How's that again, can't hear you!" A roar of pleasure as he cupped his hand to his ear. "Well come on, let me hear it!" A louder roar. Pete, Pete; a gabble of voices. "I got nothing against Fred," said the bald man earnestly in the middle of the noise, "I mean for a square he's a nice guy." "Know what you mean," said the pop-eyed man, "I mean like he doesn't *mean* it." "Sure," said the bald man, "but Jesus that sweaty undershirt and all. . . ." The pop-eyed man shrugged. "What are

you gonna do?'' Then they both burst out laughing as the big man made a comic face, tongue lolling, eyes crossed. Pete, Pete, Pete; the room was really jumping; it was a great party, and everything was all right, far into the night.

Topics for Discussion

1. Why does the atmosphere of the party change when Fred emerges? Why does it change when he dissolves into Pete?

2. Do you conclude from personal observation that people have "inner" and "outer" selves? Do you find "inner" or "outer" self reflected in any of the characters of this story?

3. In paragraph 17, why does Knight have Pete congratulate the three-fingered band leader?

4. In paragraph 19, why does the girl leave?

5. In paragraph 31, Fred says, "Thought I'd take it easy for a while." What is the symbolic meaning of this comment?

6. Fred seems very insecure but can become secure in the character of Pete. What is the basis for his insecurity? Do you feel insecure at times? When? Why?

7. Do you find yourself playing different roles in life? How do people react? Are their reactions similar to those of the people in this story?

Rhetorical Considerations

1. Why does Knight leave the setting of the story rather indistinct?

2. How does Knight use physical description as a device for indirectly revealing some of his central themes? See especially paragraph 19.

3. Compare Pete's language with Fred's. How does Knight use contrast of tone to emphasize the difference between inner and outer self? See especially paragraphs 17 and 18 and 21–29.

4. Why does Knight make Pete's language transparent and hollow? Why does he make Fred sound sincere?

5. What does this story teach you about the relationship between the language of direction and the language of indirection?

Rhetorical Analysis

Bertrand Russell: What I Have Lived For

You may not have realized it, but the short piece of writing at the beginning of this section, Bertrand Russell's introduction to his *Autobiography,* is an *argument.* In a quick, pointed sketch of his feelings about his past, this ninety-year-old man is trying to convince us that life is indeed worth living. Take it from someone who knows, he says, life can actually glow with a mellow sort of joy for the person who kindles the few sparks of love, knowledge, or pity which he finds in himself or in the world.

Most arguments we are familiar with are very unlike Russell's. A lawyer *arguing* a case in civil court, for example, relies on statistics, precedents, cold hard facts. The lawyer angles for a clear-cut decision by the judge—a basic acceptance or rejection of the case. Despite elements of degree (in tort suits, for example), the issue is basically win or lose, and a smart attorney will marshall every bit of evidence and every precedent to win.

Russell argues for a basic acceptance of his case too, but he does so much differently than does our lawyer. The stuff of which Russell speaks is so intimately intertwined with the whole history of human experience that the pettiness of courtroom speech would seem out of place here. Can you imagine Russell trying to *prove* that love is an overwhelmingly strong human emotion—"87.6 percent of the people interviewed at a Columbus, Ohio, shopping center reported that *love* held an important place in their lives. 8.3 percent reported that it did not, while 4.1 percent had no opinion." Statistics like this may have a great deal to tell us about how people view the world, perhaps, ultimately, much more than what some people might view as Russell's impressionistic and naive display of emotion. But Russell does not choose to rely on *empirical proof* to make his case. He appeals instead to our emotional attitudes toward what most of us have been taught is essential and unchanging in human experience, to what he believes to be the ethical essence of the inner person.

Russell does not appeal to our reason but to our feelings and to our general *sense* of justice, implying that *love* and the

97

desire for *knowledge* make human beings more human, and that *pity* characterizes individuals who act with justice and compassion. This appeal to our emotions can be quite convincing. On the whole, *love, knowledge,* and *pity* are words which seem to go well with the good that has happened in the world. Moreover, these words acquire a special ethical authenticity when spoken by a man whose life has reflected their meaning. But you have heard emotional appeals before, and you have probably been taught to be wary of them. You have heard the appeal to "patriotism," perhaps, which has been honestly employed to move people to fight for freedom and independence but which has also been used by tyrants from Napoleon to Hitler and beyond to rouse people of ordinary good sense to fight senseless wars and to allow their neighbors to be taken to concentration camps. You have perhaps learned that appeals to religious faith cannot satisfactorily end arguments, that in the Middle Ages and Renaissance army fought against army, each with God on its side. The appeal to emotion ought to move, but it ought not to convince—every argument must ultimately pass the test of reason. That is, every proposition must be studied in terms of its causal connection with other phenomena. Russell does not attempt to offer his comments directly on life for rational analysis—he knows that we already feel that there is something distasteful about dissecting human emotions, about slicing apart such a deeply emotional essay as this. But let's get our sharp scalpels of reason and do it anyway. Perhaps Russell intends after all to let his argument stand in the face of reason, knowing that even though he has not used reason, logic, or demonstrable argument to *make* his case, reason, logic, and demonstrable argument cannot be effectively employed against it.

If Russell had attempted to rationally prove his point, without relying on the inductive statistical proof of the lawyer's case, he might have said something like the following:

> There exist in the minds of men certain abstract principles which ought to govern the actions of men. These principles have their foundation in the basic inner nature of man, something we call *human nature.* But ever since man can remember—that is, throughout recorded history—human nature, which is essentially noble, honest, and good, has been tainted. It seems that individuals relate to their fellow human

beings on the basis of *greed, hate,* and *pride*, perversions of what *should* characterize the nature of man—*generosity, love,* and *friendship*. To raise human nature from its fallen state, we should cultivate ideas which bring people together. To reach this end, therefore, *love,* as an abstract principle, should govern our activities. Also, since human beings fight each other especially when the material things they seek are scarce, we should cultivate *knowledge*. The pursuit of knowledge moves us toward a world of abundance where fighting will be unnecessary, and this pursuit provides as well an activity which one soon learns is of more value than many of the material things over which we fight. *Pity* is perhaps the most important motivating force in the restoration of a noble and dignified human nature, for it directs our wills not toward what is good for the individual self but toward what is good for the other. Only when people become as interested in the other as they are in themselves will men begin to live in peace and harmony with each other.

All of this sounds quite reasonable, if less poetic than Russell's original essay. One can logically conclude, therefore, that Russell, if he had desired, could have made at least a reasonable case for himself. But it remains to be asked whether we can make a reasonable case *against* Russell, against *love, knowledge,* and *pity* as motivating forces for human activity. Russell's argument needs to be tested by a counterargument. One such counterargument might go as follows:

> *Love, knowledge,* and *pity* are ideas which exist in the human mind, and as such they have a certain degree of power to move people to action. But the mind is not some abstract, totally unchanging world unto itself. It is generated and conditioned by the material world around it, and the ideas it acquires are nothing more than a reflection of concrete relationships within that world. Since the world changes, it is reasonable to expect that the meaning and effect of certain ideas in the world will also change. *Love* can, for example, mean refusing to shoot another human being, but that refusal can have very different consequences depending on the context. A policeman raises his pistol and aims it at a fourteen-year-old boy who has just looted a single six-pack of beer from a burned-out liquor store. Do you urge him in the name of *love* not to shoot? A colonial guerrilla fighter waits in ambush for foreign soldiers who come

to burn his village, to rape and kill his family. Do you urge him in the name of *love* not to shoot? Answer these questions for yourself, but in answering ask yourself whether or not *love by itself* means anything. Ask yourself the same question about *knowledge*. You would probably agree that people should seek after *knowledge* in the search for a cure for cancer, but how about *knowledge* in the search for better germ warfare? What about germ warfare for the "other side"? Is the *search for knowledge* always so unequivocally noble? *Pity* can be very debilitating for the person who receives it. Do you constantly show your pity for a disabled person and thereby imply that he is somehow a lesser human being than you? Does not the whole notion of *pity* imply a power relationship, with the person being pitied on the bottom? In the name of *love,* should we not seek the elimination of *pity*?

These short counterarguments do not destroy Russell's case, but they do give us a perspective on the matters he talks about which is quite removed from his emotional appeal.

Half of the business of rhetoric is making arguments reasonable enough to convince people of the truth of some proposition or of the validity of some conclusion deduced from a given set of propositions. The other half involves the technical business of making your case in an orderly, effective way. Complex problems cannot, of course, always be explained in language which eliminates confusion and doubt. In fact, as we have just observed in Russell's case, grand simplicity in a piece of writing often tends to obscure an essay's internal logic. Nevertheless, Russell's short essay is a masterpiece of technical construction. Here are some of the reasons:

1. *General Structure.* The first word of the essay predicts a very simple, solid structure. The reader knows, as soon as Russell says "three," that some very concrete statements are going to be made and that they will be made in a very systematic way. What follows is a diagrammatical representation of that simple structure:

INTRODUCTION	(Paragraph 1)
SUBTOPIC 1	(Paragraph 2)
SUBTOPIC 2	(Paragraph 2)
SUBTOPIC 3	(Paragraph 3)
CONCLUSION	(Paragraph 5)

2. *Commitment and Response.* Good writers deliver what they promise, and, unless they are intent on providing suspense or bringing the reader to a surprise conclusion, they also explicitly promise what they plan to deliver. Russell does this in the essay when he specifically names *love, knowledge,* and *pity* as the topics he will cover. This point may seem to be so simple as not to require mention, yet, surprisingly enough, it is something often forgotten by students.

3. *Coherence I.* In terms of structure, note how Russell moves from *love,* which he has "found," to *knowledge,* which he has achieved "a little" of, to *pity,* which "cannot" alleviate the suffering he finds in the world. The structural movement from affirmation to negation, from hope to sorrow, exists simultaneously with and within a larger structural movement from negation to affirmation. Russell begins his essay with a paragraph ending with the word *despair* and ends the essay with strong notes of affirmation and hope. This structural *interlace* cannot be reduced to a simple diagram without losing the largest part of its effectiveness, but perhaps the following illustration will help you to better understand the principles of organization and coherence which Russell has chosen to use:

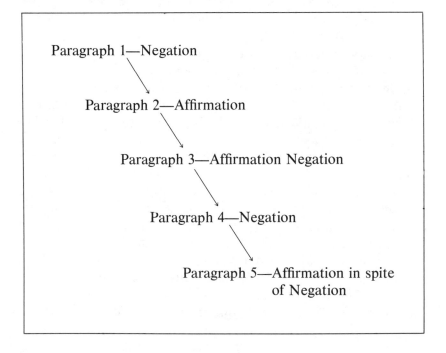

4. *Coherence II.* The word *simple* in the essay's first line describes the overall structure we find in these five brief paragraphs. Yet, as we have just seen, there are some techniques used by Russell which go beyond mere simplicity. Notice how he juxtaposes opposites in several places to create a kind of continuous echo—a sort of *tone coherence.* Russell's passions are "simple" but "strong." He has been brought to the "edge of despair," but he has decided to live. Love is too good for this world, but he has found it. He has also found a little knowledge but not enough to satisfy him totally. *Love* and *knowledge* led his thoughts into abstraction, but *pity* brought him back to concrete reality. He wants to change the world but realizes that he cannot. The final paragraph's note of affirmation is not qualified by a *but.*

5. *Variation from Expected Patterns.* Sometimes, in an attempt to achieve clarity, a writer bores the reader by setting up easily predictable rhetorical patterns which contain no surprises. But, like the composer of a good symphony, Russell has small surprises for all throughout the essay. The first time he mentions the three basic components of his structural pattern—*love, knowledge, pity*—neither *love* nor *knowledge* is qualified by an adjective. However, he qualifies *pity* with the word *unbearable,* thereby indicating that this emotion perhaps has less in common with the first two than those two do with each other. Look for other pattern variations throughout the essay.

6. *Metaphor.* Metaphor is the implied or stated comparison of one thing with another. Some metaphors are dead clichés— "My love is like a rose." Others are more interesting—Eldridge Cleaver's comparison of the Holy Trinity to 3-in-1 Oil. The metaphors in Russell's essay are not all original. Passions have been compared to great winds before (see Canto V of Dante's *Inferno*). The "lifeless abyss" of existential despair is a commonplace throughout modern literature—if you have not heard the phrase before, you'll hear it soon in one context or another around the campus. "Shivering consciousness" seems at least OK, but the business of heaven and the saints seem a bit gushy and romantic. Maybe you disagree, though. Maybe these metaphors move you. Think about this—reread the essay.

7. *Sentence Structure.* Russell uses a combination of *periodic, balanced, simple,* and mainly *cumulative* sentences.

He constructs his sentences in such a way as to achieve parallelism and arranges them to provide variety and intense, immediate effect. Here is an outline of his sentence patterns:

    I. 1. Main Clause
             Expansion
             Expansion
             Expansion (CS)
      2. Main Clause
             Expansion
               Expansion
                  Expansion (CS)

   II. 1. Main Clause
             Expansion
             Expansion
               Expansion
                  Expansion (CS)
      2. Main Clause
             Expansion
             Expansion
               Expansion
                  Expansion (CS)
      3. Main Clause
             Expansion
             Expansion (Embedded exp)
               Expansion (CS)
      4. Main Clause—QUALIFIER—Main Clause (BS)

  III. 1. Qualifier
             Main Clause (PS)
      2. Main Clause (SS)
      3. Main Clause (SS)
      4. Main Clause (SS)
      5. Inverted Main Clause (Embedded exp) (SS)

  IV. 1. Main Clause (Embedded exp)
             —Expansion (CS)
      2. Main Clause (SS)
      3. Item
         Item   Main Clause (SS)
         Item
         Item Verb Complement
      4. Main Clause—Main Clause—Main Clause (BS)

V. 1. Main Clause (SS)
    2. Main Clause
        Expansion (CS)

8. You can, we are sure, find other things to say about this essay in terms of rhetoric, especially in terms of tone and style.

What is love? 'Tis not hereafter.
Present mirth hath present laughter;
What's to come is still unsure.
In delay there lies no plenty;
Then come kiss me, sweet and twenty,
Youth's a stuff will not endure.

Twelfth Night, II, iii

2

YOUTH

Recently the United States Congress decided to extend the right to vote in all federal elections to eighteen-year-old citizens. For some people this step simply represented a logical development in a country inordinately fond of young people. Others considered it simply a long-overdue recognition of the maturity of young people. Your view on this probably has a great deal to do with your own age group. In any event, the lowering of the voting age had far-reaching effects not only on young people between the ages of eighteen and twenty-one, but on society as a whole as well. Many states, following the lead of Congress, lowered the voting age in state and local elections. Then some states lowered the age of majority to eighteen, and suddenly eighteen-year-olds were adults.

Youth, obviously, is a difficult term to define because its limits are so imprecise. You may, in some uneasy sense, object to being included in this category. Some of you may prefer the term *young adult* while others may insist upon the term *adult* since you are legally adults. But whatever term you use or prefer, the reality of things is that you are at what has often been termed the most difficult stage of life—the passage from childhood to adulthood.

We do not pretend to know any more than anyone else about the problems, concerns, and feelings of young people today, and we recognize that in attempting to suggest that most young people share common interests and perspectives we run the risk of making oversimplifications and drawing stereotypes. But we do know that youth is not the golden, carefree existence adults often make it out to be. We do know that by the age of seventeen a young woman or man has experienced joy and anguish as deeply felt as the emotions of a person much older. We do know that to be young is not entirely to be innocent.

It is not easy to be young. Your first love, your first job, your first college course, all these experiences thrust you into new, complex, and sometimes harsh realities. Because these experiences are firsts, they figure large in your life. For the person of seventeen, the basic stuff of life is still a bit fresh, a bit raw, a bit more capable of hurting. A man or woman of thirty is probably better acquainted with his or her strengths and weaknesses. The person of seventeen has just begun to test himself as adult. Are these vast generalizations? Of course. Some people of seventeen are very old, and some people of thirty have not yet grown up, whatever that means. But the fact remains that young people by and large are more totally engaged in defining the contours of the road before them than are older people. To make things more simple than they are, we might say that young people are guilty of being young.

Again at the risk of making a generalization, let us say that the greatest distinction between youth and adults, perhaps we should say older people, is the realization of death. "No young man believes he shall ever die," said William Hazlitt. It is just this unawareness of death that gives youth an apparently innocent character—this and youth's concern with life and living and the future. One does not find young people worrying about Social Security or pension plans. The culture of the young is the culture of life. Look at the music, clothing, and entertainment of the young. What are the concerns of young people—not death but the prolongation of life, the preservation of life, the enjoyment of life. Life is immediate and real to the young.

You may wonder, then, why we begin this section with two essays by young people who are concerned with looking back on their lives. It is, of course, always good for people to examine their lives and determine where they are going and how they will get there. Better this than to look back with regret on a seemingly wasted life. Bertrand Russell in the first section of this book looked back with no regret on his life.

Most of the essays in this section deal with the most immediate experience of young people—school. If anything is central in the lives of young people it is school and all the pain and sometimes joy it causes. Indeed, you are probably reading this right now not because you really want to but because it is part of an assignment for school. Perhaps you have never really thought about the whole process of education. Now might be a good time to do a little critical thinking about school and what education is all about. Other selections in this section touch on other topics which we hope will interest you—drugs, politics, religion.

Read the selections carefully and critically. Do not be quick to pass over an essay lightly just because you agree with what the author says. Nor should you dismiss an essay because you disagree with it. Because the material in this section is so much a part of your life you may tend to read casually and uncritically. Instead, you should make a concentrated effort to question, probe, and criticize, for then you will be able to form a judgment based on informed opinion and not uncritical acceptance.

The Rhetorical Analysis at the end of this section deals with Deborah Perry's essay *Because I Am Black*. Be sure to read Perry's essay before reading the Rhetorical Analysis.

Kids' Country

Shana Alexander

Shana Alexander (b. 1925) has written extensively for Harper's
Bazaar, Life, *and* McCall's. *Since 1971 she has appeared as a
radio and television commentator for CBS. In 1969 she received
the Golden Pen Award of the American Newspaper Women's
Club. Her book,* The Feminine Eye, *was published in 1970.*

1 Children are a relatively modern invention. Until a few
hundred years ago they did not exist. In medieval and Renaissance
painting you see pint-size men and women, wearing grown-up
clothes and grown-up expressions, performing grown-up tasks.
Children did not exist because the family as we know it had not
evolved. In the old days most people lived on the land, and life was a
communal affair.

2 Children today not only exist; they have taken over. God's
Country has to an astonishing degree become Kids' Country—in no
place more than in America, and at no time more than now. Once
more 'tis the season, holiday time has begun, the frantic family
skedaddle from pumpkin to holly when Kids' Country runs in its
jumpingest high gear.

3 But it is always Kids' Country here. Our civilization is child-
centered, child-obsessed. A kid's body is our physical ideal.
Weightwatchers grunt and pant. Sages jog from sea to shining sea.
Plastic surgeons scissor and tuck up. New hair sprouts, transplanted, on wisdom's brow. One way or another we are determined
to "keep in shape," and invariably this means keeping a kid's
shape—which we then outfit in baby-doll ruffles, sneakers and blue
jeans.

4 The food we live on is kids' food: pizza, hot dogs, fried
chicken, ice cream, hamburgers. This bizarre diet is the reason we
have such trouble maintaining our kids' bodies.

5 The stuff we now drink has thrown the beverage industry into
turmoil. Our consumption of soft drinks has risen 80 percent in a
decade. Americans not only are switching *en masse* from hot coffee
to iced tea, and bitter drinks to sweet. The popularity of alcoholic
soda pop—the so-called "fun" wines like Thunderbird and apple
wine has jumped 168 percent in five years!

6 Children hate spinach, vitamins and *haute cuisine*. They like

their food kooked, not cooked: you pop, thaw, dissolve or explode it into eatability. To buy it you push around a wire perambulator, and at the end of the supermarket line you get prizes of colored stamps.

7   In Kids' Country, every day must be prize day. Miss America, Miss Teen-Age America, Miss Junior Miss America and probably Miss Little Miss America trample each other down star-spangled runways. Volume mail-order giveaways will shortly silt up our postal system entirely. All day long TV shows like "Concentration," "Dating Game," "Hollywood Squares" and "Jackpot" hand out more toys: wrist watches, washing machines, trips to Hawaii.

8   The rest of the world may be in fee to the Old Boy Network, carried on to the point of senility, but here there are no elder statesmen left. Seniority in an American politician no longer denotes wisdom, only power or tenure. The old age of the present Congress is a major hindrance. No one considers the Héberts and Eastlands as Athenian men.

9   Our contemporary heroes are a series of golden boys. A direct line links Charles Lindbergh to Billy Graham to the astronauts to John F. Kennedy—and to his kid brothers.

10   The philosopher-kings of Kids' Country are professors like Erich Segal and Charles Reich, who saw in Woodstock and the flower children a new golden age of innocence he called Consciousness III. The totem animal in Kids' Country just now is a talking, philosophizing seagull who soars on vast updrafts of hot air, and the beloved bogeyman is a wicked movie *mafioso* with a heart of gold.

11   The ideal of American parenthood is to be a kid with your kid. Take him to Disneyland; take him fishing, take him out to the ball game. Our national pastimes are kids' games, and we are all hooked. When the Redskins are blacked out in Washington, the President holes up in New York so as not to miss the big game. Bobby Fischer, the quintessential smart boy of every school, turns the whole country on to chess. "The Boys of Summer" becomes a best seller. In nostalgia's golden haze, we forget the poet's full line, "I see the boys of summer in their ruin."

12   In Kids' Country we do not permit middle age. Thirty is promoted over 50, but 30 knows that soon his time to be overtaken will come. Middle-aged man must appear to run, even if it is only running in place. Often the big kid outruns his heart. In our over-60 population there are ten widows for every man.

13   Like a child's room, Kids' Country is a mess. New York City seems about to disappear under its load of litter, graffiti and dog droppings. How is it that China can eliminate the house fly, and we can't even clean up Central Park?

14   In Kids' Country, not so ironically, Mommy and Daddy are household gods, and so we have two immense national holidays, elsewhere virtually unknown, called "Mother's Day" and "Father's Day."

15   We are the first society in which parents expect to learn from their children. Such a topsy-turvy situation has come about at least in part because, unlike the rest of the world, ours is an immigrant society, and for immigrants the *only* hope is in the kids. In the Old Country, hope was in the father, and how much family wealth he could accumulate and pass along to his children. In the growth pattern of America and its ever-expanding frontier, the young man was ever advised to Go West; the father was ever inheriting from his son: the topsy-turviness was built-in from the beginning. In short, a melting pot needs a spoon. Kids' Country may be the inevitable result.

16   Kids' Country is not all bad. America is the greatest country in the world to grow up in *because* it's Kids' Country. We not only wear kids' clothes and eat kids' food; we dream kids' dreams, and make them come true. It was, after all, a boys' game to go to the moon.

17   Certainly as a people we thrive. By the time they are 16, most American kids today are bigger, stronger—and smarter—than Mommy and Daddy ever were. And if they are not precisely "happier," they may well be more "grown up." But being a civilization with no genuine rites of passage, what we are experiencing now seems in many ways the exact opposite of medieval and Renaissance life. If in the old days children did not exist, it seems equally true today that adults, as a class, have begun to disappear, condemning all of us to remain boys and girls forever, jogging and doing push-ups against eternity.

Vocabulary

communal	skedaddle	bizarre
en masse	*haute cuisine*	
perambulator	quintessential	

Topics for Discussion

1. When Alexander says, "Children are a relatively modern invention. Until a few hundred years ago they did not exist," what does she mean?

2. Do you agree that "our civilization is child-centered, child-obsessed"? Can you cite any arguments to support your answer?

3. What is *haute cuisine*? Why would children hate it?

4. Do you agree that "our contemporary heroes are a series of golden boys"? Who are your contemporary heroes?

5. Does Alexander see anything good in "Kids' Country"?

6. What role do the old have in "Kids' Country"?

Rhetorical Considerations

1. How effective is the opening sentence of the essay in attracting your attention?

2. Alexander writes very short paragraphs. How fully developed are her paragraphs?

3. What effect do her short paragraphs have on the structure and development of the essay as a whole? Could some short paragraphs be joined together effectively?

4. Many of Alexander's references are very topical. How many such references are unknown to you? Does this in any way lessen the impact of the essay?

5. To what audience is Alexander speaking?

How I Won Bruce, Ruth, and Acapulco

Judy Fayard

Judy Fayard was the Los Angeles correspondent for Life *magazine, from which this article is taken.*

1   The first time I was ever a contestant on a quiz show, it was on radio, in 1949, and I was 6 years old. I was unable to answer the question, "What is a baby tadpole?" (I knew a tadpole was a baby frog, but what was a baby tadpole?) I didn't win the $25 U.S. savings bond, and was taken home in tears. The next time I played a

game show was this summer, when I became a contestant on *The Dating Game* to find out what it's like to be a performer in television's daytime game show carnival.

2   Like a mutant phoenix, the TV game show has risen from the ashes of *The $64,000 Question* and has proliferated, filling the hours between Mr. Greenjeans and the afternoon news, challenging the ratings supremacy of those once all-channel champions, the soap operas. For those of us who spend our days in offices, daytime TV game shows are a sometime thing, accompaniment to chicken soup and cold pills. A week of watching them in good health, head clear and sneezeless, left me awed by their monumental, impossibly magnificent, *brontosaurian* vacuity. They are games of mental tiddledywinks, snake oil to embalm dead midafternoons.

3   The object of a game show is to entertain the viewer as inexpensively as possible between blocks of highly profitable commercials. The contestant is simply an unpaid volunteer actor in a very particular kind of situation comedy. The fun of waving at Mom from the TV screen, and winning at least a consolation prize, might be enough to attract contestants to *Concentration* or *Password*. But what murky urge for self-ridicule could ever possess anyone to make himself a willing victim of *Let's Make a Deal?* How can a new marriage be eagerly offered up to the sniggering jokes of a coast-to-coast shivaree for the price of a household appliance on *The New-lywed Game?* And why would anyone want to win a "romantic" weekend *anywhere on earth* with a blind date and a chaperon by playing *The Dating Game?*

4   Dating was always a purely American phenomenon, an artificial bridge across the artificial separation of the sexes that began in early childhood. In my small southern city dating was the only game in town. All that mattered was that you had one, because by our Noah's Ark etiquette there were parties and places you couldn't go without one. Social status rose and fell according to the quantity and quality of the dates, and for that we endured all the attendant little rites: getting fixed up, getting stood up, bringing a date or breaking a date, late dates and double dates and how far would you go on a first date; the tears when you didn't have a date for the senior dance, and the tears when you did but it wasn't the right one.

5   As formal social ritual, dating is pretty well washed up today; kids don't date anymore, they have "meaningful relationships," or at least ways of getting together that are much more loosely prescribed. But there are seven million daily daytime viewers whose prurient interest is still piqued by pitting the boys *against* the girls in the good old-fashioned way. For them, the remains of the rites are

all there, mummified and preserved in maraschino, on display Monday through Friday afternoons at 2:30 P.M. EST.

6   Like its sibling *The Newlywed Game* (both produced by Chuck Barris), *The Dating Game* adds a pinch of sex—of the hint-and-wink variety—to the basic game show formula. A female contestant has three minutes in which to ask questions of three unseen male contestants; on the basis of their answers (or voices, or whim) she chooses one as her ''date.'' The newly coupled strangers are then sent off, in company of a chaperon, on their date—anything from four glorious days on the beach at Waikiki to a table for two at Liberace's opening night in Las Vegas. The female automatically wins a trip; her only risk is *whom* she picks.

7   Roughly 14,000 of us have played *The Dating Game* in the seven years the show has been on the air. Since the producers agreed to let me go on, my experience was something less than typical, but, judging from my adventures, no significant alterations were made in my honor. Any applicant who is (1) reasonably attractive or at least not ugly, (2) not more than modishly long-haired, and (3) deemed unlikely to engage in on-the-air lewdness, profanity, sacrilege, political commentary or acts of physical or emotional violence—or complete silence—has a pretty good chance of being accepted as a contestant.

8   Because neither dating nor daytime TV is particularly fashionable among today's youth, it is harder than it used to be to scrape up enough willing contestant fodder for the voracious eight-contestants-a-day five-days-a-week show. Some, like me, volunteer, but most are recruited by a 500-calls-a-day squad of telephone ''bandits.'' Once recruited, potential contestants are processed by the 30-odd, mostly young *Dating Game* staffers with breezy, fraternity-rush courtesy and the smooth mechanical efficiency found at a discount dentist's.

9   The double door to the *Dating Game* studio has ''Male'' and ''Female'' halves, and the reception room behind them is divided into the boys' side and the girls' side by a partition covered with snapshots of happy couples. The receptionist, her desk straddling the line between the sexes, smilingly hands out application forms—pink for girls and blue for boys.

10   Slumped into one of the schoolroom desks in the corner, next to the door that says ''Bachelorettes,'' I bury my head in the form. Rejecting a momentary urge to fudge it—everyone else in the room looks 12—I resolutely put 30 after ''Age.'' I wrestle with ''Special Achievements (awards, titles, etc.)'' and ''Anything Interesting about Yourself.'' (Joe Jefferson Players Mobile Alabama Best Ac-

tress 1959? I can't.) I skip down to sign the affidavit that I am "not married, engaged nor legally separated from any spouse . . . single and not in any way involved in the state of matrimony." Certainly does sum it up.

11   I lean over to see what my neighbor is writing. We compare the lists of questions we've been asked to submit ("DO NOT ASK ABOUT NAME, AGE, INCOME, RELIGION OR POLITICS. ASK FUN-TYPE QUESTIONS"), and I learn that she is older even than I, divorced, and here at the insistence of her 13-year-old-daughter. We laugh about the silliness of what we are doing, but later, after we stand against the height marks on the wall to be snapped in Polaroid, she confides, "It really is hard to meet people in L.A., don't you think?"

12   Eventually we are shepherded into the next room to play a sample game. Although staff writers tailor the questions used on the air, most of my sister applicants have already captured the particular rhythm of *Dating Game* questions—a personal statement followed by query, i.e., "I love little feathered creatures. Can you make a noise like a little feathered creature that will convince me to go out with you?" My friend the divorcée hastily scribbles out new questions, suddenly realizing that "What is your idea of happiness?" is off on the wrong track. This sample game is the first big sieve, giving the staff a chance to weed out the uglies and the really impossibles right away. As we play, the smiling young man casually encodes little notations on our forms, and then we are cheerily dismissed to await a summons to play in the Saturday finals.

13   On Saturday the receptionist stops me on my way in, returning my application because of the unfilled blanks. "We need more information for your introduction if you get on the show," she smiled. Still unable to think of any awards or titles more recent than "University of Colorado Homecoming Queen Runner-up 1962," I invent a trip to Africa for "Anything Interesting."

14   There are six of us on each side of the bundling board in the finalists' round, and three staffers on the judges' panel. "Now no questions about how much money he makes. Remember this is not *Let's Make a Deal*. And no questions about politics. It's not *Face the Nation* either."

15   Barely a week after the Saturday finals I am invited to appear on the show. I had hoped it would take longer to find three willing and available bachelors old enough for me. (Contestants are more or less carefully matched by age and height and *very* carefully matched by race. There are black games and white games, but never integrated games. After all, it's not *Issues and Answers*.)

16   The show coordinator makes an appointment for me with the writers, and dictates instructions for the taping. Bring three outfits—but nothing white, glittery, checked, plaid, paisley or Day-Glo. Also no rings on the left hand.

17   "One more thing," he continues. "You haven't filled your form out completely enough."

18   "I have been through this before."

19   "Well, it says here you're a reporter. What kinds of stories do you do?"

20   "Entertainment and movie stuff, generally, but I do almost anything."

21   "Well, we wouldn't wanna put *that* down now, would we? Heh, heh, heh."

22   The objective of the question writers is, of course, to come up with questions that will entertain their audience—typically questions with just enough naughty innuendo to tickle the fantasies of the folks at home and give them that same giggly-wicked feeling they get by eating the cherry out of somebody else's Tom Collins. "We live in an age of automation. If we were alone in a car together what would you automatically do with your hands?" (Oddly, nobody ever says "grope.")

23   My objective, on the other hand, is to refrain from saying anything about which I will later be mortified. Working at such crossed purposes, our question session takes quite some time.

24   To my surprise they do not have a ready grab bag of possible questions from which to pluck. But they are unflaggingly good-natured as I reject any suggestions starting with "Make a noise like . . ." or "Describe your body as if . . ." (They usually get in at least one "body" question a show.) They in turn reject any offerings for which nobody in the room can imagine a possible "cute" answer.

25   Of my final list of nine, four are altered versions of my own questions, three are theirs entirely, and two joint efforts. They decide the *order*, however, and when I get my question card the day of the taping, their three are all in the crucial first five.

26   I had lots of company in the female-contestant waiting room: three teen-age girls and three ruffled tots with their mothers. ("The little girls? Oh, they're gonna do a show with a little *guy*.") One of the teen-agers asks my age. I tell her and she is shocked and then sympathetic. "Oh, gee, I hope you don't get any old 45-year-old fag bachelors."

27   One of the writers handles our pregame coaching: "Don't try to walk off with an Emmy or an Oscar. And don't stop to think. If a guy gives you an answer that's interesting and you'd like to

think about it for a while, that's wonderful, but it creates DEAD AIR. But the most important thing to remember, in big capital letters, is this . . ." he sums up. "Have . . ." and he draws big letters in the air: F-U-N.

28   On that encouraging note I am led away to the offstage isolation booth. My booth mate is "Moosie," a 6-year-old regular on *Laugh-In*, who is performing for the other half of the show, the Little League game. I am suddenly gripped by panic, finally realizing that I am about to manhunt on coast-to-coast television. I offer to settle for Moosie and run, but neither Moosie nor our guard will go along.

29   I don't remember much of my three minutes on the air The lights were so blinding that I couldn't see the audience at all, much less my friends ready with hand signals to guide me to Mr. Wonderful. (Contestants' guests are all tucked together in a far corner to prevent just that.) My questions seemed interminable and all the answers dreary and I just kept laughing at everything. ("Hadda coupla belts before you went on, huh, Jude?" a friend later chided.) Finally the gong goes off and I am given a minute to make my choice. I stare at my question card trying to remember who said what but I can't. In the end the studio audience makes my decision. They obviously liked No. 2—he got more applause and there was more *feeling* in it—and since they can see him and I can't, I figure I might as well go along. That's how I won Bruce and three days in Acapulco.

30   While Moosie is winning Little Miss Garden Grove and a trip to the magic kingdom of Disneyland, I have three minutes to talk to this man with whom I am going to Mexico, Bruce Oughterson, 35, once a nightclub singer but now a merchandising manager for a department store chain. He was on the show because he filled out an application for kicks while waiting to watch a girl friend appear on the show weeks before. That's as far as we get when they call us back onstage to throw our sign-off kisses—me and Bruce and Moosie and Moosie's date and a bobbing man in a Mickey Mouse suit representing the Magic Kingdom.

31   The chaperon has the right to terminate the trip if . . . my conduct is without due regard to social conventions or public morals or decency, or if I commit any act tending to bring me into public disrepute or tending to shock, insult, or offend the community, or tending to reflect unfavorably upon Chuck Barris Projects, the American Broadcasting Company or the sponsors or their advertising agencies, if any, or programs of *The Dating Game* series.

32   "Ruth will be sharing a room with you," the trip coordinator smiles at me. "That's how we make sure that Bruce doesn't go

visiting in your room and you don't go visiting in . . ." She pauses, sensing some small gap in the logic. "Anyway, there'll be no visiting between rooms."

33   It starts out well enough. We meet at the airport, buoyant and excited about Mexico. I have one bad moment when I notice that Ruth carries a big shoulder bag emblazoned *The Dating Game*. I have a flash vision of introductions and explanations that I do not relish. ("So you're a *Dating Game* couple. My, how big you've grown!") But we have a drink in the airport lounge and toast our adventure and by the time we toast again on the plane, we are having a wonderful time. Little do I realize that this will be the high point of the trip.

34   Four days in Acapulco turn out to be four days in a hotel in Acapulco, which is not precisely the same thing. We overlook one of the most beautiful bays in the world, but we cannot go boating, skin diving or water-skiing, for "insurance reasons." No tours or excursions are planned, no sightseeing arrangements, and we are not allowed to rent a car. Rather, we can rent one, but we are not allowed to drive it.

35   Our meals are paid for—if we take them at the hotel—and we are allotted two drinks before dinner and two after. The hotel is pure Miami Beach, the Musak in the rooms is American pop, and there is only one Mexican dish on the menu. The only clue to our location is the word "Acapulco" on the funny hats in the gift shop.

36   According to our "itinerary" we can go "swimming, shopping, sunning, etc." The first day we try to shop in the street market in the central city. But the temperature and humidity in off-season Acapulco are in the upper 90s. Besides, the city drainage system is enduring off-season repair, and the sections of the main street not flooded are not there at all.

37   Swimming? A tropical storm the week before has turned the water an uninviting muddy ocher—when the water can be seen at all between the throngs of tourists lured there by off-season rates. The hotel pool, meantime, has been commandeered by an army of children, most of them dive-bombing off the sides.

38   So we lie in the scalding sun. walk on the beach, and are hustled by hordes of peddlers. We lunch together, later each day, and struggle for conversation, three perfectly mismatched strangers trying very hard to be nice to one another. Bruce says it is like being in jail in paradise.

39   Nights are better. We have dinner, one night downstairs, one night upstairs. We have our after-dinner drinks upstairs, where there is good music and a Dutch singer named Andrik. The second night Ruth tells Andrik about *The Dating Game* and we are introduced

and get to tell our hometowns, and Bruce is asked to sing, which he does very well indeed. Bruce and I do have dancing in common, so we cha-cha with all the unused energy of the day and stay up until the early hours, as if, having spent all day waiting for something to happen, we are unwilling to give up the vigil. And Ruth, bless her, stays right with us.

40   *Dating Game* chaperons come in both sexes and all ages over 21. They are staffers, ex-staffers, relatives or friends of staffers. Ruth is a kind and generous mother of four, tripping with *The Dating Game* for the sixth time. She earns $5 a day for minding kids like us, and her only disciplinary power is that she holds the tickets home. That, and the fact that she is too nice for anyone to make her life difficult by sneaking off to go water-skiing or anything else. (No *Dating Game* ''date'' so far has had to be terminated by the chaperon.)

41   There have been more than 3,000 *Dating Game* ''dates'' in the last seven years, and I don't know how many of them were like ours. Surely not all, because the show has matchmade 11 marriages. I can't even speak for Bruce or Ruth, although I suspect that, gallantly as he stuck it out, Bruce would have preferred to be elsewhere. But I do know what it was like for me, because as we all said goodbye, I realized I'd been there before. It was a blind date for the Dartmouth Winter Carnival in 1959.

42   I did win some luggage, though. And I waved at Mom from the TV screen. But my mother missed the show.

Vocabulary

mutant	phoenix	proliferate
brontosaurian	vacuity	shivaree
prurient	pique	sacrilege
voracious	query	innuendo
mortify	interminable	terminate
emblazon	itinerary	

Topics for Discussion

1. Have you ever wanted to be a contestant on a quiz show? What do you think about being a contestant on a quiz show after reading this essay?

2. Fayard calls dating "an artificial bridge across the artificial separation of the sexes." What do you think is the function of dating? Do you agree that "as formal social ritual, dating is pretty well washed up today"?

3. Fayard asks, "Why would anyone want to win a 'romantic' weekend *anywhere on earth* with a blind date and a chaperon by playing *The Dating Game?*" Does she ever answer this question? Why do you think people become contestants on such a quiz show?

4. How much fun does Fayard have in Acapulco with Bruce and Ruth? Could she have expected the trip to be any different?

5. Do quiz shows such as *The Dating Game, Let's Make a Deal,* and *The Newlywed Game* reveal anything about our culture?

6. Why are all the people associated with *The Dating Game* young and smiling?

7. While you may not want to be a contestant on *The Dating Game*, would you ever sign up with a computer dating service?

Rhetorical Considerations

1. In the first paragraph of the essay Fayard mentions the two times she has been a contestant on a quiz show. What comparison is made here? What point about quiz shows does the comparison make?

2. Explain the following terms: mutant phoenix, *brontosaurian* vacuity, games of mental tiddledywinks, shivaree, and Noah's Ark etiquette.

3. What is the effect of the last paragraph? How does it fit in with the tone of the essay?

4. How is this essay structured? How does Fayard work in her observations on such things as dating customs and quiz shows?

5. Why is there a change in diction in paragraph 31?

The Ungreening of Our Children

Margot Hentoff

*Margot Hentoff is a writer living in Greenwich Village,
New York, with her husband and four children who range in age
from 10 to 22.*

1   Chance being what it is, despite weighty prophecies from the
futurists, we are rarely prepared for what actually does happen.
During the fevered latter half of the '60s, spokesmen for the youth
movement warned that we must make immediate plans for a new
evolutionary breed of young. America had greened, we were told.
New generations would never share old values, old expectations.
Margaret Mead proclaimed that from now on the old would learn
from the young. If you think we're radical, some of the college
students predicted, just wait till you see our younger brothers and
sisters—they'll make *us* look tame.

2   About this time, I overheard a conversation between two
bright 7-year-olds who were indeed the younger brothers of the
revolutionary young:

3   "I wouldn't want to run for President," one of them said, "it's
too dangerous a kind of job."

4   "Yes," said the other, "I think a very good job would be
Secretary of the Treasury."

5   I didn't need a weatherman to tell me which way the wind was
blowing. Nonetheless, the futurists kept insisting on the imminence
of a new order. In the years since, parents, teachers, social theorists
and those who actually run our institutions have been gearing up
for this promised generation. However, I have long suspected that
they are building a kind of institutional Maginot Line—perfectly
equipped to deal with the past. The kind of youngsters I see and
speak to now seem extraordinarily familiar. Sort of like I was as a
child. Why, these middle-class children are just a bunch of good old
kids.

6   My 10-year-old son goes to a school where, for the first time
this year, dress regulations allow blue jeans. He tells me blue jeans
are uncomfortable—too cold in winter. He was disappointed to hear
that his school is thinking of substituting comments for grades. How

will he know when he gets an "A"? How will anyone else know? One of his few demands is that I drop him off at the barbershop at regular intervals so that his hair doesn't straggle too far below his baseball cap.

7   Last week, I listened to a 13-year-old complain to his mother about having been sent to a permissive elementary school. He had just gotten the results of his high-school entrance exams. "Did you see the rotten scores I had on the grammar? And on the spelling?" He went on, "Why didn't you send me to a school where they made sure I knew all this stuff at the beginning? I'll never catch up now."

8   I asked him what he thought his parents' reasons had been for sending him to such a school. "I guess they thought it would be too hard for me in a regular school," he said disgustedly. He is annoyed because he suspects he has already lost part of his edge in the race. If he doesn't get into the kind of college that leads to a top law school, how will be ever be able to join a successful corporate law firm like his father's?

9   Even those a little older, who swung with it when the good times rolled, begin to sound less and less like a new breed. I recently talked to a couple of girls who have been out of college for a year. One of them said, "I'm so sick of hearing girls say about their boyfriends, 'We're living together.' *Living together!* It always sounds to me as if what they're really saying is, 'We're living together and it's just great, but we have a little problem—one of us here doesn't want to get married.'"

10   Lately newspapers and magazines have been running stories about the new obsession with grades in colleges, the new willingness of the students to be agreeable to elders in power. It seems that just as the institutions have finally prepared themselves to bend to the kids, the kids have announced themselves ready to conform to any institution that will get them what they want—and what they want is what the middle class has traditionally wanted: comfort, security, status and order.

11   I drove a group of sixth- and eighth-graders home from school last week and listened to them talk about what their school should have done about a student who was found with a joint in his pocket. The only disagreement between them was the question of whether the student should have been instantly expelled or merely subjected to suspension and probation. "After all," one of the kids who held out for expulsion said indignantly, "it's not like smoking cigarettes. It's *illegal!*"

12   Even the clothes of the young look different today from the costumes of a few years ago. No more peacock splendor and

attention-drawing style. The kids look sort of drab—as if they want to be faceless, to blend in with the crowd in a way appropriate to apprentices, trainees and applicants.

13   Perhaps what really happened on the way to the forecast was that the middle-class kids now reaching adolescence were frightened by the chaos of the '60s that surrounded them as young children—the demonstrations, the bombings, the assassinations of political figures, the drug-ruined panhandlers they passed on city streets. Even the music was too wild for them (they listen now to '50s rock) and their early exposure to the new sexual freedom could well have made them pull back. If you had seen the pictures in Screw on the newsstand when you were 6, at 13 what dirty books would be worth secretly passing around?

14   In any case, I rather think that those who have been busy dismantling our traditional institutions for the training of the young (although I haven't heard much about "de-schooling" lately) ought to get on with rebuilding them. Otherwise they're going to be sitting alone in their schools without walls, contemplating their alternative systems, and waiting, waiting, for a children's crusade that never comes.

Vocabulary

imminence   obsession

Topics for Discussion

1. Do you agree with Hentoff that the changes that began in the 1960s have ended? Do you think her description of contemporary young people is accurate? Do you agree with her description?

2. Are students today obsessed with grades?

3. Do you agree that what students want today is "comfort, security, status and order"?

4. Why does Hentoff feel that institutions today are perfectly equipped to deal with the past and are out of step with today's youth?

5. What reasons does Hentoff offer for the change in young people? Do you agree with her reasons?

6. In what ways do your perceptions differ from Hentoff's? In what ways are they the same? Do you think she would have a different perception of things if she were a college student today?

Rhetorical Considerations

1. In what paragraph does Hentoff state the main idea of her essay? Does she state her thesis in one sentence or does she use more than one?

2. Hentoff cites many of her experiences with children to support and illustrate her thesis. How valid are her examples? How appropriate are they for her argument?

3. How appropriate is the image of the Maginot Line in paragraph 5? How does it fit with Hentoff's thesis?

4. How typical is the boy Hentoff describes in paragraphs 7 and 8? In what way does this boy's attitude illustrate and support Hentoff's thesis? How do these paragraphs relate to paragraph 10?

Because I Am Black

Deborah L. Perry

Deborah Perry was a freshman student at Barnard College when she wrote this essay.

1   During my first week as a Barnard freshman I was infused with a spirit of adventure, of anticipation at being in New York—that legendary metropolis where all things are possible. I had chosen Barnard because I was enraptured by the thought of New York City, and the idea of a small college within a large university appealed to me. I would, I thought, be able to do all those things I'd dreamed about, and read about, and heard about—all the things that other girls in America were doing. Those "other" girls, however, happened to be white.

2   My goal, from junior high on, had been to go to a big college in a big city, major in English, and, presto—become a rich and famous writer. I was unaware at that time how utterly unrealistic these goals were, how childish—not simply because I was expecting success to come so easily, but because I am black, and these things that I dreamed about were white dreams. I did not admit it to myself, but I was saying, in effect: "Well, I may not be good enough for them (white people) now, but when I'm rich and famous, they can't help

but respect me.'' The things that I wanted when I came to Barnard were products of the white-oriented books, movies, and television that I had been brought up on and the urgings of my white teachers in junior and senior high school, and, in fact, everyone else around me.

3   My background—black middle-class comfortable—dictated that I should strive for this kind of success. My parents thought, and still think, that a degree would open up all the doors that I wanted to open—and I agreed with them. I had very little contact with whites, except as teachers, and I staunchly supported the idea that only through integration and communication between the races could we ever have harmony. Still, I worried about assimilation and acceptance here at Barnard. From the very first, I had felt uncomfortable and uneasy with the white girls I met. I felt that I had nothing to say to them, and vice versa, but I ignored the feeling, chalking it up to ''the period of adjustment.'' This feeling persisted, though, and I began to feel overwhelmed and surrounded. The social life— freshman orientation programs, floor parties, mixers, luncheons, teas—was geared to the incoming white freshman, completely ignoring the different needs of the black students. We were treated as whites too. This may sound fine and dandy, but it is a kind of racism in itself. The administration, the student sponsors, everyone was so willing to ''overlook'' the fact that we were black and to ignore the different cultural and social background that is black people's. Barnard's lily-white faculty and courses of study emphasized even more the lack of concern or interest on the part of the ''powers that be'' about the needs or interests of blacks. There were courses in the lives of Ancient Greeks and Romans, in Russian history, in Oriental Studies, but the contributions and considerations of black people in history, in literature, in everything that had to do with the shaping of this country, were skillfully omitted.

4   It has been put forth as an excuse that the white administration and students know nothing about us and therefore cannot possibly understand what it is that we want, or why we are dissatisfied; in other words, their treatment of us results from ignorance and is not their fault. I contend, however, that it is their fault. They have taken neither the time nor the initiative heretofore to learn anything about black people because the ''subject'' either did not interest them or did not seem important. Black people, on the other hand, know just about everything there is to know about white people.

5   At this particular point in history, when suddenly everyone and his brother wants to know what the black person is thinking and why, we have been accused of shutting off the communication lines.

"How are we to know what you want us to do, unless you talk to us?" is the cry that I and other black students have heard time and again from administration, faculty, and students here. The answer is, I think, that we no longer want to have things done "for" us; we want to do them ourselves. We are willing to have dialogue, but to protect ourselves, we must dictate the terms.

Vocabulary

infuse   enrapture   staunch

Topics for Discussion

1. In paragraph 2 Perry says that being black prevents her from achieving status in her chosen profession. Do you think she has made a correct analysis here, or is this an excuse? To what extent might her position be a little of both?

2. Do you think that your college curriculum takes into account the contributions of black people to government, sciences, and the arts? If not, what might be done to remedy the situation?

3. Do you think that some black students may have over-reacted to the exclusion of things black from college curricula by ignoring important contributions made by whites? Do you perceive a tendency for students of all races to use "relevancy" as a cloak for taking only those courses which immediately interest them and in which they are likely to secure a good grade? Comment as objectively as you can.

4. Perry restricts her discussion to conditions at Barnard. Would most black people, or poor whites for that matter, think the issues she mentions are in any way significant for them? What might these people say?

Rhetorical Considerations

1. Perry lets the reader know that race will be a topic in two places early in the essay: the title and the last word of the first paragraph. Do you think the opening would have been more effective without the title? Why?

2. Perry says at one point that she comes from a middle-class background, yet she castigates the Barnard administration for ignoring the "social background that is black people's." Is she logical here? Why? Why not?

3. From your knowledge of what it takes for people to successfully communicate, do you think it likely that any "dialogue" will evolve out of Perry's insistence that blacks "dictate the terms"? Evaluate Perry's diction in terms of her audience.

4. Comment on the number and kinds of examples Perry uses to support her contentions.

5. Read the Rhetorical Analysis at the end of this section.

The Campus Revisited: Classes Can Be Exciting, but the Kids Don't Like to Read

Susan Jacoby

Susan Jacoby, a graduate of Michigan State University, is a free-lance writer who has contributed to the Saturday Review *and other magazines.*

1   It has always been difficult to determine how most students at a large university feel about the education to which presumably they are being exposed. Although I was a reporter while I was a student at Michigan State, no consensus of values ever emerged from my interviews with hundreds of fellow undergraduates. Then, as now, the university was too big and too fragmented for anyone to draw valid conclusions about "student opinion."

2   I do remember what we thought about our own classes. We were interested mainly in liberal arts; many of us had been lured to Michigan State by the promise of complete freedom in choosing our courses if we maintained a high grade-point average. When I returned to the campus this year, I sought out students with similar interests. The humanistic orientation is still there, but one vital element has changed: Today's students, however bright, seem indifferent to anything that smacks of intellectual discipline.

3   Michigan State today seems to be a much better place for a liberal arts student than it was ten years ago, primarily because the administration realized it had neglected the humanities in its headlong drive to create a science-research complex. The Justin Morrill College, founded in 1965, is a case in point.

4   Justin Morrill is a residential college with about 800 students; they live in the same dormitories during their freshman and sophomore years. The college brings together outstanding faculty members from different departments—something that seems to be administratively impossible throughout most of the university. Classes are small—usually fewer than fifteen students—and a term of independent study, generally in a foreign country, is required for graduation.

5   The intellectual atmosphere at Justin Morrill is exciting; there was nothing like it when I was a student. I sat enthralled in one class as a freshman compared Dante's view of hell with the ideas of earlier Christian writers and theologians; in my own college experience such discussions were found only in senior or graduate seminars. Then I listened as Dean Gordon Rohman, dressed in undeanlike fashion in an electric-blue jacket, tie, and shirt, described some of the independent study projects. One of his favorites: A student bought a boat in England, sailed it to Spain, kept a diary, and wrote poetry as he sailed home across the Atlantic. Was that at all unusual? I asked the dean. He said it was, but he believed in unusual projects if the students were able to plan them and if they could carry them through.

6   Later a quiet eighteen-year-old told me how pleased she was with Justin Morrill. "I know it sounds corny," she said, "but the personal contact with fine teachers is really inspiring." She added, however, that she plans to transfer to another college within the university at the end of her sophomore year.

7   I asked her why. "There's a two-year foreign-language requirement," she explained. "I started French last term, and it was just too much work. So I'm going to transfer to a college that doesn't make a language compulsory." I met dozens of older students who had dropped out of Justin Morrill for the same reason. Yet many of them said they wanted to live abroad. What, I wondered, in their catchword, could be more "relevant" to living abroad than a foreign language?

8   With a few memorable exceptions, the students' opinions were expressed in almost identically worded clichés. "We want practical learning, not book learning. . . . History just doesn't seem relevant to me. After all, it's in the past and you can't change it. . . . Even if a course requirement does make sense, I don't want it shoved down

my throat." Most seemed puzzled as to why the statement "history is past" should elicit a mild chuckle from the interviewer.

9   One of the hopeful exceptions—an editor of the campus newspaper—was disturbed by other students' attitudes toward "book learning." He said he had been enthusiastic about Free University classes but gave them up when it became apparent that many students were not willing to do the work required for critical discussion. "They just didn't want to be bothered with the reading," he said, "and success of the Free University idea depended on voluntary work by everyone."

10   The shaky intellectual discipline of many students raised serious questions in my mind about the willingness of faculty members to accede to student demands for the elimination of course requirements. The College of Liberal Arts, for example, was considering abolition of its own foreign-language requirement—not because faculty members believed the move was right, but because they were afraid of losing students to social science departments that have no foreign-language requirements.

11   "I personally am geared to what I'm interested in right now," said a nineteen-year-old sociology major. "I'm not looking ahead ten years, five years, or even one year. I'm only interested in today."

Vocabulary

elicit

Topics for Discussion

1. What is your immediate reaction to the final sentence of the second paragraph? Do you take it as a challenge, or do you generally agree?

2. Do you think you would enjoy studying at Justin Morrill College? Do you think enjoyment should be the main point of studying?

3. What do you know about Dante? Do you think it is important to know anything about Dante? Is it important to study history?

4. Do you think it is important to learn languages other than English? Evaluate the perspective of the woman described in paragraphs 6 and 7.

5. Evaluate the attitudes of the student quoted in the final paragraph. What reason might he/she have for thinking only of today? Do you think members of other generations might have had similar reasons?

6. Discuss the purpose of your education. Try to be as candid and honest as you can, without relying on clichés.

Rhetorical Considerations

1. There is an implicit comparison in this essay between what Jacoby considers the purpose of education and what the students think it is. Find instances in which she uses negative examples to put forth her views.

2. How does Jacoby use examples to structure her essay? Using the same examples can you structure the essay differently?

3. Do you think Jacoby uses the best examples available to describe anti-intellectualism in student life? Can you supply better examples? How would you use them to expand this essay?

4. To what extent does Jacoby rely on adjectives for evaluation—"memorable, hopeful, exciting"? Does her use of such adjectives strengthen or weaken the essay?

5. Why does Jacoby mention the dean's electric-blue jacket?

Where College Fails Us

Caroline Bird

Caroline Bird (b. 1915) has frequently contributed articles to national magazines. She is author of The Invisible Sear *(1966) and* Born Female *(1968).*

1   The case *for* college has been accepted without question for more than a generation. All high school graduates ought to go, says Conventional Wisdom and statistical evidence, because college will help them earn more money, become "better" people, and learn to be more responsible citizens than those who don't go.

2   But college has never been able to work its magic for everyone. And now that close to half our high school graduates are attending, those who don't fit the pattern are becoming more numerous, and more obvious. College graduates are selling shoes and driving taxis; college students sabotage each other's experiments and forge letters of recommendation in the intense competition for admission to graduate school. Others find no stimulation in their studies, and drop out—often encouraged by college administrators.

3   Some observers say the fault is with the young people themselves—they are spoiled, stoned, overindulged, and expecting too much. But that's mass character assassination, and doesn't explain all campus unhappiness. Others blame the state of the world, and they are partly right. We've been told that young people have to go to college because our economy can't absorb an army of untrained eighteen-year-olds. But disillusioned graduates are learning that it can no longer absorb an army of trained twenty-two-year-olds, either.

4   Some adventuresome educators and campus watchers have openly begun to suggest that college may not be the best, the proper, the only place for every young person after the completion of high school. We may have been looking at all those surveys and statistics upside down, it seems, and through the rosy glow of our own remembered college experiences. Perhaps college doesn't make people intelligent, ambitious, happy, liberal, or quick to learn new things—maybe it's just the other way around, and intelligent, ambitious, happy, liberal, and quick-learning people are merely the ones who have been attracted to college in the first place. And perhaps all those successful college graduates would have been successful whether they had gone to college or not. This is heresy to those of us who have been brought up to believe that if a little schooling is good, more has to be much better. But contrary evidence is beginning to mount up.

5   College graduates say that they don't want to work "just" for the money: They want work that matters. They want to help people and save the world. But the numbers are stacked against them. Not only are there not enough jobs in world-saving fields, but in the current slowdown it has become evident that there never were, and probably never will be, enough jobs requiring higher education to go around.

6   Students who tell their advisers they want to help people, for example, are often directed to psychology. This year the Department of Labor estimates that there will be 4,300 new jobs for

psychologists, while colleges will award 58,430 bachelor's degrees in psychology.

7   Sociology has become a favorite major on socially conscious campuses, but graduates find that social reform is hardly a paying occupation. Male sociologists from the University of Wisconsin reported as gainfully employed a year after graduation included a legal assistant, sports editor, truck unloader, Peace Corps worker, publications director, and a stockboy—but no sociologist per se. The highest paid worked for the post office.

8   Other fields most popular with college graduates are also pathetically small. Only 1,900 foresters a year will be needed during this decade, although schools of forestry are expected to continue graduating twice that many. Some will get sub-professional jobs as forestry aides. Schools of architecture are expected to turn out twice as many as will be needed, and while all sorts of people want to design things, the Department of Labor forecasts that there will be jobs for only 400 new industrial designers a year. As for anthropologists, only 400 will be needed every year in the 1970's to take care of all the college courses, public health research, community surveys, museums, and all the archaeological digs on every continent. (For these jobs graduate work in anthropology is required.)

9   Many popular occupations may seem to be growing fast without necessarily offering employment to very many. "Recreation work" is always cited as an expanding field, but it will need relatively few workers who require more special training than life guards. "Urban planning" has exploded in the media, so the U.S. Department of Labor doubled its estimate of the number of jobs to be filled every year in the 1970s—to a big, fat 800. A mere 200 oceanographers a year will be able to do all the exploring of "inner space"—and all that exciting underwater diving you see demonstrated on television—for the entire decade of the 1970s.

10   Whatever college graduates *want* to do, most of them are going to wind up doing what *there is* to do. During the next few years, according to the Labor Department, the biggest demand will be for stenographers and secretaries, followed by retail-trade salesworkers, hospital attendants, bookkeepers, building custodians, registered nurses, foremen, kindergarten and elementary-school teachers, receptionists, cooks, cosmetologists, private-household workers, manufacturing inspectors, and industrial machinery repairmen. These are the jobs which will eventually absorb the surplus archaeologists, urban planners, oceanographers, sociologists, editors, and college professors.

11   A diploma saves the employer the cost of screening candidates and gives him a predictable product: He can assume that those who have survived the four-year ordeal have learned how to manage themselves. They have learned how to budget their time, meet deadlines, set priorities, cope with impersonal authority, follow instructions, and stick with a task that may be tiresome without direct supervision.

12   The employer is also betting that it will be cheaper and easier to train the college graduate because he has demonstrated his ability to learn. But if the diploma serves only to identify those who are talented in the art of schoolwork, it becomes, in the words of Harvard's Christopher Jencks, "a hell of an expensive aptitude test." It is unfair to the candidates because they themselves must bear the cost of the screening—the cost of college. Candidates without the funds, the academic temperament, or the patience for the four-year obstacle race are ruled out, no matter how well they may perform on the job. But if "everyone" has a diploma, employers will have to find another way to choose employees and it will become an empty credential.

13   College is an ideal place for those young adults who love learning for its own sake, who would rather read than eat, and who like nothing better than writing research papers. But they are a minority, even at the prestigious colleges, which recruit and attract the intellectually oriented.

14   The rest of our high school graduates need to look at college more closely and critically, to examine it as a consumer product, and decide if the cost in dollars, in time, in continued dependency, and in future returns, is worth the very large investment each student—and his family—must make.

Vocabulary

heresy   *per se*   pathetically
prestigious

Topics for Discussion

1. In what way does Bird believe that colleges have failed?
2. Why do you think people go to college? Is getting a better job the only reason for going to college?
3. Is there anything wrong with someone having a Ph.D. and driving a taxi for a living?

4. Do you think there is a surplus of teachers and other college-educated professionals? Couldn't you argue instead that there is a shortage of money to hire all the teachers, doctors, nurses, and others who are needed?

5. Is college only a "consumer product" as Bird claims? What else do you think college might be?

6. What is Bird's basic attitude toward college as revealed in paragraph 13? How is this attitude revealed in other places in the essay?

Rhetorical Considerations

1. Bird cites numerous figures as part of her evidence. How well does she integrate these numbers into her sentences? Note, for example, paragraphs 6 and 8.

2. As Bird admits in her opening paragraph, the case for college has been accepted without question. How effectively does Bird argue against this "conventional wisdom"? What kinds of arguments does she use? How has she arranged her evidence?

3. How objective is Bird? What tone does Bird use to create the impression her essay is an objective one? Does Bird shift her tone at any point in the essay?

The Intellectual Taxicab Company

Peter Carlson

Peter Carlson is a 21-year-old college graduate who has held a great variety of jobs, none of which were in the area he majored in while attending college.

1   My friend Danny hung his Boston University diploma below the hack license in his cab.

2   After seventeen years of education in the finest schools in America, Danny, at 22, couldn't fix his stopped sink, repair a burnt

connection in his fuse box, replace a pane of glass in his kitchen or locate the carburetor in his car.

3   Danny is an educated man. He is a master of writing research papers, taking tests, talking and filling out forms. He can rattle off his social-security number as easily as he can his name because it was also his student identification number. He can analyze Freud from a Marxian viewpoint and he can analyze Marx from a Freudian viewpoint.

4   In short, Danny is an unskilled worker and he has a sociology degree to prove it. He is of very little use to American industry.

5   This is nothing new. Colleges have been turning out unskilled workers for decades. Until five years ago, most of these unskilled workers took their degrees in sociology, philosophy, political science or history and marched right into the American middle class. Some filled executive positions in business and government but many, if not most, went into education, which is the only thing they knew anything about. Once there, they taught another generation the skills necessary to take tests and write papers.

6   But that cycle broke down. Teachers are overabundant these days, college applications are down, plumbers are making $12 an hour and liberal-arts graduates are faced with a choice—graduate school or the taxicab.

7   Danny chose the taxicab because driving was about the only marketable skill he possessed. Danny refers to his job as "Real World 101." He has been shot at, punched, sideswiped and propositioned. But he has also acquired some practical skills—he can get his tickets fixed; he knows how to cheat the company out of a few extra dollars a week; he found his carburetor and he can fix it.

8   Soon, I will be in the same position. I'll graduate from Boston University with a B.S. in journalism. Whatever skills that degree symbolizes are not currently in demand. I suppose I could go to graduate school but, Christ, I've been doing the same thing for seventeen years and I'm getting a little tired of it. Besides, there are a lot of grad-school graduates who are driving cabs, too.

9   And that brings me to the Intellectual Taxicab Company.

10   Danny and I were discussing the hack business recently and we came up with the idea. It is the simple answer to a simple question: why should all that college education go to waste reading road signs when masses of people are looking for knowledge and riding in cabs?

11   What America needs is a system to bring together all the knowledgeable cabbies and the undereducated rest of the country. The system we propose is the Intellectual Taxicab Company.

12   The Intellectual Taxicab Company would consist of a dispatcher and a fleet of cabs driven by recent college graduates. When you need a ride, you call the company and say something like: "I'd like to go from Wall Street over to East 83rd and I'd like to discuss the world monetary situation."

13   "All right, sir, we'll have an NYU economics graduate over in five minutes."

14   Or: "Hello, I'm in Central Square and I'd like to go to Brookline and discuss whether or not there is a God."

15   "You're in luck, madame, we have a Harvard philosophy graduate who minored in Comparative Religions right in the neighborhood."

16   The educational possibilities of this plan are staggering. English and Drama graduates could take the after-theater run, explaining the literary ramifications of the shows. Political Science graduates could hack around Capitol Hill or City Hall. Regular bus runs could be set up to conduct seminars on popular topics.

17   The Intellectual Taxicab Company would bring adult education to the streets. It would also give all those alienated college graduates a feeling that they didn't waste four years and all that tuition money. And it would elevate the snotty cabdriver to an art form: cabbies would quote Voltaire while they rant about how bad the mayor is.

18   Surely there must be some foundation money or unimpounded Federal funds available to begin such a noble experiment in education. If there is, Danny and I are ready to start immediately. In fact, Danny is licking his lips in anticipation. "Just think how much my tips will go up," he said.

Vocabulary

hack	sociology	overabundant
carburetor	ramifications	alienated

Topics for Discussion

1. If the point of going to college is to get a good job, what does this essay say to you about college as a worthwhile pursuit?

2. Is getting a good job the main reason for going to college? If

everybody received a higher education, some highly educated people would be collecting garbage, cleaning public toilets, and catching dogs. Would it be worthwhile for everyone to have such education?

3. Can you think of any rational solution to the problem of unemployment among college-educated people? What changes in the structure of society would have to be made in order to implement your solution?

4. To what extent do Danny's experiences in paragraph 7 apply to you? Have you ever taken "Real World 101"? Do you think that high schools and colleges should teach such a course?

5. Do you expect something other than job training in your education? What is that something? How do you expect to get it?

Rhetorical Considerations

1. Carlson follows the classical argumentative structure according to which the writer (1) demonstrates the need for some change and (2) sets before us a plan designed to explicitly meet that need. But Carlson only implies a need, and his plan is presented in ironic terms. What social needs do you think are really being discussed by Carlson?

2. Why does Carlson speak ironically about the scarcity of jobs for college graduates? What would have to be deleted, and what would have to be added, to remove irony from the essay? To what extent would the new essay be more or less effective than the present one?

3. Examine the diction in the first four paragraphs. Do these paragraphs seem to have anything stylistically in common with newspaper reporting? Why is such diction especially suitable for the introductory part of the essay?

4. How does the figure of Danny contribute to unity in the essay?

5. Do the specific references in paragraphs 12–16 add to the essay's effectiveness?

6. What is especially ironic about the last sentence in the essay?

Long Live Intelligence

Harry Brent

Harry Brent (b. 1943) is an assistant professor of English and former Director of Freshman English at Rutgers University in Camden, New Jersey.

1   During the Spanish Civil War, the Rector of the University of Salamanca, the writer and philosopher Miguel de Unamuno, came to the window of his study to find a fascist demonstration in the courtyard. "Down with intelligence," shouted the fascists. "Long live death." Unamuno responded to the demonstrators, "No. Long live intelligence." There are few real fascists in the courtyards of our universities today, but a trail for them is being blazed, most obviously and notoriously, by the men and women of intellect who sell the legacy of intellect to the CIA and the Pentagon. Much less noticeable are their accomplices, the innocent students, pitiful in their eighteen-year-old cynicism, the offspring of a society where youth no longer enjoys the luxury of the cheapest idealism.

2   As an assistant professor of English, I have little contact with the first of these groups, and much contact with the second. I know about Henry Kissinger only from the *New York Times*; I know my freshmen from their papers in English 101, from their responses to my questions in class. But whether Kissinger knows it, or whether my students know it, there exists an informal alliance between him and them, a pact neither sealed by champagne toasts nor solemnized at state banquets, an agreement, nowhere written down, whose essence is that education shall exist primarily to serve the practical needs of the state and the career aspirations of the individual as defined by those with power and money. Economists do research not to determine how the greatest number of people may have access to the abundance of the earth, but to determine how to "destabilize" freely elected socialist governments. Freshmen, if they have heard of Plato, do not bother to study his ideas on justice, but instead flock to courses in the practical "science" of criminology, a promising field with good pay. Politics no longer serves the human ends of art and science; art and science instead serve politics, the artist the candidate's makeup man, the scientist the defoliation expert.

3   What is to be expected of college students at a time when pragmatism is officially sanctioned as the highest character of intellect, when Kissinger attempts to duplicate Metternich? Should students be expected to view the four years of their education as a time to forget the bottom line of their bank accounts and turn to learning for its own sake? When the minority-group revolutionaries of yesterday have become the minority-group entrepreneurs of today, should students be expected to embody the social concern and commitment traditionally characteristic of youth? I suppose I must think that they still should, for I was startled three years ago when for the first time in my experience a freshmen student baldly admitted in front of his classmates that his central goal in coming to college consisted in getting a good job. In the very early sixties, before the protest movements, when I was an undergraduate, even the business majors would assert that, while they certainly hoped that a B.S. would land them a moderate salary, an expense account, and a company car, they also hoped that college would give them some insights into life which could not be provided by the sales department at Xerox. My classmates were grade conscious, but more often than occasionally they took courses simply because the courses were interesting, and they frequently sought out their professors, not only to grub grades, but also to find out what the professors really thought about formalist criticism or the origin of the universe.

4   Perhaps I have a bad case of *O tempora, O mores* (look that one up if you took Relevancy 101 instead of Latin 102), and I certainly am being a bit flippant, but I do not think that I am wrong. There is a noticeable decline in enthusiasm for learning among young people today, and a decidedly lower capability to cope with what ought to be learned. Some examples:

> (1) Of the fifteen students in my Introduction to Linguistics class, not one knew, until a few days ago, what the term "passive voice" means. This in itself may or may not be important, but it becomes very difficult to teach a course dealing with the nature and structure of language when the students lack any terminology with which to talk about language.
>
> (2) In a writing course which I taught two years ago, admittedly a remedial course, the class discussed an essay in which Adolph Hitler was mentioned. Eleven of the eighteen students did not know who Hitler was (fourteen had never heard of Stalin). Anyone who says that this may or may not be important shouldn't complain when the Brownshirts (whom none of the students had ever heard of) start marching again.

(3) In a class discussion recently, the majority took the position that William Calley was correct in his treatment of the population of My Lai. After all, it was argued, Calley had his own career to think of, and an officer who does not follow orders, even implied orders (*populum occidere nolite temere bonum est*), will not go far. This is pretty damn serious to my mind. Success in a career has become so important for students that it justifies the crimes of Herod. This is not to say that the study of twelfth-century English history or the plays of Christopher Marlowe guarantees that one will refuse to carry out immoral orders (there were learned officers in the SS), but such study does mean that there is no excuse for not making a choice between what seems morally right and what is simply expedient, the kind of choice that Unamuno was forced to make and which demands courage.

5   I suspect that the decline of interest in the morality of mass murder, the history of modern Germany, and the grammar of English is not restricted to classrooms where I teach. My friends tell me that students more and more frequently ask questions like "How is it possible to write a five-page paper on a three-page short story?" At least these students ask. You don't worry about them as much as you do about the ones who don't ask and who drift out of your class and into somebody else's seminar in "meaningful life experiences." It is not unusual for students taking the English Placement Test at the university where I teach to complain that the section of the test requiring them to write a five-hundred-word composition in one hour is absurd. Of course it's absurd if, for four years of high school, you've been taught to look upon a five-hundred-word essay as a major term assignment in an English course. Our student teachers are routinely advised by high school administrators not to require writing, or at least only a minimal amount of writing, from their students. After all, if you graded these students on their writing, most of them would flunk, and that would hardly build the good relations with parents necessary for the advancement of one's career as an educator. Better to assume that the students have already learned to write in grammar school and that there is no need for them to prove it in high school. But in grammar school, at least in the first-grade class where I recently observed the practice teaching of one of our English majors, about a third of the class spent its time in what the teacher called "remedial alphabet."

6   What are the roots of the problem? Television? The argument goes that since kids stopped reading books and more or less stayed glued to the tube, literacy levels went down. Students became more interested in the practical concerns of life as defined by television

(commercials included). Some truth to this? Yes. But essentially a *post hoc, ergo propter hoc* argument? I think so. For one thing, the children of the wealthy still make it into Yale and Harvard in greater numbers than the bulk of this country's youth. Their parents have televisions—and I bet there are lots of televisions at Deerfield Academy. For another, television was around when I was growing up, and the literacy rate wasn't falling then (or at least there was no hue and cry about it). When I was eight or nine years old, in about 1952, my family acquired a television. I remember watching Saturday morning junk, but the junk didn't weaken my appetite for reading in the evenings or watching television programs like *Omnibus* and *You are There* on Sunday afternoons. The radio, which I spent a good deal of time listening to before the television came, didn't have cultural enrichment like that—unless you're moved by the current craze for nostalgia to call *Tom Mix, The Lone Ranger,* or *Teddy Bear's Picnic Time* cultural enrichment.

7　　　　Maybe it was just good fortune for me, though. I had a father wise enough to get me a library card when I was five, and a mother concerned enough to take me there on Saturday afternoons. And my grandfather, an Irish immigrant who had been a blacksmith, gave me a good role model—smoking his pipe in his rocking chair in the tenement kitchen deep into the night, occasionally nodding off toward the spitoon, and reading. When I got a little older, I ran his cowboy westerns back and forth to the library. That gave me an excuse to invade the adult section and browse in the travel and history departments where I learned that great cathedrals were built in France during the Middle Ages and that some unspeakable things happened to the Jews in Germany during the Second World War. When Grampa had finished all the westerns on the library's open shelves, I had to learn to use the card catalogue (standing on a stool) to find the westerns in the closed stacks. So maybe I was lucky, an exception; but other kids from backgrounds similar to mine, lots of them, learn to like to read and write in grammar school—and they all knew who Hitler was before they were eighteen.

8　　　　If television, then, is not the main enemy of literacy, who or what is? One might suggest that people of great wealth and power may not keep their wealth and power very long if the poor and powerless come to acquire the expertise and eloquence necessary for initiating basic social change. But to many minds this is a truism, and it becomes inportant to ask who else is complicit. In no small part, I think, the decline of literacy, of intelligence, is the fault of the guardians of literacy themselves, the experts in education who define what a person's literacy level ought to be according to that person's social background, the educators who see to it that children in the third grade shall not open the covers of books "designed" for children in the eighth grade, the people who are fond of talking about the first year on one's university education as the "thirteenth grade." If one of these individuals had caught me roaming around upstairs in the "adult" section of my hometown library when I was ten, he or she, I'm sure, would have taken me by the hand and led me to the "fifth grade" collection in the basement. He or she would probably have looked with extreme displeasure upon the efforts of the Sisters of St. Joseph to teach Latin declensions to working-class boys and girls in my freshman class in high school (heaven forbid trying to teach what rich kids learn as a matter of course to the "nontraditional" student). He or she would not share my belief that *education* means what its Latin roots imply—to be led out of ignorance. And he or she would probably not understand that the study of Latin at thirteen (while apparently quite irrelevant in acquiring the skills that go with being a dental assistant or a cop) may teach one that languages work in remarkably different, yet similar, ways, that different realities can be analyzed for what they have in common, and that the large issues of life can be viewed from remarkably different perspectives.

9   The case for retarding intellectual stimulation is consciously made not only with respect to high-school freshmen, but to college freshmen as well. In my field, English, there is an emerging tendency among professors to expect that most entering students are much less literate than their counterparts of ten years ago. This tendency should not surprise us, for it is based on accurate observation. What is surprising, and quite astounding, is the notion, implicitly held by many teachers of writing, that these students have little capacity for learning, that given the opportunity to learn, and the guidance of a good teacher, they simply wouldn't be able to cope. This attitude most recently came to my attention in an article in one of the leading journals in my field. The article[1] reviewed two prominent rhetoric handbooks[2] widely used in freshman writing courses and faulted them for supposedly being much too sophisticated for most college freshmen. Much of the criticism in the article

[1] Harvey S. Wiener, "Selecting the Freshman English Textbook," *College English,* 37, No.1 (September, 1975), pp. 28–34.

[2] John C. Hodges and Mary E. Whitten, *Harbrace College Handbook,* 7th edition (New York: Harcourt Brace Jovanovich, 1972). James M. McCrimmon, *Writing With a Purpose,* 5th edition (Boston: Houghton Mifflin, 1974).

is directed at dull examples used as models for student writing, and such criticism, I think, is well put. However, here is one piece of advice which I believe may well serve to retard students of teachers who take it seriously:

> Instructors of freshman English at community colleges (at any colleges, in fact, with open admissions audiences) need books written in understandable vocabulary and clear sentences, books with handy charts and lists, books rich in exclusions: *no* [original emphasis] material on advanced research techniques, *no* [original emphasis] information on linguistics and transformations, *no* [original emphasis] glossary of grammatical terminology, *no* [original emphasis] information on the history of the language, on the relative merits of dictionaries, on neutral voices or nominative absolutes. We need books . . . that *do* [original emphasis] eviscerate content if the content has no relationship to the problems or needs of the student in the composition class.[3]

10   The author of the article quotes an example from one of the books he reviews:

> Most of the topically inspired writing of the thirties has long since receded into the past, but Agee's book survives because he lifted a topical issue out of its particular time and place and gave it universal significance through his individual way of experiencing and communicating it. In his insistence on working out his own relationships to his age . . . he forfeited contemporary acceptance, but he wrote a book that has spoken across the years to a later and more receptive generation of critics and readers.[4]

and he comments:

> . . . "forfeited contemporary acceptance"—indeed. If these are supposed to be typical student research papers, they are typical of a group in hiding on many campuses. One wonders how the massive numbers who take remedial English (45% at the University of California) are served by such instruction.[5]

To what purpose this sortie against the expansion of one's vocabulary? Does the author really mean that students should get past the freshman year of college without having learned what the words *forfeited, contemporary,* and *acceptance* mean? No. He means

[3] Wiener, p. 32.
[4] McCrimmon (p. 303) quoted in Wiener, pp. 30–31.
[5] Wiener, p. 31.

something quite different and, to my mind, much worse. He means that teachers have a duty to assume that a large number of entering college freshmen, notably those from "nontraditional" backgrounds, are not capable of learning what such words mean, that unlike the educational bill of fare served up to the children of the rich, the intellectual diet of such students should be one "rich in exclusions." "Rich in exclusions"—indeed. Bread and water is a meal rich in exclusions—it provides little nourishment and less delight. At one point this writer says that the "use of the word omniscient" is "tough even for gifted writers."[6] Yet he himself uses the word *eviscerate*. When, let me ask, is it too early for a college student to learn such words? Or, and I suspect this may be the case, is there the underlying assumption in this article that none of the students at community colleges, that none of the students who enter universities only because those universities have open-admissions programs, will (or *should*?) ever become regular readers of journals like *College English,* that their education, unlike the education of the children of the rich, *should not* prepare them for even middle-level positions of responsibility in society, that their education should not prepare them to change this society?

11   And thus we return to Henry Kissinger and the defense of ignorance. American education, as I see it, is becoming repolarized. Democracy has kept its promise to the American people—everybody gets an education; everybody is admitted to college, and most of those who are admitted do graduate. Only, beneath the surface, some big differences remain—and the people in power know it. The heirs of the powerful learn what *omniscient* means, and they learn it in high school—or, for "underachievers," in prep school. They leave college educated enough to read articles in journals assigned at the Wharton Business School or at Cal Tech, and ultimately they may come to wield the power of their parents. Their counterparts from the slums, and increasingly from middle-class suburbia—are passed along and given degrees by liberal-minded educators. They may even get into law school or Wharton on minority admittance programs (unless they happen to be poor white males) and end up as window dressing at IBM, comfortably ensconced behind the portals of power, but without power, waiting to join their brothers and sisters who have been taught the irrelevancy of intellect in taking up the banner of some new leader, waiting to follow him or her into the future, shouting "Down with intelligence; long live death."

[6] Wiener, p. 29.

Vocabulary

fascist	cynicism	aspiration
pragmatism	sanction	duplicate
entrepreneurs	flippant	expedient
absurd	nostalgia	browse
expertise	eloquence	initiate
truism	complicit	perspective
declension	implicit	sophisticated
eviscerate	sortie	polarized
wield	ensconsed	

Topics for Discussion

1. Brent speaks of knowing college freshmen through contact with them in his classes. Do you agree with his impressions of today's college freshmen?

2. Do you think college should prepare you for a career? What does Brent think college should do for students?

3. Brent says that Plato, Latin, history, and philosophy are "relevant" areas of study. In what ways are they relevant? Do you think they are relevant? Do you intend to study these subjects while you are in college? Why or why not?

4. Do you believe it is the function of education to challenge students intellectually or to meet them at their own level? What does Brent believe education should do?

5. Is there a difference between the education a student receives at Harvard and the education a student receives at a state college? What are these differences? Should there be differences?

6. According to Brent, how does education serve to reinforce and perpetuate a class and economic stratification in America?

7. Brent dismisses television as the cause for the decline of literacy among students. What other causes does he suggest? Can you think of any other possible causes?

Rhetorical Considerations

1. How does Brent's use of the quotation in the first and last paragraphs of the essay serve as a method of unification?

2. In paragraph 3 Brent begins with three questions. How

does this question-and-answer technique serve to organize and structure the paragraph?

3. Brent uses many examples throughout his essay. How effective are these examples in illustrating and clarifying the thesis idea in the paragraph? See, for example, paragraphs 4 and 6.

4. What shift in structure is signalled in the first sentence of paragraph 8?

5. How effectively does Brent use the three quotations in paragraph 9? Could he have simply paraphrased the information in the quotations? What effect does he achieve by the use of the quotation and not paraphrasing?

6. How does the first sentence in paragraph 11 signal a shift in structure? What is the rhetorical function of paragraph 11?

Style: The Decline of

Marya Mannes

Marya Mannes is a nationally syndicated columnist in major United States newspapers and author of two books: Message from a Stranger *(1948) and* But Will It Sell? *(1964).*

1   Dismiss "fashion," which is ephemeral and external. Dispose of "mode" or "flair," both inadequate. Discard "stylish," the word itself a turn-of-the-century evocation of ladies with very small waists, very large hats, and very narrow minds. These have nothing to do with style, which I see as a way of speaking, walking, behaving, creating, and *being,* which is both highly personal and yet—through its commanding presence—able to color the social and cultural climate of others.

2   It has to do with "life-style," the climate of a new generation, only in that a few in the vast multitude of young conformists managed to emerge with that special signature which is part of style. In so soing they were timeless, conjuring visions of Regency dandies, medieval princes, Renaissance rakes. (Forget the fake Navajos, the handcraft shawls and the poverty patches.)

3   All right,who had style? Fred Astaire, Franklin D. Roosevelt, Emily Dickinson, Aldous Huxley, Richard Brinsley Sheridan, François Villon—a wildly disparate few of history's many. In trying to find out what they had in common, I would include form, clarity, grace and that clear consciousness of self without which none can affect the quality of life.

4   Finally, people with style have managed to distill the essence of their gifts by imposing upon themselves certain disciplines that refine rather than smother their instincts.

5   Listening to a recent revival of Cole Porter's "Out of This World," the pristine and lovely lilt of his lyrics made me all the more conscious of what we miss today. The common language of school or street is an inchoate mess of "like I said" and "y'know" and "like, man"—interspersed with obscenities and other substitutes for thought.

Aping the Ignorant

6   Blame this on several things: a steep decline in reading as a result of laziness, the substitution of television, film and visual distractions for language, and the assumption that brotherhood consists of aping the ignorant.

7   At the other end, the jargons of sociology, psychiatry and other inexact sciences (including business) are arid, tedious and without savor. The language of government and its leaders is a waste of platitudes and declarations, so void of pace, inflection, vitality and form that the listening mind drifts before closing. Even our pornography lacks style.

8   A French philosopher, Joseph de Maistre, observed that "every individual or national degeneration is immediately revealed by a directly proportional degradation in language."

9   He would find further evidence in a nationwide survey made three years ago to find out how well Johnny can write. It was based on uniform writing exercises administered to 86,000 children aged 9, 13 and 17 in 2,500 schools in every section of the country, and to nearly 8,000 young adults.

        Herewith some findings:

10   Nine-year-old Americans show almost no command of the basic writing mechanics of grammar, vocabulary, spelling, sentence structure and punctuation.

11   Even the best of the 17-year-olds seldom displayed any flair or facility by moving beyond commonplace language.

12   Only four or five people in the whole assessment, the survey found, had a really good command of the English language. They could write adequate business letters and personal notes, but their writing usually "lacked imagination, vitality and detail."

13   (Personal footnote: style in the writing of letters—a specific and valued art for centuries—killed by the telephone?)

14   As for public prose, particularly in fiction, coherence, clarity and rhythmic line (in all but a few acknowledged masters of these) are as contemptuously dismissed or ignored as the phrase "well-made" applied to a play.

15   On the contrary (and no thanks to McLuhan), most lavishly praised today is the non-style: an electric circus of schizoid images and fragmented sequence that is supposed to indicate powerful talent. The starts and stutters and wild inversions of a spastic mind are highly praised by critics bored by simplicity and easy reading.

16   As for legitimate boredom, what about architecture? Look at your cities: what style exists except for the few new skyscrapers with swoop and elegance or the few residential streets where houses survive from an era of dignity and proportion? And the rest? Vast cubes of commerce, purely functional, great blocks of apartments with filing cabinets for living and "balconies" for breathing carbon monoxide.

Deserts and Clutter

17   And the rest? Deserts of parking lots intercepted by the cluttered sprawl of gas stations, snack bars, motels and shopping centers.

18   Style? Form? Grace? Conspicuous waste, not even worth recycling.

19   And what about people themselves? Beings? In style, a prime index is manners. Indeed, they do make the man or woman. How have we managed at last to achieve a graceless society?

20   Partly because a new generation, rejecting deception, came to think of "manners" as a form of hypocrisy. Why ask "How are you?" when you don't give a damn? Why give up your bus seat to an old bag who can stand? "Please," "thank you," "excuse me"—who's kiddin', man?

21   In more and more adults, whatever manners they once possessed have been eroded by the sheer pressures of daily living: crowds, noise, brutality on a massive scale in life, on screen, in print

. . . all these and the daily hassle of job and transport have murdered those small amenities: the social lubricant.

22   Style is one thing more: bearing. The way you hold yourself, how you use your body. Stance: what you see in all good dancers, actors, acrobats. The way a solo violinist stands before lifting his bow. The way someone in equilibrium enters a room. A combination of tension, pride, balance—standards.

23   (Standards . . . Ah, those things they still teach at the small conservatories of music and theater, starved for money . . .)

24   Style: without which we all slouch not toward Bethlehem but toward the town dump; brothers and sisters to beer cans and the immortal shapes of plastic.

Vocabulary

inchoate	ephemeral	flair
pristine	platitude	schizoid
amenity		

Topics for Discussion

1. How does Mannes define style? Do you agree with her definition? Would you define style differently? If so, how?

2. What difference, if any, is there between ''style'' and ''life-style''?

3. Mannes mentions some people who had style. Do you agree with Mannes's selections? Who do you think has style? Why?

4. Mannes believes that there is a decline in style. What does this decline consist of? Can the decline be reversed?

5. There is, according to Mannes, a degradation of language which contributes greatly to the decline of style. Why is the proper use of language so important to style? Do you agree with Mannes that reading and writing are so important?

Rhetorical Considerations

1. Examine the first three sentences of this essay. What do you notice about their structure? What effect does this structure create? Where else in the essay is this sentence structure used?

2. This is an essay in definition. How clearly has Mannes defined the term *style*? What method of definition is used?

3. How would you characterize the prose style of this essay? What are some of the dominant aspects of the prose? Do you like the style of this essay?

4. What evidence does Mannes use in her essay? How does this evidence help structure the essay?

Never Lose Your Cool

Paul Friedman

> *Paul Friedman, a native of New York City, is an assistant professor of English at the University of Illinois in Urbana. His short stories and essays have appeared in a wide variety of publications including* New Directions *and the* Quarterly Review of Literature.

I

1   He turned an unfamiliar corner and heard footsteps quickly coming up on him. He started to run. He ran, people saw him run, they saw the two boys chasing him. The people did not try to stop the chase. William saw a vacant lot and started to cut through it, fell, was overtaken. When he got up they were standing right in front of him, two long haired, long sideburned boys, about his age, in their middle teens.

2   Although the two boys had been running hard, when they spoke it was as if they had not exerted themselves in the chase; they were not out of breath, they were not panting.

3   "Okay man, all I want is your wallet, hand it across."

4   "I don't have any bread."

5   "That ain't what I asked Jack. I just want to see your wallet."

6   "I don't have one."

7   "Sure Ace, but I'm going to take a look."

8   "Look man, why don't you just cool it and do like he says? There won't be trouble that way."

9   "That's right Ace, what do you want trouble for? You're just

asking for trouble. What are you going to do with trouble when you get it?

10   "Yeah, we want the wallet," explained the boy. "We don't want trouble. How come you want trouble?"

11   "Man, I can't understand these cats that go around looking for trouble."

12   "Well, I guess some cats just got eyes for trouble. I can't understand it either."

13   They talked slowly, clearly, so deliberately. As they took a step toward him he took two steps back. They came in slowly, seemingly carelessly yet actually carefully. They were positioning for the attack: craftsmen working at their craft, sharp, delicate, not one crude step, not one faulty movement. William kept backing up. He was about five feet from the wall when he pulled out his knife.

14   William did not carry the knife for protection and he didn't carry it for fun, although he used it for both; he carried it because he liked to put his hand inside his pocket and feel it.

15   The two boys stopped. They didn't turn and run when they saw the knife. William was frightened. They did not look at him any more. They ignored him almost completely. They paid no attention to the people on the street who could see everything. They spread out a little and while talking between themselves they forced him to back up, even more, even with his knife, even though they acted as if he were not there; back up, back up, more, ever so slowly.

16   "What do you think of a cat that pulls a blade?"

17   "I think he might be forcing someone to get cut."

18   "Yeah, that's what I think. Do you want to get cut?"

19   "Well, to tell you the truth, no, I don't think that I want to get cut."

20   "Man, I *know* I don't want to get cut."

21   "Yeah, that's right, I definitely don't want to get cut."

22   "Don't look like we'll get cut on then, does it?"

23   "No. I'll tell you something man, now that I've thought about it I'm damn glad that I'm not going to get cut because that can really be nasty, you know what I mean?"

24   "Man, I've seen some cats that look so ugly they hurt my eyes." He waited a moment then continued. "Do you know why?"

25   "Because they got cut on?"

26   "Right where people could see the scars."

27   "That's awful. But if there's a blade and if I'm not going to get cut, and you say you're not going to get cut, and it looks like someone might get cut, who do you figure is going to get cut on?"

28   "Well, it might be that cat that started all the action with the blade in the first place."

29   "That's just what I was thinking."

30   Slow, soft talk, purring, almost velvet talk, almost comical talk but talk that is electric and serious and adult. Walking in on William, spreading out on him, closing in a little, shuffling, positioning, forcing William back, all the way back now, still ignoring him.

31   "If the man had any smart he'd just drop the blade. He'd drop the blade and give us his bread."

32   "But if the man had any smart he never would have shown the blade, ain't that so?"

33   "Yeah, that's right."

34   "I guess the cat just don't have any smart."

35   Then one of the boys, with his head slightly down, lifted his eyes and looked at William. Directly. William could no longer move.

36   "C'mon my man, you made a couple of mistakes so far, you going to make another one now? Now what are you going to do?"

37   William could not keep his knees still; his nose started to run, his eyes were watering and his cheek twitched. He wanted to urinate; a few drops escaped and slid down his leg.

38   "Look man, you're holding a blade, you don't want to do anything with it, why don't you just drop it?"

39   "Yeah, no one's going to help you. I'm not, he's not. You're going to have to help yourself because you're the only one on your side. Now, what are you going to do?"

40   William dropped his knife. As he did this the boy slapped him in the face, gently, playfully, like he'd pat a puppy. William felt a knee blast his stomach, then a thunderous blow on the back of his neck. He sagged down; not passed out. Not quite.

41   They kicked William. They took William's knife. They took the few pennies he had and then they sauntered off. He watched them walk away, unconcernedly; they walked with a certain air, an air that included pistol pockets and saddle stitching; he watched the people walking by on the street, the people who had witnessed this episode and who had walked right on by, the people who had averted their eyes after realizing what it was that they were seeing, the people who had been afraid to try and stop it, afraid to even call the police.

42   The two boys who had beaten him up were well trained, intuitively William grasped this, the people walking by were well trained, housebroken, William saw and accepted this. He was now determined that one day he too would be well trained, proficient, so proficient that he would have the power to turn strangers into sniveling and blind housebroken puppies.

43   William felt a profound admiration for those two boys. He desired their power.

44   The disdain they showed for everyone and everything; the sneer attitude they carried like a sign on their bodies and faces; the attitude that said we can do what we want and when we want and how we want and if you don't think so why don't you step up here and try to stop us; they didn't respect anything, they didn't sweat anyone.

45   The way they walked; a slight bounce to every step, a litheness, a gliding more than walking. Not one clumsy movement. Surety . . . Cool.

II

46   William felt like punching someone, anyone. Blast, hard, in the mouth. There would be blood and spitting teeth; his hand would be cut and it would be painful. He wanted to feel a part of him hurt. William wanted to strike out. He felt the knot grow in his stomach.

47   He walked down the block to his car. Some of the people he passed were aware of him. William was starting to make it. He hadn't been tested yet; before the test comes you have to be worthy of a test. He had been proving that he was.

48   William got into his car. Not a hotrod with a packed hood and dual exhausts and an aerial that extended three feet over the roof of the car. Not a new black Fleetwood either. He was just starting to move up, he was ready to prove it.

49   Eighteen years old. William felt old, mature. Out of school for a year and a half, had a few hustles going, making good money, had a hard reputation, was respected. He learned his lessons well in high school and he had learned all that high school had to teach him by the time he was thrown out.

50   He parked the car in front of the school and smoked a cigarette. His hand did not shake as he smoked but he inhaled jerkily. He finished, locked the car door, and walked toward the gymnasium.

51   William was wearing a light blue topcoat with wide lapels. A belt was loosely strung around the outside of his coat and he had a thick loose knot tied in front of him. His pants were black, slightly pegged and sharply creased; his shoes had pointed toes and were gleaming black, polished to perfection. His hair was long and slicked back. William knew that he looked cool.

52   There was a basketball game scheduled today and William knew the gymnasium would be packed. William had seen many things happen at high school athletic events; he had participated in

many of the happenings. He still retained a vivid picture of the football game he'd attended two years ago: the opposing school's side of the grandstand started to move, en masse, and like a wave they flowed from their side of the stands, through the end zone section, and toward his school's side of the stands. They met. Razor blades were shot from rubber bands. Brass knuckles appeared from back pockets. Lengths of lead pipe wrapped in tape connected with human shapes and caused dull thuds. The dull cracks of blackjacks. The screams of captured girls who were being toyed with under the grandstand. The game was forgotten, hysteria grabbed the crowd, the students surged forward, seeking the safety of the playing field. (This was a student body that was used to fights and flare-ups at athletic events, that expected and, by and large, looked forward to them, but the viciousness and savagery that were evident at that game were too much for most of them. They did not want to be involved, at all, this time.)

53   The feeling that William had (being a part of the small force that did not desert the stands) was a feeling that he could not forget. Standing there defiantly, not running, not moving, waiting, bouncing up and down confidently, trying to spot an enemy trooper within range, sensing that hundreds of people were watching him, or rather, watching all of the men who stayed in the stands, this was something he would never forget. This is what he thought about at night, in bed, alone, unable to sleep, when he wanted to think about the nicest thing that had ever happened to him.

54   On other occasions William had succeeded in partially recapturing that feeling, but never completely; either the audience was too small or the feat was not significant enough. He often imagined what it would be like if, instead of waiting for the enemy to advance, he were the aggressor, and if, instead of being a cog in the advancing machine, he were the whole machine. William spent many hours speculating on this unknown sensation, its rewards, the hazards presented by the difficulty of the task; he wondered, and he told himself that one day he would find out.

55   William was waiting, and after the wait was over, and after the feat was performed, he was going to tell the whole damn world, "Listen, I'm me and I'm the swinging cat. I'm cool, watch if you don't believe me, or ask someone who's seen me, he'll tell you, you'll find out. I'm cool, so my way is the cool way, don't try and mess up because remember what happened to the last cat who tried. I'm not a punk. I worked hard to get where I am and now I'm here baby so dig, I do what I want, you do what I want. What I say, me. I'm cool, remember that. Watch."

56   As he was on his way into the gymnasium he noticed a group of students standing in the hallway outside the gym entrance. He lit a cigarette, stopped to smoke it. The students saw him, and watched him, and their conversation slowly evaporated. The air thickened with the smoke from William's cigarette. William inhaled. One hand went into a big patch pocket on his topcoat. The other hung almost limply at his side. The cigarette hung between his lips. The smoke from the cigarette made his eyes squint. He snapped his thumb and middle finger together, rhythmically, as if keeping time to a rock tune. He nodded his head in time to the beat of his thumb and middle finger. He moved his left knee back and forth. The movement of his head, of his knee, of his whole body, was almost but not quite, imperceptible. He looked sensual, lazy, ready to uncoil, cool.

57   William walked through the crowd of students and opened the door to the gym. A boy sitting behind a desk at the entrance was collecting admissions.

58   "Half a rock pal."

59   William laughed; a low, calculated and controlled laugh.

60   "Sure." He made no move to pay. He stood right where he was, not looking at the boy, but letting his eyes rove through the crowd that was already seated.

61   The game was just starting. Not many people had their eyes on the entrance, most of them were watching the jump at mid-court, but those few who did happen to see William saw not only an ex-student but also a person who had not come to watch a basketball game. They sensed this and they prodded the person sitting next to them. Slowly the crowd's attention was transferred from the court to the entrance.

62   William was well known. To these high school people he stood for fear on one hand and freedom on the other. Freedom through defiance. The stands were full of people who nurtured the same dream he nurtured, but he was more advanced than they were. William felt the eyes on him.

63   "C'mon, it's a half a dollar."

64   William turned to face the boy. William's head bobbed slightly now. He opened his mouth wide, raised his eyebrows, sneered, and shook his head.

65   The boy did not know what to do. He wished that one of the teachers would come over. He was sure that the teachers knew what was going on. He also knew that teachers never tried to break up fights in the locker room. The teachers had been teaching in this high school long enough to know when it is wisest to stay away, when it is time to keep the eyes straight ahead and unseeing. The teachers

were hoping that William would just go and sit down. They didn't want his fifty cents. It wasn't worth it.

66   William was savoring every moment of the boy's indecision. He wanted the boy to ask him for the money, again. He wanted to hear that quivering voice, again. He felt powerful, knowing that the boy's voice did not ordinarily quiver. William knew that by now more people were watching him than were watching the game. He sensed the admiration, the adulation, the intense jealousy, the hatred. He gloried in it all. The boy's lips started to move. William wanted to expand his chest. He wanted to make his biceps bulge. Suddenly, tiring of the warm-up game, he walked away; a time-out had been called on the floor.

67   William walked out there. The cheerleaders who had run onto the court quickly headed back to the sideline. He headed for the referee. Tense inside, but loose and agile on the outside. He wished that he had a piece of gum to chew on. He felt that his walk was right. From the quiet of the crowd he knew that it was. The referee, out of a corner of his eye, could see William coming at him. He did not turn around to face William, to meet him head on, to look him in the eye, to try and stare him down, to intimidate him with age and righteousness. He did not want to. William reached him, tapped him on the shoulder, gently, two times. Very, very . . . lightly . . . politely. The referee stiffly turned. He seemed startled that it was William and not a fellow in a basketball uniform. The referee had known that William was going to force him to turn around; he had tried to hope that it was a player who was touching him.

68   No one moved. Anywhere. There were at least two hundred high school pupils. They sat, transfixed. Dreaming. Envious. The few instructors who were there sat shamed and afraid. William had everything in the palm of his hand. He knew it.

69   William pointed, almost daintily, at the whistle that hung around the referee's neck. He moved his finger back and forth, in pantomime, telling the referee and the crowd and the whole goddam world that he, William Baronofsky, wanted that silly goddam whistle that hung around that frightened goddam referee's neck. And everyone knew he wanted it. And everyone knew that he wanted it for nothing; and everyone knew that if he got it he could have everything.

70   William realized that if he made a mistake now he would have less than nothing. The referee did not know what to do. William waited, bouncing on the balls of his feet. Laughing inside a little, happy that the timekeeper would be messed up, happy that the ballplayers were not on the court even though the time-out was

over. William wondered if this extra time-out could be considered an official's time-out. William laughed a little more. He felt giddy. William still bounced on the balls of his feet. Patient so far, making everything simple. Not a complicated plan; not a complicated objective; everything was simple. The referee looked toward the benches where the coaches sat. They looked the other way. The referee waited. William bounced and waited. The crowd sat, frozen. William deliberated. Should he try and yank the whistle off the referee's neck? If the string did not break and the whistle did not come off with the first yank the picture would not appear smooth and unmarred. That flaw could change everything. It could break the spell. He decided. His hand flashed to the whistle and pulled it and the string up over the referee's head. The whistle was off and in his hand. Free. Nothing had been touched; nothing was ruptured.

71   The referee stood, paralyzed. The crowd gasped silently, in awe. The crowd did not utter a sound but the pride, and also the revulsion, they felt could be heard quite clearly. That instant they all wanted to be William, regardless of how they had felt fifteen minutes before they walked into the gymnasium, regardless of the way they felt toward adults, regardless of the way they felt toward their parents and going to church on Sunday and helping old ladies with packages; any one of them would have traded places with William right then, gladly. They all ached to be William.

72   William tossed the whistle up and down a few times. He tossed it neatly and caught it neatly. Nothing sloppy, nothing that was not clear, hard, cold. He balanced the whistle in the palm of his hand. He looked at it. And smiled. He looked at one of the baskets at the end of the court. He looked at the whistle again. Long, hard. He smiled again. William started to walk, slowly, lightly, toward the basket, with his head still down, looking at the whistle, still balanced in the palm of his hand. When he was two feet from the basket he stopped. He threw the whistle, carefully, through the hoop. He caught it, glad that it had not touched the netting. After he caught it he looked at it again. Again he smiled; with his head down he almost started to laugh. He threw the whistle straight up and down a few times. He stopped doing this and thought about throwing it through the hoop again. He decided not to; it might touch the net and somehow spoil the picture. The picture he had created. He wondered what he should do now. The crowd was straining toward him, going with him, wanting him. Being him.

73   Turning, without thinking, without realizing what he was doing, he hurled the whistle against the wall. There had been no

warning. The crowd screamed. Loud. Everyone was caught off guard, unprepared. William included. The hypnotic spell had been pierced but not completely broken. The whistle had sliced the air like a saber. The sound the whistle made when it hit the wall was like the sound of a man dying, not afraid of death, but unable to keep from crying out.

74   William had not planned on any movement as violent as the one that had just taken place. It just happened. He heard the noise and he felt his cool leaving him. He started to feel lonely and afraid. Tired and empty. He felt untidy, almost undressed. Undressed and dirty. He almost panicked and ran. He wanted to let himself panic. He wanted to run, away. He bit his tongue to keep control. He realized the faster he ran now, the longer and farther he would have to crawl later. He forced his body to move. Slowly, disconnectedly, heavily. William plodded. He was stiff instead of loose. He made an effort to walk self-assuredly. He looked up at the crowd. He was surprised to see that they were still sitting still, staring at him, watching him with care, taking in every detail. He tried to regain his loose and agile walk. His body reacted jerkily, no longer a well-oiled machine; but it did do what he wanted it to do, more or less. He was surprised.

75   William could not unlock his car door. He could not get the key into the lock. He had captivated and then fooled those people, but he knew that he had lost. He realized he had failed. He did not know why. He didn't know if it was a lack of training or a lack of ability or perhaps even a lack of desire. He did not know. He realized he had almost won.

76   He wondered why he missed.

Topics for Discussion

1. How do you think you might react if attacked by muggers like those who attacked William? Would there be any point in attempting to reason with them? If you think there might be, what would you say? How might they respond?

2. In your opinion, what is the worst thing that happens to William? What character changes does he undergo during the story?

3. In paragraph 43 Friedman tells us that William admires his attackers. Paragraph 44 gives the reasons. Can you cite any parallel experience in your own life?

4. In paragraph 51 William is described as looking "cool." What does it mean to be "cool"? Cite examples. Why, most fundamentally, do you think people try to be "cool"?

5. When William throws the whistle through the basket, he does not want it to touch the netting. Why? What do you think the spectators think about William? Are their thoughts markedly different from William's thoughts about himself?

6. Does William really fail, in your opinion? If so, how might he have succeeded?

7. In what specific ways is this story representative of social problems larger than the experience of any single person?

Rhetorical Considerations

1. Why does Friedman give his central character the formal name, *William,* rather than the more familiar *Bill?*

2. Examine the speech of the muggers who attack William. How do they use the word "trouble" to confuse him? How would you answer them in their use of this word?

3. Freidman employs a third-person narrator. What changes would have to be made to rewrite the story in the first person?

4. Note the attention that Friedman pays to William's minor body movements, for example, the precise manner in which he smokes a cigarette (paragraph 56). What do such details add to the story?

5. How often does William speak in the story? Why doesn't Friedman have him speak more?

Rhetorical Analysis

Perry: Because I Am Black

We have selected this essay for analysis for three reasons: 1. Its length. Perry's essay is about seven hundred words long, about as long as a standard college theme. 2. Its subject matter. The essay discusses the reaction of a college freshman to her new environment, a topic probably quite familiar to you. 3. Its uneven rhetoric. The essay is characterized by a combination of rhetorical successes and mistakes. We hope to show you things to imitate and things to avoid.

Perry begins by presenting a personal narrative of her experiences at Barnard, but the essay does not consist of narrative only. Much good writing is based on rhetorical strategies allowing for a combination and interpenetration of two or more different modes of rhetoric. Perry combines narration and argumentation. You will have little difficulty determining where narrative ends and argument begins if you quickly scan the middle paragraph of the essay, paragraph three, and notice the frequency of the word *I*. About halfway through that paragraph the *I*'s stop, and with their termination ends the main portion of the narrative part of the essay. After the *I*'s stop, a more objective, distant, and evaluating voice takes over, raising the level of discussion from the simple recounting of one person's experience to a complex interweaving of generalizations based on that experience. How successful is Perry in making this combination of rhetorical modes? Let us critically examine her essay's major strengths and weaknesses.

Major Strengths

Perry creates a close bond with her readers in the first paragraph by presenting herself as someone disillusioned, emotionally hurt, and perhaps oppressed. At this point in the essay Perry wants to prepare her readers, perhaps her white readers especially, for her forthright, angry statements of the final paragraph. Had she come on as angry in the first paragraph, had she made the final sentence of the essay the first, she would probably have gained sympathy and understanding only from people who agreed with her to begin with—she would neither win any converts to her position, nor would she successfully neutralize the probable arguments of her opponents. The tone created in the first paragraph puts most of the audience firmly on her side before she says anything controversial. Who cannot but feel some sense of dismay that an intelligent young woman, a skillful writer—you can tell by the sentence and paragraph structure— does not feel at home where she rightfully belongs. The second paragraph continues Perry's attempt to ingratiate herself with her readers. Who when a child, she asks, did not come to understand that all of a child's dreams are not to be realized in this tough world. But the world is tougher for some than for others, tough enough, if you're not white, to kill those dreams even before you're finished dreaming them—to be young, gifted, and black with nowhere to go save into a white man's world. And so Deborah Perry tells her story, a credible story given the history of social oppression in America. Only bigots and racists, which nobody in Perry's audience wants to be, would not be moved, even if only a little, by this story. Many black readers of this essay will find in it a correlative for their own personal experiences and will thus be moved to indignation and anger. People with a sense of justice, white and black, will be moved from uneasiness to outrage, born either of opposition to racism or a sense of guilt. The *I* of the first part of this essay does not threaten; it stands there alone waiting for support.

At the middle of the third paragraph the focus of the essay switches from *I* to *them*. *They* are those, says Perry, who are responsible for her plight, the "powers that be who govern this university and who ignore the contributions and needs of black people." *They* are those, the fourth paragraph continues, who have decided to learn something about black people only recently when it suited their fancy, and *they* are those—on to the final paragraph—who now whine and grumble when black people show no interest in *them*. If there is to be discussion then it must be black people who will decide how it is to proceed, not *them*. The cautious *I* of the first paragraph has become a self-assured *we* in the last, a change in voice oriented to leave Perry's opponents at a loss for rebuttal. Those who already agree with Perry's major contention will have their opinions reaffirmed.

Those who will want to disagree with her, still under the influence of the narrative part of the essay, will perhaps want to reconsider their positions. Perry has a neatly constructed essay here, to put it simply, a structure that sets the reader up in the first part and which grabs hold in the second. How can the reader immediately dismiss Perry's last few sentences after warmly accepting the first two-and-one-half paragraphs?

Perry's success is not limited to large structural operations in her essay. She succeeds on lesser levels as well. Some examples:

1. *Sentence Structure.* The first sentence, like a good chess move, serves more than one purpose. It sets the tone of the essay as personal, self-directed, something for the reader to identify with. Its cumulative structure sets a familiar easy personal style which works to the same end. And the last expansion in the sentence, "where all things are possible," suggests a central idea for the whole essay—What is *really* possible for a black person at a white college?

In other places Perry characteristically uses sentences frequently punctuated by interjections, nonrestrictive modifiers, and parallel variation both to clarify her ideas and to add an even, flowing quality to her prose. A few examples:

> *Interjection:* "I would, I thought, be able to"
>
> *Nonrestrictive Modifier:* "My background—black middle class comfortable."
>
> *Parallel Variation:* "dreamed about, read about, and heard about?"

In what other ways do you think Perry's sentence structure can be characterized? Note that the success of many of Perry's sentences is closely associated with her choice of short, direct words—*black, white, presto.*

2. *Paragraph Structure and Essay Coherence.* We have already analyzed the opening sentence of paragraph one. The closing sentence is no less important. Its final word, *white,* abruptly ends the harmonious, expansive quality of the sentences which precede it, just as the realities of a white world, as

we are soon to learn, abruptly shattered Perry's dreams. The second paragraph continues in parallel fashion, picking up the dream motif again in fairly lengthy, harmonious sentences until that harmony is abruptly ended by the monosyllabic word *black*. The second paragraph ends with an example to support its generalization. The fourth paragraph leaves the individual and the personal behind for a more abstract view of things, comparing and contrasting the viewpoints of whites and blacks concerning each other. The final paragraph sets up a generalization of white views and attitudes. It ends with a powerful statement placed in the face of that generalization.

Major Weaknesses

Perry's reliance on well-knit sentences and paragraphs may lead the reader to overlook the omission of convincing evidence to support her conclusions. Evidently she hopes that her readers will have read elsewhere about the difficulties black college students face, or will have faced those difficulties themselves. A writer who makes assumptions like this one will not make the best case possible and will not likely reach the people most in need of convincing.

Some suggestions: Given the short length of the essay, Perry might have included a concrete example of "indirect racism" at least by the beginning of the second paragraph. Such an example would show the reader plainly and clearly that racial oppression can and does exist in disguised forms, and might substitute well for the undemonstrated, and thus unproved, contention that Perry cannot realize her dreams simply because she is black. A counterargument specifically detailing the notable achievements of black individuals with less affluent class backgrounds and much more limited educational opportunities than Perry's would probably win out over her simple assertion in a serious debate. Because of its lack of concrete detail, the final sentence of the second paragraph also does little to advance Perry's argument. If she rejects the personal aspirations inculcated by white society, what aspirations have taken their place? Why, if she has rejected white goals, does she remain at "lily-white'' Barnard? The first half of paragraph three constitutes a good example of violating the rhetorical principle of commitment and response. Perry says she felt "uncomfortable" and "uneasy" with white students, that orientation programs did not meet black needs. The reader is primed at this point to agree with her. She needs only one or two solid examples in response to her generalizations to clinch her case—a description of a luncheon conversation about white middle-class dissatisfaction with life in the suburbs, perhaps a question put behind an artificial smile: "What's it like to be a, a, a, ne—gro?" Perry could come up with better examples than we can—but she doesn't.

Perry's failure to use concrete examples in the narrative section of her essay seriously weakens her argumentation section. Since she has not really *shown,* but simply suggested, that there exists a need to change things for black students at Barnard, she can only suggest, but not substantially argue, that certain changes ought in fact to be made.

And so the rest of the essay continues in the mode of suggestion rather than in the mode of proof. Instead of briefly outlining a black studies program and showing concretely how such an addition to the curriculum might broaden the intellectual horizons of many students, white and black, Perry uses the moral authority gained in the first part of the essay to snipe at Plato, Virgil, Lenin, and Confucius. The fourth paragraph's final sentence, a good example of understatement, puts forth an important truth hardly needing exemplification. The foregoing sentences would stand better if Perry mentioned the names of some sadly neglected black figures from history—"Have whites gathered to learn anything about Denmark Vesey, Peatie Wheatstraw, Blind Willie McTell, or George Schuyler?" A white reader has to answer either yes or no to this question. As the passage stands now, the reader can indulge in lengthy and perhaps self-serving speculations.

And so we come to the final paragraph with its heavy final sentence. For those who do not already agree with her, Perry's dictum that blacks should "dictate" to whites must surely sound harsh and abrasive. If her purpose is to tell these readers off, as it may perhaps justifiably be, she will have succeeded. If, however, she intends to inform them that changes should be made, even a harsh and abrasive term like "dictate" might go over a bit better if these readers understood the grounding for black peoples' need to define the terms of discussion about themselves. The use of examples in this essay to that end might not make "dictate" sound any less harsh or abrasive, but those examples might clearly show why such a word comes to be used in the first place.

Why should we in the compass of a pale
Keep law and form and due proportion,
Showing, as in a model, our firm estate,
When our sea-walled garden, the whole land,
Is full of weeds, her fairest flowers choked up,
Her fruit trees all unpruned, her hedges ruined,
Her knots disordered, and her wholesome herbs
Swarmed with caterpillars?

Richard II, III, iv

3

THE COMPLEX SOCIETY

One thing that we can be certain about is that things change.
Nothing remains the same. The world as we know it in the
twentieth century is far different from the world of the Mesozoic
Era, 200 million years ago, when reptiles held sway. It is also
vastly different from the feudal world only six hundred years
past when kings and queens ruled the earth. Even the United
States today is something quite other than the expanding frontier
democracy it was only a century ago. Things not only change;
they change very quickly, and the speed of social and technological change in the modern era has created enormous difficulties
for those who wish to understand or influence that change.

If you do not believe this, then try your hand at working on
some useful social project. Let's say that you and some friends
want to do something as simple as build a playground for
neighborhood kids near your university. You know that the
university owns a vacant lot in the neighborhood, a perfect site.
Do you go ahead on your next free weekend to cut weeds and lay
cement? A simple solution for a simple problem? You may
remember that when students at the University of California at
Berkeley attempted to do just that a few years ago, the univer-

sity had a cyclone fence erected to prevent use of the new "People's Park." That led to mass marches and a response by police which included the shooting to death of one James Rector, a bystander at a demonstration.

You realize that the world is different for you than it was for Daniel Boone. No longer are people free to clear unused space to build a log cabin—or a playground. A series of procedures— "the system"—has been installed by those in authority for implementing projects such as yours. You must, you realize, work through this "system" to establish your playground.

And so you start out. Since the university owns the vacant lot, you decide to visit the person whom you think might be able to give you permission to use it, the Director of Buildings and Grounds. So you wander over to his office, dressed in your customary blue jeans, for an interview. Alas, he cannot help you. He has authority to water the flowers and empty the wastebaskets, but not to give away university property. Outfitted in your only suit to project that gentlemanly or ladylike appearance, you visit the dean. But, sadly enough, you learn that he has authority only over things such as changing grades and inventing courses. He has nothing whatsoever to do with "Buildings and Grounds," the department he sends you back to.

By chance, while walking out of the administration building, you notice a sign reading, "Vice President for Planning and Development." Here at last! When you arrive for your appointment two weeks later, your clothes newly pressed, and present your plans for the playground to the middle-aged man sitting in the plush leather chair behind the mahogany desk, you feel relieved to be met with eager nods of his graying head. He does indeed understand your position, he informs you, and is most eager to see your project set in motion. There are, however, certain practical concerns which must be taken into account in evaluating your proposal. He will investigate these concerns and meet with you a month hence to discuss them. You return at the month's end in your rumpled suit to learn that:

(1) The vacant lot is not really vacant. Even though it may appear to be empty, and for the moment actually is empty, its area is potentially filled with a twenty-story luxury high-rise apartment building.

(2) The principal investor in the building is a cousin of a member of the Board of Regents.

(3) Construction is being held up because the leaders of a local minority group have threatened to file a conflict-of-interest suit against the Board of Regents. They want the land for a cultural center.

(4) The university would just as soon give the land to the minority group except that the apartment building is going to be financed by a local bank that provides the bulk of student loans for minority group members at the university.

(5) Minority-group students have threatened to strike the university if loans are not forthcoming. They have the support of the teaching assistants and physical plant workers.

(6) The bank would just as soon finance the cultural center except that the rate of return would be quicker from the apartment building.

(7) The university is attempting to get some minority-group leaders appointed to the Board of Regents so that the leaders can appreciate the complexities of the problem and thus forestall the student strike.

(8) Conservatives in the community and around the state view the attempt to have minority-group members placed on the Board of Regents as "pandering to radicals." They have launched a campaign to prevent the appointments.

(9) Any attempt by any group, no matter how idealistic in purpose, to focus attention on the vacant lot would at this time greatly exacerbate tensions in the community, possibly leading to civil strife and the breakdown of social order.

(10) But to encourage your idealism, the vice president has decided to appoint you to a university committee to study the needs of children in the university neighborhood, especially minority-group children.

You decide to write a novel using your recent experience as a metaphor for American society in general. You call the novel *The Castle, II.*

The essays in this section will not give you enough information to understand how the American society, or any other society, works. They can, however, offer some indication of the ways in which perceptive or, at least, rhetorically skillful individuals have used language to illuminate or obfuscate the contradictions present in complex social issues.

Read these essays critically, even the ones you immediately find yourself agreeing with. On one hand, you may conclude that certain writers have a tendency to oversimplify the difficulties of the problems they deal with. On the other hand, you may agree that certain complexities can in fact be resolved by relatively uncomplicated solutions, solutions which go to the roots of things. After all, Alexander the Great did untangle the Gordian Knot. Sweeping solutions sometimes do solve problems—sometimes they do not. We hope a close reading of the essays in this section will lead to a finer discrimination in your thinking and writing about social and political problems.

The Rhetorical Analysis for this section deals with John F. Kennedy's *Inaugural Address*. Be sure to read Kennedy's speech before reading the Rhetorical Analysis.

Inaugural Address

John F. Kennedy

John F. Kennedy (1917–1963), the thirty-fifth president of the United States, served less than three years of the term he began in 1961. He was assassinated in Dallas, Texas, on November 22, 1963. During his brief presidential career, the world was brought to the brink of nuclear war over the presence of Soviet missiles in Cuba.

1   We observe today not a victory of party but a celebration of freedom, symbolizing an end as well as a beginning, signifying renewal as well as change. For I have sworn before you and Almighty God the same solemn oath our forebears prescribed nearly a century and three-quarters ago.

2   The world is very different now. For man holds in his mortal hands the power to abolish all forms of human poverty and all forms of human life. And yet the same revolutionary belief for which our forebears fought is still at issue around the globe, the belief that the

rights of man come not from the generosity of the state but from the hand of God.

3 We dare not forget today that we are the heirs of that first revolution. Let the word go forth from this time and place, to friend and foe alike, that the torch has been passed to a new generation of Americans, born in this century, tempered by war, disciplined by a hard and bitter peace, proud of our ancient heritage, and unwilling to witness or permit the slow undoing of those human rights to which this nation has always been committed, and to which we are committed today at home and around the world.

4 Let every nation know, whether it wishes us well or ill, that we shall pay any price, bear any burden, meet any hardship, support any friend, oppose any foe to assure the survival and the success of liberty.

5 This much we pledge—and more.

6 To those old allies whose cultural and spiritual origins we share, we pledge the loyalty of faithful friends. United, there is little we cannot do in a host of co-operative ventures. Divided, there is little we can do, for we dare not meet a powerful challenge at odds and split asunder.

7 To those new states whom we welcome to the ranks of the free, we pledge our word that one form of colonial control shall not have passed away merely to be replaced by a far more iron tyranny. We shall not always expect to find them supporting our view. But we shall always hope to find them strongly supporting their own freedom, and to remember that, in the past, those who foolishly sought power by riding the back of the tiger ended up inside.

8 To those peoples in the huts and villages of half the globe struggling to break the bonds of mass misery, we pledge our best efforts to help them help themselves, for whatever period is required, not because the Communists may be doing it, not because we seek their votes, but because it is right. If a free society cannot help the many who are poor, it cannot save the few who are rich.

9 To our sister republics south of our border, we offer a special pledge: to convert our good words into good deeds, in a new alliance for progress, to assist free men and free governments in casting off the chains of poverty. But this peaceful revolution of hope cannot become the prey of hostile powers. Let all our neighbors know that we shall join with them to oppose aggression or subversion anywhere in the Americas. And let every other power know that this hemisphere intends to remain the master of its own house.

10 To that world assembly of sovereign states, the United Nations, our last best hope in an age where the instruments of war have

far outpaced the instruments of peace, we renew our pledge of support: to prevent it from becoming merely a forum for invective, to strengthen its shield of the new and the weak, and to enlarge the area in which its writ may run.

11   Finally, to those nations who would make themselves our adversary, we offer not a pledge but a request: that both sides begin anew the quest for peace, before the dark powers of destruction unleashed by science engulf all humanity in planned or accidental self-destruction.

12   We dare not tempt them with weakness. For only when our arms are sufficient beyond doubt can we be certain beyond doubt that they will never be employed.

13   But neither can two great and powerful groups of nations take comfort from our present course—both sides over-burdened by the cost of modern weapons, both rightly alarmed by the steady spread of the deadly atom, yet both racing to alter that uncertain balance of terror that stays the hand of mankind's final war.

14   So let us begin anew, remembering on both sides that civility is not a sign of weakness, and sincerity is always subject to proof. Let us never negotiate out of fear, but let us never fear to negotiate.

15   Let both sides explore what problems unite us instead of belaboring those problems which divide us.

16   Let both sides, for the first time, formulate serious and precise proposals for the inspection and control of arms, and bring the absolute power to destroy other nations under the absolute control of all nations.

17   Let both sides seek to invoke the wonders of science instead of its terrors. Together let us explore the stars, conquer the deserts, eradicate disease, tap the ocean depths and encourage the arts and commerce.

18   Let both sides unite to heed in all corners of the earth the command of Isaiah to "undo the heavy burdens . . . [and] let the oppressed go free."

19   And if a beachhead of co-operation may push back the jungle of suspicion, let both sides join in creating a new endeavor, not a new balance of power, but a new world of law, where the strong are just and the weak secure and the peace preserved.

20   All this will not be finished in the first one hundred days. Nor will it be finished in the first one thousand days, nor in the life of this Administration, nor even perhaps in our lifetime on this planet. But let us begin.

21   In your hands, my fellow citizens, more than mine, will rest the final success or failure of our course. Since this country was founded, each generation of Americans has been summoned to give

testimony to its national loyalty. The graves of young Americans who answered the call to service surround the globe.

22   Now the trumpet summons us again—not as a call to bear arms, though arms we need; not as a call to battle, though embattled we are; but a call to bear the burden of a long twilight struggle, year in and year out, "rejoicing in hope, patient in tribulation," a struggle against the common enemies of men: tyranny, poverty, disease and war itself.

23   Can we forge against these enemies a grand and global alliance, North and South, East and West, that can assure a more fruitful life for all mankind? Will you join in that historic effort?

24   In the long history of the world, only a few generations have been granted the role of defending freedom in its hour of maximum danger. I do not shrink from this responsibility; I welcome it. I do not believe that any of us would exchange places with any other people or any other generation. The energy, the faith, the devotion which we bring to this endeavor will light our country and all who serve it, and the glow from that fire can truly light the world.

25   And so, my fellow Americans, ask not what your country can do for you; ask what you can do for your country.

26   My fellow citizens of the world, ask not what America will do for you, but what together we can do for the freedom of man.

27   Finally, whether you are citizens of America or citizens of the world, ask of us here the same high standards of strength and sacrifice which we ask of you. With a good conscience our only sure reward, with history that final judge of our deeds, let us go forth to lead the land we love, asking His blessing and His help, but knowing that here on earth God's work must truly be our own.

Vocabulary

oath	forebearers	aggression
subversion	hemisphere	forum
invective	writ	adversary
civility	eradicate	

Topics for Discussion

1. John F. Kennedy was elected president by the smallest margin of any modern American president, and then after a long and bitter election campaign. Is this background reflected in the president's speech? How?

2. How much of real content is in the speech? That is, looking beyond the rhetoric of the speech, what concrete, specific ideas and proposals are offered by Kennedy?

3. Kennedy says that ". . . only when our arms are sufficient beyond doubt can we be certain beyond doubt that they will never be employed." In this age of ballistic missiles and antiballistic missiles, can there ever be a nation which has arms sufficient beyond doubt? Was Kennedy thus committing the United States to an unlimited arms race?

4. Idealism and hope characterize this speech. Kennedy claims that "the torch has been passed to a new generation of Americans. . . ." Given subsequent revelations about some of the covert practices of the Kennedy administration, how much of the speech do you think is just "political rhetoric"?

5. Throughout his speech, Kennedy describes the United States as "embattled" and engaged in a "long struggle." With what or whom is the United States engaged in this struggle? Cite specific references from the speech. Are there any enemies not mentioned but referred to indirectly?

Rhetorical Considerations

1. Much has been written about this speech. Yet when Kennedy delivered this address, the reception by the audience was polite and the applause restrained. Why do you think the speech is appreciated more after rereadings?

2. In the eighth paragraph, Kennedy says that "if a free society cannot help the many who are poor, it cannot save the few who are rich." What is the main clause of this sentence? What is the subordinate clause? What does this indicate is the primary concern of a free society according to Kennedy?

3. Throughout the speech Kennedy makes effective use of coordinating conjunctions, particularly at the beginning of sentences. For example, in paragraph 2 he says, "The world is very different now. For man holds in his mortal hands the power to abolish all forms of human poverty and all forms of human life." Find similar examples and evaluate their effectiveness.

4. There is great use of the "let us" formula here ("Let us . . . Let both sides . . ."). Locate all the uses of this formula. Is it overused? What effect does repetition of this structure achieve?

5. Look carefully at the diction of the speech. What kind of words appear most frequently? (Abstract, concrete, monosyllabic, polysyllabic?) What effect does the diction achieve, and how does it contribute to the tone of the speech?

6. This speech is rich in figures of speech, particularly metaphors. List some of the metaphors and discuss their effectiveness. How original are they? Are there any old metaphors used in new ways?

7. The use of antithesis (the juxtaposition of contrasting ideas) is striking throughout the speech. Perhaps the most famous example of antithesis in the speech is the sentence, "And so, my fellow Americans, ask not what your country can do for you; ask what you can do for your country." List other examples of antithesis and discuss their effectiveness.

8. Read the Rhetorical Analysis at the end of this section.

The Language of Myth and Reality

William Lutz

William Lutz (b. 1940) is an assistant professor and Director of Freshman English at Rutgers University in Camden, New Jersey.

1   Every civilization creates its own myths to sustain, strengthen, and inspire it. We are all familiar with the Greek, Roman, and Norse myths which played an important role in their cultures and continue to play an important role in our literature today. We have, too, our American myths which have played important roles in our history, and which we continue to cherish. The Horatio Alger myth and the myth of the western American frontier still evoke powerful emotions in us as a people. All of these myths—Roman, Greek, Norse, and American—may be called "positive" in the sense that they inspired nations and peoples to great actions and to endure great hardships. The collective myth of "mom, home, apple pie, and democracy" has sustained more than a few American soldiers in more than one war. But if there are "positive" myths then there are also "negative" myths. Such negative myths would include the myth of racial superiority of the Nazis and white supremacists, the myth of the will of the proletariat in totalitarian societies, and the myth of national-

ism. Any one of these myths will not strengthen, sustain, or inspire to greatness. And any one of these myths, once accepted, can control "the whole individual, who becomes immune to any other influence."[1] Once the negative myth is in control, we are led to Dachau, apartheid, crimes in the name of the people, and any endless number of wars in the name of national honor. Whether positive or negative, myth plays a powerful and significant role in our lives.

2   Before I go too much further, perhaps I should briefly define what I mean by myth. I would like to use Jacques Ellul's definition of myth as

> . . . an all-encompassing, activating image: a sort of vision of desirable objectives that have lost their material, practical character and have become strongly colored, over-whelming, all-encompassing, and which displace from the conscious all that is not related to it. Such an image pushes man to action precisely because it includes all that he feels is good, just, and true.[2]

Some of you will recognize that the myth Ellul speaks of is the myth created by the propagandist, for it is the goal of the propagandist that his "myth take possession of a man's mind so completely that his life is consecrated to it."[3] I will use this definition of myth in examining the language of Watergate, for it is my contention that all those events we gather under the name Watergate were part of an effort to create a new American myth. This new myth, once accepted, would allow for just that kind of unthinking, unconscious, reflex action which Ellul says such myths bring—the new myth that Watergate attempted to create was the myth of national security.

3   I know that national security has existed as a semi-myth since the end of World War II. The McCarthy era produced a kind of hysteria over national security. And while the Pentagon budget grew ever larger, supposedly to insure our national security, the tactics of McCarthy were exposed and rejected publicly. Watergate, however, has demonstrated that once again we are fighting the creation of the national security myth. And lest anyone doubt that the myth of national security, once accepted, can lead to unspeakable actions, I remind you that one of the most feared and vicious branches of the Nazi SS was the *Sicherheitsdienst,* or SD, the security service, the

---

[1] Jacques Ellul, *Propaganda: The Formation of Men's Attitudes* (New York: Alfred A. Knopf, 1965), p. 11.
[2] Ellul, p. 31.
[3] Ellul, p. 31.

section that ran the concentration camps and followed the conquering armies eliminating all possible security risks to the new order, as well as maintaining security within the borders of Germany.[4] Similar organizations for "state security" exist in many countries today. It is one reason we as a people have fought the establishment of any kind of national police.

4   Throughout Watergate, the theme of national security occurs again and again until it becomes an endless refrain, a continual rationale, and a last court of appeal. For example, in an official statement issued on May 22, 1973, President Nixon used the phrase "national security" twenty-five times, and the word "security" ten times, in his attempt to justify the break-in at the Democratic Party headquarters, the burglary of Ellsberg's psychiatrist's office, and the other criminal actions which had been exposed.[5] Indeed, G. Gordon Liddy still refuses to talk about his role in the whole Watergate affair because of his belief that national security is involved. Only recently did E. Howard Hunt say anything at all about his role for the same reason. Hunt now believes, however, that rather than protect national security, he was used by others to achieve completely different goals.

5   During Watergate, language has been used to create the myth of national security, to sustain and enlarge that myth, and finally to hide the ugly reality that the myth embodied. Somehow, the American people had to be made to think that burglary, wiretapping, lying, blackmail, conspiracy, subordination of perjury, and attempts to limit the constitutional freedoms of speech and the press were all done to preserve, protect, and defend the Constitution and the United States. But as the various investigations revealed more and more of Watergate, people became less and less convinced that national security was a legitimate concern of those involved.

6   I know that you are probably very familiar with much of the language of Watergate already, but let me review some of it.

7   The first thing to note in the language of Watergate is that no one did anything and therefore no one is responsible for anything. President Nixon, for example, says in his statement of May 22, 1973, that there were "three security operations initiated by my Administration."[6] Note that he did not initiate them, but his Administration

---

[4] For a full discussion of the Sicherheitsdienst's role in Nazi Germany, see Heinz Höhne, *The Order of the Death's Head* (New York: Coward, McCann & Geoghegan, 1970).

[5] Richard M. Nixon, "Watergate Speech, May 22, 1973" in John Somer and James Hoy, eds., *The Language Experience* (New York: Dell Publishing, 1974).

[6] Nixon, p. 117.

did. Even in the field of foreign affairs President Nixon did not take action, but as he says in the same statement, "by mid-1969, my Administration had begun a number of highly sensitive policy initiatives."[7] When an entire Administration initiates something it is impossible to pin the responsibility on any one person. Likewise with national security matters. President Nixon says again in this same statement that he "looked to John Ehrlichman for the supervision of this group [the White House Plumbers]."[8] However, Ehrlichman says that he put his assistant Egil Krogh in charge. But Krogh says that David Young, E. Howard Hunt, and G. Gordon Liddy also had responsibility for the plumbers group. Who, therefore, created and controlled the plumbers? From the testimony given it seems that the plumbers sprang spontaneously to life and did whatever they wanted to do with no supervision and no one to report to. And if the president only "looked to" Ehrlichman and did not order him, isn't the president absolved from all responsibility for the subsequent actions of the plumbers? In the world of Watergate, no one is responsible for anything. As Ronald Ziegler, the President's press secretary, so clearly put it, all previous White House statements were "no longer operative."

8   The language of Watergate functions also to hide reality with the use of words, to separate words from truth. Thus, as we all know, a burglary becomes a "surreptitious entry" or an "intelligence-gathering operation," burglars become "plumbers," illegal acts are "inappropriate actions," flattery is "stroking" or "puffing," subordination of perjury is "coaching," government-sponsored crimes are "White House horrors" or "dirty tricks," blackmail payments are "laundered money" or "increments . . . in the form of money," covering up a crime is "containing" or "confining a situation," conspiracy to obstruct justice is "biting the bullet," "stonewalling," or the "game plan," and conspirators become "team players." Sports metaphors are popular in the language of Watergate. There is a "game plan" with the "team players" doing the "downfield blocking" so the chief could "shoot the gap" or "throw the long bomb." And, as John Mitchell reminded us, "when the going gets tough, the tough get going." Come on team, let's get out there and commit a burglary for the gipper.

9   Then, too, technical jargon is used, or misused, in an attempt to sound important, to give substance to the wind. Much of this language is not peculiar to Watergate but is all too often heard in many other areas. Executives now "operate" within "timeframes"

[7] Nixon, p. 117.
[8] Nixon, p. 121.

within the "context" of which a "task force" will serve as the proper "conduit" for all necessary "input" to "program a scenario" that, within acceptable "parameters," will "generate" the "maximum output" for a "print-out" of "zero-defect terminal objectives." And after plans are "finalized," executives can then "deal with each other telephonically," as John Dean testified.

10   At all times the function of the language of Watergate is to remove the speaker from the event and from any responsibility for the event. Thus, people "recollect to the best of their ability" and they never lie, only "misspeak." Language does not reveal but hides, does not communicate but misdirects, does not clarify but obscures. National security means ending freedom to protect freedom. In those immortal words from the Vietnam war, "It became necessary to destroy the town to save it."[9]

11   It becomes clear upon reading the White House transcripts, the testimony of the various witnesses before the Ervin Committee, and the public statements by President Nixon that the threats to national security came from such sources as Daniel Ellsberg, the *New York Times,* students who demonstrated against President Nixon's Vietnam policies, and newspapers which reported President Nixon's foreign policy plans and intentions. All of these are cited by President Nixon as national security matters. Thus, President Nixon can "initiate" "security operations" designed to "strenghten internal security procedures." For once national security is raised to the level of myth, then the person who acts "in accord with those beliefs will experience a feeling of almost unshakable self-justification. To act in conformity with collective beliefs provides security and a guarantee that one acts properly."[10]

12   The Nixon Administration, however, did not invent the myth of national security but merely built upon all that had preceded it. I mentioned earlier the McCarthy era and the concern for both internal and national security then. As we know, President Nixon rose to prominence during that era and even then his concern with national security was well known. But other events—the Cuban Missile Crisis, the war in Vietnam, the continual tension in the Middle East, and many other problems—have heightened the national concern for security. And the Pentagon, ever eager for a larger budget, has for some years played upon our national desire for peace and security by promising us security and peace if only we give them all the money and resources they ask for. Given President Nixon's political

[9] United States Army Major quoted in an Associated Press dispatch of February 7, 1968.
[10] Ellul, p. 200.

career and background, and the state of national unrest when he took office, no one should be surprised that for the Nixon Administration national security became the myth which would sustain, strengthen, and inspire, the myth that would evoke powerful emotions, the myth that would help make sense out of the world. Once committed to this myth, anything became possible, reasonable, and justifiable. Thus, John Dean's remark to President Nixon about L. Patrick Gray is understandable in terms of the myth. Gray's nomination as director of the F.B.I. was in trouble in the Senate. Haldeman, Ehrlichman, Dean and President Nixon are discussing Gray's problems before the Senate Committee.

> Ehrlichman: He [Senator Eastland] thinks Gray is dead on the floor.
> Nixon: He's probably right—poor guy.
> Haldeman: Gray, the symbol of wisdom today and future counsel for tomorrow.
> Dean: Maybe someone will shoot him.
> *Laughter.*[11]

In a similar session in the White House, it was suggested that Gray's nomination be left hanging until the question of executive privilege was resolved. Ehrlichman commented: "Let him hang there? Well, I think we ought to let him hang there. Let him twist slowly, slowly in the wind."[12] Even good team players are expendable in the name of the myth.

13   The "inhumane and dishonest uses of language"[13] did not begin, however, with the Nixon Administration. The problem existed before Watergate. I have mentioned previously some of the conditions which I think created our concern with national security. I have also mentioned how President Nixon built on this concern in propagating the myth of national security. But it was the Pentagon's misuse of language which outraged so many English teachers and others. I would like now to look at some of the language of the Pentagon and relate it to the language of Watergate.

[11] Staff of the *New York Times, The White House Transcripts* (New York: Viking Press, 1974), pp. 194–195.
[12] Barry Sussman, *The Great Coverup: Nixon and the Scandal of Watergate* (New York: New American Library, 1974), p. 170.
[13] "On Dishonest and Inhumane Uses of Language," Resolution passed by the National Council of Teachers of English at its Sixty-first Annual Meeting, 1971. As published in Hugh Rank, ed., *Language and Public Policy* (Urbana: National Council of Teachers of English, 1974), p. vii.

14   The language of the Pentagon attempts to make death and destruction appear acceptable and respectable. It is the cool, crisp, detached language of the "professional" who is only doing his job as efficiently and as effectively as he can. As David Halberstam noted, many of these men are graduates of our best universities. They are the "best and the brightest."[14]

15   We all know that in the wonderful world of the Pentagon it is not bombing but "armed reconnaissance," "interdiction," "protective reaction strike," or "limited duration protective reaction strike." When the name "search-and-destroy mission" took on the wrong connotation it was quickly changed to "search-and-clear mission," and then finally to "reconnaissance in force." Even "defoliation" was too revealing a word so the substitute "resources control program" was invented. Of course the meaning was the same: poisonous chemicals were used to destroy crops and contaminate water, thus starving the population. "Suspected enemy troop concentrations" means that civilians got in the way of "incontinent ordinance" or bombs and artillery fire. It is never invasion but always "incursion." And if a spy should be found in a "new life hamlet," which might more properly be called a refugee camp or concentration camp, then he might be "terminated with extreme prejudice" or executed without a trial. Generals never have battle plans but an "orchestration of military moves." American troops do not retreat but are "tactically redeployed." Nor are they ever ambushed, they just "engage the enemy on all sides." There are no battlefields or enemy-controlled territory, just "contested areas." The "relocation" of people in order to "restructure local social systems" means burning the village and forcing the villagers out of their homes and into government-controlled areas, thus producing refugees who "vote with their feet." A "preemptive counterattack" means to attack first and blame it on the enemy later. And at all times alternatives are always "viable" and actions "meaningful." In the language of the Pentagon,

> The noun "damage" is modified by the adjective "progressive"; "meaningful" comes before "bombing." The "losses" are "acceptable" and "casualties" are "visible." The word "disadvantageous" here means defeated. And always there are crisp, cool words like "cumulative" and "rationale."[15]

---

[14] David Halberstam, *The Best and the Brightest* (New York: Random House, 1972).
[15] Mike McGrady, "Pentagon Papers' Air-Conditioned Lingo," *Sacramento Bee,* 11 July 1971, Section P, p. 1, cols. 3–4.

16   The language of the Pentagon has been used to justify the Vietnam war as well as the spending of huge amounts of money for national security. And the language of Watergate has been used to justify all the crimes associated with Watergate as necessary to insure and protect national security. The language of the Pentagon and the language of Watergate merge into one, with both using the same euphemisms and doublespeak to separate words from truth, words from reality. Both languages use the same devices to achieve their goals.

17   The language of the Pentagon was part of a propaganda effort by both the military and civilian government to convince the American people of the justness of their cause and that what they were doing, both in Vietnam and to the national budget, was necessary for national security. The same propaganda techniques used by the Pentagon were used also by the Nixon people in their explanation and defense of Watergate. J. A. C. Brown discusses these techniques in his book *Techniques of Persuasion.*[16] Among the techniques Brown discusses is "downright lying." Now, with benefit of hindsight, and the *Pentagon Papers* as well as the *White House Transcripts,* we know that lying was crucial to the Pentagon's defense and explanation of American actions in Vietnam and President Nixon's defense and explanation of Watergate. But a more subtle propaganda technique is assertion, wherein the propagandist does not argue but makes "bold assertions in favour of his thesis."[17] Throughout the Vietnam war and Watergate we were given not rational debate but unquestionable assertions which were designed to present one side of the picture only and deliberately limit free thought and debate. This, Brown notes, is "the essence of propaganda."[18] Joining assertion and lying creates a very effective propaganda technique known as "The Big Lie," a device used very cleverly by Josef Goebbels, the Nazi Minister of Propaganda.

18   Another technique is the appeal to authority or bandwagon technique which suggests that everyone holds a particular belief and those who don't are outsiders. Both the Pentagon and the Nixon Administration were fond of citing public opinion polls which purported to prove that their beliefs were in the majority and those who did not hold their beliefs were in a small minority. Remember all the appeals to the "Silent Majority"? And, of course, the propagandist will, "out of a mass of complex facts, select only those that are

[16] J. A. C. Brown, *Techniques of Persuasion: From Propaganda to Brainwashing* (Baltimore: Penguin Books, 1971), pp. 26–28.
[17] Brown, p. 28.
[18] Brown, p. 28.

suitable for his purpose.''[19] This is not an unusual device, but it does get in the way of honest debate seeking the truth. Remember how President Nixon continually ignored crucial facts and refused to explain important details in all of his "explanations" of Watergate? The Pentagon similarly outraged reporters during press conferences in Vietnam which reporters dubbed "the five o'clock follies." The propagandist is most effective when he can "put forth a message which is not only *for* something, but also *against* some real or imagined enemy. . . .''[20] For the Pentagon it was the "Communists," but whether it was the Communists of Russia, or China, or just North Vietnam was never made clear. For President Nixon the enemy was just about everyone, as we later found out. For quite some time, though, the media seemed to be the primary target. A wise man once said that whenever anyone pointed at someone or something and said that everyone should hate that person or thing, he always looked in the opposite direction to see what was being hidden. As Emerson said, "The louder he talked of his honor, the faster we counted the spoons.''[21] There are other propaganda techniques such as the Substitution of Names (long-haired hippie freak, college bums, and so forth), the Use of Stereotypes, and Repetition. These devices are familiar enough to you.

19   The language of Watergate is a natural outgrowth and development of the language of the Pentagon, particularly the language used by the Pentagon during the Vietnam war. And the language of the Pentagon is a language that uses the techniques of propaganda, a language that divorces words from truth and reality in an attempt to construct a false reality that people will believe and act upon. Using and extending both the language of the Pentagon and the developing myth of national security, the Nixon Administration attempted to create a new national myth of national security, a myth that could be used to justify any and all government actions. And, finally, the language of Watergate was intimately tied to the myth of national security. While the myth was dependent upon the language for existence and acceptance, the language was not and is not dependent upon the myth for existence.

20   The language of Watergate and the language of the Pentagon have infiltrated other areas of our life, but the consequences are not as serious nor the effects as far reaching as when the political misuse of language becomes, in Orwell's words, "the defence of the inde-

---

[19] Brown, p. 27.

[20] Brown, p. 28.

[21] As quoted by Arthur M. Schlesinger, "Watergate and the Corruption of Language," *Today's Education*, 63, No. 3 (1974), 26.

fensible." If we do not fight such deliberate misuse of language, then we too bear the responsibility for all the "outputs," "print-outs," "terminal objectives," and "zero-defect systems" all the Haldemans, Ehrlichmans, and Pentagon generals impose on us.

Bibliography

BROWN, J. A. C. *Techniques of Persuasion: From Propaganda to Brainwashing*. Baltimore: Penguin Books, 1971.

ELLUL, JACQUES. *Propaganda: The Formation of Men's Attitudes*. New York: Alfred A. Knopf, 1965.

HALBERSTAM, DAVID. *The Best and the Brightest*. New York: Random House, 1972.

HERZOG, ARTHUR. *The B.S. Factor: The Theory and Technique of Faking It in America*. New York: Simon and Schuster, 1973.

HÖHNE, HEINZ. *The Order of the Death's Head: The Story of Hitler's SS*. New York: Coward, McMann & Geoghegan, 1970.

McGRADY, MIKE. "Pentagon Papers' Air-Conditioned Lingo." *Sacramento Bee*, July 11, 1971.

RANK, HUGH, ed. *Language and Public Policy*. Urbana, Ill.: National Council of Teachers of English, 1974.

SCHLESINGER, ARTHUR M. "Watergate and the Corruption of Language." *Today's Education*, 63, No. 3 (1974), 25–27.

SOMER, JOHN, and JAMES HOY, eds. *The Language Experience*. New York: Dell Publishing, 1974.

Staff of the *New York Times*. *The Watergate Hearings*. New York: Viking Press, 1973.

Staff of the *New York Times*. *The White House Transcripts*. New York: Viking Press, 1974.

SUSSMAN, BARRY. *The Great Coverup: Nixon and the Scandal of Watergate*. New York: New American Library, 1974.

Vocabulary

proletariat	hysteria	rationale
initiate	surreptitious	conduit
parameters	interdiction	duration
defoliation	contaminate	incontinent
incursion	orchestration	preemptive
viable	cumulative	euphemism
crucial	infiltrated	

Topics for Discussion

1. What myths, other than those mentioned by Lutz, help sustain popular attitudes in America today? Can you point to any myths in which you believe or in which you have lost faith?

2. Do you think it possible for Americans to fall prey to myths such as those which inspired the German people to follow Hitler?

3. Can you define the term *national security* in such a way as to make it a defensible notion?

4. In paragraph 8, Lutz mentions the use of sports metaphors by figures involved in the Watergate scandal. Have you observed the use of such metaphors in your daily life? What kinds of behavior are they used to justify?

5. Lutz refers to Nixon's "concern with national security" during the 1950s. What research materials should you consult to learn more about this topic?

6. In paragraph 20, Lutz mentions areas of life affected by the language of Watergate and the Pentagon. Identify some of these areas and explain what Lutz may mean.

Rhetorical Considerations

1. How does Lutz use parallelism to advantage in the essay's opening paragraph?

2. Why is it important that Lutz define *myth* early in the essay? What consequences might follow from a failure to define the word? Is the definition from Ellul absolute or limited to the purposes of this essay?

3. What kind of tone is created by Lutz's use of the pronoun *I*? Is this tone suitable to the subject matter of the essay?

4. How does Lutz use irony in paragraphs 7 and 8? How does this use of irony serve as a unifying device for each of these paragraphs?

5. Is Watergate, or something else, the central concern of this essay? Does Lutz formulate his thesis in any single sentence? Can you write a paragraph summarizing the essay's central concerns?

6. Why in opinionated essays such as this is footnoting especially important?

The Declaration of Independence

Thomas Jefferson

Thomas Jefferson (1743–1826) was the third president of the United States. One of the most cosmopolitan men of his age, he was responsible for great and diverse achievements ranging from the Louisiana Purchase to the establishment of a decimal system of coinage for the United States. His epitaph reflects what he thought to be his most significant contributions: "Here was buried Thomas Jefferson, author of the Declaration of Independence, of the statute of Virginia for religious freedom, and father of the University of Virginia."

In CONGRESS, July 4, 1776.

THE UNANIMOUS DECLARATION OF THE THIRTEEN UNITED STATES OF AMERICA

1   When in the Course of human events, it becomes necessary for one people to dissolve the political bands which have connected them with another, and to assume among the powers of the earth, the separate and equal station to which the Laws of Nature and of Nature's God entitle them, a decent respect to the opinions of mankind requires that they should declare the causes which impel them to the separation.

2   We hold these truths to be self-evident, that all men are created equal, that they are endowed by their Creator with certain unalienable Rights, that among these are Life, Liberty and the pursuit of Happiness.

3   That to secure these rights, Governments are instituted among Men, deriving their just powers from the consent of the governed.

4   That whenever any Form of Government becomes destructive of these ends, it is the Right of the People to alter or to abolish it, and to institute new Government, laying its foundation on such principles and organizing its powers in such form, as to them shall seem most likely to effect their Safety and Happiness. Prudence, indeed, will dictate that Governments long established should not be changed for light and transient causes; and accordingly all experience hath shewn, that mankind are more disposed to suffer, while evils are sufferable, than to right themselves by abolishing the forms to which they are accustomed. But when a long train of abuses and

usurpations, pursuing invariably the same Object evinces a design to reduce them under absolute Despotism, it is their right, it is their duty, to throw off such Government, and to provide new Guards for their future security.

5   Such has been the patient sufferance of these Colonies, and such is now the necessity which constrains them to alter their former Systems of Government. The history of the present King of Great Britain is a history of repeated injuries and usurpations, all having in direct object the establishment of an absolute Tyranny over these States. To prove this, let Facts be submitted to a candid world.

6   He has refused his Assent to Laws, the most wholesome and necessary for the public good.

7   He has forbidden his Governors to pass Laws of immediate and pressing importance, unless suspended in their operation till his Assent should be obtained; and when so suspended, he has utterly neglected to attend to them.

8   He has refused to pass other Laws for the accommodation of large districts of people, unless those people would relinquish the right of Representation in the Legislature, a right inestimable to them and formidable to tyrants only.

9   He has called together legislative bodies at places unusual, uncomfortable, and distant from the depository of their public Records, for the sole purpose of fatiguing them into compliance with his measures.

10   He has dissolved Representative Houses repeatedly, for opposing with manly firmness his invasions on the rights of the people.

11   He has refused for a long time, after such dissolutions, to cause others to be elected; whereby the Legislative powers, incapable of Annihilation, have returned to the People at large for their exercise; the State remaining in the mean time exposed to all the dangers of invasion from without, and convulsions within.

12   He has endeavoured to prevent the population of these States; for that purpose obstructing the Laws for Naturalization of Foreigners; refusing to pass others to encourage their migrations hither, and raising the conditions of new Appropriations of Lands.

13   He has obstructed the Administration of Justice, by refusing his Assent to Laws for establishing Judiciary powers.

14   He has made Judges dependent on his Will alone, for the tenure of their offices, and the amount and payment of their salaries.

15   He has erected a multitude of New Offices, and sent hither swarms of Officers to harass our people, and eat out their substance.

16   He has kept among us, in times of peace, Standing Armies without the Consent of our legislatures.

17   He has affected to render the Military independent of and superior to the Civil power.

18   He has combined with others to subject us to a jurisdiction foreign to our constitution, and unacknowledged by our laws; giving his Assent to their Acts of pretended Legislation:

19   For Quartering large bodies of armed troops among us:

20   For protecting them, by a mock Trial, from punishment for any Murders which they should commit on the Inhabitants of these States:

21   For cutting off our Trade with all parts of the world:

22   For imposing Taxes on us without our Consent:

23   For depriving us in many cases, of the benefits of Trial by Jury:

24   For transporting us beyond Seas to be tried for pretended offenses:

25   For abolishing the free System of English Laws in a neighboring Province establishing therein an Arbitrary government, and enlarging its Boundaries so as to render it at once an example and fit instrument for introducing the same absolute rule into these Colonies:

26   For taking away our Charters, abolishing our most valuable Laws, and altering fundamentally the Forms of our Governments:

27   For suspending our own Legislatures, and declaring themselves invested with power to legislate for us in all cases whatsoever.

28   He has abdicated Government here, by declaring us out of his Protection and waging War against us:

29   He has plundered our seas, ravaged our Coasts, burnt our towns, and destroyed the lives of our people.

30   He is at this time transporting large Armies of foreign Mercenaries to compleat the works of death, desolation and tyranny, already begun with circumstances of Cruelty & perfidy scarcely paralleled in the most barbarous ages, and totally unworthy the Head of a civilized nation.

31   He has constrained our fellow Citizens taken Captive on the high Seas to bear Arms against their Country, to become the executioners of their friends and Brethren, or to fall themselves by their Hands.

32   He has excited domestic insurrections amongst us, and has endeavoured to bring on the inhabitants of our frontiers, the merciless Indian Savages, whose known rule of warfare, is an undistinguished destruction of all ages, sexes and conditions. In every stage of these Oppressions We have Petitioned for Redress in the most humble terms: Our repeated Petitions have been answered only by

repeated injury. A Prince, whose character is thus marked by every act which may define a Tyrant, is unfit to be the ruler of a free people. Nor have We been wanting in attentions to our British brethren. We have warned them from time to time of attempts by their legislature to extend an unwarrantable jurisdiction over us. We have reminded them of the circumstances of our emigration and settlement here. We have appealed to their native justice and magnanimity, and we have conjured them by the ties of our common kindred to disavow these usurpations, which, would inevitably interrupt our connections and correspondence. They too have been deaf to the voice of justice and of consanguinity. We must, therefore, acquiesce in the necessity, which denounces our Separation, and hold them, as we hold the rest of mankind, Enemies in War, in Peace Friends.

33   We, THEREFORE, the Representatives of the UNITED STATES OF AMERICA, in General Congress Assembled, appealing to the Supreme Judge of the world for the rectitude of our intentions, do, in the Name and by Authority of the good People of these Colonies, solemnly publish and declare, That these United Colonies are, and of Right ought to be FREE AND INDEPENDENT STATES; that they are Absolved from all Allegiance to the British Crown, and that all political connection between them and the State of Great Britain, is and ought to be totally dissolved; and that as Free and Independent States, they have full Power to levy War, conclude Peace, contract Alliances, establish Commerce, and to do all other Acts and Things which Independent States may of right do.

34   And for the support of this Declaration, with a firm reliance on the protection of divine Providence, we mutually pledge to each other our Lives, our Fortunes and our sacred Honor.

Vocabulary

unalienable	prudence	transient
usurpations	invariably	evinces
constrains	tyranny	candid
assent	utterly	relinquish
formidable	fatiguing	annihilation
convulsions	naturalization	appropriations
tenure	arbitrary	abdicated
mercenaries	perfidy	barbarous
insurrections	unwarrantable	magnanimity
conjured	consanguinity	acquiesce
rectitude	absolved	

Topics for Discussion

1. The Declaration is a justification for revolution. What circumstances must be present to justify a revolution according to the Declaration? Are similar conditions present in the United States or any place else in the world that you know of today?

2. What is the current attitude of Americans toward revolution? What is your attitude? What is the attitude of the American government toward revolutions in other countries? (For example, Cuba, China, Russia, Portugal, Guatemala, Iran, Chile.)

3. In the list of reasons for breaking away from England, the author mentions quite a few items. How many of these reasons are economic and how many are humanistic? Is there any difference between human needs and economics?

4. If you were an Englishman of the eighteenth century and you read this document, how do you think you would respond? Would you support the colonies or not? Note the specific reference in the Declaration to "our British brethren."

5. Would the American government today recognize the American people's right to revolution as enunciated in the Declaration?

Rhetorical Considerations

1. The Declaration of Independence is almost automatically treated as a political document. It is also a written document and can be examined just like any other piece of writing. The preamble to the document serves as an introduction to the argument presented in the body of the text. What information does this introduction provide? How important is it to the effectiveness of the main argument of the Declaration?

2. The Declaration is essentially a political argument. How effective is the argument it presents? Is the argument based on emotion or reason, or both?

3. How objective is the author of the Declaration? How is the evidence in the Declaration presented? Does the tone help or hinder the objectivity of the document?

4. The prose style and vocabulary of the Declaration are of the eighteenth century. Does this enhance the document as you read it, or does it make it difficult to read and understand? Would you prefer that it be written in more modern prose?

5. Certainly the Declaration presents an overwhelming case on behalf of the colonies. Do you feel the author has overstated his case? Do you think that the facts that are presented are biased? What is your opinion of King George III of England after reading the Declaration?

On the Duty of Civil Disobedience

Henry David Thoreau

Henry David Thoreau (1817–1862) was a Massachusetts writer known chiefly for his account of the two years he spent alone in a cabin in the forest, Walden. *An exponent of transcendentalist philosophy, he was a political activist as well, refusing to pay his taxes and spending a night in jail for the refusal, a situation which moved him to write the following essay.*

1   I heartily accept the motto—"That government is best which governs least"; and I should like to see it acted up to more rapidly and systematically. Carried out, it finally amounts to this, which also I believe,—"That government is best which governs not at all"; and when men are prepared for it, that will be the kind of government which they will have. Government is at best but an expedient; but most governments are usually, and all governments are sometimes, inexpedient. The objections which have been brought against a standing army, and they are many and weighty, and deserve to prevail, may also at last be brought against a standing government. The standing army is only an arm of the standing government. The government itself, which is only the mode which the people have chosen to execute their will, is equally liable to be abused and perverted before the people can act through it. Witness the present Mexican war, the work of comparatively a few individuals using the standing government as their tool; for, in the outset, the people would not have consented to this measure.

2   This American government—what is it but a tradition, though a recent one, endeavoring to transmit itself unimpaired to posterity, but each instant losing some of its integrity? It has not the vitality

and force of a single living man; for a single man can bend it to his will. It is a sort of wooden gun to the people themselves. But it is not the less necessary for this; for the people must have some complicated machinery or other, and hear its din, to satisfy that idea of government which they have. Governments show us how successfully men can be imposed on, even impose on themselves, for their own advantage. It is excellent, we must all allow. Yet this government never of itself furthered any enterprise, but by the alacrity with which it got out of its way. *It* does not keep the country free. *It* does not settle the West. *It* does not educate. The character inherent in the American people has done all that has been accomplished; and it would have done somewhat more, if the government had not sometimes got in its way. For government is an expedient by which men would fain succeed in letting one another alone; and, as has been said, when it is most expedient, the governed are most let alone by it. Trade and commerce, if they were not made of India-rubber, would never manage to bounce over the obstacles which legislators are continually putting in their way; and, if one were to judge these men wholly by the effects of their actions and not partly by their intentions, they would deserve to be classed and punished with those mischievous persons who put obstructions on the railroads.

3   But, to speak practically and as a citizen, unlike those who call themselves no-government men, I ask for, not at once no government, but *at once* a better government. Let every man make known what kind of government would command his respect, and that will be one step toward obtaining it.

4   After all, the practical reason why, when the power is once in the hands of the people, a majority are permitted, and for a long period continue, to rule is not because they are most likely to be in the right, nor because this seems fairest to the minority, but because they are physically the strongest. But a government in which the majority rule in all cases cannot be based on justice, even as far as men understand it. Can there not be a government in which majorities do not virtually decide right and wrong, but conscience— in which majorities decide only those questions to which the rule of expediency is applicable? Must the citizen ever for a moment, or in the last degree, resign his conscience to the legislator? Why has every man a conscience, then? I think that we should be men first, and subjects afterward. It is not desirable to cultivate a respect for the law so much as for the right. The only obligation which I have a right to assume is to do at any time what I think right. It is truly enough said, that a corporation has no conscience; but a corporation

of conscientious men is a corporation *with* a conscience. Law never made men a whit more just; and, by means of their respect for it, even the well-disposed are daily made the agents of injustice. A common and natural result of an undue respect for law is, that you may see a file of soldiers, colonel, captain, corporal, privates, powder-monkeys, and all, marching in admirable order over hill and dale to the war, against their will, ay, against their common sense and consciences, which makes it very steep marching indeed, and produces a palpitation of the heart. They have no doubt that it is a damnable business in which they are concerned; they are all peace-ably inclined. Now, what are they? Men at all? or small movable forts and magazines, at the service of some unscrupulous man in power? Visit the Navy-Yard, and behold a marine, such a man as an American government can make, or such as it can make a man with its black arts—a mere shadow and reminiscence of humanity, a man laid out alive and standing, and already, as one may say, buried under arms with funeral accompaniments, though it may be,—

> Not a drum was heard, not a funeral note,
>   As his corpse to the rampart we hurried;
> Not a soldier discharged his farewell shot
>   O'er the grave where our hero we buried.

5   The mass of men serve the state thus, not as men mainly, but as machines, with their bodies. They are the standing army, and the militia, jailors, constables, posse comitatus, etc. In most cases there is no free exercise whatever of the judgment or of the moral sense; but they put themselves on a level with wood and earth and stones; and wooden men can perhaps be manufactured that will serve the purpose as well. Such command no more respect than men of straw or a lump of dirt. They have the same sort of worth only as horses and dogs. Yet such as these even are commonly esteemed good citizens. Others—as most legislators, politicians, lawyers, minis-ters, and officeholders—serve the state chiefly with their heads; and, as they rarely make any moral distinctions, they are as likely to serve the Devil, without *intending* it, as God. A very few, as heroes, patriots, martyrs, reformers in the great sense, and *men,* serve the state with their consciences also, and so necessarily resist it for the most part; and they are commonly treated as enemies by it. A wise man will only be useful as a man, and will not submit to be "clay," and "stop a hole to keep the wind away," but leave that office to his dust at least:—

> I am too high-born to be propertied,
> To be a secondary at control,
> Or useful serving-man and instrument
> To any sovereign state throughout the world.

6   He who gives himself entirely to his fellow-men appears to them useless and selfish; but he who gives himself partially to them is pronounced a benefactor and philanthropist.

7   How does it become a man to behave toward this American government to-day? I answer, that he cannot without disgrace be associated with it. I cannot for an instant recognize that political organization as my government which is the *slave's* government also.

8   All men recognize the right of revolution; that is, the right to refuse allegiance to, and to resist, the government, when its tyranny or its inefficiency are great and unendurable. But almost all say that such is not the case now. But such was the case, they think, in the Revolution of '75. If one were to tell me that this was a bad government because it taxed certain foreign commodities brought to its ports, it is most probable that I should not make an ado about it, for I can do without them. All machines have their friction; and possibly this does enough good to counterbalance the evil. At any rate, it is a great evil to make a stir about it. But when the friction comes to have its machine, and oppression and robbery are organized, I say, let us not have such a machine any longer. In other words, when a sixth of the population of a nation which has undertaken to be the refuge of liberty are slaves, and a whole country is unjustly overrun and conquered by a foreign army, and subjected to military law, I think that it is not too soon for honest men to rebel and revolutionize. What makes this duty the more urgent is the fact that the country so overrun is not our own, but ours is the invading army. . . .

> A drab of state, a cloth-o'-silver slut,
> To have her train borne up, and her soul trail in the dirt

Practically speaking, the opponents to a reform in Massachusetts are not a hundred thousand politicians at the South, but a hundred thousand merchants and farmers here, who are more interested in commerce and agriculture than they are in humanity, and are not prepared to do justice to the slave and to Mexico, *cost what it may*. I quarrel not with far-off foes, but with those who, near at home, coöperate with, and do the bidding of, those far away, and without whom the latter would be harmless. We are accustomed to say, that the mass of men are unprepared; but improvement is slow, because the few are not materially wiser or better than the many. It is not so important that many should be as good as you, as that there be some absolute goodness somewhere; for that will leaven the whole lump. There are thousands who are *in opinion* opposed to slavery and to the war, who yet in effect do nothing to put an end to them; who, esteeming themselves children of Washington and Franklin, sit down with their hands in their pockets, and say that they know not what to do, and do nothing; who even postpone the question of freedom to the question of free-trade, and quietly read the prices-current along with the latest advices from Mexico, after dinner, and, it may be, fall asleep over them both. What is the price-current of an honest man and patriot to-day? They hesitate, and they regret, and sometimes they petition; but they do nothing in earnest and with effect. They will wait, well disposed, for others to remedy the evil, that they may no longer have it to regret. At most, they give only a cheap vote, and a feeble countenance and God-speed, to the right, as it goes by them. There are nine hundred and ninety-nine patrons of virtue to one virtuous man. But it is easier to deal with the real possessor of a thing than with the temporary guardian of it.

9   All voting is a sort of gaming, like checkers or backgammon, with a slight moral tinge to it, a playing with right and wrong, with moral questions; and betting naturally accompanies it. The character of the voters is not staked. I cast my vote, perchance, as I think right; but I am not vitally concerned that that right should prevail. I am willing to leave it to the majority. Its obligation, therefore, never exceeds that of expediency. Even voting *for the right* is *doing* nothing for it. It is only expressing to men feebly your desire that it should prevail. A wise man will not leave the right to the mercy of chance, nor wish it to prevail through the power of the majority. There is but little virtue in the action of masses of men. When the majority shall at length vote for the abolition of slavery, it will be because they are indifferent to slavery, or because there is but little slavery left to be abolished by their vote. *They* will then be the only slaves. Only *his* vote can hasten the abolition of slavery who asserts his own freedom by his vote.

10   I hear of a convention to be held at Baltimore, or elsewhere, for the selection of a candidate for the Presidency, made up chiefly of editors, and men who are politicians by profession; but I think, what is it to any independent, intelligent, and respectable man what decision they may come to? Shall we not have the advantage of his wisdom and honesty, nevertheless? Can we not count upon some

independent votes? Are there not many individuals in the country who do not attend conventions? But no: I find that the respectable man, so called, has immediately drifted from his position, and despairs of his country, when his country has more reason to despair of him. He forthwith adopts one of the candidates thus selected as the only *available* one, thus proving that he is himself *available* for any purposes of the demagogue. His vote is of no more worth than that of any unprincipled foreigner or hireling native, who may have been bought. O for a man who is a *man,* and, as my neighbor says, has a bone in his back which you cannot pass your hand through! Our statistics are at fault: the population has been returned too large. How many *men* are there to a square thousand miles in this country? Hardly one. Does not America offer any inducement for men to settle here? The American has dwindled into an Odd Fellow,—one who may be known by the development of his organ of gregariousness, and a manifest lack of intellect and cheerful self-reliance; whose first and chief concern, on coming into the world, is to see that the Almshouses are in good repair; and, before yet he has lawfully donned the virile garb, to collect a fund for the support of the widows and orphans that may be; who, in short, ventures to live only by the aid of the Mutual Insurance Company, which has promised to bury him decently.

11   It is not a man's duty, as a matter of course, to devote himself to the eradication of any, even the most enormous wrong; he may still properly have other concerns to engage him; but it is his duty, at least, to wash his hands of it, and, if he gives it no thought longer, not to give it practically his support. If I devote myself to other pursuits and contemplations, I must first see, at least, that I do not pursue them sitting upon another man's shoulders. I must get off him first, that he may pursue his contemplations too. See what gross inconsistency is tolerated. I have heard some of my townsmen say, "I should like to have them order me out to help put down an insurrection of the slaves, or to march to Mexico;—see if I would go"; and yet these very men have each, directly by their allegiance, and so indirectly, at least, by their money, furnished a substitute. The soldier is applauded who refuses to serve in an unjust war by those who do not refuse to sustain the unjust government which makes the war; is applauded by those whose own act and authority he disregards and sets at naught; as if the state were penitent to that degree that it hired one to scourge it while it sinned, but not to that degree that it left off sinning for a moment. Thus, under the name of Order and Civil Government, we are all made at last to pay homage to and support our own meanness. After the first blush of sin comes

its indifference; and from immoral it becomes, as it were, unmoral, and not quite unnecessary to that life which we have made.

12   The broadest and most prevalent error requires the most disinterested virtue to sustain it. The slight reproach to which the virtue of patriotism is commonly liable, the noble are most likely to incur. Those who, while they disapprove of the character and measures of a government, yield to it their allegiance and support are undoubtedly its most conscientious supporters, and so frequently the most serious obstacles to reform. Some are petitioning the state to dissolve the Union, to disregard the requisitions of the President. Why do they not dissolve it themselves—the union between themselves and the state,—and refuse to pay their quota into its treasury? Do not they stand in the same relation to the state that the state does to the Union? And have not the same reasons prevented the state from resisting the Union which have prevented them from resisting the state?

13   How can a man be satisfied to entertain an opinion merely, and enjoy *it?* Is there any enjoyment in it, if his opinion is that he is aggrieved? If you are cheated out of a single dollar by your neighbor, you do not rest satisfied with knowing that you are cheated, or with saying that you are cheated, or even with petitioning him to pay you your due; but you take effectual steps at once to obtain the full amount, and see that you are never cheated again. Action from principle, the perception and the performance of right, changes things and relations; it is essentially revolutionary, and does not consist wholly with anything which was. It not only divides states and churches, it divides families; ay, it divides the *individual,* separating the diabolical in him from the divine.

14   Unjust laws exist: shall we be content to obey them, or shall we endeavor to amend them, and obey them until we have succeeded, or shall we transgress them at once? Men generally, under such a government as this, think that they ought to wait until they have persuaded the majority to alter them. They think that, if they should resist, the remedy would be worse than the evil. But it is the fault of the government itself that the remedy is worse than the evil. *It* makes it worse. Why is it not more apt to anticipate and provide for reform? Why does it not cherish its wise minority? Why does it cry and resist before it is hurt? Why does it not encourage its citizens to be on the alert to point out its faults, and *do* better than it would have them? Why does it always crucify Christ, and excommunicate Copernicus and Luther, and pronounce Washington and Franklin rebels?

15   One would think, that a deliberate and practical denial of its

authority was the only offense never contemplated by government; else, why has it not assigned its definite, its suitable and proportionate penalty? If a man who has no property refuses but once to earn nine shillings for the state, he is put in prison for a period unlimited by any law that I know, and determined only by the discretion of those who placed him there; but if he should steal ninety times nine shillings from the state, he is soon permitted to go at large again.

16   If the injustice is part of the necessary friction of the machine of government, let it go, let it go: perchance it will wear smooth,— certainly the machine will wear out. If the injustice has a spring, or a pulley, or a rope, or a crank, exclusively for itself, then perhaps you may consider whether the remedy will not be worse than the evil; but if it is of such a nature that it requires you to be the agent of injustice to another, then, I say, break the law. Let your life be a counter friction to stop the machine. What I have to do is to see, at any rate, that I do not lend myself to the wrong which I condemn.

17   As for adopting the ways which the state has provided for remedying the evil, I know not of such ways. They take too much time, and a man's life will be gone. I have other affairs to attend to. I came into this world, not chiefly to make this a good place to live in, but to live in it, be it good or bad. A man has not everything to do, but something; and because he cannot do *everything,* it is not necessary that he should do *something* wrong. It is not my business to be petitioning the Governor or the Legislature any more than it is theirs to petition me; and if they should not hear my petition, what should I do then? But in this case the state has provided no way: its very Constitution is the evil. This may seem to be harsh and stubborn and unconciliatory; but it is to treat with the utmost kindness and consideration the only spirit that can appreciate or deserves it. So is all change for the better, like birth and death, which convulse the body.

18   I do not hesitate to say, that those who call themselves Abolitionists should at once effectually withdraw their support, both in person and property, from the government of Massachusetts and not wait till they constitute a majority of one, before they suffer the right to prevail through them. I think that it is enough if they have God on their side, without waiting for that other one. Moreover, any man more right than his neighbors constitutes a majority of one already.

19   I meet this American government, or its representative, the state government, directly, and face to face, once a year—no more—in the person of its tax-gatherer; this is the only mode in which a man situated as I am necessarily meets it; and it then says distinctly, Recognize me; and the simplest, most effectual, and, in

the present posture of affairs, the indispensablest mode of treating with it on this head, of expressing your little satisfaction with and love for it, is to deny it then. My civil neighbor, the tax-gatherer, is the very man I have to deal with,—for it is, after all, with men and not with parchment that I quarrel,—and he has voluntarily chosen to be an agent of the government. How shall he ever know well what he is and does as an officer of the government, or as a man, until he is obliged to consider whether he shall treat me, his neighbor, for whom he has respect, as a neighbor and well-disposed man, or as a maniac and disturber of the peace, and see if he can get over this obstruction to his neighborliness without a ruder and more impetuous thought or speech corresponding with his action. I know this well, that if one thousand, if one hundred, if ten men whom I could name,—if ten *honest* men only,—ay, if *one* HONEST man, in this State of Massachusetts, *ceasing to hold slaves,* were actually to withdraw from this copartnership, and be locked up in the county jail therefor, it would be the abolition of slavery in America. For it matters not how small the beginning may seem to be: what is once well done is done forever. But we love better to talk about it: that we say is our mission. Reform keeps many scores of newspapers in its service, but not one man. If my esteemed neighbor, the State's ambassador, who will devote his days to the settlement of the question of human rights in the Council Chamber, instead of being threatened with the prisons of Carolina, were to sit down the prisoner of Massachusetts, that State which is so anxious to foist the sin of slavery upon her sister,—though at present she can discover only an act of inhospitality to be the ground of a quarrel with her,—the Legislature would not wholly waive the subject the following winter.

20   Under a government which imprisons any unjustly, the true place for a just man is also a prison. The proper place to-day, the only place which Massachusetts has provided for her freer and less desponding spirits, is in her prisons, to be put out and locked out of the State by her own act, as they have already put themselves out by their principles. It is there that the fugitive slave, and the Mexican prisoner on parole, and the Indian come to plead the wrongs of his race should find them; on that separate, but more free and honorable ground, where the State places those who are not *with* her, but *against* her,—the only house in a slave State in which a free man can abide with honor. If any think that their influence would be lost there, and their voices no longer afflict the ear of the State, that they would not be as an enemy within its walls, they do not know by how much truth is stronger than error, nor how much more eloquently

and effectively he can combat injustice who has experienced a little in his own person. Cast your whole vote, not a strip of paper merely, but your whole influence. A minority is powerless while it conforms to the majority; it is not even a minority then; but it is irresistible when it clogs by its whole weight. If the alternative is to keep all just men in prison, or give up war and slavery, the State will not hesitate which to choose. If a thousand men were not to pay their tax-bills this year, that would not be a violent and bloody measure, as it would be to pay them, and enable the State to commit violence and shed innocent blood. This is, in fact, the definition of a peaceable revolution, if any such is possible. If the tax-gatherer, or any other public officer, asks me, as one has done, "But what shall I do?" my answer is, "If you really wish to do anything, resign your office." When the subject has refused allegiance, and the officer has resigned his office, then the revolution is accomplished. But even suppose blood should flow. Is there not a sort of blood shed when the conscience is wounded? Through this wound a man's real manhood and immortality flow out, and he bleeds to an everlasting death. I see this blood flowing now.

21   I have contemplated the imprisonment of the offender, rather than the seizure of his goods,—though both will serve the same purpose—because they who assert the purest right, and consequently are most dangerous to a corrupt State, commonly have not spent much time in accumulating property. To such the State renders comparatively small service, and a slight tax is wont to appear exorbitant, particularly if they are obliged to earn it by special labor with their hands. If there were one who lived wholly without the use of money, the State itself would hesitate to demand it of him. But the rich man—not to make any invidious comparison—is always sold to the institution which makes him rich. Absolutely speaking, the more money, the less virtue; for money comes between a man and his objects, and obtains them for him; and it was certainly no great virtue to obtain it. It puts to rest many questions which he would otherwise be taxed to answer; while the only new question which it puts is the hard but superfluous one, how to spend it. Thus his moral ground is taken from under his feet. The opportunities of living are diminished in proportion as what are called the "means" are increased. The best thing a man can do for his culture when he is rich is to endeavor to carry out those schemes which he entertained when he was poor. Christ answered the Herodians according to their condition. "Show me the tribute-money," said he;—and one took a penny out of his pocket;—if you use money which has the image of Caesar on it and which he has made current

and valuable, that is, *if you are men of the State,* and gladly enjoy the advantages of Caesar's government, then pay him back some of his own when he demands it. "Render therefore to Caesar that which is Caesar's, and to God those things which are God's,"— leaving them no wiser than before as to which; for they did not wish to know. . . .

22   I have paid no poll-tax for six years. I was put into a jail once on this account, for one night; and, as I stood considering the walls of solid stone, two or three feet thick, the door of wood and iron, a foot thick, and the iron grating which strained the light, I could not help being struck with the foolishness of that institution which treated me as if I were mere flesh and blood and bones, to be locked up. I wondered that it should have concluded at length that this was the best use it could put me to, and had never thought to avail itself of my services in some way. I saw that, if there was a wall of stone between me and my townsmen, there was a still more difficult one to climb or break through before they could get to be as free as I was. I did not for a moment feel confined, and the walls seemed a great waste of stone and mortar. I felt as if I alone of all my townsmen had paid my tax. They plainly did not know how to treat me, but behaved like persons who are underbred. In every threat and in every compliment there was a blunder; for they thought that my chief desire was to stand the other side of that stone wall. I could not but smile to see how industriously they locked the door on my meditations, which followed them out again without let or hindrance, and *they* were really all that was dangerous. As they could not reach me, they had resolved to punish my body; just as boys, if they cannot come at some person against whom they have a spite, will abuse his dog. I saw that the State was half-witted, that it was timid as a lone woman with her silver spoons, and that it did not know its friends from its foes, and I lost all my remaining respect for it, and pitied it.

23   Thus the State never intentionally confronts a man's sense, intellectual or moral, but only his body, his senses. It is not armed with superior wit or honesty, bit with superior physical strength. I was not born to be forced. I will breathe after my own fashion. Let us see who is the strongest. What force has a multitude? They only can force me who obey a higher law than I. They force me to become like themselves. I do not hear of *men* being *forced* to live this way or that by masses of men. What sort of life were that to live? When I meet a government which says to me, "Your money or your life," why should I be in haste to give it my money? It may be in a great strait, and not know what to do: I cannot help that. It must

help itself; do as I do. It is not worth the while to snivel about it. I am not responsible for the successful working of the machinery of society. I am not the son of the engineer. I perceive that, when an acorn and a chestnut fall side by side, the one does not remain inert to make way for the other, but both obey their own laws, and spring and grow and flourish as best they can, till one, perchance, over-shadows and destroys the other. If a plant cannot live according to its nature, it dies; and so a man. . . .

24   When I came out of prison,—for some one interfered, and paid that tax,—I did not perceive that great changes had taken place on the common, such as he observed who sent in a youth and emerged a tottering and gray-headed man; and yet a change had to my eyes come over the scene,—the town, and State, and country,—greater than any that mere time could effect. I saw yet more distinctly the State in which I lived. I saw to what extent the people among whom I lived could be trusted as good neighbors and friends; that their friendship was for summer weather only; that they did not greatly propose to do right; that they were a distinct race from me by their prejudices and superstitions, as the Chinamen and Malays are; that in their sacrifices to humanity they ran no risks, not even to their property; that after all they were not so noble but they treated the thief as he had treated them, and hoped, by a certain outward observance and a few prayers, and by walking in a particular straight though useless path from time to time, to save their souls. This may be to judge my neighbors harshly; for I believe that many of them are not aware that they have such an institution as the jail in their village.

25   It was formerly the custom in our village, when a poor debtor came out of jail, for his acquaintances to salute him, looking through their fingers, which were crossed to represent the grating of a jail window. "How do ye do?" My neighbors did not thus salute me, but first looked at me, and then at one another, as if I had returned from a long journey. I was put into jail as I was going to the shoemaker's to get a shoe which was mended. When I was let out the next morning, I proceeded to finish my errand, and, having put on my mended shoe, joined a huckleberry party, who were impa-tient to put themselves under my conduct; and in half an hour,—for the horse was soon tackled,—was in the midst of a huckleberry field, on one of our highest hills, two miles off, and then the State was nowhere to be seen. . . .

26   I have never declined paying the highway tax, because I am as desirous of being a good neighbor as I am of being a bad subject; and as for supporting schools, I am doing my part to educate my fellow-

countrymen now. It is for no particular item in the tax-bill that I refuse to pay it. I simply wish to refuse allegiance to the State, to withdraw and stand aloof from it effectually. I do not care to trace the course of my dollar, if I could, till it buys a man or a musket to shoot with,—the dollar is innocent,—but I am concerned to trace the effects of my allegiance. In fact, I quietly declare war with the State, after my fashion, though I will still make what use and get what advantage of her I can, as is usual in such cases.

27   If others pay the tax which is demanded of me, from a sympathy with the State, they do but what they have already done in their own case, or rather they abet injustice to a greater extent than the State requires. If they pay the tax from a mistaken interest in the individual taxed, to save his property, or prevent his going to jail, it is because they have not considered wisely how far they let their private feelings interfere with the public good.

28   This, then, is my position at present. But one cannot be too much on his guard in such a case, lest his action be biased by obstinacy or an undue regard for the opinions of men. Let him see that he does only what belongs to himself and to the hour.

29   I think sometimes, Why, these people mean well, they are only ignorant; they would do better if they knew how: why give your neighbors this pain to treat you as they are not inclined to? But I think again. This is no reason why I should do as they do, or permit others to suffer much greater pain of a different kind. Again, I sometimes say to myself, When many millions of men, without heat, without ill will, without personal feeling of any kind, demand of you a few shillings only, without the possibility, such is their constitution, of retracting or altering their present demand, and without the possibility, on your side, of appeal to any other millions, why expose yourself to this overwhelming brute force? You do not resist cold and hunger, the winds and the waves, thus obstinately; you quietly submit to a thousand similar necessities. You do not put your head into the fire. But just in proportion as I regard this as not wholly a brute force, but partly a human force, and consider that I have relations to those millions as to many millions of men, and not of mere brute or inanimate things, I see that appeal is possible, first and instantaneously, from them to the Maker of them and, secondly, from them to themselves. But if I put my head deliberately into the fire, there is no appeal to fire or to the Maker of fire, and I have only myself to blame. If I could convince myself that I have any right to be satisfied with men as they are, and to treat them accordingly, and not according, in some respects, to my requisitions and expectations of what they and I ought to be, then, like a good Mussulman and

fatalist, I should endeavor to be satisfied with things as they are, and say it is the will of God. And, above all, there is this difference between resisting this and a purely brute or natural force, that I can resist this with some effect; but I cannot expect, like Orpheus, to change the nature of the rocks and trees and beasts.

30   I do not wish to quarrel with any man or nation. I do not wish to split hairs, to make fine distinctions, or set myself up as better than my neighbors. I seek rather, I may say, even an excuse for conforming to the laws of the land. I am but too ready to conform to them. Indeed, I have reason to suspect myself on this head; and each year, as the tax-gatherer comes round, I find myself disposed to review the acts and position of the general and State governments, and the spirit of the people, to discover a pretext for conformity.

> We must affect our country as our parents,
> And if at any time we alienate
> Our love or industry from doing it honor,
> We must respect effects and teach the soul
> Matter of conscience and religion,
> And not desire of rule or benefit.

I believe that the State will soon be able to take all my work of this sort out of my hands, and then I shall be no better a patriot than my fellow-countrymen. Seen from a lower point of view, the Constitution, with all its faults, is very good; the law and the courts are very respectable; even this State and this American government are, in many respects, very admirable, and rare things, to be thankful for, such as a great many have described them; but seen from a point of view a little higher, they are what I have described them; seen from a higher still, and the highest, who shall say what they are, or that they are worth looking at or thinking of at all?

31   However, the government does not concern me much, and I shall bestow the fewest possible thoughts on it. It is not many moments that I live under a government, even in this world. If a man is thought-free, fancy-free, imagination-free, that which *is not* never for a long time appearing *to be* to him, unwise rulers or reformers cannot fatally interrupt him.

32   I know that most men think differently from myself; but those whose lives are by profession devoted to the study of these or kindred subjects content me as little as any. Statesmen and legislators, standing so completely within the institution, never distinctly and nakedly behold it. They speak of moving society, but have no

resting-place without it. They may be men of a certain experience and discrimination, and have no doubt invented ingenious and even useful systems, for which we sincerely thank them; but all their wit and usefulness lie within certain not very wide limits. They are wont to forget that the world is not governed by policy and expediency. Webster never goes behind government, and so cannot speak with authority about it. His words are wisdom to those legislators who contemplate no essential reform in the existing government; but for thinkers, and those who legislate for all time, he never once glances at the subject. I know of those whose serene and wise speculations on this theme would soon reveal the limits of his mind's range and hospitality. Yet, compared with the cheap professions of most reformers, and the still cheaper wisdom and eloquence of politicians in general, his are almost the only sensible and valuable words, and we thank Heaven for him. Comparatively, he is always strong, original, and, above all, practical. Still, his quality is not wisdom, but prudence. The lawyer's truth is not Truth, but consistency or a consistent expediency. Truth is always in harmony with herself, and is not concerned chiefly to reveal the justice that may consist with wrongdoing. He well deserves to be called, as he has been called, the Defender of the Constitution. There are really no blows to be given by him but defensive ones. He is not a leader, but a follower. His leaders are the men of '87. "I have never made an effort" he says "and never propose to make an effort; I have never countenanced an effort, and never mean to countenance an effort, to disturb the arrangement as originally made, by which the various States came into the Union." Still thinking of the sanction which the Constitution gives to slavery, he says, "Because it was a part of the original compact,—let it stand." Notwithstanding his special acuteness and ability, he is unable to take a fact out of its merely political relations, and behold it as it lies absolutely to be disposed of by the intellect,—what, for instance, it behooves a man to do here in America to-day with regard to slavery,—but ventures, or is driven, to make some such desperate answer as the following while professing to speak absolutely, and as a private man,—from which what new and singular code of social duties might be inferred? "The manner," says he, "in which the governments of those States where slavery exists are to regulate it is for their own consideration, under their responsibility to their constituents, to the general laws of propriety, humanity, and justice, and to God. Associations formed elsewhere, springing from a feeling of humanity, or other cause, have nothing whatever to do with it. They have never received any encouragement from me, and they never will."

33   They who know of no purer sources of truth, who have traced
up its stream no higher, stand, and wisely stand, by the Bible and the
Constitution, and drink at it there with reverence and humility; but
they who behold where it comes trickling into this lake or that pool,
gird up their loins once more, and continue their pilgrimage towards
its fountainhead.

34   No man with a genius for legislation has appeared in America.
They are rare in the history of the world. There are orators, politicians, and eloquent men, by the thousand; but the speaker has not
yet opened his mouth to speak who is capable of settling the much-
vexed questions of the day. We love eloquence for its own sake, and
not for any truth which it may utter, or any heroism it may inspire.
Our legislators have not yet learned the comparative value of free-
trade and of freedom, of union, and of rectitude, to a nation. They
have no genius or talent for comparatively humble questions of
taxation and finance, commerce and manufactures and agriculture.
If we were left solely to the wordy wit of legislators in Congress for
our guidance, uncorrected by the seasonable experience and the
effectual complaints of the people, America would not long retain
her rank among the nations. For eighteen hundred years, though
perchance I have no right to say it, the New Testament has been
written; yet where is the legislator who has wisdom and practical
talent enough to avail himself of the light which it sheds on the
science of legislation?

35   The authority of government, even such as I am willing to
submit to,—for I will cheerfully obey those who know and can do
better than I, and in many things even those who neither know nor
can do so well,—is still an impure one: to be strictly just, it must
have the sanction and consent of the governed. It can have no pure
right over my person and property but what I concede to it. The
progress from an absolute to a limited monarchy, from a limited
monarchy to a democracy, is a progress toward a true respect for the
individual. Even the Chinese philosopher was wise enough to regard
the individual as the basis of the empire. Is a democracy, such as we
know it, the last improvement possible in government? Is it not
possible to take a step further towards recognizing and organizing
the rights of man? There will never be a really free and enlightened
State until the State comes to recognize the individual as a higher
and independent power, from which all its own power and authority
are derived, and treats him accordingly. I please myself with imagining a State at last which can afford to be just to all men, and to treat
the individual with respect as a neighbor; which even would not
think it inconsistent with its own repose if a few were to live aloof

from it, not meddling with it, nor embraced by it, who fulfilled all the duties of neighbors and fellow-men. A State which bore this kind of fruit, and suffered it to drop off as fast as it ripened, would prepare the way for a still more perfect and glorious State, which also I have imagined, but not yet anywhere seen.

Vocabulary

expedient	prevail	liable
unimpaired	integrity	vitality
din	alacrity	fain
whit	admirable	palpitation
magazines	unscrupulous	rampart
benefactor	philanthropist	commodities
ado	countenance	tinge
demagogue	hireling	inducement
gregariousness	virile	insurrection
naught	penitent	scourge
disinterested	aggrieved	effective
perception	proportionate	friction
unconciliatory	convulse	parchment
impetuous	foist	waive
parole	eloquently	exorbitant
superfluous	strait	inert
obstinancy	fatalist	alienate
indred	prudence	sanction
acuteness	rectitude	aloof

Topics for Discussion

1. "Civil Disobedience" is the classic essay on the relation-ship between the people and government. Thoreau's argument for the rights of the individual to be free and for the individual's duty to actively resist injustice contains a multitude of questions about the nature of government, law, and public responsibility. Here are a few questions which a reading of the essay may help you to answer.
A. Is there a difference between breaking a law in a totalitarian state and breaking a law in a supposedly democratic state?
B. Even in a state that is truly democratic, whose laws represent the will of the majority of the people, are there some individual pre-

rogatives which should remain beyond the rule of law? What personal and property rights do you believe belong in this category?

C. Even if one is in fundamental agreement with Thoreau, is it not in the best interests of society to tolerate some injustice, perhaps procedural injustice like court delays, for the general welfare of the social order?

2. It is difficult to put a political label on Thoreau. He seems a partisan of social revolution in various places in the essay, yet he says, "I came into this world not chiefly to make this a good place to live in, but to live in it, be it good or bad." This sounds more like a dropout from society than a social activist. In the final paragraph of the essay he calls for a form of government beyond American "democracy," yet he does not sketch what political program might lead to the establishment of that government. Given this, and the aphorism about the government which governs least, what do you think the program of a political movement in the 1970s would contain were it to try to reflect Thoreau's philosophy? What points of agreement and disagreement would you have with that program?

3. Thoreau called for civil disobedience to end the Mexican war. What part has civil disobedience played in recent American history? Could movements against war or for civil rights have been formed without the catalyst of civil disobedience?

Rhetorical Considerations

1. Examine the tone of Thoreau's essay. At one point he says, "All men recognize the right of revolution." This is certainly a bold statement, but the language of the paragraph in which it appears, and the language of the essay as a whole, provides a context which makes these words sound almost moderate. Why? Compare the tone used by Thoreau to that found in the speeches and writings of modern revolutionaries and would-be revolutionaries.

2. Thoreau has the ability to compress complex ideas into short sentences which drive those ideas home forcefully. For example: "I think that we should be men first, and subjects afterward." Find other examples of this kind of sentence in the essay. What other kinds of sentence structure does Thoreau typically use? Do you find that many of his sentences initially present an idea which turns out not to be the main idea of the sentence after all?

3. How does Thoreau handle words subject to vague interpretation? One would expect that the terms *hero, patriot,* and *martyr*

would be used in essays opposing Thoreau's ideas, yet he manages to use them to advantage. How does he do this?

4. Whether or not you agree with Thoreau, inspect his argument for logical flaws and misplaced reliance on emotion. What do you think of the sentence, "I think it is enough if they have God on their side. . . ."?

Lessons of the Street

Bruce Jay Friedman

Bruce Jay Friedman (b. 1930) is a novelist and playwright. His works include Stern *(1962),* From the City of Class *(1963), and* A Mother's Kisses *(1964).*

1   John is a New York City plainclothes detective whose clothes are not all that plain. He wears webbed belts, bell-bottom slacks, and all-in-one suede and corduroy suits of a type purchasable at what the radio commercials refer to as "in" shops. This fondness for mod outfits makes him a bit unusual in his profession, most detectives favoring baggy slacks and white anklets or what John politely refers to as "period dress." But the clothing helps John blend into the background when he is at work in certain "swinging" neighborhoods, particularly those along Manhattan's upper East Side. He also keeps a conservative gray double-breasted suit on hand for Wall Street operations, and in a flash he can get himself up as a junkie when called upon for a narcotics caper.

2   John has ten years as a detective under his belt and sees the city with a certain shrewd streetwise vision; it was for this reason that a mutual friend suggested I meet and hang around with him since I would be amazed at how different detectives' eyes are from anyone else's. Well, actually, I wasn't going to be that amazed: I'd written about detectives before: a few articles, stories, a novel called *The Dick*. But my fascination, not so much with crime as with detectives, continues to operate on a high burner—the guns, the hair-raising amount of power, their ability to keep a grip of their sanity, however razor-thin. John is a lonely fellow, I was told, and would be happy to meet a new friend, particularly a literary type.

3   I keep an office apartment in Manhattan's East sixties and it was agreed that we would get our project under way at my place. John showed up punctually at eight one night, almost as though he'd been crouched at the door to make sure his arrival was right on the dot. As advertised, he turned out to be a dapper young man with a constant look of incredulity on his face, as though all his life someone had been whispering a long, amazing story in his ear. At times he seemed handsome, at other times quite snotty-looking; on appearance alone, it would not be surprising if he was revealed to be yet another Kennedy brother, long hidden away in some obscure religious order.

4   Halfway through the door, John began to fiddle with my lock, asking if it was the original one assigned to me by the building. I had to admit it was, and John, with a sad shake of his head, said that not changing it was a bad move on my part since the contractors had doubtless sold the basic key pattern to the rackets people, making my flat a pushover for burglars.

5   I told John that the building seemed to have pretty good security, with squadrons of attendants guarding each of the entrances. But John said they would all be sitting ducks for Argentinian husband-and-wife teams who would cut through a building of this sort like locusts through a wheatfield. "They are very fine-looking people who can walk through the front door on dignity alone. The husband breaks-and-enters and the wife's skirts are the stash. They have schools for these people in Argentina, training them in assorted con games."

6   John patted his breast pocket and said, "Here, incidentally, is the best place to carry your money." Tapping his backside, he said, "Here's the worst." Moving deeper into the apartment, John spotted the wraparound glass windows and said, "A voyeur's paradise, I see. I'd like to lock up nine perverts in a place like this. What you'd wind up with is one fat man and a bag of bones." Like other detectives I've known (and many Air Force officers) John is obsessed with the subject of homosexuality. Given the slightest conversational opportunity—or none at all—he will work in a fag reference or girlish imitation of some sort.

7   I offered him a drink, which he declined in favor of coffee, explaining that he never imbibes while carrying a gun, which is always. The weapon is a .38, and he has mastered the art of wearing it in his mod slacks so that no bulge shows beneath his jacket. When his slacks are a bit too tight, the gun is difficult to draw, and on one occasion, a homosexual interpreted his wriggling about to get the weapon as an overture. A .38 is the only weapon John carries,

although several months before he had been assigned a back-up man who wore a pair of guns at the waist, one attached to his back, another in the crotch, and a long, saberlike knife tucked into his boots. John wears his one gun both on and off duty and on occasion has been criticized by girls who've run across it during amorous encounters. He has killed two men he knows of and a vague number of others in shoot-outs when all hell broke loose and exactly who killed whom was unclear. As to the drinking, John tries to stay away from bars where he is known. "They will slide ninety-six free drinks my way and then, invariably, there will be a six-foot-nine goon pushing people around, and I will be expected to deposit him outside on his ass."

8   Moving across to the windows, John was reminded of his work with "leapers"—suicidal jumpers from high buildings. As he told it, the one thing such dry-divers forget is that at some point they are going to hit the ground. "They just think about the flying-through-the-air part. And if you've ever heard the sound of a leaper coming in for a landing, you'll never forget it. It's like two tons of wet laundry dropped from a plane."

9   Still, John would rather deal with a leaper any day of the week than be assigned to a "roast-toastie"—a rackets victim who is burned up in a building or car. There is a requirement that little plastic tags be affixed to each section of the victim's body, a particular problem when "toasties" are involved. "You'll be standing there with an ear in one hand and a foot in the other, and the supervisor will be hollering, 'All right you men, get those ninety-five tags on.' " A standard procedure for a detective who is tagging bodies is to put a rag in his mouth to keep himself from throwing up.

10   Turning to an only slightly lighter topic, John scanned the street below and informed me that I lived on Old Fag Row, five blocks that aging homosexuals had marked off as their turf. "You can put numbers on their backs and chart their course, like salmon going upstream." But, in any case, he said, the entire East Side deviate scene was fun and games compared to a certain West Side section of Central Park referred to by detectives as "Gobbler's Nook."

11   "There it really gets vicious," said John. "One step inside is like going into the jaws of death. A girl who passed by would get killed for her insolence. Many of the fags are actually junkies in disguise so they can take someone off. The trees whisper to you. You look up and see a huge 'gorilla fag' with white teeth and wash-and-wear hair, standing on a branch and grinning at you." John, who turned out to have many unique ideas for ending the

Vietnam war, said one quick method would be to turn 200 or so Central Park "gorilla fags" loose on the Cong.

12   "All right," said John, leaping to his feet, "time to go out and harass the public."

A Junk Cop Has the Supreme Mix

13   On the way downstairs, John proudly filled me in on the fact that he had made detective after only three years on the beat, and without the help of a "rabbi"—a friend in city government. Further upward movement, however, was going to be rocky without influence. "The police commissioner can expose himself in the middle of 42nd Street and no one'll pay attention to him. Yet all you need is one dum dum in the mayor's office pointing to a cop and saying, 'I like that boy,' and the next day he's got a promotion." Despite this beef, John felt the department was a virtual playpen now, compared to a period in recent memory when police internal security men had more power than the Gestapo. "If they knocked on your door at three in the morning and said you were out, that's exactly what you were—out. It didn't matter if you were Spellman's nephew. No phone calls, no hearing, no nothing. It's still a department run on Catholic morality—for Catholics, by Catholics, and for the benefit of Catholics." Actually, it had been a long time since I'd met anyone who was as strenuously Catholic as John was—and for a moment I thought of a time when I passed St. Angela Merici's each day on the way to public school, afraid of being whisked inside and forced to wear a parochial school uniform.

14   John broke my reverie as he, for some reason, next turned his anger to the FBI, which he and his fellow detectives regard with the same contempt that combat infantrymen reserve for the boys back at Headquarters. "Do you know those guys actually believe the movies and TV shows. An agent with his suit and striped tie will rap on a door and say, 'Open up in the name of the FBI!' The only trouble is, the junkie inside hasn't seen the movie, so he fires a round through the door. The FBI guy feels all this blood coming out of his suit and can't believe it. 'How could he *do* that,' he says. 'I *told* him I was with the FBI.' "

15   By the time we reached the street, John was in a total lather over the federal agency, sticking a finger at my nose and saying, "And they'll get you, too, don't worry, if they want you for something. If they say you're a murderess, then you're a murderess if they got to dig up a corpse and stick one in your lap. If they want

you for junk, they'll run into your apartment and start scaling bags of heroin off the walls, one kilo for you, one kilo for you over there, and one for the baby. And you're all under arrest for possession of dangerous drugs.''

16   Once on the subject of drugs, John was off to the races, most of his years on the street having been spent as a "junk cop," which he regarded as a thankless, dreary job, but one possessed of a certain grubby nobility. "We're at the bottom of the toilet bowl, but for reliability, dependability, give me a junk cop any day of the week. It's the supreme mix—with everything coming down on us— rape, burglary, arson, homicide. The department can't exist without the junk cop and his fresh street information. A detective is only as good as his informants—and the junk man has the most, since every junkie is an informant.''

17   Since I'd first met John, I'd been waiting for this kind of "commercial." Throughout my experience with the police, I'd never met a vice cop who didn't claim that vice work was the only place there was any real action, or a homicide dick who didn't insist that murder was the only aspect of crime worth bothering about.

18   When we reached my car, I held John off for a moment to ask if the vehicle's security was in good shape: it had door locks, an ignition lock, and a third little lock-switch of which I was particularly proud, tucked away at the base of the steering column. "You're fair against amateurs, a dead duck against a professional." Well, then, was a burglar alarm system worth installing? Not really. The only surefire path to absolute security in a city-parked car was to unscrew the rotor and take it along. "It's a bit messy," said John, "but you'd be surprised—more and more people are walking into restaurants with them.''

A Trained Dick Sees the Hits

19   Once in my car, John suggested we drive over to Manhattan's West Side, where we would be sure to see junkies in action, although he quickly apologized for its not being as heavy a dope scene as the East Bronx. "Up there, it's just one big syringe, with more glassine wrappers on the street than cigarette butts. The only man ever reported for suspicious behavior is a guy who's not a junkie.''

20   Briefing me as he drove, John said that until five years ago and the arrival of stiff federal laws, Italians controlled the heroin market. And it wasn't all that bad since at least the traffic was orderly and the prices firm. The dons would decide to import 150 keys (kilos)

one year and hold it at that. But now that the Cubans are in command, all bets are off and the traffic in junk is wild. The footloose South Americans are independent operators, with no controlling network, and you might have as much as 800,000 keys a year coming into the country. As we moved along upper Broadway and then turned onto a bleak and sourly cast section of Columbus and then Amsterdam, John said he would soon be pointing out some junkies "on the set." Rolling down the window to wink at an effeminate young man, John said, "Hi there, Holly Golightly," and when a car up ahead blocked our path momentarily, John quickly marked its driver down as an out-of-towner on the hunt for an assignation. "Look at him, so horny he can hardly turn the wheel. If the radio cars spent as much time prowling as he does, they'd be no crime in the city. He'll pick up a little guppy, contract a dose and bring it home as a present for his family in Topeka. They'll spend all their lives looking for a cure."

21   We passed another corner which John described as a notorious nesting place for female impersonators, most of them Puerto Rican, the ex-islanders being especially philosophical about this aberration. "They'll say, 'Poor José, what a shame, but that is the way it goes.' Amazingly, these people make as much money off tourists as regular pross [prostitutes]. The guy goes back to his hotel dreaming happy dreams and it never occurs to him that he's been worked over by a Puerto Rican third baseman in drag."

22   On a particularly forlorn corner of Columbus Avenue, John double-parked, dug a finger in my ribs, and pointed to what he described as a group of junkies "on the set." I turned to look and he said, "Don't just wheel around that way. If they see two of us staring, it's all over. Pretend you're talking to me and use the car mirror." Feeling very Paul Newman, I did so and saw a group of stooped-over people not having very much to do with one another. "A junkie 'hanging' that way means either one, he's had his shot; two, he's steering people to a connection; or three, he's actually holding something. Watch, and you'll see some shit go down." After a moment or so, one of the men ambled over to another. "Closer," said John, "closer, closer—" The two men exchanged a Harlem "take five" slap of hands and John said, "That was it."

23   "That was it?"

"That was it," he repeated.

"I don't really think I saw anything,"

"Of course you didn't," said John. "Neither would a radio car, circling the corner for hours. It takes a trained junk dick to see a hit like that."

24   Feeling as though I'd slowed the march of justice, I asked John if, under normal circumstances, he would have made an arrest in a case like that. He said no—the department doesn't have enough personnel to bother with one-bag transactions. "What you're after is your half-load and full-load twenty-five bags of heroin collar. When you get one, you immediately turn the man into a confidential informer. 'You give us X number of collars and we'll write a letter to the D.A. to get you a suspended sentence.' The trick, though, is always to work up, getting a half-load man to lead you to a one-key man.

25   "And then one day," he said, swallowing hard, "you make that fifteen-key collar."

26   The thought of pulling off a coup of such proportions put John in a jovial mood. Doubling back to Amsterdam, we came across a parked car with a man leaning in, talking to the driver and slipping him a package. As far as I was concerned, it might have been two fellows discussing a recent Mets game. John slowed up, then stepped on the gas, and with genuine anger, said, "Damn! Of all nights not to be traveling with my partner. There goes one of the top collars of my career."

27   I told John I wasn't sure I was following him and he said, "What do you think was in that box—Fanny Farmer chocolates? That was at least a two-key pinch. We'll circle 'round and five gets you ten they'll be gone. The driver took one look at my face and did you see him turn white? He knew I was The Man, all right." In total honesty, I hadn't seen any of this, but we circled the block and sure enough, the street-corner talkers had disappeared. "That was what we call a telephone delivery: swift, punctual, every half hour on the hour. Check your watch." I did and had to admit it was 10:30 on the dot. "No offense about before," said John, tapping me on the knee, "but I really did need at least one more gun."

28   "How come?" I asked.

"Because there were four more sitting in the back that you didn't see. On a two-key pinch, it's going to be guns and knives, D'Artagnan and the O.K. Corral.

29   "Oh, Jesus!" he said. "What a collar that would have been! The guy in the car was colored. He can get all the weed he wants uptown. So the fact that he was dealing with a Cuban—they hate each other—can only mean heroin.

30   "Well," he said with a sigh, "till we meet again." He then rattled off a detailed description of the car, its color, year, condition, plate number, and a precise physical rundown on the two men we'd observed, right down to a small scar over the left eye of the Cuban.

This struck me as amazing since we'd sailed past them in a matter of seconds.

31   "Training," said John. "Getting used to surprise, vibrations, the rhythm of the street. Besides," he said, "the Cuban is a dead ringer for the chef in a restaurant I love to eat at."

Watch for the Tip-Offs

32   Traveling about with a detective, it strikes me, is like being in a mild accident or a fistfight. You feel fine while it's going on, even elated, and the shock of what has happened—or worse, what might have happened—doesn't set in until a bit later. I enjoyed John's company, and since writers are actors too, mimics, role-players of a kind, I felt a little detectivelike myself for the next few days, looking people over more carefully and attributing the very worst possible motives to their behavior. As for John himself, I was able somehow to block out the fact that he carried a loaded gun at all times and indeed was paid, when the circumstances fit, to blow people's heads off with it.

33   We kicked off our next meeting at Frankie and Johnny's, a favorite steak restaurant of mine, John dapper as ever but still grumbling about the fabulous collar he'd missed. A medium-rare sirloin distracted him somewhat, and two attractive women sitting alone helped things along even more. There was a hint that John fancied himself to be a ladies' man. I asked if women were fascinated by men in police work. "There's an old saying," said John. "Put a uniform on a hanger and it'll get laid by itself."

34   John expressed a certain sympathy for women who lived alone in the city; just in case I had a lady-love in this circumstance, he advised that she never allow a man to follow her at night at less than a five-foot margin. And if she ever got into an elevator with a male tenant, it was wise to let him push his floor button first—even if she knew the fellow. "And for God's sakes," said John, "tell her to make sure she locks her door each time she leaves the apartment, even if it's just to take the garbage to the incinerator. That brief moment with the door open is the worst—Freaksville Time."

35   Feeling a bit overdressed, John suggested we go back to his bachelor apartment on the West Side, where he could change clothes, and I could look at his scrapbook. He lived in a small building on a quiet street. Because there had been some indiscreet passage of junk in the halls, he had let it be known that he was a

detective. "Now, there's a guy six-foot-nine who bows down to me every morning on the way to work."

36   The first thing to greet the visitor to John's pad is a large, comic drawing of what used to be known as a "yegg," pointing a pistol straight at the door. This is a police target and John said he has to qualify in marksmanship twice each year. Was he a good shot? He wasn't sure, since most shoot-outs are held at less than ten feet and the winner tends to be the one who gets his gun out fastest. The apartment was glum, temporary—the lighting faded in the style of some of the West Side street corners we'd surveyed. John never stopped apologizing about it. I leafed through his scrapbook, on the first page of which was an empty shell, secured with Scotch tape and proudly inscribed, "My First Round—With Many More To Come." John sneaked up alongside me, aimed a .45 at my eyes and pulled the trigger shouting, "Bang! Bang!" The gun turned out to be an almost perfect replica of the real thing, complete with gun clip. John had taken it from a junkie stick-up man whose victims, presumably, would actually be able to hear the clip being inserted in case they had doubts about the weapon's authenticity. I asked John if he would mind not doing that again and he said, "Okay, okay."

37   An hour later, driving along the East River, I was prompted to ask about the relationship between crime and the city's rivers. John said that most "floaters" were a signal from the organized crime people that they were still in business and not to mess around with them. The particular style of the killing was always significant. "We find a drowning victim with his tongue cut out, it's not because he's skipped confession." Thus, a body found in the river was generally meant to be discovered. If there was a need to dispose of a body totally, the syndicate would use either car-crushing machinery or lime pits.

38   "Now *there's* something wrong," said John, as we bounced along the quiet and seemingly crime-free upper East Side, my new friend having promised to give me further examples of his instinct for smoking out breaks in the rhythm of the streets. All I saw was a moving van parked in front of a luxurious seven-story building. "Fine," said John, "except when was the last time you've heard of someone in this neighborhood moving at eleven at night? If it was over on the West Side, it would be perfectly natural, you'd know it was a 'Midnight Mover,' some Puerto Rican guy ducking out on the rent." In other words, what was normal behavior in one section of the city was a dead giveaway to wrongdoing in another. A group of men—even one man—parked in a car at night on the East Side was

suspicious. Something, someone was probably being cased. The same group parked on the rundown West Side meant someone had probably said, "Let's go sit in John's car," the vehicle being much more comfortable than the apartment of anyone in the crowd.

39   As we headed downtown to the East Village, John flipped his gun into a new position, between his legs, whipping it out quickly to demonstrate how he'd be able to gain an extra second in case he had to fire off a round through the windshield. As we got into the twenties, on Second Avenue, two young men sprinted by and John asked me what I saw. "Two fellows running," I said.

40   "Without jackets?" he said. "In this weather? Here's where my eyes are different from yours. What I saw was two pair of hands looking for a purse to snatch." The two young men disappeared into what seemed like a small dance hall. "They've got their coats in there and, if questioned, can say they've been there all along. It's not much of an alibi, but it's something." Suddenly, everyone on the street looked a little fishy to me. I pointed to a man carrying a stick and said, "How about him? He doesn't look right to me."

41   "Nice going," said John. "You're getting the hang of it. The stick is a tip-off that the fellow's a junkie. Also the stooped walk. To avoid being taken off, junkies always carry something, a stick, umbrella, or a rolled-up newspaper. Not for the editorials. It's got a knife inside."

42   John said that most people were under the false impression that the majority of junkie crime was committed against the public. "Negative," he said. "It's committed on one another, strong junkies smelling out weak ones and sticking it to them."

You Can Tell a Man by His Walk

43   Before long, we were double-parked on St. Marks Place in a colorful swirl of head shops and ice cream stores, advertising such flavors as Acapulco Gold and Panama Red. A pretty young girl skipped out of a clothing store and approached a late-model car with a group of men inside. "Where'd you get the car, boys?" we heard her ask. "You gonna help me cut that bitch?" Seemingly intrigued by the proposal, one of the men opened the car door, and she hopped inside. "We're in luck." said John. "That's one of the toughest little chicks on the Eastern seaboard. Pisses icewater. She's obviously jumped bail and the car she got into is a stolen job. Let's give them a light tail and see what happens."

44   Since I'm always at one of a half-dozen bars and restaurants

and keep seeing the same people, I'd always had the feeling that the colossus-of-New-York was a myth—and that the city was actually quite small in size. But John, who rarely passed a corner without seeing something or someone he recognized, made it seem even smaller.

45   He waited until the car had turned a corner, then zipped off in pursuit, explaining that on a tail it was always a good idea to keep two cars between yours and the one you were following. "I think they've spotted us," said John, gunning the accelerator and racing off after them, going through red light after red light. That was my favorite part, a boyhood dream. I knew that detectives were underpaid, but it seemed to me that getting to go through red lights and park in front of fireplugs was worth at least five grand a year in salary. Before long a radio car, with sirens howling and a cigar-smoking sergeant at the wheel, pulled up alongside and cut us off. The cigar was against regulations.

46   "Where you off to, chaps?" asked the driver.

47   "Nowhere, now," said John, flashing his tin. "You just caused us to lose our tail."

48   "Sorry, brother," said the driver.

49   "Enjoying the smoke?" John asked.

50   "Just fine," said the driver, considering whether to dump the cigar in the ashtray and then deciding to risk a grand, Joe Levine-style puff to show he trusted John not to turn him in.

51   "Dum dum," said John, driving off. He apologized for our losing the bail-jumper, but assured me that before the night was gone we'd come up with something.

52   A block from the Police Academy, true to his word, John spotted two bearded men in their twenties, pacing up and back on a street corner and shooting suspicious glances over their shoulders. "They're going to try to boost that little Volks on the corner," said John. "I'm going after them. Observe my walk as I make my approach. It will be a street-style movement, so as not to put them on the alert." Before he left, John explained that he was a student of walks and could tell exactly what New York neighborhood a man was from by the nature of his walk, even pinning it down to an Italian kid who grew up in a black neighborhood or a black youth who grew up in a Jewish one. "You are what you walk," said John, leaving the car and moving toward his prey with a jaunty, turkey-like stride that reminded me of Ray Bolger's movements in a Forties' musical called *By Jupiter*. I followed behind, trying to do a Bolger myself, but giving it up quickly—no one could truly imitate the great dancing star—and going back to my normal slouching

style. In a flash, John had both men against a wall, frisking them for weapons, finding only a "roach" in one man's cigarette pack. "A roach, eh?" said John. "Don't do that again."

53   Driving back uptown, John said, "Maybe now you're getting some idea of what this job means to me. The hunt. The defense reading the offense, constantly moving your linebackers around. When I'm doing work like this, I'm as hooked as any junkie."

Criminals May Want to be Caught

54   As a special and final indoctrination, John called and said he was going to take me on a nighttime tour of Harlem. At the same time, he cautioned me that it might get a little hairy, and that we would have to stay on the alert and keep our doors and windows locked. "We are not visiting the College of Cardinals," he said.

55   Several nights later, doors and windows battened down, we made our way uptown, John a bit sorry I was going to miss Harlem's nine o'clock Sunday morning "Bryn Mawr Show." All up and down Lenox Avenue, according to John, you'd see pretty little blond finishing school girls staggering out of Harlem tenements, dazed, their stockings rolled down around their ankles. The previous night, on the West Side, or in the Village, someone had invited them to a party. "What the guy neglected to tell them is they were the party."

56   We slipped into Harlem through its side door, a small tidy upper East Side Italian section known as "Northern Mulberry Street," one I had somehow missed in my previous travels about the city. John agreed that the streets were quiet and orderly but said that most of the big-time criminals escapades were being planned inside the many "social clubs" that lined the streets.

57   John, who was quite democratic in his ethnic slurs, dealing them out good-naturedly to Jews, Irish, and blacks alike, now took a swipe at the Italians. "I just don't see why they're supposed to be so smart. If you have an organized crime group lit up, the idea is to find the big man, the don, right? With the Italians, they do all the work for you. You've got the binoculars on them, six guys in undershirts playing pinochle, another six doing a John Wayne bicep number in the corner. Then in comes this little old nothing-looking mozzarella-head you'd ordinarily pay no attention to. Except that everybody in the place jumps to their feet and practically salutes and you know who your man is."

58   But John felt that was true of all criminals, the need to be caught. "A guy commits a crime in a purple shirt and orange pants

and insists he's all upset about being collared. 'Why the bizarre attire?' you ask. 'I just wanted to wear something nice.' he tells you.''

59   We drove into Harlem proper now, John crouching down behind the wheel, on the alert, for all practical purposes in enemy territory. "All right, this is it," he said. "A white man comes up here there has got to be some sort of crime committed on his person—his wallet goes, his jacket is swiped, his throat cut, something. When I see a white man get out of his car, my only interest is that he has left a next-of-kin note on the front seat and instructions on where to ship the body. If you ever come up here alone, make sure your speedometer starts at fifty. A red light is the signal for an ambush.''

60   As we moved through the sad, bleary-eyed neighborhoods of Lenox and St. Nicholas Avenues, John went into some kind of weird inverse Lenny Bruce monologue. I'd been with detectives before, and the grim attitude toward blacks came as no great surprise to me. But I'd never before seen the revulsion-fascination machinery in operation. "All right, folks, up here it's wall-to-wall junk. Open the window you get stoned by osmosis. See that building, fifteen junkies out in front? On Park Avenue you pay $750 a month and get one doorman. Here you get fifteen. . . . It's ten o'clock at night now, that's like ten in the morning in the rest of the city. These people are just waking up to start the day. . . . There's a guy doing karate in the wind. He's trying to impress some dingbat chick in the bar and hasn't executed one movement properly. . . . There's a guy with a golfing hat. Now I ask you, did that man ever pick up a nine iron? . . . See that phone booth on the corner? It's fine except there's no floor in it. Go in to drop a dime, you wind up on a banana boat going to Panama. . . .''

61   What really drove John wild were the hats worn by Harlem's residents. To him, the area was just one big hat show and he couldn't seem to get over it. Hats were "toilet bowls," "inverted spittoons.''

62   "Will you *look* at that chapeau!" John said about one particularly flamboyant topper. "He don't know his hat's goin' north and his head's goin' south. Will you look at that man dig himself. He takes a perfectly good Panama number, stomps on it, chews on it, pours on a little rib sauce, and thinks it looks groovy. The skinnier the guy the bigger the brim. The fatter the guy the smaller the brim. Maybe I'm wrong?" I decided John wanted secretly to jump out of the car and start trying on all the hats in Harlem.

63   Before we left the neighborhood, John pointed out a

restaurant-hangout where criminals obeyed the strictest of social hierarchies, the pimps sitting in one section, disdainful of the stick-up men who are sitting in another and are in turn contemptuous of the pickpockets and small-time con men who are also cordoned off by themselves.

64   As a final piece of advice, John said the time you know you are in trouble in Harlem is when someone asks you the size of your shoes. If you give the right answer, your questioner will undoubtedly say, "Hey man. That's my size too. Put your hands in the air." And you're on your way back home, barefoot.

65   Driving downtown once again, John said that one good thing about detective work is that you get rid of your violent urges in the day's work.

66   But then we passed a magnificent Bentley limousine, waiting for a green light, with some almost parodically rich and social Peter Arno types inside.

67   "Just once," said John, "I'd like to sail into a car like that, going around eighty miles an hour. Get 'em right in the grill."

68   "Maybe I'm wrong." This phrase had the slightest trace of poignance each time John used it. After I'd left him, I had to wonder what it would be like to grow up as a nice Catholic boy in a nice Catholic New York neighborhood, taught to honor God, home, and country. Everything neat. Mother cooks the stew, the corner cop's your friend, Jews are sissies, the flag makes your eyes water, and only mentally retarded girls put out. And then suddenly absolutely nothing fits; every step you take, another sacred vessel explodes in your face like a flashbulb—the flag is used to roll joints, veterans fling their medals at the White House, star pass receivers get arrested for indecent exposure, blacks get elected mayor all over the place, even appointed admiral, for Christ's sake.

69   Detectives are one group with a legitimate right to paranoia—there really are a lot of bad people hiding in the bushes—but what in the world was next—Nixon joining a commune? Hoover opening a microbiotic restaurant?

70   It was enough to make a man go out and . . . well, write a book or something, which, as it turns out, is what John was doing the last time I talked to him on the phone. I thanked him for the glimpse he'd given me of the city through a detective's eyes, and much to my surprise he thanked me for the glimpse I'd given him of the same city through a writer's eyes. Then, with the tentative clack of a typewriter in the background, he excused himself and said he

had to get back to his first chapter. And besides, the phone was probably bugged.

Vocabulary

mod	junkie	caper
shrewd	streetwise	obscure
fag	deviate	kilo
arson	homicide	rotor
syringe	glassine	dons
coup	elated	mimic
intrigued	colossus	battened
mozzarella	revulsion	fascination
osmosis	dingbat	nine iron
chapeau	flamboyant	topper
dig	number	hierarchies
pimps	contemptuous	cordoned
poignance	paranoia	commune
microbiotic		

Topics for Discussion

1. How does Friedman's description of a policeman compare with your conception of what a policeman is?

2. John is a New York City detective. Do you think detectives in other cities would be different? Why?

3. What is John's attitude toward criminals? Toward the police department? Toward the public?

4. How true do you think it is that "you are what you walk," as John says? Do you think your style of walking can reveal that much about you? Why are such things important to John?

5. Do you agree with John that all criminals want to be caught? Does John really believe this, or is it a rationale for his job and conduct?

6. What is the "revulsion-fascination machinery" that operates in John?

7. Do you agree with Friedman that "detectives are one group with a legitimate right to paranoia"? Why would detectives have this right?

Rhetorical Considerations

1. Friedman quotes John as comparing his job to a football game with offense, defense, and linebackers. How is this comparison extended throughout the essay?

2. Examine the essay and determine how Friedman implies the differences between himself and John. How does this contrast contribute to the structure of the essay?

3. John is the central character in this essay, yet Friedman himself plays an important role. What is the role Friedman plays? How does this role help the reader with the essay?

4. What is the device that unifies all of the different experiences that John and Friedman have?

5. What is the tone of the essay? How is this tone achieved? What does the tone contribute to the essay?

The Criminal Type

Jessica Mitford

Jessica Mitford (b. 1917) contributes articles to Esquire *and* The Nation. *She is author of* The American Way of Death *(1963) and of* Daughters and Rebels *(1960).*

1   Time was when most crimes were laid at the door of the Devil. The English indictment used in the last century took note of Old Nick's complicity by accusing the defendant not only of breaking the law but of "being prompted and instigated by the Devil," and the Supreme Court of North Carolina declared in 1862: "To know the right and still the wrong pursue proceeds from a perverse will brought about by the seductions of the Evil One."

2   With the advent of the new science of criminology toward the end of the nineteenth century, the Devil (possibly to his chagrin) was deposed as primary cause of crime by the hand of an Italian criminologist, one of the first of that calling, Cesare Lombroso. Criminals, Lombroso found, are born that way and bear physical stigmata to show it (which presumably saddles God with the respon-

sibility, since He created them). They are "not a variation from a norm but practically a special species, a subspecies, having distinct physical and mental characteristics. In general all criminals have long, large, projecting ears, abundant hair, thin beard, prominent frontal sinuses, protruding chin, large cheekbones." Furthermore, his studies, consisting of exhaustive examination of live prisoners and the skulls of dead ones, enabled him to classify born criminals according to their offense: "Thieves have mobile hands and face; small, mobile, restless, frequently oblique eyes; thick and closely set eyebrows; flat or twisted nose; thin beard; hair frequently thin." Rapists may be distinguished by "brilliant eyes, delicate faces" and murderers by "cold, glassy eyes; nose always large and frequently aquiline; jaws strong; cheekbones large; hair curly, dark and abundant." Which cause a contemporary French savant to remark that Lombroso's portraits were very similar to the photographs of his friends.

3   A skeptical Englishman named Charles Goring, physician of His Majesty's Prisons, decided to check up on Lombroso's findings. Around the turn of the century he made a detailed study of the physical characteristics of 3,000 prisoners—but took the precaution of comparing these with a group of English university students, impartially applying his handy measuring tape to noses, ears, eyebrows, chins of convicts and scholars alike over a twelve-year period. His conclusion: "In the present investigation we have exhaustively compared with regard to many physical characteristics different kinds of criminals with each other and criminals as a class with the general population. From these comparisons no evidence has emerged of the existence of a physical criminal type."

4   As the twentieth century progressed, efforts to pinpoint the criminal type followed the gyrations of scientific fashions of the day with bewildering results. Studies published in the thirties by Gustav Aschaffenburg, a distinguished German criminologist, show that the pyknic type (which means stout, squat, with large abdomen) is more prevalent among occasional offenders, while the asthenic type (of slender build and slight muscular development) is more often found among habitual criminals. In the forties came the gland men, Professor William H. Sheldon of Harvard and his colleagues, who divided the human race into three: endomorphs, soft, round, comfort-loving people; ectomorphs, fragile fellows who complain a lot and shrink from crowds; mesomorphs, muscular types with large trunks who walk assertively, talk noisily, and behave aggressively. Watch out for those.

5   Skull shape, glands, IQ, and deviant personality aside, to get a more pragmatic view of the criminal type one merely has to look at the composition of the prison population. Today the prisons are filled with the young, the poor white, the black, the Chicano, the Puerto Rican. Yesterday they were filled with the young, the poor native American, the Irish or Italian immigrant.

6   Most studies of the causes of crime in this decade, whether contained in sociological texts, high-level government commission reports, or best-selling books like Ramsey Clark's *Crime in America,* lament the disproportionately high arrest rate for blacks and poor people and assert with wearing monotony that criminality is a product of slums and poverty. Mr. Clark invites the reader to mark on his city map the areas where health and education are poorest, where unemployment and poverty are highest, where blacks are concentrated—and he will find these areas also have the highest crime rate.

7   Hence the myth that the poor, the young, the black, the Chicano are indeed the criminal type of today is perpetuated, whereas in fact crimes are committed, although not necessarily punished, at all levels of society.

8   There is evidence that a high proportion of people in all walks of life have at some time or other committed what are conventionally called "serious crimes." A study of 1,700 New Yorkers weighted toward the upper income brackets, who had never been arrested for anything, and who were guaranteed anonymity, revealed that 91 percent had committed at least one felony or serious misdemeanor. The mean number of offenses per person was 18. Sixty-four percent of the men and 27 percent of the women had committed at least one felony, for which they could have been sent to the state penitentiary. Thirteen percent of the men admitted to grand larceny, 26 percent to stealing cars, and 17 percent to burglary.

9   If crimes are committed by people of all classes, why the near-universal equation of criminal type and slumdweller, why the vastly unequal representation of poor, black, brown in the nation's jails and prisons? When the "Italian bandit, bloodthirsty Spaniard, bad man from Sicily," and the rest of them climbed their way out of the slums and moved to the suburbs, they ceased to figure as an important factor in crime statistics. Yet as succeeding waves of immigrants, and later blacks, moved into the same slum area the rates of reported crime and delinquency remained high there.

10   No doubt despair and terrible conditions in the slums give rise

to one sort of crime, the only kind available to the very poor: theft, robbery, purse-snatching; whereas crimes committed by the former slum-dweller have moved up the scale with his standard of living to those less likely to be detected and punished: embezzlement, sale of fraudulent stock, pricefixing. After all, the bank president is not likely to become a bank robber; nor does the bank robber have the opportunity to embezzle depositors' funds.

11   Professor Theodore Sarbin suggests the further explanation that police are conditioned to perceive some classes of persons (formerly immigrants, now blacks and browns) as being actually or potentially "dangerous," and go about their work accordingly: "The belief that some classes of persons were 'dangerous' guided the search for suspects. . . . Laws are broken by many citizens for many reasons: those suspects who fit the concurrent social type of the criminal are most likely to become objects of police suspicion and of judicial decision-making." The President's Crime Commission comments on the same phenomenon: "A policeman in attempting to solve crimes must employ, in the absence of concrete evidence, circumstantial indicators to link specific crimes with specific people. Thus policemen may stop Negro and Mexican youths in white neighborhoods, may suspect juveniles who act in what the policemen consider an impudent or overly casual manner, and may be influenced by such factors as unusual hair styles or clothes uncommon to the wearer's group or area. . . . Those who act frightened, penitent, and respectful are more likely to be released, while those who assert their autonomy and act indifferent or resistant run a substantially greater risk of being frisked, interrogated, or even taken into custody."

12   An experiment conducted in the fall of 1970 by a sociology class at the University of California at Los Angeles bears out these observations. The class undertook to study the differential application of police definitions of criminality by varying one aspect of the "identity" of the prospective criminal subject. They selected a dozen students, black, Chicano, and white, who had blameless driving records free of any moving violations, and asked them to drive to and from school as they normally did, with the addition of a "circumstantial indicator" in the shape of a phosphorescent bumper sticker reading "Black Panther Party." In the first 17 days of the study these students amassed 30 driving citations—failure to signal, improper lane changes, and the like. Two students had to withdraw from the experiment after two days because their licenses were suspended; and the project soon had to be abandoned because the

$1,000 appropriation for the experiment had been used up in paying bails and fines of the participants.

13   As anyone versed in the ways of the criminal justice system will tell you, the screening process begins with the policeman on the beat: the young car thief from a "nice home" will be returned to his family with a warning. If he repeats the offense or gets into more serious trouble, the parents may be called in for a conference with the prosecuting authorities. The well-to-do family has a dozen options: they can send their young delinquent to a boarding school, or to stay with relatives in another part of the country, they can hire the professional services of a psychiatrist or counselor—and the authorities will support them in these efforts. The Juvenile Court judge can see at a glance that this boy does not belong in the toils of the criminal justice system, that given a little tolerance and helpful guidance there is every chance he will straighten out by the time he reaches college age.

14   For the identical crime the ghetto boy will be arrested, imprisoned in the juvenile detention home, and set on the downward path that ends in the penitentiary. The screening process does not end with arrest, it obtains at every stage of the criminal justice system.

15   To cite one example that any observer of the crime scene—and particularly the black observer—will doubtless be able to match from his own experience: a few years ago a local newspaper reported horrendous goings-on of high school seniors in Piedmont, a wealthy enclave in Alameda County, California, populated by executives, businessmen, rich politicians. The students had gone on a general rampage that included arson, vandalism, breaking and entering, assault, car theft, rape. Following a conference among parents, their lawyers, and prosecuting authorities, it was decided that no formal action should be taken against the miscreants; they were all released to the custody of their families, who promised to subject them to appropriate discipline. In the very same week, a lawyer of my acquaintance told me with tight-lipped fury of the case of a nine-year-old black ghetto dweller in the same county, arrested for stealing a nickel from a white classmate, charged with "extortion and robbery," hauled off to juvenile hall, and, despite the urgent pleas of his distraught mother, there imprisoned for six weeks to wait for his court hearing.

16   Thus it seems safe to assert that there is indeed a criminal type—but he is not a biological, anatomical, phrenological, or anthropological type; rather, he is a social creation, etched by the dominant class and ethnic prejudices of a given society.

Vocabulary

perverse	seductions	chagrin
stigmata	norm	oblique
savant	gyrations	pyknic
endomorphs	mesomorphs	ectomorphs
disproportionately	perpetuated	weighted
anonymity	felony	embezzlement
fraudulent	differential	Chicano
circumstantial	psychiatrist	ghetto
penitentiary	rampage	assert
anatomical	phrenological	anthropological
ethnic		

Topics for Discussion

1. In your daily life, do you divide people into types? Is this process conscious or unconscious? Do you make divisions on any rational basis?

2. On your way home from a party, you're mugged. To what racial group does the mugger belong? What does your answer to this question tell you about our tendencies to stereotype people?

3. What is "white collar crime"? Why does such crime frequently go unpunished?

4. Does your personal experience confirm or deny the results of the experiment outlined in paragraph 12?

5. Do the courts and police really treat criminals differently according to race and social class? Does equal justice under law really exist, in your opinion?

6. Identify common stereotypes other than those mentioned in this essay. How does stereotyping differ from logical classification?

Rhetorical Considerations

1. The phrase, "Time was . . ." sets up an informal tone for the essay. Does the author move away from this tone at any point? Look at paragraphs 7, 14, and 16. Determine how these paragraphs differ in tone from paragraph 1 and from each other.

2. Mitford suggests logical and illogical ways of classifying criminals. Determine three logical classifications for human beings and human behavior.

3. Of what value is the historical introduction of paragraphs 1–4? How does this introduction prepare the reader for the central idea implied in paragraph 5 and stated in paragraph 7? Can you explicitly state that central idea?

4. How is comparison and contrast used as an argumentative device? See especially paragraphs 7–9.

5. How does Mitford handle the interplay between example and statistical evidence? Which does she rely on more? See especially paragraphs 8, 12, and 15.

6. Is the conclusion of Mitford's argument (paragraph 16) well substantiated? List the argumentative devices she uses.

To Tell the Truth, the Price Is Right

Stephanie Harrington

Stephanie Harrington is a television critic and a contributor to the New York Times Magazine.

1   To critics, game shows are a vulgar expression of American materialism. To an enthusiast, they are a passion that drives someone in its throes to appear on national television dressed as a baked Alaska in hopes of winning a Vega Hatchback or a color TV or, at least, a nuclear-powered potato masher by AEC, Inc., and a week's supply of Blue Luster Carpet Shampoo. To broadcasters, this low-budget format is such an inexpensive schedule filler that, during daytime and early evening hours, they have given viewers little else to choose from. And the game shows' ratings are more than healthy enough to indicate that millions of viewers seem to find them an entertaining way to pass the time.

2   What is the appeal of game shows? One of the least charitable explanations has been offered by a man who has made millions from some of the most exploitive examples of the genre, independent producer Chuck Barris, who has given us "The Newlywed Game,"

"The Dating Game" and "The New Treasure Hunt." Barris, an assiduous *enfant terrible,* who has referred to himself as "the King of Slob Culture," told a TV Guide interviewer that the elements of a game show are "emotions and tensions . . . you must bring out those hidden hostilities in your contestants. You can actually watch them temporarily lose their sanity on the air. We prompt them to do that. Thus, audiences are being entertained, whether in awe or shock or horror or joy, over someone going bananas in public."

3   But perhaps the most profoundly manipulative aspect of the game-show business is the kind of financial calculation that leads broadcasters and producers not just to offer enough game shows to satisfy audiences who enjoy them but to blanket certain stretches of viewing time with game shows to the point that television consumers have little other choice. As one former network programer, who now works for an independent producer, observed, "It isn't really a public demanding a trend, but responding to a trend in offerings." And what is being offered is:

4   "Wheel of Fortune," on which contestants spin a roulette wheel to win guesses at the letters in a word puzzle, and winners must use their cash earnings to "shop" among "showcases" of prizes. Richard, winner of the *largest three-day total* in the program's *history* (more than $16,000), is beaming and rubbing his hands and saying, "I gotta go shopping." "That video cassette is really fabulous," volunteers host Chuck Woolery, who has been pushing the video cassette as if his brother-in-law had manufactured it. "Or do you want another car?" "For $170 I'd love the camera," says Richard, "and the wine and cheese for $50 and the Tiffany gift certificate for $1,000." Losers go home worse than bankrupt, with the consolation promise of a generous supply of Days Ease Air Freshener and Tabby Treat, "every meal a banquet for your cat."

5   And then there is the hardcore experience of fun and games in the consumer society, "The Price Is Right," which demands neither more nor less than precise knowledge of the famous Speigel mail-order catalogue, containing more than 50,000 quality items. If, as sociologist David Riesman observed, childhood in America is being a consumer trainee, "The Price Is Right" is the final exam.

6   On this show, contestants compete to see who can come closest to guessing the retail value of merchandise without guessing higher than the exact price. Here, the chance to win a front-loading portable dishwasher, a refrigerator-freezer with activated-charcoal air filter and "meat keeper" temperature control, and a heavy-duty garbage compactor-disposer with one-half-horsepower motor depends on the contestant's certain knowledge that the retail price of

four sets of "thick and thirsty famous St. Mary's towels," plus the retail price of a craft set plus the retail price of 15 cans of Lucite paint add up to more than the retail price of a Sunbeam 1,000-watt hair dryer with four speed settings and styling stand plus the retail price of a Schick Fresh Air Machine plus the retail price of a leather bag plus the price of a pollinium-proof pollywog terrarium with infrared heating device and southern exposure. With this kind of information, you can price your way to a shot at pricing—and thereby *winning—the Don Quixote Showcase!* Which includes "a trip to the land of Don Quixote," where you will stay in the *Eurobuilding Hotel* "in the heart of Madrid's Generalissimo Quarter!"

7   This side of that supershowcase in the sky, what could match this brand of Dionysian transport, except maybe a weekend at Friendly Frost, or dressing up like a macaroon to be sure you will be noticed and picked out of the studio audience to be a contestant on "Let's Make A Deal," which is such a big deal that admission to the studio audience is booked up for the next two years and host-producer Monty Hall was elected honorary Mayor of *Hollywood.* Here you can compete with the couple dressed in matching his and hers Lhasa Apso skins and the guy in the skirt who is supposed to be a cheerleader and the couple impersonating a pair of shoes and waving a sign that says, "Let's lace up a deal." Here you can experience the ecstasy of selling Monty the contents of your grungy old handbag for $150 and then agreeing to spend the $150 on a box, the contents of which you do not know, but which turns out to be . . . a *$759.95 refrigerator-freezer stocked with $25 worth of Breakstone's Cottage Cheese! And a $479.75 sewing machine!* Which means that you've traded *$150* and an old purse for a *deal,* the total retail value of which is *$1,264.70!* And you can compound your ecstasy by being smart enough *not* to trade it all back for your old purse and whatever amount of money Monty has put in it (which turns out to be a measly 27 bucks), or for the solid wall of frozen chopped chives from Armanino and the real clunker of a prize behind it. And then, after all this . . . the *agony* of *not* knowing when to stop and trying for the really *big* deal by agreeing to trade your $1,264.70 deal in for whatever is behind Door No. 3. Which turns out to be three bicycles and a $50 gift certificate to Dairy Queen.

8   But when it comes to sheer sado-masochism, the master of the medium is Barris, whose "The New Treasure Hunt" opens with the boast that it is the show that offers "more prizes and more cash than any other show in the world." (It is also a show that, according to Barris, grosses at least $2-million a year.) A stripped-down witless

version of "Let's Make A Deal," "New Treasure Hunt" reached a pitch of manipulative frenzy with one contestant who traded in a prize of $1,850 for one clunker after another (each related to the word "tire")—a unicycle, a bicycle, the humiliating experience of being tied up on stage by four human *ti-ers*. Her emotions were pushed and pulled until she was crying and pleading like a victim in a trap. When at last she was presented with a Rolls-Royce, she fainted. (Later she had to sell the Rolls to pay the taxes on it.)

9   Barris amuses himself with fantasies about a game show he would call "Greed." "As I see it," he explains, "you would have this horrendous situation in which an arthritic 85-year-old man would come in on crutches and contestants would bid down to see how little money they would take to kick the crutches out. . . ." But he is not beyond turning irony on himself. He is writing a novel in which a failing game-show producer, in a desperate effort to boost his ratings, figures out a way to kill contestants on the air.

Vocabulary

materialism	throes	assiduous
enfant terrible	Dionysian	exploitive

Topics for Discussion

1. Have you watched many game shows on television? Do you agree or disagree that they "are a vulgar expression of American materialism"? What do you find appealing or repulsive in game shows?

2. According to Harrington, why are there so many game shows on television?

3. Did so many game shows get on television because the public demanded them? Which came first, the public's interest in such shows or the shows themselves?

4. What are the appeals of the game shows? What do these appeals reveal about the audience that watches these shows?

5. What are the elements of a successful game show?

6. What do you think game shows reveal about American culture?

7. Design a game show that would be new and completely different and appeal to an audience on a different basis than those

currently on television. What is the basis of your show? Why would people want to watch it?

Rhetorical Considerations

1. In the opening paragraph Harrington cites three groups—critics, enthusiasts, broadcasters—who are interested in television game shows. How does this opening paragraph suggest the structure of the entire essay?

2. What is the effect of citing so many of the prizes that contestants win on game shows? What do these details contribute to the argument of the essay?

3. How is the writer's attitude revealed in the essay? Cite specific examples.

4. Some of the shows Harrington cites are no longer on television. Why doesn't this detract from the effectiveness of her argument?

5. Is Barris serious when he describes his game show "Greed" in paragraph 9? How do you know that he is or isn't?

6. Harrington says (in paragraph 9) that the book Barris is writing is ironic. Why is it ironic?

Time Is Power, Money, and Sex

Michael Korda

Michael Korda is a contributor to the New York Times *and has published books dealing with strategies for social mobility.*

1   Time broods heavily over New York, affecting its very essence. My good friend Jonathan Dolger, managing editor of Simon and Schuster, when promoted to a massive and luxurious office in Rockefeller Center, found himself being driven to distraction by the fact that his expansive windows permit him to see the flashing digital clocks of both the I.B.M. and the Newsweek buildings simultaneously. This was not only distracting because the clocks remind him

of the passing time every minute on the minute, but even more so because they don't always agree just exactly what time it really *is*.

2   I was never a time-conscious person until I moved to New York, and even then, in my first months here, I moved with primordial sluggishness, conscious there was a tempo of speed and anxiety around me, but untouched by it. I lounged in the Village and spent my afternoons in bars, and didn't wear a wrist watch, or even own one. Then I got a job, and met a girl, and quite soon became married and ambitious and—beep!—at the tone, standard time was anxiety, and has been ever since. I had become a New Yorker.

3   Even children are programmed early into time-consciousness, at any rate in the executive class, where the school bus schedule is the perfect Skinnerian conditioning for future life as a New Yorker. Only the other day, I found a small, blond moppet weeping under the canopy of my building in the early morning because her school bus was nowhere in sight, and hopelessly moaning, "I shall be late, I shall be late," for all the world like the White Rabbit in *Alice in Wonderland*. My own son's schedule, which includes school, riding lessons, and swimming, is so complex that it resembles the plan for an Army maneuver, and requires concentration, an ability to change clothes quickly, and reckless driving and parking on the part of any number of people. At age eleven, he knows that Second Avenue is Bad News (the city is apparently using large stretches of it to test earthmoving equipment or dig a hole to China), and that it's faster to come up First Avenue than to take the F.D.R. Drive. On the way down to school the other day, his mother (at the wheel of our VW) saw him hunch over in frustration at the sight of a traffic jam north of the Midtown Tunnel and mutter, "Come on, *move* it!" like any taxi-driver or businessman who knows he's going to be late. It's not so much that he wants to get to school, you understand, as the fact that he views time as the enemy, as most New Yorkers do, and has been caught up in our deadly combat with it, spurred on by the car radio's constant announcement of the time signal and by the relayed reports of those godlike helicopter pilots who warn the stranded motorists of disasters it is already too late to avoid ("Overheating cars on the F.D.R., things look real bad down there. . .").

4   Not surprisingly, these children of ours turn into the kind of adult who can be seen glancing furtively at his watch at his own mother's funeral, wondering if there's any way to leave before the end of the service and get back to the office in time to read the four o'clock mail and answer the calls, and who keeps his watch on even while making love.

5   Time is money for people who make an hourly wage, as any-

one can tell who has ever had a painter or a carpenter or an air-conditioner repairman set to work on an hourly basis, and for most of the trades and crafts in New York, work is something to be spread out over as much time as possible. Others, more highly paid, automatically divide their lives into regular segments. Psychoanalysts, for example, see the day as divisible into sessions at so much an hour (or rather 50 minutes, since the patient is always short-changed by ten minutes). Doctors are of course chronically over-scheduled, rising at dawn to be in the hospitals, or, in the case of many pediatricians, setting aside an hour from 7:30 to 8:30 a.m. to receive telephone calls. Time is as real for them as it is for a plumber, but for the power player, time is an element in the game, more symbolic than real. The greatest compliment a busy executive can pay to a visitor is to take off his watch ostentatiously and place it—face down—on the desk. It's a way of saying, "My time belongs to you, for as long as you need me," and time, as we all know, is the ultimate gift. Alternatively, taking off your wrist watch and placing it face *up* on your desk is a way of announcing that you're a busy man and can't spare much time for your visitor's business, that he'd better damn well state his case and get out, because you count your time in minutes.

6   This business of making yourself important by means of time is very easily noticed. One financial adviser I know has a huge digital clock, the kind that is made of shiny green plastic in the shape of a sacred mushroom, in which a transparent window reveals big white leaves with black Bauhaus numbers that click over to signify passing time. It is arranged so that it faces his visitor squarely, thus announcing that his time is more important than yours, and has the same effect on most people as the writing on the wall at Belshazzar's unfortunate feast ("God hath numbered thy kingdom, and finished it"). This somewhat oppressive effect can be reinforced by arranging to have his secretary come in at intervals to announce that he's running behind schedule.

7   Lawyers, who usually charge on the basis of time, have their own ways of establishing their importance. At the lowest level, they have clocks that face toward them, status being set by the kind of clock it is. A round, wedge-topped battery-operated clock that sits flat on the desk and is only visible to the lawyer himself seems to be this year's favorite, though I greatly admired one lawyer who has a complicated Swiss "Atmos" clock in a glass case on his desk with the dial facing him, leaving the client to be mesmerized by the restless swing of the brass pendulum and the endless clicking of the gears and wheels, without, of course, ever being able to see what

time it is. At this stage of power, the lawyer wants to know how long the client has been there, but would just as soon the client didn't know. More important lawyers announce that their time is expensive by having the clock face the client, digital clocks being favored by corporation lawyers and ancient, noisy railroad clocks by the more traditional old-line lawyers. Roy Grutman, a very powerful laywer, favors a beautiful antique English clock, while Murray Ramson, a very energetic lawyer who manages to ride, fence, and practice law successfully, has a ship's clock "with chimes that can really startle people." Some older lawyers have no clocks at all, the implication being that everyone they see is on a retainer basis anyway, and if they're not, there's a secretary outside to keep the log.

8   Just as there are fashions in clocks, there are fashions in watches, which can tell you a good deal about the people who wear them. The West Coast watch power symbol is to have the letters of your name painted on the dial instead of numbers, though this only works when your name has twelve letters, like Ernest Lehman, the producer, unless you can abbreviate your first name, like Irving Mansfield, Jacqueline Susann's protean husband, whose watch reads "Irv Mansfield." This fashion does not seem to have made it to New York, where the status watch is still the old Cartier tank with one of those Cartier hinged gold buckles that are almost invisible except to the connoisseur, who *knows*. On the whole, though, watch wearers are divided into two basic categories: those who like watches that are impossible to read, either having no numbers or four almost invisible dots, and those who like the kind of watches astronauts, pilots, and skindivers wear, with enormous luminous dials and bezel rings that allow you to compute how much air you have left or what G.M.T. is, in case you need to know.

9   One executive I know wears a watch that actually tells the time in London and New York simultaneously at the push of a button, but my own experience is that the less powerful the executive, the more intricate the watch. The lowest power rating goes to those who wear little miniature calendars on their watchbands, thus indicating both that they can't afford an automatic date-adjusting watch and that they need to be reminded what day it is. A complicated watch like a Rolex "Submariner" usually shows the wearer is prey to extreme time anxiety, and thus fairly far down the scale of power. More powerful executives wear watches that hardly even show the time, so thin are the hands and so obscure the marks on the face, and people who are really secure in their power, like Robert Gottlieb, the president of Alfred A. Knopf, rarely wear watches at

all. They rely on the fact that nothing important can happen without them anyway.

10   Styles of wearing wrist watches are pretty limited—after all, we only have two wrists—but I have noticed that a good many men wear their wrist watch on the *inside* of the left wrist, a New York affectation that puzzled me for some time. In my youth it was one of those mysterious British military customs, like a rolled-up handkerchief in one's right coat sleeve, and indicated membership in the professional officer caste. I think officers wore their watches on the inside wrist so that the luminous dial wouldn't be visible to the enemy at night, or possibly so that you could look at the time while keeping the reins of your horse in the left hand (most military affectations are cavalry inspired). None of these reasons seemed to me to apply to modern New Yorkers, who could hardly have been inculcated with the sartorial traditions of Sandhurst and Cranwell, but close observation has shown that this habit has its purpose in the modern world. A man with a watch on the inside of his left wrist can put his arm around a woman and kiss her while looking at his watch, which will then be facing him at about the level of her left ear, invisible to her. This custom can be observed in a great many midtown bars and restaurants at lunchtime, when men are making the difficult decision whether to stay and suggest an afternoon in bed or go back to the office and answer their telephone calls. It is obviously callow to look at one's watch openly; still, at a certain point, say 1:45 P.M., or just about the time one is thinking of ordering coffee, it's necessary to know what time it is and move accordingly. An arm around the shoulder and a kiss will quickly establish whether a proposition is likely to succeed and at the same time, if one's watch is in the correct position, whether one has time to follow through.

11   The people follow the style of their kings. At the Court of Louis XV, the court circular always announced the king's daily activities. Some days it would simply say, "Today His Most Christian Majesty hunted," or "His Majesty met with his Council of State." When neither of these events took place, the court circular bluntly announced, "Today His Majesty did nothing." We have come a long way since then. Our leaders can admit to anything except laziness and unpunctuality. For them, as for us, time is money and power, inflexible in its demands, dubious in its rewards and gratifications, infinitely productive of anxiety.

12   The energy crisis may well put us back on Daylight Saving Time permanently, and I'm not against it, but I am in favor of a more radical innovation. A kind of urban consciousness-raising pro-

gram in which for one day a week, we stop the clocks, agree not to wear watches, unplug the digital desk clocks, and navigate for that day on inner time for a change. Shall we pencil it in for next week?

Vocabulary

luxurious	simultaneously	primordial
moppet	furtively	chronically
ostentatiously	mesmerized	protean
affectation	sartorial	callow
dubious	inculcated	inflexible

Topics for Discussion

1. How conscious of time are you? Do you run your life by the clock? Do you have a regular schedule that you follow? Do you own and wear a wrist watch? Could you go for a day without looking at a clock? For two days? A week?

2. Korda's discussion centers on the importance of time to people who live in New York. Do you think this is a phenomenon peculiar to New York, or do you think concern with time is common to most Americans? Cite specific examples of the concern, or lack of concern, with time shown by people you know in their everyday lives.

3. Do you agree that ours is a society run by the clock? In what way is it true that "time is money"? Could we reconstruct our society so we would not be ruled by the clock? If so, how?

4. How would you classify yourself according to Korda's list of time-conscious people?

5. What does Korda mean when he says that time is power?

Rhetorical Considerations

1. How do paragraphs 1 and 2 serve to introduce the essay? Note particularly the last sentence of paragraph 2.

2. How do the examples in paragraphs 3 to 5 function to make the abstract concept of time concrete for the reader?

3. How would you characterize the tone of this essay? Cite specific devices which contribute to the tone. You might note, for example, the frequent use of quotations and what they contribute to the tone.

4. Paragraphs 11 and 12 not only conclude the essay but restate the essay's main idea. What is that idea? How do these paragraphs not only conclude the essay but continue the development of the main idea?

Business as Usual

Bruno Bettelheim

Bruno Bettelheim (b. 1903) is a psychologist, educator, and author. His works include Truants from Life *(1954),* Love is Not Enough *(1950), and* The Informed Heart *(1960).*

1   A few words about the world's reaction to the concentration camps: The terrors committed in them were experienced as uncanny by most civilized persons. It came as a shock to their pride that supposedly civilized nations could stoop to such inhuman acts. The implication that modern man has such inadequate control over his cruelty was felt as a threat. Three different psychological mechanisms were most frequently used for dealing with the phenomenon of the concentration camp: (a) its applicability to man in general was denied by asserting (contrary to available evidence) that the acts of torture were committed by a small group of insane or perverted persons; (b) the truth of the reports was denied by ascribing them to deliberate propaganda. This method was favored by the German government which called all reports on terror in the camps horror propaganda (*Greuelpropaganda*); (c) the reports were believed, but the knowledge of the terror was repressed as soon as possible.

2   All three mechanisms could be seen at work after liberation. At first, after the "discovery" of the camps, a wave of extreme outrage swept the Allied nations. It was soon followed by a general repression of the discovery. It may be that this reaction of the general public was due to something more than the shock dealt their narcis-

sism by the fact that cruelty is still rampant among men. It may also be that the memory of the tortures was repressed out of some dim realization that the modern state now has available the means for changing personality. To have to accept that one's personality may be changed against one's will is the greatest threat to one's self respect. It must therefore be dealt with by action, or by repression.

3   The universal success of the *Diary of Anne Frank* suggests how much the tendency to deny is still with us, while her story itself demonstrates how such denial can hasten our own destruction. It is an onerous task to take apart such a humane and moving story, arousing so much compassion for gentle Anne Frank. But I believe that its world-wide acclaim cannot be explained unless we recognize our wish to forget the gas chambers and to glorify attitudes of extreme privatization, of continuing to hold on to attitudes as usual even in a holocaust. Exactly because their going on with private life as usual brought destruction did it have to be glorified, in that way we could overlook the essential fact of how destructive it can be under extreme social circumstances.

4   While the Franks were making their preparations for going passively into hiding, thousands of other Jews in Holland and elsewhere in Europe were trying to escape to the free world, the better to survive or to be able to fight their executioners. Others who could not do so went underground—not simply to hide from the SS, waiting passively, without preparation for fight, for the day when they would be caught—but the to fight the Germans, and with it for humanity. All the Franks wanted was to go on with life as nearly as possible in the usual fashion.

5   Little Anne, too, wanted only to go on with life as usual, and nobody can blame her. But hers was certainly not a necessary fate, much less a heroic one; it was a senseless fate. The Franks could have faced the facts and survived; as did many Jews living in Holland. Anne could have had a good chance to survive, as did many Jewish children in Holland. But for that she would have had to be separated from her parents and gone to live with a Dutch family as their own child.

6   Everybody who recognized the obvious knew that the hardest way to go underground was to do it as a family; that to hide as a family made detection by the SS most likely. The Franks, with their excellent connections among gentile Dutch families should have had an easy time hiding out singly, each with a different family. But instead of planning for this, the main principle of their planning was to continue as much as possible with the kind of family life they were accustomed to. Any other course would have meant not merely

giving up the beloved family life, but also accepting as reality man's inhumanity to man. Most of all it would have forced them to accept that going on with life as usual was not an absolute value, but can sometimes be the most destructive of all attitudes.

7   There is little doubt that the Franks, who were able to provide themselves with so much, could have provided themselves with a gun or two had they wished. They could have shot down at least one or two of the "green police" who came for them. There was no surplus of such police. The loss of an SS with every Jew arrested would have noticeably hindered the functioning of the police state. The fate of the Franks wouldn't have been any different, because they all died anyway except for Anne's father, though he hardly meant to pay for his survival with the extermination of his whole family. But they could have sold their lives dearly instead of walking to their death.

8   There is good reason why the so successful play ends with Anne stating her belief in the good in all men. What is denied is the importance of accepting the gas chambers as real so that never again will they exist. If all men are basically good, if going on with intimate family living no matter what else is what is to be most admired, then indeed we can all go on with life as usual and forget about Auschwitz. Except that Anne Frank died because her parents could not get themselves to believe in Auschwitz. And her story found wide acclaim because for us too, it denies implicitly that Auschwitz ever existed. If all men are good, there was never an Auschwitz.

Vocabulary

implication   narcissism   onerous
holocaust

Topics for Discussion

1. How much do you know about the German concentration camps of World War II? Of the three psychological mechanisms for dealing with knowledge of these camps listed by Bettelheim, which do you think you use?

2. Do you agree with Bettelheim that the members of the Frank family contributed to their own destruction by insisting that they stay together? Would you willingly leave your family for six years?

3. Bettelheim says that people want "to hold on to attitudes as usual even in a holocaust." Do you think this is true? Can you cite any examples of human behavior during natural disasters such as floods, tornadoes, and hurricanes that tend to prove or disprove Bettelheim's contention?

4. Bettelheim implies that by denying or repressing the knowledge of the existence of the concentration camps people are making it possible for such camps to exist again. How important do you think it is for all people to confront the fact that the concentration camps existed? Do you think there is a chance such camps could ever again exist? Where?

5. Do you think people believe, as Anne Frank believed, that all men are good? Is there any danger in believing this? What dangers does Bettelheim see in maintaining such a belief?

6. Of the three psychological mechanisms people use for dealing with knowledge of the concentration camps, which one explains the success of the play, *The Diary of Anne Frank?*

7. Does Bettelheim find the play *The Diary of Anne Frank* a positive or a negative influence?

Rhetorical Considerations

1. How closely does Bettelheim follow in the rest of the essay the structure outlined in paragraph 1?

2. How would you characterize the tone in Paragraph 7? Is it any different from the tone of the rest of the essay? Cite specific details in the paragraph which indicate its tone.

3. In what way does the example of Anne Frank fit into the structure of the essay? How does Bettelheim's use of this example illustrate his main idea as stated in paragraph 1?

4. Bettelheim uses adjectives such as "gentle" and "little" when he talks about Anne Frank. What effect does this create? How does it support his thesis?

The New Barbarism

Günter Grass

*Günter Grass (b. 1927) is a West German writer. His works in-
clude* The Tin Drum, Cat and Mouse, *and* Dog Years.

1   Unlike our limited knowledge of the extermination camps during the Nazi period, today we know everything. The daily news
reports inform us immediately how many are starving where. The
rough estimates lend themselves to simple addition at the end of the
year. Television has made misery photogenic. Science, on the other
hand, is served by impeccable statistics. We know in which countries a particular vitamin is lacking. Every schoolchild can talk
intelligently about the global protein deficiency. The subject is as
much a part of the curriculum as the theory of relativity. It starts
early. Think of the terrible European practice of inspiring listless
children to eat their soup by reminding them of the starving children
in India and elsewhere.

2   Hunger somewhere else has thus become a part of our daily
lives. No one can again say, "I didn't know what was going on."
This is hunger, caused not by floods or natural disasters but by the
hand of man; or put bluntly, by the hand of man stayed. Nothing can
absolve us. We try to rationalize the growing misery by cynically
hoping for the survival of the fittest. Entire peoples and nations are
written off as conceptual failures, a pattern which by comparison
makes Orwell's *1984* appear a paradise.

3   I am an author by profession. I attempt to capture a passing
moment so that that which is past is not forgotten. At present I am
writing a book that reaches back into the Middle Ages and beyond to
describe eating, cooking, and starving people. The story of food and
nourishment must be continued. Past hunger must be described. Yet
the future has already overtaken us and past barbarism returns as a
mirror image. We set out to look back and instead come face to face
with the future. Progress, it appears, lies behind us.

4   I recently visited India as a guest and talked to its people about
their problems. To a European, India is no longer the romantic
country it once may have been, mysterious and inscrutable, no
longer a tourist's goal. We know about the exploding population.
Are there 570 or 600 million? We hear about hunger in Bihar and
other states. Rough estimates give us a variety of figures. Among us

242

are our own young people wrapped up in the cult of Hare Krishna and the concept of Nirvana. There are picturebooks which describe India's cultural heritage. Newspapers, busy with scandals within Germany, make short shrift of political corruption in India.

5   All of this is somewhat out of focus and through it we tend to say: Only Mao can help in a case like this. The Chinese have done it. We at home are well fed and have no desire to feel sated with a guilty conscience. Help? Well, we'd like to. But how? India? That's a bottomless pit, a drop of water on a hot stone.

6   Is the Indian misery, I ask myself and you, beyond help because of fate or Karma? Or is the Indian misery, like so much other misery in the world, attributable to class and caste structures, faulty economic planning and corruption? If so there is hope for a solution, for it is misery caused by the hand of man.

Vocabulary

photogenic	impeccable	protein
curriculum	cynically	inscrutable
caste		

Topics for Discussion

1. In what sense has poverty become photogenic? How would you characterize people who enjoy taking photographs of the poor and hungry? Would you enjoy looking at such photographs? Does the photographer's intention make a difference?

2. Is there any just reason for talking about human beings as statistics? Or is such discussion inherently dehumanizing?

3. Explain Grass's notion about the past and the present as he outlines it in paragraph 3. Do you agree?

4. Are there social remedies to the problem of hunger and poverty? What does Grass suggest in paragraph 5?

5. Read the essay entitled "On Enjoying Food while Millions Starve" by Waverly Root. What might Root say in response to Grass?

6. Do you think that people still generally recall the Nazi concentration camps with horror? What do you think a person's attitude about those camps says about him or her?

Rhetorical Considerations

1. What is Grass trying to persuade us about? Paragraph 6 is not at all specific in its conclusions. What are some of the implied conclusions?

2. Is the order of exposition inductive or deductive? What is the central idea of the essay? Is this idea ever directly stated?

3. What purpose does the allusion to concentration camps serve? How does this allusion prepare the reader to accept the central idea of paragraph 2?

4. Why is the use of words like *I, we, our, myself* appropriate to the subject matter of the essay? Would the essay be more persuasive, or less so, if it were written in the third person?

On Enjoying Food
While Millions Starve

Waverly Root

Waverly Root (b. 1903), an Officer of the Legion of Honor of France, is the author of several books in diverse fields. These include The Truth about Wagner *(1929),* The Secret History of the War *(1945-46),* Contemporary French Cooking *(1962),* The Cooking of Italy *(1968), and* Paris Dining Guide *(1969).*

1   Last winter I contributed to this magazine an article, "Taste is falling! Taste is falling!" A dissenting opinion was published shortly afterward in the Letters columns. The writer did not dispute the fact that taste *is* falling; he maintained simply, if I read him aright, that it is immoral to object to this fact.

2   "With a worldwide food shortage," the letter read, "one can scarcely give thought to diverting additional grains and proteins to make meat more flavorful. To cater to the taste of an élite while millions waste away would be absurd, if not criminal."

3   This American attitude toward food has been formed by . . . our Puritanism. The Puritan nourishes himself (grudgingly), for God has so organized the universe that he must. Possibly he suspects that

the chore of eating was imposed on him as a penance for his disgraceful *gourmandise* in connection with an apple. "Because thou hast . . . eaten of the tree, of which I commanded thee, saying, Thou shalt not eat of it," reads Genesis, iii, 17, "cursed is the ground for thy sake; in sorrow shalt thou eat of it all the days of thy life." Obviously man was not intended to enjoy eating, and the Puritan obediently disapproves of taking pleasure in food. He eats to maintain strength in order to get on with the serious business of earning his bread by the sweat of his brow, the only permissible seasoning; to take pains to make his food tasty would be abandonment to sensual self-indulgence, to gluttony—a deadly sin. Wasting time and attention on the preparation and serving of food, and above all dawdling in euphoric leisure over one's meals, conduces to another mortal sin, sloth.

4   Eve, who, we have it on scriptural authority, was guiltier than Adam in this matter, has remained consistently incorrigible. When she has the neighbors in for dinner, she offers them the best she can provide, thus surrendering to a third deadly sin, pride. The Puritan, accordingly, distrusts food, an insidious tempter, leading the weak down the primrose path to eternal damnation. Obviously only tempting food can do this. Therefore, a proper concern for our salvation demands that we avoid tastiness. Bad food is good food— or at least, virtuous food. Fortunately, the Puritan has a potent ally in the American restaurant operator, a Puritan, too, as we know by his works, and a good Christian, for he does his best to lead us not into temptation.

5   A large part of the American public has been brainwashed by the Puritan, who holds gastronomy in horror, and the he-man, who holds it in contempt. Conditioned for generations by such thinking, a considerable number of Americans simply do not like to eat and are suspicious of those who do. They have become so many preprogramed, scorn-powered missiles, ready to spring toward their destined target, the gourmet, whenever the subject of food comes up.

6   To the Puritan who would advise cooks to forsake the search for tastiness and concentrate on nourishment, it can be answered that the two are one. Tastier food is more nourishing food; tastier food is healthier food. We all remember that lesson in elementary physiology which demonstrated that the stomach refuses to perform its functions when its possessor is angry or otherwise emotionally disturbed. The lesson usually stops there, but it would be underestimating the stomach's subtlety to assume it is incapable of responding to positive as well as to negative stimuli. Or that it requires emotions as gross or violent as anger to induce it to react. When we

are confronted with tasty food, our digestive processes are titillated into taking the first step to convert it to our uses—salivation. Popular wisdom has recognized this by dubbing tasty food "mouth-watering." Saliva is only the first of several secretions that promote digestion. The various gastric juices which take over from the saliva are stimulated in particular by such foods as herbs and spices—the seasoners.

7   Taste, after all, is the sense which enables us to recognize foods that are good for us, the ones whose content in proteins, vitamins, mineral salts and other elements are necessary for health. All our senses require education to function efficiently; but we have been dissuaded from educating the sense of taste, remaining to a large extent a nation gastronomically illiterate because of the Puritan distrust of food, especially tasty food.

8   Puritanism has been eroding our eating habits for three and a half centuries now, and we will not easily be rid of its ravages. "Food preferences, like languages, are obstinate cultural traits," Naomi Bliven wrote recently; and nearly half a century earlier the famous chef, Auguste Escoffier, had told us that "the culinary art depends on the psychological state of a society. It follows naturally, unable to free itself of them, the impulses it receives from that psychology." A few sentences later in the same passage he added another observation which seems to fit our society:

> Wherever life and its cares preoccupy the mind of man, he will not be able to give good cheer more than a limited place. Usually the need to nourish themselves appears to those caught up in the whirlpool of business not as a pleasure, but as a burden. They look upon the time passed at the table as time lost, and demand only one thing: not to have to wait to be served."

And yet Escoffier died before the era of fast foods.

9   One idea that never entered Escoffier's head was that there was anything reprehensible about providing or enjoying good cheer. He would have reproached nobody for listening to the Ninth Symphony while some cities were without concert halls, nor for appreciating the Blue Period while some cities were without art museums, nor for reading "War and Peace" while some cities were without libraries. Would he have suspected, in fact, that the person who criticized some people for enjoying Beethoven, Picasso or Tolstoy because other people can't was really objecting to anybody enjoying himself at all?

10   It is not so long ago that we still had Puritans among us who held that any music more intricate than hymns, any paintings above

the level of religious-art chromos, any literature except the Bible and collections of sermons, was superfluous, sensual and sinful. They have given up so far as the major arts are concerned (though there are still countries where any art that does not serve the current political philosophy risks being branded antisocial if not criminal). It has been conceded that it is permissible, even praiseworthy, to appreciate music, art and literature.

11　　But gastronomy is still suspect. I assume that one day it will be admitted to the list of honored activities, for the desire to give us good cooking instead of bad stems from one of man's most admirable traits; his tendency to add an esthetic element to anything he undertakes.

12　　As for the ill-fed, from whom may they expect the most sympathy—from those who like to eat or from those who don't?

Vocabulary

dissenting	Puritan	cater
élite	gluttony	dawdling
euphoric	conduces	sloth
incorrigible	gastronomy	gourmet
physiology	salivation	secretions
gastric	dissuaded	chromos
superfluous	esthetic	

Topics for Discussion

1. Do you accept the analogy in paragraph 9 between food and art? What major criticism might be made of this analogy?

2. Do you think that Puritanism is still a major force in American life? If so, to what extent do Puritan attitudes influence matters other than the consumption of food? What is your definition of Puritanism?

3. What factors in American life other than Puritanism influence the way people eat?

4. Do you agree or disagree with Root that Americans take a negative attitude, collectively, toward good food? If you do agree, do you think this attitude has anything in common with anti-intellectualism?

5. Do you think that perhaps both Root and his antagonist, whom he mentions in paragraphs 1 and 2, miss some of the major reasons for starvation in the world? What might some of these reasons be?

6. What kinds of food do you like? Do your parents like similar or different foods? Account for the similarities or differences.

7. Read the selection in this book by Günter Grass. How might Grass respond to Root?

8. If you disagree with Root's central thesis and own a pet, what do you think of the morality of feeding your pet while millions starve?

Rhetorical Considerations

1. Note Root's use of the word "obviously" in paragraph 3. What kind of tone is conveyed by this word? How does Root manipulate this tone to advantage in other parts of the essay?

2. Does Root ever explicitly respond to the argumentative challenge of paragraph 2? Does Root skillfully sidestep some serious issues?

3. Where does Root use allusion in this essay? What different kinds of allusions does he employ?

4. Are Root's common-sense biological arguments (paragraphs 6 and 7) very effective? How might such arguments be refuted?

5. Evaluate the final sentence of the essay. Is Root insensitive?

A Modest Proposal

Jonathan Swift

Jonathan Swift (1667-1745) was an Anglo-Irish writer known principally for his use of satire. His works include Gulliver's Travels *(1726) and* A Tale of a Tub *and* The Battle of the Books, *both published in 1704.*

1   It is a melancholy object to those who walk through this great town, or travel in the country, when they see the streets, the roads, and cabin-doors crowded with beggars of the female sex, followed by three, four, or six children, *all in rags,* and importuning every passenger for an alms. These mothers, instead of being able to work for their honest livelihood, are forced to employ all their time in strolling, to beg sustenance for their helpless infants, who, as they grow up, either turn thieves for want of work, or leave their dear Native Country to fight for the Pretender in Spain, or sell themselves to the Barbadoes.

2   I think it is agreed by all parties that this prodigious number of children, in the arms, or on the backs, or at the heels of their mothers, and frequently of their fathers, is in the present deplorable state of the kingdom a very great additional grievance; and therefore whoever could find out a fair, cheap, and easy method of making these children sound useful members of the common-wealth would deserve so well of the public as to have his statue set up for a preserver of the nation.

3   But my intention is very far from being confined to provide only for the children of professed beggars; it is of a much greater extent, and shall take in the whole number of infants at a certain age who are born of parents in effect as little able to support them as those who demand our charity in the streets.

4   As to my own part, having turned my thoughts, for many years, upon this important subject, and maturely weighed the several schemes of other projectors, I have always found them grossly mistaken in their computation. It is true a child, just dropped from its dam, may be supported by her milk for a solar year with little other nourishment, at most not above the value of two shillings, which the mother may certainly get, or the value in scraps, by her lawful occupation of begging, and it is exactly at one year old that I propose to provide for them, in such a manner as, instead of being a

charge upon their parents, or the parish, or wanting food and raiment for the rest of their lives, they shall, on the contrary, contribute to the feeding and partly to the clothing of many thousands.

5   There is likewise another great advantage in my scheme, that it will prevent those voluntary abortions, and that horrid practice of women murdering their bastard children, alas, too frequent among us, sacrificing the poor innocent babes, I doubt, more to avoid the expense than the shame, which would move tears and pity in the most savage and inhuman breast.

6   The number of souls in this kingdom being usually reckoned one million and a half, of these I calculate there may be about two hundred thousand couple whose wives are breeders, from which number I subtract thirty thousand couple who are able to maintain their own children, although I apprehend there cannot be so many under the present distresses of the kingdom, but this being granted, there will remain an hundred and seventy thousand breeders. I again subtract fifty thousand for those women who miscarry, or whose children die by accident or disease within the year. There only remain an hundred and twenty thousand children of poor parents annually born: The question therefore is, how this number shall be reared, and provided for, which, as I have already said, under the present situation of affairs, is utterly impossible by all the methods hitherto proposed, for we can neither employ them in handicraft, or agriculture, we neither build houses (I mean in the country), nor cultivate land: they can very seldom pick up a livelihood by stealing till they arrive at six years old, except where they are of towardly parts, although I confess they learn the rudiments much earlier, during which time they can however be properly looked upon only as *probationers*, as I have been informed by a principal gentleman in the County of Cavan, who protested to me that he never knew above one or two instances under the age of six, even in a part of the kingdom so renowned for the quickest proficiency in that art.

7   I am assured by our merchants that a boy or a girl, before twelve years old, is no saleable commodity, and even when they come to this age, they will not yield above three pounds, or three pounds and half-a-crown at most on the Exchange, which cannot turn to account either to the parents or the kingdom, the charge of nutriment and rags having been at least four times that value.

8   I shall now therefore humbly propose my own thoughts, which I hope will not be liable to the least objection.

9   I have been assured by a very knowing American of my acquaintance in London, that a young healthy child well nursed is at a year old a most delicious, nourishing, and wholesome food, whether

stewed, roasted, baked, or boiled, and I make no doubt that it will equally serve in a fricassee, or a ragout.

10   I do therefore humbly offer it to public consideration, that of the hundred and twenty thousand children already computed, twenty thousand may be reserved for breed, whereof only one fourth part to be males, which is more than we allow to sheep, black-cattle, or swine, and my reason is that these children are seldom the fruits of marriage, a circumstance not much regarded by our savage, therefore one male will be sufficient to serve four females. That the remaining hundred thousand may at a year old be offered in sale to the persons of quality, and fortune, through the kingdom, always advising the mother to let them suck plentifully in the last month, so as to render them plump, and fat for a good table. A child will make two dishes at an entertainment for friends, and when the family dines alone, the fore or hind quarters will make a reasonable dish, and seasoned with a little pepper or salt will be very good boiled on the fourth day, especially in winter.

11   I have reckoned upon a medium, that a child just born will weigh 12 pounds, and in a solar year if tolerably nursed increaseth to 28 pounds.

12   I grant this food will be somewhat dear, and therefore very proper for landlords, who, as they have already devoured most of the parents, seem to have the best title to the children.

13   Infant's flesh will be in season throughout the year, but more plentiful in March, and a little before and after, for we are told by a grave author, an eminent French physician, that fish being a prolific diet, there are more children born in Roman Catholic countries about nine months after Lent than at any other season; therefore reckoning a year after Lent, the markets will be more glutted than usual, because the number of Popish infants is at least three to one in this kingdom, and therefore it will have one other collateral advantage by lessening the number of Papists among us.

14   I have already computed the charge of nursing a beggar's child (in which list I reckon all cottagers, labourers, and four-fifths of the farmers) to be about two shillings *per annum,* rags included, and I believe no gentleman would repine to give ten shillings for the carcass of a good fat child, which, as I have said, will make four dishes of excellent nutritive meat, when he hath only some particular friend or his own family to dine with him. Thus the Squire will learn to be a good landlord, and grow popular among his tenants, the mother will have eight shillings net profit, and be fit for work till she produces another child.

15   Those who are more thrifty (as I must confess the times

require) may flay the carcass; the skin of which, artificially dressed, will make admirable gloves for ladies, and summer boots for fine gentlemen.

16   As to our City of Dublin, shambles may be appointed for this purpose, in the most convenient parts of it, and butchers we may be assured will not be wanting, although I rather recommend buying the children alive, and dressing them hot from the knife, as we do roasting pigs.

17   A very worth person, a true lover of this country, and whose virtues I highly esteem, was lately pleased, in discoursing on this matter, to offer a refinement upon my scheme. He said that many gentlemen of this kingdom, having of late destroyed their deer, he conceived that the want of venison might be well supplied by the bodies of young lads and maidens, not exceeding fourteen years of age, nor under twelve, so great a number of both sexes in every country being now ready to starve, for want of work and service: and these to be disposed of by their parents if alive, or otherwise by their nearest relations. But with due deference to so excellent a friend, and so deserving a patriot, I cannot be altogether in his sentiments; for as to the males, my American acquaintance assured me from frequent experience that their flesh was generally tough and lean, like that of our schoolboys, by continual exercise, and their taste disagreeable, and to fatten them would not answer the charge. Then as to the females, it would, I think with humble submission, be a loss to the public, because they soon would become breeders themselves: And besides, it is not improbable that some scrupulous people might be apt to censure such a practice (although indeed very unjustly) as a little bordering upon cruelty, which, I confess, hath always been with me the strongest objection against any project, however so well intended.

18   But in order to justify my friend, he confessed that this expedient was put into his head by the famous Psalmanazer, a native of the island Formosa, who came from thence to London, above twenty years ago, and in conversation told my friend that in his country when any young person happened to be put to death, the executioner sold the carcass to persons of quality, as a prime dainty, and that, in his time, the body of a plump girl of fifteen, who was crucified for an attempt to poison the emperor, was sold to his Imperial Majesty's Prime Minister of State, and other great Mandarins of the Court, in joints from the gibbet, at four hundred crowns. Neither indeed can I deny that if the same use were made of several plump girls in this town, who, without one single groat to their fortunes, cannot stir abroad without a chair, and appear at the

playhouse, and assemblies in foreign fineries, which they never will pay for, the kingdom would not be the worse.

19   Some persons of a desponding spirit are in great concern about that vast number of poor people, who are aged, diseased, or maimed, and I have been desired to employ my thoughts what course may be taken to ease the nation of so grievous an encumbrance. But I am not in the least pain upon that matter, because it is very well known that they are every day dying, and rotting, by cold, and famine, and filth, and vermin, as fast as can be reasonably expected. And as to the younger labourers they are now in almost as hopeful a condition. They cannot get work, and consequently pine away for want of nourishment, to a degree, that if at any time they are accidentally hired to common labour, they have not strength to perform it; and thus the country and themselves are happily delivered from the evils to come.

20   I have too long digressed, and therefore shall return to my subject. I think the advantages by the proposal which I have made are obvious and many, as well as of the highest importance.

21   For first, as I have already observed, it would greatly lessen the number of Papists, with whom we are yearly over-run, being the principal breeders of the nation, as well as our most dangerous enemies, and who stay at home on purpose with a design to deliver the kingdom to the Pretender, hoping to take their advantage by the absence of so many good Protestants, who have chosen rather to leave their country than stay at home, and pay tithes against their conscience to an Episcopal curate.

22   Secondly, the poorer tenants will have something valuable of their own, which by law be made liable to distress, and help to pay their landlord's rent, their corn and cattle being already seized and *money a thing unknown*.

23   Thirdly, Whereas the maintenance of an hundred thousand children, from two years old, and upwards, cannot be computed at less than ten shillings a piece *per annum*, the nation's stock will be thereby increased fifty thousand pounds *per annum*, besides the profit of a new dish, introduced to the tables of all gentlemen of fortune in the kingdom, who have any refinement in taste, and the money will circulate among ourselves, the goods being entirely of our own growth and manufacture.

24   Fourthly, The constant breeders, besides the gain of eight shillings sterling *per annum*, by the sale of their children, will be rid of the charge of maintaining them after the first year.

25   Fifthly, This food would likewise bring great custom to taverns, where the vintners will certainly be so prudent as to pro-

cure the best receipts for dressing it up to perfection, and consequently have their houses frequented by all the fine gentlemen, who justly value themselves upon their knowledge in good eating; and a skillful cook, who understands how to oblige his guests, will contrive to make it as expensive as they please.

26   Sixthly, This would be a great inducement to marriage, which all wise nations have either encouraged by rewards, or enforced by laws and penalties. It would increase the care and tenderness of mothers toward their children, when they were sure of a settlement for life, to the poor babes, provided in some sort by the public to their annual profit instead of expense. We should see an honest emulation among the married women, which of them could bring the fattest child to the market, men would become as fond of their wives, during the time of their pregnancy, as they are now of their mares in foal, their cows in calf, or sows when they are ready to farrow, nor offer to beat or kick them (as it is too frequent a practice) for fear of a miscarriage.

27   Many other advantages might be enumerated: For instance, the addition of some thousand carcasses in our exportation of barrelled beef; the propagation of swine's flesh, and improvement in the art of making good bacon, so much wanted among us by the great destruction of pigs, too frequent at our tables, which are no way comparable in taste or magnificence to a well-grown, fat yearling child, which roasted whole will make a considerable figure at a Lord Mayor's feast, or any other public entertainment. But this and many others I omit, being studious of brevity.

28   Supposing that one thousand families in this city would be constant customers for infants' flesh, besides others who might have it at merry-meetings, particularly weddings and christenings, I compute that Dublin would take off annually about twenty thousand carcasses, and the rest of the kingdom (where probably they will be sold somewhat cheaper) the remaining eighty thousand.

29   I can think of no one objection that will possibly be raised against this proposal, unless it should be urged that the number of people will be thereby much lessened in the kingdom. This I freely own, and it was indeed one principal design in offering it to the world. I desire the reader will observe, that I calculate my remedy for this one individual *Kingdom of Ireland, and for no other that ever was, is, or, I think, ever can be upon earth. Therefore let no man talk to me of other expedients: Of taxing our absentees at five shillings a pound: Of using neither clothes, nor household furniture, except what is of our own growth and manufacture: Of utterly rejecting the materials and instruments that promote foreign luxury:*

Of curing the expensiveness of pride, vanity, idleness, and gaming in our women: Of introducing a vein of parsimony, prudence, and temperance: Of learning to love our Country, wherein we differ even from LAPLANDERS, *and the inhabitants of* TOPINAMBOO: *Of quitting our animosities and factions, nor act any longer like the Jews, who were murdering one another at the very moment their city was taken: Of being a little cautious not to sell our country and consciences for nothing: Of teaching landlords to have at least one degree of mercy toward their tenants. Lastly, of putting a spirit of honesty, industry, and skill into our shopkeepers, who, if a resolution could now be taken to buy only our native goods, would immediately unite to cheat and exact upon us in the price, the measure, and the goodness, nor could ever yet be brought to make one fair proposal of just dealing, though often and earnestly invited to it.*

30   Therefore I repeat, let no man talk to me of these and the like expedients, till he hath at least some glimpse of hope that there will ever be some hearty and sincere attempt to put them in practice.

31   But as to myself, having been wearied out for many years with offering vain, idle, visionary thoughts, and at length utterly despairing of success, I fortunately fell upon this proposal, which as it is wholly new, so it hath something solid and real, of no expense and little trouble, full in our own power, and whereby we can incur no danger in *disobliging* ENGLAND. For this kind of commodity will not bear exportation, the flesh being too tender a consistence to admit a long continuance in salt, *although perhaps I could name a country which would be glad to eat up our whole nation without it.*

32   After all I am not so violently bent upon my own opinion as to reject any offer, proposed by wise men, which shall be found equally innocent, cheap, easy, and effectual. But before something of that kind shall be advanced in contradiction to my scheme, and offering a better, I desire the author, or authors, will be pleased maturely to consider two points. First, as things now stand, how they will be able to find food and raiment for an hundred thousand useless mouths and backs. And secondly, there being a round million of creatures in human figure, throughout this kingdom, whose whole subsistence put into a common stock would leave them in debt two millions of pounds sterling; adding those, who are beggars by profession, to the bulk of farmers, cottagers, and labourers with their wives and children, who are beggars in effect. I desire those politicians, who dislike my overture, and may perhaps be so bold as to attempt an answer, that they will first ask the parents of these mortals whether they would not at this day think it a great happiness to have been sold for food at a year old, in the manner I prescribe,

and thereby have avoided such a perpetual scene of misfortunes as they have since gone through, by the oppression of landlords, the impossibility of paying rent without money or trade, the want of common sustenance, with neither house nor clothes to cover them from the inclemencies of the weather, and the most inevitable prospect of entailing the like, or greater miseries upon their breed for ever.

33   I profess in the sincerity of my heart that I have not the least personal interest in endeavoring to promote this necessary work, having no other motive than the *public good of my country, by advancing our trade, providing for infants, relieving the poor, and giving some pleasure to the rich.* I have no children by which I can propose to get a single penny; the youngest being nine years old, and my wife past childbearing.

Vocabulary

melancholy	importuning	sustenance
prodigious	dam	bastard
towardly	rudiments	probationers
proficiency	fricassee	eminent
prolific	Popish	collateral
cottagers	venison	sentiments
expedient	dainty	Mandarins
gibbet	groat	desponding
grievous	encumbrance	vermin
vintners	inducement	miscarriage
studious	parsimony	temperance
factions	visionary	

Topics for Discussion

1. What is Swift actually proposing? How serious is he about his proposal?

2. Does Swift suggest any other possible solutions to the problem of poverty in Ireland? What is his opinion of these other solutions?

3. What does Swift suggest can be done with the aged, diseased, or maimed poor?

4. Who are the Papists Swift refers to? Why does he mention them so often?

5. What does Swift say are some of the advantages of his proposal?

6. How carefully has Swift presented his argument? Can you find any flaws in his reasoning?

7. This essay was first published in 1729. Do you think it is relevant today?

Rhetorical Considerations

1. What is the tone of this essay? How is it achieved? Is the tone appropriate to the subject matter of the essay?

2. Where does Swift state his thesis? Why does he wait so long before stating it?

3. What effect does Swift's last paragraph achieve?

4. Swift's essay is a famous satire. What are some of the elements of satire?

5. What effect does Swift achieve by citing so many facts and figures?

"Repent, Harlequin!" Said the Ticktockman

Harlan Ellison

Harlan Ellison (b. 1934) is mainly known for his science fiction short stories and novels. These include Perhaps Impossible *(1967) and* Love Ain't Nothing but Sex Misspelled *(1968). The following short story received the Hugo Award for the best science fiction short story of 1965.*

1   There are always those who ask, what is it all about? For those who need to ask, for those who need points sharply made, who need to know "where it's at," this:

"The mass of men serve the state thus, not as men mainly, but as machines, with their bodies. They are the standing army, and the militia, jailors, constables, posse comitatus, etc. In most cases there is no free exercise whatever of the judgment or of the moral sense; but they put themselves on a level with wood and earth and stones; and wooden men can perhaps be manufactured that will serve the purpose as well. Such command no more respect than men of straw or a lump of dirt. They have the same sort of worth only as horses and dogs. Yet such as these even are commonly esteemed good citizens. Others—as most legislators, politicians, lawyers, ministers, and office-holders— serve the state chiefly with their heads; and as they rarely make any moral distinctions, they are as likely to serve the Devil, without intending it, as God. A very few, as heroes, patriots, martyrs, reform- ers in the great sense, and *men,* serve the state with their consciences also, and so necessarily resist it for the most part; and they are commonly treated as enemies by it."

Henry David Thoreau
Civil Disobedience

2   That is the heart of it. Now begin in the middle, and later learn the beginning; the end will take care of itself.

3   But because it was the very world it was, the very world they had allowed it to *become,* for months his activities did not come to the alarmed attention of The Ones Who Kept The Machine Functioning Smoothly, the ones who poured the very best butter over the cams and mainsprings of the culture. Not until it had become obvious that somehow, someway, he had become a notori- ety, a celebrity, perhaps even a hero for (what Officialdom inescap- ably tagged) "an emotionally disturbed segment of the populace," did they turn it over to the Ticktockman and his legal machinery. But by then, because it was the very world it was, and they had no way to predict he would happen—possibly a strain of disease long- defunct, now, suddenly, reborn in a system where immunity had been forgotten, had lapsed—he had been allowed to become too real. Now he had form and substance.

4   He had become a *personality,* something they had filtered out of the system many decades before. But there it was, and there *he* was, a very definitely imposing personality. In certain circles— middle-class circles—it was thought disgusting. Vulgar ostentation. Anarchistic. Shameful. In others, there was only sniggering: those strata where thought is subjugated to form and ritual, niceties, proprieties. But down below, ah, down below, where the people always needed their saints and sinners, their bread and circuses, their heroes and villains, he was considered a Bolivar; a Napoleon; a Robin Hood; a Dick Bong (Ace of Aces); a Jesus; a Jomo Kenyatta.

5   And at the top—where, like socially-attuned Shipwreck Kel-
lys, every tremor and vibration threatens to dislodge the wealthy,
powerful, and titled from their flagpoles—he was considered a
menace; a heretic; a rebel; a disgrace; a peril. He was known down
the line, to the very heartmeat core, but the important reactions
were high above and far below. At the very top, at the very bottom.

6   So his file was turned over, along with his time-card and his
cardioplate, to the office of the Ticktockman.

7   The Ticktockman: very much over six feet tall, often silent, a
soft purring man when things went timewise. The Ticktockman.

8   Even in the cubicles of the hierarchy, where fear was generated, seldom suffered, he was called the Ticktockman. But no one
called him that to his mask.

9   You don't call a man a hated name, not when that man, behind
his mask, is capable of revoking the minutes, the hours, the days and
nights, the years of your life. He was called the Master Timekeeper
to his mask. It was safer that way.

10   "This is *what* he is," said the Ticktockman with genuine
softness, "but not *who* he is? This time-card I'm holding in my left
hand has a name on it, but it is the name of *what* he is, not *who* he is.
This cardioplate here in my right hand is also named, but not whom
named, merely what named. Before I can exercise proper revocation, I have to know who this what is."

11   To his staff, all the ferrets, all the loggers, all the finks, all the
commex, even the mineez, he said. "Who is this Harlequin?"

12   He was not purring smoothly. Timewise, it was jangle.

13   However, it *was* the longest single speech they had ever heard
him utter at one time, the staff, the ferrets, the loggers, the finks, the
commex, but not the mineez, who usually weren't around to know,
in any case. But even they scurried to find out.

14   Who is the Harlequin?

15   High above the third level of the city, he crouched on the
humming aluminum-frame platform of the air-boat (foof! air-boat,
indeed! swizzleskid is what is was, with a tow-rack jerryrigged) and
stared down at the neat Mondrian arrangement of the buildings.

16   Somewhere nearby, he could hear the metronomic left-right-
left of the 2:47 P.M. shift, entering the Timkin roller-bearing plant in
their sneakers. A minute later, precisely, he heard the softer right-
left-right of the 5:00 A.M. formation, going home.

17   An elfin grin spread across his tanned features, and his dimples
appeared for a moment. Then, scratching at his thatch of auburn
hair, he shrugged within his motley, as though girding himself for
what came next, and threw the joystick forward, and bent into the
wind as the air-boat dropped. He skimmed over a slidewalk, pur-

posely dropping a few feet to crease the tassels of the ladies of fashion, and—inserting thumbs in large ears—he stuck out his tongue, rolled his eyes, and went wugga-wugga-wugga. It was a minor diversion. One pedestrian skittered and tumbled, sending parcels everywhichway, another wet herself, a third keeled slantwise and the walk was stopped automatically by the servitors till she could be resuscitated. It was a minor diversion.

18   Then he swirled away on a vagrant breeze, and was gone. Hi-ho.

19   As he rounded the cornice of the Time-Motion Study Building, he saw the shift, just boarding the slidewalk. With practiced motion and an absolute conservation of movement, they sidestepped up onto the slowstrip and (in a chorus line reminiscent of a Busby Berkeley film of the antediluvian 1930s) advanced across the strips ostrich-walking till they were lined up on the expresstrip.

20   Once more, in anticipation, the elfin grin spread, and there was a tooth missing back there on the left side. He dipped, skimmed, and swooped over them; and then, scrunching about on the air-boat, he released the holding pins that fastened shut the ends of the home-made pouring troughs that kept his cargo from dumping prematurely. And as he pulled the trough-pins, the air-boat slid over the factory workers and one hundred and fifty thousand dollars' worth of jelly beans cascaded down on the expresstrip.

21   Jelly beans! Millions and billions of purples and yellows and greens and licorice and grape and raspberry and mint and round and smooth and crunchy outside and soft-mealy inside and sugary and bouncing jouncing tumbling clittering clattering skittering fell on the heads and shoulders and hardhats and carapaces of the Timkin workers, tinkling on the slidewalk and bouncing away and rolling about underfoot and filling the sky on their way down with all the colors of joy and childhood and holidays, coming down in a steady rain, a solid wash, a torrent of color and sweetness out of the sky from above, and entering a universe of sanity and metronomic order with quite-mad coocoo newness. Jelly beans!

22   The shift workers howled and laughed and were pelted, and broke ranks, and the jelly beans managed to work their way into the mechanism of the slidewalks after which there was a hideous scraping as the sound of a million fingernails rasped down a quarter of a million blackboards, followed by a coughing and a sputtering, and then the slidewalks all stopped and everyone was dumped thisawayandthataway in a jackstraw tumble, and still laughing and popping little jelly bean eggs of childish color into their mouths. It was a holiday, and a jollity, an absolute insanity, a giggle. But. . . .

23   The shift was delayed seven minutes.

24   They did not get home for seven minutes.

25   The master schedule was thrown off by seven minutes.

26   Quotas were delayed by inoperative slidewalks for seven minutes.

27   He had tapped the first domino in the line, and one after another, like chik chik chik, the others had fallen.

28   The System had been seven minutes worth of disrupted. It was a tiny matter, one hardly worthy of note, but in a society where the single driving force was order and unity and promptness and clocklike precision and attention to the clock, reverence of the gods of the passage of time, it was a disaster of major importance.

29   So he was ordered to appear before the Ticktockman. It was broadcast across every channel of the communications web. He was ordered to be *there* at 7:00 dammit on time. And they waited, and they waited, but he didn't show up till almost ten-thirty, at which time he merely sang a little song about moonlight in a place no one had ever heard of, called Vermont, and vanished again. But they had all been waiting since seven, and it wrecked *hell* with their schedules. So the question remained: Who is the Harlequin?

30   But the *unasked* question (more important of the two) was: how did we get *into* this position, where a laughing, irresponsible japer of jabberwocky and jive could disrupt our entire economic and cultural life with a hundred and fifty thousand dollars' worth of jelly beans. . . .

31   *Jelly* for God's sake beans! This is madness! Where did he get the money to buy a hundred and fifty thousand dollars' worth of jelly beans? (They knew it would have cost that much, because they had a team of Situation Analysts pulled off another assignment, and rushed to the slidewalk scene to sweep up and count the candies, and produce findings, which disrupted *their* schedules and threw their entire branch at least a day behind.) Jelly beans! Jelly . . . *beans*? Now wait a second—a second accounted for—no one has manufactured jelly beans for over a hundred years. Where did he get jelly beans?

32   That's another good question. More than likely it will never be answered to your complete satisfaction. But then, how many questions ever are?

33   The middle you know. Here is the beginning. How it starts:

34   A desk pad. Day for day, and turn each day. 9:00—open the mail. 9:45—appointment with planning commission board. 10:30—discuss installation progress charts with J. L. 11:45—pray for rain. 12:00—lunch. *And so it goes.*

35   "I'm sorry, Miss Grant, but the time for interviews was set at 2:30, and it's almost five now. I'm sorry you're late, but those are the rules. You'll have to wait till next year to submit application for this college again." *And so it goes.*

36   The 10:10 local stops at Cresthaven, Galesville, Tonawanda Junction, Selby, and Farnhurst, but not at Indiana City, Lucasville, and Colton, except on Sunday. The 10:35 express stops at Galesville, Selby, and Indiana City, except on Sunday & Holidays, at which time it stops at . . . *and so it goes.*

37   "I couldn't wait, Fred. I had to be at Pierre Cartain's by 3:00, and you said you'd meet me under the clock in the terminal at 2:45, and you weren't there, so I had to go on. You're always late, Fred. If you'd been there, we could have sewed it up together, but as it was, well, I took the order alone. . . ." *And so it goes.*

38   Dear Mr. and Mrs. Atterley: in reference to your son Gerold's constant tardiness, I am afraid we will have to suspend him from school unless some more reliable method can be instituted guaranteeing he will arrive at his classes on time. Granted he is an exemplary student and his marks are high, his constant flouting of the schedules of this school makes it impractical to maintain him in a system where the other children seem capable of getting where they are supposed to be on time *and so it goes.*

39   YOU CANNOT VOTE UNLESS YOU APPEAR AT 8:45 A.M.

40   "I don't care if the script is *good,* I need it Thursday!"

41   CHECK-OUT TIME IS 2:00 P.M.

42   "You got here late. This job's taken. Sorry."

43   YOUR SALARY HAS BEEN DOCKED FOR TWENTY MINUTES' TIME LOST.

44   "God, what time is it, I've gotta run!"

45   And so it goes. And so it goes. And so it goes. And so it goes goes goes goes goes tick tock tick tock tick tock and one day we no longer let time serve us, we serve time and we are slaves of the schedule, worshippers of the sun's passing, bound into a life predicated on restrictions because the system will not function if we don't keep the schedule tight.

46   Until it becomes more than a minor inconvenience to be late. It becomes a sin. Then a crime. Then a crime punishable by this:

47   EFFECTIVE 15 JULY 2389, 12:00:00 midnight, the office of the Master Timekeeper will require all citizens to submit their timecards and cardioplates for processing. In accordance with Statute 555-7-SGH-999 governing the revocation of time per capita, all cardioplates will be keyed to the individual holder and—

48   What they had done was devise a method of curtailing the

amount of life a person could have. If he was ten minutes late, he lost ten minutes of his life. An hour was proportionately worth more revocation. If someone was consistently tardy, he might find himself, on a Sunday night, receiving a communique from the Master Timekeeper that his time had run out, and he would be ''turned off'' at high noon on Monday, please straighten your affairs, sir, madame or bisex.

49 And so, by this simple scientific expedient (utilizing a scientific process held dearly secret by the Ticktockman's office) the System was maintained. It was the only expedient thing to do. It was, after all, patriotic. The schedules had to be met. After all, there *was* a war on!

50 But, wasn't there always?

51 "Now that is really disgusting," the Harlequin said, when Pretty Alice showed him the wanted poster. "Disgusting and *highly* improbable. After all, this isn't the days of desperadoes. A *wanted* poster!"

52 "You know," Alice noted, "you speak with a great deal of inflection."

53 "I'm sorry," said the Harlequin, humbly.

54 "No need to be sorry. You're always saying 'I'm sorry.' You have such massive guilt, Everett, it's really very sad."

55 "I'm sorry," he repeated, then pursed his lips so the dimples appeared momentarily. He hadn't wanted to say that at all. "I have to go out again. I have to *do* something."

56 Alice slammed her coffee-bulb down on the counter. "Oh for God's *sake,* Everett, can't you stay home just *one* night! Must you always be out in that ghastly clown suit, running around *annoying* people?"

57 "I'm—" he stopped, and clapped the jester's hat onto his auburn thatch with a tiny tingling of bells. He rose, rinsed out his coffee-bulb at the spray, and put it into the drier for a moment. "I have to go."

58 She didn't answer. The faxbox was purring, and she pulled a sheet out, read it, threw it toward him on the counter. "It's about you. Of course. You're ridiculous."

59 He read it quickly. It said the Ticktockman was trying to locate him. He didn't care, he was going out to be late again. At the door, dredging for an exit line, he hurled back petulantly, "Well, *you* speak with inflection, *too!*"

60 Alice rolled her pretty eyes heavenward. "You're ridiculous." The Harlequin stalked out, slamming the door, which sighed shut softly, and locked itself.

61 There was a gentle knock, and Alice got up with an exhalation

of exasperated breath, and opened the door. He stood there. "I'll be back about ten-thirty, okay?"

62   She pulled a rueful face. "Why do you tell me that? Why? You *know* you'll be late! You *know it!* You're *always* late, so why do you tell me these dumb things?" She closed the door.

63   On the other side, the Harlequin nodded to himself. *She's right. She's always right. I'll be late. I'm always late. Why do I tell her these dumb things?*

64   He shrugged again, and went off to be late once more.

65   He had fired off the firecracker rockets that said: I will attend the 115th annual International Medical Association Invocation at 8:00 P.M. precisely. I do hope you will all be able to join me.

66   The words had burned in the sky, and of course the authorities were there, lying in wait for him. They assumed, naturally, that he would be late. He arrived twenty minutes early, while they were setting up the spiderwebs to trap and hold him. Blowing a large bullhorn, he frightened and unnerved them so, their own moisturized encirclement webs sucked closed, and they were hauled up, kicking and shrieking, high above the amphitheater floor. The Harlequin laughed and laughed, and apologized profusely. The physicians' gathered in solemn conclave, roared with laughter, and accepted the Harlequin's apologies with exaggerated bowing and posturing, and a merry time was had by all, who thought the Harlequin was a regular foofaraw in fancy pants; all, that is, but the authorities, who had been sent out of the office of the Ticktockman; they hung there like so much dockside cargo, hauled up above the floor of the amphitheater in a most unseemly fashion.

67   (In another part of the same city where the Harlequin carried on his "activities," totally unrelated in every way to what concerns us here, save that it illustrates the Ticktockman's power and import, a man named Marshall Delahanty received his turn-off notice from the Ticktockman's office. His wife received the notification from the gray-suited minee who delivered it, with the traditonal "look of sorrow" plastered hideously across his face. She knew what it was, even without unsealing it. It was a billet-doux of immediate recognition to everyone these days. She gasped, and held it as though it were a glass slide tinged with botulism, and prayed it was not for her. Let it be for Marsh, she thought, brutally, realistically, or one of the kids, but not for me, please dear God, not for me. And then she opened it, and it *was* for Marsh, and she was at one and the same time horrified and relieved. The next trooper in the line had caught the bullet. "Marshall," she screamed. "Marshall! Termination. Marshall! OhmiGod, Marshall, whattl we do, whattl we do, Mar-

shall omigodmarshall . . . " and in their home that night was the sound of tearing paper and fear, and the stink of madness went up the flue and there was nothing, absolutely nothing they could do about it.

68   (But Marshall Delahanty tried to run. And early the next day, when turn-off time came, he was deep in the Canadian forest 200 miles away, and the office of the Ticktockman blanked his cardio-plate, and Marshall Delahanty keeled over, running, and his heart stopped, and the blood dried up on its way to his brain, and he was dead that's all. One light went out on the sector map in the office of the Master Timekeeper, while notification was entered for fax re-production, and Georgette Delahanty's name was entered on the dole roles till she could re-marry. Which is the end of the footnote, and all the point that need be made, except don't laugh, because that is what would happen to the Harlequin if ever the Ticktockman found out his real name. It isn't funny.)

69   The shopping level of the city was thronged with the Thursday-colors of the buyers. Women in canary yellow chitons and men in pseudo-Tyrolean outfits that were jade and leather and fit very tightly, save for the balloon pants.

70   When the Harlequin appeared on the still-being-constructed shell of the new Efficiency Shopping Center, his bullhorn to his elfishly-laughing lips, everyone pointed and stared, and he berated them:

71   "Why let them order you about? Why let them tell you to hurry and scurry like ants or maggots? Take your time! Saunter a while! Enjoy the sunshine, enjoy the breeze, let life carry you at your own pace! Don't be slaves of time, it's a helluva way to die, slowly, by degrees . . . down with the Ticktockman!"

72   Who's the nut? most of the shoppers wanted to know. Who's the nut oh wow I'm gonna be late I gotta run. . . .

73   And the construction gang on the Shopping Center received an urgent order from the office of the Master Timekeeper that the dangerous criminal known as the Harlequin was atop their spire, and their aid was urgently needed in apprehending him. The work crew said no, they would lose time on their construction schedule, but the Ticktockman managed to pull the proper threads of governmental webbing, and they were told to cease work and catch that nitwit up there on the spire; up there with the bullhorn. So a dozen and more burly workers began climbing into their construction platforms, releasing the a-grav plates, and rising toward the Harlequin.

74   After the debacle (in which, through the Harlequin's attention to personal safety, no one was seriously injured), the workers tried

to reassemble, and assault him again, but it was too late. He had vanished. It had attracted quite a crowd, however, and the shopping cycle was thrown off by hours, simply hours. The purchasing needs of the system were therefore falling behind, and so measures were taken to accelerate the cycle for the rest of the day, but it got bogged down and speeded up and they sold too many float-valves and not nearly enough wegglers, which meant that the popli-ratio was off, which made it necessary to rush cases and cases of spoiling Smash-O to stores that usually needed a case only every three or four hours. The shipments were bollixed, the transshipments were misrouted, and in the end, even the swizzleskid industries felt it.

75   "Don't come back till you have him!" the Ticktockman said, very quietly, very sincerely, extremely dangerously.

76   They used dogs. They used probes. They used cardioplate crossoffs. They used teepers. They used bribery. They used stiktytes. They used intimidation. They used torment. They used torture. They used finks. They used cops. They used search&seizure. They used fallaron. They used betterment incentive. They used fingerprints. They used Bertillon. They used cunning. They used guile. They used treachery. They used Raoul Mitgong, but he didn't help much. They used applied physics. They used techniques of criminology.

77   And what the hell: they caught him

78   After all, his name was Everett C. Marm, and he wasn't much to begin with, except a man who had no sense of time.

79   "Repent, Harlequin!" said the Ticktockman.

80   "Get stuffed!" the Harlequin replied, sneering.

81   "You've been late a total of sixty-three years, five months, three weeks, two days, twelve hours, forty-one minutes, fifty-nine seconds, point oh three six one one one microseconds. You've used up everthing you can and more. I'm going to turn you off."

82   "Scare someone else. I'd rather be dead than live in a dumb world with a bogeyman like you."

83   "It's my job."

84   "You're full of it. You're a tyrant. You have no right to order people around and kill them if they show up late."

85   "You can't adjust. You can't fit in."

86   "Unstrap me, and I'll fit my fist into your mouth."

87   "You're a non-conformist."

88   "That didn't used to be a felony."

89   "It is now. Live in the world around you."

90   "I hate it. It's a terrible world."

91   "Not everyone thinks so. Most people enjoy order."

92   "I don't, and most of the people I know don't."
93   "That's not true. How do you think we caught you?"
94   "I'm not interested."
95   "A girl named Pretty Alice told us who you were."
96   "That's a lie."
97   "It's true. You unnerve her. She wants to belong, she wants to conform, I'm going to turn you off."
98   "Then do it already, and stop arguing with me."
99   "I'm not going to turn you off."
100   "You're an idiot!"
101   "Repent, Harlequin!" said the Ticktockman.
102   "Get stuffed."
103   So they sent him to Coventry. And in Coventry they worked him over. It was just like what they did to Winston Smith in "1984," which was a book none of them knew about, but the techniques are really quite ancient, and so they did it to Everett C. Marm, and one day quite a long time later, the Harlequin appeared on the communications web, appearing elfin and dimpled and bright-eyed, and not at all brainwashed, and he said he had been wrong, that it was a good, a very good thing indeed, to belong, to be right on time hip-ho and away we go, and everyone stared up at him on the public screens that covered an entire city block, and they said to themselves, well, you see, he was just a nut after all, and if that's the way the system is run, then let's do it that way, because it doesn't pay to fight city hall, or in this case, the Ticktockman. So Everett C. Marm was destroyed, which was a loss, because of what Thoreau said earlier, but you can't make an omelet without breaking a few eggs, and in every revolution a few die who shouldn't but they have to, because that's the way it happens, and if you make only a little change, then it seems to be worthwhile. Or, to make the point lucidly:
104   "Uh, excuse me, sir, I, uh, don't know how to uh, to uh, tell you this, but you were three minutes late. The schedule is a little, uh, bit off."
105   He grinned sheepishly.
106   "That's ridiculous!" murmured the Ticktockman behind his mask. "Check your watch." And then he went into his office, going mrmee, mrmee, mrmee, mrmee.

Vocabulary

militia	posse comitatus	notoriety
anarchistic	sniggering	heretic

generated	cardioplate	hierarchy
loggers	revocation	ferrets
mineez	finks	commex
joystick	metronomic	motley
vagrant	servitors	resuscitated
prematurely	antediluvian	expresstrip
domino	carapaces	inoperative
flouting	jabberwocky	jive
desperadoes	predicated	expedient
faxbox	inflection	thatch
minee	dredging	foofaraw
chitons	billet-doux	botulism
jade	pseudo	Tyrolean
bogeyman	debacle	guile
omelet		

Topics for Discussion

1. Are you invariably late for dates and classes? Is it as important to be punctual as it is to retain your individuality? Is too much emphasis put on "being on time" in our society today? Does time clock scheduling serve the individual or the System? Are human beings made subservient to the System by such rigors?[1]

2. What kind of a society does Ellison portray in this story? How different is it from our present society? Are there any similarities between the society in the story and our society?

3. Has the Ticktockman been clever or made a serious mistake in keeping the Harlequin alive, rather than simply eradicating him? Discuss the impact of martyrs. What happens to their causes? How many parallels in history can you find, starting with Jesus?

4. Pretty Alice finked on the Harlequin. But she isn't a bad person, she's merely doing what most people do: looking out after "number one." Is this a moral and ethical attitude? Do you have the same philosophy of survival? Discuss it, but be honest if you can.

5. Is the Harlequin brave, a coward, or just a damn fool? Consider courage and the reasons for performing courageous acts, particularly when you know you'll be clobbered for them. Is it worth it? If so, try to relate three courageous acts you've performed; not grandstanding, but genuine acts of courage by which you had something important to lose.

---

[1] Topics for Discussion 1, 3, 4, and 5 have been supplied by Harlan Ellison.

Rhetorical Considerations

1. Is the quotation from Thoreau too obvious a way to begin the story? Could Ellison have made the allusion to Thoreau more indirectly?
2. How does the fate of Marshall Delahanty illustrate concretely the kind of society which the Ticktockman rules? How does Delahanty's fate contrast with the Harlequin's fate?
3. What does it mean to be sent to Coventry?
4. What is the allusion to Winston Smith in *1984*?
5. Does the story end on a note of hope or despair? How do you know?

Rhetorical Analysis

John F. Kennedy: Inaugural Address

Unlike most selections which appear in this book, John F. Kennedy's inaugural address is not a formal, written essay, but a formal, spoken speech. As such, it was delivered to a particular audience for a particular occasion—Kennedy's inauguration as president of the United States on January 20, 1961. In assuming this office, Kennedy found himself in the position of having to make far-reaching pronouncements regarding the course of America's role in world affairs for what was then the foreseeable future. He spoke not only to all the people of the United States but to all the people of the world. Moreover, Kennedy spoke to them as the youngest man ever to assume this powerful office, as the first Catholic president, and as the president elected by the smallest margin of votes in the history of the United States—a young man speaking brave words and who spoke them by necessity. Kennedy needed to create a sense of faith and trust in his worldwide audience, and he used specific rhetorical devices as his tools to create that trust. Here is an analysis of some of those devices.

The speech is brief, simple; it has an elegance which contrasts with and yet reinforces the grandeur and importance of the occasion for which it was written. Yet it is a careful speech, very consciously divided into four sections. The first section (paragraphs 1–4), Kennedy's introduction, attempts to heal the wounds of the campaign which has brought him victory. Kennedy wants to appear a generous winner and desires also to make supporters out of former opponents. He does not gloat over the defeat of his opposition, but calls the members of that opposition to join with him as equals in a "celebration" of the ideals and values which they hold sacred and dear in common with members of his party, foremost among these the idea of "freedom." The basis of his appeal is the heritage of the presidency, that just as he is the successor to a long line of distinguished American presidents, the American people are collectively the successors of a tradition of liberty dating as far back as that office—to the American Revolution. Just as he is committed to upholding that office, so the American people ought to be committed to upholding those principles which guided early presidents in making that revolution. Therefore, Kennedy wishes his audience to believe that he and they share the same traditions, that they are united by a common past and share a common future, and that they shall make that future together, despite whatever differences they have had in the immediate past. He wishes, so to speak, to tell them that he and they are one.

Based on the assumption that America is not a divided but a united nation, Kennedy proceeds in the second section of the speech (paragraphs 5–13) to let other nations know that the American people, in this unity, renew old promises to old friends and plan to make new pledges for the defense of "liberty" to old and new friends alike. He also makes the pledge to potential enemies of the United States that the American people in this new-found unity will reject isolationism and national chauvinism in a new quest for peace.

Up to this point in the speech, Kennedy has spoken in quite general terms. He now (paragraphs 14–20) speaks more specifically concerning the future of his presidency and the future of America's role in the world. As political parties in America must heal the wounds of differences which appeared during the election campaign, so too must the nations of the world heal their differences in the interest of peace. It is time, Kennedy says, to begin to remedy those divisions which have for so long separated the nations of the world. As Americans come together in a united effort to mend the wounds of their country, so too should the peoples and nations of the world come together to build a just and lasting unity of purpose.

In his final section (paragraphs 21–27), Kennedy restates the task before all of us: to build a world of freedom and peace where people will no longer have to fear tyranny, poverty, disease, and war. And it is not merely the citizens of the United States upon whom the burden of this great task rests but upon all persons of all nations. The struggle facing the world is truly monumental, Kennedy reminds us, but just such a test will prove our worth as a nation and as a world determined to rise above our baser instincts.

This admittedly brief summation of the general organization of Kennedy's speech leaves many gaps, which we will attempt to fill in with a more careful look at the speech section by section and rhetorical device by rhetorical device.

The brevity of the speech is reflected in the dominance of brief paragraphs. There are twenty-seven paragraphs in the speech, and the majority are brief—the shortest paragraph is one sentence long (there are ten of these), and the longest paragraph is only four sentences long (there are only two of these). The effect of this paragraph structure is to create an almost litany-like listing of principles and policies. Yet this does not become dull because Kennedy carefully varies his paragraph construction. Then too, the speech was delivered with all the brilliance of the Kennedy style.

In keeping with the brevity of the speech as a whole and the brevity of the majority of the paragraphs, most of the sentences are also brief. And as with his paragraphs, Kennedy carefully mixes his sentences. The shortest sentence is only four words ("But let us begin"), while the longest is eighty words ("Let the word go forth from this time and place . . ."). But the majority of sentences in the speech are less than twenty words long. The short sentences more effectively communicate with a listening audience than long complicated sentences. Kennedy undoubtedly had this in mind when he wrote the speech. The short sentences also serve to compress ideas and create the tone of high seriousness appropriate to such a speech.

Although the majority of sentences in the speech are brief, the predominant grammatical sentence type is the complex sentence. Yet rarely do two or more sentences of the same type follow one another. The use of complex sentence structure as the dominant type reveals Kennedy's reliance upon subordination, rather than coordination, as his main device for expanding his basic sentence pattern.

Kennedy's speech is rich in its use and variety of rhetorical patterns. We cannot exhaustively catalog all of the types here, but we can look at some of the more important. Even the most cursory examination of the speech will reveal that the dominant rhetorical pattern is *antithesis*. The opening sentence of the speech sets the theme and style of the speech: "We observe today not a victory of party but a celebration of freedom, symbolizing an end as well as a beginning, signifying renewal as well as change." This *juxtaposition of contrasting ideas* continues throughout the speech both in sentence style and in the thematic structure of the speech. Other examples of the use of antithesis are:

> United, there is little we cannot do in a host of co-operative ventures. Divided, there is little we can do, for we dare not meet a powerful challenge at odds and split asunder.

> If a free society cannot help the many who are poor, it cannot save the few who are rich.

> Let both sides explore what problems unite us instead of belaboring those problems which divide us.

> My fellow citizens of the world, ask not what America will do for you, but what together we can do for the freedom of man.

Then, too, there is the most memorable line of the speech, which is also a perfect example of antithesis:

> And so, my fellow Americans, ask not what your country can do for you; ask what you can do for your country.

This contrasting of opposite ideas is the theme of the speech, for Kennedy's speech is a speech of hope, of hope for a new beginning and a new era of peace and friendship. In order to achieve this beginning, opposing forces and ideas in the world must be reconciled. Thus his speech, in both sentence style and thematic structure, reflects this concern with reconciliation of opposites: old-new, rich-poor, friend-enemy, tyranny-freedom, war-peace, fear-hope.

Closely allied to, and often confused with, antithesis is the device of *parallelism*, setting forth equivalent items in coordinate grammatical structure. Many of the examples of antithesis we have mentioned are also examples of parallelism in grammatical structure. Antithesis, of course, lends itself to parallelism, but there are other forms of parallelism such as enumeration and specification:

> Together let us explore the stars, conquer the deserts, eradicate disease, tap the ocean depths and encourage the arts and commerce.

> Let every nation know, whether it wishes us well or ill, that we shall pay any price, bear any burden, meet any hardship, support any friend, oppose any foe to assure the survival and the success of liberty.

This last example is probably most familiar to you as a listing of items in a series. But it is important to note that in these examples the parallel items must be expressed in coordinate grammatical structure.

Of the fifty-two sentences in Kennedy's speech, the overwhelming majority are *declarative;* that is, they make a statement. While Kennedy also uses both the rhetorical question and the imperative, there are only two rhetorical questions and three imperative sentences in the speech:

> Can we forge against these enemies a grand and global alliance, North and South, East and West, that can assure a more fruitful life for all mankind? Will you join in that historic effort?

> And so, my fellow Americans, ask not what your country can do for you; ask what you can do for your country.

> My fellow citizens of the world, ask not what America will do for you, but what together we can do for the freedom of man.

> Finally, whether you are citizens of America or citizens of the world, ask of us here the same high standards of strength and sacrifice which we ask of you.

The *rhetorical question* does not really ask a question but instead either asserts or denies something indirectly. In this instance Kennedy is using the rhetorical question to elicit support from his audience for his statements. Of course the rhetorical question is never directly answered. All Kennedy wishes to achieve is an appropriate internal response from his audience. The *imperative* sentences all occur at the end of Kennedy's speech. Since imperative sentences give commands or directions, Kennedy is no longer suggesting or urging his audience to action; he is directing them to act.

Next to the declarative sentence, the *hortative* occurs most frequently. The hortative is used to exhort or urge to action; it seeks to persuade or induce action, in contrast to the imperative. Kennedy uses the hortative throughout his speech ("Let the word go forth. . . ." "Let every nation know. . . ." "But let us begin.") In paragraphs 14 through 20 Kennedy uses the hortative both to suggest and to urge a plan of action. He carefully avoids the use of the declarative, which simply states a fact, and the imperative, which commands action. The effect Kennedy hopes to achieve with this extended use of the hortative is that of a reasonable man seeking to solve problems which can be solved, and to solve those problems through reason, understanding, and cooperation and not through force.

A few words should also be said about the *diction,* or word choice, of the speech. Kennedy uses quite a few monosyllabic words and avoids using polysyllabic words. This word usage gives the speech the impression of strength and simplicity. Yet there are very few concrete words (*stars, deserts, disease, graves, huts, villages*). The real weight of the speech is carried by abstract words, most of which are also polysyllabic and Latinate (*tyranny, loyalty, freedom, celebration, agression, tribulation, invective*). The use of abstract words is to be expected in a speech in which Kennedy is mainly concerned with broad statements about his programs and is carefully avoiding any specific suggestions. One final note about the diction of the speech is the use of *archaic diction* to give the speech a formal quality. Kennedy uses such words as *forebears, foe, writ, anew, adversary*. The overall effect of the diction of the speech is to sound uncomplicated and convey simplicity while at the same time remaining broad and general in the statement of ideas.

But the entire speech is not abstract. If that were so, Kennedy would not have made the impression he did with the speech. While the diction of the speech may lack concreteness, the *metaphors* he uses do not. A metaphor is an implied comparison of two things of unlike nature. The use of metaphor gives the speech the concreteness it lacks in its diction. Kennedy uses such metaphors as:

> *The torch has been passed*
> *riding the back of the tiger*
> *the bonds of mass misery*
> *the chains of poverty*
> *a beachhead of co-operation may push back*
>   *the jungle of suspicion*
> *corners of the earth*
> *glow from that fire can truly light the world*

There are more metaphors in the speech, and you should look at it again and see how many you can locate. You should also see whether the metaphors function well and whether they are aptly chosen. But you will not fail to notice that all the metaphors give concreteness to otherwise abstract ideas. And this is precisely the use Kennedy intended for them.

You can also find other points to make about the rhetorical aspect of this speech. You might, for example, look at Kennedy's use of subordinating conjunctions (such as *for, if, although, because*), particularly at the beginning of sentences.

> Though the will of the majority is in all cases to prevail, that will, to be rightful, must be reasonable; the minority possess their equal right, which equal laws must protect, and to violate would be oppression.
>
> Thomas Jefferson, *Inaugural Address*

4

MINORITIES AND MAJORITIES

Depending on how you look at it, everyone is a member of one minority group or another. When you place someone in a minority group you are classifying that person, and therefore you are engaging in the process of classification. If you are a woman or white you are a member of a majority group, but if you are black, Puerto Rican, American Indian, or Chicano you are a member of a minority group. Two more minority groups in the United States would be the rich and the poor. This classification is true, however, only if you are speaking in terms of the population of the United States. If you are speaking in terms of the world population, whites are a minority group, and blacks, Chinese, and women are majority groups. In fact, the largest majority group in the world is young, female Chinese, and white males are just another minority group. As you can see from all this, the terms *minority* and *majority* are dependent upon how you are classifying your subject. What constitutes a majority group in one context can be a minority in another context.

Take this situation. A telephone company has two hundred jobs for repair workers. Of these two hundred employees, 97 percent are white males with the remaining 3 percent women and racial minorities. However, the surrounding communities are made up of 50 percent women and 40 percent racial minorities. Through expansion, fifty new jobs are created. Because of high unemployment in the area, the company receives many job applications from skilled white male workers. However, pressure groups of women and minorities begin to agitate to have equal representation in the telephone company's labor force. Women demand that all fifty new jobs go to them as a step toward an ultimate goal of a half male and half female working force. The minorities demand that all fifty jobs go to them as a step toward an ultimate goal of 40 percent of the working force. There are further complexities. Several prominent spokespersons of the minority groups say that all fifty jobs should go to minority males because these are the breadwinners of the black, Chicano, Puerto Rican, and American Indian families. Women's liberation, they argue, comes after freedom for their men. Some women minority group leaders argue that twenty-five new jobs should go to minority group men and twenty-five to minority group women and none should go to white males or females. Obviously there is a problem here. What would you do if you were the personnel director of this telephone company?

There are questions that we all do not like to face, problems with no easy solutions, that we wish would go away. But problems never go away if just ignored. Unpleasant and difficult though they may be, problems demand solutions. The problem outlined above is certainly complex and, one is almost tempted to say, insoluble. But if our society is to survive we must not only face such problems but solve them.

The first step in solving any problem is a thorough understanding of the problem itself. Do you really understand the situation outlined above? Do you understand all of the ramifications and emotions involved? Before you attempt any solution at all, make sure you study all aspects and understand the full meaning of the problem. And in the process of study you will have to examine many unpleasant things about yourself, your attitudes and beliefs, and our society. You will have to make some very fundamental decisions about what kind of a society you want to live in. In order to solve any problem you must make basic decisions and commitments.

During the past decade, three groups have begun to face the problems that confront them and have begun to take action to solve these problems. More women, because of new laws against job discrimination, are entering traditionally male-dominated professions such as law and medicine. And more women are also entering such job areas as bartending, engineering, and news reporting. More than ever we find blacks and other racial minorities taking an increasing role in the American political process, on both a community and a national level. Lately, American blue collar workers have become aware that they too are confronted by serious problems which go beyond the traditional concerns of wages, working hours, and job security. Each of these groups is in its own way confronting and attempting to solve those problems that they perceive as immediate and real. However, the great problem facing our society is the conflict that arises when the legitimate goals and aspirations of these groups clash, as illustrated in our example above.

The readings in this section do not attempt to offer possible solutions for the problems facing minority and majority groups in America. Indeed, all we hope to do is clarify those issues so that through a better understanding of them more progress can be made toward possible solutions.

The Rhetorical Analysis at the end of this section deals with Anne Roiphe's *Confessions of a Female Chauvinist Sow*. Be sure to read Roiphe's essay before you read the Rhetorical Analysis.

Women Discourage Other Women's Ambitions

Susan Brownmiller

Susan Brownmiller has frequently contributed articles to The Village Voice *and is the author of* Against Our Will: Men, Women, and Rape.

1   One of the hardest things for a woman with aspirations to do in our society is to admit, first to herself and then to others, that she has ambitions that go beyond the routine—a good marriage, clever children. Early on, we learn that men don't take kindly to the notion

of a woman entering the competitive lists. It is in the nature of power and position that those who have it do not relinquish it graciously, as all colonial peoples and all minority groups discover at a certain stage in their development. Well, O.K. so be it. But infinitely more damaging to our psyche is the realization that our ambitions are met with equal hostility—pooh-poohed, sniffed at, scoffed at, ignored, or worse, not taken seriously—by mothers, sisters, cousins, aunts and friends, who won't believe that we have set our sights on a different sort of goal than they have envisioned, preferring instead to believe that our ambition is merely a "passing phase"—which, unfortunately, it often is because of lack of encouragement.

2   Psychologists talk a great deal about the importance of the approbation or approval of a peer group upon the individual. It is human nature to want to fit in. The senior at college who sends away for law-school catalogues while her dormitory mates down the corridor are sending away for catalogues of silver patterns is already conscious of swimming against the tide. (How different the atmosphere must be in a man's dormitory!) The magazine researcher who took her job as a stepping-stone to become a writer, but discovers that girl researchers are not encouraged to write by the magazine's male editors, will find little sympathy and understanding from other researchers who have taken the job to mark time until their proper engagements are properly announced in *The New York Times*. The peer-group pressure on a young woman in her 20s—as opposed to the pressure on a young man in his 20s—is decidedly against career.

Vocabulary

psyche   approbation   peer

Topics for Discussion

1. Do you agree with Brownmiller that women are discouraged by men from having ambitions other than marriage and children? What forms does this discouragement take?

2. What peer group pressures do women experience?

3. How can your psyche be damaged by the disapproval of others?

4. Do you agree with Brownmiller that men do not like to compete against women?

Rhetorical Considerations

1. This is a very short essay, only two paragraphs long. Does Brownmiller make her point in this brief space?
2. What use does Brownmiller make of specific examples? Are the examples effectively chosen and used?
3. At six different points in this essay Brownmiller uses dashes. What other punctuation marks could she have used? Which punctuation do you think is more effective?
4. Brownmiller states her thesis in the first sentence of the essay. Is this the best place? Would it have been more effective to place it somewhere else in the essay?

Confessions of a Female Chauvinist Sow

Anne Roiphe

Anne Roiphe (b. 1935) is a novelist and essayist whose publications include Up the Sandbox *(made into a successful movie starring Barbra Streisand) and* Long Division.

1   I once married a man I thought was totally unlike my father and I imagined a whole new world of freedom emerging. Five years later it was clear even to me—floating face down in a wash of despair—that I had simply chosen a replica of my handsome daddy-true. The updated version spoke English like an angel but—good God!—underneath he was my father exactly: wonderful, but not the right man for me.

2   Most people I know have at one time or another been fouled up by their childhood experiences. Patterns tend to sink into the unconscious only to reappear, disguised, unseen, like marionette strings,

pulling us this way or that. Whatever ails people—keeps them up at night, tossing and turning—also ails movements no matter how historically huge or politically important. The women's movement cannot remake consciousness, or reshape the future, without acknowledging and shedding all the unnecessary and ugly baggage of the past. It's easy enough now to see where men have kept us out of clubs, baseball games, graduate schools; it's easy enough to recognize the hidden directions that limit Sis to cake-baking and Junior to bridge-building; it's now possible for even Miss America herself to identify what *they* have done to us, and, of course, *they* have and *they* did and *they* are. . . . But along the way we also developed our own hidden prejudices, class assumptions and an anti-male humor and collection of expectations that gave us, like all oppressed groups, a secret sense of superiority (co-existing with a poor self-image—it's not news that people can believe two contradictory things at once).

3   Listen to any group that suffers materially and socially. They have a lexicon with which they tease the enemy: ofay, goy, honky, gringo. "Poor pale devils," said Malcolm X loud enough for us to hear, although blacks had joked about that to each other for years. Behind some of the women's liberation thinking lurk the rumors, the prejudices, the defense systems of generations of oppressed women whispering in the kitchen together, presenting one face to their menfolk and another to their card clubs, their mothers and sisters. All this is natural enough but potentially dangerous in a revolutionary situation in which you hope to create a future that does not mirror the past. The hidden anti-male feelings, a result of the old system, will foul us up if they are allowed to persist.

4   During my teen years I never left the house on my Saturday night dates without my mother slipping me a few extra dollars—mad money, it was called. I'll explain what it was for the benefit of the new generation in which people just sleep with each other: the fellow was supposed to bring me home, lead me safely through the asphalt jungle, protect me from slithering snakes, rapists and the like. But my mother and I knew young men were apt to drink too much, to slosh down so many rye-and-gingers that some hero might well lead me in front of an oncoming bus, smash his daddy's car into Tiffany's window or, less gallantly, throw up on my new dress. Mad money was for getting home on your own, no matter what form of insanity your date happened to evidence. Mad money was also a wallflower's rope ladder; if the guy you came with suddenly fancied someone else, well, you didn't have to stay there and suffer, you could go home. Boys were fickle and likely to be unkind; my mother

and I knew that, as surely as we knew they tried to make you do things in the dark they wouldn't respect you for afterwards and in fact would spread the word and spoil your rep. Boys liked to be flattered; if you made them feel important they would eat out of your hand. So talk to them about their interests, don't alarm them with displays of intelligence—we all knew that, we groups of girls talking into the wee hours of the night in a kind of easy companionship we thought impossible with boys. Boys were prone to have a good time, get you pregnant, and then pretend they didn't know your name when you came knocking on their door for finances or comfort. In short, we believed boys were less moral than we were. They appeared to be hypocritical, self-seeking, exploitative, untrustworthy and very likely to be showing off their precious masculinity. I never had a girl friend I thought would be unkind or embarrass me in public. I never expected a girl to lie to me about her marks or sports skill or how good she was in bed. Altogether—without anyone's directly coming out and saying so—I gathered that men were sexy, powerful, very interesting, but not very nice, not very moral, humane and tender, like us. Girls played fairly while men, unfortunately, reserved their honor for the battlefield.

5   Why are there laws insisting on alimony and child support? Well, everyone knows that men don't have an instinct to protect their young and, given half a chance, with the moon in the right phase, they will run off and disappear. Everyone assumes a mother will not let her child starve, yet it is necessary to legislate that a father must not do so. We are taught to accept the idea that men are less than decent; their charms may be manifold but their characters are riddled with faults. To this day I never blink if I hear that a man has gone to find his fortune in South America, having left his pregnant wife, his blind mother and taken the family car. I still gasp in horror when I hear of a woman leaving her asthmatic infant for a rock group in Taos because I can't seem to avoid the assumption that men are naturally heels and women the ordained carriers of what little is moral in our dubious civilization.

6   My mother never gave me mad money thinking I would ditch a fellow for some other guy or that I would pass out drunk on the floor. She knew I would be considerate of my companion because, after all, I was more mature than the boys that gathered about. Why was I more mature? Women just are people-oriented; they learn to be empathetic at an early age. Most English students (students interested in humanity, not artifacts) are women. Men and boys—so the myth goes—conceal their feelings and lose interest in anybody else's. Everyone knows that even little boys can tell the difference

between one kind of a car and another—proof that their souls are mechanical, their attention directed to the non-human.

7   I remember shivering in the cold vestibule of a famous men's athletic club. Women and girls are not permitted inside the club's door. What are they doing in there, I asked? They're naked, said my mother, they're sweating, jumping up and down a lot, telling each other dirty jokes and bragging about their stock market exploits. Why can't we go in? I asked. Well, my mother told me, they're afraid we'd laugh at them.

8   The prejudices of childhood are hard to outgrow. I confess that every time my business takes me past that club, I shudder. Images of large bellies resting on massage tables and flaccid penises rising and falling with the Dow Jones average flash through my head. There it is, chauvinism waving its cancerous tentacles from the depths of my psyche.

9   Minorities automatically feel superior to the oppressor because, after all, they are not hurting anybody. In fact, they feel they are morally better. The old canard that women need love, men need sex—believed for too long by both sexes—attributes moral and spiritual superiority to women and makes of men beasts whose urges send them prowling into the night. This false division of good and bad, placing deforming pressures on everyone, doesn't have to contaminate the future. We know that the assumptions we make about each other become a part of the cultural air we breathe and, in fact, become social truths. Women who want equality must be prepared to give it and to believe in it, and in order to do that it is not enough to state that you are as good as any man, but also it must be stated that he is as good as you and both will be humans together. If we want men to share in the care of the family in a new way, we must assume them as capable of consistent loving tenderness as we.

10   I rummage about and find in my thinking all kinds of anti-male prejudices. Some are just jokes and others I will have a hard time abandoning. First, I share an emotional conviction with many sisters that women given power would not create wars. Intellectually I know that's ridiculous; great queens have waged war before; the likes of Lurleen Wallace, Pat Nixon and Mrs. General Lavelle can be depended upon in the future to guiltlessly condemn to death other people's children in the name of some ideal of their own. Little girls, of course, don't take toy guns out of their hip pockets and say "Pow, pow" to all their neighbors and friends like the average well-adjusted little boy. However, if we gave little girls the six-shooters, we would soon have double the pretend body count.

11   Aggression is not, as I secretly think, a male-sex-linked

characteristic: brutality is masculine only by virtue of opportunity. True, there are 1,000 Jack the Rippers for every Lizzie Borden, but that surely is the result of social forms. Women as a group are indeed more masochistic than men. The practical result of this division is that women seem nicer and kinder, but when the world changes, women will have a fuller opportunity to be just as rotten as men and there will be fewer claims of female moral superiority.

12   Now that I am entering early middle age, I hear many women complaining of husbands and ex-husbands who are attracted to younger females. This strikes the older woman as unfair, of course. But I remember a time when I thought all boys around my age and grade were creeps and bores. I wanted to go out with an older man: a senior or, miraculously, a college man. I had a certain contempt for my coevals, not realizing that the freshman in college I thought so desirable, was some older girl's creep. Some women never lose that contempt for men of their own age. That isn't fair either and may be one reason why some sensible men of middle years find solace in young women.

13   I remember coming home from school one day to find my mother's card game dissolved in hysterical laughter. The cards were floating in black rivers of running mascara. What was so funny? A woman named Helen was lying on a couch pretending to be her husband with a cold. She was issuing demands for orange juice, aspirin, suggesting a call to a specialist, complaining of neglect, of fate's cruel finger, of heat, of cold, of sharp pains on the bridge of the nose that might indicate brain involvement. What was so funny? The ladies explained to me that all men behave just like that with colds, they are reduced to temper tantrums by simple nasal conges-tion, men cannot stand any little physical discomfort—on and on the laughter went.

14   The point of this vignette is the nature of the laughter—us laughing at them, us feeling superior to them, us ridiculing them behind their backs. If they were doing it to us we'd call it male chauvinist pigness; if we do it to them, it is inescapably female chauvinist sowness and, whatever its roots, it leads to the same isolation. Boys are messy, boys are mean, boys are rough, boys are stupid and have sloppy handwriting. A cacophony of childhood memories rushes through my head, balanced, of course, by all the well-documented feelings of inferiority and envy. But the important thing, the hard thing, is to wipe the slate clean, to start again without the meanness of the past. That's why it's so important that the women's movement not become anti-male and allow its most preju-diced spokesmen total leadership. The much-chewed-over abortion

issue illustrates this. The women's-liberation position, insisting on a woman's right to determine her own body's destiny, leads in fanatical extreme to a kind of emotional immaculate conception in which the father is not judged even half-responsible—he has no rights, and no consideration is to be given to his concern for either the woman or the fetus.

15   Woman, who once was abandoned and disgraced by an unwanted pregnancy, has recently arrived at a new pride of ownership or disposal. She has traveled in a straight line that still excludes her sexual partner from an equal share in the wanted or unwanted pregnancy. A better style of life may develop from an assumption that men are as human as we. Why not ask the child's father if he would like to bring up the child? Why not share decisions, when possible, with the male? If we cut them out, assuming an old-style indifference on their part, we perpetuate the ugly divisiveness that has characterized relations between the sexes so far.

16   Hard as it is for many of us to believe, women are not really superior to men in intelligence or humanity—they are only equal.

Vocabulary

marionette	lexicon	vestibule
canard	masochistic	coeval
vignette	cacophony	

Topics for Discussion

1. Roiphe says that most people she has known "have at one time or another been fouled up by their childhood experiences." Did anything happen to you as a child that might affect your present behavior?

2. Is this essay against women's liberation? What does the title of the essay imply?

3. What does Roiphe mean when she says that women must "create a future that does not mirror the past"?

4. Much has been made of the so-called sexual double standard which allows men but not women sexual freedom. To believe in this double standard, Roiphe says, is to believe that men are "not very nice, not very moral, humane and tender, like us." Do you agree with this?

5. What does Roiphe mean by "female chauvinist sowness"?

Rhetorical Considerations

1. Is Roiphe directing this essay to men or women?
2. What use does Roiphe make of humor?
3. Would you characterize Roiphe's style as formal or casual? What evidence would you offer to support your choice? How would you characterize her diction?
4. This essay is about women's liberation. Do you find any of the terminology normally associated with women's liberation in this essay?
5. How do you react to the first sentence of the essay? Do you think this is the effect Roiphe intended?
6. Does Roiphe effectively make use of evidence to support her contentions?
7. Where is the central idea of the essay stated?

The Average American Househusband

Robert Claiborne

Robert Claiborne (b. 1919) is a writer and editor whose works include Climate, Man and History *and* On Every Side the Sea.

1   What started the whole thing was my wife's orthopedic surgery. The result for her: seven weeks of plaster and crutches. For me: seven weeks in which—with a little help from our friends—I kept house.

2   It is tempting to say that I faced this prospect with apprehension, having read the allegations of certain militant feminists that houskeeping (a) occupies the Average American Housewife for approximately eighty hours a week and (b) is degrading. To be honest, however, my wife and I had both long ago concluded that these writers knew even less about housework than about human nature. We were well aware, for example, that she, despite being saddled with a major share of our domestic burdens, normally manages to spend all her weekday mornings writing and most of her weekday

afternoons in such nondomestic pursuits as working for the peace movement and chatting and shopping with friends. It did occur to me, however, to keep a rough count of my own housekeeping hours and see how near they came to eighty a week. Or how far.

3   In round numbers, it worked out about like this. Making breakfast and dinner and doing dishes for same: 1½ hours a day, or 10½ a week. Fixing lunch and washup on weekends, one-half hour a day, or 1 hour a week. Shopping, taking out and collecting laundry and miscellaneous: 3 hours a week. Total: 14½ hours a week.

4   Thus far my own contribution, to which must be added an allowance for "outside" labor. Fixing lunch on working days (performed by relays of friends): one-half hour a day or 2½ a week. Shopping by same: 1 hour a week. Ironing: 1 hour a week, by our friendly Chinese laundryman. Cleaning: 8 hours a week by our West Indian houseworker. Total outside work: 12½ hours a week. Grand total: 27 hours a week.

5   My portion of this, though coming on top of a full-time writing job, got done without grossly fatiguing me—or, of course, degrading me.

6   I do not, obviously, claim that this schedule typifies seven weeks in the life of the Average American Housewife. In particular, as most readers will already have spotted, there are no kids figured into the equation. My own two did in fact visit us during that time, as they regularly do, but I have omitted them to avoid complicating the story. More broadly, I would note that a sizable proportion of American housewives—a third to a half—have either no children or grown children. I would note further that of those who have children, a goodly number have them of an age to take over a portion of the extra work they generate, as my own two routinely do when they visit us—though not without a certain amount of equally routine sparring over who clears and who washes.

7   But there is more to the story than numbers. My wife's immobilization meant that we watched TV more than we normally do, including commercials and their leading character, the Average American Housewife.

8   I do not know how successful these all-too-visible persuaders are in selling their housekeeping mystique to the Average American Housewife. That they must be at least reasonably successful seems implicit in their annual expenditure of tens of millions in peddling this particular bill of goods; surely somebody must be buying it. And those who do are undoubtedly well on their way to a 50- or 60-hour week, if not an 80-hour one. Housekeeping, as Betty Friedan long ago noted, follows Parkinson's law, expanding to fill the time avail-

able for it. And it will clearly expand most inexorably for those unfortunate women who have been brainwashed into accepting the inhuman standards of the housekeeping mystique.

9   Don't get me wrong. I do not suggest that because the difficulties of housekeeping have been grossly exaggerated—by writers of both TV commercials and feminist tracts—it is therefore lots of fun. Though many women (my wife included) find some aspects of homemaking—cooking and preserving, for instance—rewarding at least part of the time, much of it is incontestably dull. Though no duller, I would wager, than working in a typing pool or on an assembly line. Nor, dull or not, can I see it as "degrading"—at least not until someone explains to me why it is degrading for a woman to sweep a floor but not for a man to sweep a street.

10   Least of all am I suggesting that woman's place is in the home; her place is wherever her tastes, talents and luck can get her. I do say, however, that for those who approach the home with common sense, free from the manufactured obsessions of the housekeeping mystique, there are a lot worse places a woman could be. Or a man, for that matter.

Vocabulary

orthopedic	degrading	domestic
sparring	immobilization	inexorably
mystique	tracts	incontestably

Topics for Discussion

See "Topics for Discussion" following the next essay in this book, "The Househusband's Son Replies."

Rhetorical Considerations

1. Claiborne begins his essay with a wordy and awkward sentence, the kind of sentence we would not recommend for imitation. Why do you think he chooses this kind of sentence? Is his intent, perhaps, to sacrifice conciseness for tone? Note also the sentence fragment at the end of paragraph 2. Is it appropriate?

2. How does Claiborne use parallelism and repetition for effect in paragraph 3?

3. How do paragraphs 2, 3, and 4 work as a unit? Does Claiborne answer all the questions he raises? Can you spot holes in his argument?

4. In paragraph 6, does Claiborne skirt some central questions related to his topic?

5. Does Claiborne succeed in winnning the reader emotionally, if not through reason? If not, how might he have done so?

The Househusband's Son Replies

Sam Claiborne

1   My father, Robert Claiborne, wrote an article that appeared on the Op-Ed Page Jan. 21 and in which he calculated that during the seven weeks of his wife's disability from surgery all housekeeping chores consumed only 27 hours a week.

2   It is particularly sad, and also fairly annoying, to realize that so many men (including my father) fail to recognize what is involved in housekeeping.

3   My father's calculation is perfectly correct if you fail to take into account that (a) he neglected to mention that what he called breakfast is coffee, period. In many families breakfast is a big meal that is cooked, served and cleaned up by the mother of the house. The reason I say mother, instead of Ms., is that a lot of families have children and many of the jobs associated with children are also associated with housekeeping.

4   This brings me to point (b). In his article, my father said that of the families that have children "a goodly number have them of an age to take over a portion of the extra work they generate, as my own two routinely do when they visit us." During my stepmother's illness, his children (my sister, Amanda, and I) not only took over a portion of the extra work we generated, we have calculated that we also did five hours of work a week that we didn't generate. This included afterschool trips by my sister and me to shop, make dinner and clean up, as well as weekend work.

5   But, point (c), there are many jobs that children can't do, such as replacement and maintenance of children's clothing, entertainment of children's friends, arranging children's doctor and dental appointments, arranging birthday parties, toy-shopping, chauffeur-

ing children to a variety of activities ranging from emergency hospital visits to soccer practice—the list goes on and on.

6   Moreover, perhaps the most important job of all is just being there to listen to ideas, exchange thoughts, and help out with problems (including homework. In my family, my father as well as my mother does help me with homework and listen to my problems, but in most families this vital function of parenthood is laid in the mother's hands.)

7   Now to point (d). My father allowed a total of one and a half hours' work a day for breakfast and dinner, while my sister and I think that those meal-time jobs took at least three hours; the houseworker my father mentioned is a superefficient person whose eight hours would be 16 for anybody else.

8   So the grand total is a lot more than 27 hours. In fact, just the things he mentioned, put into more realistic terms, add up to more than 40 hours a week. When you add the things I mentioned (and the things I didn't mention) I can see those hours climbing into the fifties, sixties and seventies.

9   I do agree with my father that there is a housekeeping mystique to the Average American Housewife, though I do not agree that it is as widespread as he implies. The mystique is the idea that a woman should be completely preoccupied with becoming the flawless homemaker. This idea has been passed from mother to daughter, and television has greatly amplified it.

10   All the commercials about "ring around the collar" and "perfect rice" are all designed to make the woman viewer feel guilty. Undoubtedly, the women who are affected by them do end up spending more time housekeeping since being a flawless homemaker involves being a master launderer and housecleaner as well as being a cordon bleu chef.

11   But even without the housekeeping mystique most women end up doing much more than 27 hours of housework a week, and I didn't even mention all the jobs that are not generated by children, such as replacing kitchen utensils, household gadgets, towels and sheets.

Vocabulary

annoying	generate	routinely
maintenance	chauffeuring	implies
mystique	flawless	amplified
cordon bleu	utensils	

Topics for Discussion

1. Whom do you think has the better argument, Claiborne or his son? On which particular points of debate did you make your decision? Are some matters in the discussion more important than others? Why?

2. Is housework really a demeaning occupation, generally? Without lapsing into sentimentality, explain why housework is or is not as important an occupation as other significant jobs.

3. Why are there so many housewives, and so few househusbands? Can the problem of housework as an occupation best be dealt with by changing or sharing sex roles, by changing the character of housework, or by some other solution?

4. What experience have you had with housework and its complexities? Are there difficulties or advantages connected with this occupation which neither writer mentions?

5. Given your choice between becoming a housewife/househusband and entering a more prestigious career, which road would you choose? Why?

6. Examine Sam Claiborne's paragraph 10. Do you agree that advertising gives women (and perhaps men also) a false picture of what is important and valuable in life? Cite examples other than those mentioned by Claiborne.

7. Do you agree with the elder Claiborne that the case against housework is sometimes overstated? Whether you agree or not, do you think that individuals with legitimate complaints often overstate those complaints? Cite examples from your experience.

Rhetorical Considerations

1. Read the essay by Sam Claiborne's father which comes immediately before Sam's in this book. Does the younger Claiborne adequately deal with all of his father's arguments?

2. Sam Claiborne enumerates the major points of his argument (a, b, c, d). Would his essay have been more effective or less if he had used a different organizing device? What other devices can you think of?

3. Does the author achieve a balanced tone? Is he critical without being abrasive? See paragraph 6.

4. Is the article better or worse for not having a formal conclusion? Can you supply an effective conclusion?

5. What do these two articles tell you about the uses of evidence? Can even well-supported arguments sometimes be misleading? Cite examples both from the material here and from your own experience.

In Defense of "Mere" Women

Marjorie Proops

Marjorie Proops received the Order of the British Empire and was named Woman Journalist of the year in 1969. She has written for British newspapers including the Daily Herald *and the* Daily Mirror.

1   What has a woman toiling on a factory workbench got in common with Mrs. Margaret Thatcher, working on the Opposition front bench? Skipping the obvious physical similarities, the answer is that both are wage earners. One big difference between them is that the take-home pay of the woman on the factory bench is $60 a week while Mrs. Thatcher's weekly pay is $530.

2   Those who saw Margaret Thatcher's dramatic elevation to the top of the Tory pile as a great leap forward for women in this International Women's Year—Barbara Castle (Secretary of State for Social Services in the Labor Party Cabinet) was the first to tell me that this was the way she saw it—are misguided in their applause for what they regard as a triumph for feminism.

3   International Women's Year is no more than a token gesture, a public sop to relieve male guilt and detract from the real issues—the inequalities which exist and will continue to exist long after this year has ended. The paltry sum allocated by Britain for International Women's Year is $25,000. We allocate $20 million for sport. A year designated Women's Year and dedicated to the cause of raising our status is unlikely to produce much more than a reiteration of all the old clichés about our second-class rating and sexploitation by male chauvinist pigs.

4   What will Margaret Thatcher's victory really do for the countless women who tell me of their problems, the women who describe themselves as "mere" housewives, whose lifelong vision of them-

selves and their daughters can indeed be described as "mere"? Will it change their lifestyle in a flash—or in a year? Will it make their husbands kinder, their children less demanding, their chores easier, their sex lives more fulfilling? Will they dream of glory on the front bench, musing, as they fantasize with the duster in their hands, that Margaret's achievement could be theirs?

5   One woman's success does nothing for the expectation of "mere" women: There have always been a few outstanding women who could never be labeled "mere," however humble their beginnings. They are the ones who have the mysterious plus element, the X factor, which spurs them—as the same X factor spurs successful men—toward their glittering goals. Fine. We need leaders of both sexes, and good luck to them, male and female. But one bright female star does not mean that the rest of womankind suddenly takes on a new and glorious image of a petticoat army marching to victory over the bloodied corpses of the sexist enemy.

6   Mere women are not fighters. Aggressive with the butcher when he overcharges, perhaps, indignant when fishticks cost more. Cross when milk goes up. Angry when their husbands lose their jobs. And resigned when they have to go out to work to help the family budget. When I listen to pompous talk about the condition of women, the career fulfillment of women, the new role of women in society, I wonder whom people are talking about. They cannot be talking about the women I know, about the 30,000 or so who write to me every year.

7   The are, I imagine, talking about the tiny elite group of women—the thin layer of rich cream at the top of the bottle—who have career fulfillment and a new role (whatever that is) and expectations of being a leader. The rest of the women, the "mere" ones, simply plod on with their lives. And it is these women who are being got at by all the propaganda that is mounted.

8   No wonder the mere women are beginning to feel miserable and inadequate and are rushing off to their doctors to beg for tranquilizers and sleeping pills so that they can forget that they are supposed to feel guilty if they are not fulfilled the way the propagandists for women's rights suggest they should be. It has come to something when a young mother of three says she feels guilty because all she does with her life is stay home and look after the children and try to make the place decent for her husband when he comes in at night. Or when a working woman feels guilty because she has no ambition to be the boss, only to take home enough to pay the installments on the TV and the new three-piece suite.

9   If we are not careful in the Year of the Woman, we shall end up with millions of defensive neurotic females trying to live up to all the propaganda that puts so much pressure on them to take on more than they can cope with and more than they ever want to do. All this may make me anti–Women's Lib and reactionary and opposed to the advancement of women. But I am not knocking Women's Lib. Or not very hard.

10   Of course it is right to fight, as I do, for equality of opportunity and education, for justice in an unjust world, and against the exploitation of women and the discrimination that blocks their enterprise. Of course it is right to demand recognition of the fact that we are not second-class citizens. What is wrong is promoting the idea that all women the world over had better aim to be superstars. And feel deprived and guilty and inferior if they do not make it. Or cannot make it. Or do not even want to try. After all, not many men are going to get to the front bench, either.

Vocabulary

reiteration   cliché   chauvinist
reactionary

Topics for Discussion

1. Proops says she is close to becoming anti–Women's Liberation. What has caused this reaction in her?

2. This essay was written by an Englishwoman discussing conditions and problems in England. Do you find it difficult to understand the essay or relate to the problems discussed in the essay? What might this suggest about the fundamental issues of Women's Liberation?

3. Why does Proops maintain that Margaret Thatcher's election as leader of the Conservative Party in England was not a victory for women?

4. Who are the "mere" women Proops is concerned about? What are some of their problems?

5. Why does Proops feel International Women's Year will achieve no real progress for women?

Rhetorical Considerations

1. In her opening paragraph Proops asks and then answers a question. How does this question and its answer predict the structure of the rest of the essay?
2. Throughout the essay Proops uses sentence fragments. Are they effective?
3. Proops invents the term "mere women" for this essay. How does the use of this term unify the essay?
4. Is Proops's use of informal diction appropriate?

Is Gloria Steinem Dead?

Annette K. Baxter

Annette Baxter (b. 1926) is a professor of history and chairwoman of the history department at Barnard College. She has published widely in scholarly journals as well as Harper's *and other magazines.*

1   In his first address as President to the joint session of Congress, Gerald Ford said that he would be the President of all Americans, and proceeded to illustrate with a list embracing different ages, races, religions, occupations, backgrounds and economic means. In this heartwarming declaration, there was one grouping that surely would not have appeared in any previous President's list: "women's liberationists and male chauvinists and all the rest of us in between."

2   It was a striking concession to the political impact of the women's movement. But more significant was the addition of the phrase "and all the rest of us in between." Coming from a former star center on the University of Michigan football team, the acknowledgement that he counted himself as one of those "in between" ought to gladden the hearts of all but the most diehard partisans on either side of the feminist controversies of recent years.

Indeed, behind the playful humor of his remarks may have lurked
some friendly criticism of extremists in either camp. As a man noted
for his skill at conciliation, President Ford could be hoping to effect
a truce even in the troubled area of sexual politics.

3   Certainly many Americans have recently been indicating that
they are eager for such a truce. Employers and government agencies
have been searching for women to fill upper-echelon jobs. The
courts have been struggling with old prejudices on matters ranging
from abortion to the Little League. And husbands have become less
resistant to domestic responsibilities. Meanwhile, women with no
previous ambitions beyond their family and the PTA have ventured
increasingly into the working world. The shriller and more aggressive feminists have become less audible and visible. All signs point
to the end of a revolution. In proclaiming Women's Equality Day,
President Ford has suggested that the time has now come to in-
stitutionalize the gains of the past five years.

4   Is this, then, the final import of the women's movement? Are
Gloria Steinem and Kate Millett already figures out of our past,
useful as revolutionary catalysts but no longer needed when the
average American's outlook has to a greater or lesser degree been
purged of rampant sexism? The answer depends on what we thought
the women's movement was about in the first place. Higher-status
jobs, plentiful role models, fairer household sharing and quality day
care—all imply that women deserve both more opportunity and
more freedom than they have enjoyed in the past. But to my mind,
the women's movement is part of a much larger change, a change
away from stereotyped thinking in our national life.

5   Like the civil-rights movement of the 1960s, the women's
movement of the 1970s means more than simply the broadened
participation within American life of a formerly disadvantaged
group. What seems to me of overarching importance is the deflation
of stereotypes that has accompanied both movements. It is easier to
provide better jobs for women and blacks or to establish day-care
centers and youth-corps programs than it is to overcome the fixed
images people harbor of others, whether out of ignorance and fear,
or out of philistinism and a lack of imagination. As blacks entered
the mainstream in recent years, they had to struggle simultaneously
to overcome these images and to recover in all its variety and
complexity the authenticity of their own past. For women, too, this
has been the urgent task. How far, then, have women really come?

6   Not far enough. Shortly before President Ford's address, Sen.
Barry Goldwater was quoted as responding to the possibility of a
woman Vice President in these words: ''I have nothing against a

woman, just so she can cook and get home on time.'' When will the American male cease not only to speak such thoughts but to think them? Here is where feminists face their toughest challenge. No one would wish Senator Goldwater to be deprived of free speech, although political pressure may exact from him a measure of caution in the future. (The Arizona Women's Political Caucus promptly wired President Ford, asking for Senator Goldwater's own removal from the list of Vice Presidential candidates.) But a genuine conversion in the thinking of most American males will be the product of frequent exposure to a variety of life-patterns, tastes and accomplishments in both sexes, and thus it will be a while before chauvinism is voluntarily surrendered.

7   Though psychologists have repeatedly demonstrated that innate sexual characteristics are extremely difficult, if not impossible, to assign, the belief persists that a shift in the familiar roles of men and women will somehow threaten the natural polarity of the sexes. The richness and mystery of human personality are continually underrated by those who fear a sexual Armageddon in the wake of female liberation.

8   For this fear the best remedy may be a strong dose of women's history. Like black history, which strikes at the roots of the white man's stereotypes, women's history has opened unexpected vistas into the feminine psyche. When enough Americans learn that Emerson's friend Margaret Fuller, journalist, teacher and philosopher, possessing one of the most brilliant minds America ever produced, was once the helpless victim of infatuation and later married a man intellectually far beneath her, the stereotype of the bluestocking suffers a severe blow. When they discover that Elizabeth Cady Stanton, a central force within the nineteenth-century American feminist movement, raised seven children, had a happy and fulfilling family life, yet wrote and lectured on laws unjust to married women and ended by attacking prevailing Biblical interpretations of sexual roles, the stereotype of the contented housewife invites revision.

9   When they look into such later controversial figures as Jane Addams, Emma Goldman, Margaret Sanger and Gertrude Stein, they will have to reject the ruling stereotypes of women altruists, radicals, reformers and bohemians. Ultimately, this will require the rejection of feminine stereotypes of any kind.

10   In the past, only the exceptionally strong or talented or contentious woman could hope to transform her life into a feminist parable. The study of those exceptional lives, together with the daily challenging of stereotypes by contemporary feminists, should convince men like Goldwater to adopt a more sophisticated, as well as a more

humane, view of what women are. It was cheering to read, on the same day that the senator's remarks were reported, that President Ford enjoys cooking. An ex-football star who likes to cook may be just the President feminists have been looking for.

Vocabulary

chauvinists	concession	partisans
extremists	conciliation	echelon
ventured	shriller	catalysts
rampant	stereotyped	overarching
philistinism	simultaneously	authenticity
assign	Armageddon	vistas
infatuation	altruists	bohemians
contentious	parable	

Topics for Discussion

1. Do you notice in your own life that attitudes toward the expected social roles of women have been changing? Define, precisely, some of these changes.

2. Do you think that the greater visibility given to women professionals (news reporters, for example) has helped provide more opportunities for women generally? See especially the end of paragraph 6.

3. How many of the women mentioned in paragraph 8 are you familiar with? Should schools and colleges modify their curricula to emphasize the contributions of women?

4. Why do you think the president identified himself as neither a women's liberationist nor a male chauvinist? Do you think that Ford's fondness for cooking necessarily implies anything about his attitude toward the position of women in society? What has happened since this essay was written to support your view?

5. In your opinion, what are the most worthwhile goals for the women's liberation movement? What methods should be used to reach these goals?

6. What is your opinion of preferential hiring for women and members of minority groups? Is this practice essentially discrimination in reverse, or is it necessary for genuine equality? Defend your view.

Rhetorical Considerations

1. Are the references in paragraph 4 to Gloria Steinem and Kate Millett somewhat obscure? What does Baxter assume about her audience in making these references?

2. Are the comparisons between the women's movement and the civil rights movement (paragraphs 5 and 8) helpful to the thesis of the essay? Should these comparisons be developed further?

3. How do the references to President Ford in paragraphs 1 and 10 help to unify the essay?

4. How do the references to Senator Goldwater contribute to the essay's coherence?

5. Which paragraphs provide a definition of the women's liberation movement? How satisfactory is this definition?

A Talk With Simone de Beauvoir

Caroline Moorehead

Caroline Moorehead is a staff writer for the London Times *and contributes articles to the* New York Times.

1   Freedom for women is a basic theme in her work, the notion that women must be true to themselves, and not live as women through men. She based "The Second Sex" on the ethics of existentialism, the moral imperative that every human being must have the right to engage in freely chosen activity. And she frequently attacks any relationship in which both parties are not equally free, or in which women are treated as objects rather than equal human beings.

2   In "The Second Sex" she wrote that the principle of marriage was obscene because it transformed into rights and duties an exchange which should be founded on spontaneous attraction. She says now: "I don't think the whole social system should be based on marriage. It's hard to say what should be put in its place, but the fact that one criticizes it doesn't mean that one has to find something to replace it. After all, the American slaves didn't ask themselves what was going to happen to the American economy when they won their freedom.

3 "I think marriage is a very alienating institution, for men as well as for women. I think it's a very dangerous institution— dangerous for men, who find themselves trapped, saddled with a wife and children to support; dangerous for women, who aren't financially independent and end up by depending on men who can throw them out when they are 40; and very dangerous for children, because their parents vent all their frustrations and mutual hatred on them. The very words 'conjugal rights' are dreadful. Any institution which solders one person to another, obliging people to sleep together who no longer want to is a bad one."

4 Mlle. de Beauvoir has never denied that there is a great difference between men and women; but she insists that it is culturally determined.

5 "I think the difference begins immediately, at birth. Even such a ridiculous thing as choosing a pink or a blue blanket means that the parents start discriminating," she said to me. "By the age of 1 the little boy has already been turned into a boy, the little girl into a girl. I was very struck by a psychoanalyst I read recently who said that if masculinity isn't built up in a little boy then he turns out just as feminine—if you can call it that—as a little girl."

6 It is not enough, she points out, for parents to try to provide an identical upbringing for boys and girls, because everything with which children come into contact—the stories they read, the clothes they wear, the toys they are given—show them clearly that they are meant to be unalike. "To achieve perfect equality you would have to start at the very roots, reconstruct an entire educational system, and, to do that, a totally new society. Boys and girls should be given exactly the same experience, as I hear they are trying in nursery schools in Sweden and Denmark.

7 "Cleanliness, for instance, should not just be handled by mother or women teachers. Fathers should do just as much cleaning up. Just as there should be men nursery teachers, so that boys grow up thinking that a man looks after children, too. But all this is terribly difficult without a basic change in society. . . . To change the mentality of women one would also need to change that of men, so as to create a person in which is combined the best of man and the best of woman."

Vocabulary

spontaneous	alienating	mutual
conjugal	solders	psychoanalyst

Topics for Discussion

1. To what extent are women treated as objects in this society? What kinds of objectification do you think are most harmful, personally and socially?

2. Do you think that, perhaps, men are degraded in this society by being treated as objects? In what ways are men treated as objects, by women and by other men?

3. Do you agree or disagree with de Beauvoir's views on marriage (paragraphs 2 and 3)? If you agree, what kinds of relationships would you like to see replace marriage?

4. Does your generation, in your opinion, have a view of marriage different from that of your parents' generation? What observations in your personal life lead you to your conclusions?

5. Do you think that marriages that are not "alienating" or "dangerous" do, or can, exist? Without discussing your parents' marriage, explain what such a relationship might entail.

6. Evaluate de Beauvoir's comments in paragraph 5 concerning the socialization of children. Should socialization into sex roles be discouraged? What might be some of the results of this change?

7. In what ways do you think men will have to change their attitudes as women more and more come to occupy positions traditionally held by men? How might our social structure have to change?

Rhetorical Considerations

1. Do Moorehead's comments interfere with the clear exposition of de Beauvoir's ideas, or do those comments serve for better organization and clarity in the essay?

2. Evaluate the interplay between editorial comment and quotation in paragraph 2. What purpose does the use of the word *obscene* serve?

3. Why does de Beauvoir introduce the example of the American slaves in paragraph 2?

4. How does the author indicate her agreement or disagreement with de Beauvoir's views? Examine the tone of paragraph 4.

5. Examine de Beauvoir's use of parallelism in paragraph 3.

Monogamy

Brigid Brophy

Brigid Brophy (b. 1929) lives in London, England, where she has won prizes for her writings, which include Hackenfeller's Ape, The Finishing Touch, *and* The Snow Bull. *She is also a frequent contributor to the* New Statesman, London Magazine, *and other journals.*

1   There is a belief, widely held among both sexes, that whereas men are irked by monogamy women are suited to it by nature.

2   Even on the face of it, this seems fishy. After all, monogamy is what we actually have; and the social, religious and legal systems which gave it to us were all invented, and until recently run, by men. I can well believe men were masochistic enough to impose monogamy on themselves as a hairshirt, but I find it a touch implausible that the hairshirt designed for the husband just happened to be a comfortable and perfectly fitting garment for the wife.

3   And indeed I suspect that, if you scrutinize the notion that women are naturally monogamous, it turns out to be based on no sounder authority than that rhyme which begins "higamus hogamus, woman is monogamous," and no more cogent evidence than a one-eyed view of biology which is in fact about as good science as "higamus hogamus" is good Latin.

4   The "biological" argument goes like this. A man can, if pressed for time, beget a child in twenty-five seconds flat, but a woman can't bring it to birth in less than nine months (seven if it's premature). A woman can therefore, the argument proceeds, be set up in the reproductive business and kept fully occupied at it by the expenditure of only a tiny fraction of a man's time and sexual capacity; he, on the other hand, will have so much of both those to spare that a natural impulse will drive him to distribute them among several other women. Thus, the argument concludes, a woman is so constituted by nature that she can be made happy and "fulfilled" by the part-time attentions of one man, but if a man is not allowed to pay his attentions to several women he will be frustrated and unhappy.

5   What is one-eyed about this view is that it sees nothing in biology but reproduction. It is also remarkably ignorant of women. In point of fact, biology endows women not only with the ability and

an instinct to bear children but also with the ability to experience pleasure and an instinct to seek it. Close the eye which sees nothing but reproduction and open instead the eye which sees the overriding biological instinct towards pleasure, and you get a very different biological argument. A man is sexually excited on small provocation, satisfied quickly, and often so exhausted by the process that he falls straight asleep. A woman, on the other hand, requires long and skilled wooing if she is to be satisfied at all; when she is, she is often ready to start being wooed again within half a minute. The needs of a man can, therefore, be satisfied to exhaustion point by one woman, but she will still retain capacities and desires which will be frustrated unless she has further men to go on to. Indeed, what her biology really requires is a large number of lovers, from whom she will discard those whose love-making doesn't suit her, and will pick out and keep not one—who would be too quickly exhausted—but three or four permanent husbands. Thus, higamus hogamus, it is man who is monogamous and, hogamus higamus, woman who is, by her biological nature, polygamous.

6   There is of course no reason why we should be bound by nature and biology at all. Much of civilization consists of overcoming them and setting ourselves free to choose. Many people of both sexes choose monogamy, overcoming their biological tendency to polygamy. But it is unreasonable of society to—without good cause—impose monogamy on the ones who have not chosen it. Above all, there is no reason why, human relationships being almost infinitely various, we should impose any one pattern on all marriages—especially when it so often doesn't work.

7   At present, monogamy is the corset into which we try to fit every married couple—a process which has on so many occasions split the seams that we have had to modify the corset. There used to be a social modification which, excused by the erroneous belief that men were naturally more polygamous than women, gave the sort of glancing blow that is really an approving pat to men who broke out of monogamy but seriously and cruelly disapproved of women who did. The injustice of this "double standard" is now pretty clear to everyone, and in its place we have introduced a legal modification of monogamy. Divorce is a device which makes polygamy permissible, but only nonsimultaneous polygamy. In practice, even this is modified. The law sometimes insists that a divorcée remain a man's wife economically though she is no longer so in name or in bed. The result is that just as in Mohammedan countries the number of wives a man may legally have simultaneously is often whittled down in practice to the number he can support, so in Europe and the United

States, under our modified monogamy, the number of ex-wives a man may legally have simultaneously is often limited to the number of *those* he can support.

8   Apart from this economic bias against men, divorce is much fairer than the double standard, since it is equally available, on the same grounds, to men and women. Its unfairness starts with the grounds. Divorce is an excellent solution when both married people want to say goodbye. But let them admit that that's what they both want, and English law refuses them a divorce. Often they have to pretend an adultery—which is, legally considered, the best and, rationally considered, the worst conceivable grounds for divorce. Nothing could be more wasteful of that rare and rarely beautiful quality, married love, than that a marriage should break simply because one of the partners would like to enlarge it by co-opting a third.

9   To be sure, the whole business of love and people's behaviour under its stress is irrational in itself; but that is all the more reason to be as rational as we can in coping with our most irrational area. Sexual jealousy is one of the most painful emotions on earth. But in coping with it society licenses us to indulge in a two-year-old's tantrum. To divorce your mate because he has mated with someone else is to cut off your nose to spite the face you suddenly feel holds less attraction for him; it is to act on the principle that no bread is better than half a loaf. In some countries an unwritten law even permits the slighted spouse to kill the adulterous one. Here you may merely make him dead as far as you are concerned, by cutting him out of your life by divorce. This is probably the most perverse approach you could make to what, if you love him, you want, which is to have him living, and with you.

10   The obvious remedy is at least respectabilised and for preference legalised polygamy. No one in his senses could suppose it would be easy or painless to work. But it would give less pain than either of the other courses: to stand on your full monogamous rights and insist that the person you love forgo the company of someone he loves; or to avail yourself of the legal modification to monogamy and insist on yourself forgoing the company of the person you love.

Vocabulary

monogamy	masochistic	scrutinize
instinct	polygamous	nonsimultaneous

Topics for Discussion

1. How true is the contention in paragraph 1? Do most women still believe that they ought to be less sexually alive than men? In your opinion, are women naturally more monogamous than men?

2. Evaluate Brophy's contention in the first two sentences of paragraph 6. What relationship does she posit between civilization and nature? Do you agree?

3. Is monogamy a characteristic only of marriage, or does it also characterize many premarital relationships (e.g., engagement, going steady)? Do you think premarital monogamous relationships help or hinder personal growth?

4. What are some of the advantages and disadvantages of monogamy for both men and women?

5. Suggest some alternatives to monogamy other than the general "polygamy" mentioned by Brophy.

6. In your opinion, does the institution of marriage make duties of things which ought to be freely and spontaneously given? If so, can, or should, marriage, as an institution, be changed in some important ways?

Rhetorical Considerations

1. In paragraph 9, Brophy uses clichés to support her contentions. Identify these clichés. Are they rhetorically justified? Is the colloquialism at the beginning of paragraph 1 justified?

2. Analyze the relationship between the argument in paragraph 4 and the argument in paragraph 5. What techniques are used in each? Does one successfully answer the other?

3. What is Brophy's contention in paragraph 6? How do paragraphs 4 and 5 prepare the reader to accept Brophy's views?

4. Why is the metaphor in the first sentence of paragraph 7 specifically appropriate to the topic? Create two or three similarly appropriate metaphors.

5. Paragraph 9 contains sentences far more formally structured than those found in most of the rest of the essay. Does this formality work to the writer's advantage, or do you think it a slip into turgid prose? If you think these sentences need changing, how should they be changed?

The 21st-Century Woman—Free at Last?

Clare Boothe Luce

Clare Boothe Luce (b. 1903) is an author and playwright whose works include The Women, Margin for Error, Child of the Morning, *and* Slam the Door Softly.

1   Anyone—feminist or anti-feminist—who reads the above title knows that the author intends to speculate on the "gut" feminist question: the chances of overthrowing male supremacy in our social order and achieving equality of the sexes.

2   Will the male, in America, still be considered superior to the female a half-century from now? Will the American woman's political, economic, and social status still be inferior? Will her individual social status—the respect given to her in her community—still largely derive from the respect accorded to her husband or other male relatives? Will her chief claim to a place in history still consist in being, or having been, some famous man's wife or mother? Will woman still be only a consumer of goods and a spender of money, or will she also be a co-equal producer of goods and a co-equal maker of money?

3   What is there for a feminist, in the year 1974, to cheer about? And why did an intelligent and sensitive editor tell me recently that he foresaw "a tidal wave" of feminism rising in the land which, if taken at the flood, would lead women on to fame and fortune?

4   I suspect that he, like so many other men of goodwill and large mind, is exaggerating the importance of three breakthroughs for the female sex that have more or less recently occurred.

5   The first is the advance made by medical technology in giving woman control over her own reproductive function. The availability (to American women) of reliable contraceptives, especially the Pill, is *potentially* of great help in her struggle for equality.

6   The talk about what "nature intended" in respect of the social roles of the male and the female is a lot of nonsense. Roles are character parts played by the *dramatis personae* in the human tragedy. Roles are, by definition, assignable—and *re-assignable*—at

the discretion of society. People play them well, or badly, willingly or unwillingly. It is, of course, always to the best interests of society that the roles which its members play should be well and willingly played. In a truly participatory democracy, all its characters or citizens would be free to choose their own roles.

7   It is a historic fact that there is no social role that has not, at some time, somewhere, been played by a woman. Women have been absolute monarchs and heads of states. They have also been (outside of the West) priests. Tinker, tailor, soldier, sailor—women in one culture or another have played every masculine role. And vice versa. Women were once the vintners, the farmers, the weavers, the animal breeders of society. Now men are. Is cooking today a male or a female role? The cook who cooks for nothing is a female—or a housewife. The cook who cooks for $25,000 is a male—or a chef.

8   Even the so-called female nursing role is often played by men. The American male who rises at 2:00 A.M. to feed baby his bottle is playing a "woman's role."

9   Nature assigns no "roles" to her creatures. She endows them with instincts and functions, which are not re-assignable. And she lets her role-playing human children take it from there. Nature intended them to procreate, since it endowed them—and heavily—with the copulative instinct. (In view of the fate of the once-dominant dinosaurs, whether nature *intended* any particular species to survive—including humans—is an open question.) Nature also endowed the sexes with different procreative organs and programmed them for different functions. It programmed a healthy male with the capacity to copulate tens of thousands of times (the spirit moving him) in the course of a lifetime. It programmed a healthy female with the capacity to bear between 20 and 30 children. I venture to suggest that there are few American men today who think that women should stick with nature's program—or, as the expression goes, "play the role of mother, for which nature intended them."

10   For centuries, women had no control (except abortion) over nature's programming of their procreative function. Consequently, owing to successive pregnancies, they were unable to play many of the social roles that they otherwise could have performed quite ably.

11   Thanks to contraceptives and the Pill, woman no longer is forced to choose between no sex or the once-inevitable 9-months, 9-pounds consequences of the sex act. For the first time in history, she is—*almost*—as free as man to opt for the roles she wishes to

play in society. Motherhood has now become a role that she can assign to herself or refuse to have assigned to her even by her husband. The social consequences of this new freedom, however, await the verdict of history. For the past 50 years woman has used her political freedom badly. It remains to be seen whether she will make any better use of her sexual freedom. But the opportunity of using it to her own best interests is there.

12   A human's "best years," in the role-playing market, are between the ages of 18 and 65. Depending on how many children a woman chooses to have, she can make herself available today as a role-player for all, or part, of these years. *If* (and this is a point I will come to later) she is determined to get a particular role, and *if* society's historic role-assigner—the male of her species—can be made to give it to her, there is no longer any reason why she should not play it.

13   The second great breakthrough favoring the goal of sex equality is the opening of the doors of higher education to women. Today a girl who can make it to college can get the same education as a boy—right through the Ph.D. level. Today she is free to study for any "masculine" career that her own ambition suggests. But as matters stand, her ambition is understandably dampened by the knowledge that even if she graduates at the top of her class, she will not find it easy to translate her well-earned degree into an upward mobility job. Nevertheless, the educational opportunities and facilities that have been opened to women in the last decade are one valid cause of the recent breeze of optimism that is blowing in feminist circles. The ranks of the feminist leaders are being swelled every day by the female graduates of the universities.

14   A third cause for feminist optimism is the progress that is being made in the legal area. Groups of well-organized professional women and feminists are taking skillful advantage of the civil-rights bills and government regulations originally designed to end discrimination against black *males* and are applying them to end discrimination against females. Too much credit cannot be given to the organized groups of feminists for the vigorous pressure they are putting on the government and the courts.

15   I now reach, somewhat reluctantly, for my crystal ball. I am sorry to say that the picture I see there is *not* one of Woman sitting in the Oval Room of the White House in 2024. I see her playing many more roles that were once considered masculine. I see her making a little more money than she is making now. But I see her still trying to make her way up—in a man's world—and not having

very much more success than she is having now. There may be, and probably will be, great political and technological changes in the world in the next half-century. But I venture to suggest that none of them will greatly affect the relatively inferior status of the American woman.

16   Several years ago, Edward A. Shaw, dean of job placement at the Career-Planning Center of U.C.L.A., explained to a woman interviewer that although women now have many jobs in which they sit apart and analyze, identify, and solve business, industrial, political, and scientific problems ("think jobs"), they are still not getting jobs with upward mobility in "line management." "There is," Mr. Shaw said, *"an underlying cultural reluctance to have women bossing men."* And this is the very heart of the matter.

17   Throughout recorded history, in all civilizations at all times and in all places, the underlying culture in respect of the *most important of all human relationships*—the male-female relationship—has been patriarchal: the male has had dominion over the female throughout recorded history. It is much too late in this article to point out that the prehistoric cultures were matriarchies or to argue the question of whether patriarchy is what "nature intended." (However, I have already indicated that I think it is not.)

18   But there is, perhaps, time to make three quick points: first, feminists who are bent on knocking out a worldwide underlying culture, which shows no great signs of collapse, are taking on a pretty large assignment.

19   Second, the very durability of the superior male–inferior female relationship is reasonably good proof that it has *so far* served the best interests of human society. It has certainly permitted the survival of woman, inferior and unhappy though her lot has been. Despite man's undeniable inhumanity to woman, she not only has survived but represents today half of the world's population. Indeed, woman has not only survived her treatment as an inferior in greater numbers than her "superiors"; in modern times she survives some five years longer. Male supremacy has kept her down. It has not knocked her out.

20   Third, and last, the fact that male superiority has lasted so long is not in itself proof that it will survive even another century. (Though the odds are certainly that it will.)

21   The institution of slavery (oppression by the use of overt force) existed at the dawn of history and lasted, with social approval in almost all civilizations, right down to the middle of the nineteenth century. (As forced labor, it still exists in Soviet Russia.) Our own

Founding Fathers, as enlightened, scholarly, liberty-loving, and God-fearing a group of males as ever lived, did not question either the religious or political morality of black slavery. In America the institution of slavery was brought to an end only a century ago. And it took the bloodiest war on our soil to do it. Nevertheless—*it ended.*

22   The oppressed (the enslaved, the politically imprisoned, the exploited, the discriminated against) are oppressed because oppression is to the oppressor's interests, and because the oppressed lack the physical, political, economic, and psychological means to resist and throw them off. The oppressed never free themselves—they do not have the necessary strengths. They become free only when their oppressors lose the strength or the will to oppress them. A white President emancipates the black man. A male Congress grants woman the vote. A male-dominated Congress passes the equal-rights amendment.

23   The dominating, or oppressor, class relinquishes its position of superiority either when another dominant class collapses it (the anti-slavery white North defeats the white slave-holding South), or when oppression no longer serves the political, economic, and psychological needs of the oppressors.

24   Today it is certain that the centuries-old underlying culture of male supremacy no longer serves *man's* best interests, if for no other reason than that the political and economic arithmetic of sex-discrimination, like the arithmetic of slavery, is increasingly written in red ink. And although the majority of men are not yet themselves aware of it, there are many evidences that the superior male–inferior female relationship is no longer serving their psychological needs. The American male is not yet ready to take his foot off the female's neck. He has believed for too many centuries that that is what nature intended his foot and her neck for. But as a liberal, a humanitarian, and a democrat, he is not really happy in the ancient posture. Nor, he has begun to see, is she. It is not exactly a posture in which she has much of a chance to enjoy her life, her liberty, or the pursuit of her happiness. Also, she has begun to struggle and cry out in anger and in pain. She is not looking up *to* him with the eyes of a loving dog any more. She is looking up *at* him with eyes that are full of contempt for the person who looks down on any other human being as his inferior.

25   Altogether, the psychological satisfactions are going out of the scene. But it may take him another 50 years to admit it. A hundred years from now she may be on her own feet, in the dawn of the Age of Equality.

Vocabulary

dramatis personae   vintner   patriarchal
matriarchy   overt

Topics for Discussion

1. Do you share Luce's pessimism about the present and future status of women? Why or why not?

2. How significant has medical technology been in advancing the status of women? What advances can you mention that Luce doesn't?

3. Do you agree that there is "an underlying cultural reluctance to have women bossing men"? What effect does such a reluctance have on advancing the status of women? Can anything be done to overcome such reluctance?

4. Do you agree with Luce that "nature assigns no roles to her creatures"? If you disagree with Luce, can you then accept the rest of her arguments? If you believe in roles, what arguments would you use to disprove Luce's thesis?

5. What are the three causes for feminine optimism in progress that Luce cites?

6. What changes do you think would occur in our society if the fundamental patriarchal male-female relationship were altered? Would you like such changes?

Rhetorical Considerations

1. Luce announces her thesis in the first three paragraphs of her essay. What is that thesis? Is stating an essay's thesis in the opening paragraphs an effective rhetorical device? Suggest at least three alternate introductions Luce could have used.

2. A transition occurs in paragraph 15. How does Luce indicate this transition? What shift in the structure and development of the essay occurs at this point?

3. Throughout the essay Luce enumerates her various arguments by simply listing them with the words "first, second, third." See paragraphs 18 to 20, for example. Is this an effective rhetorical device? What effect does Luce achieve by using it?

4. Luce's conclusion in paragraphs 24 and 25 both summarizes and presents new arguments. What is the tone of her conclusion? Does it fit with the tone of the rest of the essay?

5. What part of Luce's argument is fact and what part opinion? How does she use the two to build an effective argument?

Where Did Their Revolution Go?

J. K. Obatala

J. K. Obatala is an associate professor and Chairman of Black Studies at Long Beach State University, California, and was a founding member of the Black Student Union at California State College, Los Angeles.

1   A tall, muscular figure rose slowly and deliberately from the lunchroom table, his semi-clenched fist wavering anxiously in the dimly lighted space above his head; he motioned as if to place a devastating blow in the attentive face of one of the seated students. From the cashier's booth where I was standing, the vague symmetry of the student's body appeared silhouette-like against the pale white background of the Venetian blinds which concealed the card players from the brightness of the world outside.

2   Although the near-rhythmic rumble of uninhibited voices which came from the darkened corner had now subsided momentarily, elsewhere in the cafeteria the drone of meal-time chatter continued unbroken: even after the wavering black fist, which had probably held an ace of spades, or perhaps a deuce, came slamming down upon the table with a thunderous crash, evoking jubilant cries of "Boston!, Boston!" from the small cluster of black spectators who had huddled around the table.

3   To the mass of white students this was—so it must have appeared—simply another game of Afro-American-style Bid Whiz being brought once again to its melodramatic conclusion. But to the small group of Afro-American students who gather in the cafeteria at Cal State, Los Angeles, almost every day, a "Boston" is much more than just a flawless card game. It is something in which to immerse

oneself, a social ritual, a ''trip'' whereby participants try to extricate themselves from the humdrum that has once again become life on the college campus.

4   To be sure, many blacks on college and university campuses manage to find other equally satisfying diversions. Indeed, the chronic card players represent only a small minority of Afro-American students. Yet their reappearance in the cafeterias and lounges on a regular basis is an important indicator of the state of political affairs among black students. For during the heyday of the black student movement, many of the card players could be seen among the rank and file of the protesters and demonstrators; and it is no accident that this and other forms of black student escapism come at a time when political activism among blacks on campus is at the lowest ebb since its emergence in the early 1960s.

5   Aside from the resurgence of black student escapism, the most important index of the decline of black political activity on campus is the withering away of many of the once ubiquitous Black Student Unions (BSUs) and the stagnant, almost impotent posture of those which manage to survive. This can be seen not only in the case of Cal State University at Los Angeles, where the Black Student Union has been dissolved, but the same phenomenon is also evident on other campuses throughout Southern California (and perhaps the nation). At Cal State, Dominguez Hills, for example, the once militant BSU is gone and in its place is the ''Black Caucus,'' which is nothing more than a negotiating committee, a black students' version of the NAACP. All is calm at the University of Southern California, while at UCLA, the BSU is still intact but has adopted a relatively moderate program of action, one that resembles liberal Republicanism more than revolutionary change. For example:

> Our direction for the *past quarter and the quarter to come* is towards meeting the educational, social, political, and service needs of black students in relation to self-help and co-ordination. Our programs and projects are designed primarily to service the black family *at UCLA* in the most constructive ways we can. The black Student Union's programs are: Sickle Cell Anemia; Prison Project; Ethnic Film Series; Black Culture Week. [Emphasis added.]

Thus spoke the chairman of UCLA's BSU in a recent issue of the black student newspaper, *Nommo*. It could very well have been Robert Finch.

6   Whatever happened to the black campus revolution? Whatever happened to the gun-toting nationalist, the uncombed hair, the dem-

onstrations, the handbills, the placards, the protests, the black leather jackets and Malcolm X sweat shirts that came to be symbols of black student militancy in the 1960s? One answer is, of course, that the "true revolutionaries" have either been killed, jailed, driven underground or just plain suppressed by the forces of law and order. In a few instances, this has indeed been the case.

7   However, a more realistic explanation would be that there simply never was a "black revolution." There was militancy, as well as anger, hate and racial frustration, but—except for radical rhetoric—never much of a genuine revolutionary conviction on the part of most black students. Ironically, if indeed there had been a meaningful degree of revolutionary commitment and understanding among the black student population, much of the chaos and confusion that was generated out of the black campus rebellion in its later stages might never have occurred. For the mature revolutionary understands that real revolutions aren't made in a day and that violence is an important but not an *all-important* part of revolutionary strategy; that there comes a time in any protracted struggle when thought is much more important than action.

8   Yet the black campus mood today is not one of revolutionary reflection and regroupment; in fact, the black "revolution" has become its opposite: many Afro-Americans on campuses where yesterday blacks declared their willingness to "wipe out the white race" if their demands were not met, seem now prepared to "wipe out" half the black race if the gains from those demands are threatened. Thus it has been reported that a high administration official at UCLA, put there in response to the militant demands of black students, has cautioned the Economic Opportunities Program (EOP) workers on campus against admitting lower-income students with jail records because the latter might "cause trouble"! And strange though it may at first seem, many black students are in sympathy with this conservative approach to student admissions. This is demonstrated, implicitly, by the fact that there has been little opposition from black students—including the BSUs—on the various Southern California campuses to EOP policies which are clearly biased against lower-income students.

9   Nor should the lingering, if somewhat stale, separatist rhetoric of "blackness" and "nation building" be allowed to obscure the essentially conservative outlook of the Afro-American student population. Even during the peak years of the black campus "revolt"—the middle to late 1960s—such verbiage was nothing more than a fudge coating, beneath which lay the frozen social drives, the frustrated goals and unrealized ideals of an essentially

patriotic, pro-American and white-oriented black middle class. Indeed, as the training ground for the Afro-American elite, the colleges and university campuses—not only in Southern California but throughout the nation—have always been the strongholds of black conservatism.

10   Thus the black world to which the Afro-American student "revolutionary" supposedly declared his allegiance in the 1960s was, in reality, the white world of the 1950s: a world from which the Afro-American middle class was disbarred by the dogs, fire hoses and night sticks of the white-dominated American ruling class. Denied entrance into the white world around whose periphery it had been anxiously pacing since Reconstruction, the black bourgeoisie, led by a radicalized student sector, turned against its white liberal mentors and stormed angrily into the ranks of the growing "separatist" movement. Here they drew crude sketches of an alternative black world—a fantasy world, devoid of hypocritical white liberals, decidely more humane and, most important, controlled by blacks. This new world of the black bourgeoisie remained without any concrete expression except that it was supposed to be a manifestation of "blackness."

11   This vagueness, of course, was an attempt to hide the fact that the Afro-American bourgeoisie had little in common with the masses of black people with whom it had formed a temporary and somewhat shaky alliance. The brief alliance between the Afro-American elite and the masses—who, because of their social conditions are frequently susceptible to separatist agitation—expressed itself socially and politically as the Black Power movement.

12   Though few would dare admit it at the time, Black Power meant totally different things to different people. For the masses, the struggle for power had truly revolutionary implications, in that such a struggle must necessarily concern itself with a redistribution of goods and income and a change in the ownership of productive capacity. This was shown by the fact that looting was a main preoccupation of the ghetto rebellions that erupted among the masses in Watts, Harlem, Detroit and other American cities.

13   On the other hand, when the Afro-American middle class—including the black student elite—spoke of power, it was, with a few exceptions, speaking mainly in terms of social recognition and social mobility within the present system. Therefore, the vague and abstract nature of the bourgeois ideologies of "blackness" and Black Power was its main strength: it helped to conceal the divergent and contradictory interest of the masses and the Afro-American middle class.

14   However, in the last half of the 1960s, the Afro-American student community—its ranks swollen by converted integrationists returned from the civil rights struggles in the Southeast—started to organize itself under the umbrella of Black Power. The key issues around which most of the Black Student Unions were organized were the basically elitist notions of black studies, EOP and more black professors on the faculties.

15   Although these essentially reformist demands were clothed in the rhetorical garb of black nationalism, they were not qualitatively different from the demands Dr. Martin Luther King, Jr. had made upon transit authorities in Montgomery, Ala. more than a decade earlier, when he demanded black bus drivers for the black community. Thus the "separatism" of the black campus elite was, for the most part, back-door integrationism. The programs of the Black Student Unions consisted of nothing more than the deferred dreams of the integrationist movement, transformed by frustrated minds into the surrealistic imagery which flowed so profusely from the pens and lips of petit-bourgeois intellectuals whose influence came to dominate the unions: Blackness! Soul! Negritude! Redneck! House Niggers! White Racist! Indeed, the black student elite cursed the white man with a thousand tongues and, at the same time, implicitly, worshipped his institutions: Miss *Black* America! The *Black* Madonna! Miss *Black* Homecoming! The *Black* Church! *Black* History! *Black* Capitalism! The *Black* University! All of these were the militant harangues of a socially frustrated and alienated people, provocative symbolism which tended to obscure the essentially conservative political and institutional outlook of the Afro-American nationalist movement on campus.

16   Finally, it should be pointed out that Black Student Unions, as the vehicles of this political and institutional conservatism, contained within themselves the germs of their own destruction. If the unions moved too far to the left, i.e., if they substituted political radicalism for racial militancy—as was the case with the now defunct Black Student Alliance which was based in Southern California—the BSUs would lose their conservative black student following as did the Alliance. On the other hand, if the unions managed to achieve their goals of acceptance for EOP, black studies and other integrationist demands by college and university officials, the BSUs would deprive themselves of further meaningful issues around which to organize and thus remove the need for their own existence. The latter—and, in a few instances, the former—development has already resulted in the decline or disappearance of Black Student Unions on campuses in Southern California.

Vocabulary

extricate	chronic	ubiquitous
verbiage	periphery	bourgeoisie
susceptible		

Topics for Discussion

1. What differences does Obatala see between revolutionary and reformist demands?

2. In what way did the Black Student Unions contain the seeds of their own destruction?

3. What does Obatala mean when he calls demands for black studies and more black professors "basically elitist notions"?

4. Do you agree with Obatala that "there simply never was a 'black revolution' "?

5. If, as Obatala says, the black campus mood is not revolutionary, what is the mood?

6. Why does Obatala feel that looting during a ghetto riot is a manifestation of revolutionary tendencies in the masses? Do you agree with his opinion?

Rhetorical Considerations

1. What do the following terms mean: *masses, petit-bourgeois, Afro-American bourgeoisie, redistribution of goods and income*? What does the use of such terms tell you about the author's viewpoint?

2. Where does Obatala state his thesis?

3. What supporting evidence and arguments does Obatala offer? How is his argument organized?

4. What does Obatala assume about his audience? How are these assumptions evident in the essay?

Custer Died for Your Sins

Vine Deloria, Jr.

Vine Deloria (b. 1933) is a writer, lawyer, social activist, and South Dakota Sioux who is a leading spokesman for the cause of the American Indian. His works include We Talk, You Listen; God Is Red; Custer Died For Your Sins; *and* Behind the Trail of Broken Treaties.

1   Into each life, it is said, some rain must fall. Some people have bad horoscopes; others take tips on the stock market. McNamara created the TFX and the Edsel, American politics has George Wallace. But Indians have been cursed above all other people in history. Indians have anthropologists.

2   Every summer when school is out, a stream of immigrants heads into Indian country. The Oregon Trail was never as heavily populated as Route 66 and Highway 18 in the summertime. From every rock and cranny in the East, *they* emerge, as if responding to some primeval migratory longing, and flock to the reservations. They are the anthropologists—the most prominent members of the scholarly community that infests the land of the free and the homes of the braves. Their origin is a mystery hidden in the historical mists. Indians are certain that all ancient societies of the Near East had anthropologists at one time, because all those societies are now defunct. They are equally certain that Columbus brought anthropologists on his ships when he came to the New World. How else could he have made so many wrong deductions about where he was? While their origins are uncertain, anthropologists can readily be identified on the reservations. Go into any crowd of people. Pick out a tall, gaunt white man wearing Bermuda shorts, a World War Two Army Air Corps flying jacket, an Australian bush hat and tennis shoes and packing a large knapsack incorrectly strapped on his back. He will invariably have a thin, sexy wife with stringy hair, an I.Q. of 191 and a vocabulary in which even the prepositions have 11 syllables. And he usually has a camera, tape recorder, telescope and life jacket all hanging from his elongated frame.

3   This odd creature comes to Indian reservations to make *observations*. During the winter, these observations will become books by which future anthropologists will be trained, so that they can come out to reservations years from now and verify the observations in

more books, summaries of which then appear in the scholarly journals and serve as a catalyst to inspire yet other anthropologists to make the great pilgrimage the following summer. And so on.

4   The summaries, meanwhile, are condensed. Some condensations are sent to Government agencies as reports justifying the previous summer's research. Others are sent to foundations, in an effort to finance the following summer's expedition West. The reports are spread through the Government agencies and foundations all winter. The only problem is that no one has time to read them. So $5000-a-year secretaries are assigned to decode them. Since these secretaries cannot comprehend complex theories, they reduce the reports to the best slogans possible. The slogans become conference themes in the early spring, when the anthropological expeditions are being planned. They then turn into battle cries of opposing groups of anthropologists who chance to meet on the reservations the following summer.

5   Each summer there is a new battle cry, which inspires new insights into the nature of the "Indian problem." One summer Indians will be greeted with the joyful cry "Indians are bilingual!" The following summer this great truth will be expanded to "Indians are not only bilingual, they are *bicultural!*" Biculturality creates great problems for the opposing anthropoligical camp. For two summers, they have been bested in sloganeering and their funds are running low. So the opposing school of though breaks into the clear faster than Gale Sayers. "Indians," the losing anthros cry, "are a *folk* people!" The tide of battle turns and a balance, so dearly sought by Mother Nature, is finally achieved. Thus go the anthropological wars, testing whether this school or that school can long endure. The battlefields, unfortunately, are the lives of Indian people.

6   The anthro is usually devoted to *pure research.* A 1969 thesis restating a proposition of 1773, complete with footnotes to all material published between 1773 and 1969, is pure research. There are, however, anthropologists who are not clever at collecting footnotes. They depend on their field observations and write long, adventurous narratives in which their personal observations are used to verify their suspicions. Their reports, books and articles are called *applied research.* The difference, then, between pure and applied research is primarily one of footnotes. Pure has many footnotes, applied has few footnotes. Relevancy to subject matter is not discussed in polite company.

7   Anthropologists came to Indian country only after the tribes had agreed to live on reservations and had given up their warlike ways. Had the tribes been given a choice of fighting the cavalry or

the anthropologists, there is little doubt as to who they would have chosen. In a crisis situation, men always attack the biggest threat to their existence. A warrior killed in battle could always go to the happy hunting grounds. But where does an Indian laid low by an anthro go? To the library?

8 　　The fundamental thesis of the anthropologist is that people are objects for observation. It then follows that people are considered objects for experimentation, for manipulation and for eventual extinction. The anthropologist thus furnishes the justification for treating Indian people like so many chessmen, available for anyone to play with. The mass production of useless knowledge by anthropologists attempting to capture real Indians in a network of theories has contributed substantially to the invisibility of Indian people today. After all, who can believe in the actual existence of a food-gathering, berrypicking, seminomadic, fire-worshiping, high-plains-and-mountain-dwelling, horse-riding, canoe-toting, bead-using, pottery-making, ribbon-coveting, wickiup-sheltered people who began flourishing when Alfred Frump mentioned them in 1803 in *Our Feathered Friends*?

9 　　Not even Indians can see themselves as this type of creature—who, to anthropologists, is the "real" Indian. Indian people begin to feel that they are merely shadows of a mythical super-Indian. Many Indians, in fact, have come to parrot the ideas of anthropologists, because it appears that they know everything about Indian communities. Thus, many ideas that pass for Indian thinking are in reality theories originally advanced by anthropologists and echoed by Indian people in an attempt to communicate the real situation. Many anthros reinforce this sense of inadequacy in order to further influence the Indian people.

10 　　Since 1955, there have been a number of workshops conducted in Indian country as a device for training "young Indian leaders." Churches, white Indian-interest groups; colleges and, finally, poverty programs have each gone the workshop route as the most feasible means for introducing new ideas to younger Indians, so as to create leaders. The tragic nature of the workshops is apparent when one examines their history. One core group of anthropologists has institutionalized the workshop and the courses taught in it. Trudging valiantly from workshop to workshop, from state to state, college to college, tribe to tribe, these noble spirits have served as the catalyst for the creation of workshops that are identical in purpose and content and often in the student body itself.

11 　　The anthropoligical message to young Indians has not varied a jot or a title in ten years. It is the same message these anthros

learned as fuzzy-cheeked graduate students in the post-War years—Indians are a folk people, whites are an urban people and never the twain shall meet. Derived from this basic premise are all the other sterling insights: Indians are between two cultures, Indians are bicultural, Indians have lost their identity and Indians are warriors. These theories, propounded every year with deadening regularity and an overtone of Sinaitic authority, have become a major mental block in the development of young Indian people. For these slogans have come to be excuses for Indian failures. They are crutches by which young Indians have avoided the arduous task of thinking out the implications of the status of Indian people in the modern world.

12   If there is one single cause that has importance today for Indian people, it is tribalism. Against all odds, Indians have retained title to some 53,000,000 acres of land, worth about three and a half billion dollars. Approximately half of the country's 1,000,000 Indians relate meaningfully to this land, either by living and working on it or by frequently visiting it. If Indians fully recaptured the idea that they are tribes communally in possession of this land, they would realize that they are truly impoverished. But the creation of modern tribalism has been stifled by a ready acceptance of the Indians-are-a-folk-people premise of the anthropologists. This premise implies a drastic split between folk and urban cultures, in which the folk peoples have two prime characteristics: They dance and they are desperately poor. Creative thought in Indian affairs has not, therefore, come from the younger Indians who have grown up reading and talking to anthropologists. Rather, it has come from the older generation that believes in tribalism—and that the youngsters mistakenly insist has been brainwashed by Government schools.

13   Because other groups have been spurred on by their younger generations, Indians have come to believe that, through education, a new generation of leaders will arise to solve the pressing contemporary problems. Tribal leaders have been taught to accept this thesis by the scholarly community in its annual invasion of the reservations. Bureau of Indian Affairs educators harp continuously on this theme. Wherever authority raises its head in Indian country, this thesis is its message. The facts prove the opposite, however. Relatively untouched by anthropologists, educators and scholars are the Apache tribes of the Southwest. The Mescalero, San Carlos, White Mountain and Jicarilla Apaches have very few young people in college, compared with other tribes. They have even fewer people in the annual workshop orgy during the summers. If ever there was a distinction between folk and urban, this group of Indians characterizes it.

14   The Apaches see themselves, as neither folk nor urban but *tribal*. There is little sense of a lost identity. Apaches could not care less about the anthropological dilemmas that worry other tribes. Instead, they continue to work on massive plans for development that they themselves have created. Tribal identity is assumed, not defined, by these reservation people. Freedom to choose from a wide variety of paths of progress is a characteristic of the Apaches; they don't worry about what type of Indianism is real. Above all, they cannot be ego-fed by abstract theories and, hence, unwittingly manipulated.

15   With many young people from other tribes, the situation is quite different. Some young Indians attend workshops over and over again. Folk theories pronounced by authoritative anthropologists become opportunities to escape responsibility. If, by definition, the Indian is hopelessly caught between two cultures, why struggle? Why not blame all one's lack of success on this tremendous gulf between two opposing cultures? Workshops have become, therefore, summer retreats for nonthought rather than strategy sessions for leadership. Therein lies the Indian's sin against the anthropologist. Only those anthropologists who appear to boost Indian ego and expound theories dear to the hearts of workshop Indians are invited to teach at workshops. They become human recordings of social confusion and are played and replayed each summer, to the delight of a people who refuse to move on into the real world.

16   The workshop anthro is thus a unique creature, partially self-created and partially supported by the refusal of Indian young people to consider their problems in their own context. The normal process of maturing has been confused with cultural difference. So maturation is cast aside in favor of cult recitation of great truths that appear to explain the immaturity of young people.

17   While the anthro is thus, in a sense, the victim of the Indians, he should, nevertheless, recognize the role he has been asked to play and refuse to play it. Instead, the temptation to appear relevant to a generation of young Indians has clouded his sense of proportion. Workshop anthros often ask Indians of tender age to give their authoritative answers to problems that an entire generation of Indians is just now beginning to solve. Where the answer to reservation health problems may be adequate housing in areas where there has never been adequate housing, young Indians are shaped in their thinking processes to consider vague doctrines on the nature of man and his society.

18   It is preposterous that a teenaged Indian should become an instant authority, equal in status to the Ph.D. interrogating him. Yet the very human desire is to play that game every summer, for the

status acquired in the game is heady. And since answers can be given only in the vocabulary created by the Ph.D., the entire leadership-training process internalizes itself and has no outlet beyond the immediate group. Real problems, superimposed on the ordinary problems of maturing, thus become insoluble burdens that crush people of great leadership potential.

19   Let us take some specific examples. One workshop discussed the thesis that Indians were in a terrible crisis. They were, in the words of friendly anthro guides, "between two worlds." People between two worlds, the students were told, "drank." For the anthropologists, it was a valid explanation of drinking on the reservation. For the young Indians, it was an authoritative definition of their role as Indians. Real Indians, they began to think, drank; and their task was to become real Indians, for only in that way could they re-create the glories of the past. So they *drank*. I've lost some good friends who drank too much.

20   Abstract theories create abstract action. Lumping together the variety of tribal problems and seeking the demonic principle at work that is destroying Indian people may be intellectually satisfying, but it does not change the situation. By concentrating on great abstractions, anthropologists have unintentionally removed many young Indians from the world of real problems to the lands of make-believe.

21   As an example of a real problem, the Pyramid Lake Paiutes and the Gila River Pima and Maricopa are poor because they have been systematically cheated out of their water rights, and on desert reservations, water is the single most important factor in life. No matter how many worlds Indians straddle, the Plains Indians have an inadequate land base that continues to shrink because of land sales. Straddling worlds is irrelevant to straddling small pieces of land and trying to earn a living.

22   Along the Missouri River, the Sioux used to live in comparative peace and harmony. Although land allotments were small, families were able to achieve a fair standard of living through a combination of gardening and livestock raising and supplemental work. Little cash income was required, because the basic necessities of food, shelter and community life were provided. After World War Two, anthropologists came to call. They were horrified that the Indians didn't carry on their old customs, such as dancing, feasts and giveaways. In fact, the people did keep up a substantial number of customs, but they had been transposed into church gatherings, participation in the county fairs and tribal celebrations, particularly fairs and rodeos. The people did Indian dances. But they didn't do them all the time.

23   Suddenly, the Sioux were presented with an authority figure who bemoaned the fact that whenever he visited the reservations, the Sioux were not out dancing in the manner of their ancestors. Today, the summers are taken up with one great orgy of dancing and celebrating, as each small community of Indians sponsors a weekend powwow for the people in the surrounding communities. Gone are the little gardens that used to provide fresh vegetables in the summer and canned goods in the winter. Gone are the chickens that provided eggs and Sunday dinners. In the winter, the situation becomes critical for families who spent the summer dancing. While the poverty programs have done much to counteract the situation, few Indians recognize that the condition was artificial from start to finish. The people were innocently led astray, and even the anthropologists did not realize what had happened.

24   One example: The Oglala Sioux are perhaps the most well known of the Sioux bands. Among their past leaders were Red Cloud, the only Indian who ever defeated the United States in a war, and Crazy Horse, most revered of the Sioux war chiefs. The Oglala were, and perhaps still are, the meanest group of Indians ever assembled. They would take after a cavalry troop just to see if their bowstrings were taut enough. When they had settled on the reservation, the Oglala made a fairly smooth transition to the new life. They had good herds of cattle, they settled along the numerous creeks that cross the reservation and they created a very strong community spirit. The Episcopalians and the Roman Catholics had the missionary franchise on the reservation and the tribe was pretty evenly split between the two. In the Episcopal Church, at least, the congregations were fairly self-governing and stable.

25   But over the years, the Oglala Sioux have had a number of problems. Their population has grown faster than their means of support. The Government allowed white farmers to come into the eastern part of the reservation and create a county, with the best farmlands owned or operated by whites. The reservation was allotted—taken out of the collective hands of the tribe and parceled out to individuals—and when ownership became too complicated, control of the land passed out of Indian hands. The Government displaced a number of families during World War Two by taking a part of the reservation for use as a bombing range to train crews for combat. Only last year was this land returned to tribal and individual use.

26   The tribe became a favorite subject for anthropological study quite early, because of its romantic past. Theories arose attempting to explain the apparent lack of progress of the Oglala Sioux. The true issue—white control of the reservation—was overlooked com-

pletely. Instead, every conceivable intangible cultural distinction was used to explain the lack of economic, social and educational progress of a people who were, to all intents and purposes, absentee landlords because of the Government policy of leasing their lands to whites.

27   One study advanced the startling proposition that Indians with many cattle were, on the average, better off than Indians without cattle. Cattle Indians, it seems, had more capital and income than did noncattle Indians. Surprise! The study had innumerable charts and graphs that demonstrated this great truth beyond the doubt of a reasonably prudent man. Studies of this type were common but unexciting. They lacked that certain flair of insight so beloved by anthropologists. Then one day a famous anthropologist advanced the theory, probably valid at the time and in the manner in which he advanced it, that the Oglala were "warriors without weapons."

28   The chase was on. Before the ink had dried on the scholarly journals, anthropologists from every library stack in the nation converged on the Oglala Sioux to test this new theory. Outfitting anthroplogical expeditions became the number-one industry of the small off-reservation Nebraska towns south of Pine Ridge. Surely, supplying the Third Crusade to the Holy Land was a minor feat compared with the task of keeping the anthropologists at Pine Ridge.

29   Every conceivable difference between the Oglala Sioux and the folks at Bar Harbor was attributed to the quaint warrior tradition of the Oglala Sioux. From lack of roads to unshined shoes, Sioux problems were generated, so the anthros discovered, by the refusal of the white man to recognize the great desire of the Oglala to go to war. Why expect an Oglala to become a small businessman, when he was only waiting for that wagon train to come around the bend? The very real and human problems of the reservation were considered to be merely by-products of the failure of a warrior people to become domesticated. The fairly respectable thesis of past exploits in war, perhaps romanticized for morale purposes, became a spiritual force all its own. Some Indians, in a tongue-in-cheek manner for which Indians are justly famous, suggested that a subsidized wagon train be run through the reservation each morning at nine o'clock and the reservation people paid a minimum wage for attacking it.

30   By outlining this problem, I am not deriding the Sioux. I lived on that reservation for 18 years and know many of the problems from which it suffers. How, I ask, can the Oglala Sioux make any headway in education when their lack of education is ascribed to a desire to go to war? Would not, perhaps, an incredibly low per-capita income, virtually nonexistent housing, extremely inadequate

roads and domination by white farmers and ranchers make some difference? If the little Sioux boy or girl had no breakfast, had to walk miles to a small school and had no decent clothes nor place to study in a one-room log cabin, should the level of education be comparable with that of Scarsdale High?

31   What use would roads, houses, schools, businesses and income be to a people who, everyone expected, would soon depart on the warpath? I would submit that a great deal of the lack of progress at Pine Ridge is occasioned by people who believe they are helping the Oglala when they insist on seeing, in the life of the people of that reservation only those things they want to see. Real problems and real people become invisible before the great romantic and nonsensical notion that the Sioux yearn for the days of Crazy Horse and Red Cloud and will do nothing until those days return.

32   The question of the Oglala Sioux is one that plagues every Indian tribe in the nation, if it will closely examine itself. Tribes have been defined; the definition has been completely explored; test scores have been advanced promoting and deriding the thesis; and, finally, the conclusion has been reached: Indians must be redefined in terms that white men will accept, even if that means re-Indianizing them according to the white man's idea of what they were like in the past and should logically become in the future.

33   What, I ask, would a school board in Moline, Illinois—or Skokie, even—do if the scholarly community tried to reorient its educational system to conform with outmoded ideas of Sweden in the glory days of Gustavus Adolphus? Would they be expected to sing *"Ein' feste Burg"* and charge out of the mists at the Roman Catholics to save the Reformation every morning as school began? Or the Irish—would they submit to a group of Indians coming to Boston and telling them to dress in green and hunt leprechauns?

34   Consider the implications of theories put forward to solve the problem of poverty among the blacks. Several years ago, the word went forth that black poverty was due to the disintegration of the black family, that the black father no longer had a prominent place in the home. How incredibly shortsighted that thesis was. How typically Anglo-Saxon! How in the world could there have been a black family if people were sold like cattle for 200 years, if there were large plantations that served merely as farms to breed more slaves, if white owners systematically ravaged black women? When did the black family unit ever become integrated? Herein lies a trap into which many Americans have fallen: Once a problem is defined and understood by a significant number of people who have some relation to it, the fallacy goes, the problem ceases to exist. The rest of America had better beware of having quaint mores that attract

anthropologists, or it will soon become a victim of the conceptual prison into which blacks and Indians, among others, have been thrown. One day you may find yourself cataloged—perhaps as a credit-card-carrying, turnpike-commuting, condominium-dwelling, fraternity-joining, churchgoing, sports-watching, time-purchase-buying, televison-watching, magazine-subscribing, politically inert transmigrated urbanite who, through the phenomenon of the second car and the shopping center, has become a golf-playing, wife-swapping, etc., etc., etc., suburbanite. Or have you already been characterized—and caricatured—in ways that struck you as absurd? If so, you will understand what has been happening to Indians for a long, long time.

35   In defense of the anthropologists, it must be recognized that those who do not publish perish. Those who do not bring in a substantial sum of research money soon slide down the scale of university approval. What university is not equally balanced between the actual education of its students and a multitude of small bureaus, projects, institutes and programs that are designed to harvest grants for the university?

36   The effect of anthropologists on Indians should be clear. Compilation of useless knowledge for knowledge's sake should be utterly rejected by the Indian people. We should not be objects of observation for those who do nothing to help us. During the critical days of 1954, when the Senate was pushing for termination of all Indian rights, not one scholar, anthropologist, sociologist, historian or economist came forward to support the tribes against the detrimental policy. Why didn't the academic community march to the side of the tribes? Certainly the past few years have shown how much influence academe can exert when it feels compelled to enlist in a cause. Is Vietnam any more crucial to the moral stance of America than the great debt owed to the Indian tribes?

37   Perhaps we should suspect the motives of members of the academic community. They have the Indian field well defined and under control. Their concern is not the ultimate policy that will affect the Indian people, but merely the creation of new slogans and doctrines by which they can climb the university totem pole. Reduction of people to statistics for purposes of observation appears to be inconsequential to the anthropologist when compared with the immediate benefits he can derive—the acquisition of further prestige and the chance to appear as the high priest of American society, orienting and manipulating to his heart's desire.

38   Roger Jourdain, chairman of the Red Lake Chippewa tribe of Minnesota, casually had the anthropologists escorted from his reservation a couple of years ago. This was the tip of the iceberg. If

only more Indians had the insight of Jourdain. Why should we continue to provide private zoos for anthropologists? Why should tribes have to compete with scholars for funds, when their scholarly productions are so useless and irrelevant to life?

39   Several years ago, an anthropologist stated that over a period of some 20 years he had spent, from all sources, close to $10,000,000 studying a tribe of fewer than 1000 people. Imagine what that amount of money would have meant to that group of people had it been invested in buildings and businesses. There would have been no problems to study.

40   I sometimes think that Indian tribes could improve relations between themselves and the anthropologists by adopting the following policy: Each anthro desiring to study a tribe should be made to apply to the tribal council for permission to do his study. He would be given such permission only if he raised as a contribution to the tribal budget an amount of money equal to the amount he proposed to spend on his study. Anthropologists would thus become productive members of Indian society, instead of ideological vultures.

41   This proposal was discussed at one time in Indian circles. It blew no small number of anthro minds. Irrational shrieks of "academic freedom" rose like rockets from launching pads. The very idea of putting a tax on useless information was intolerable to the anthropologists we talked with. But the question is very simple. Are the anthros concerned about freedom—or license? Academic freedom certainly does not imply that one group of people has to become chessmen for another group of people. Why should Indian communities be subjected to prying non-Indians any more than other communities? Should any group have a franchise to stick its nose into someone else's business?

42   I don't think my proposal ever will be accepted. It contradicts the anthropologists' self-image much too strongly. What is more likely is that Indians will continue to allow their communities to be turned inside out until they come to realize the damage that is being done to them. Then they will seal up the reservations and no further knowledge—useless or otherwise—will be created. This may be the best course. Once, at a Congressional hearing, someone asked Alex Chasing Hawk, a council member of the Cheyenne Sioux for 30 years, "Just what do you Indians want?" Alex replied, "A leave-us-alone law."

43   The primary goal and need of Indians today is not for someone to study us, feel sorry for us, identify with us or claim descent from Pocahontas to make us feel better. Nor do we need to be classified as semiwhite and have programs made to bleach us further. Nor do we need further studies to see if we are "feasible." We need,

instead, a new policy from Congress that acknowledges our intelligence, and our dignity.

44   In its simplest form, such a policy would give a tribe the amount of money now being spent in the area on Federal schools and other services. With this block grant, the tribe itself would communally establish and run its own schools and hospitals and police and fire departments—and, in time, its own income-producing endeavors, whether in industry or agriculture. The tribe would not be taxed until enough capital had accumulated so that individual Indians were getting flat dividends.

45   Many tribes are beginning to acquire the skills necessary for this sort of independence, but the odds are long: An Indian district at Pine Ridge was excited recently about the possibility of running its own schools, and a bond issue was put before them that would have made it possible for them to do so. In the meantime, however, anthropologists visiting the community convinced its people that they were culturally unprepared to assume this sort of responsibility; so the tribe voted down the bond issue. Three universities have sent teams to the area to discover why the issue was defeated. The teams are planning to spend more on their studies than the bond issue would have cost.

46   I would expect an instant rebuttal by the anthros. They will say that my sentiments do not represent the views of all Indians—and they are right, they have brainwashed many of my brothers. But a new day is coming. Until then, it would be wise for anthropologists to climb down from their thrones of authority and pure research and begin helping Indian tribes instead of preying on them. For the wheel of karma grinds slowly, but it does grind fine. And it makes a complete circle.

Vocabulary

catalyst   franchise   caricature

Topics for Discussion

1. What are the main problems confronting Indians today, according to Deloria?

2. Deloria says that "the fundamental thesis of the anthropologist is that people are objects for observation. It then follows

that people are considered objects for experimentation, for manipulation and for eventual extinction." Do you agree with this view of anthropologists? How would you answer Deloria?

3. According to Deloria, tribalism is the "one single cause that has importance today for Indian people." What does he mean by tribalism? Why is it so important?

4. Deloria rejects the idea that Indians are bicultural. Why? What is meant by *bicultural*?

5. What does Deloria see as the primary goal and need of Indians today? Why does Deloria believe that education is not the answer to Indian problems?

6. What possible solutions to Indian problems does Deloria offer? Evaluate these solutions if you think you have enough information to make such an evaluation.

Rhetorical Considerations

1. What does the title of the essay mean? How does the title relate to the essay?

2. Throughout the essay Deloria refers to anthropologists as "anthros." What does this contribute to the tone of the essay? Can you cite similar devices in the essay?

3. Deloria's introduction certainly gets your attention quickly. What else does the introduction do?

4. How objective is this essay? What subjective elements can you locate? How do these subjective elements operate? Are they effective?

5. How does Deloria use geographical references? Do these references create a tone of universality?

A Study of *La Vida*

Oscar Lewis

Oscar Lewis (1914-1970) was a writer who received the National Book Award in 1967 for his book La Vida.

Summary of Major Findings in New York

1   Although the majority of our sample families has lost track of relatives who had gone to New York, when our informants were planning to migrate, they usually managed somehow to get into contact with at least one relative there. Upon arrival, the first thing most Puerto Ricans did was look up a kinsman. Some 48 percent of our New York and Puerto Rican families were related by sibling ties; two-thirds of the New York families came from the same slum as their Puerto Rican relatives.

2   The majority of the migrants lived with a relative when they first arrived, but friction often developed, ending in the establishment of an independent residence. There was a strong general feeling that the family in New York was not as close or as helpful as in Puerto Rico.

3   The predominant type of household among our New York families was nuclear, but 20 percent of the households were extended, usually horizontally; that is, including a person of the same generation, such as a brother or sister who might contribute income to the household. However, a relatively small number of migrants were in their most productive years; over half of the New York sample was under age twenty. When they went to New York, 44 percent were between fifteen and twenty-four; the average age at the time of migration was twenty-eight.

4   The average household size was four. Whereas 44 percent of the household heads were legally married and 22 percent lived in free unions, 26 percent were separated, abandoned, or divorced, 6 percent were single, and 2 percent were widows.

5   The Puerto Ricans in our New York sample lived in Puerto Rican neighborhoods that formed little islands within the city, perpetuating their native language and many of their customs. The process of adjustment and of assimilation was slow and difficult. Contacts with North Americans were few and often limited to landlords, government officials, and other functionaries. Most of the

migrants were disillusioned when they arrived because of the cold, the ugliness of the city, and the difficulties of finding employment and a decent place to live. Many retained a negative attitude toward the city, its people, and its customs even after many years of residence.

6   The motives for migration to New York were generated by low incomes and unemployment, but often the precipitating factor in leaving Puerto Rico was not directly economic in nature but rather psychological or personal. Most informants denied that their New York relatives had influenced their decision to migrate. Higher welfare payments in New York did not appear to be an important factor in migration.

7   Migration from Puerto Rico to New York usually involved two stages. The New York families were mostly of rural origin and had left their place of birth during their younger years to move to San Juan. Most of them had lived in a city slum for a number of years before leaving for New York. Of the families in our New York sample 82 percent had come from a Puerto Rican slum.

8   The Puerto Rican migrants did not look upon the decision to migrate to the United States as irrevocable. Only one of every four migrants in our sample stated that he planned to remain in New York permanently. Often, they came to work and save money in order to go back and buy a house or establish a small business, but they usually discovered that this was not easy. The majority of migrants were able only to make one or more return visits to their native land. Nevertheless, for the most part, they were glad they had come to New York.

9   The migrants changed dwellings in the city fairly frequently (an average of four moves per family), but the moves were restricted in geographical area, usually within the same borough and often within a block or two of the previous residence.

10   All the migrants lived in apartments, usually in dilapidated tenement buildings, but some had acquired leases in public housing projects. All but four families lived in unfurnished apartments. The median rent was $62.50 a month. Adjustment to apartment living was often difficult for the Puerto Rican migrants, who were accustomed to living in free communication with their neighbors in open-door, open-window, slum dwellings.

11   Most of the Puerto Ricans worked in factories in New York, and all but a few held low-prestige jobs. A higher proportion (40.6 percent) of the wives worked, also mostly in factories. Some 80 percent of the working adults belonged to a union. Occupationally, the families in our sample ranked at the very bottom of the scale,

being in an even worse position than the New York Puerto Rican community as a whole.

12   The median annual income of the sample families was $3,678, a figure that again placed them in the lowest rank in New York.[1] The per capita monthly income was a little over $100.

13   Unemployment was about 9 percent, and 20 percent of the families were on relief. The jobs acquired by the migrants lasted an average of only three years. The lowest income families in our New York sample had an associated history of separation, abandonment, and divorce.

14   The educational achievement of the migrants was low, an average of 6.5 years completed by each adult. This is the lowest educational level of any of the major ethnic groups in New York. In general, there was a correlation between income and education.

15   "Dropouts" were a problem in New York; very few of the younger generation went beyond the ninth grade. In our sample of adults above eighteen years of age, over 90 percent had not completed high school. The majority of these had dropped out of school in Puerto Rico. The advantages to attaining a high school diploma were outweighed in most cases by the advantages of immediate employment. Almost no one had gone to night school.

16   The family heads complained about problems in disciplining the children and the fear, sometimes realized, that their youngsters were joining gangs. This delinquency was attributed to working wives whose absence from the home affected the ability of the parents to control their children.

17   Marital conflict increased in New York as a result of the changing role of the Puerto Rican wife. The working wife was less subject to the close surveillance of her husband, family, and neighbors and had greater financial independence. Their independence was resented by husbands and led to quarrels and sometimes to physical violence. The strict sanctions in New York against wife beating only increased the men's deep feelings of frustration.

18   The household inventories revealed that the families owned an average of $1,664 worth of household and related goods (not including clothing), most of which had been purchased in the five-year period preceding the study. Installment buying and the purchase of new, rather than secondhand, goods was the general pattern. The annual indebtedness averaged $128 per family. Clothing represented a large investment. Complete inventories of the clothing of selected families showed that a third more was spent on clothing than on all other household possessions.

[1] The median income would have been lower had we not included two families with annual incomes of over $10,000.

19   English was learned more quickly by the men and children than by the women. Over half the men had achieved some degree of fluency in English, but two out of every three women in the sample knew little or no English, even though they might be employed. English was used by all informants almost exclusively as a utilitarian tool, to communicate with the foreman, to get about the city, and to make themselves understood in visits to hospitals and similar situations. Many purchased an English-language newspaper in addition to a Spanish newspaper. Little English was spoken in the home, but there was much concern that the children were forgetting Spanish. Since almost all the children attended New York public schools, most of them were bilingual to some degree. There was a tendency to give American names to children born in New York City.

20   Visiting relatives in the city was fairly frequent and regular, depending upon the distance of their homes. However, there was a general feeling among our informants that kin ties had weakened in the United States. We also found a reluctance to take *compadres* in New York, although many families still felt obligated to do so.

21   Church attendance, the practice of spiritualism, and the use of herbs declined in New York.

22   In general, the migrants believed that they had changed little since living in New York City. Our data tended to corroborate this. To most of them, the main advantages of living in New York were of an economic nature. The disadvantages were high rents and poor housing conditions, lawlessness in the city, racial or ethnic discrimination, and climate. There was marked hostility toward American Negroes and a strong resistance to being classified with them. Puerto Ricans seemed to be well aware of their competition with Negroes for a higher status in the city. On the other hand, there was a lack of unity among the Puerto Ricans and an inability to organize for common goals.

Vocabulary

irrevocable   dilapidated

Topics for Discussion

1. What does Lewis mean by *nuclear* as opposed to *extended* families? How would you characterize your family when you were growing up? Do you think the character of the family is changing in America?

2. What are *compadres?* Do American minority groups have different family characteristics than whites? Do minority groups differ in this respect from each other? Are there differing family structures among whites according to ethnic and socioeconomic groupings?

3. Lewis does not mention some of the important issues in the Puerto Rican community today. What do you think about local control of the Puerto Rican community? Do you have a position on independence, statehood, or commonwealth status for Puerto Rico?

4. Given that Lewis's studies are widely acclaimed as revealing of oppressive social conditions, do you think this essay is in any way demeaning to minority groups? Why not a similar study on the shopping habits of the rich?

Rhetorical Considerations

1. Do you think that Lewis's almost-technical style betrays an insensitivity to the needs of the Puerto Rican community, or do you think that his presentation contains an objectivity which could not be achieved by taking a more personal rhetorical stance?

2. Does Lewis overuse the verb *to be?*

3. Lewis's essay is a good example of the kind of writing that students may be required to do for social science courses. How and why is this kind of writing different from the casual, familiar essay?

4. Do you think that all the conclusions in Lewis's final paragraph are justified on the basis of information presented earlier in the essay?

5. Is choppy paragraphing necessary for the "sociological" or "objective" style? See, for example, paragraphs 12–14.

Children of the Barrio

Ronald Arias

Ronald Arias writes articles dealing with the social situation of Spanish-speaking America.

1   "Why did he cut your hair?"

2   "He said it was too long."

3   Shamefaced and almost in tears, Mexico-born John Garcia took his seat in class. His head was bald in spots. He tried to hide the black tufts of hair that stuck out all over. There was an awkward silence. Garcia's humiliation was to serve as a warning to the other boys.

4   "Haircutting never works," Miss Maria Talavera, Garcia's English teacher, complained later. "All this does is force them out of school. They've had this kind of treatment since the first grade. Why should they want to stay in?" she added.

5   Miss Talavera teaches ninth grade in a largely Mexican-American junior high school in East Los Angeles. She pointed out that Anglo youngsters are never given such treatment as the one Garcia received from the vice-principal. "There's one blond and freckled kid in my class with longer hair than any of the Mexican kids. Nobody will ever touch him, though," Miss Talavera said.

6   When questioned about the incident, a downcast Garcia said he hated most of his teachers. "If they're out to get me, why should I like them? Why should I like the math teacher who called me a dirty Mexican?" Miss Talavera, 22 and also a Mexican-American, explained that most classes were overcrowded—about 40 pupils to a teacher. Attention is consequently poor or harsh.

7   "Most of the teachers take an unsympathetic attitude towards these kids and their cultural background," she said. "Poor students in this atmosphere become worse and eventually drop out. Of course, nearly all are poor to begin with."

8   John Garcia will probably drop out. Or else he will transfer to another school "for disciplinary reasons." His situation is typical in the crowded *barrios* (ghettos). In the city's two predominantly Mexican-American high schools the average drop-out rate is above 20 percent. And average transfer rates are far above 50 percent of the student body. This means that a teacher will face essentially a

different class at the end of the school year than he faced at its beginning.

9   In predominantly Anglo schools these averages are generally reduced by half or more. "Forced-out" is another term often applied to the *barrio* school drop-out. Usually beginning school with little more than a pidgin-grasp of English, he works slowly in class and rarely catches up to the "Anglo norm." All textbooks, exams, and I.Q. tests are geared for the Anglo student, which presents other stumbling blocks. After failing several grades and accepting the image of inferiority, the Mexican-American youth will long to be free of school.

10   "They don't respect me at school," one student complained. "Why should I stay in a place that calls me dumb?"

11   Miss Talavera emphasized the tendency of many teachers to stereotype the Mexican-American child. "Right off, he's considered stupid. And the only remedy is to keep him busy in manual arts or shop classes," she explained. "All this, because he can't speak English well and maybe comes from a broken home."

12   It is hardly a surprise that a high drop-out rate exists throughout the Southwest among Mexican-Americans. This has a telling effect on their earning capacities. Results of the Mexican-American Study Project at UCLA show a startling pattern concerning education and income. The study found that on the average, Spanish-surnamed persons (88% Mexican-American) had much less schooling and income than white Anglos. In California, for example, those of Spanish surnames receive a median education of 8.5 years and go on to receive an average yearly income of $4,381. The corresponding figures for the Anglo group are 12.1 and $5,806. In Texas, Spanish-surnamed persons finish an average of 4.8 years of school and receive an income of $2,400. For the Anglo population the figures are 10.8 years and $4,768. The severest cases of low income and education are found among rural migrant workers. In the Southwest and Pacific states alone, these workers total over 75,000—almost entirely of Mexican descent. Their average annual income drops below $1,000 and their schooling is generally from one to four years.

13   Admittedly, the plight of the migrant's child is the worst. He rejoices with little more than some shade and a handful of strawberries. School is still something he knows during summers only. In most cases he remains illiterate. Theodore W. Parsons, in a 1966 Stanford doctoral dissertation, gives some distressing examples of discrimination in an agricultural town. After 40 days of personal observation in a 58% Mexican-American elementary school in central California, Parsons cites:

A teacher, asked why she had called on "Johnny" to lead five Mexicans in orderly file out of the schoolroom, explained: "His father owns one of the big farms in the area and . . . one day he will have to know how to handle the Mexicans."

Another teacher, following the general practice of calling on the Anglos to help Mexican pupils recite in class, said in praise of the system: "It draws them (Anglos) out and gives them a feeling of importance."

The president of the Chamber of Commerce declared in praise of the school principal: "He runs a good school. We never have any trouble in our school. Every kid knows his place . . . we believe that every kid has to learn to respect authority and his betters."

The principal stated: "Once we let a Mexican girl give a little talk of some kind and all she did was mumble around. She had quite an accent too. Afterwards we had several complaints from parents, so we haven't done anything like that since. . . . That was about 12 years ago."

14   Discrimination goes beyond the schools. Especially in cities, this unwritten rule of the majority envelops entire communities. Housing segregation is often the direct cause for ghetto school-zoning. The harsh truth of this system is that the most up-to-date facilities are designed for middle and upper class Anglo districts. Can the quality of a school, then, be disregarded? Can a new approach to teaching the Mexican-American youth be taken? Can a curriculum—perhaps bilingual in part—be scaled for him and not just the Anglo student? If the children of the *barrio* are ever to be released from the poverty traps of the ghetto, they must first be given full opportunity for education of good quality.

Vocabulary

pidgin

Topics for Discussion

1. This is an essay about racial discrimination. What prejudices do Mexican-Americans suffer from? Are these prejudices similar to those suffered by black Americans?

2. What does this essay reveal about school systems?

3. Why is attention "poor or harsh" in an overcrowded classroom?

4. How true do you think it is that "the most up-to-date facilities are designed for middle and upper class Anglo districts"? If this is true, what does it reveal about American society?

5. Are the problems of Mexican-Americans shared by any other minority groups?

6. Is it the function of a school to teach children to respect authority?

Rhetorical Considerations

1. Arias begins his essay by recounting an incident. How effective is this opening? How does it set the tone of the essay? How does Arias integrate this incident into the rest of his essay? How does it help to develop his thesis?

2. The concluding paragraph of this essay includes three questions. Do the questions weaken or strengthen the conclusion?

3. Arias uses many quotations throughout this essay. How well are these quotations integrated into the essay? How effectively does he use his quotations? Do his quotations stand alone or need more support? Are quotations a substitute for the author's assertions?

4. Paragraph 12 is filled with statistics. How easily does this paragraph read? Does it fit in with the style of the rest of the essay? What is the value of these statistics as evidence?

The Issue of Cultural Pluralism in America Today

Nathan Glazer

Nathan Glazer (b. 1923) is a sociologist whose works include The
Lonely Crowd, Faces in the Crowd, *and* Beyond the Melting Pot.

1   Two questions are paramount, I believe, in talking about the
current wave of ethnic feeling in America. One is, is it honest? And
by that, people mean, is it a cover for racism? Is it a way of
justifying anti-Negro prejudice? Is it simply a defensive reaction to
black pride? All these are important questions.

2   And the second is, what does it mean for a decent and harmonious relationship between ethnic and racial groups in America?
Does it mean a better America or a worse one? Does it mean more
emphasis on group differences, on conflict, on prejudice? And if it
does, how are we to avoid these consequences?

3   I recall when Martin Luther King marched in Chicago and
Groppi marched in Milwaukee, both in largely working class, low-
income, ethnic areas, and were met with screams and posters and
hatred, "We want to save our homes," or "Get out of our neighborhoods." It was very difficult to make the case that there was any
motivation for such action but a simple racial hatred. No blacks
allowed; they will reduce the value of the property, bring in crime,
ruin the schools.

4   These incidents—and many like them—raise the question, is
ethnic feeling honest, in the sharpest form possible. What was there
to the Polish or Lithuanian or Italian group and its "culture" that
could justify such behavior?

5   Liberals answered, nothing. The South said it was protecting
white culture and white womanhood, something else was said in the
North, but it was all the same—racism.

6   I thought at the time this was an inadequate analysis of what
was going on. Let me say at the outset that I do not deny there was
some admixture of simple racial prejudice. I won't say how much,
and would accept any estimate from 10 to 90 percent. But there was
something else. There was a sense that a valued way of life was
being threatened. And that kind of motivation for that kind of
behavior was different from racism and different from racial prejudice. It had to be understood—conceivably it had to be protected.

7   One argument of those who insisted it was only racism went; after all, how much of Polish or Lithuanian or Italian culture actually existed in these areas? Who read Mickiewicz, or Dante, in such areas? If there was no real commitment to the heights of culture, how could one claim that a positive motivation in favor of maintaining a community and its culture dominated, as against a negative hatred of outsiders? The fact is, however, we confuse the meanings of the word culture.

8   It has always meant, on the one hand, the high culture. But it also means, as anthropologists use it, simply the way of life—the customs: the language, or if the language goes, the accent, the food, the stores, the weddings, the street life, the comfortable expectation that you know what will happen next in your own group, that you know how to approach a person on the street or how to address someone. All this is culture too.

9   It think it reflects snobbery to take the position that some communities have a right to protect their culture because it is high and others do not because we refuse to accept it as valuable. A known and experienced way of life is always of value to those who have been raised in it, and a reflexive effort to defend it demands at the least sympathy and understanding, if not acquiescence. Because every value may be inferior to a superior value, the Lithuanian neighborhood may have to go to give justice to another group. But we don't know that in advance and it is worth taking the initial claim seriously and sympathetically.

10   We have proceeded through two phases in the effort to cope positively with a multi-ethnic America. In the first phase, inspired by the black revolution, our chief concern was to solve the problem of what groups owed to each other. Except we did not see it quite that way. We thought of it in terms of what ''whites'' owed to ''blacks.'' The agenda was long, created by 300 years of oppression. As the more outrageous inequalities were overcome—those dealing with access to public facilities, with the right to vote, with inequality in the courts, with direct discrimination by major institutions, public and private—the problem of what the races owed to one another became ever more complicated. Did whites owe blacks, for example, precedence in civil service appointments, and how much? Did they owe sending their children to black schools for certain benefits to be achieved by the mixture? Did they owe silence when black leaders denounced them as racists and called for violence? These were all painful and difficult decisions.

11   They became more complex when we began to see the issue not in terms of what whites owed to blacks, but as one of what

groups of many kinds owed to one another. Black militancy inspired Chicanos, American Indians, others. Whites, on the other hand, began to openly recognize, despite the black-white rhetoric, that there was really no one "white" group. It was one thing for whites to say they owed Negroes more places with support in institutions of higher education. It was another thing for Poles and Italians or the white working classes—who also had few supported places in higher education—to say that they owed blacks more places with support in institutions of higher education. As Leonard Fein has pointed out, "white" made up a single average—of rich groups and poor, and of richer parts of groups and poorer parts of groups. Wealthy Jews who lived in the East Side of New York and sent their children to private schools and never dreamed of having their children become school teachers were quite happy to give up the positions of teachers in the public schools to blacks. Poor working-class Jews in Brooklyn who hoped their children would become teachers were by no means so happy to graciously surrender these posts.

12   The period in which groups thought of what they owed each other has been replaced by one in which groups considered what they owed themselves. The black experience, and black behavior, convinced many groups they owed more to themselves than they originally thought they did. The black demand for black studies convinced Chicanos they should have Chicano studies. Even rather modest and self-effacing Japanese and Chinese students became convinced that they should have Asian studies. Black assertion convinced many groups that they too had been robbed of their heritage by American society. Many argued the demand for English, for public school attendance, for conformity to middle class standards, had effectively destroyed their culture.

13   Now the blacks undoubtedly had a much better basis to this claim than any other group. They had been brought unwillingly as slaves. But the Chicanos pointed out that they had been conquered, the Native Americans and Puerto Ricans likewise, the Chinese and Japanese pointed out that poverty had forced them to come as indentured servants, and even the free white immigrants from Europe could point to religious, political, and economic deprivation and insist that they too had been forced into an unfair bargain, the bargain of Anglo-conformity. They now wanted their heritage back, along with full rights in the American society, economy, and polity. They too insisted that they had sold themselves too cheaply and now demanded what the larger society owed them.

14   Some of the demands on the face of it appear comical. Some of the protestors are not clear just what the culture was that they gave

up, and wouldn't want it if it were given back to them. The immigrants also fled from their cultures—it was not only a matter of being forced into conformity. But the black rhetoric is overwhelming. Young Jews now attack their "Uncle Jakes" as blacks attack their "Uncle Toms." I think it is that phase we now find ourselves in, the phase in which everyone asks, what do we owe ourselves as a group, while we are still trying to remember, what do we owe the more deprived groups?

15   Both of these phases have some validity, but both also have their pathology.

16   Let me describe some of the problems that arise when we focus only on the question of what one group owes to another. One reads in *The New York Times* a story about a woman who has to walk one block in Harlem, from a meeting to a subway station. She is robbed of her pocketbook in the course of her one block walk by black children. The purpose of her article is not to decry crime. If it were, of course, *The New York Times* would hardly find it worth publishing. It is to explain that the proper response, in place of her initial anger and distress at the loss of her money, papers and keys, is sympathy—sympathy with young boys who unfortunately will lead, even with her pocketbook, a worse life than she will.

17   Clearly in focussing on the question of what one group owes to another, this woman's perceptions have become distorted. Presumably the mothers and fathers of these children are trying to teach them not to rob the pocketbooks of women, even of white women, their ministers and teachers are doing the same. Her understanding—which might be suitable in some analytical framework—can only serve to undermine the behavior—the minimal behavior—that underlies any civilized society, and any multi-group society.

18   There is also a pathology to the position which emphasizes what we owe to ourselves and our own group. We have all become students of the blacks, and the unashamed insistence on self-interest has legitimated the same kind of behavior in many of us—not that we have needed one group to teach us selfishness. It is a natural human failing. A few days ago, a black student who was a candidate for chairman of the Stanford Student Senate was being questioned by the Senators. In answer to the question would he be impartial, he said, no, he would be partial to blacks. He was elected to the position.

19   At what point does the perfectly legitimate interest in one's self and one's group become illegitimate? I think we have become very confused about this point. I believe that when all the positions of power or high income or influence are withheld from members of a

substantial and numerous group, it is unjust and it is also unstable. We have long lived with such a society. I believe—more than others—that we have made impressive efforts in the past half dozen years to change this unjust and dangerous situation, efforts revealed when we look at the enormous increase in the numbers of blacks— and to some lesser extent of other deprived groups—in college, in high civil service positions, in white collar and professional positions, in elected and appointed political posts, and the like. But I also believe that in this phase we have not come up with any sound standard which both defends the interests of all groups and advances the interests of deprived groups. Rather we have a naive and childish ideology which insists there are no standards, there is no justice, there is only brute power. I do not believe this was the case in the United States in the past—otherwise it is hardly to be explained how some groups, white and nonwhite, achieved income, property, influence and respect, when they clearly lacked brute power. It is not true now. The fostering of this dangerous and delusive ideology is one of the serious challenges to a decent society in this country that we now face. I have given one example of this dangerous and delusive ideology in the case of the black Stanford student. Maybe only college students are still so guilt ridden that they are willing to accept as their chairman someone who openly confesses that he will not be impartial. Adult voters will not be so silly.

20   We have been strong in insisting to many groups that they could not defend their interests as they conceived them to the exclusion of the rights of others. They could not band together to deny Negroes homes. They could not keep them out of schools. They could not keep them out of jobs. This battle is scarcely won—I imagine it will never be in any simple sense "won." But thousands of people are engaged in the battle to defend these rights, and powerful legislation exists to defend them. But in all honesty I believe the greater danger to this country today is not in the denial of the rights of the minority groups with an officially recognized status of deprivation, but in ignoring the rights of groups without such a recognized status.

21   San Francisco offers now one of the major cases we have of such a reverse denial of rights. It is well known that a very substantial part of the Chinese population of this city did not want its children bussed to other schools. It is well known that many of the Spanish surname community of the Mission district did not want its children bussed to other sections. A good part of the black community felt the same way. Parents in all groups found some virtue in having their children near them. These virtues were not only those

that any parent might see in having children attend school nearby. They also had a community aspect. There was a positive desire to maintain a degree of group togetherness which busing would to some degree dissipate. The Chinese pointed out their system of afternoon schools in Chinatown would suffer if their children were widely dispersed. Many argued that all groups owed to the blacks an integrated school setting, and to provide it their children were needed. But more and more of us, as I said, believe we—as members of groups—owe something to ourselves. What groups owe to themselves in San Francisco—their desire to maintain themselves, their desire to freely select an option which permits group maintenance—was denied because it was insisted the interests of one deprived group was paramount. Now, if it is true that there was one and only one way in which the education of black children could be improved—and that was to distribute them evenly among the children of other groups—then conceivably some aspect of desired group maintenance had to be given to overcome a greater evil. But there is no clear and unambiguous demonstration of this fact in our research. Even if there were, there were ways of achieving this aim without the destructive, and it appears to me narrow-minded, insistence that whatever elements of group homogeneity existed, because of residential concentration and free individual choices, should be disrupted.

22   Once again, the tragic fact is that these impulses to group maintenance were denounced as racist, and those who defended them did not have the language or the ideology or sophistication to explicate their desires and to put them in a framework in which the charge of racist could be lifted. I think it is critical to explicate such a point of view, one which indeed takes into account what we owe to each other—to deprived groups—but which also takes into account what each group owes to itself, and which finally takes into account what we owe the nation.

Vocabulary

paramount	ethnic	admixture
acquiescence	agenda	precedence
polity	pathology	delusive
ideology	dissipate	homogeneity
explicate	naive	

Topics for Discussion

1. What does Glazer mean by "liberal guilt"? Does he give any examples of what he means by this term?

2. How does Glazer define *culture*? What difference does he see between "high culture" and "a way of life"? How would you define *culture*? Do you agree with Glazer's distinction between two definitions for the word *culture*?

3. Does Glazer see any conflict between a social group's self-interest and the interest it owes to other social groups?

4. What does Glazer find so important and so significant in the San Franciso case of Chinese parents objecting to busing their children to other schools? How does this case fit in with Glazer's views on cultural pluralism and what social groups owe each other?

5. Glazer cites an incident related in a letter to the *New York Times*. What does he find significant about the letter? Do you agree with Glazer's reaction to the letter or with the woman who wrote the letter? Why?

6. The ideology of brute power is dangerous and delusive, according to Glazer. What is this ideology? Why is it dangerous and delusive? Cite at least one example of such an ideology not mentioned by Glazer.

7. What is your cultural heritage? How conscious of it are you? Do you think it is important or unimportant for people to feel strongly about their ethnic background? Would America be a better or worse country if everyone forgot his or her cultural background?

Rhetorical Considerations

1. How effective is the third paragraph of the essay? Does Glazer develop the ideas presented in paragraph 3 in subsequent paragraphs? Are paragraphs 4 and 5 adequately developed or are they choppy and too brief?

2. Throughout the essay Glazer uses the rhetorical question. Does he rely too much on this rhetorical device? Examine, for example, paragraphs 1, 2, 4, 7, and 10. Can you see any rhetorical reason for using the question structure so often?

3. Glazer outlines the structure of his essay in the first two paragraphs. Does he follow this outline?

4. Glazer uses examples both to illustrate and to develop his

arguments. Note particularly the examples in paragraphs 3, 16, 18, and 21. In what ways does he use his examples?

5. How much of this essay is fact and how much opinion? For example, does the last sentence of paragraph 7 state a fact? Is all of paragraph 9 only opinion? How does Glazer use fact and opinion in his essay? Does he always distinguish between the two so the reader knows which is which?

6. What is the basis of Glazer's argument—moral or factual? Does he make any appeals to emotion?

Confessions of a Working Stiff

Patrick Fenton

Patrick Fenton is a 31-year-old cargo handler at John F. Kennedy Airport in New York where he has worked for seven years.

1   The Big Ben is hammering out its 5:45 alarm in the half-dark of another Tuesday morning. If I'm lucky, my car down in the street will kick over for me. I don't want to think about that now; all I want to do is roll over into the warm covers that hug my wife. I can hear the wind as it whistles up and down the sides of the building. Tuesday is always the worst day—it's the day the drudgery, boredom, and fatigue start all over again. I'm off from work on Sunday and Monday, so Tuesday is my blue Monday.

2   I make my living humping cargo for Seaboard World Airlines, one of the big international airlines at Kennedy Airport. They handle strictly all cargo. I was once told that one of the Rockerfellers is the major stockholder for the airline, but I don't really think about that too much. I don't get paid to think. The big thing is to beat that race with the time clock every morning of your life so the airline will be happy. The worst thing a man could ever do is to make suggestions about building a better airline. They pay people $40,000 a year to come up with better ideas. It doesn't matter that these ideas never work, it's just that they get nervous when a guy from South Brooklyn or Ozone Park acts like he actually has a brain.

3   I throw a Myadec high-potency vitamin into my mouth to ward off one of the ten colds I get every year from humping mailbags out in the cold rain at Kennedy. A huge DC-8 stretch jet waits impatiently for the 8,000 pounds of mail that I will soon feed its empty belly. I wash the Myadec down with some orange juice and grab a brown bag filled with bologna and cheese. Inside the lunch bag there is sometimes a silly note from my wife that says, "I Love You—Guess Who?" It is all that keeps me going to a job that I hate.

4   I've been going there for seven years now and my job is still the same. It's weary work that makes a man feel used up and worn out. You push and you pull all day long with your back. You tie down pallets loaded with thousands of pounds of freight. You fill igloo-shaped containers with hundreds of boxes that all look the same. If you're assigned to work the warehouse, it's really your hard luck. This is the job all the men hate most. You stack box upon box until the pallet resembles the exact shape of the inside of the plane. You get the same monotonous feeling an adult gets when he plays with a child's blocks. When you finish one pallet, you find another and start the whole dull process over again.

5   The airline pays me $192 a week for this. After they take out taxes and $5.81 for the pension, I go home with $142. Once a month they take out $10 for term life insurance, and $5.50 for union dues. The week they take out the life insurance is always the worst: I go home with $132. My job will never change. I will fill up the same igloos with the same boxes for the next 34 years of my life, I will hump the same mailbags into the belly of the plane, and push the same 8,000-pound pallets with my back. I will have to do this until I'm 65 years old. Then I'll be free, if I don't die of a heart attack before that, and the airline will let me retire.

6   In winter the warehouse is cold and damp. There is no heat. The large steel doors that line the warehouse walls stay open most of the day. In the cold months, wind, rain and snow blow across the floor. In the summer the warehouse becomes an oven. Dust and sand from the runways mix with the toxic fumes of fork lifts, leaving a dry, stale taste in your mouth. The high windows above the doors are covered with a thick, black dirt that kills the sun. The men work in shadows with the constant roar of jet engines blowing dangerously in their ears.

7   Working the warehouse is a tedious job that leaves a man's mind empty. If he's smart he will spend his days wool-gathering. He will think about pretty girls that he once knew, or some other daydream of warm, dry places where you never had a chill. The worst thing he can do is to think about his problems. If he starts to

think about how he is going to pay the mortgage on the $30,000 home that he can't afford, it will bring him down. He will wonder why he comes to the cargo airline every morning of his life, and even on Christmas Day. He will start to wonder why he has to listen to the deafening sound of the jets as they rev up their engines. He will wonder why he crawls on his hands and knees, breaking his back a little bit more every day.

8   To keep his kids in that great place in the country in the summer, that great place far away from Brooklyn and the South Bronx, he must work every hour of overtime that the airline offers him. If he never turns down an hour, if he works some 600 hours over, he can make about $15,000. To do this he must turn against himself, he must pray that the phone rings in the middle of the night, even though it's snowing out and he doesn't feel like working. He must hump cargo late into the night, eat meatball heroes for supper, drink coffee that starts to taste like oil, and then hope that his car starts when it's time to go home. If he gets sick—well, he better not think about that.

9   All over Long Island, Ozone Park, Brooklyn, and as far away as the Bronx, men stir in the early morning hours as a new day begins. Every morning is the same as the last. Some of the men drink beer for breakfast instead of coffee. Way out in Bay Shore a cargoman snaps open a can of Budweiser. It's 6 A.M., and he covers the top of the can with his thumb in order to keep down the loud hiss as the beer escapes. He doesn't want to awaken his children as they dream away the morning in the next room. Soon he will swing his Pinto wagon up onto the crowded Long Island Expressway and start the long ride to the job. As he slips the car out of the driveway he tucks another can of beer between his legs.

10   All the men have something in common: they hate the work they are doing and they drink a little too much. They come to work only to punch a timecard that has their last name on it. At the end of the week they will pick up a paycheck with their last name on it. They will never receive a bonus for a job well done, or even a party. At Christmastime a card from the president of the airline will arrive at each one of their houses. It will say Merry Christmas and have the president's name printed at the bottom of it. They know that the airline will be there long after they are dead. Nothing stops it. It runs non-stop, without sleep, through Christmas Day, New Year's Eve, Martin Luther King's birthday, even the deaths of Presidents.

11   It's seven in the morning and the day shift is starting to drift in. Huge tractors are backing up to the big-mouth doors of the warehouse. Cattle trucks bring tons of beef to feed its insatiable

appetite for cargo. Smoke-covered trailers with refrigerated units packed deep with green peppers sit with their diesel engines idling. Names like White, Mack, and Kenworth are welded to the front of their radiators, which hiss and moan from the overload. The men walk through the factory-type gates of the parking lot with their heads bowed, oblivious of the shuddering diesels that await them.

12   Once inside the warehouse they gather in groups of threes and fours like prisoners in an exercise yard. They stand in front of the two time clocks that hang below a window in the manager's office. They smoke and cough in the early morning hour as they await their work assignments. The manager, a nervous-looking man with a stomach that is starting to push out at his belt, walks out with the pink work sheets in his hand.

13   Eddie, a young Irishman with a mustache, has just bolted in through the door. The manager has his timecard in his hand, holding it so no one else can hit Eddie in. Eddie is four minutes late by the time clock. His name will now go down in the timekeeper's ledger. The manager hands the card to him with a ''you'll be up in the office if you don't straighten out'' look. Eddie takes the card, hits it in, and slowly takes his place with the rest of the men. He has been out till four in the morning drinking beer in the bars of Ozone Park; the time clock and the manager could blow up, for all he cares. ''Jesus,'' he says to no one in particular, ''I hope to Christ they don't put me in the warehouse this morning.''

14   Over in another group, Kelly, a tall man wearing a navy knit hat, talks to the men. ''You know, I almost didn't make it in this morning. I passed this green VW on the Belt Parkway. The girl driving it was singing. Jesus, I thought to myself, it must be great going somewhere at 6:30 in the morning that makes you want to sing.'' Kelly is smiling as he talks. ''I often think, why the hell don't you keep on going, Kelly? Don't get off at the cargo exit, stay on. Go anywhere, even if it's only Brooklyn. Christ, if I was a single man I think I would do just that. Some morning I'd pass this damn place by and drive as far away as Riverhead. I don't know what I'd do when I got there—maybe I'd pick up a pound of beefsteak tomatoes from one of those roadside stands or something.''

15   The men laugh at Kelly but they know he is serious. ''I feel the same way sometimes,'' the man next to him says. ''I find myself daydreaming a lot lately; this place drives you to that. I get up in the morning and I just don't want to come to work. I get sick when I hit that parking lot. If it wasn't for the kids and the house I'd quit.'' The men then talk about how hard it is to get work on ''the outside.'' They mention ''outside'' as if they were in a prison.

16   Each morning there is an Army-type roll call from the leads. The leads are foremen who must keep the men moving; if they don't, it could mean their jobs. At one time they had power over the men but as time went by the company took away their little bit of authority. They also lost the deep interest, even enjoyment, for the hard work they once did. As the cargo airline grew, it beat this out of them, leaving only apathy. The ramp area is located in the backyard of the warehouse. This is where the huge jets park to unload their 70,000-pound payloads. A crew of men fall in behind the ramp lead as he mopes out of the warehouse. His long face shows the hopelessness of another day.

17   A brutal rain has started to beat down on the oil-covered concrete of the ramp as the 306 screeches in off the runway. Its engines scream as they spit off sheets of rain and oil. Two of the men cover their ears as they run to put up a ladder to the front of the plane. The airline will give them ear covers only if they pay for half of them. A lot of the men never buy them. If they want, the airline will give them two little plugs free. The plugs don't work and hurt the inside of the ears.

18   The men will spend the rest of the day in the rain. Some of them will set up conveyor belts and trucks to unload the thousands of pounds of cargo that sit in the deep belly of the plane. Then they will feed the awkward bird until it is full and ready to fly again. They will crawl on their hands and knees in its belly, counting and humping hundreds of mailbags. The rest of the men will work up topside on the plane, pushing 8,000-pound pallets with their backs. Like Egyptians building a pyramid, they will pull and push until the pallet finally gives in and moves like a massive stone sliding through sand. They don't complain too much; they know that when the airline comes up with a better system some of them will go.

19   The old-timers at the airline can't understand why the younger men stay on. They know what the cargo airline can do to a man. It can work him hard but make him lazy at the same time. The work comes in spurts. Sometimes a man will be pushed for three hours of sweat, other times he will just stand around bored. It's not the hard work that breaks a man at the airline, it's the boredom of doing the same job over and over again.

20   At the end of the day the men start to move in off the ramp. The rain is still beating down at their backs but they move slowly. Their faces are red and raw from the rain-soaked wind that has been snapping at them for eight hours. The harsh wind moves in from the direction of the city. From the ramp you can see the Manhattan skyline, gray- and blue-looking, as it peeks up from the west wall of the warehouse. There is nothing to block the winter weather as it

rolls in like a storm across a prairie. They head down to the locker room, heads bowed, like a football team that never wins.

21   With the workday almost over, the men move between the narrow, gray rows of lockers. Up on the dirty walls that surround the lockers someone has written a couple of four-letter words. There is no wit to the words; they just say the usual. As they strip off their wet gear the men seem to come alive.

22   "Hey, Arnie! You want to stay four hours? They're asking for overtime down in Export," one of the men yells over the lockers.

23   Arnie is sitting about four rows over, taking off his heavy winter clothing. He thinks about this for a second and yells back, "What will we be doing?"

24   "Working the meat trailer." This means that Arnie will be humping huge sides of beef off rows of hooks for four hours. Blood will drip down onto his clothes as he struggles to the front of the trailer. Like most of the men, he needs the extra money, and knows that he should stay. He has Master Charge, Korvettes, Times Square Stores, and Abraham & Straus to pay.

25   "Nah, I'm not staying tonight. Not if it's working the meat trailer. Don wanted to stop for a few beers at The Owl; maybe I'll stay tomorrow night."

26   It's four o'clock in the afternoon now—the men have twelve minutes to go before they punch out. The airline has stopped for a few seconds as the men change shifts. Supervisors move frantically across the floor pushing the fresh lot of new men who have just started to come in. They hand out work sheets and yell orders: "Jack, get your men into their rain gear. Put three men in the bellies to finish off the 300 flight. Get someone on the pepper trailers, they've been here all morning."

27   The morning shift stands around the time clock with three minutes to go. Someone says that Kevin Delahunty has just been appointed to the Fire Department. Kevin, a young Irishman from Ozone Park, has been working the cargo airline for six years. Like most of the men, he has hated every minute of it. The men are openly proud of him as they reach out to shake his hand. Kevin has found a job on "the outside." "Ah, you'll be leaving soon," he tells Pat. "I never thought I'd get out of here either, but you'll see, you're going to make it."

28   The manager moves through the crowd handing out timecards and stops when he comes to Kevin. Someone told him Kevin is leaving. "Is that right, Delahunty? Well I guess we won't expect you in tomorrow, will we? Going to become a fireman, eh? That means you'll be jumping out of windows like a crazy man. Don't act like you did around here," he adds as he walks back to his office.

29   The time clock hits 4:12 and the men pour out of the warehouse. Kevin will never be back, but the rest of them will return in the morning to grind out another eight hours. Some of them will head straight home to the bills, screaming children, and a wife who tries to understand them. They'll have a Schaefer or two, then they'll settle down to a night of television.

30   Some of them will start to fill up the cargo bars that surround Kennedy Airport. They will head to places like Gaylor's on Rockaway Boulevard or The Dew Drop Inn down near Farmers Boulevard. They will drink deep glasses of whiskey and cold mugs of Budweiser. The Dew Drop has a honky-tonk mood of the Old West to it. The barmaid moves around like a modern-day Katie Elder. Like Brandy, she's a fine girl, but she can out-curse any cargoman. She wears a low-cut blouse that reveals most of her breasts. The jukebox will beat out some Country & Western as she says, "Ah, hell, you played my song." The cargomen will hoot and holler as she substitutes some of her own obscene lyrics.

31   They will drink late into the night, forgetting time clocks, Master Charge, First National City, Korvettes, mortgages, cars that don't start, and jet engines that hurt their ears. They will forget about damp, cold warehouses, winters that get longer and colder every year, minutes that drift by like hours, supervisors that harass, and the thought of growing old on a job they hate. At midnight they will fall dangerously into their cars and make their way up onto the Southern State Parkway. As they ride into the dark night of Long Island they will forget it all until 5:45 the next morning—when the Big Ben will start up the whole grind all over again.

Vocabulary

insatiable   oblivious   pallet

Topics for Discussion

1. Patrick Fenton's job does not seem appealing. In fact, it is the kind of job most people would avoid if at all possible. Why do you think he continues to work for the airline company? What reason does he give for staying on the job?

2. Someone once observed that most of the jobs in our society are dull, uncreative, boring, and often physically and psychologically

debilitating. Can you think of any job that does not fit this description? If there are so many jobs that fit this description, why do people want to work?

3. In what ways could Fenton's job be humanized, or at least made more bearable? Would it be difficult to make the job easier on the men? Why do you think the airline company doesn't take these steps?

4. Why would officials of the airline get uncomfortable if one of the warehouse workers "acts like he actually has brains"?

5. Fenton says all the men share a common hate for the work they do, and all drink a little too much. What does this sense of sharing do for the men? Could this feeling be expressed in other ways besides hating their jobs and drinking?

6. What is Fenton's attitude toward the company he works for? Do you think his attitude is typical of what most workers feel toward their employers?

7. Have you ever had a job that gave you attitudes similar to Fenton's? If you have, compare your job and your attitudes with Fenton's. What are the sources of your attitudes? Do they have a common source with Fenton's attitudes? Does this comparison lead you to any observations about the nature of work and the employer-employee relationship?

Rhetorical Considerations

1. In keeping with the title of the essay, Fenton uses the first person pronoun "I" throughout his "confession." What similar rhetorical devices does he use as part of his "confession" or personal narrative essay?

2. Tone is very important in this essay. What is the tone, and what devices does Fenton use to achieve this tone? Note particularly the vocabulary in the essay.

3. Fenton concentrates on concrete detail throughout his essay. Note the detail in paragraphs 3, 4, 6, 18, and 30. What effect does he achieve with his use of detail? How well has he selected and presented his details?

4. Compare the first and last paragraphs of the essay. How do they indicate the principle of organization used in the essay? Does the final paragraph really conclude the essay?

5. The sentence structure of the essay is simple, almost repetitious. How does it contribute to the theme of the essay? How do the sentence structure and vocabulary work together to reinforce the essay's theme?

Work in an Alienated Society

Erich Fromm

Erich Fromm (b.1900) is an author, psychoanalyst, and social philosopher whose published works include The Art of Loving, May Man Prevail, The Sane Society, *and* Escape From Freedom.

1   What becomes the meaning of *work* in an alienated society? . . . Since this problem is of utmost importance, not only for the understanding of present-day society, but also for any attempt to create a saner society, I want to deal with the nature of work separately and more extensively in the following pages.

2   Unless man exploits others, he has to work in order to live. However primitive and simple his method of work may be, by the very fact of production, he has risen above the animal kingdom; rightly has he been defined as "the animal that produces." But work is not only an inescapable necessity for man. Work is also his liberator from nature, his creator as a social and independent being. *In the process of work, that is, the molding and changing of nature outside of himself, man molds and changes himself.* He emerges from nature by mastering her; he develops his powers of cooperation, of reason, his sense of beauty. He separates himself from nature, from the original unity with her, but at the same time unites himself with her again as her master and builder. The more his work develops, the more his individuality develops. In molding nature and re-creating her, he learns to make use of his powers, increasing his skill and creativeness. Whether we think of the beautiful paintings in the caves of Southern France, the ornaments on weapons among primitive people, the statues and temples of Greece, the cathedrals of the Middle Ages, the chairs and tables made by skilled craftsmen, or the cultivation of flowers, trees or corn by peasants— all are expressions of the creative transformation of nature by men's reason and skill.

3   In Western history, craftsmanship, especially as it developed in the thirteenth and fourteenth centuries, constitutes one of the peaks in the evolution of creative work. Work was not only a useful activity, but one which carried with it a profound satisfaction. The main features of craftsmanship have been very lucidly expressed by C. W. Mills. "There is no ulterior motive in work other than the product being made and the processes of its creation. The details of

daily work are meaningful because they are not detached in the worker's mind from the product of the work. The worker is free to control his own working action. The craftsman is thus able to learn from his work; and to use and develop his capacities and skills in its prosecution. There is no split of work and play, or work and culture. The craftsman's way of livelihood determines and infuses his entire mode of living."

4   With the collapse of the medieval structure, and the beginning of the modern mode of production, the meaning and function of work changed fundamentally, especially in the Protestant countries. Man, being afraid of his newly won freedom, was obsessed by the need to subdue his doubts and fears by developing a feverish activity. The outcome of this activity, success or failure, decided his salvation, indicating whether he was among the saved or the lost souls. *Work, instead of being an activity satisfying in itself and pleasureable, became a duty and an obsession.* The more it was possible to gain riches by work, the more it became a pure means to the aim of wealth and success. Work became, in Max Weber's terms, the chief factor in a system of "inner-worldly asceticism," an answer to man's sense of aloneness and isolation.

5   However, work in this sense existed only for the upper and middle classes, those who could amass some capital and employ the work of others. For the vast majority of those who had only their physical energy to sell, work became nothing but forced labor. The worker in the eighteenth or nineteenth century who had to work sixteen hours if he did not want to starve was not doing it because he served the Lord in this way, nor because his success would show that he was among the "chosen" ones, but because he was forced to sell his energy to those who had the means of exploiting it. The first centuries of the modern era find the meaning of work divided into that of *duty* among the middle class, and that of *forced labor* among those without property.

6   The religious attitude toward work as a duty, which was still so prevalent in the nineteenth century, has been changing considerably in the last decades. Modern man does not know what to do with himself, how to spend his lifetime meaningfully, and he is driven to work in order to avoid an unbearable boredom. But work has ceased to be a moral and religious obligation in the sense of the middle-class attitude of the eighteenth and nineteenth centuries. Something new has emerged. Ever-increasing production, the drive to make bigger and better things, have become aims in themselves, new ideals. Work has become alienated from the working person.

7   What happens to the industrial worker? He spends his best

energy for seven or eight hours a day in producing "something." He needs his work in order to make a living, but his role is essentially a passive one. He fulfills a small isolated function in a complicated and highly organized process of production, and is never confronted with "his" product as a whole, at least not as a producer, but only as a consumer, provided he has the money to buy "his" product in a store. He is concerned neither with the whole product in its physical aspects nor with its wider economic and social aspects. He is put in a certain place, has to carry out a certain task, but does not participate in the organization or management of the work. He is not interested, nor does he know why one produces this, instead of another commodity—what relation it has to the needs of society as a whole. The shoes, the cars, the electric bulbs, are produced by "the enterprise," using the machines. He is a part of the machine, rather than its master as an active agent. The machine, instead of being in his service to do work for him which once had to be performed by sheer physical energy, has become his master. Instead of the machine being the substitute for human energy, man has become a substitute for the machine. *His work can be defined as the performance of acts which cannot yet be performed by machines.*

8   Work is a means of getting money, not in itself a meaningful human activity. P. Drucker, observing workers in the automobile industry, expresses this idea very succinctly: "For the great majority of automobile workers, the only meaning of the job is in the pay check, not in anything connected with the work or the product. Work appears as something unnatural, a disagreeable, meaningless and stultifying condition of getting the pay check, devoid of dignity as well as of importance. No wonder that this puts a premium on slovenly work, on slow-downs, and on other tricks to get the same pay check with less work. No wonder that this results in an unhappy and discontented worker—because a pay check is not enough to base one's self-respect on."

9   This relationship of the worker to his work is an outcome of the whole social organization of which he is a part. Being "employed," he is not an active agent, has no responsibility except the proper performance of the isolated piece of work he is doing, and has little interest except the one of bringing home enough money to support himself and his family. Nothing more is expected of him, or wanted from him. He is part of the equipment hired by capital, and his role and function are determined by this quality of being a piece of equipment. In recent decades, increasing attention has been paid to the psychology of the worker, and to his attitude toward his work, to the "human problem of industry"; but this very formulation is

indicative of the underlying attitude, there is a human being spending most of his lifetime at work, and what should be discussed is the *"industrial problem of human beings,"* rather than *"the human problem of industry."*

10　　Most investigations in the field of industrial psychology are concerned with the question of how the productivity of the individual worker can be increased, and how he can be made to work with less friction; psychology has lent its services to "human engineering," an attempt to treat the worker and employee like a machine which runs better when it is well oiled. Rather than being primarily concerned with a better organization of the technical use of the worker's physical powers, most industrial psychologists are mainly concerned with the manipulation of the worker's psyche. The underlying idea can be formulated like this: if he works better when he is happy, then let us make him happy, secure, satisfied, or anything else, provided it raises his output and diminishes friction. In the name of "human relations," the worker is treated with all devices which suit a completely alienated person; even happiness and human values are recommended in the interest of better relations with the public. Thus, for instance, according to *Time* magazine, one of the best-known American psychiatrists said to a group of fifteen hundred supermarket executives: "It's going to be an increased satisfaction to our customers if we are happy. . . . It is going to pay off in cold dollars and cents to management, if we could put some of these general principles of values, human relationships, really into practice." One speaks of "human relations" and one means the most in-human relations, those between alienated automatons; one speaks of happiness and means the perfect routinization which has driven out the last doubt and all spontaneity.

11　　The alienated and profoundly unsatisfactory character of work results in two reactions: one, the ideal of complete *laziness*; the other a deep-seated, though often unconscious *hostility* toward work and everything and everybody connected with it.

12　　It is not difficult to recognize the widespread longing for the state of complete laziness and passivity. Our advertising appeals to it even more than to sex. There are, of course, many useful and labor saving gadgets. But this usefulness often serves only as a rationalization for the appeal to complete passivity and receptivity. A package of breakfast cereal is being advertised as *"new—easier to eat."* An electric toaster is advertised with these words: ". . . the most distinctly different toaster in the world! Everything is done *for* you with this new toaster. You need not even bother to lower the bread. Power-action, through a unique electric motor, *gently takes the bread right out of your fingers!''* How many courses in languages, or other subjects are announced with the slogan "effortless learning, no more of the old drudgery." Everybody knows the picture of the elderly couple in the advertisement of a life-insurance company, who have retired at the age of sixty, and spend their life in the complete bliss of having nothing to do except just travel.

13   Radio and television exhibit another element of this yearning for laziness: the idea of "push-button power"; by pushing a button, or turning a knob on my machine, I have the power to produce music, speeches, ball games, and on the television set, to command events of the world to appear before my eyes. The pleasure of driving cars certainly rests partly upon this same satisfaction of the wish for push-button power. By the effortless pushing of a button, a powerful machine is set in motion; little skill and effort is needed to make the driver feel that he is the ruler of space.

14   But there is far more serious and deep-seated reaction to the meaninglessness and boredom of work. It is a hostility toward work which is much less conscious than our craving for laziness and inactivity. Many a businessman feels himself the prisoner of his business and the commodities he sells; he has a feeling of fraudulency about his product and a secret contempt for it. He hates his customers, who force him to put up a show in order to sell. He hates his competitors because they are a threat; his employees as well as his superiors, because he is in a constant competitive fight with them. Most important of all, he hates himself, because he sees his life passing by, without making any sense beyond the momentary intoxication of success. Of course, this hate and contempt for others and for oneself, and for the very things one produces, is mainly unconscious, and only occasionally comes up to awareness in a fleeting thought, which is sufficiently disturbing to be set aside as quickly as possible.

Vocabulary

asceticism   stultify   fraudulent

Topics for Discussion

1. Fromm implies that meaningful work is necessary for a happy existence. How can work become meaningful?

2. What else besides meaningful work is necessary for human fulfillment?

3. Do you think there exist some kinds of work which of their nature could never be meaningful?

4. Why doesn't everybody simply choose to peform the work most meaningful to them?

5. What bores you? Why? Can you control it? Can you compensate for boredom? Can you imagine or describe a life without boredom?

6. What is alienation? Do you find alienation in your own life? How do you deal with it?

7. Reformers argue that the present economic system can be modified to significantly reduce or eliminate alienation. Some critics, on the other hand, contend that only a radical change in the economic and social structure will make human happiness possible. Which argument do you favor?

8. Is "total freedom" ever possible? Do you suspect that given "total freedom," most people would be afraid of it? Why? Have you ever experienced what you think is "total freedom"?

Rhetorical Considerations

1. Of what value is Fromm's historical introduction? What is he trying to tell us about the nature of work and the fact of change? Note that one of the essay's three italicized sentences comes in this section. What is the significance of that sentence for the whole essay? Would the essay have been more informative had it said more about the history of work?

2. In paragraph 8, does the final sentence flow logically from those that come before it?

3. Does Fromm tend needlessly to depart from his central subject? See paragraph 13, for example.

4. Does the conclusion of the essay satisfactorily answer all of the questions the essay raises?

5. Would the essay have communicated better were it written in more precise and less familiar prose? Why?

Survival Ship

Judith Merril

Judith Merril (b. 1923) is a science fiction writer, editor, and teacher. As an editor of science fiction she is best known for the anthology series The Year's Best Science Fiction, *which she began editing in 1956.*

1   Half a million people actually made the round trip to Space Station One that day to watch the take-off in person. And back on Earth a hundred million video screens flashed the picture of Captain Melnick's gloved hand waving a dramatic farewell at the port, while the other hand slowly pressed down the lever that would fire the ship out beyond the orbit of the artificial satellite, past the Moon and the planets, into unknown space.

2   From Station One, Earth, and Moon, a hundred million winged wishes added their power to the surge of the jets, as a rising spiral of fire inside the greatest rocket tower ever built marked the departure of the thrice-blessed ship, *Survival.* In the great churches, from pole to pole, services were held all day, speeding the giant vessel on its way, calling on the aid of the Lord for the Twenty and Four who manned the ship.

3   At mountain-top telescopes a dozen cameras faithfully transmitted the messages of great unblinking glass eyes. Small home sets and massive pulpit screens alike looked to the sky to follow the flare dimming in the distance, to watch the man-made star falling away.

4   Inside the great ship Melnick's hand left the firing lever, then began adjusting the chin rest and the earphones of the acceleration couch. The indicator dashboard, designed for prone eye level, leaped into focus. Securing the couch straps with the swift competence of habit, the captain intently watched the sweep of the big second hand around the take-off timer, aware at the same time that green lights were beginning to glow at the other end of the board. The indicator reached the first red mark.

5   "The show's over, everybody. We're in business!" The mike built into the chin rest carried the captain's taut voice all over the ship. "Report, all stations!"

6   "Number one, all secure!" Melnick mentally ticked off the first green light, glowing to prove the astrogator's couch was in use.

7   "Number two, all secure!"

8   "Number three . . ." "Four . . ." "Five." The rhythmic sing-song of pinpoint timing in take-off was second nature by now to the whole crew. One after another, the green lights glowed for safety, punctuating the litany, and the gong from the timer put a period neatly in place after the final "All secure!"

9   "Eight seconds to black out," the captain's voice warned. "Seven . . . six . . . stand by." The first wave of acceleration shock reeled into twenty-four helmet-sheathed heads on twenty-four individually designed head rests. "Five——" *It's got to work,* Melnick was thinking, fighting off unconsciousness with fierce intensity. "Four——" *It's got to . . . got to . . .* "Three——" *got to . . . got to . . .* "Two——" *got to . . .*

10   At the space station, a half-million watchers were slowly cleared from the giant take-off platform. They filed in long orderly lines down the ramps to the interior, and waited there for the smaller Earth rockets that would take them home. Waiting, they were at once elated and disappointed. They had seen no more than could be seen at the same place on any other day. The entire rocket area had been fenced off, with a double cordon of guards to make sure that too-curious visitors stayed out of range. Official explanations mentioned the new engine, the new fuel, the danger of escaping gases—but nobody believed it. Every one of the half-million visitors knew what the mystery was: the crew, and nothing else. Giant video screens all over the platform gave the crowd details and closeups, the same they would have seen had they stayed comfortably at home. They saw the captain's gloved hand, at the last, but not the captain's face.

11   There was muttering and complaining, but there was something else too. Each man, woman, and child who went to the station that day would be able to say, years later, "I was there when the *Survival* took off. You never saw anything so big in your life."

12   Because it wasn't just another planet hop. It wasn't just like the hundreds of other take-offs. It was the *Survival,* the greatest spaceship ever engineered. People didn't think of the *Survival* in terms of miles-per-second; they said "Sirius in fifteen years!"

13   From Sunday supplements to dignified periodicals, nearly every medium of communication on Earth had carried the story. Brightly colored graphs made visibly simple the natural balance of life forces in which plants and animals could maintain a permanently fresh atmosphere as well as a self-perpetuating food supply. Lecture demonstrations and videocasts showed how centrifugal force would replace gravity.

14   For months before take-off, the press and video followed the

preparations with daily intimate accounts. The world over, people knew the nicknames of pigs, calves, chickens, and crew members—and even the proper botanical name of the latest minor masterpiece of the biochemists, a hybrid plant whose root, stems, leaves, buds, blossoms, and fruit were all edible, nourishing, and delicious, and which had the added advantage of being the thirstiest CO_2 drinker ever found.

15   The public knew the nicknames of the crew, and the proper name of the plant. But they never found out, not even the half million who went to the field to see for themselves, the real identity of the Twenty and Four who comprised the crew. They knew that thousands had applied; that it was necessary to be single, under twenty-five, and a graduate engineer in order to get as far as the physical exam; that the crew was mixed in sex, with the object of filling the specially equipped nursery and raising a second generation for the return trip, if, as was hoped, a lengthy stay on Sirius's planet proved possible. They knew, for that matter, all the small characteristics and personal idiosyncrasies of the crew members—what they ate, how they dressed, their favorite games, theaters, music, books, cigarettes, preachers, and political parties. There were only two things the public didn't know, and couldn't find out: the real names of the mysterious Twenty and Four, and the reason why those names were kept secret.

16   There were as many rumors as there were newsmen or radio reporters, of course. Hundreds of explanations were offered at one time or another. But still nobody knew—nobody except the half hundred Very Important Persons who had planned the project, and the Twenty and Four themselves.

17   And now, as the pinpoint of light faded out of the screens of televisors all over Earth, the linear and rotary acceleration of the great ship began to adjust to the needs of the human body. "Gravity" in the living quarters gradually approached Earth-normal. Tortured bodies relaxed in the acceleration couches, where the straps had held them securely positioned through the initial stage, so as to keep the blood and guts where they belonged, and to prevent the stomach from following its natural tendency to emerge through the backbone. Finally, stunned brain cells awoke to the recognition that danger signals were no longer coming through from shocked, excited tissues.

18   Captain Melnick was the first to awake. The row of lights on the board still glowed green. Fumbling a little with the straps, Melnick watched tensely to see if the indicator lights were functioning properly, sighing with relief as the one at the head of the board

went dead, operated automatically by the removal of body weight from the couch.

19   It was right—it was essential—for the captain to wake up first. If any of the men had showed superior recuperative powers, it could be bad. Melnick thought wearily of the years and years ahead during which this artificial dominance had to be maintained in defiance of all Earth conditioning. But of course it would not be that bad, really. The crew had been picked for ability to conform to the unusual circumstances; they were all without strong family ties or prejudices. Habit would establish the new castes soon enough, but the beginning was crucial. Survival was more than a matter of plant-animal balance and automatic gravity.

20   While the captain watched, another light went out, and then another. Officers, both of them. Good. Three more lights died out together. Then men were beginning to awaken, and it was reassuring to know that their own couch panels would show them that the officers had revived first. In any case, there was not more time for worrying. There were things to be done.

21   A detail was sent off immediately to attend to the animals, release them from the confinement of the specially prepared acceleration pens, and check them for any possible damage incurred in spite of precautions. The proportions of human, animal, and plant life has been worked out carefully beforehand for maximum efficiency and for comfort. Now that the trip had started, the miniature world had to maintain its status quo or perish.

22   As soon as enough of the crew were awake, Lieutenant Johnson, the third officer, took a group of eight out to make an inspection of the hydroponic tanks that lined the hull. Nobody expected much trouble here. Being at the outermost part of the ship, the plants were exposed to high "gravity." The outward pull exerted on them by rotation should have held their roots in place, even through the tearing backward thrust of the acceleration. But there was certain to be a large amount of minor damage, to stems and leaves and buds, and whatever there was would need immediate repair. In the ship's economy the plants had the most vital function of all—absorbing carbon dioxide from dead air already used by humans and animals, and deriving from it the nourishment that enabled their chlorophyll systems to release fresh oxygen for re-use in breathing.

23   There was a vast area to inspect. Row upon row of tanks marched solidly from stem to stern of the giant ship, all around the inner circumference of the hull. Johnson split the group of eight into four teams, each with a biochemist in charge to locate and make

notes of the extent of the damage, and an unclassified man as helper, to do the actual dirty work, crawling out along the catwalks to mend each broken stalk.

24   Other squads were assigned to check the engines and control mechanisms, and the last two women to awake got stuck with the booby prize—first shift in the galley. Melnick squashed their immediate protests with a stern reminder that they had hardly earned the right to complain; but privately the captain was pleased at the way it had worked out. This first meal on board was going to have to be something of an occasion. A bit of ceremony always helped; and above all, social procedures would have to be established immediately. A speech was indicated—a speech Melnick did not want to have to make in the presence of all twenty-four crew members. As it worked out, the Four would almost certainly be kept busy longer than the others. If these women had not happened to wake up last . . .

25   The buzzing of the intercom broke into the captain's speculations. "Lieutenant Johnson reporting, sir." Behind the proper, crisp manner, the young lieutenant's voice was frightened. Johnson was third in command, supervising the inspection of the tanks.

26   "Having trouble down there?" Melnick was deliberately informal, knowing the men could hear over the intercom, and anxious to set up an immediate feeling of unity among the officers.

27   "One of the men complaining, sir." The young lieutenant sounded more confident already. "There seems to be some objection to the division of work."

28   Melnick thought it over quickly and decided against any more public discussion on the intercom. "Stand by. I'll be right down."

29   All over the ship airducts and companionways led from the inner-level living quarters "down" to the outer level of tanks; Melnick took the steps three at a time and reached the trouble zone within seconds after the conversation ended.

30   "Who's the troublemaker here?"

31   "Kennedy—on assignment with Petty Officer Giorgio for plant maintenance."

32   "You have a complaint?" Melnick asked the swarthy, dungareed man whose face bore a look of sullen dissatisfaction.

33   "Yeah." The man's voice was deliberately insolent. The others had never heard him speak that way before, and he seemed to gain confidence from the shocked surprise they displayed. "I thought I was supposed to be a pampered darling this trip. How come I do all the dirty work here, and Georgie gets to keep so clean?"

34   His humor was too heavy to be effective. "Captain's orders,

that's why," Melnick snapped. "Everybody has to work double time till things are squared away. If you don't like the job here, I can fix you up fine in the brig. Don't worry about your soft quarters. You'll get 'em later and plenty of 'em. It's going to be a long trip, and don't forget it." The captain pointed significantly to the chronometer built into the overhead. "But it's not much longer to dinner. You'd better get back to work if you want to hit the chow line while it's hot. Mess call in thirty minutes."

35   Melnick took a chance and turned abruptly away, terminating the interview. It worked. Sullen but defeated, Kennedy hoisted himself back up on the catwalk, and then began crawling out to the spot Giorgio pointed out. Not daring to express their relief, lieutenant and captain exchanged one swift look of triumph before Melnick walked wordlessly off.

36   In the big control room that would be mess hall, social hall, and general meeting place for all of them for fifteen years to come—or twice that time if Sirius's planet turned out to be uninhabitable—the captain waited for the crew members to finish their checkup assignments. Slowly they gathered in the lounge, ignoring the upholstered benches around the sides and the waiting table in the center, standing instead in small awkward groups. An undercurrent of excitement ran through them all, evoking deadly silences and erupting in bursts of too-noisy conversation, destroying the joint attempt at an illusion of nonchalance. They all knew—or hoped they knew—what the subject of the captain's first speech would be, and behind the facade of bronzed faces and trimly muscled bodies they were all curious, even a little afraid.

37   Finally there were twenty of them in the room, and the captain rose and rapped for order.

38   "I suppose," Melnick began, "you will all want to know our present position and the results of the checkup." Nineteen heads turned as one, startled and disappointed at the opening. "However," the captain continued, smiling at the change of expressions the single word brought, "I imagine you're all as hungry and—er—impatient as I am, so I shall put off the more routine portions of my report until our other comrades have joined us. There is only one matter which should properly be discussed immediately."

39   Everyone in the room was acutely conscious of the Four. They had all known, of course, how it would be. But on Earth there had always been other, ordinary men around to make them less aware of it. Now the general effort to maintain an air of artificial ease and disinterest was entirely abandoned as the captain plunged into the subject most on everyone's mind.

40   "Our ship is called the *Survival*. You all know why. Back on

Earth, people think they know why too; they think it's because of our plants and artificial gravity, and the hundreds of other engineering miracles that keep us going. Of course, they also know that our crew is mixed, and that our population is therefore''—the captain paused, letting an anticipatory titter circle the room—''is therefore by no means fixed. What they don't know, naturally, is the division of sexes in the crew.

41   "You are all aware of the reason for the secrecy. You know that our organization is in direct opposition to the ethical principles on which the peace was established after World War IV. And you know how the planners of this trip had to struggle with the authorities to get this project approved. When consent was granted, finally, it was only because the highest prelates clearly understood that the conditions of our small universe were in every way different from those on Earth—and that the division proposed was *necessary for survival.*''

42   The captain paused, waiting for the last words to sink in, and studying the attitudes of the group. Even now, after a year's conditioning to counteract earthly mores, there were some present who listened to this public discussion of dangerous and intimate matters with flushed faces and embarrassed smiles.

43   "You all realize, of course, that this consent was based, finally, on the basic principle itself." Automatically, out of long habit unbroken by that year's intensive training, the captain made the sign of the olive branch. *"Survival of the race is the first duty of every ethical man and woman.''* The command was intoned meaningfully, almost pontifically, and brought its reward as confusion cleared from some of the flushed faces. "What we are doing, our way of life now, has the full approval of the authorities. We must never forget that.

44   "On Earth, survival of the races is best served by the increasing strength of family ties. It was not thought wise to endanger those ties by letting the general public become aware of our—unorthodox—system here on board. A general understanding, on Earth, of the true meaning of the phrase, 'the Twenty and the Four,' could only have aroused a furor of discussion and argument that would, in the end, have impeded survival both there and here.

45   "The knowledge that there are twenty of one sex on board, and only four of the other—that children will be born outside of normal family groups, and raised jointly—I need not tell you how disastrous that would have been." Melnick paused, raising a hand to dispel the muttering in the room.

46   "I wanted to let you know, before the Four arrive, that I have

made some plans which I hope will carry us through the initial period in which difficulties might well arise. Later, when the groups of six—five of us, and one of them in each—have been assigned their permanent quarters, I think it will be possible, in fact necessary, to allow a greater amount of autonomy within those groups. But for the time being, I have arranged a —shall we call it a dating schedule?" Again the captain paused, waiting for tension to relieve itself in laughter. "I have arranged dates for all of you with each of them during convenient free periods over the next month. Perhaps at the end of that time we will be able to choose groups; perhaps it will take longer. Maternity schedules, of course, will not be started until I am certain that the grouping is satisfactory to all. For the time being, remember this:

47   "We are not only more numerous than they, but we are stronger and, in our social placement here, more fortunate. We must become accustomed to the fact that they are our responsibility. It is because we are hardier, longer-lived, less susceptible to pain and illness, better able to withstand, mentally, the difficulties of a life of monotony, that we are placed as we are—and not alone because we are the bearers of children."

48   Over the sober silence of the crew, the captain's voice rang out. "Lieutenant Johnson," Melnick called to the golden-haired, sun-tanned woman near the door, "will you call the men in from the tank rooms now? They can finish their work after dinner."

Vocabulary

competence	cordon	centrifugal
hybrid	carbon dioxide	idiosyncrasy
hydroponic	chlorophyll	swarthy
chronometer	nonchalance	prelate
mores		

Topics for Discussion

1. What is so unusual about the crew of the spaceship *Survival*? Why was the public kept ignorant of the composition of the crew?

2. Do you find the composition of the crew unusual? Why? What social restrictions does the composition of the crew violate? Would such a crew be acceptable today?

3. Were you startled by the end of the story? Why? What does your reaction reveal about your attitudes toward the relationship between men and women, and the role of women in society?

4. Were you surprised to learn that Captain Melnick is a woman? What does your reaction reveal about your attitude toward women?

5. Would you fly in a commercial airliner piloted by a woman? Discuss your answer in relation to your answers to questions 3 and 4.

6. How factual is Captain Melnick being when she says that women "are hardier, longer-lived, less susceptible to pain and illness, better able to withstand, mentally, the difficulties of a life of monotony . . ."?

Rhetorical Considerations

1. Since Merril does not reveal the sex of any of the characters in the story until the end, how does she handle the problem of gender in pronouns? Are there any grammatical clues in the story as to the sexual composition of the crew?

2. Why is the crew called the Twenty and Four? Why capitalize the numbers?

3. Examine the dialogue in the story, particularly the exchange between Melnick and Kennedy in paragraphs 30 to 34. Is there anything in the rhetoric of each character's speech to indicate his or her sex? How do you know Kennedy is a man?

4. Look at the use of the word *men* in the second sentence of paragraph 19. What is the meaning of the word? How does the meaning of the word change once you know the ending of the story?

5. Only two characters are described according to their physical characteristics, Lieutenant Johnson and crewman Kennedy. Locate each description and discuss whether such descriptions are necessary. That is, is it important to emphasize the physical characteristics of men and women?

Rhetorical Analysis

Anne Roiphe: Confessions of a Female Chauvinist Sow

Anne Roiphe deals with an issue of contemporary concern, women's liberation. She presents an argument, an attempt to persuade her audience. But unlike other argumentative essays in this book, Roiphe's essay does not present the arguments one would expect on the particular issue. Indeed, she chooses instead to assume the acceptance of women's liberation by her readers. Roiphe's goal in this essay is to reveal women's "hidden prejudices, class assumptions and an anti-male humor and collection of expectations that gave [women] . . . a secret sense of superiority. . . ." And in revealing this she hopes to uncover women's hidden anti-male feelings, which are largely a result of childhood experiences and which will hinder women's drive for equality if they are allowed to continue unrecognized and unchecked.

Roiphe chooses to present her argument not in a formal but in a personal, reflective essay. Basing all her observations, criticisms, and arguments upon her experiences, she draws upon her life to illustrate what she feels all women should realize and be aware of. The appeal of her essay is not rooted in emotion or theory but in the writer's experience and, by inference, the reader's experience.

Roiphe begins with the premise that just as people can be affected throughout their lives by unremembered experiences, so, too, can social movements. Thus, an adult can unconsciously act a certain way because of some experience dimly remembered, and these individual experiences together can affect a movement such as women's liberation. Roiphe's personal example of her marriage that failed illustrates the effect of these unremembered experiences. Indeed, this episode in her life provides one framework for her argument that women do have hidden anti-male feelings.

After setting up her premise and giving her example of how unconscious patterns of behavior are established in an individual, Roiphe moves on to futher illustrations involving herself and her childhood. Subtly, indirectly, girls were given the impression that boys were indeed different. Not only did boys take shop in school and play football while girls took homemaking and were cheerleaders, but boys did not behave like girls. Boys were fickle, unkind, didn't like intelligent girls, wanted to seduce girls and then leave them pregnant, and in general were less moral than girls. In short, boys were "hypocritical, self-seeking, exploitative, untrustworthy," and all the other things that girls were not. And all of these beliefs are reflected in our society and in our attitudes toward men and women. Child support and alimony laws exist, says Roiphe, because basically we believe that men don't care about their children nor the women they may have loved at one time. No such laws exist for women because we believe that women would never do the things men would do, such as abandon their children or their spouses. Men just don't have the same feelings as women, and if they do they don't show them. It is up to women to be the preservers and defenders of the family.

The reader may want to protest as the essay progresses, but Roiphe moves quickly to her next arguments. Again recalling her childhood, Roiphe points out that her attitudes toward men were acquired from other women. "Boys are messy, boys are mean, boys are rough, boys are stupid and have sloppy handwriting." Such attitudes are inculcated in childhood and then carried into adulthood, and it is upon such attitudes that women's relations with men are based.

Woman must recognize the assumptions about men that are drawn from their childhood experiences. Just as men may have antifemale attitudes based upon their previous experiences, so too women may have anti-male attitudes based upon their experiences. And if a man can be labeled a *male chauvinist pig* for his attitudes toward women, then a woman can be labeled a *female chauvinist sow*. The resolution of this problem, and the resolution of Roiphe's argument and essay, is to operate from the assumption that men are just as human as women—that just as men are not superior to women, so women are not superior to men.

This summary of Roiphe's arguments is, of course, brief,

but it gives an idea of the general movement of the essay. Now let us look at the essay in more detail.

The opening sentence sounds something like a fairy tale: "I once married a man. . . ." This appeal to childhood is the basis of the essay, as Roiphe clearly points out in the first sentence of the second paragraph. To understand ourselves as adults, we must look to our childhood. And so it is with movements both political and social; before any movement can affect the present or alter the future it must rid itself of "all unnecessary and ugly baggage of the past." And what is this baggage and how did women acquire it? The baggage is "hidden anti-male feelings," and it was acquired indirectly.

In paragraph 4, the longest paragraph in the essay, Roiphe discusses some of her childhood experiences and points out how they have helped shape her attitudes toward men. She recounts her experiences in some detail and at some length. The final two sentences of the paragraph present her conclusions based upon her discussion. Thus the paragraph is structured inductively: the detailed evidence leads to the conclusion.

Paragraph 5 points out how the attitudes acquired in childhood begin to operate in society in the form of laws and assumptions about the behavior of men and women. And even though we may be perfectly aware of how our attitudes have been shaped and how wrong they might be, we still cannot help but react as we do. Thus, Roiphe finds herself expecting a woman to stay always by her children but is not shocked when a man abandons his family.

Paragraphs 6 and 7 continue the accounts of childhood experiences that have shaped the mind of the adult. And, as Roiphe says in paragraph 8, "the prejudices of childhood are hard to outgrow."

Paragraphs 9, 10, and 11 point out that women must reject the anti-male prejudices of their childhood if the divisions that now exist between men and women are ever to be eradicated. False notions about female moral superiority only prolong the oppression of women.

Paragraphs 12 through 15 again recall childhood experiences that helped shape the mind of the adult and how they contribute to the divisions between men and women. All of these examples demonstrate why it is so important to "wipe the slate clean" and start again without the ugliness of the past burdening the present. And, in view of what she has just said, Roiphe suggests that women rethink some of the current issues of women's liberation such as abortion and childrearing. Perhaps suggest Roiphe, if women were to deal with men more as human beings and less as creatures they were prejudiced against as children a better style of life might emerge.

And finally, in the sixteenth paragraph, Roiphe sums up her arguments in one sentence: Women are only equal to men, not superior.

Throughout her essay, Roiphe balances personal accounts of incidents of her childhood with comments on the present relations between men and women. She makes her experiences relevant to these relations and to her contention that women have hidden anti-male attitudes. Rather than present all her reminiscences at once at the beginning of the essay, she chooses the approach of alternating her experiences with more general comments. Thus her experiences become the basis for observations on the interactions between men and women. She states her thesis twice in the essay: at the end of the second paragraph and again in the last paragraph. And in paragraph 9 she restates her main idea differently. Roiphe thus directs her reader's attention to her central idea and does not allow any straying from the issue at hand. This restatement of the thesis lends organization and structure to the essay while at the same time reinforcing the argument.

The prose style of the essay, along with the vocabulary and tone, is relaxed and casual. This is not the formal writing of a selection in this book such as Kennedy's inaugural address. Throughout her essay, Roiphe achieves an easy flow in her sentences by the frequent use of internal sentence breaks, particularly dashes. These frequent breaks in the sentences, along with the use of parallelism and elliptical clauses, contribute a casualness to the sentences which in turn helps create an informal, personal tone in the whole essay. And this is in keeping with the subject matter and approach of the essay. Roiphe is calling upon her experiences, and thus her tone and style must communicate her informality. It would be incongruous for her to take a stiff, formal, and aloof approach to her own childhood.

What she seeks instead is a personal, direct immediacy in the essay. She wants her readers to remember their own childhoods and to examine their own beliefs just as she does. Everything in the style of the essay is calculated to draw the readers out of themselves and into the essay—to explore Roiphe's mind and their own as well.

Roiphe might have made her point more effectively with a formal essay, but she chose not to appeal to abstraction or scientific facts and figures. Rather she presents herself as example and invites her readers to make similar examinations of their own beliefs and their origins. Her argument thus rests both on her own experiences and on her readers' identification with those experiences. It is a risky approach she has chosen, but she has aimed for more than persuasion; she has aimed for involvement and commitment. Whether she has succeeded, only her readers can answer.

> Nothing endures but change.

Heraclitus

5

SOURCES OF PERMANENCE AND CHANGE

As I write this introduction, I am looking at the faces of two women on the cover of this week's *New York Times Magazine* (and I tell my students not to allow distractions to interfere with their writing—better to incorporate them, perhaps). I am also listening to Beethoven's *Fifth Piano Concerto.* The younger woman has long pigtails with red bows on the end—red bows of yarn—and light brown hair. The caption says she is a student at Radcliffe College. The woman with her has very black hair with a touch of grey at the right temple. She is an accomplished professor of psychology and is also the president of Radcliffe College, and she is thirty-three years old. Her name is Matina Horner. You may not know this, but since the time Matina Horner and I were undergraduates, universities have undergone dramatic changes. Coed dorms? Student-faculty committees? A focus on women and minorities? Experimental curricula? Jeans and T-shirts in class? A thirty-three-year-old university president? These were our fantasies. For many of you they are reality. Things, you see, do change. And by the time the woman with the pigtails gets ready to become a university president or to write the introduction to section 5 of her own rhetoric reader, they will, no doubt, have changed again.

But what about Beethoven's *Fifth Piano Concerto*? That has not changed—not one note of it—since it was first performed on November 28, 1811. Nor has one note changed of Igor Stravinsky's *Le Sacre du Printemps,* which I heard the Philadelphia Orchestra perform last night—not since 1913. So you see, things remain the same.

The program for last night's concert contains this sentence: "*Le Sacre du Printemps* is universally acknowledged as the work which did more than any other to *change* the course of twentieth-century music." 1913 marked a revolution in music, a big change, and this is perhaps the hard part to understand—the music that made and marked that change has come down to us as something which itself cannot be essentially changed, something which must be reacted to in order for change to take place, perhaps by the new electronic music of Stockhausen or perhaps—how sacrilegious!—by the Rolling Stones.

If history continues the way it always has, then things in music, like all things else, are sure to change again. And yet after they have changed again, Beethoven, Mozart, Haydn, Schubert, Berlioz, Stravinsky, and Mick Jagger will remain fixed in history as having created works of art, each of which, in its uniqueness born of taking new directions, tells us permanently something vital and essential about the permanent direction of humanity.

The point, if you should still wonder, is that the vital energetic things of the present, the stuff of change, will someday become the stuff of permanence, changing thus into its opposite as all things do. And thus, the title of this section—not "Sources of Permanence and Sources of Change," not *permanence* and *change* separately, but *permanence* and *change* together. "Nothing endures," as Heraclitus observed, "but change"; so it is with all things, and nowhere more noticeably so than in the most playful and elegant creations of human work—in myth, symbol, and art.

The Rhetorical Analysis in this section deals with Charlton Laird's essay, *Folk Roots of Civilization—and Thereby Hangs a Tale.* Be sure to read Laird's essay before reading the Rhetorical Analysis.

The Reach of Imagination

Jacob Bronowski

Jacob Bronowski (1908-1975) was a British mathematician and au-
thor whose works include Science and Human Values, The Common Sense of Science, *and* The Poet's Defense.

1   For three thousand years, poets have been enchanted and
moved and perplexed by the power of their own imagination. In a
short and summary essay I can hope at most to lift one small corner
of that mystery; and yet it is a critical corner. I shall ask, What goes
on in the mind when we imagine? You will hear from me that one
answer to this question is fairly specific: which is to say, that we can
describe the working of the imagination. And when we describe it as
I shall do, it becomes plain that imagination is a specifically *human*
gift. To imagine is the characteristic act, not of the poet's mind, or
the painter's, or the scientist's, but of the mind of man.

2   My stress here on the word *human* implies that there is a clear
difference in this between the actions of men and those of other
animals. Let me then start with a classical experiment with animals
and children which Walter Hunter thought out in Chicago about
1910. That was the time when scientists were agog with the success
of Ivan Pavlov in forming and changing the reflex actions of dogs,
which Pavlov had first announced in 1903. Pavlov had been given a
Nobel prize the next year, in 1904; although in fairness I should say
that the award did not cite his work on the conditioned reflex, but on
the digestive gland.

3   Hunter duly trained some dogs and other animals on Pavlov's
lines. They were taught that when a light came on over one of three
tunnels out of their cage, that tunnel would be open; they could
escape down it, and were rewarded with food if they did. But once
he had fixed that conditioned reflex, Hunter added to it a deeper
idea: he gave the mechanical experiment a new dimension,
literally—the dimension of time. Now he no longer let the dog go to
the lighted tunnel at once; instead, he put out the light, and then kept
the dog waiting a little while before he let him go. In this way Hunter
timed how long an animal can remember where he has last seen the
signal light to his escape route.

4   The results were and are staggering. A dog or a rat forgets
which one of three tunnels has been lit up within a matter of

seconds—in Hunter's experiment, ten seconds at most. If you want such an animal to do much better than this, you must make the task much simpler: you must face him with only two tunnels to choose from. Even so, the best that Hunter could do was to have a dog remember for five minutes which one of two tunnels had been lit up.

5   I am not quoting these times as if they were exact and universal: they surely are not. Hunter's experiment, more than fifty years old now, had many faults of detail. For example, there were too few animals, they were oddly picked, and they did not all behave consistently. It may be unfair to test a dog for what he *saw,* when he commonly follows his nose rather than his eyes. It may be unfair to test any animal in the unnatural setting of a laboratory cage. And there are higher animals, such as chimpanzees and other primates, which certainly have longer memories than the animals that Hunter tried.

6   Yet when all these provisos have been made (and met, by more modern experiments) the facts are still startling and characteristic. An animal cannot recall a signal from the past for even a short fraction of the time that a man can—for even a short fraction of the time that a child can. Hunter made comparable tests with six-year-old children, and found, of course, that they were incomparably better than the best of his animals. There is a striking and basic difference between a man's ability to imagine something that he saw or experienced, and an animal's failure.

7   Animals make up for this by other and extraordinary gifts. The salmon and the carrier pigeon can find their way home as we cannot: they have, as it were, a practical memory that man cannot match. But their actions always depend on some form of habit: on instinct or on learning, which reproduce by rote a train of known responses. They do not depend, as human memory does, on calling to mind the recollection of absent things.

8   Where is it that the animal falls short? We get a clue to the answer, I think, when Hunter tells us how the animals in his experiment tried to fix their recollection. They most often pointed themselves at the light before it went out, as some gun dogs point rigidly at the game they scent—and get the name *pointer* from the posture. The animal makes ready to act by building the signal into its action. There is a primitive imagery in its stance, it seems to me; it is as if the animal were trying to fix the light on its mind by fixing it in its body. And indeed, how else can a dog mark and (as it were) name one of three tunnels, when he has no such words as *left* and *right,* and no such numbers as *one, two, three*? The directed gesture of attention and readiness is perhaps the only symbolic device that the

dog commands to hold on to the past, and thereby to guide himself into the future.

9   I used the verb *to imagine* a moment ago, and now I have some ground for giving it a meaning. *To imagine* means to make images and to move them about inside one's head in new arrangements. When you and I recall the past, we imagine it in this direct and homely sense. The tool that puts the human mind ahead of the animal is imagery. For us, memory does not demand the preoccupation that it demands in animals, and it lasts immensely longer, because we fix it in images or other substitute symbols. With the same symbolic vocabulary we spell out the future—not one but many futures, which we weigh one against another.

10   I am using the word *image* in a wide meaning, which does not restrict it to the mind's eye as a visual organ. An image in my usage is what Charles Peirce called a *sign,* without regard for its sensory quality. Peirce distinguished between different forms of signs, but there is no reason to make his distinction here, for the imagination works equally with them all, and that is why I call them all images.

11   Indeed, the most important images for human beings are simply words, which are abstract symbols. Animals do not have words, in our sense: there is no specific center for language in the brain of any animal, as there is in the human being. In this respect at least we know that the human imagination depends on a configuration in the brain that has only evolved in the last one or two million years. In the same period, evolution has greatly enlarged the front lobes in the human brain, which govern the sense of the past and the future; and it is a fair guess that they are probably the seat of our other images. (Part of the evidence for this guess is that damage to the front lobes in primates reduces them to the state of Hunter's animals.) If the guess turns out to be right, we shall know why man has come to look like a highbrow or an egghead: because otherwise there would not be room in his head for his imagination.

12   The images play out for us events which are not present to our senses, and thereby guard the past and create the future—a future that does not yet exist, and may never come to exist in that form. By contrast, the lack of symbolic ideas, or their rudimentary poverty, cuts off an animal from the past and the future alike, and imprisons him in the present. Of all the distinctions between man and animal, the characteristic gift which makes us human is the power to work with symbolic images: the gift of imagination.

13   This is really a remarkable finding. When Philip Sidney in 1580 defended poets (and all unconventional thinkers) from the Puritan charge that they were liars, he said that a maker must imagine things

that are not. Halfway between Sidney and us, William Blake said, "What is now proved was once only imagined." About the same time, in 1796, Samuel Taylor Coleridge for the first time distinguished between the passive fancy and the active imagination, "the living Power and prime Agent of all human Perception." Now we see that they were right, and precisely right: the human gift is the gift of imagination—and that is not just a literary phrase.

14 Nor is it just a literary gift; it is, I repeat, characteristically human. Almost everything that we do that is worth doing is done in the first place in the mind's eye. The richness of human life is that we have many lives: we live the events that do not happen (and some that cannot) as vividly as those that do: and if thereby we die a thousand deaths, that is the price we pay for living a thousand lives. (A cat, of course, has only nine.) Literature is alive to us because we live its images, but so is any play of the mind—so is chess: the lines of play that we foresee and try in our heads and dismiss are as much a part of the game as the moves that we make. John Keats said that the unheard melodies are sweeter, and all chess players sadly recall that the combinations that they planned and which never came to be played were the best.

15 I make this point to remind you, insistently, that imagination is the manipulation of images in one's head; and that the rational manipulation belongs to that, as well as the literary and artistic manipulation. When a child begins to play games with things that stand for other things, with chairs or chessmen, he enters the gateway to reason and imagination together. For the human reason discovers new relations between things not by deduction, but by that unpredictable blend of speculation and insight that scientists call induction, which—like other forms of imagination—cannot be formalized. We see it at work when Walter Hunter inquires into a child's memory, as much as when Blake and Coleridge do. Only a restless and original mind would have asked Hunter's questions and could have conceived his experiments, in a science that was dominated by Pavlov's reflex arcs and was heading toward the behaviorism of John Watson.

16 Let me find a spectacular example for you from history. What is the most famous experiment that you had described to you as a child? I will hazard that it is the experiment that Galileo is said to have made in Sidney's age, in Pisa about 1590, by dropping two unequal balls from the Leaning Tower. There we say, is a man in the modern mold, a man after our own hearts: he insisted on questioning the authority of Aristotle and St. Thomas Aquinas, and seeing with his own eyes whether (as they said) the heavy ball would reach the ground before the light one. Seeing is believing.

17   Yet seeing is also imagining. Galileo did challenge the authority of Aristotle, and he did look at his mechanics. But the eye that Galileo used was the mind's eye. He did not drop balls from the Leaning Tower of Pisa—and if he had, he would have got a very doubtful answer. Instead, Galileo made an imaginary experiment in his head, which I will describe as he did years later in the book he wrote after the Holy Office silenced him: the *Discorsi . . . intorno a due nuove scienze,* which was smuggled out to be printed in the Netherlands in 1638.

18   Suppose, said Galileo, that you drop two unequal balls from the tower at the same time. And suppose that Aristotle is right—suppose that the heavy ball falls faster, so that it steadily gains on the light ball, and hits the ground first. Very well. Now imagine the same experiment done again, with only one difference: this time the two unequal balls are joined by a string between them. The heavy ball will again move ahead, but now the light ball holds it back and acts as a drag or brake. So the light ball will be speeded up and the heavy ball will be slowed down; they must reach the ground together because they are tied together, but they cannot reach the ground as quickly as the heavy ball alone. Yet the string between them has turned the two balls into a single mass which is heavier than either ball—and surely (according to Aristotle) this mass should therefore move faster than either ball? Galileo's imaginary experiment has uncovered a contradiction; he says trenchantly, "You see how, from your assumption that a heavier body falls more rapidly than a lighter one, I infer that a (still) heavier body falls more slowly." There is only one way out of the contradiction: the heavy ball and the light ball must fall at the same rate, so that they go on falling at the same rate when they are tied together.

19   This argument is not conclusive, for nature might be more subtle (when the two balls are joined) than Galileo has allowed. And yet it is something more important: it is suggestive, it is stimulating, it opens a new view—in a word, it is imaginative. It cannot be settled without an actual experiment, because nothing that we imagine can become knowledge until we have translated it into, and backed it by, real experience. The test of imagination is experience. But then, that is as true of literature and the arts as it is of science. In science, the imaginary experiment is tested by confronting it with physical experience; and in literature, the imaginative conception is tested by confronting it with human experience. The superficial speculation in science is dismissed because it is found to falsify nature; and the shallow work of art is discarded because it is found to be untrue to our own nature. So when Ella Wheeler Wilcox died in 1919, more people were reading her verses than Shakespeare's;

yet in a few years her work was dead. It had been buried by its poverty of emotion and its trivialness of thought: which is to say that it had been proved to be as false to the nature of man as, say, Jean Baptiste Lamarck and Trofim Lysenko were false to the nature of inheritance. The strength of the imagination, its enriching power and excitement, lies in its interplay with reality—physical and emotional.

20   I doubt if there is much to choose here between science and the arts: the imagination is not much more free, and not much less free, in one than in the other. All great scientists have used their imagination freely, and let it ride them to outrageous conclusions without crying "Halt!" Albert Einstein fiddled with imaginary experiments from boyhood, and was wonderfully ignorant of the facts that they were supposed to bear on. When he wrote the first of his beautiful papers on the random movement of atoms, he did not know that the Brownian motion which it predicted could be seen in any laboratory. He was sixteen when he invented the paradox that he resolved ten years later, in 1905, in the theory of relativity, and it bulked much larger in his mind than the experiment of Albert Michelson and Edward Morley which had upset every other physicist since 1881. All his life Einstein loved to make up teasing puzzles like Galileo's, about falling lifts and the detection of gravity; and they carry the nub of the problems of general relativity on which he was working.

21   Indeed, it could not be otherwise. The power that man has over nature and himself, and that a dog lacks, lies in his command of imaginary experience. He alone has the symbols which fix the past and play with the future, possible and impossible. In the Renaissance, the symbolism of memory was thought to be mystical, and devices that were invented as mnemonics (by Giordano Bruno, for example, and by Robert Fludd) were interpreted as magic signs. The symbol is the tool which gives man his power, and it is the same tool whether the symbols are images or words, mathematical signs or mesons. And the symbols have a reach and a roundness that goes beyond their literal and practical meaning. They are the rich concepts under which the mind gathers many particulars into one name, and many instances into one general induction. When a man says *left* and *right,* he is outdistancing the dog not only in looking for a light; he is setting in train all the shifts of meaning, the overtones and the ambiguities, between *gauche* and *adroit* and *dexterous,* between *sinister* and the sense of right. When a man counts *one, two, three,* he is not only doing mathematics: he is on the path to the mysticism of numbers in Pythagoras and Vitruvius and Kepler, to the Trinity and the signs of the Zodiac.

22   I have described imagination as the ability to make images and to move them about inside one's head in new arrangements. This is the faculty that is specifically human, and it is the common root from which science and literature both spring and grow and flourish together. For they do flourish (and languish) together; the great ages of science are the great ages of all the arts, because in them powerful minds have taken fire from one another, breathless and higgledy-piggledy, without asking too nicely whether they ought to tie their imagination to falling balls or a haunted island. Galileo and Shakespeare, who were born in the same year, grew into greatness in the same age; when Galileo was looking through his telescope at the moon, Shakespeare was writing *The Tempest* and all Europe was in ferment, from Johannes Kepler to Peter Paul Rubens, and from the first table of logarithms by John Napier to the Authorized Version of the Bible.

23   Let me end with a last and spirited example of the common inspiration of literature and science, because it is as much alive today as it was three hundred years ago. What I have in mind is man's ageless fantasy, to fly to the moon. I do not display this to you as a high scientific enterprise; on the contrary, I think we have more important discoveries to make here on earth than wait for us, beckoning, at the horned surface of the moon. Yet I cannot belittle the fascination which that ice-blue journey has had for the imagination of men, long before it drew us to our television screens to watch the tumbling astronauts. Plutarch and Lucian, Ariosto and Ben Jonson wrote about it, before the days of Jules Verne and H. G. Wells and science fiction. The seventeenth century was heady with new dreams and fables about voyages to the moon. Kepler wrote one full of deep scientific ideas, which (alas) simply got his mother accused of witchcraft. In England, Francis Godwin wrote a wild and splendid work, *The Man in the Moone,* and the astronomer John Wilkins wrote a wild and learned one, *The Discovery of a New World.* They did not draw a line between science and fancy; for example, they all tried to guess just where in the journey the earth's gravity would stop. Only Kepler understood that gravity has no boundary, and put a law to it—which happened to be the wrong law.

24   All this was a few years before Isaac Newton was born, and it was all in his head that day in 1666 when he sat in his mother's garden, a young man of twenty-three, and thought about the reach of gravity. This was how he came to conceive his brilliant image, that the moon is like a ball which has been thrown so hard that it falls exactly as fast as the horizon, all the way round the earth. The image will do for any satellite, and Newton modestly calculated how long therefore an astronaut would take to fall round the earth once. He

made it ninety minutes, and we have all seen now that he was right; but Newton had no way to check that. Instead he went on to calculate how long in that case the distant moon would take to round the earth, if indeed it behaves like a thrown ball that falls in the earth's gravity, and if gravity obeyed a law of inverse squares. He found that the answer would be twenty-eight days.

25   In that telling figure, the imagination that day chimed with nature, and made a harmony. We shall hear an echo of that harmony on the day when we land on the moon, because it will be not a technical but an imaginative triumph, that reaches back to the beginning of modern science and literature both. All great acts of imagination are like this, in the arts and in science, and convince us because they fill out reality with a deeper sense of rightness. We start with the simplest vocabulary of images, with *left* and *right* and *one, two, three,* and before we know how it happened the words and the numbers have conspired to make a match with nature: we catch in them the pattern of mind and matter as one.

Vocabulary

perplexed	summary	critical
conditioned reflex	digestive	dimension
primates	chimpanzees	salmon
preoccupation	manipulation	deduction
trenchantly	conception	superficial
mystical	mnemonics	gauche
adroit	dexterous	sinister
inverse		

Topics for Discussion

1. Is artistic experience necessary for the psychic survival of mankind? Do you think you could be very happy if you could not project yourself into the world of other people, real or imagined, through art? What would the world be like with no books, newspapers, movies, symphony orchestras, or museums?

2. Evaluate Bronowski's parallel between the testing of scientific hypotheses and the testing of artistic creation (paragraph 19).

3. Find out something about recent experiments in animal communication. Does the fact that dolphins can "talk" to each other and that chimps can "talk" to computers diminish the impact of Bronowski's speculation about the uniqueness of human beings?

4. Do you think that today's education is directed toward giving people the quality of mind that prompted Galileo to perform his experiments? What would have to change for education to more actively pursue this goal?

5. Do you think there are fundamental differences between the ways scientists and artists think, or do you hold, as Bronowski seems to suggest, that the differences are mainly superficial?

6. What important insights can be gained from everyday events? Can you see beneath the surface of things as Bronowski does? Mention two examples, one pertaining to science, the other to art.

Rhetorical Considerations

1. Examine Bronowski's sentence structure. What gives sentence 3 of paragraph 14 its appeal? How do the two main clauses of the final sentence of paragraph 14 complement each other? Examine parallelism as a device for development in paragraph 15.

2. Does a definition of humanity emerge from this essay? What faculty of the human being does Bronowski define which, in turn, defines the species? See paragraph 22. Using this technique, attempt to define an abstract notion such as love or art.

3. Bronowski alludes to over two dozen important figures in the history of art and science. In making these allusions, what must he assume about his audience?

4. Is the use of the first-person pronoun an effective device in this essay? Why does Bronowski use it sparingly?

5. What devices does Bronowski use to inject his presence into the reader's? See especially the first few paragraphs.

History is Bunk

Peter Steinfels

Peter Steinfels is a professor of history who contributes to Commonweal *and to various scholarly journals.*

1   There have recently been complaints that young people are not sufficiently interested in history, that they feel the study of the past

to be "irrelevant" and to have no connection with the problems we face today.

2   Of course these young people are absolutely right. Let me give you an example. I have wasted (as it turns out) a small but significant portion of my life studying the history of modern Germany. One of the most general conclusions of such study, reached by almost anyone who undertakes it for more than 15 minutes, is that a nation can achieve the pinnacle of material, intellectual and artistic civilization and yet, because of deep flaws in its political culture, perpetrate unthinkable evils. Obviously that is the kind of lesson that has no relevance to us. You can see how my time has been wasted.

3   But let me illustrate the matter in more detail. Students of German history are forced by their pedantic professors to pay attention to something known as the Prussian "Constitutional Crisis." This episode began in 1862 when the Prussian Chamber of Deputies, dissatisfied with King William I's proposed strengthening of the military and believing that the constitution meant what it said about the budget's having to be approved by the Chamber, refused to vote the funds the king's ministers requested. In turn, the feudal upper house, at the government's behest, threw out the Chamber's budget; and so there was no budget at all.

4   In a constitutional regime, one would think that the government would then have resubmitted a compromise to the Chamber or simply have abided by the Chamber's will. But constitutional theorists are never at a loss for cleverness. Those in Prussia pointed out that, yes, the constitution did seem to insist on the Chamber's approval for the budget, but, on the other hand, the constitution also gave the government the right to collect the current taxes and duties until ordered otherwise. Therefore, a "gap" existed in the constitution: and necessity being the mother of invention for constitutional theorists as for everyone else, it was decided that in the unresolved situation created by the gap, the necessity of maintaining the state implied the government could pretty much do what it pleased.

5   Such a conclusion was obviously not to everyone's taste, and in the midst of the resulting tumult, the king called a brash, 47-year-old nobleman, politician and diplomat to head the government. This was Otto von Bismarck. (In the midst of this kind of useless study, it is nice to have a familiar personality on which to hang your hat.) Mr. Bismarck was not well received. He immediately defied the Chamber, proclaiming that power—blood and iron—would resolve the great questions of the day. The moderates and liberals replied

that the legal and moral order was not violated with impunity. The historian Heinrich von Treitschke termed Bismarck's defiance a shallow and ridiculous vulgarity. But government without a budget continued.

6   Meanwhile, Bismarck dissolved the Chamber and called new elections. In the intervening period, when there was no Chamber to counter his moves, he attacked the press, obtaining a royal order allowing the suppression of critical newspapers. He further maligned his opponents as unpatriotic and even as traitors. When the elected deputies wished to question Bismarck about a semisecret agreement that allowed Russian troops to cross into Prussia to exterminate fugitive Polish rebels, Bismarck refused even to explain his policy publicly.

7   By now, you must be convinced that none of these ridiculous goings-on has the slightest relevance to our own politics; but it is too late—you have to hear the story out, so you will know exactly what we inflict upon our poor students.

8   None of these maneuvers—censorship, public disparagement of the character and loyalty of his opponents and even intimidation through the courts—had obtained for Bismarck the pliable legislative majority that he desired. The constitutional crisis remained unresolved.

9   But Bismarck was to find the solution in international politics. He adroitly manipulated a series of international crises in a pyrotechnic display of diplomatics; waged two swift and successful wars, against Denmark and Austria; and successfully united all of northern Germany under the Prussian crown. He was the hero of the hour.

10   That part of the tale, I admit, possesses a certain melodrama, but now we descend to the truly dry-as-dust details. In the wake of his victory, Bismarck submitted to the Chamber an indemnity bill, legalizing his government's three years of illegal rule. Who could resist the successful Bismarck? Certainly not the German liberals. Had he not demonstrated that ruthlessness and toughness are crowned with success, whereas moral principles count for naught? Had he not stolen the cause of German unity from the liberals' own agenda, and even admitted the liberal principle of universal suffrage into the new constitution for the North German Confederation?

11   The liberals did more than vote Bismarck his indemnity. They fell over themselves to recant the naïve and impractical ideals of their former liberalism. They learned a new "realism" at Bismarck's school. "It does not become the German," wrote

Treitschke, "to repeat the commonplaces of the apostles of peace
. . . or to shut his eyes to the cruel truth that we live in an age of
war."

12   The tale, as you can see, not only is boring and useless, it is
rather sad. The backbone of German liberalism, never much to
boast about, was now broken for good. Bismarck was no Nazi: he
accomplished his ends with a minimum of bloodshed, in a diplomatic
performance that has been justly admired ever since. But the heritage he left Germany was one of submission to the strong and
decisive leader, faith in power, cynicism about political principles
and contempt for public and parliamentary accountability. Brutality
and force were rendered respectable, adorned with a certain mystique. The opposition always cringed in fear of being branded dis-
loyal. The results eventually were tragic for Germany, and for the
rest of the world.

13   But the young people are right; none of this has anything to do
with us.

Vocabulary

flaws	perpetrate	pedantic
regime	impunity	maligned
fugitive	disparagement	intimidation
pliable	adroitly	pyrotechnic
melodrama	indemnity	ruthlessness
suffrage	naïve	commonplaces
submission	cynicism	

Topics for Discussion

1. Before your reading of this essay, did you see much value in
the study of history? Has the essay changed your mind? In what way?

2. If humanity were completely cut off from the memory of its
past, do you think the human race would be better or worse off?

3. Can you point to recent historical events which might serve
as guideposts for future generations? Specify.

4. Is there a tendency among college students to seek out the
popular, the "relevant" at the expense of studying "boring" topics
like the German Constitutional Crisis or Aristotle's thoughts on
tragedy? What consequences might such a tendency have for society?

5. What relevance does the German Constitutional Crisis have to your situation in life?

6. Indicate historical events which Steinfels might have used instead of the one he chose.

Rhetorical Considerations

1. How does Steinfels's ironic tone function as a persuasive device? Examine especially paragraphs 1, 2, 7, 10, 12, and 13.

2. Why is Steinfels's example of the German Constitutional Crisis appropriate to his purposes? What later historical events does that crisis prefigure? Why does the subject at first seem to have little appeal?

3. How does Steinfels use narrative for purposes of persuasion? Does your attitude about the German Constitutional Crisis, and about history in general, change as you read the essay?

4. How does Steinfels use understatement (litotes) to advantage?

5. Is the essay any less effective in making its point if the reader knows little about twentieth-century German history?

Knowledge Dethroned

Robert Nisbet

Robert Nisbet (b. 1913) is Albert Schweitzer Professor in Humanities at Columbia University and is widely respected for his investigations of the basic premises of modern sociology. The author of ten books in the history of ideas, Nisbet reportedly credits De Tocqueville's Democracy in America *and Edmund Burke's* Reflections on the Revolution in France *with having shaped his thinking.*

1   Through the application of science, human beings in America and other parts of the world have been liberated from plagues,

pestilences, threats of famine, hardship and torment that once seemed an unalterable part of the human condition. One need only rummage through the letters of our grandparents to be reminded of the debilitating, commonly fatal illnesses, physical pains, cripplings and disfigurements of body that we are so largely spared. It is hard to think of an area of modern physical welfare that cannot be traced in some way to science and technology. Nor, would I argue, can we deny that the social scientist and humanist have made their very genuine contributions, too, to improving the administration of government and business and to a general rise in standards of citizenship, taking that term in its widest sense.

2   And until recently, all of this was rewarded by public and governmental respect. In all the polls and surveys of prestige in American society, the scientist and scholar ranked high. In fact, in the period beginning with the end of World War II, the scientist-scholar became a very real hero in American society, joining a circle that had, with rarest exceptions, been limited to politicians, generals, explorers, artists and sports luminaries.

3   In the past few years, however, disenchantment has set in, with the public concluding that the post-war promises of learning were inflated and misleading. If he was a hero in the public eye only a decade or two ago, the scientist-scholar today seems more a combination ne'er-do-well and enemy of both nature and the human community. Some recognition of this is already forthcoming from scientists themselves. Philip Handler, president of the National Academy of Sciences, has noted that the image of infallibility the sciences had acquired over many decades is, to say the least, tarnished. "A few years ago, people regarded science and technology as a huge cornucopia that was going to enrich everyone's life. Now many people feel that science and technology have done as much harm as good." And in a recent interview Dr. Jerome Wiesner, president of M.I.T. and himself a distinguished scientist, declared that we have "outrun our technological base and certainly our intellectual base." The United States, Dr. Wiesner continued, is now seeing "the consequences of becoming too cavalier about what we do and trying to do too many things."

4   The disenchantment takes a number of forms. There is the feeling that science and scholarship, in meeting one problem, too often create other, worse problems. DDT, nuclear reactors, nuclear testing, pollution by technology quickly come to mind. Cyclamates were first declared beneficial because they can be used to control weight and thus heart disease, and then attacked as possible causes

of cancer. The so-called "war" on cancer, involving years of work and billions of dollars in research funds, has so far produced only conflicting statistics and reports on actual gains; it may be on the way to creating the greatest disillusionment of all. For whatever reasons, however improperly held, the sense of failure of knowledge begins to hover over the landscape. Publicly vented controversies among scientists, so often rancorous and shrill, do little to help the situation.

5   In many ways, public disillusionment with science and scholarship is unfair, for there is much we take for granted. As recently as 175 years ago, Elting Morison tells us, craftsmen in this country did not know how to construct a lock to join Wood Creek with the Mohawk River. Today we send men to the moon, and assume machines can be constructed for almost any purpose. How easily we forget antibiotics, pesticides, fertilizers, polio vaccines, the pill and all the wonders of nuclear and solid-state technology. And how easily we overlook the fact that in large part because of the expansion of social science and the humanities in recent decades, the modern citizen of a Western democracy is better educated and understands more about his life and his problems than at any time in history. It is indeed unfair in a great many ways.

6   But the disillusionment is not the less real as a state of mind. And often in history it is but a short step from disillusionment to outright hostility. The experience of the Christian church in the 16th century is a fair illustration. Many a prelate in Rome must have shaken his head in disbelief as he looked out on all that the church had done for man and society, only to draw on itself such widespread hatred and gathering revolt. Could the Church of Knowledge in our century be succumbing to analogous reactions from an ungrateful populace?

7   It may be said that this, like most parallels, is suspect. After all, it can be argued, no society can exist except on the basis of continuity and development of its knowledge, and the sheer complexity of our civilization makes certain the resumption of the high status of knowledge and of its practitioners.

8   But as William James pointed out many years ago, there is "knowledge-of" and there is "knowledge-about." Every civilized language except our own, James noted, has two common words for knowledge: *connaitre* and *savoir,* to go no farther than the French. The first is knowledge-by-acquaintance, the knowledge one finds in every occupation, skill, profession or role. Truly "knowledge-of" is indispensable to any culture. The second, "knowledge-about," is

the result of sustained, systematic study, of reflection, logic and abstract thinking. It is this kind of knowledge we associate with science and scholarship. *This* kind of knowledge is hardly indispensable; rather, it is quite recent in human history and still precarious in foundation. Often, tragically, it appears to be in conflict with "knowledge-of," the pride of businessmen, citizens, housewives and the rest of us.

9   To revert to my Reformation analogy: A large body of theologians in the West were convinced that their knowledge about God was crucial to the soul of Everyman. The whole point of the Protestant Reformation was Luther's and Calvin's insistence that such knowledge was *not* crucial. In our time, a rising number of environmentalists, nature-worshipers, proponents of the mystical and bizarre and consciousness-raisers are ready to argue comparably with respect to the scientist's knowledge about man, society and the cosmos.

10   Two general causes lie, I suggest, behind the present fallen estate of the man of knowledge. The first has to do with the general cultural climate that began to overtake American society in the nineteen-sixties. The second is very much embedded in the behavior of men of knowledge during the last quarter-century and in the whole structure of what came to be called, so pretentiously, the knowledge industry.

11   The decade of the nineteen-sixties was indeed a Reformation-like period. Analogous eruptions of the occult, mystical, subjective, even of the magical and demonological took place. Bizarre forms of belief, fundamentalist, pentecostal, Eastern in their diverse character, could be seen tumbling across the landscape in America, most notably on college campuses. The upsurge of ethnicity, symbolized by what is called "Negritude" and described by the motto "Black is beautiful," often implied that there is a kind of knowledge beyond the reach of science, indeed of reason, logic and research. Fascination with individual self, with internal consciousness and the evocation of reflexive states spread rapidly and widely, often becoming a substitute for established curriculums.

12   There was even a kind of *trahison des clercs:* the well-publicized turning to irrationalism by some of the leading lights of the American academic and intellectual community. Who will soon forget those philosophers, psychologists and sociologists, even biologists, historians and classicists who for more than a decade issued embarrassingly solemn gush about reflexive awareness, crises of ego-identity, the intrinsic nobility of rock music, the wisdom to be found in schizophrenic states, the higher community of a

Woodstock, repressive tolerance, the greening of America and so on? Science and scholarship inevitably suffered.

13   Why this eruption occurred I do not know for sure. Perhaps in some part its roots lie in the way middle-class children were being brought up during the age of affluence that followed World War II. Massive dosages of affection, adulation, devotion, permissiveness, incessant and instant recognition of youthful "brightness" by parents, a constantly relaxing curriculum in the schools under the ministrations of those who claimed, but did not understand, John Dewey as prophet, a whole national mood not only of indulgence but of almost awed, perhaps guilt-ridden, adoration of the young and of youthful pursuits—all of this created a setting that would in due time dissolve some of the motivation toward hard intellectual pursuits, which require unremitting discipline, constantly invoked criteria of excellence, and even (so hateful a word in the fifties and sixties) conformity.

14   How much more attractive, given this setting, were pursuits that involve little more than exploration of self. Through sheer demographic mass—the result of the now-historic baby boom—they dominated an entire culture for a couple of decades. So it is hardly a matter for wonder that disciplines like physics, chemistry, history, literature (I mean, of course, real literature, not the meanderings in print of the primitive and half-literate who have managed to achieve prophetic status) and the hard areas of the social sciences suffered.

15   The second cause of the diminished luster of the scientist and scholar in the last decade is inseparable from the learned disciplines themselves: It is the deflation that has followed an unprecedented inflation of claims by men of knowledge and, hence, of public expectations. An alien spirit of pride, even arrogance, seized the learned disciplines, the universities and institutes after World War II. In part a reflection of the discovery of atomic energy, it was also based on the belief that the New Deal's use of men of knowledge from the university in the nineteen-thirties had gotten us out of the Great Depression. It hadn't, not by a long shot. It was World War II alone that got us out of the Depression. But at the time, many of the scholars and scientists involved in the New Deal were taking credit for new prosperity, and assumed the role of priests in the new church of knowledge. "We have the knowledge, O Lord," they said; "we need only the will to accept."

16   With the Kennedy Administration, the inflation of claims and expectations reached its highest levels. The Eisenhower Government had been pilloried for eight years for its alleged insensitivity to all that the "knowledge industry" might provide to solve the innum-

erable crises that, it was said—so often by men of knowledge themselves—tormented the nation.

17   The dawn of Camelot was rosy-fingered indeed for scientists, scholars and intellectuals. Of a sudden they were the New Aristocracy in America, many of them holders of key roles in government, fulfillers of Plato's dream of the philosopher-statesman. At one royal banquet, Kennedy likened the man of knowledge to Thomas Jefferson himself. The whole academic profession basked in the warmth of Kennedy flattery. It was indeed Camelot.

18   It was also destined to end—in both a bang and a whimper. I will always be persuaded that American entry as an all-out military power in Vietnam, entry that began in earnest under Kennedy in 1963, was overwhelmingly the result of counsel given by academic intellectuals who were convinced that we had the scholarly, scientific and technical knowledge to win that war and thus score a huge success for Kennedy and, not least, the House of Intellect.

19   So much for the bang. The whimper was the retreat from the scene of the selfsame intellectuals. Under the lashes of the New Left, the retreat of the intellectual from the war he had helped create became very nearly a rout.

20   Perhaps the Muse is to be more pitied than blamed. After all, America is an intensely political and commercial civilization. If the man of knowledge remained for a long time more or less immune, such immunity could not reasonably have been expected to last forever. Starting out with the historic intention of doing good, he wound up doing very well. He cannot really be blamed for yielding to the temptations of marketplace or throne.

21   Nevertheless, there remains the problem of maintaining, even invigorating, the roots of knowledge, of *knowledge-about,* of restoring the confidence of the public, of once again attracting the best-endowed minds to the hard areas of knowledge—of, in short, restoring luster to the very difficult disciplines of science.

22   This can be done, I believe, if we can somehow restore, in the mind of scientist and layman alike, a sense of science's true purpose—the search for truth, the discovery of data, principles and laws that enlarge our understanding of man and his cosmos. Its purpose is *not* to advise governments, save mankind, make public policy or build empires.

23   Let physicists and biologists who find themselves fascinated by political power abandon the laboratory and run for office. Let there be what the late Jacob Bronowski called a "disestablishment" of science, taking science out of government and, in all hope, government out of science. Let Presidents and Congresses quit declar-

ing wars on things like pollution and cancer, enlisting scientists like so many foot soldiers. Let science get back to its genuinely nurturing contexts.

24   It is astonishing, viewed historically, what science and scholarship have done for mankind and its material advancement by obeying their own motivations, itches and rhythms. The Muse has indeed been benign. But men of knowledge can't have the Muse both ways: shy and virginal one day, denizen of the marketplace the next.

Vocabulary

cavalier	debilitating	luminary
cornucopia	prelate	indispensable
precarious	crucial	bizarre
cosmos	pretentiously	analogous
demonological	pentecostal	ethnicity
pilloried	intrinsic	schizophrenic
incessant	demographic	politicized
benign	denizen	

Topics for Discussion

1. Do you agree that scientists are no longer as honored as they once were?

2. According to Nisbet, what are some of the reasons for the disillusionment the public has with science and scientists?

3. What is "knowledge-of"? What is "knowledge-about"? What are some of the differences between the two? Which of the two is more important?

4. In what way is the experience of the 16th-century Christian church like the present experience of science and scientists?

5. What was Plato's dream of the philosopher-statesman? Why did intellectuals and scientists feel they were fulfilling this dream during the Kennedy Administration?

6. What are some of the reasons Nisbet gives for the bizarre forms of belief and fascination with self that broke out during the 1960s? Why did science and scholarship suffer during this period?

7. What is science's true purpose according to Nisbet?

8. Why is it necessary to disestablish science? What does Nisbet mean by this? Do you think it is possible?

9. What does Nisbet mean when he says that the Muse cannot be shy and virginal one day and a denizen of the marketplace the next?

Rhetorical Considerations

1. How effective is Nisbet's analogy in paragraphs 6 and 9? How does this analogy serve to clarify Nisbet's argument?

2. In paragraph 17 Nisbet refers to a "royal banquet" President Kennedy held at the White House. What does he imply by using the word *royal*? How does this reference serve to reinforce the Camelot image in the paragraph?

3. In paragraph 8 Nisbet compares and contrasts two definitions. How does this rhetorical technique help clarify the definitions?

4. Nisbet says in paragraph 10 that two causes lie behind "the present fallen estate of the man of knowledge." How well does he specifically develop this generalization in the following paragraphs (11–19)?

5. This is an essay written by a scholar about scholars. Examine the diction of the essay. What does it reveal about the author? About his audience?

6. Explain the image in the first sentence of paragraph 17. What does it contribute to the structure and tone of the paragraph?

The Lesson of the Mask

Joseph Campbell

Joseph Campbell (b. 1904) is an author and researcher whose works include the three volume Masks of God *covering primitive, oriental, and occidental mythology.*

1   The artist's eye, as Thomas Mann has said, has a mythical slant upon life: therefore, the mythological realm—the world of the gods and demons, the carnival of their masks and the curious game

of "as if" in which the festival of the lived myth abrogates all the laws of time, letting the dead swim back to life, and the "once upon a time" become the very present—we must approach and first regard with the artist's eye. For, indeed, in the primitive world, where most of the clues to the origin of mythology must be sought, the gods and demons are not conceived in the way of hard and fast, positive realities. A god can be simultaneously in two or more places—like a melody, or like the form of a traditional mask. And wherever he comes, the impact of his presence is the same: it is not reduced through multiplication. Moreover, the mask in a primitive festival is revered and experienced as a veritable apparition of the mythical being that it represents—even though everyone knows that a man made the mask and that a man is wearing it. The one wearing it, furthermore, is identified with the god during the time of the ritual of which the mask is a part. He does not merely represent the god; he *is* the god. The literal fact that the apparition is composed of A, a mask, B, its reference to a mythical being, and C, a man, is dismissed from the mind, and the presentation is allowed to work without correction upon the sentiments of both the beholder and the actor. In other words, there has been a shift of view from the logic of the normal secular sphere, where things are understood to be distinct from one another, to a theatrical or play sphere, where they are accepted for what they are *experienced* as being and the logic is that of "make believe"—"as if."

2   We all know the convention, surely! It is a primary, spontaneous device of childhood, a magical device, by which the world can be transformed from banality to magic in a trice. And its inevitability in childhood is one of those universal characteristics of man that unite us in one family. It is a primary datum, consequently, of the science of myth, which is concerned precisely with the phenomenon of self-induced belief.

3   "A professor," wrote Leo Frobenius in a celebrated paper on the force of the daemonic world of childhood, "is writing at his desk and his four-year-old little daughter is running about the room. She has nothing to do and is disturbing him. So he gives her three burnt matches, saying, 'Here! Play!' and, sitting on the rug, she begins to play with the matches. Hansel, Gretel, and the witch. A considerable time elapses, during which the professor concentrates upon his task, undisturbed. But then, suddenly, the child shrieks in terror. The father jumps. 'What is it? What has happened?' The little girl comes running to him, showing every sign of great fright. 'Daddy, Daddy,' she cries, 'take the witch away! I can't touch the witch any more!' "

4   "An eruption of emotion," Frobenius observes,

is characteristic of the spontaneous shift of an idea from the level of the sentiments (*Gemüt*) to that of sensual consciousness (*sinnliches Bewusstsein*). Furthermore, the appearance of such an eruption obviously means that a certain spiritual process has reached a conclusion. The match is not a witch; nor was it a witch for the child at the beginning of the game. The process, therefore, rests on the fact that the match has *become* a witch on the level of the sentiments and the conclusion of the process coincides with the transfer of this idea to the plane of consciousness. The observation of the process escapes the test of conscious thought, since it enters consciousness only after or at the moment of completion. However, inasmuch as the idea *is* it must have *become*. The process is creative, in the highest sense of the word; for, as we have seen, in a little girl a match can become a witch. Briefly stated, then: the phase of *becoming* takes place on the level of the sentiments, while that of *being* is on the conscious plane.

5   This vivid, convincing example of a child's seizure by a witch while in the act of play may be taken to represent an intense degree of the daemonic mythological experience. However, the attitude of mind represented by the game itself, before the seizure supervened, also belongs within the sphere of our subject. For, as J. Huizinga has pointed out in his brilliant study of the play element in culture, the whole point, at the beginning, is the *fun* of play not the rapture of seizure. "In all the wild imaginings of mythology a fanciful spirit is playing," he writes, "on the border-line between jest and earnest." "As far as I know, ethnologists and anthropologists concur in the opinion that the mental attitude in which the great religious feasts of savages are celebrated and witnessed is not one of complete illusion. There is an underlying consciousness of things 'not being real.' " And he quotes, among others, R. R. Marett, who, in his chapter on "Primitive Credulity" in *The Threshold of Religion*, develops the idea that a certain element of "make-believe" is operative in all primitive religions. "The savage," wrote Marett, "is a good actor who can be quite absorbed in his role, like a child at play; and also, like a child, a good spectator who can be frightened to death by the roaring of something he knows perfectly well to be no 'real' lion."

6   "By considering the whole sphere of so-called primitive culture as a play-sphere," Huizinga then suggests in conclusion, "we pave the way to a more direct and more general understanding of its peculiarities than any meticulous psychological or sociological analysis would allow." And I would concur wholeheartedly with this judgment, only adding that we should extend the consideration to the entire field of our present subject.

7   In the Roman Catholic mass, for example, when the priest, quoting the words of Christ at the Last Supper, pronounces the formula of consecration—with utmost solemnity—first over the wafer of the host (*Hoc est enim Corpus meum:* "for this is My Body"), then over the chalice of the wine (*Hic est enim Calix Sanguinis mei, novi et aeterni Testamenti: Mysterium fidei: qui pro vobis et pro multis effundetur in remissionem peccatorum:* "For this is the Chalice of My Blood, of the new and eternal testament: the mystery of faith: which shall be shed for you and for many unto the remission of sins"), it is to be supposed that the bread and wine become the body and blood of Christ, that every fragment of the host and every drop of the wine is the actual living Savior of the world. The sacrament, that is to say, is not conceived to be a *reference,* a mere sign or symbol to arouse in us a train of thought, but is God himself, the Creator, Judge, and Savior of the Universe, here come to work upon us directly, to free our souls (created in His image) from the effects of the Fall of Adam and Eve in the Garden of Eden (which we are to suppose existed as a geographical fact).

8   Comparably, in India it is believed that, in response to consecrating formulae, deities will descend graciously to infuse their divine substance into the temple images, which are then called their throne or seat (*pītha*). It is also possible—and in some Indian sects even expected—that the individual himself should become a seat of deity. In the *Gandharva Tantra* it is written, for example, "No one who is not himself divine can successfully worship a divinity"; and again, "Having become the divinity, one should offer it sacrifice."

9   Furthermore, it is even possible for a really gifted player to discover that everything—absolutely everything—has become the body of a god, or reveals the omnipresence of God as the ground of all being. There is a passage, for example, among the conversations of the nineteenth-century Bengalese spiritual master Ramakrishna, in which he described such an experience. "One day," he is said to have reported, "it was suddenly revealed to me that everything is Pure Spirit. The utensils of worship, the altar, the door frame—all Pure Spirit. Men, animals, and other living beings—all Pure Spirit. Then like a madman I began to shower flowers in all directions. Whatever I saw I worshiped."

10   Belief—or at least a game of belief—is the first step toward such a divine seizure. The chronicles of the saints abound in accounts of their long ordeals of difficult practice, which preceded their moments of being carried away; and we have also the more spontaneous religious games and exercises of the folk (the amateurs) to illustrate for us the principle involved. The spirit of the festival,

the holiday, the holy day of the religious ceremonial, requires that the normal attitude toward the cares of the world should have been temporarily set aside in favor of a particular mood of dressing up. The world is hung with banners. Or in the permanent religious sanctuaries—the temples and cathedrals, where an atmosphere of holiness hangs permanently in the air—the logic of cold, hard fact must not be allowed to intrude and spoil the spell. The gentile, the "spoil sport," the positivist, who cannot or will not play, must be kept aloof. Hence the guardian figures that stand at either side of the entrances to holy places: lions, bulls, or fearsome warriors with uplifted weapons. They are there to keep out the "spoil sports," the advocates of Aristotelian logic, for whom A can never be B; for whom the actor is never to be lost in the part; for whom the mask, the image, the consecrated host, tree, or animal cannot become God, but only a reference. Such heavy thinkers are to remain without. For the whole purpose of entering a sanctuary or participating in a festival is that one should be overtaken by the state known in India as "the other mind" (Sanskrit, *anya-manas:* absent-mindedness, possession by a spirit), where one is "beside oneself," spellbound, set apart from one's logic of self-possession and over-powered by the force of a logic of "indissociation"—wherein A is B, and C also is B.

11   "One day," said Ramakrishna, "while worshiping Shiva, I was about to offer a bel-leaf on the head of the image, when it was revealed to me that this universe itself is Shiva. Another day, I had been plucking flowers when it was revealed to me that each plant was a bouquet adorning the universal form of God. That was the end of my plucking flowers. I look on man in just the same way. When I see a man, I see that it is God Himself, who walks on earth, rocking to and fro, as it were, like a pillow floating on the waves."

12   From such a point of view the universe is the seat (*pītha*) of a divinity from whose vision our usual state of consciousness excludes us. But in the playing of the game of the gods we take a step toward that reality—which is ultimately the reality of ourselves. Hence the rapture, the feelings of delight, and the sense of refresh-ment, harmony, and re-creation! In the case of a saint, the game leads to seizure—as in the case of the little girl, to whom the match revealed itself to be a witch. Contact with the orientation of the world may then be lost, the mind remaining rapt in that other state. For such it is impossible to return to this other game, the game of life in the world. They are possessed of God; that is all they know on earth and all they need to know. And they can even infect whole societies, so that these, inspired by their seizures, may likewise

break contact with the world and spurn it as delusory, or as evil. Secular life then may be read as a fall—a fall from Grace, Grace being the rapture of the festival of God.

13   But there is another attitude, more comprehensive, which has given beauty and love to the *two* worlds: that, namely, of the *līlā,* "the play," as it has been termed in the Orient. The world is not condemned and shunned as a fall, but voluntarily entered as a game or dance, wherein the spirit plays.

14   Ramakrishna closed his eyes. "Is it only this?" he said. "Does God exist only when the eyes are closed, and disappear when the eyes are opened?" He opened his eyes. "The Play belongs to Him to whom Eternity belongs, and Eternity to Him to whom the Play belongs. . . . Some people climb the seven floors of a building and cannot get down; but some climb up and then, at will, visit the lower floors."

15   The question then becomes only: How far down or up the ladder can one go without losing the sense of a game? Professor Huizinga, in his work already referred to, points out that in Japanese the verb *asobu,* which refers to play in general—recreation, relaxation, amusement, trip or jaunt, dissipation, gambling, lying idle, or being unemployed—also means to study at a university or under a teacher; likewise, to engage in a sham fight; and finally, to participate in the very strict formalities of the tea ceremony. He continues:

> The extraordinary earnestness and profound gravity of the Japanese ideal of life is masked by the fashionable fiction that everything is only play. Like the *chevalerie* of the Christian Middle Ages, Japanese *bushido* took shape almost entirely in the play-sphere and was enacted in play-forms. The language still preserves this conception in the *asobase-kotoba* (literally play-language) or polite speech, the mode of address used in conversation with persons of higher rank. The convention is that the higher classes are merely playing at all they do. The polite form for "you arrive in Tokyo" is, literally, "you play arrival in Tokyo"; and for "I hear that your father is dead," "I hear that your father has played dying." In other words, the revered person is imagined as living in an elevated sphere where only pleasure or condescension moves to action.

16   From this supremely aristocratic point of view, any state of seizure, whether by life or by the gods, must represent a fall or drop of spiritual *niveau,* a vulgarization of the play. Nobility of spirit is the grace—or ability—to play, whether in heaven or on earth. And this, I take it, this *noblesse oblige,* which has always been the quality of aristocracy, was precisely the virtue (ἀρετή) of the Greek

poets, artists, and philosophers, for whom the gods were true as poetry is true. We may take it also to be the primitive (and proper) mythological point of view, as contrasted with the heavier positivistic; which latter is represented, on the one hand, by religious experiences of the literal sort, where the impact of a daemon, rising to the plane of consciousness from its place of birth on the level of the sentiments, is taken to be objectively real, and, on the other, by science and political economy, for which only measurable facts are objectively real. For if it is true, as the Greek philosopher Antisthenes (born c. 444 B.C.) has said, that "God is not like anything: hence no one can understand him by means of an image," or, as we read in the Indian Upanishad,

> It is other, indeed, than the known
> And, moreover, above the unknown!

then it must be conceded, as a basic principle of our natural history of the gods and heroes, that whenever a myth has been taken literally its sense had been perverted; but also, reciprocally, that whenever it has been dismissed as a mere priestly fraud or sign of inferior intelligence, truth has slipped out the other door.

17   And so what, then, is the sense that we are to seek, if it be neither here nor there?

18   Kant, in his *Prolegomena to Every Future System of Metaphysics,* states very carefully that all our thinking about final things can be only by way of *analogy.* "The proper expression for our fallible mode of conception," he declares, "would be: that we imagine the world *as if* its being and inner character were derived from a supreme mind" (italics mine).

19   Such a highly played game of "as if" frees our mind and spirit, on the one hand, from the presumption of theology, which pretends to know the laws of God, and, on the other, from the bondage of reason, whose laws do not apply beyond the horizon of human experience.

20   I am willing to accept the word of Kant, as representing the view of a considerable metaphysician. And applying it to the range of festival games and attitudes just reviewed—from the mask to the consecrated host and temple image, transubstantiated worshiper and transubstantiated world—I can see, or believe I can see, that a principle of release operates throughout the series by way of the alchemy of an "as if"; and that, through this, the impact of all so-called "reality" upon the psyche is transubstantiated. The play state and the rapturous seizures sometimes deriving from it repre-

sent, therefore, a step rather *toward* than away from the ineluctable truth; and belief—acquiescence in a belief that is not quite belief—is the first step toward the deepened participation that the festival affords in that general will to life which, in its metaphysical aspect, is antecedent to, and the creator of, all life's laws.

21   The opaque weight of the world—both of life on earth and of death, heaven, and hell—is dissolved, and the spirit freed, not *from* anything, for there was nothing from which to be freed except a myth too solidly believed, but *for* something, something fresh and new, a spontaneous act.

22   From the position of secular man (Homo sapiens), that is to say, we are to enter the play sphere of the festival, acquiescing in a game of belief, where fun, joy, and rapture rule in ascending series. The laws of life in time and space—economics, politics, and even morality—will thereupon dissolve. Whereafter, re-created by that return to paradise before the Fall, before the knowledge of good and evil, right and wrong, true and false, belief and disbelief, we are to carry the point of view and spirit of man the player (Homo ludens) back into life; as in the play of children, where, undaunted by the banal actualities of life's meager possibilities, the spontaneous impulse of the spirit to identify itself with something other than itself for the sheer delight of play, transubstantiates the world—in which, actually, after all, things are not quite as real or permanent, terrible, important, or logical as they seem.

Vocabulary

abrogates	banal	opaque
spontaneous	veritable	meager
trice	ritual	secular
self-induced	precisely	literal
supervened	daemonic	phenomenon
operative	ethnologists	anthropologists
fragment	concur	chalice
amateurs	utensils	altar
rapture	positivist	Aristotelian
vulgarization	delusory	condescension
analogy	*noblesse oblige*	perverted
theology	fallible	presumption
alchemy	consecrated	transubstantiated
antecedent	ineluctable	acquiescence

Topics for Discussion

1. Campbell owes much of what he says in this selection to Johan Huizinga's characterization of man as essentially a player of games (*Homo ludens*). To what extent do you think this characterization is true? Cannot man be defined as essentially something else—Hannah Arendt has called him *Homo faber,* man the maker, the creative worker. Can you suggest one or more similar definitions?

2. Do you think that most people in their daily lives engage in a variety of "games" without acknowledging that they do? Describe in detail one such game.

3. Is it necessary in the modern world to wear one or more "masks" in order to survive? Explain why you think it necessary for an individual to change identities several times in one day. If you think "masks" are unnecessary, explain why.

4. What is the essential point of this essay? What is the lesson of the mask?

5. Do you agree with Campbell's conclusion that man must live "as if"?

Rhetorical Considerations

1. Read the first sentence of this essay very carefully and answer two questions:

   A. How is this sentence structured? Note the first three words, the final three words.

   B. Does this sentence contain any of the essay's major ideas? Where do those ideas come in this sentence? Why are they placed there?

2. This is an essay rich in interesting and detailed examples. Are there different kinds of examples? What purpose do they serve? Which ones do you think more central than others? Why? How do the examples relate to Campbell's ideas and his development of those ideas? Do the examples add to or detract from the orderly progression and development of the essay?

3. In paragraphs 3 and 4 why does Campbell juxtapose a childhood experience with a scholarly quotation?

4. How does Campbell use comparison and contrast in this essay (examine paragraphs 7 and 8, for example)?

5. What is the importance of paragraph 17 in the structure of the essay?

6. Comment on Campbell's use of the dash throughout the essay, especially in the first paragraph and in the final three paragraphs. What purpose does this kind of punctuation serve?

The Concept of the Collective Unconscious

Carl Jung

Carl Jung (1875–1961) was a founder of analytical psychology. His published works include The Psychology of the Unconscious *and* Psychology and Alchemy.

1   Probably none of my empirical concepts has met with so much misunderstanding as the idea of the collective unconscious. In what follows I shall try to give (1) a definition of the concept, (2) a description of what it means for psychology, (3) an explanation of the method of proof, and (4) an example.

1. Definition

2   The collective unconscious is a part of the psyche which can be negatively distinguished from a personal unconscious by the fact that it does not, like the latter, owe its existence to personal experience and consequently is not a personal acquisition. While the personal unconscious is made up essentially of contents which have at one time been conscious but which have disappeared from consciousness through having been forgotten or repressed, the contents of the collective unconscious have never been in consciousness, and therefore have never been individually acquired, but owe their existence exclusively to heredity. Whereas the personal unconscious consists for the most part of *complexes,* the content of the collective unconscious is made up essentially of *archetypes.*

3   The concept of the archetype, which is an indispensable correlate of the idea of the collective unconscious, indicates the existence of definite forms in the psyche which seem to be present always and

everywhere. Mythological research calls them "motifs"; in the psychology of primitives they correspond to Lévy-Bruhl's concept of "représentations collectives," and in the field of comparative religion they have been defined by Hubert and Mauss as "categories of the imagination." Adolf Bastian long ago called them "elementary" or "primordial thoughts." From these references it should be clear enough that my idea of the archetype—literally a pre-existent form—does not stand alone but is something that is recognized and named in other fields of knowledge.

4   My thesis, then, is as follows: In addition to our immediate consciousness, which is of a thoroughly personal nature and which we believe to be the only empirical psyche (even if we tack on the personal unconscious as an appendix), there exists a second psychic system of a collective, universal, and impersonal nature which is identical in all individuals. This collective unconscious does not develop individually but is inherited. It consists of preexistent forms, the archetypes, which can only become conscious secondarily and which give definite form to certain psychic contents.

2. The Psychological Meaning of the Collective Unconscious

5   Medical psychology, growing as it did out of professional practice, insists on the *personal* nature of the psyche. By this I mean the views of Freud and Adler. It is a *psychology of the person,* and its aetiological or causal factors are regarded almost wholly as personal in nature. Nonetheless, even this psychology is based on certain general biological factors, for instance on the sexual instinct or on the urge for self-assertion, which are by no means merely personal peculiarities. It is forced to do this because it lays claim to being an explanatory science. Neither of these views would deny the existence of *a priori* instincts common to man and animals alike, or that they have a significant influence on personal psychology. Yet instincts are impersonal, universally distributed, hereditary factors of a dynamic or motivating character, which very often fail so completely to reach consciousness that modern psychotherapy is faced with the task of helping the patient to become conscious of them. Moreover, the instincts are not vague and indefinite by nature, but are specifically formed motive forces which, long before there is any consciousness, and in spite of any degree of consciousness later on, pursue their inherent goals. Consequently they form very close analogies to the archetypes, so close, in fact, that there is good

reason for supposing that the archetypes are the unconscious images of the instincts themselves, in other words, that they are *patterns of instinctual behaviour.*

6   The hypothesis of the collective unconscious is, therefore, no more daring than to assume there are instincts. One admits readily that human activity is influenced to a high degree by instincts, quite apart from the rational motivations of the conscious mind. So if the assertion is made that our imagination, perception, and thinking are likewise influenced by inborn and universally present formal elements, it seems to me that a normally functioning intelligence can discover in this idea just as much or just as little mysticism as in the theory of instincts. Although this reproach of mysticism has frequently been levelled at my concept, I must emphasize yet again that the concept of the collective unconscious is neither a speculative nor a philosophical but an empirical matter. The question is simply this: are there or are there not unconscious, universal forms of this kind? If they exist, then there is a region of the psyche which one can call the collective unconscious. It is true that the diagnosis of the collective unconscious is not always an easy task. It is not sufficient to point out the often obviously archetypal nature of unconscious products, for these can just as well be derived from acquisitions through language and education. Cryptomnesia should also be ruled out, which it is almost impossible to do in certain cases. In spite of all these difficulties, there remain enough individual instances showing the autochthonous revival of mythological motifs to put the matter beyond any reasonable doubt. But if such an unconscious exists at all, psychological explanation must take account of it and submit certain alleged personal aetiologies to sharper criticism.

7   What I mean can perhaps best be made clear by a concrete example. You have probably read Freud's discussion of a certain picture by Leonardo da Vinci: St. Anne with the Virgin Mary and the Christ-child. Freud interprets this remarkable picture in terms of the fact that Leonardo himself had two mothers. This causality is personal. We shall not linger over the fact that this picture is far from unique, nor over the minor inaccuracy that St. Anne happens to be the grandmother of Christ and not, as required by Freud's interpretation, the mother, but shall simply point out that interwoven with the apparently personal psychology there is an impersonal motif well known to us from other fields. This is the motif of the *dual mother,* an archetype to be found in many variants in the field of mythology and comparative religion and forming the basis of numerous "représentations collectives." I might mention, for in-

stance, the motif of the *dual descent,* that is, descent from human and divine parents, as in the case of Heracles, who received immortality through being unwittingly adopted by Hera. What was a myth in Greece was actually a ritual in Egypt: Pharaoh was both human and divine by nature. In the birth chambers of the Egyptian temples Pharaoh's second, divine conception and birth is depicted on the walls; he is "twice-born." It is an idea that underlies all rebirth mysteries, Christianity included. Christ himself is "twice-born": through his baptism in the Jordan he was regenerated and reborn from water and spirit. Consequently, in the Roman liturgy the font is designated the "uterus ecclesiae," and, as you can read in the Roman missal, it is called this even today, in the "benediction of the font" on Holy Saturday before Easter. Further, according to an early Christian-Gnostic idea, the spirit which appeared in the form of a dove was interpreted as Sophia-Sapientia—Wisdom and the Mother of Christ. Thanks to this motif of the dual birth, children today, instead of having good and evil fairies who magically "adopt" them at birth with blessings or curses, are given sponsors—a "godfather" and a "godmother."

8   The idea of a second birth is found at all times and in all places. In the earliest beginnings of medicine it was a magical means of healing; in many religions it is the central mystical experience; it is the key idea in medieval, occult philosophy, and, last but not least, it is an infantile fantasy occurring in numberless children, large and small, who believe that their parents are not their real parents but merely foster-parents to whom they were handed over. Benvenuto Cellini also had this idea, as he himself relates in his autobiography.

9   Now it is absolutely out of the question that all the individuals who believe in a dual descent have in reality always had two mothers, or conversely that those few who shared Leonardo's fate have infected the rest of humanity with their complex. Rather, one cannot avoid the assumption that the universal occurrence of the dual-birth motif together with the fantasy of the two mothers answers an omnipresent human need which is reflected in these motifs. If Leonardo da Vinci did in fact portray his two mothers in St. Anne and Mary—which I doubt—he nonetheless was only expressing something which countless millions of people before and after him have believed. The vulture symbol (which Freud also discusses in the work mentioned) makes this view all the more plausible. With some justification he quotes as the source of the symbol the *Hieroglyphica* of Horapollo, a book much in use in Leonardo's time. There you read that vultures are female only and symbolize the

mother. They conceive through the wind (*pneuma*). This word took on the meaning of "spirit" chiefly under the influence of Christianity. Even in the account of the miracle at Pentecost the pneuma still has the double meaning of wind and spirit. This fact, in my opinion, points without doubt to Mary, who, a virgin by nature, conceived through the pneuma, like a vulture. Furthermore, according to Horapollo, the vulture also symbolizes Athene, who sprang, unbegotten, directly from the head of Zeus, was a virgin, and knew only spiritual motherhood. All this is really an allusion to Mary and the rebirth motif. There is not a shadow of evidence that Leonardo meant anything else by his picture. Even if it is correct to assume that he identified himself with the Christ-child, he was in all probability representing the mythological dual-mother motif and by no means his own personal prehistory. And what about all the other artists who painted the same theme? Surely not all of them had two mothers?

10   Let us now transpose Leonardo's case to the field of the neuroses, and assume that a patient with a mother complex is suffering from the delusion that the cause of his neurosis lies in his having really had two mothers. The personal interpretation would have to admit that he is right—and yet it would be quite wrong. For in reality the cause of his neurosis would lie in the reactivation of the dual-mother archetype, quite regardless of whether he had one mother or two mothers, because, as we have seen, this archetype functions individually and historically without any reference to the relatively rare occurrence of dual motherhood.

11   In such a case, it is of course tempting to presuppose so simple and personal a cause, yet the hypothesis is not only inexact but totally false. It is admittedly difficult to understand how a dual-mother motif—unknown to a physician trained only in medicine—could have so great a determining power as to produce the effect of a traumatic condition. But if we consider the tremendous powers that lie hidden in the mythological and religious sphere in man, the aetiological significance of the archetype appears less fantastic. In numerous cases of neurosis the cause of the disturbance lies in the very fact that the psychic life of the patient lacks the co-operation of these motive forces. Nevertheless a purely personalistic psychology, by reducing everything to personal causes, tries its level best to deny the existence of archetypal motifs and even seeks to destroy them by personal analysis. I consider this a rather dangerous procedure which cannot be justified medically. Today you can judge better than you could twenty years ago the nature of the forces

involved. Can we not see how a whole nation is reviving an archaic symbol, yes, even archaic religious forms, and how this mass emotion is influencing and revolutionizing the life of the individual in a catastrophic manner? The man of the past is alive in us today to a degree undreamt of before the war, and in the last analysis what is the fate of great nations but a summation of the psychic changes in individuals?

12   So far as a neurosis is really only a private affair, having its roots exclusively in personal causes, archetypes play no role at all. But if it is a question of a general incompatibility or an otherwise injurious condition productive of neuroses in relatively large numbers of individuals, then we must assume the presence of constellated archetypes. Since neuroses are in most cases not just private concerns, but *social* phenomena, we must assume that archetypes are constellated in these cases too. The archetype corresponding to the situation is activated, and as a result those explosive and dangerous forces hidden in the archetype come into action, frequently with unpredictable consequences. There is no lunacy people under the domination of an archetype will not fall a prey to. If thirty years ago anyone had dared to predict that our psychological development was tending towards a revival of the medieval persecutions of the Jews, that Europe would again tremble before the Roman fasces and the tramp of legions, that people would once more give the Roman salute, as two thousand years ago, and that instead of the Christian Cross an archaic swastika would lure onward millions of warriors ready for death—why, that man would have been hooted at as a mystical fool. And today? Surprising as it may seem, all this absurdity is a horrible reality. Private life, private aetiologies, and private neuroses have become almost a fiction in the world of today. The man of the past who lived in a world of archaic "représentations collectives" has risen again into very visible and painfully real life, and this not only in a few unbalanced individuals but in many millions of people.

13   There are as many archetypes as there are typical situations in life. Endless repetition has engraved these experiences into our psychic constitution, not in the form of images filled with content, but at first only as *forms without content,* representing merely the possibility of a certain type of perception and action. When a situation occurs which corresponds to a given archetype, that archetype becomes activated and a compulsiveness appears, which, like an instinctual drive, gains its way against all reason and will, or else produces a conflict of pathological dimensions, that is to say, a neurosis.

3. Method of Proof

14   We must now turn to the question of how the existence of archetypes can be proved. Since archetypes are supposed to produce certain psychic forms, we must discuss how and where one can get hold of the material demonstrating these forms. The main source, then, is *dreams,* which have the advantage of being involuntary, spontaneous products of the unconscious psyche and are therefore pure products of nature not falsified by any conscious purpose. By questioning the individual one can ascertain which of the motifs appearing in the dream are known to him. From those which are unknown to him we must naturally exclude all motifs which *might* be known to him, as for instance—to revert to the case of Leonardo—the vulture symbol. We are not sure whether Leonardo took this symbol from Horapollo or not, although it would have been perfectly possible for an educated person of that time, because in those days artists were distinguished for their wide knowledge of the humanities. Therefore, although the bird motif is an archetype par excellence, its existence in Leonardo's fantasy would still prove nothing. Consequently, we must look for motifs which could not possibly be known to the dreamer and yet behave functionally in his dream in such a manner as to coincide with the functioning of the archetype known from historical sources.

15   Another source for the material we need is to be found in "active imagination." By this I mean a sequence of fantasies produced by deliberate concentration. I have found that the existence of unrealized, unconscious fantasies increases the frequency and intensity of dreams, and that when these fantasies are made conscious the dreams change their character and become weaker and less frequent. From this I have drawn the conclusion that dreams often contain fantasies which "want" to become conscious. The sources of dreams are often repressed instincts which have a natural tendency to influence the conscious mind. In cases of this sort, the patient is simply given the task of contemplating any one fragment of fantasy that seems significant to him—a chance idea, perhaps, or something he has become conscious of in a dream—until its context becomes visible, that is to say, the relevant associative material in which it is embedded. It is not a question of the "free association" recommended by Freud for the purpose of dream-analysis, but of elaborating the fantasy by observing the further fantasy material that adds itself to the fragment in a natural manner.

16   This is not the place to enter upon a technical discussion of the method. Suffice it to say that the resultant sequence of fantasies

relieves the unconscious and produces material rich in archetypal images and associations. Obviously, this is a method that can only be used in certain carefully selected cases. The method is not entirely without danger, because it may carry the patient too far away from reality. A warning against thoughtless application is therefore in place.

17   Finally, very interesting sources of archetypal material are to be found in the delusions of paranoiacs, the fantasies observed in trance-states, and the dreams of early childhood, from the third to the fifth year. Such material is available in profusion, but it is valueless unless one can adduce convincing mythological parallels. It does not, of course, suffice simply to connect a dream about a snake with the mythological occurrence of snakes, for who is to guarantee that the functional meaning of the snake in the dream is the same as in the mythological setting? In order to draw a valid parallel, it is necessary to know the functional meaning of the individual symbol, and then to find out whether the apparently parallel mythological symbol has a similar context and therefore the same functional meaning. Establishing such facts not only requires lengthy and wearisome researches, but is also an ungrateful subject for demonstration. As the symbols must not be torn out of their context, one has to launch forth into exhaustive descriptions, personal as well as symbological, and this is practically impossible in the framework of a lecture. I have repeatedly tried it at the risk of sending one half of my audience to sleep.

18   But as to whether this supra-individual psychic activity actually exists, I have so far given no proof that satisfies all the requirements. I should now like to do this once more in the form of an example. The case is that of a man in his thirties, who was suffering from a paranoid form of schizophrenia. He became ill in his early twenties. He had always presented a strange mixture of intelligence, wrongheadedness, and fantastic ideas. He was an ordinary clerk, employed in a consulate. Evidently as a compensation for his very modest existence he was seized with megalomania and believed himself to be the Saviour. He suffered from frequent hallucinations and was at times very much disturbed. In his quiet periods he was allowed to go unattended in the corridor. One day I came across him there, blinking through the window up at the sun, and moving his head from side to side in a curious manner. He took me by the arm and said he wanted to show me something. He said I must look at the sun with eyes half shut, and then I could see the sun's phallus. If I moved my head from side to side the sun-phallus would move too, and that was the origin of the wind.

19   I made this observation about 1906. In the course of the year 1910, when I was engrossed in mythological studies, a book of Dieterich's came into my hands. It was part of the so-called Paris magic papyrus and was thought by Dieterich to be a liturgy of the Mithraic cult. It consisted of a series of instructions, invocations, and visions. One of these visions is described in the following words: "And likewise the so-called tube, the origin of the ministering wind. For you will see hanging down from the disc of the sun something that looks like a tube. And towards the regions westward it is as though there were an infinite east wind. But if the other wind should prevail towards the regions of the east, you will in like manner see the vision veering in that direction." The Greek word for "tube," $\alpha\nu\lambda\acute{o}\varsigma$, means a wind-instrument, and the combination $\alpha\dot{\upsilon}\lambda\grave{o}\varsigma$ $\pi\alpha\chi\dot{\upsilon}\varsigma$ in Homer means "a thick jet of blood." So evidently a stream of wind is blowing through the tube out of the sun.

20   The vision of my patient in 1906, and the Greek text first edited in 1910, should be sufficiently far apart to rule out the possibility of cryptomnesia on his side and of thought-transference on mine. The obvious parallelism of the two visions cannot be disputed, though one might object that the similarity is purely fortuitous. In that case we should expect the vision to have no connections with analogous ideas, nor any inner meaning. But this expectation is not fulfilled, for in certain medieval paintings this tube is actually depicted as a sort of hose-pipe reaching down from heaven under the robe of Mary. In it the Holy Ghost flies down in the form of a dove to impregnate the Virgin. As we know from the miracle of Pentecost, the Holy Ghost was originally conceived as a mighty rushing wind, the $\pi\nu\epsilon\hat{\upsilon}\mu\alpha$, "the wind that bloweth where it listeth." In a Latin text we read: "Animo descensus per orbem solis tribuitur" (They say that the spirit descends through the disc of the sun). This conception is common to the whole of late classical and medieval philosophy.

21   I cannot, therefore, discover anything fortuitous in these visions, but simply the revival of possibilities of ideas that have always existed, that can be found again in the most diverse minds and in all epochs, and are therefore not to be mistaken for inherited ideas.

Vocabulary

correlate	psyche	primordial
aetiological	*a priori*	analogies

hypothesis	cryptomnesis	mysticism
autochthonous	traumatic	catastrophic
fasces	swastika	phallus
impregnate		

Topics for Discussion

1. Look up the meaning of *archetype* in a dictionary or encyclopedia. Do you find manifestations of various kinds of archetypes in the world about you?

2. To what extent do you think archetypes are reflected in religious and civic ceremonies? Do some religious ceremonies seem to be more archetypally oriented than others?

3. Jung points out that the same archetype may be present in several religions. Does this fact serve to strengthen or weaken the importance of religions in our world?

4. To what extent do you think Nazism was an expression of a collective unconscious? Do you agree with Jung that neuroses are more often social rather than individual?

5. Do you see any connection between the occult and science? Are the two fundamentally at odds, or do they move along parallel paths?

6. Can you think of any literature (short stories, poems, plays) that you have read in which archetypes were significant?

Rhetorical Considerations

1. What is the organization of this essay? How is the essay structured? Does this essay provide a good organizational model for any of the papers you might write in this or other classes? How does the first paragraph serve to prepare the reader for Jung's discussion?

2. What methods of definition are employed by Jung? Are these methods adequate for his purposes? Could he have used other methods to advantage?

3. Evaluate Jung's reasoning in his discussion of Leonardo's painting. Can you detect any flaws? Is the same reasoning used in his discussion throughout the essay?

4. How suitable is Jung's example for his purposes? Is it positioned in the essay for maximum rhetorical advantage? Why does he use only one example? How does this example affect the structure of the essay?

The Truth About Cinderella

Sam Rosenberg

Sam Rosenberg is an author. His latest book is Naked is the Best Disguise, *a study of Sherlock Holmes.*

1   Once upon an actual time, when I first arrived in "Baghdad-on-the-Hudson" to seek my fortune (through shrewd trading in jackasses and molasses I'm now richer than Croesus or Jackie Onassis), a mighty Warner Brothers vizier phoned me.

2   "O learned but lowly one," he said, "it has been whispered into our corporate ear that you are a free-lance Broadway stage manager and play editor who privately delves into the hidden origins of literary ideas. You have been recommended as one who might assist us in a literary plagiarism matter. Are your interested? Good! Please come see me here tomorrow morning at 8:45."

3   At the appointed time next morning the lawyer wasted no time with chitchat or the ceremonial sipping of lukewarm coffee from Dixie cups. He merely pointed to a chair and said abruptly, "What do *you* know about Cinderella?"

4   As I made a soft moon landing on the red leather chair, I thought, quite irritably: "Cinderella? At this ungodly hour? I've just squeezed my way through subway trains *filled* with Cinderellas, lovely Princesses, Pusses in Boots to get here . . . expecting to talk about Jimmy Cagney, George Raft, Bette Davis, Errol . . . and this, this barrister throws *Cinderella* at me! What's a nice mythological kid like *her* doing in a rough, tough place like Warner Brothers?"

5   But I wanted that job and I answered brightly: "Cinderella? I know only what I remember from the fairy tale. But I did read recently that the famous, magical 'glass slipper' dropped by Cinderella when she fled from the royal palace at midnight was the result of a mistranslation from the original French story."

6   The lawyer stared at me expressionlessly as I continued: "In the seventeenth-century fairy tale the wonderful slipper was actually made of *fur,* but the French word for 'fur' closely resembles their word for '*glass*'—and the English translator goofed. In one way the mistranslation improved the story, because, obviously, a highly rigid, inflexible slipper made of *glass* would be much harder to fit than an elastic one made of *fur*. But, on the other hand, Prince Charming's obsessive erotic search, and his frantic fitting of a *fur*

slipper is a more precise Freudian sexual symbol—since a cute little fur-lined slipper more closely resembles a cute little female va—''

7   The Warner Brothers executive interrupted me hastily. ''I see that you do indeed delve into the—uh—*hidden* origins of—uh—cliterary ideas! We already know that a *'pantoufle en vair'* (fur slipper) verbally resembles a *pantoufle en verre,'* or glass slipper, but we've found that such fascinating—uh—tidbits are regarded in the courtroom as 'irrelevant' and 'immaterial.' As for the Freudian interpretations! Even when they are valid—as this one of yours is—they embarrass judges and juries, who find them hard to understand. I myself always look for the psychological elements in these cases because they help our strategy of analysis. But, you see, I'm a Freudian, too.''

8   The lawyer made a 360-degree turn in his rotating chair, stopping in midrevolution to stare for a moment at the bleak skyline. When he returned from orbit he smiled and said, ''O.K., you're hired! The research and written report will take you about six to eight weeks, and we'll pay you $150.00 weekly. O.K.? We'll begin work today. But first: have you seen our recent release, *Princess O'Rourke*? That's what we need the Cinderella background for. The opposing lawyer says our writer *stole* the idea for *Princess O'Rourke* from a story by his client, but actually, we think they *both* lean pretty heavily on the Cinderella fairy tale. We'll screen the movie for you tomorrow morning at 9:00. You'll probably have to look at it a half-dozen times.''

9   He handed me a thick folder. ''Here is your homework. It's the summary of the opposing lawyer's brief detailing our alleged theft of his client's ideas. You will also find a copy of the screenplay of *Princess O'Rourke*. You'll want to make your first preliminary study of the two properties before you look at our film tomorrow. Good luck!''

10   Next day the lawyer's secretary conducted me to the luxurious executive projection room, closed the door, and left me to watch the ''million-dollar superproduction'' entirely alone. The tiny theater darkened, ''Princess O'Rourke'' flashed onto the screen, and the film's orchestral fanfare filled the little auditorium. Deranged by my quick elevation in status, I suddenly remembered and identified completely with one of my favorite historical characters, Ludwig II of Bavaria. Before he was dragged off to the insane asylum in an ermine straitjacket, ''Mad'' Ludwig once expressed his mania for complete solitude by ordering a major Wagnerian opera performed in a huge opera house for himself alone. Now, through the stirring racket of the film's fanfare, I shouted exultantly, ''You weren't so cuckoo, Ludwig! This is *wonderful!*''

11   But my instant delusions of grandeur faded quickly, replaced by a more lasting feeling of anxiety as I watched the rapidly unfolding film and tried to compare it with the voluminous legal and script material I'd studied on the previous day.

12   This is the plot of *Princess O'Rourke*: In this charming film (it won an Oscar for its writer, Norman Krasna), Olivia de Havilland is the princess apparent of a mythical country who has arrived in Washington as a White House guest of President Roosevelt. While en route to the United States she meets, falls in love with, and decides to marry a plebeian American airplane chauffeur named O'Rourke, played by Robert Cummings. But her mean old pig-eyed uncle and guardian (Charles Coburn) vetoes the marriage, forbids any further contact between the young lovers, and then locks her Highness in her bedroom—which just *happens* to be the room in which Abraham Lincoln wrote the Emancipation Proclamation.

13   Inspired by the spiritual presence of the Great Emancipator, the imprisoned princess decides to liberate herself from the Ruritanian conventions that enslave her. She has already made friends with President Roosevelt's famous little dog, Fala, and at three o'clock in the morning the adorable little dog senses her dilemma and arrives at her door to scratch and bark for admittance. The spirit of Lincoln stands by, invisibly, as the princess hastily scribbles her own little Emancipation Proclamation and slips it under the door.

14   At once smart little Fala seizes the note in his teeth, races down the hallway to the President's office, scoots through the legs of the Secret Service guards, and delivers it to the President, who is still ("while the nation sleeps") working at his desk!

15   Enter the *deus ex machina!* Let me digress for a minute to explain the character of the *deus ex machina*. It descended to us from the ancient Greek dramatists, who usually solved their plays' dilemmas by sending messengers to Zeus. The rescuing king of the gods (*deus*) immediately responded by coming down to earth in a chariot (*machina*). Now, nearly two thousand years later, a clever American screenwriter was doing the very same thing: His *deus ex machina* (Roosevelt in his wheelchair) in turn sends *his* machines— and motorcycles—to fetch a bewildered O'Rourke and a benign Justice of the Supreme Court (Brandeis) to the White House. Minutes later, with Franklin and Eleanor (and tail-wagging Fala!) as witnesses, the commoner is married to his Princess Charming, after which they presumably live happily into eternity.

16   But as I watched this charming, modernized version of the Cinderella fairy tale, I became increasingly worried for Warner Brothers because of the strong resemblance between the two "properties" (both, in their way, based on the Cinderella legend)

now locked in litigation. Not only did the two contending literary scripts *both* hinge on the *reversal* of the Cinderella story, but, extraordinarily, it was a *little dog* in each story that carried the message begging for help to the rescuing *deus ex machina* figure!

17   The movie over, I nervously expressed my anxiety to my employer, who said quite calmly: "I appreciate your concern, but we haven't hired you to worry about Warner Brothers. You must stay entirely objective and unconcerned. If we are innocent of plagiarism we want to know it. But if one of our producers has consciously—or unconsciously—stolen his ideas from someone else, we'd like to know that, too. As for these similarities . . . in dozens of such litigations we've found that extremely similar details turn up which are later found in *other* well-known literary works published long before *either* of the litigating properties. You now enter stage two of your work: the search for the common literary ancestor of the two scripts you've been working with. But," he cautioned, "try to find your literary ancestors in a source that a judge or jury will recognize as easily available. Like encyclopedias or reference works found in any home or public library."

18   Following his instructions I opened my own Britannica (the eleventh, or "scholar's edition"), and, with remarkable beginner's luck, hit a magnificent jackpot at my very first try!

The brief reference read:

> *Cinderella* (i.e., cinder girl), the heroine of an almost universal fairy tale. Its essential features are: (1) the persecuted maiden whose youth and beauty bring upon her the jealousy of her stepmother and sisters, (2) the intervention of a fairy godmother or other supernatural instrument on her behalf, (3) the prince who falls in love with her and marries her.

But it was the tiny footnote at the end of this brief summary that was pure treasure trove: "See Marian R. Cox, 1893. *Three Hundred and Forty-Five Variants of Cinderella,* English Folklore Society."

19   What a find! Without even looking at the book I knew that most of the laborious research had already been done *for* me. It must have taken Marian Cox many *years* to find and synopsize the 345 variants of the Cinderella tale, and this priceless book had been found in one of the most readily available places.

20   An immediate search of Cox's book, which defined the classic story as "basically that of a poor girl who makes a good marriage with the help of a supernatural friend," revealed a number of variations in which they were *male* Cinderellas; and the folklorist

indicated that *Princess Charmings* had existed since the beginning of recorded history, and presumably before that.

21   I was also delighted to learn from the same book that in many versions of the perennially told tale the "supernatural friend" was frequently an animal—a dog, cat, bird, or cow—and that several ancient stories even used a *little black dog* to carry begging messages for help from the persecuted girl to a rescuing god or monarch. Eureka! As a result of this lucky book-find, I was quickly able to submit my opinion that both of the contending "properties" had been derived by their respective authors from many early literary ancestors now in the public domain, or common treasury of ideas that belong to everyone. (My employer expressed his gratitude for my work by hiring me for similar work for several years. I never learned what his company *did* with my reports and, mysteriously, I was never told the legal outcome of Cinderella-in-reverse, *Princess O'Rourke,* or *any* of the cases. "It's better if you don't know" was the answer to my first and only inquiry!)

22   But as I continued to explore the Cinderella stories (I was hooked on the lady by now and continued a personal investigation), I also noticed that considerable changes in the classic tale had been made at the end of the seventeenth century. Now, all myths and folklore undergo certain revisions as they are told and retold through the ages, but the revisions in the Cinderella story were so drastic I wondered *why* they were made and *who* made them. And although Marian R. Cox had delineated 345 different versions of "Cinderella," there was no Marian R. Cox to tell me why the original story had been so tampered with. Recalling recent discoveries by folklorist Robert Graves and others that the famous Mother Goose nursery rhymes all referred to early *historical* and political events, I thought I might strike pay dirt on Cinderella's behalf by delving a bit into *history.* Once again, with fine beginner's luck, I succeeded in finding some plausible answers to my little mystery.

23   First of all, as I had avidly devoured the fascinating material in the Cox book, an intriguing and puzzling fact had emerged: the dominant form of the Cinderella myth as it had been told from the third century A.D. until the end of the seventeenth century was usually entitled, "*The King Who Would Marry His Daughter*"! Here, in synopsis and composite, uncensored form, is that clearly incestuous *original Cinderella fairy tale:*

24   Once upon a time there was a mighty king who fell in love with and married a damsel whom he believed to be the most beautiful woman in the world. They were very, very happy together until she gave birth to a daughter and, in so doing, lost her life. At her

deathbed the grief-maddened king made the very rash promise to his dying wife that he would never again make love to or marry any other woman. But he added the curious proviso: "Unless she is just as beautiful as you."

25   In the long years that followed, the desperately lonely and sex-starved widower actually kept his promise until one day, when his daughter reached the age of puberty, he saw that she was the "spitting image" of her beautiful mother. At once the king told his daughter that fate had decreed *she* must become his wife, and told her to prepare for an early wedding. The terrified girl then prayed for help and immediately her dead mother returned in the guise of her "fairy godmother." (Incidentally, in many such stories the well-known "fairy godmother" is *usually* the transformation of a dead mother who always hovers invisibly over her daughter as a guardian angel.)

26   The transmogrified mother, or godmother, advises Cinderella: "Tell that father of yours that you have 'absolutely nothing to wear for the wedding' and that you refuse to be married in anything but a gown 'made of the light of the stars.' In other words, ask for the *impossible*. That might cool off his incestuous madness."

27   But, through his own clever supernatural technicians, the raunchy king actually succeeds in *procuring* a wedding gown made of the evanescent "light of the stars," and the consultant fairy godmother then advises her daughter to flee to a neighboring kingdom and hide where her lustful daddy will never find her.

28   After many exciting adventures the fugitive girl reaches a nearby sanctuary, trades her beautiful gown for the rags worn by a beggar girl, hides her lovely hair under a frumpy hat, and blackens her face with *cinders*. In this pioneer-hippie disguise she then obtains a job as a scullery maid in the kitchen of the royal palace, where she hides successfully for many months. But each night, like our own modern hippies who (several mothers have told me) are spotlessly clean beneath their disguises of sackcloth and ashes, the princess secretly bathes in a secluded pond near the palace.

29   One night the prince of the neighboring kingdom returns from a hunt and sees her at her bath, nude and sparkling clean, and instantly falls in love with her. When she sees him approaching, Cinderella runs back to the kitchen and quickly resumes her slovenly disguise. But the prince finds a shoe—or ring—she's left behind at her bathing spot and immediately begins a nation-wide search for the foot—or finger—that will fit the talismanic object.

30   The fugitive princess has—of course!—also fallen in love with the royal shoe fetishist, but is afraid to reveal her identity lest her father find her; but, when the prince becomes mortally ill from

frustration and is about to die, Cinderella washes her face, gets rid of those awful rags, and comes out of the kitchen to reveal her true identity. The lost-and-found shoe fits perfectly, of course, and the young lovers become man and wife and live happily ever after.

31   As you have observed, the differences between the earlier and later versions of the Cinderella stories are considerable; and one notices in particular that the main feature of an incestuous, daughter-grabbing king has been censored completely out of the version we all grew up with.

32   But may you also have noticed that the earlier incest version of "Cinderella" contains *absolutely no trace of any stepmother or sisters*? When I noted this revolutionary change in the myth of the persecuted scullery maid in the later versions of "Cinderella," I asked myself these questions: Why are the villainy and guilt transferred from the person of the father and king to the three unpleasant females who were presumably invented for that purpose? Then, again, the corollary question: If this is so, *who* was responsible for the change?

33   The answers to this problem evaded me for quite a while until one day, while pursuing the questions in a biography of the "author" of the Cinderella version we now know, I came upon some plausible answers.

34   This author, you may be interested to learn, was Charles Perrault (who wrote fairy tales under the name of his son, Perrault d'Armancour), a member of a highly influential family in the seventeenth century. Perrault's brother Claude was the architect and builder of the Louvre, constructed in Paris as a residence of Louis XIV. Charles Perrault was Louis' superintendent of public works and artistic adviser to Jean Baptiste Colbert, hated oppressor of the French lower classes. As chief henchman to Colbert, Perrault was a ranking member of the ruthless top brass of the Court. When Colbert died in 1683, the Perrault family lost its influence and position, and Charles Perrault spent the remaining decades of his life writing obscure religious and political tracts. He never revealed how he *came* to write the collections of fairy tales still published and read everywhere. But his biographers agree that he probably acquired his taste for such stories from his long residence at the court of Louis XIV, where, according to Madame de Sévigné, there was a considerable vogue for fairy tales, Oriental tales, and classical romantic ballets based on such material.

35   Anyway, a careful reading of the Perrault anthologies reveals that the author carefully collected and transcribed many traditional stories, like "Little Red Riding Hood," "Sleeping Beauty," and "Puss and Boots," quite accurately. But he *felt impelled to make*

drastic changes in the story entitled "The King Who Would Marry His Daughter."

36   It isn't hard to guess why he did so . . . and now, finally, comes the unraveling of my mystery. As a once-prominent member of the intrigue-ridden, notoriously immoral court of Louis XIV, Perrault was not about to risk his neck by publishing a story about a king who incestuously desires his own daughter! Consequently, Perrault simply rewrote the ancient fairy tale and eliminated the character of the king entirely. But the story requires a "villain," so he substituted a wicked stepmother and her daughters, recruited from the despised new bourgeoisie, and from the already disenfranchised female minority!

37   And that, dear friends, is the reconstructed account of the story of little Cinderella and her stepsisters and stepmother—who were together the victims of an ancient legendary king and of a very real seventeenth-century revisionist and male chauvinist.

38   To be sure, Cinderella emerges triumphant in the charming story—in all of its versions down through the ages—for she always, after much suffering, finds true happiness with Prince Charming. But it is the "ugly relatives-by-marriage" who have suffered most since they were invented by Perrault. After being ridiculed in every telling of the story, they then go down into humiliating defeat as perpetual victims within the fantasy mind of their creator and his audience. (Stepmothers have had a very bad public image ever since.)

39   Several hard moral questions arise from this set of discoveries about Cinderella. They are: (1) Shall we continue to tell the beloved story as it was told to us? (2) Shall we tell it in its original form? (3) Shall we explain the antifeminist metamorphosis of the story itself to our children? or (4) Shall we forget the matter entirely?

40   My experience tells me that probably Number 4 will prevail! But I shall, of course, remain confident that we will all meet *this* little moral test as perfectly as we have met every other moral test we've had to face. And may we all live happily ever after!

THE END

Vocabulary

vizier	erotic	mania
eureka	plausible	avidly
sackcloth		

Topics for Discussion

1. Now that you know the truth about the Cinderella fairy tale, have you changed your opinion of it? What is the truth about the story?

2. This essay implies that fairy tales change and are changed over a period of time. How significant are the changes in the Cinderella story? Have these changes altered the basic meaning of the story?

3. Why does Rosenberg refer to "the Cinderella stories"? In what way can there be more than one story?

4. Do you tend to believe Rosenberg's explanation of why Charles Perrault included the evil stepmother and sisters? How reasonable do you find this explanation? What proof does Rosenberg offer to support his reasoning?

5. Rosenberg raises four "hard moral questions" at the end of the essay. How hard are these questions, and how moral are they? How would you answer these questions? Do you agree with his answer to question four?

6. Rosenberg mentions a Freudian interpretation of the Cinderella story. What is meant by a Freudian interpretation? Do you think that fairy tales are symbolic? Choose a fairy tale and give your interpretation of its symbolic meaning.

Rhetorical Considerations

1. The first paragraph of the essay sounds something like the opening of a fairy tale. Why does Rosenberg call New York the "Baghdad-on-the-Hudson"? Why does he refer to a "mighty Warner Brothers vizier"? Examine the first two paragraphs carefully. Based on these paragraphs and your knowledge of fairy tales can you say there is such a thing as a rhetoric of fairy tales? What would be some of the elements of this rhetoric?

2. Throughout the essay Rosenberg uses dashes, ellipsis (three periods in a row), and other devices to break up sentences internally. What effect does this create?

3. Examine the beginnings of paragraphs in the essay. How does Rosenberg achieve variety in the first sentences of his paragraphs? Where does he use the opening sentence of a paragraph to achieve a transition? How effectively does he bridge his paragraphs?

4. What is the tone of this essay? Does the tone in any way detract from the scholarly information Rosenberg provides? Is the tone consistent throughout the essay?

5. What unexpected details do you find in paragraphs 3 and 4? What do you expect to find in the rest of the essay after reading these paragraphs?

Folk Roots of Civilization—And Thereby Hangs a Tale

Charlton Laird

Charlton Laird (b. 1901), Professor Emeritus of English at the University of Nevada, Reno, is an essayist, novelist, and lexicographer whose works include Laird's Thesaurus, The Miracle of Language, Language in America, *and* Thunder on the River.

1   ''Once upon a time there was a wicked old witch who lived in a dark wood . . . '' (or a beautiful princess whose stepmother kept her locked up so that she was very lonely, or a poor little lame boy who had only one shoe, which fitted the foot he couldn't walk on). Or what you will. Children love stories, and for that matter, adults love stories, albeit more sophisticated tales than those of beautiful princesses with improbable stepmothers. People liked stories during the long childhood of the race, and this fondness has more than childish interest, for childish stories have defied time as human flesh and human conduct could not. Men have loved and hated and feared and wondered; we know they must have, though much of their love and wonder died with them. Their stories did not die, and the stories carried with them something of the loves and hates and hopes and fears of the storytellers, and of the folk for whom the tales were told.

2   We have been pretty stupid about naive stories. Some of them, of course, got used for sophisticated purposes, and we were charmed to learn that King Lear and his daughters came out of an old Celtic tale and that Portia and her caskets came out of an old Italian one. But we were a long time taking simpleminded stories seriously. We patronizingly banished them to the nursery, and turned to the philosophers to tell us about the nature of man, not recognizing that a profound philosopher is very far from a primitive

man, but that a prattling child is in some ways very close to him. And even when sober savants like the Brothers Grimm realized that lost testimony to truth lurked in the tales that delighted simple people, children, and funny little old Igorots, nobody knew much how to study this truth.

3   We know more, now, or think we do, and if this is no place to write the history of the study of folklore, we might notice something of the new study of the old tale. First, of course, we needed the stories themselves—we could not work with them until we had them. For some centuries there had been somewhat casual collection of tales, mostly as pleasant curiosities, but for the past century or so folklorists have been very industriously, and very soberly, collecting every scrap of genuine old tales they can uncover, and tucking the tales away in scholarly journals. Now we have a treasury of them.

4   We have, also, excellent means of working with stories. A number of techniques have been developed, most of them semi-literary and semi-scientific, which produce tolerably orderly, measurable, and interpretable results. Notable is the method of the Finnish Folklore Fellows, worked up in Finland, and in modified forms used throughout the learned world. Roughly, the method works like this.[1]

5   The folklorist selects a popular tale, say the Widow of Ephesus, and collects all the variants of this story that have been recorded anywhere. Then he tries to break the story into its parts, studying the parts and the distribution of the various versions of the story. Let us say that he has one version that runs about as follows:

6   A good woman had a jealous husband who became unduly suspicious of her friendliness with a wealthy neighbor, and when they got into an argument because the neighbor's goats had eaten the husband's cabbages, the husband killed the neighbor, robbed him, and tried to dispose of the body by chopping it up and feeding it to the pigs. But he was found out, and hung. In that country the law required that the body of any murderer hang for seven days, and to prevent the relatives from cutting down the body and burying it, a

---

[1] Scholars will not need to be told that I have greatly simplified a complicated operation. The classic statements are those of Antti Aarne, *Leitfaden der ver-gleichenden Märchensforschung,* FF Communications 13, Hamina, 1913, and Kaarle Krohn, *Die folkloristische Arbeitsmethode,* Oslo, 1926. Aarne and Krohn called the method historic-geographic, and endeavored to be as objective as possible. Subsequent scholars have given more attention to the logical importance of key motifs, and less to determining the original form of the story, the archetype. An excellent statement in English will be found in Stith Thompson, *The Folktale* (New York: 1946), pp. 430–48.

soldier was kept on guard. Now, the widow had loved her husband very much, and accordingly she went to the soldier and begged him to let her have the body to bury. He refused, pointing out that he would be punished. The next night the widow came again, and told the solider she would work for him for the rest of his days, but he still refused. Then she offered to kiss and fondle him, and he agreed that that would be a pleasant way to while away a chilly night, but that as to relinquishing the body, he would have to think about that while the kissing progressed. Later, in spite of kisses, he still refused the body. On the third night, the widow offered him her ultimate favors, partly because her husband would not need them any more anyhow, and during the course of providing these favors she became so pleased with the soldier that she suggested they run away together. He was willing, but penniless. Then the widow remembers that when her husband feared he would be found out, he had swallowed the gold he had stolen from the neighbor, and that he had been executed so quickly that the gold must still be inside him. Accordingly the two of them disembowelled the body, found the gold, and fled to a far country, where they lived in wealth and splendor.

7   What can the folklorist do with this story? First he can break it down into parts and examine the parts. Some are more nearly essential than others. The story concerns the fact that amorous inclinations, supposedly especially in women, can overcome grief and even decency. For this story, some objects and actions are imperative. There must be, for instance, the body of a dead husband, or at least of a dead lover. Other details are not so essential. The husband need not have been angry because the neighbor's goats ate his cabbages rather than his carrots, and his victim need not have been a neighbor. The husband need not have been jealous, or he need not have been guilty of murder. He may have been hung as a heretic, or for breaking a tabu against paring his nails in the presence of his sister's son's mother-in-law, or he need not have been hung. In short, the details (or motifs, as folklorists prefer to call the important details) can be assorted into something like categories. Some, like the corpse of the husband, are essential. Some, like the widow trying three nights and not winning until the third night, sound like traditional themes which would readily attach themselves to any story. Some, like the goats eating the cabbages or the soldier saying he wouldn't mind because it was a chilly night, sound like the sort of verisimilitude that any good raconteur will add, just to make his tale more convincing or more engaging to his particular audience.

8   By now the folklorist is well started. He can extract a plot

which must resemble the essential story of the Widow of Ephesus, approximately the following: a man dies leaving a fond widow or mistress, who endeavors to recover the body, which is guarded by another man; in trying to indulge her own grief and pay the respects due to her dead lover she becomes so enamored of the guard that she marries him and desecrates the corpse. These are the elements of the story; without these the story cannot exist in its entirety, and these elements must have been in the original story. Or at least most of them must have; the detail about the mutilation of the body could have been dispensed with, relying only upon copulation in the presence of the corpse, but the folklorist would probably suspect this of being a very early addition if not part of the original tale.

9   The folklorist is now ready to compare his hypothetical reconstruction of the story with the occurrence of the tale throughout the world. He notices which versions are clearly old. Do versions exist in the Old Testament, in an Egyptian papyrus, in Aesop's Fables or in the great Hindu collections like the *Panchatantra* and the *Jatakas*? What is the geographical distribution of the tales? He analyses all his variants, breaking them into parts, and plotting on maps the occurrences of the various motifs. He may note, for instance, that the tale is common in Russia, but that there the guard is posted to protect the corpse from wolves, that the theme of the three nights appears in no early versions of the story, but became common in certain areas. Gradually, the whole history of the tale takes shape. If the folklorist is smart and his materials plentiful enough, he will be able to tell about where and when the story got started, where it wandered, and how it changed as it went. He will be able to demonstrate which of the versions are archaic, even though they may not have been discovered until they cropped up recently in some obscure corner of the world, where they have been kept alive by simple people.

10   Now that we have a history of the tale and a chart of its wanderings we can begin to use it to understand mankind, his nature and his dim past, what he was doing with his mind and his emotions. Of course the original plot does not tell us much except that mankind has always loved stories and has always been ingenious. These facts we could have guessed, although we may be a bit surprised to find out how much he loved stories and how ingenious he could be. But granted that we know the original form of the story, and where it wandered we know what individual people were doing to it. We know how these people changed a story, and knowing what they did we can see into them. If the Blackfoot Indians tell the Christ story to explain why the jackass has long ears, we do not know more about

Christ but we do know something more about the Blackfoot and perhaps something more about many of our forgotten ancestors, and even something about the way we became what we are. When the same story of the Christ child (even though Christ has here become a girl) is told among the Zuni to account for sterility in the mule, we know nothing new about mules but we may know something of the devotion of the Zuni to fertility.

11   For instance, the story of the flood occurs not only in the Old Testament, but among primitive peoples the world over. It must have been such an old story that it was spread by mankind in their original dissemination over the earth, or at least it must have been so early that it spread everywhere, overcoming the obstacles of space and foreign tongues as it went. On the other hand, tales involving the evil eye, which are very common in Europe, are almost unknown in the native tales of the Americas. The concept must be later.

12   Do these tales have historical value also? Only of a limited sort. Consider the story of the embattled vagina, for instance, the tale of a female creature who appears as an enticing young woman, but uses her toothy organs of Venus to devour her suitors. This tale is certainly deeply psychological, but it probably does not tell us anything of the history of anatomy. On the other hand, the female usually entertains her suitors in some kind of dwelling which is local in the time and place of the narrator. If the story is told by a Bannock Indian, the men wait their turn outside a Bannock wickiup, but if the tale comes from a Crow Indian, the line forms outside a teepee. That is, the core of the tale, the directions of the elaboration of the tale, reveal man's inner fears and longings; the superficial details reveal the society of the teller and the audience for which the tale was told. They reveal little about the history of the first teller of the story or of his people. In the Tar Baby story, we know that the tale must have originated in a climate where pitchy substances become sticky, not in the Arctic, but we would know that anyhow, and much more accurately from the Finnish method of analysis. The Uncle Remus version of the story may tell us something, if we needed the information, about the briar patches of the Old South, but not of the briar patches of ancient India whence the type tale spread. Mainly, such stories are interesting for what they tell us of minds and emotions, of art and essential idea.

13   These tales from the folk are legion. Even those which have survived in hundreds of variants spread half way around the globe are numerous—The Great Fool, The Little Tailor, The Master Thief, Potiphar's Wife, The Judgment of Solomon, The Faithful

Mongoose, The External Soul, Sleeping Beauty, The Swan Maiden, The Golden Fleece. They have been named for famous individual stories involving the tale, have by now mostly been charted at least roughly, and some have been analysed and reanalysed in great detail. But since we are interested at the moment not in the patterns of taletelling but in the revelation of the mind and the manners of people as they are preserved in tales, let us examine two that are closely involved in our own tradition.

14   This first concerns an Irish monk, a genial old fellow whose duty was to copy manuscripts. He was so kind that the little creatures which were his companions in his lonely cell wanted to help him and thus show their love of the good man and their worship of the good God. In the warm afternoon the monk would become drowsier and drowsier until finally he slumbered, and the ink-laden pen slipped from his fingers. That was the chance for his little friends. The bird, who had been sitting patiently on the window sill for this to happen, would dart in and grasp the pen in her beak, lest it smirch the precious vellum. The knowing fly would buzz down upon the manuscript and mark the place where the monk had left off, lest awaking he make an error, and the mouse would sit quietly in his corner until the proper moment for his turn. When the monk had slept long enough to revive himself, but not yet to be guilty of sloth, the mouse would come out and nibble his toe to wake him up.

15   In folktales animal helpers are countless, and this particular story is obviously a variant of the well-known tales of St. Francis and his birds, but there is a play of fancy over it which suggests that the tellers and the hearers of the tales—for one should remember, no appreciative audience, few good stories—had a liveliness of imagination and a sense of lightness and charm which must have been unusual. The Irish were Celts, and one notices similar qualities in other Celtic tales. The Welsh, for instance, were culturally close cousins of the Irish, and their tales flower with fancy. Take the tale of *Kulhwch* (also spelled *Kilhwch*) and *Olwen,* for instance, from the great collection known as the *Mabinogion.* Summarizing the quality of a story is not easy, especially if the quality to be summarized is the variety, wealth, and elaboration of detail, but we shall try a few samples. Kulhwch wishes to marry Olwen, who is not reluctant, but she has an ogre of a father, the Giant Yspaddaden, an inhospitable fellow who speeds the parting guest by hurling spears after him. From Kulhwch he gets the spears back; one "pierced him through the eyeball, until it came out through the nape of his neck. 'A cursed savage son-in-law,'" Yspaddaden observed, "'whilst I am left alive, worse will be the sight of my eyes. When I go against the wind

they will boil; my head will always ache, and giddiness will be upon me before every noon.' "

16   Under such persuasion the old man does not deny the suit, but he pretends to be a stickler for suitable weddings and to have peculiarities about his private toilet. The bridegroom must provide a staggering array of impossible necessities, and as for Father's toilet, he will need a haircut and a shave, but his hair is so tough and bristly that he can get a beard trim only with the comb and scissors between the ears of the Twrch Trwyth. Now this brute was an uncommonly difficult wild pig, that could be hunted only with the help of a man nobody had ever heard of, leading a vile hound nobody can ever master except with an inaccessible collar and an unattainable leash, and the hunting cannot go forward without the aid of dozens of helpers, none to be had through love, money, or military might, and each with various other restrictions without which he is useless. Of course the necessary scissors, comb, and razor are the old fellow's external soul, as he very well knows, for he is a relatively sophisticated giant. He cannot be killed except with these barbering implements, which he has prudently stashed where nobody can get at them. While he lives he will not relinquish his daughter.

17   With the help of King Arthur, who is conveniently Kulhwch's uncle, the world is ransacked and the island of Britain laid waste during the hunting of the Twrch Trwyth, the barbering tools are retrieved from between the Trwyth's ears before the brute plunges into the sea, and the wedding party arrives. To prepare the father of the bride they "shave his beard, flesh, and skin to the bone, and the two ears entirely. And Kulhwch said, 'are you shaved, Man?' 'I am shaved,' said he. 'Is your daughter mine now?' 'Yours,' said he . . . 'And it is high time to take my life.' " which they do by beheading him.

18   Essentially, of course, this is a very common tale. It employs the theme of the quest for extremely difficult objects, known in the classical story of Jason and the Golden Fleece and in dozens of Grimm's fairy tales. It supplements this theme with the motif of the external soul, the secret of life which has been hidden somewhere, a tale which crops up in an ancient Egyptian papyrus and dozens of later places. The story gains its charm not from the freshness of its plot. In spite of difficulties the reader is never in doubt as to who will wed whom and whose head is to be tossed on the dung pile. But the story gains its charm—and it is charming, and not only to children—from the exotic play of Celtic imagination over it.

19   The Celts, of course, were early inhabitants of Britain (the island got its name from the Brythonic Celts), but the core of early

English culture was certainly Germanic. The Angles and the Saxons, who came to the island of Britain sometime after A.D. 350, when the Romans withdrew, participated in a great culture complex which dominated north central Europe. What were these people like? Did their minds work differently, did their feelings rise differently, than did those of the Celts? It is not easy to know. There was no Anglian Boswell telling us what he thought when he came home from an assignation. We have no case histories of Saxon juvenile delinquents. There was no *New Anglian Times* with Sunday news reviews. A Roman by the name of Tacitus wrote a politico-social sketch called *Germania,* but he obviously did not know much, and even the little he recorded, valuable though it is, is not very reliable. How can we get at the minds and feelings of these people?

20   Like everybody else they told stories, and some stories have survived. Take, for instance, the Anglo-Saxon epic, *Beowulf.* Roughly, the tale breaks into two parts. In the first part, a great hero, Beowulf, a Geat (the Geats lived in what is now Southern Sweden) goes on an errand of mercy to what is modern Denmark, where the Spear Danes were in trouble. In two fights he rids his hosts of a pestiferous monster called Grendel and the brute's dam. In the latter half of the story he returns to Geatland, becomes king, destroys a dragon that has been plaguing his people, seizes its hoard of gold, and dies from his wounds, believing he has provided his people with the wealth that will bring them protection.

21   The poem is a longish work of more than three thousand lines, and although it is highly adorned, it is also told with narrative rapidity, so that we can here examine only a small portion of it, the more because we shall need to bring other works to bear upon it. We might take the fights with Grendel and his dam. The Spear Danes have left their great hall, since they dare not spend the night there. Beowulf has boasted to his companions that he has more strength in his handgrip than any man living, and that he will not deign to use weapons on a beast that knows not the cunning of arms. Soon Grendel comes, "the Shadowgoer gliding under the misty slopes," tears the iron-bound door from its hinges, drags one of the finest young Geats from his bed, and devours him, "feet and hands"—that is, he began with the softer middle parts and finally cleaned up the scraps.

22   Meanwhile Beowulf has been leaning on his elbow, watching the fight, for he alone had been too angry,—"bulging in his mind" the poet puts it—to go to sleep. We are told he has been studying his opponent's tactics. Grendel tries to seize him, too, but Beowulf clamps an armlock on the monster and starts smashing up the

furniture with him, "tearing down the mead-benches," for this is a drinking hall. Grendel tries to break loose, but cannot do so until he tears his own arm out of the socket, or gets it torn out for him, and disappears into the night. In the morning the Geats find a neighboring pool, Grendel's supposed home, stained with blood. The Spear Danes spend the day rejoicing and that night occupy the great hall again.

23   The next morning Beowulf, sleeping in guest quarters, is routed out early. A young Spear Dane has been slaughtered, supposedly by Grendel's mother, and the king, Hrothgar, is distraught. Beowulf prepares at once to go after the mother, but takes time off to give the king some good advice, saying, "Sorrow not, Prudent One. Better it is for anyone to avenge his friend than to mourn him much." He dives to the bottom of the lake, finds a cave with a fire in it, Grendel's body, and the furious mother herself. Though he had refused to use weapons on Grendel, his chivalry does not prevent him from burying his sword in the lady, nor does hospitality prevent the mother, in her hot blooded and magical wrath, from melting his sword for him. That leaves him protected only by his armor, and he is getting the worst of the fight until he sees an old sword hanging on the walls, "giants' work," with which he finishes off the old lady, breaking her "bonehinges."

24   In the original this is an exciting story, if the reader is not too skeptical, and presumably the Anglo-Saxons for whom it was composed, hearing it with the night howling outside, would not have been skeptical. But we can scarcely avoid asking why Beowulf allowed Grendel to eat his good friend (the poet's explanation that he wished to observe the brute's tactics seems too lame), how the fire was getting on under the lake, and why the sportsmanlike Beowulf attacked the old lady without a qualm and with the best sword he could get. The answers are rooted in the folkloristic background of the story. They were presumably not known to the Anglo-Saxon poet, who was retelling a story which he supposed to be history, but modern scholarship has found them out.[2]

25   This portion of the epic shows strong resemblances to a group of Germanic folktales of the Bear's Son (*Beowulf* means bee wolf, that is, bear), which are in turn a form of the tale of the Great Fool, the fellow who does not know his own strength, so that when he is told to mow the "upper field" mows the mountain clean of its

[2] I am relying especially upon the work of Friedrich Panzer as revised by William Witherle Lawrence, *Beowulf and Epic Tradition,* (Cambridge, Mass.: 1928) The analogues cited below are excerpted in Lawrence, pp. 179–203; see also *Beowulf and the Fight at Finnsburgh* (New York: 1922), 3d. ed., with supplements (1950).

forests. Beowulf was the miraculous son of a polar bear, a totemic god, and he thus had cause to boast that he had more strength in his handgrip than any other man living and was the world's champion swimmer, which he also boasted. His exploits in the Grendel fights are paralleled in various other northern accounts, but we may as well use that in the Icelandic *Saga of Grettir the Strong* (also called the *Gretissaga*).

26   We are told that Beowulf was thought in his youth to be backward, and so it was with Grettir, at least mentally. A hugh oaf, he meant well, but if he lost his temper, always somebody was dead. Even in tolerant Iceland this habit irritated the neighbors. Grettir was exported to Norway, where he got a job with a widow and tried to behave. Christmas came and the widow wanted him to go to church. He declined. She urged him, and when he still refused, begged him, and finally explained why. It seemed that evil spirits were at work in her home. One Christmas Eve her husband had disappeared, the next Christmas Eve the hired man, and in fact she had hired Grettir because none of the local people would work for her.

27   Now Grettir knew he was not going to church. He had been spoiling for a fight for months, and here was one. About midnight a huge she-troll came in, and Grettir grappled with her, making the place a shambles until she dragged him outside, taking the door-frame with them as they went. She snaked him to a river cliff, where they wrestled until Grettir cut off her arm with his knife. She plunged into the waterfall and he went home to bed.

28   By daylight Grettir went after her, saw that there was a cave under the waterfall—there always is, more or less, because the water dashes backward as well as forward when it strikes—and reached the cave by diving under the waterfall. A fire was burning there, and by its light Grettir saw a giant thrusting at him with a pike. Grettir whacked off the head of the pike, and when he saw the giant reach for a sword hanging on the wall he disembowelled the brute. He recovered some treasure and the bones of his predecessors.

29   Now the problems we posed ourselves a few paragraphs back clear up at once. In the first place we should not be much perturbed about variations in sex among these trolls; sex is notably inconstant among supernatural monsters. The cave was not at the bottom of a lake, but under a waterfall, the favorite home of trolls. Grendel and his dam, in the folktale original of the episode, had been trolls. Beowulf does not engage Grendel at once because he was the Great Fool, the third son who essayed an adventure, and he had to give his older brothers (reduced from two to one) the first chance at the

adventure. Grendel's mother was protected by all sorts of magic and charms; her sword-melting blood would protect her from all but the one sword with which she could be killed, which hung on her own wall, that is, it was her external soul.

30   Thus the first half of *Beowulf* is a handsome retelling, with contemporary coloring, of an old folktale of the Bear's Son. Even more obviously, the second half is a retelling of the famous story of the hero who slays a fire-breathing dragon and brings a curse upon his people by acquiring the cursed gold that the dragon has been brooding over. This is an extremely widely spread tale, best known to modern music lovers in Wagner's version of Siegfried and Fafnir in *The Ring Cycle*. Of course *Beowulf* is very much more than a refurbishing of old popular tales. It is a highly wrought work of art, one of the great poems of all time, in whatever language one seeks great literary monuments, and in its day it was probably philosophy and theology as well. The author was a Christian, probably not a priest, more likely a court poet, but he was a cultured man as culture was reckoned in England in the seventh or eighth century—the poem cannot be dated exactly—and he would have been familiar with the widely held belief that God revealed his truth by levels of meanings. The poet was probably not aware that in Beowulf he was dealing with a degraded minor mythical deity; he must have believed he was honoring a national hero, a sort of George Washington of the Angles; and a modern scholar can scarely doubt that the poet saw Beowulf as a Christ figure. In fact, the poet quite probably thought that was the reason the story was particularly worth telling, that Beowulf on a historical level was Christ on another level. . . . One might notice that when Beowulf killed Grendel and his dam he was overcoming the powers of sin and evil—Grendel was of the brood of Cain, and his family heritage probably included miscegenation with devils—and in dying by the blasting flame of a hell-breathing dragon Beowulf was saving his people as Christ had saved mankind by dying on the cross. . . .

31   What does it profit us to know that behind *Beowulf* skulk old folktales, ancient time out of mind? Artistically, very little, except that a few inconsistencies are accounted for; the Anglo-Saxon poet was doing his best to make plausible story elements which he had to respect, but which made very little sense to him. To the historian of art, especially literary art, this knowledge is extremely valuable, because it shows us that *Beowulf* was built up by slow processes from primitive folktale to artistic epic. Accordingly, the critic will suspect that the *Odyssey,* the *Ramayana,* the *Chanson de Roland,* and a good many other epics and epic-like tales have grown in the

same way. . . . What good does it do us to know that beneath the polished exterior, the brooding horror of *Beowulf* is a scramble of old folktale?

32　　At least this, the knowledge provides us, that when we can isolate what the Anglo-Saxons had to work with we can see more clearly what they did. Presumably poet after poet reworked the old tales concerning dragons and bear's sons, reshaping them nearer to their own desires and the desires of their hearers, until only the mis-articulated bones of the original remained, and the character of the story has become the character of the Anglo-Saxons themselves. And what was this character? It is revealed pretty clearly, apparently, in *Beowulf*, but we can pause for only a few glimpses of it here.

33　　Notice, for instance, Beowulf's remark to Hrothgar, quoted above, "Sorrow not, Prudent One. Better it is for any man to avenge his friend than to mourn him much." These were men who did things, but they did them knowing that man's fate is sure and probably soon, that the light of the fire can cast its cheer but a little way, and outside are always the misty slopes and the Grendels of the world. And this same man would take a grim delight in brooding horror—and one suspects that that is one reason he is a hero, that he could delight in the macabre. When, before the first fight with Grendel, he offered to defend the hall he added, in effect, "I shall not cause you great inconvenience. If I don't cleanse your hall for you, I won't expect you to get me breakfast." He knew, and his audience knew why he would not need breakfast. He would have been devoured, "feet and hands." Then, on the second night, everyone is rejoicing, celebrating the death of Grendel. But the hearers of *Beowulf* (which must have been recited to listeners who knew the story as well as you know the story of the Christ child) would have anticipated that before morning Grendel's dam would continue the slaughter. And as if this were not enough, the poet makes clear that even a larger doom hangs over these people. He describes the great hall, and goes into raptures over its size and elegance, and then asks, "What could ever harm such a building?" Immediately he answers, "Unless, indeed, it should burn down." His audience knew that it had. The Spear Danes had been butchered in a terrible fight, during which their enemies burned the great hall Heorot over their heads. And the Geats, what of them? Doom hung over them, too, and everybody knew it. Beowulf died supposing he had won his people so much wealth that they could buy themselves out of any trouble. Instead, he had won them cursed gold, which would bring destruction to anyone who held it. Not long after that they fought the Swedes, and took refuge behind a lake; but the lake froze over, the Swedes came upon them, and wiped them out. The Geats do not appear again in history.

34   This is a far cry—and a moving, haunting one—from simpleminded Grettir and his she-troll, and the difference is presumably provided by the theological lesson, hinted at above, and the essential quality, the pervading spirit, or what you will, of our Germanic ancestors. It is a spirit, one notices, quite different from that observable in those other ancestors of ours, the Celts. Where the Celts loved gaity and exuberance the German gloried in a sense of impending gloom held off by the courage of man, man who recognized his own inadequacy, an inadequacy which he faced with heroic courage and a grim jest, grimly understated. Or, at least, so the Germanic hero appears in Germanic literature, for one must always remember that literary heroes may represent social ideals rather than social fact. The Celts had their sense of sadness, too, of course; the tales of *Dierdre* and of *Tristram and Isolde* are among the sad and beautiful stories of the world, but there is a difference between the deep moans of Dierdre and the haunting, light-struck gloom of *Beowulf.* Just what that difference is I shall not endeavor to express too exactly; it is all so evanescent that nobody could be expected to agree with me entirely, and for the moment I am interested in agreement.

35   My point is this, and it seems to me a clear one. People, including relatively primitive people, do take on characters of their own. This character may be difficult to describe, is never simple, is variously apparent and always shifting. And yet something very important is there. The Celts differed from the Germans, differed in tribal or national ways, even as individual Celts or Germans differed from each other. And these different ideas and attitudes, wherever they grew from, whether from race, climate, cultural borrowings, or whatever, have been deeply pervading in making us what we are, in determining what we did with our bodies, our brains, and our feelings.

Vocabulary

naive	endeavored	motifs
archetype	amorous	imperative
indulge	vile	inaccessible
oaf	miscegenation	skulk

Topics for Discussion

1. Certainly you remember some fairy tales from your child-hood. Reflecting upon these now, do you find more meaning in them than you once did?
2. Laird implies that the tales he recounts tell us something basic about humanity. What for you is that basic something?
3. Because of the proliferation of mass media, folktales have ceased to be a central source of entertainment in our culture. Do they survive, however, in any modified form? Explain.
4. Do you think that the principles of folklore study explained here could be effectively employed to study the culture of a large urban community or a small rural town?
5. If you were to make up a folktale reflecting the experience of your own cultural group, what might you say? Discuss this topic with other members of the class.

Rhetorical Considerations

1. Why does Laird begin the essay with a sentence written in the language of children? Do you think the essay is meant for specialists in folklore or for the general public? In this context, discuss the rhetorical stratagem in Laird's first sentence.
2. Analyze the structure and juxtaposition of Laird's sentences. What patterns do his larger sentences follow? Where and why does he use short sentences?
3. Does the writer reveal anything about himself in this essay—his background, major interests, attitudes toward history, scholarship, life?
4. Can you classify this essay as belonging to any single one of the four types—narration, description, exposition, argumentation? Or is it a combination?
5. Read the rhetorical analysis at the end of this section.

Needed—A Myth For Our Time

Ruth Whitney

Ruth Whitney (b. 1928) has edited Seventeen *magazine and is currently the editor of* Glamour.

1   A teen-age girl we know recently saw Bing Crosby in *Going My Way,* a 1944 movie, on television. She loved it. And the reason she loved it was, she said, because it was "realistic."

2   Realistic? Have you ever *seen Going My Way?* During the course of it, Bing Crosby, as a jaunty young priest, manages to straighten out a runaway teen-ager by teaching her to sing, turn the local gang into a boys' choir, straighten out crotchety old Father Fitzgibbon by getting him out on the golf course, pay off the mortgage on St. Dominic's by selling a song he has written (with the help of an old girl friend who happens to be a reigning star of the Metropolitan Opera), marry off the teen-age singer to the mortgage man's son—well, need we go on?

3   Charming, heartwarming, OK. But realistic is the precise word this girl used. And we know what she meant.

4   She sees a lot of movies. She loved *The Graduate, Bonnie and Clyde, Faces, Joanna.* But these films she didn't find "realistic." *Going My Way* she did.

5   "I don't mean it was true to life," she explained. "How often do priests write hit songs? I mean that people acted in ways that made sense. You could understand why they did what they did."

6   What she was getting at, although she didn't realize it, was that she found in this film an interweaving of myths—myths that our society once accepted and that we remember with nostalgia. Talent is always financially rewarded. Virtue always triumphs. A boy's best friend is his mother. The film makes all these points. You know exactly how everything is going to come out, and it's a reassuring feeling.

7   They don't make movies like *Going My Way* anymore. Perhaps because we don't have myths anymore. And this is a discomforting thought.

8   Myths are the stories that societies tell themselves to make the world make sense. They are not necessarily false. In fact, functioning myths are based on profound truths about the society that embraces them. (If not, they wouldn't function for long.) "A myth,"

says psychoanalyst Rollo May, ". . . is a description of a pattern of life . . . that carries the values for a society and gives a person the ability to handle anxiety, to face death, to deal with guilt. It gives him an identity."

9   Every civilization has had its myths. The Greeks explained their lives to themselves in terms of their gods. At the core of every great religion is a myth that has sustained the society it serves. There are secular myths, too. Our own Horatio Alger myth, the frontier myth, worked to sustain this country while it was growing. The workers'-paradise myth helped a lot to push the Soviet Union along from an agrarian civilization to a major power in fifty years. Nationalist myths, throughout history, have been powerful enough to persuade men to give up their lives in their name. The present American generation is the first in modern history to challenge in conspicuous numbers the nationalist myth—which is why their stance is emotionally outrageous to many of their elders.

10   We have rejected many of the myths of the past because they have little relevance to the present. Much of the chaos of contemporary society, the alienation and fragmentation we feel, is because, as Dr. May says, we've rejected the old myths and have no new ones to replace them.

11   There's no denying we miss them. How else to explain the pleasure of escaping into old movies on TV, whether it's Dick Powell and Ruby Keeler achieving stardom overnight on Broadway or the heroic gallantries of World War II. And if you think the frontier myth is dead, check the ratings of any of those hardy perennials, the TV Westerns.

12   Yet once we've switched off the set, these myths are of small comfort. They're just not convincing anymore.

13   At present, our one real, contemporary working myth is black power. The black power myth is, in essence, a revival of older American myths. In its community spirit and emphasis on do-it-yourself, it reflects the frontier spirit that built the West: in its emphasis on individual entrepreneurship, there are echoes of Horatio Alger. (And the militant stance is a new nationalistic myth.) This is a positive myth and can give great strength to the black community. But not the total community.

14   We haven't much going for us in terms of overall, unifying myths. (The current emphasis of our churches on secular affairs diminishes somewhat the emphasis on the mythic aspects of religion—although the powerful impact of Col. Borman's simple Christmas Eve message from the Apollo 8 makes one wonder if anything can diminish that particular myth.)

15   There have been, however, some beginning myths. There was the Camelot myth that died with the Kennedys. There was the hippie myth of love, communal living and doing your own thing—but that had a built-in self-destruction: drugs. There was the student-revolution myth—that mounting the barricades will change the world. That myth worked, to a degree, inside the university walls; but outside the university walls it lost its power, because in our open society, with its diffusion of authority, there's no focal point of attack, no one logical point at which to erect the barricades.

16   Yet, looking at all these beginning myths, a pattern emerges. Myths happen because society needs them, and these myths provide lots of clues as to what it is we're looking for. We want a sense of social purpose, a sense of belonging, a sense of being able as individuals to change things for the better. That was the appeal of the student-revolution myth. We want to love each other. That's the appeal of the hippie myth. And we want to feel that somebody, not only up there but down in Washington, likes us. That was the magic of the Camelot myth.

17   These myths didn't take root in themselves. But the elements that gave them their appeal are worth pondering and hanging onto. The needs that they point out are a tall order for any society to fulfill. However, nothing's impossible; knowing what you want is a big step toward getting it. And that's the thing about myths. Believing in them is the biggest part of making them happen.

Vocabulary

entrepreneurship   barricades   focal point
sustained

Topics for Discussion

1. Whitney defines myths as "the stories that societies tell themselves to make the world make sense." Is this a better definition than the one she quotes by Rollo May? Why?

2. Have you seen a movie lately that you would call "realistic"? Why would you call it realistic?

3. Whitney says that "at the core of every great religion is a myth that has sustained the society it serves." If this is true, what is the myth at the core of Christianity? of Judaism? of Islam?

4. The black power myth is a revival of old myths, according to Whitney. What are these myths? Do you agree with this analysis?

5. We may have rejected many of our old myths, but what will we substitute for them? Can you cite a really new myth that serves our present need for one?

6. Whitney mentions some "beginning" myths. What are they? Do you agree with her that they are just myths?

Rhetorical Considerations

1. What is your reaction to Whitney's plot summary of the movie *Going My Way*? How does this reaction prepare you for the rest of the essay?

2. Whitney is careful to define her terms. How clear and useful are her definitions?

3. How would you characterize the sentence style of this essay—formal or casual? How well does the style fit the subject?

4. Is Whitney's use of short, undeveloped paragraphs, and of sentence fragments, appropriate?

The Myth of Sisyphus

Albert Camus

Albert Camus (1913–1960) was a noted French existentialist novelist, essayist, and playwright whose works include The Stranger, The Fall, *and* The Rebel. *He was awarded the Nobel Prize for literature in 1957.*

1   The gods had condemned Sisyphus to ceaselessly rolling a rock to the top of a mountain, whence the stone would fall back of its own weight. They had thought with some reason that there is no more dreadful punishment than futile and hopeless labor.

2   If one believes Homer, Sisyphus was the wisest and most prudent of mortals. According to another tradition, however, he was

disposed to practice the profession of highwayman. I see no contradiction in this. Opinions differ as to the reasons why he became the futile laborer of the underworld. To begin with, he is accused of a certain levity in regard to the gods. He stole their secrets. Ægina, the daughter of Æsopus, was carried off by Jupiter. The father was shocked by that disappearance and complained to Sisyphus. He, who knew of the abduction, offered to tell about it on condition that Æsopus would give water to the citadel of Corinth. To the celestial thunderbolts he preferred the benediction of water. He was punished for this in the underworld. Homer tells us also that Sisyphus had put Death in chains. Pluto could not endure the sight of his deserted, silent empire. He dispatched the god of war, who liberated Death from the hands of her conqueror.

3   It is said also that Sisyphus, being near to death, rashly wanted to test his wife's love. He ordered her to cast his unburied body into the middle of the public square. Sisyphus woke up in the underworld. And there, annoyed by an obedience so contrary to human love, he obtained from Pluto permission to return to earth in order to chastise his wife. But when he had seen again the face of this world, enjoyed water and sun, warm stones and the sea, he no longer wanted to go back to the infernal darkness. Recalls, signs of anger, warnings were of no avail. Many years more he lived facing the curve of the gulf, the sparkling sea, and the smiles of earth. A decree of the gods was necessary. Mercury came and seized the impudent man by the collar and, snatching him from his joys, led him forcibly back to the underworld, where his rock was ready for him.

4   You have already grasped that Sisyphus is the absurd hero. He *is*, as much through his passions as through his torture. His scorn of the gods, his hatred of death, and his passion for life won him that unspeakable penalty in which the whole being is exerted toward accomplishing nothing. This is the price that must be paid for the passions of this earth. Nothing is told us about Sisyphus in the underworld. Myths are made for the imagination to breathe life into them. As for this myth, one sees merely the whole effort of a body straining to raise the huge stone, to roll it and push it up a slope a hundred times over; one sees the face screwed up, the cheek tight against the stone, the shoulder bracing the clay-covered mass, the foot wedging it, the fresh start with arms outstretched, the wholly human security of two earth-clotted hands. At the very end of his long effort measured by skyless space and time without depth, the purpose is achieved. Then Sisyphus watches the stone rush down in a few moments toward that lower world whence he will have to push it up again toward the summit. He goes back down to the plain.

5   It is during that return, that pause, that Sisyphus interests me. A face that toils so close to stones is already stone itself! I see that man going back down with a heavy yet measured step toward the torment of which he will never know the end. That hour like a breathing-space which returns as surely as his suffering, that is the hour of consciousness. At each of those moments when he leaves the heights and gradually sinks toward the lairs of the gods, he is superior to his fate. He is stronger than his rock.

6   If this myth is tragic, that is because its hero is conscious. Where would his torture be, indeed, if at every step the hope of succeeding upheld him? The workman of today works every day in his life at the same tasks, and this fate is no less absurd. But it is tragic only at the rare moments when it becomes conscious. Sisyphus, proletarian of the gods, powerless and rebellious, knows the whole extent of his wretched condition: it is what he thinks of during his descent. The lucidity that was to constitute his torture at the same time crowns his victory. There is no fate that cannot be surmounted by scorn.

7   If the descent is thus sometimes performed in sorrow, it can also take place in joy. This word is not too much. Again I fancy Sisyphus returning toward his rock, and the sorrow was in the beginning. When the images of earth cling too tightly to memory, when the call of happiness becomes too insistent, it happens that melancholy rises in man's heart: this is the rock's victory, this is the rock itself. The boundless grief is too heavy to bear. These are our nights of Gethsemane. But crushing truths perish from being acknowledged. Thus, Œdipus at the outset obeys fate without knowing it. But from the moment he knows, his tragedy begins. Yet at the same moment, blind and desperate, he realizes that the only bond linking him to the world is the cool hand of a girl. Then a tremendous remark rings out: "Despite so many ordeals, my advanced age and the nobility of my soul make me conclude that all is well." Sophocles' Œdipus, like Dostoevsky's Kirilov, thus gives the recipe for the absurd victory. Ancient wisdom confirms modern heroism.

8   One does not discover the absurd without being tempted to write a manual of happiness. "What! by such narrow ways—?" There is but one world, however. Happiness and the absurd are two sons of the same earth. They are inseparable. It would be a mistake to say that happiness necessarily springs from the absurd discovery. It happens as well that the feeling of the absurd springs from happiness. "I conclude that all is well," says Œdipus, and that remark is sacred. It echoes in the wild and limited universe of man. It teaches that all is not, has not been, exhausted. It drives out of this world a

god who had come into it with dissatisfaction and a preference for futile sufferings. It makes of fate a human matter, which must be settled among men.

9   All Sisyphus' silent joy is contained therein. His fate belongs to him. His rock is his thing. Likewise, the absurd man, when he contemplates his torment, silences all the idols. In the universe suddenly restored to its silence, the myriad wondering little voices of the earth rise up. Unconscious, secret calls, invitations from all the faces, they are the necessary reverse and price of victory. There is no sun without shadow, and it is essential to know the night. The absurd man says yes and his effort will henceforth be unceasing. If there is a personal fate, there is no higher destiny, or at least there is but one which he concludes is inevitable and despicable. For the rest, he knows himself to be the master of his days. At that subtle moment when man glances backward over his life. Sisyphus returning toward his rock, in that slight pivoting he contemplates that series of unrelated actions which becomes his fate, created by him, combined under his memory's eye and soon sealed by his death. Thus, convinced of the wholly human origin of all that is human, a blind man eager to see who knows that the night has no end, he is still on the go. The rock is still rolling.

10   I leave Sisyphus at the foot of the mountain! One always finds one's burden again. But Sisyphus teaches the higher fidelity that negates the gods and raises rocks. He too concludes that all is well. This universe henceforth without a master seems to him neither sterile nor futile. Each atom of that stone, each mineral flake of that night-filled mountain, in itself forms a world. The struggle itself toward the heights is enough to fill a man's heart. One must imagine Sisyphus happy.

Vocabulary

futile	levity	abduction
pivoting	fidelity	negates
henceforth		

Topics for Discussion

1. Sisyphus is a romantic, mythical figure as well as an absurd one, and for that reason it is very difficult not to personally identify with him. In what ways do you identify with him? What does

Sisyphus's rock represent for you? Do you think Camus's mention of the modern worker is accurate?

2. It has been asserted that recognition of the human condition leads to a tragic sense of life; yet Camus says that we must imagine Sisyphus happy—and that all is well in the world. Can you explain this contradiction?

3. Camus writes in another place, "There is but one truly serious philosophical problem, and that is suicide." How does this statement relate to what you have read of Sisyphus?

4. Can you define what Camus means by "absurd"?

Rhetorical Considerations

1. Myths are really metaphors for human experience, but in this essay a myth is used as a metaphor for rhetorical purposes. Is Camus successful in his attempt? Can you think of another myth available for use in a similar way?

2. Examine point of view in this essay. Camus flows back and forth between a rather impersonal "If one believes" and a very personal "I." Would the essay have been better had he written it strictly in either the first or third person?

3. Examine Camus's sentences for structure and juxtaposition. You will notice that many sentences are less than fifteen words long, each containing a philosophical nugget. Camus builds with these nuggets, especially in the essay's final paragraph, as a bricklayer builds a wall. Is his edifice as solid as the artisan's?

4. When does myth become cliché? Why, apart from subject matter, is Sisyphus a better choice as a methaphorical vehicle than David and Goliath?

The Decline of the West

Walter Lippmann

Walter Lippman (1889–1974) was a Pulitzer-Prize-winning columnist who published numerous books and who founded the New Republic *magazine.*

1   What I am going to say is the result of a prolonged exposure to the continuing crisis of our Western society—to the crisis of the democratic governments and of free institutions during the wars and revolutions of the twentieth century. Now it does not come easily to anyone who, like me, has breathed the soft air of the world before the wars that began in 1914—who has known a world that was not divided and frightened and full of hate—it does not come easily to such a man to see clearly and to measure coolly the times we live in. The scale and scope and the complexity of our needs are without any precedent in our experience, and indeed, we may fairly say, in all human experience.

2   In 1900 men everywhere on earth acknowledged, even when they resented, the leadership of the Western nations. It was taken for granted that the liberal democracies were showing the way toward the good life in the good society, and few had any doubts of the eventual, but certain, progress of all mankind toward more democracy and a wider freedom.

3   The only question was when—the question was never whether—the less fortunate and the more backward peoples of the world would have learned to use not only the technology of the West but also the political institutions of the West. All would soon be learning to decide the issues which divided them by free and open and rational discussion; they would soon learn how to conduct free and honest elections, to administer justice. Mankind would come to accept and comprehend the idea that all men are equally under the laws and all men must have the equal protection of the laws.

4   At the beginning of this century the acknowledged model of a new government, even in Russia, was a liberal democracy in the British or the French or the American style. Think what has happened to the Western world and to its ideas and ideals during the forty years since the World Wars began. The hopes that men then took for granted are no longer taken for granted. The institutions and the way of life which we have inherited, and which we cherish, have lost their paramount, their almost undisputed, hold upon the allegiance and the affections and the hopes of the peoples of the earth. They are no longer universally accepted as being the right way toward the good life on this earth. They are fiercely challenged abroad; they are widely doubted and they are dangerously violated even here at home.

5   During this half century the power of the Western democratic nations has been declining. Their influence upon the destiny of the great masses of people has been shrinking. We are the heirs of the proudest tradition of government in the history of mankind. Yet we

no longer find ourselves talking now—as we did before the First World War—about the progress of liberal democracy among the awakening multitudes. We are talking now about the defense and the survival of liberal democracy in its contracted area.

6   We are living in an age of disorder and upheaval. Though the United States has grown powerful and rich, we know in our hearts that we have become, at the same time, insecure and anxious. Our people enjoy an abundance of material things, such as no large community of men has ever known. But our people are not happy about their position or confident about their future. For we are not sure whether our responsibilities are not greater than our power and our wisdom.

7   We have been raised to the first place in the leadership of the Western society at a time when the general civilization of the West has suffered a spectacular decline and is gravely threatened. We, who have become so suddenly the protecting and the leading power of that civilization, are not clear and united among ourselves about where we are going and how we should deal with our unforeseen responsibilities, our unwanted mission, our unexpected duties.

8   It is an awe-inspiring burden that we find ourselves compelled to bear. We have suddenly acquired responsibilities for which we were not prepared—for which we are not now prepared—for which, I am very much afraid, we are not now preparing ourselves.

9   We have had, and probably we must expect for a long time to have, dangerous and implacable enemies. But if we are to revive and recover, and are to go forward again, we must not look for the root of the trouble in our adversaries. We must look for it in ourselves. We must rid ourselves of the poison of self-pity. We must have done with the falsehood that all would be well were it not that we are the victims of wicked and designing men.

10   In 1914, when the decline of the West began, no one had heard of Lenin, Trotsky, Mussolini, Hitler, Stalin, and Mao Tse-tung. We have not fallen from our pre-eminence because we have been attacked. It would be much truer to say, and it is nobler to say it, that we have been attacked because our capacity to cope with our tasks had begun to decline.

11   We shall never have the spirit to revive and to recover so long as we try to console ourselves by shutting our eyes, and by wringing our hands and beating our breasts and filling the air with complaints that we have been weakened because we were attacked, and that we have been making mistakes because we were betrayed.

12   We must take the manly view, which is that the failure of the Western democracies during this catastrophic half of the twentieth

century is due to the failings of the democratic peoples. They have been attacked and brought down from their pre-eminence because they have lacked the clarity of purpose and the resolution of mind and of heart to cope with the accumulating disasters and disorders. They have lacked the clarity of purpose and the resolution of mind and of heart to prevent the wars that have ruined the West, to prepare for these wars they could not prevent, and, having won them at last after exorbitant sacrifice and at a ruinous cost, to settle those wars and to restore law and order upon the face of the globe.

Vocabulary

eventual   acknowledged   contracted
implacable

Topics for Discussion

1. What is "the continuing crisis of our Western society" that Lippmann mentions in the first paragraph?
2. According to Lippmann, in what ways is the West declining? How long has this decline been going on? What has caused the decline?
3. What is the "awe-inspiring burden" that the United States is compelled to bear? Do you agree that the United States must bear this burden? Do you agree that it is a burden?
4. Does Lippmann see any hope for the Western democracies?
5. What date does Lippmann give for the decline of the West? Why does he choose that date?

Rhetorical Considerations

1. In the first paragraph Lippmann begins by using the pronoun "I," but he ends the paragraph using the pronoun "we." Is there any significance to this shift?
2. How specifically and concretely does Lippmann present his argument that the West is declining?

3. This selection is a speech given by Lippmann. Does it read like a speech? What differentiates a speech from an essay to be read? Can you locate any of these differences here?

4. Does Lippmann leave some of his assumptions unsupported (see, for example, paragraph 6)?

5. Lippmann uses parallelism in paragraph 12. Why is this structure particularly appropriate for the conclusion of an essay?

Good English Ain't What We Thought

Sydney J. Harris

Sydney J. Harris is a newspaper columnist whose work is syndicated in a number of newspapers throughout the United States.

1   Lemme recommend a swell new book that has been in the works for 27 years and has just been finalized—no kidding—by the G. & C. Merriam Co. in Springfield, Mass.

2   It's Webster's Third New International Dictionary. Unabridged, and wordwise it's a gasser. In this new edition, it turns out that good English ain't what we thought it was at all—good English, man, is whatever is popular.

3   This is a nifty speak-as-you-go dictionary. Not like that moldy fig of a Second Edition, which tried to separate "standard English" from slang, bastardized formations, colloquialisms, and all the passing fads and fancies of spoken English.

4   This here edition is for the people, who decide how a language is going to be spoken, or misspoken. It's all relative, anyway; there are no rules or laws to language, just custom. So there's no point in yakking about "tradition" when Webster's Third offers up some juicy quotes from such authorities as Art Linkletter, Polly Adler, Willie Mays and Mickey Spillane.

5   If this column begins using the Third Edition as a reference source, instead of my old Oxford Dictionary, don't be surprised if I start playing footsie with 100,000 new words that have just been admitted to membership in the club. And if I make a boo-boo, just call me a schlemiel.

6   What's the point in any writer's trying to compose clear and graceful prose, to avoid solecisms, to maintain a sense of decorum and continuity in that magnificent instrument, the English language, if that peerless authority, Webster's Unabridged, surrenders abjectly to the permissive school of speech?

7   Relativism is the reigning philosophy of our day, in all fields. Not merely in language, but in ethics, in politics, in every field of human behavior. There is no right and wrong—it is all merely custom and superstition to believe so. If the majority behave a certain way, that is the way to behave. Popularity gives sanction to everything.

8   Our attitude toward language merely reflects our attitude toward more basic matters. It is not terribly important whether we use "ain't," or "like" instead of "as"—except as symptoms of a general decay in values. If everything is a matter of taste and preference and usage, then we are robbing ourselves of all righteous indignation against evil. For what is evil, in the modern canon, except somebody else's equally valid conception of "good"?

Vocabulary

colloquialism	schlemiel	solecism
decorum	continuity	

Topics for Discussion

1. What is the role of the dictionary according to Harris? How has *Webster's Third* failed to fill that role?

2. Why does Harris object to citing such people as Art Linkletter and Willie Mays in a dictionary? How does this objection fit in with his idea of what a dictionary should be?

3. Take your dictionary and look up the following words: *boo-boo, schlemiel, finalize, ain't, footsie.* Are any of them listed? Should such words be listed in a dictionary?

4. What do you think a dictionary is for? What do you use a dictionary for?

5. Do you agree or disagree with Harris's contention that *Webster's Third* is just another sign of decay in our society?

Rhetorical Considerations

1. What is Harris's main argument? What evidence does he cite to support his thesis? Is his argument based on fact or opinion?

2. What is the tone of this essay? How is this tone clearly indicated? Where does the tone shift in the essay? How is this shift clearly indicated? What is the purpose of this shift?

3. Are the paragraphs in the essay too brief and choppy? Could Harris have developed them to any greater length?

4. This essay is really in two parts, paragraphs 1–5 and 6–8. How do the two parts fit together? Which part do you find more effective?

The Library of Babel

Jorge Luis Borges

Jorge Luis Borges (1899-1974) is an Argentinian author who shared the International Pulitzer Prize with Samuel Beckett in 1961. His works include Antologia Personal *and* Labyrinths.

By this art you may contemplate the variation of the 23 letters . . .
The Anatomy of Melancholy,
part 2, sec. II, mem. IV

1   The universe (which others call the Library) is composed of an indefinite and perhaps infinite number of hexagonal galleries, with vast air shafts between, surrounded by very low railings. From any of the hexagons one can see, interminably, the upper and lower floors. The distribution of the galleries is invariable. Twenty shelves, five long shelves per side, cover all the sides except two; their height, which is the distance from floor to ceiling, scarcely exceeds that of a normal bookcase. One of the free sides leads to a narrow hallway which opens onto another gallery, identical to the first and to all the rest. To the left and right of the hallway there are two very small closets. In the first, one may sleep standing up; in the other, satisfy one's fecal necessities. Also through here passes a

spiral stairway, which sinks abysmally and soars upwards to remote distances. In the hallway there is a mirror which faithfully duplicates all appearances. Men usually infer from this mirror that the Library is not infinite (if it really were, why this illusory duplication?); I prefer to dream that its polished surfaces represent and promise the infinite . . . Light is provided by some spherical fruit which bear the name of lamps. There are two, transversally placed, in each hexagon. The light they emit is insufficient, incessant.

2   Like all men of the Library, I have traveled in my youth; I have wandered in search of a book, perhaps the catalogue of catalogues; now that my eyes can hardly decipher what I write, I am preparing to die just a few leagues from the hexagon in which I was born. Once I am dead, there will be no lack of pious hands to throw me over the railing; my grave will be the fathomless air; my body will sink endlessly and decay and dissolve in the wind generated by the fall, which is infinite. I say that the Library is unending. The idealists argue that the hexagonal rooms are a necessary form of absolute space or, at least, of our intuition of space. They reason that a triangular or pentagonal room is inconceivable. (The mystics claim that their ecstasy reveals to them a circular chamber containing a great circular book, whose spine is continuous and which follows the complete circle of the walls; but their testimony is suspect; their words, obscure. This cyclical book is God.) Let is suffice now for me to repeat the classic dictum. *The Library is a sphere whose exact center is any one of its hexagons and whose circumference is inaccessible.*

3   There are five shelves for each of the hexagon's walls; each shelf contains thirty-five books of uniform format; each book is of four hundred and ten pages; each page, of forty lines, each line, of some eighty letters which are black in color. There are also letters on the spine of each book; these letters do not indicate or prefigure what the pages will say. I know that this incoherence at one time seemed mysterious. Before summarizing the solution (whose discovery, in spite of its tragic projections, is perhaps the capital fact in history) I wish to recall a few axioms.

4   First: The Library exists *ab aeterno*. This truth, whose immediate corollary is the future eternity of the world, cannot be placed in doubt by any reasonable mind. Man, the imperfect librarian, may be the product of chance or of malevolent demiurgi; the universe, with its elegant endowment of shelves, of enigmatical volumes, of inexhaustible stairways for the traveler and latrines for the seated librarian, can only be the work of a god. To perceive the distance between the divine and the human, it is enough to compare

these crude wavering symbols which my fallible hand scrawls on the cover of a book, with the organic letters inside: punctual, delicate, perfectly black, inimitably symmetrical.

5   Second: *The orthographical symbols are twenty-five in number.*[1] This finding made it possible, three hundred years ago, to formulate a general theory of the Library and solve satisfactorily the problem which no conjecture had deciphered: the formless and chaotic nature of almost all the books. One which my father saw in a hexagon on circuit fifteen ninety-four was made up of the letters MCV, perversely repeated from the first line to the last. Another (very much consulted in this area) is a mere labyrinth of letters, but the next-to-last page says *Oh time thy pyramids.* This much is already known: for every sensible line of straightforward statement, there are leagues of senseless cacophonies, verbal jumbles and incoherences. (I know of an uncouth region whose librarians repudiate the vain and superstitious custom of finding a meaning in books and equate it with that of finding a meaning in dreams or in the chaotic lines of one's palm . . . They admit that the inventors of this writing imitated the twenty-five natural symbols, but maintain that this application is accidental and that the books signify nothing in themselves. This dictum, we shall see, is not entirely fallacious.)

6   For a long time it was believed that these impenetrable books corresponded to past or remote languages. It is true that the most ancient men, the first librarians, used a language quite different from the one we now speak; it is true that a few miles to the right the tongue is dialectal and that ninety floors farther up, it is incomprehensible. All this, I repeat, is true, but four hundred and ten pages of inalterable MCV's cannot correspond to any language, no matter how dialectal or rudimentary it may be. Some insinuated that each letter could influence the following one and that the value of MCV in the third line of page 71 was not the one the same series may have in another position on another page, but this vague thesis did not prevail. Others thought of cryptographs; generally, this conjecture has been accepted, though not in the sense in which it was formulated by its originators.

7   Five hundred years ago, the chief of an upper hexagon[2] came

[1] The original manuscript does not contain digits or capital letters. The punctuation has been limited to the comma and the period. These two signs, the space and the twenty-two letters of the alphabet are the twenty-five symbols considered sufficient by this unknown author. (*Editor's note.*)

[2] Before, there was a man for every three hexagons. Suicide and pulmonary diseases have destroyed that proportion. A memory of unspeakable melancholy: at times I have traveled for many nights through corridors and along polished stairways without finding a single librarian.

upon a book as confusing as the others, but which had nearly two pages of homogeneous lines. He showed his find to a wandering decoder who told him the lines were written in Portuguese; others said they were Yiddish. Within a century, the language was established: a Samoyedic Lithuanian dialect of Guarani, with classical Arabian inflections. The content was also deciphered: some notions of combinative analysis, illustrated with examples of variation with unlimited repetition. These examples made it possible for a librarian of genius to discover the fundamental law of the Library. This thinker observed that all the books, no matter how diverse they might be, are made up of the same elements: the space, the period, the comma, the twenty-two letters of the alphabet. He also alleged a fact which travelers have confirmed: *In the vast Library there are no two identical books.* From these two incontrovertible premises he deduced that the Library is total and that its shelves register all the possible combinations of the twenty-odd orthographical symbols (a number which, though extremely vast, is not infinite): in other words, all that it is given to express, in all languages. Everything: the minutely detailed history of the future, the archangels' autobiographies, the faithful catalogue of the Library, thousands and thousands of false catalogues, the demonstration of the fallacy of those catalogues, the demonstration of the fallacy of the true catalogue, the Gnostic gospel of Basilides, the commentary on that gospel, the commentary on the commentary on that gospel, the true story of your death, the translation of every book in all languages, the interpolations of every book in all books.

8   When it was proclaimed that the Library contained all books, the first impression was one of extravagant happiness. All men felt themselves to be the masters of an intact and secret treasure. There was no personal or world problem whose eloquent solution did not exist in some hexagon. The universe was justified, the universe suddenly usurped the unlimited dimensions of hope. At that time a great deal was said about the Vindications: books of apology and prophecy which vindicated for all time the acts of every man in the universe and retained prodigious arcana for his future. Thousands of the greedy abandoned their sweet native hexagons and rushed up the stairways, urged on by the vain intention of finding their Vindication. These pilgrims disputed in the narrow corridors, proffered dark curses, strangled each other on the divine stairways, flung the deceptive books into the air shafts, met their death cast down in a similar fashion by the inhabitants of remote regions. Others went mad . . . The Vindications exist (I have seen two which refer to persons of the future, to persons who perhaps are not

imaginary) but the searchers did not remember that the possibility of a man's finding his Vindication, or some treacherous variation thereof, can be computed as zero.

9   At that time it was also hoped that a clarification of humanity's basic mysteries—the origin of the Library and of time—might be found. It is verisimilar that these grave mysteries could be explained in words: if the language of philosophers is not sufficient, the multiform Library will have produced the unprecedented language required, with its vocabularies and grammars. For four centuries now men have exhausted the hexagons . . . There are official searchers, *inquisitors*. I have seen the performance of their function: they always arrive extremely tired from their journeys; they speak of a broken stairway which almost killed them; they talk with the librarian of galleries and stairs; sometimes they pick up the nearest volume and leaf through it, looking for infamous words. Obviously, no one expects to discover anything.

10   As was natural, this inordinate hope was followed by an excessive depression. The certitude that some shelf in some hexagon held precious books and that these precious books were inaccessible, seemed almost intolerable. A blasphemous sect suggested that the searches should cease and that all men should juggle letters and symbols until they constructed, by an improbable gift of chance, these canonical books. The authorities were obliged to issue severe orders. The sect disappeared, but in my childhood I have seen old men who, for long periods of time, would hide in the latrines with some metal disks in a forbidden dice cup and feebly mimic the divine disorder.

11   Others, inversely, believed that is was fundamental to eliminate useless works. They invaded the hexagons, showed credentials which were not always false, leafed through a volume with displeasure and condemned whole shelves: their hygienic, ascetic furor caused the senseless perdition of millions of books. Their name is execrated, but those who deplore the "treasures" destroyed by this frenzy neglect two notable facts. One: the Library is so enormous that any reduction of human origin is infinitesimal. The other: every copy is unique, irreplaceable, but (since the Library is total) there are always several hundred thousand imperfect facsimiles: works which differ only in a letter or a comma. Counter to general opinion, I venture to suppose that the consequences of the Purifiers' depredations have been exaggerated by the horror these fanatics produced. They were urged on by the delirium of trying to reach the books in the Crimson Hexagon: books whose format is smaller than usual, all-powerful, illustrated and magical.

12   We also know of another superstition of that time: that of the Man of the Book. On some shelf in some hexagon (men reasoned) there must exist a book which is the formula and perfect compendium *of all the rest:* some librarian has gone through it and he is analogous to a god. In the language of this zone vestiges of this remote functionary's cult still persist. Many wandered in search of Him. For a century they exhausted in vain the most varied areas. How could one locate the venerated and secret hexagon which housed Him? Someone proposed a regressive method: To locate book A, consult first a book B which indicates A's position; to locate book B, consult first a book C, and so on to infinity . . . In adventures such as these, I have squandered and wasted my years. It does not seem unlikely to me that there is a total book on some shelf of the universe;[3] I pray to the unknown gods that a man—just one, even though it were thousands of years ago!—may have examined and read it. If honor and wisdom and happiness are not for me, let them be for others. Let heaven exist, though my place be in hell. Let me be outraged and annihilated, but for one instant, in one being, let Your enormous Library be justified. The impious maintain that nonsense is normal in the Library and that the reasonable (and even humble and pure coherence) is an almost miraculous exception. They speak (I know) of the "feverish Library whose chance volumes are constantly in danger of changing into others and affirm, negate and confuse everything like a delirious divinity." These words, which not only denounce the disorder but exemplify it as well, notoriously prove their authors' abominable taste and desperate ignorance. In truth, the Library includes all verbal structures, all variations of absolute nonsense. It is useless to observe that the best volume of the many hexagons under my administration is entitled *The Combed Thunderclap* and another *The Plaster Cramp* and another *Axaxaxas mlö.* These phrases, at first glance incoherent, can no doubt be justified in a cryptographical or allegorical manner; such a justification is verbal and, *ex hypothesi,* already figures in the Library. I cannot combine some characters

dhcmrlchtdj

which the divine Library has not foreseen and which in one of its secret tongues do not contain a terrible meaning. No one can articulate a syllable which is not filled with tenderness and fear, which is

---

[3] I repeat: it suffices that a book be possible for it to exist. Only the impossible is excluded. For example: no book can be a ladder, although no doubt there are books which discuss and negate and demonstrate this possibility and others whose structure corresponds to that of a ladder.

not, in one of these languages, the powerful name of a god. To speak is to fall into tautology. This wordy and useless epistle already exists in one of the thirty volumes of the five shelves of one of the innumerable hexagons—and its refutation as well. (An *n* number of possible languages use the same vocabulary; in some of them, the symbol *library* allows the correct definition *a ubiquitous and lasting system of hexagonal galleries,* but *library* is *bread* or *pyramid* or anything else, and these seven words which define it have another value. You who read me, are You sure of understanding my language?)

13   The methodical task of writing distracts me from the present state of men. The certitude that everything has been written negates us or turns us into phantoms. I know of districts in which the young men prostrate themselves before books and kiss their pages in a barbarous manner, but they do not know how to decipher a single letter. Epidemics, heretical conflicts, peregrinations which inevitably degenerate into banditry, have decimated the population. I believe I have mentioned the suicides, more and more frequent with the years. Perhaps my old age and fearfulness deceive me, but I suspect that the human species—the unique species—is about to be extinguished, but the Library will endure: illuminated, solitary, infinite, perfectly motionless, equipped with precious volumes, useless, incorruptible, secret.

14   I have just written the word "infinite." I have not interpolated this adjective out of rhetorical habit; I say that it is not illogical to think that the world is infinite. Those who judge it to be limited postulate that in remote places the corridors and stairways and hexagons can conceivably come to an end—which is absurd. Those who imagine it to be without limit forget that the possible number of books does have such a limit. I venture to suggest this solution to the ancient problem: *The Library is unlimited and cyclical.* If an eternal traveler were to cross it in any direction, after centuries he would see that the same volumes were repeated in the same disorder (which, thus repeated, would be an order: the Order). My solitude is gladdened by this elegant hope.[4]

Translated by J.E.I.

[4] Letizia Alvarez de Toledo has observed that this vast Library is useless: rigorously speaking, *a single volume* would be sufficient, a volume of ordinary format, printed in nine or ten point type, containing an infinite number of infinitely thin leaves. (In the early seventeenth century, Cavalieri said that all solid bodies are the superimposition of an infinite number of planes.) The handling of this silky vade mecum would not be convenient: each apparent page would unfold into other analogous ones; the inconceivable middle page would have no reverse.

Vocabulary

hexagonal	interminably	invariable
fecal	abysmally	incessant
pentagonal	inconceivable	prefigure
incoherence	malevolent	fallible
cacophonies	uncouth	dictum
dialectal	inalterable	cryptographs
Yiddish	vindications	apology
sect	mimic	hygienic
ascetic	perdition	infinitesimal
facsimiles	depredations	venerated
regressive	annihilated	impious
abominable	peregrinations	incorruptible
elegant	vade mecum	

Topics for Discussion

1. What do you think the Library stands for? Is Borges's construction totally imaginary or does there exist a phenomenon like the Library? What is that phenomenon?

2. Why do none of the inquisitors ever expect to discover anything? Does Borges actually mean "anything of significance?" What would he take to be significant?

3. Why have suicides increased in the Library as time has passed? What basic cause might there be for unhappiness in the Library, what cause for happiness? Why does the persona of the story ultimately seem fulfilled?

4. Why does Borges make the fixtures of the Library so spartan?

5. Why does Borges include a mirror on each floor of the Library?

Rhetorical Considerations

1. Borges's story is a model of neat, tight narrative prose, suggesting correspondences with mathematics and music. Can you find places in the story where Borges seems for a moment to depart from his main course? What happens when he does this?

2. This story contains many good models of descriptive writing, especially in the beginning. Select what you think are the best descriptive passages and analyze them. Do the descriptive passages relate in any way to the central idea of the story? Why does not Borges make greater mention of color?

3. Is this story better for being told in the first person rather than by an omniscient narrator? Why?

4. What is the philosophical argument of this story? Why is fictional narrative appropriate for Borges's ideas?

Rhetorical Analysis

Charlton Laird: Folk Roots of Civilization—And Thereby Hangs a Tale

Imagine yourself standing outside the entrance to a very special kind of garden, one made entirely out of ten-foot-high hedgerows, each interlocking with another to form a complex series of pathways leading either nowhere or to the center—one of Borges's labyrinths, a maze, like the "buried treasure" puzzles you worked out in the back of comic books as a kid. You enter the garden and walk about leisurely for five minutes, choosing paths at random, turning new corners all the while, refreshingly at your ease. Then you stop—you must stop because you have reached a dead end not yet the center. The garden is more complexly constructed than you had thought; you must go with greater care and closer attention to reach the middle. When you finally arrive there, you find a tower, and you climb to its top. Surveying the garden from this vantage point, you discover its symmetry. You see that the pathways in the various sections repeat one another almost as if each section *meant* something, that each section interlocks with another to form a symmetrical whole. You observe now a great complex unity where once you entered a simple garden gate.

Professor Laird's essay "Folk Roots of Civilization—And Thereby Hangs a Tale" is similar in construction to our garden. The beginning is deceptively simple; the main going is quite complicated, forcing you to pay attention; and at the end, everything fits together neatly.

Let's begin at the beginning. "Once upon a time there was a wicked old witch. . . ." The language here is that of a child, an invitation to simplicity.[1] As you wander on through the garden, the paths twist and turn just a bit at first. Laird refers to Portia. You hesitate, but you have heard of her, as a freshman in high

[1] Professor Laird himself has remarked about a similar sentence in another of his essays, an essay from which several of the ideas in this analysis are taken. See "Goldilocks and the Three or More Rhetorics" in *And Gladly Teche: Notes on Instructing The Natives in the Native Tongue* by Charlton Laird. Englewood Cliffs, N.J.: Prentice-Hall, 1970.

school when you read *The Merchant of Venice,* and you've of course heard of the Brothers Grimm. But who are these Fellows of Finnish Folklore who write books with titles you can't pronounce? Laird protests that he still speaks in oversimplifications, but you did not bargain for this—an exposition of critical method in Folklore Study—when you began with "Once upon a time."

Perhaps at this point you get a notion to put the essay aside—it is not exactly light reading. But you give Professor Laird the benefit of the doubt. You decide to continue for one more paragraph in hope of finding something less complicated. Behold, you read, "A good woman had a jealous husband. . . ." This time Laird tells the whole tale, in summary form, but fast paced and exciting. Then he says something about the tale, separating the essential elements from the accidental, charting its origins and appearance throughout various lands at different times. Thus the strategy continues through the essay. "Let me tell you a story," says Laird. "But let me add to my telling a bit of analysis," he always continues. So it goes as he tells us about the embattled vagina and about *Beowulf.* We are alternately entertained and informed, the alternation between these two modes of discourse so well manipulated that we soon forget the difference. By the time we come to the end of the essay, we see all the pieces of Laird's discourse fitting together like the sections of our labyrinthian garden. And without much reflection we sense that this speaker with two voices has both entertained and enlightened us.

Laird's success is hardly confined to the large structural concerns of rhetoric. He is also a master of detail, a master of tone. We think it worthwhile here to speak specifically about some of Laird's most successful turns with words in a few specific paragraphs of his essay.

Paragraph 1: Note the deceptively simple opening to an essay complex in theme and form—"Once upon a time." "Children love stories . . ." and the echo of *children* in "childhood of the race" raises a commentary on fairy tales to the level of an essay on humanity—a complex and lofty topic, but the word choices accent simplicity. *Child* appears again in this same sentence, this time as *"childish,"* and finds an appropriate echo in the monosyllabic *"flesh."* The theme begins to be formed here.

We are not quite sure what it is yet, but whatever, the word choices indicate it will have to do with the basic stuff of life, with *love* and *hate, fear* and *wonder,* words used not only once by Laird but as many times as he can effectively employ them, strengthening the essay's basic notion and simultaneously lending a reverberating, rhythmic quality to the paragraph, the same quality achieved with the repetition of *die* and the echo of *love, hate, fear* and *wonder* in *loves, hates, hopes,* and *fears.* Laird chooses words here not with only one sentence in mind. Most of the sentences in this paragraph contain words forming bridges to other sentences—a complex interlacing of simple words giving the paragraph tight coherence and creating a paragraph which very clearly informs the reader about the essay's central concerns.

Paragraph 6: This is good example of narrative writing within an expository essay. Since this narrative does not exist here for its own sake but as an example to illustrate several points in the exposition, Laird must be brief, but in that brevity he must include enough information to spark the reader's interest. No room here for useless words and phrases, verbal clutter. The first sentence begins almost as the full story itself might and is more lengthy than it might be for such a short summary. Laird might have said "The jealous husband of a good woman . . ." and thereby omitted the colorless *had,* but he leaves the verb in, we think, to create a leisurely pace, like the beginning of any good story. The pace quickens soon, however—the second sentence is short, to the point. Note for yourself how this combination of ease and pointedness continues through the essay and is employed in an especially powerful way in the final sentence. But notice also Laird's careful selection of phrases and economic interweaving of words. Read again the sentence beginning "Then she . . ." Note how the last phrase tells us something about the quality of the story itself: it has something that Laird has neither time nor appropriate room to tell us directly—irony. We know from Laird's corrections in the original manuscript that this was not the first version of the sentence. It originally read:

> Then she offered to kiss and fondle him, and he agreed that that would be a pleasant way to while away a chilly night, but that he would have to think about relinquishing the body.

The slight modification tells us indirectly something about the tale we might otherwise not know or which a whole sentence would be needed to tell. Laird observes well a general rhetorical principle: Rarely use a whole sentence when a simple phrase will do—never say something abstractly when you can use a concrete example, a good metaphor, or a short pointed phrase.

Paragraph 7: Notice the parallelism with the sentences beginning with *Some*. Try to imitate this in the next essay you write.

Paragraph 21: A more or less typical paragraph for this essay, it illustrates several rhetorical techniques. Note, first of all, the early juxtaposition of a long, cumulative sentence with a short, simple one. The cumulative sentence states the purpose of the paragraph and its relation to other paragraphs, and it tells us something about *Beowulf* too. The second sentence provides focus for what the paragraph and the section of the essay it introduces are more particularly about—Grendel, his mother, and Beowulf's battle with the two. Note the variation in adjective position two sentences later: "man living" instead of "living man." Note the description of Grendel quoted directly from the poem. Laird does not quote at length, just enough to whet your appetite as he tells you something about Grendel's eating habits with that almost offhand comment at the end much like the morbid humor of the Middle Ages. Again something of the mood and tone of the poem is recreated in the language of the person who writes about it.

There is more, of course, to say about this essay and of the others in this section. We hope you have gained some helpful advice toward constructing an analysis of your own.

6

SCIENCE
AND THE FUTURE

What does the future hold for humanity? Whatever our future might be, it is certain that science will play a major role in determining it. Science has become so pervasive in our society that we are no longer aware of it. We are a scientifically jaded country. No longer do we gasp in amazement at the latest scientific discovery. No longer do we doubt the predictions of scientists. No longer do we put our faith and trust in science to solve our problems.

While men walk on the moon, others battle crowds of commuters on partially functioning public transportation lines. While surgeons transplant hearts and kidneys, people still catch colds and infants die in their cribs seemingly without cause. While automobile manufacturers produce bigger, more comfortable cars, the highways become ever more clogged and the air ever more polluted. Science has blessed and cursed humanity.

Of course it is not the scientist's fault that we have not used knowledge as wisely as we might. But science has reached the point where the misuse of such knowledge is no longer a simple mistake that with some effort can be corrected. The knowledge and power which humanity now possesses is not just awesome but frightening. Everyone is aware of the threat of atomic weapons. But how many people are aware of the even greater threat posed by bacterial and biological weapons? Or what of the new chemical weapons that can kill almost instantly and are practically undetectable? The list can go on.

Environmentalists believe that the future is problematical at best, even without considering the possibility of atomic, chemical, biological, or bacteriological warfare. We will destroy ourselves, they believe, through the misuse of our environment. If civilization simply continues in its present manner without change, the end of humanity is clearly in sight. Or so the environmentalists predict.

Is there any hope, then, for us? What is humanity's future? We believe that humanity does have a future and that this future is not as bleak as some would have us believe. But in order to have a future and, more than that, a livable and enjoyable future, people and science must cooperate better than they have in the past.

But there are other threats to our future besides science and the misuse of its knowledge. As some of the selections in this section point out, people face problems in their urban environment. Cities were once among our greatest achievements, but today the great cities of the world are sick. Overcrowding, pollution, slums and decay, streets clogged with automobiles, and rising crime rates threaten to make many cities unlivable. To save our cities, we must do more than apply scientific knowledge. But what we must do is not clear.

Then, too, we face what Alvin Toffler has termed *future shock*. Science has so accelerated change in our daily life that many of our common points of reference are no longer stable. Change has become a daily fact of our lives and we must adjust and adapt to it. For those who cannot accept future shock, life becomes traumatic. Traditional points of reference and stability become fluid and unreliable, and the individual feels lost. To survive in the future, humanity will have to learn how to conquer future shock not only on the individual level but on the community and national level as well.

The selections in this section deal with a great variety of problems facing science, humanity, and its future. The writers do not offer solutions because they know that solutions are not possible at this time. But they do offer insights and suggest tentative lines of investigation. As you read the selections, remember that people can shape their future; try to formulate your own predictions, and remember that the future these writers discuss is yours.

The Rhetorical Analysis at the end of this section deals with Loren Eisley's *The Cosmic Prison*. Be sure you read Eisley's essay before you read the Rhetorical Analysis.

Nuclear Power: What Can Go Wrong Will Go Wrong

James Davidson

James Davidson is a writer on the staff of Penthouse *magazine, from which this article is taken.*

1   Ever since the Babylonians constructed the Tower of Babel, man has been trying to use technology to get into heaven. The Babylonians' plan was admirably straightforward. They thought that heaven was in the clouds, and if they built a staircase high enough they could walk right in. Of course, they never quite made it.

2   Our knowledge of engineering is better than the Babylonians'. But our judgment may not be. We're using atomic technology in the hope of attaining a very diminished version of heaven on earth. What we are striving for isn't even paradise. All we expect to achieve through our atomic projects is a slightly cheaper way of generating electricity.

3   That's not nearly as lofty a goal as the Babylonians aspired to. And because it is less lofty, it is ironic that we are risking more for it. When the Tower of Babel fell, its builders ended up back on the ground where they began. They may have been bruised and broken, but at least their failure was harmless. Not so with us. When our atomic projects fail we will end up with a flesh-and-blood version of a biblical afterlife. We have it within our power to create hell on earth.

4   An Atomic Energy Commission study of possible nuclear accident scenarios shows that failure of even a middling atomic power
plant could kill 45,000 people. (That means a slow, painful death, as
the victims' insides rot out with radiation poisoning.) And it could
render an area the size of Pennsylvania an uninhabitable wasteland.
There are fifty-five reactors capable of this sort of destruction dotted
across America today. Sixty-three additional reactors are presently
under construction, while 117 more are on the drawing boards.

5   But these are the more benign atomic reactors. An even more
deadly liquid-metal, fast-breeder reactor is in the works. The "fast
breeder," as it is known to the burgeoning atomic energy trade, has
a fuel core of about one ton of concentrated plutonium. Plutonium is
so toxic that one pound of it, evenly distributed in the atmosphere,
would be sufficient to give lung cancer to everyone on earth.

6   An explosion in a fast breeder could pollute thousands of
square miles and kill millions of people. Yet the Atomic Energy
Commission, recently sanitized as the Energy Research and Development Administration, is agitating to have as many as two
thousand breeders in operation in the United States by the year
2020. Think what that means. Just to haul away the radioactive
waste produced daily by such a system would require one hundred
railroad cars. But that's the simple part. Where would the deadly
waste be hauled? It wouldn't be a question of dumping into a
sanitary landfill. Experts agree that it would have to be kept under
protective storage for roughly a half-million years.

7   Another Ice Age could come and go during that time. But the
government "planners" expect to still be sitting there, guarding
mountains of plutonium waste during the transition through another
glacial epoch.

8   There are other solutions under consideration by the government for disposing of its atomic poison. Secretary of Defense James
Schlesinger came up with one. He said it might be better to get rid of
the waste once and for all by packing it into rockets and blasting it
off to the stars. That would be a way of rekindling interest in the
space program. Every time a garbage rocket was launched, the
whole world would be on the edge of its seat like the victim in a
game of Russian roulette.

9   Our own government is not the only one which is impressed
with the illusion of infallible science. The Shah of Iran has been
interested in newfangled ways of generating energy—and after Lock-
heed and Pan Am, what he has wanted most to purchase in
America are nuclear power plants. Since the Shah is a cash-and-
carry customer, there are more than enough American proponents

of nuclear power lining up to sell anything he might need to set up a few installations. Negotiations have been under way with the U.S. government for provision of the necessary nuclear fuel. The only hitch in the emerging agreement is that Congress is insisting upon safeguards so the Shah can't turn the plutonium he gets into bombs.

10   Let's hope that the Shah's deal falls through. Perhaps that way he'll decide to take revenge by hiring the entire staff of ERDA right out from under the U.S. government. He could make them all millionaires and move them to the Iranian desert where they could set about building the "fast breeder." We can also hope that it works better than the first one they attempted near Detroit. *It* suffered a "meltdown" and had to be sealed and abandoned. We can wish that they fare better than the Russians did. (Their experimental fast breeder blew up unexpectedly early in 1974.) We can wish them all the best, hoping that—unlike the builders of the Tower of Babel—they don't make a mistake. And if they do make a mistake, what better place to turn into a desert than a desert?

Vocabulary

diminished	lofty	aspired
ironic	scenarios	middling
benign	sanitized	infallible
newfangled	proponents	

Topics for Discussion

1. Name some major technological advances which have taken place since your birth. What negative effects have these advances produced?

2. It has become a commonplace to blame technology for the ills of the world. Can you point to some technological advances of this century which are hard to imagine doing without?

3. How does economics play a role in the development of new technology? Do you think that economics may play the primary role? See especially paragraph 9.

4. Discuss the possibility of abandoning modern technology altogether. What difficulties would be encountered by an individual, or a small group, deciding to do this?

5. After reading this essay, would you live next to a nuclear power plant? Would you rather live next to a conventional power plant? Why?

Rhetorical Considerations

1. Why does Davidson use the word *sanitized* in reporting the assignment of a new name to the Atomic Energy Commission?

2. The references to the Tower of Babel in paragraphs 1, 2, 3, and 10 serve as both introductory and concluding devices. In what way do these references help to unify the structure of the essay? How do they provide coherence among paragraphs? How do they work as metaphor?

3. How does Davidson use humor as an argumentative device? See especially paragraphs 1, 8, and 10. Can humor sometimes be grim?

4. What principles of organization operate in the essay? Why does Davidson develop some examples more extensively than others? For what rhetorical purpose does he develop the examples in paragraphs 9 and 10?

A Solution to the Population Boom

Russell Baker

Russell Baker is a syndicated columnist appearing in the New York Times.

1   It was midnight by the television set and John Carradine was turning a woman into an ape. Or was he turning an ape into a woman? I can't remember, but it makes no difference since John Carradine probably did it both ways during his long career at mad science. I seem to recall him at one stage turning Lon Chaney into Count Dracula, which is really big-time mad science, in a class with George Zucco's achievement in turning Maria Montez into an Egyptian mummy, or vice versa.

2   In any case, Carradine was wearing surgical gown and cap and he was working in what looked to be a well-built stone cellar fitted with expensive operating-room equipment. A good stone cellar is the surest warning that you are in the presence of a mad scientist. True, they always put on surgical gowns, too, but by that time it is usually too late. The time to run for the woods is when you look into the cellar and see that beautiful masonry.

3   As Carradine fiddled with scalpels and showed too much white eyeball, I realized that I knew everything that was going to happen in this movie. So did everybody who had paid good money to see it at a movie house years ago.

4   It was like Chinese opera. We all loved it for its utter predictability. Someone was going to ask Carradine why he was conducting this fiendish experiment, and Carradine would say that he was doing it for the pure hell of it, and then somebody would tell Carradine he was mad, and Carradine would strap this party to the operating table and show too much white eyeball, and so on.

5   It is hard to believe that movies of this genre ever really scared audiences, or that they were even intended to. The appeal is not to our love of horror, but to some bigotry about scientists that probably lurks in most of us.

6   Watching Carradine at work, I realized that he would have seemed a thoroughly admirable character if the filmmakers had not loaded the dice against him. The rolling eyeballs, the stone cellar. These irrelevancies were what made him Mr. Bad Guy. If the action had been switched to a busy hospital and Carradine had smiled instead of grimacing, he would have seemed a perfectly admirable, even heroic figure.

7   What, after all, is so mad about turning an ape into a woman? A British scientist says he recently started a human being growing in a test tube, and Carradine's project was surely more sensible than this. In a time of dwindling planetary resources, Carradine's project—turning apes into people—wisely compensates the human population increase by causing an equal reduction in the ape population.

8   Making new people out of whole cloth, as it were, as the British experimenter claims to have done, accelerates population growth when the real need is to stop it. Carradine's science is far saner because it opens doors on a possible solution to population problems; namely, the possibility of disposing humanely of excess people by transferring them into the ape kingdom.

9   I did not sit up to see Carradine reach the dreadful end that would deny us the fruits of his genuis. I knew his work would be

destroyed and that he would be killed by his ape-woman when she inevitably went berserk. This violent end would be representative of victory for justice. The fitting reward for all mad scientists who toy with the unknown for the pure hell of it.

10   What a betrayal of reason. Scientists are always toying with the unknown for the pure hell of it. They can no more stop themselves from toying with the unknown than a horse player can stop phoning his bookie. What's more, while they are occasionally destroyed by their works, so are coal miners and chemical-plant laborers.

11   They often give us horror shows. Hiroshima. The air of Los Angeles. Carradine's stone cellar is a place of serene civilization compared with the horrors of a large city hospital. This movie convention of isolating the scientist from any social setting makes it easier for the audience to loathe him, whereas if he is set in a modern hospital and given the dimples of Dr. Kildare the audience is compelled to admire him for his struggle to make apes and women interchangeable, for in the hospital grouping he is a servant of society.

12   Well, obviously a lot of us fear and dislike science, but don't dare admit it. The movies know it, however. They give us the mad scientist whom we can fear and despise without feeling bigoted and anti-intellectual, even though, truth to tell, his work is often saner than that of sane scientists.

Vocabulary

masonry	predictability	fiendish
genre	irrelevancy	grimace
dwindle	compensate	beserk
serene	loathe	

Topics for Discussion

1. Who is John Carradine? Why does Baker choose him as the mad scientist?

2. Are you bigoted about scientists? Why does Baker say most people are bigoted about scientists? Do you "fear and dislike science"?

3. In what ways is Carradine's science saner than modern science? Do you agree that the work of the mad scientist in the movies is saner than the work of the modern scientist in the respectable laboratory?

4. Do you agree that scientists toy with the unknown "for the pure hell of it"? What other reasons might there be that Baker doesn't mention?

5. What is Baker's attitude toward modern science as implied in this essay?

6. What are some of the horror shows modern scientists have given us, according to Baker? Can you cite any other examples?

Rhetorical Considerations

1. What is the main idea in this essay? Is it explicitly stated anywhere in the essay?

2. The tone and style of this essay are very relaxed and informal. What are some of the characteristics of the tone and style? See especially paragraphs 3 and 6.

3. How effective is Baker's use of the example of John Carradine as a mad scientist in illustrating the essay's thesis? Is any effectiveness lost if you don't know who John Carradine is?

4. How does the concluding paragraph relate back to the opening paragraph? What has happened between them in the body of the essay?

5. Baker says that scientists "toy" with the unknown. What does his use of the word *toy* reveal about his attitude toward scientists? What other words could he have used that would have revealed different attitudes?

Looking Backward from 2000 A.D.

Paul R. Ehrlich

Paul Ehrlich (b. 1932) is a population biologist who has constantly warned about the dangers of overpopulation. The Population Bomb, Process of Evolution, and Project Survival are some of his books.

DEPARTMENT OF POPULATION AND ENVIRONMENT
FIFTH ANNUAL REPORT TO THE PRESIDENT
JANUARY 1, 2000

Summary

1   *1. Population: Size.* The 1999 midyear population of the United States of North America was estimated to be 22.6 million, with a standard error of 3.2 million. The policy of special reproducer rations appears to have made significant inroads into the frequency of stillbirth, and child-health squads seem to be effectively reducing post-weaning child mortality. With the crude birth rate now standing at 30.7 and the death rate at 31.6, we are now clearly within striking distance of stabilizing our population. If present trends continue, the population will cease to decline early in 2001, and a slow rise in population size may be expected to commence thereafter. Approximately thirty-four percent of the population now resides in SRU (Standard Reorganized Urban) Areas, and the redistribution program has returned to the inactive mode. The Division of Optimum Population is expected to recommend next year a program target of a stable population of thirty-two million by 2075.

2   *2. Population: Quality.* The consequences of the release of radioactivity in the 1981 reactor disaster at the Seaborg plant, combined with the overall increase in environmental radioactivity permitted before the Gofman-Tamplin Act of 1976 restricted emissions, are still causing serious repercussions in our population. The leukemia rate is still 740 percent higher than the 1960 base rate, and that of chondrodystrophic dwarfism is now 890 percent of base. Estimates of the degree to which radiation is responsible for the present levels of embryonic, neonatal, infant, and childhood deaths are difficult to obtain because of confounding with nutritional effects and the disorganization of our medical apparatus. Similarly, it is still

impossible to sort out the causative factors for the present high level of carcinomas of all types in all age groups, but a substantial portion is thought to result from radiation damage.

3   It is encouraging that surviving molecular biologists and human geneticists are now relocated, and that research and training are proceeding as well as can be expected. Efforts are, of course, being heavily concentrated on the problem of repair of radiation damage in DNA (the genetic material).

4   The genetic variability inventory is nearing completion. Preliminary results indicate that the reduction of population size has not resulted in serious loss. The heterogeneity of the American population is considered by many specialists to have been responsible for its high survival rate relative to that of many other overdeveloped countries. It is suggested that in your State of the System address you emphasize, in layman's terms, the critical role played by "minorities" in our survival. The level of racial tension is now lower than at any previous date in our history, and positive efforts should be made to eliminate such tension entirely.

5   *3. Population: Health.* It is clear that lowered population density is a primary factor in preventing a resurgence of Marburgvirus B. Another factor is the recovery of the average diet to 2400 calories per day, and the increase of the high quality protein ration to almost forty grams daily. Famine has been estimated to have been directly or indirectly responsible for sixty-five million American deaths in the decade 1980–1989; the chances of a substantial hunger component in the next decade is now judged to be very small, unless another dramatic change in the climate occurs.

6   In addition, of course, the continual improvement of the quality of the atmosphere since the Great Die-Off has resulted in a population much less weakened by circulatory and respiratory diseases, and will thus lessen mortality due to interactions between malnutrition and cardiovascular and respiratory disorders. In the past eighteen years the turbidity of the atmosphere at all reporting points has shown almost continual decline except in areas affected locally by uncontrolled forest fires and dust from unattended farm land. (Even such local effects have been almost non-existent since 1992.) Finally, the restoration of relatively pure water supplies in many areas has further improved the epidemiological situation, although nitrate levels remain unacceptable in some areas where ground water was badly polluted.

7   Radiation still seems to be a factor in the continued susceptibility of some of the population to Marburgvirus B and in continued

low resistance to some other diseases. However, the level of chlorinated hydrocarbons stored in human body tissues has dropped until
this factor is now thought to be negligible in lowering resistance.
Remember that although about 125 million American deaths were
attributed to Marburgvirus B during the Great Die-Off, it is clear
that as many as sixty million of these would not have occurred if the
population had not been weakened by environmental deterioration.
Therefore the estimate of ten million deaths due to environmental
problems other than famine and disease is undoubtedly too low.

8   Rumors that Marburgvirus A (the strain which first infected 30
laboratory workers in 1967, killing seven, and which was only prevented from becoming epidemic by a stroke of luck) has been
causing deaths in Central African populations are unconfirmed, but
the Immigration and Carrier Act of 1996 will probably provide
protection for the population of the United States, if the presence of
that strain in the human population is confirmed.

9   *4. Resources: Food.* For the first time since these reports
were initiated the Department can report progress on a broad front
at restoring the productivity of American farms. The soil restoration
program of the Department of Agriculture is now well out of the
development stage, and trained extension workers are expected to
be in contact with approximately twenty-five percent of farmers
working five acres or more during the next growing season. Acceptance of both humus building and integrated pest control techniques is extremely high in farmers who survived the disaster years
of the mid-80's and, of course, it will be even higher among the
graduates of the new Federal Agricultural University. Monitoring of
all agricultural inputs by the Department of Population and Environment has completely eliminated the abuses of the agri-business
swindles of the 1970s. With care it should be possible to return the
American diet to the 1960 nutritional base level by 2010, as programs
developing satisfactory substitutes for dairy products and sea foods
are showing remarkable progress.

10   Food distribution is now considerably more equitable than in
the base year 1960, and considering the broad support of the population redistribution program and the rapid recovery of the national
railways it is confidently predicted that serious dietary inequities
will not occur in the foreseeable future.

11   *5. Resources: Energy.* The Energy-Demand Control Act of
1998 has established the basis for rational utilization of the energy
resources of the United States. In view of the great reduction in

population size, fossil fuel supplies will be more than adequate (in combination with hydroelectric power) to sustain our economy over the next century. It is now estimated that Deuterium-He fusion will be operational, producing pollution-free power by 2050, which will allow about fifty years to complete the transition to all-electric power.

12   *6. Resources: Mineral.*   Small population size, and continued availability of salvageable materials in Los Angeles and other cities which have not been reoccupied, have greatly eased the pressure on our reserves of nonrenewable resources. The projected non-renewable resource crisis is now about 100 years into the future, although, if international trade is not firmly reestablished in the next decade, shortages of certain materials such as industrial diamonds may be serious. We must emphasize that national and international planning for resources husbandry and substitution must be organized as soon as possible. We must not let the lessons of the '70s and '80s go unheeded. Needless to say, the planning of the Stable Economy Commission must go ahead with all deliberate speed.

13   *7. Environment.*   As indicated above, air and water quality have now both exceeded the 1960 base level by a considerable amount. Movement of chlorinated hydrocarbon residues into oceanic sinks is now estimated to have reached eighty-three percent of completion. The Department concurs, however, with estimates of Eastbloc monitoring stations that the restoration of oceanic productivity is problematical. Fears of oxygen depletion are still present in certain segments of the population, and it is essential that they be reassured. Large terrestrial areas have reverted to green plants since the Die-Off, and even if oceanic ecosystems cannot be reestablished for several centuries no significant oxygen shortage is anticipated.

14   Whether or not weather patterns will eventually return to those of the early part of the Twentieth Century cannot be determined at this time. Those few atmospheric physicists who survived the Die-Off have not reached a consensus on the exact cause of the jet stream shifts of 1978–84. Much more basic research on turbulent flow will be necessary before any attempt to reestablish previous patterns by artificial means can be made, and any such program is clearly beyond our current capability. While a rapid spontaneous return is conceivable, it would clearly be foolish to plan on that basis. It is important to remember also that a *rapid* return now would cause serious disruption in the new agricultural programs which have been established, and might result in a return of famine.

Major Recommendations

15   1. The continuation of present pronatalist policies will be necessary for the foreseeable future. It is important, however, that the public be continually reminded that the fundamental role of this Department is not to encourage population growth, but to *regulate* the size of the population for the benefit of all our citizens. The public should be prepared for the institution of antinatalist policies whenever conditions require them.

16   2. The Congress should immediately ratify the population convention of the United Nations World System Treaty.

17   3. Increased support of research in molecular biology, even in the face of extreme fiscal difficulties, is necessary in view of the severe genetic and metabolic difficulties faced by our population. The need to rebuild this area of science is made doubly urgent by the possible presence in the human population of Marburgvirus A and by the persistence of foci of Marburgvirus B in spite of the universal distribution of the Hsui vaccine. The reasons for the partial failure of the vaccine are as yet undetermined, but a larger cadre of trained scientists is clearly needed to help with this and related problems. Some slowdown in training programs of the National Ecology Institute could be accepted and the funds shifted to molecular biology. Ecology is now recruiting more talented students than can be usefully employed.

18   4. Appeals for loosening of restrictions under the Immigration and Carrier Act should be ignored for at least one more year.

19   5. No changes in the activities of the Department of Agriculture are recommended except in the Wheatlands Holding Unit. In view of the small probability of weather changes permitting the Wheatlands Reserve to be cultivated in the near future, the funds expended on this unit would better be reallocated to the South Coastal unit.

20   6. The remaining restrictions on the use of internal combustion engines in agriculture may now be safely lifted, with of course the provision that pre-disaster leaded fuel stocks remain under bond.

21   7. As the climatic changes of the last quarter century appear to be more or less permanent, it is recommended that a new climatic base be established as of this date.

22   8. The Department recommends that the President's Human Survival Medal be awarded posthumously to Dr. John W. Gofman and Dr. Arthur R. Tamplin. These scientists, while employed by the Lawrence Radiation Laboratory, which was supported by Atomic Energy Commission (AEC) funds, challenged the AEC guidelines for permissible levels of radiation exposure. Their courage and determination in the face of ill-founded bureaucratic opposition from the AEC eventually led to the landmark Federal Radiation Emissions Act of 1976, popularly known as the Gofman-Tamplin Act. As you know, untold human suffering has been avoided because of the enforcement of the act. The Department feels that further recognition of Gofman and Tamplin at this time will drive home to our new government agencies the need both for extreme care in dealing with environmental problems, and your direct concern for the rights of individuals within those agencies to be heard.

Conclusions

23   This is the first report of the Department in which the prognosis for the United States is mildly positive. In spite of this, a cautionary note must be added. In the national press there has been some comment to the effect that the environmental and public health disasters of the 1970s and 1980s were the result of "bad luck" or "Acts of God." As you know, Mr. President, if we had any luck it was good—for with bad luck the famines, disease, and competition for resources could have precipitated a thermonuclear war. It is only because most of the physical apparatus and records of our culture survived intact that recovery to the present point has been possible. We now can say with certainty that a major thermonuclear war in the 1970s or 1980s would have ended civilization permanently.

24   The Department urges you to remind our citizens that all of the trends leading to disaster were clear twenty years before the end came, and that we and the rest of mankind did nothing substantive to avert it. As a single example, the vulnerability of the world population to epidemic disease, due to large population size (overcrowding), hunger, and environmental deterioration was repeatedly pointed out by scientists. No substantial action was taken to correct the situation by a nation addicted to economic growth and ignorant of the limits of technology.

25   The cost of inaction, apathy, and unwarranted optimism has been the payment of nearly four billion human lives over a fifteen

year period—and we are still paying. We cannot permit a repetition of such a disaster. Mr. President, it is imperative that this generation and those to follow be kept mindful of mankind's recent history.

Respectfully submitted, (Signed)

L. Page Kennedy, Secretary

Vocabulary

optimum	neonatal	carcinoma
turbidity	deterioration	humus
ecosystems		

Topics for Discussion

1. Ehrlich mentions several contemporary conditions that he thinks might contribute to an ecological disaster. Comment on the condition that you think most immediately needs attention.

2. Ehrlich mentions the president's "State of the System" address. In substituting "system" for "union," what implications is Ehrlich making about both government and physical reality?

3. Can you understand this essay even if you do not know about Marburgvirus and chlorinated hydrocarbons?

4. Do you think, as Ehrlich indirectly suggests, that a Department of Population ought to be established by the federal government?

5. Do you think that Ehrlich overlooks some important social changes which might come about if a catastrophe of the magnitude he implies were really to occur? What changes in government would be necessary in order to carry out the remedies he suggests?

6. If the study of ecological systems is as important as Ehrlich suggests, why do many people look upon it as a fad?

Rhetorical Considerations

1. What is the structure of this essay? In what college courses might you write a paper structured like this one? The first word in the paper is *summary*. What might the paper be a summary of?

2. Ehrlich discusses enormous natural and human catastrophes in language precisely scientific, almost icy at times. What reasons does he have for using this tone? In what ways is his language icy?

3. Does Ehrlich overstate his case at points by using terms like "the Great Die-Off"? Does he sound more like a sincere student of the future or like a classical "prophet of doom"?

4. What special irony is there in Ehrlich's suggestion that "pronatalist" policies may someday come to be in the best interests of society?

5. How persuasive is Ehrlich here? What evidence in the essay is particularly forceful and effective?

The Paper Wedding Gown

Alvin Toffler

Alvin Toffler (b. 1928) is an author who has contributed frequently to Fortune, Life, New Republic, Saturday Review, *and other magazines. Among his books are* The Culture Consumers *and* Future Shock.

1   That man-thing relationships are growing more and more temporary may be illustrated by examining the culture surrounding the little girl who trades in her doll. This child soon learns that Barbie dolls are by no means the only physical objects that pass into and out of her young life at a rapid clip. Diapers, bibs, paper napkins, Kleenex, towels, non-returnable soda bottles—all are used up quickly in her home and ruthlessly eliminated. Corn muffins come in baking tins that are thrown away after one use. Spinach is encased in plastic sacks that can be dropped into a pan of boiling water for heating, and then thrown away. TV dinners are cooked and often served on throw-away trays. Her home is a large processing machine through which objects flow, entering and leaving, at a faster and faster rate of speed. From birth on, she is inextricably embedded in a throw-away culture.

2   The idea of using a product once or for a brief period, and then replacing it, runs counter to the grain of societies or individuals

steeped in a heritage of poverty. Not long ago Uriel Rone, a market researcher for the French advertising agency Publicis, told me: "The French housewife is not used to disposable products. She likes to keep things, even old things, rather than throw them away. We represented one company that wanted to introduce a kind of plastic throw-away curtain. We did a marketing study for them and found the resistance too strong." This resistance, however, is dying all over the developed world.

3   Thus a writer, Edward Maze, has pointed out that many Americans visiting Sweden in the early 1950's were astounded by its cleanliness. "We were almost awed by the fact that there were no beer and soft drink bottles by the roadsides, as, much to our shame, there were in America. But by the 1960's, lo and behold, bottles were suddenly blooming along Swedish highways . . . What happened? Sweden had become a buy, use and throw-away society, following the American pattern." In Japan today throw-away tissues are so universal that cloth handkerchiefs are regarded as old fashioned, not to say unsanitary. In England for sixpence one may buy a "Dentamatic throw-away toothbrush" which comes already coated with toothpaste for its one-time use. And even in France, disposable cigarette lighters are commonplace. From cardboard milk containers to the rockets that power space vehicles, products created for short-term or one-time use are becoming more numerous and crucial to our way of life.

4   The recent introduction of paper and quasi-paper clothing carried the trend toward disposability a step further. Fashionable boutiques and working-class clothing stores have sprouted whole departments devoted to gaily colored and imaginatively designed paper apparel. Fashion magazines display breathtakingly sumptuous gowns, coats, pajamas, even wedding dresses made of paper. The bride pictured in one of these wears a long white train of lace-like paper that, the caption writer notes, will make "great kitchen curtains" after the ceremony.

5   Paper clothes are particularly suitable for children. Writes one fashion expert: "Little girls will soon be able to spill ice cream, draw pictures and make cutouts on their clothes while their mothers smile benignly at their creativity." And for adults who want to express their own creativity, there is even a "paint-yourself-dress" complete with brushes. Price: $2.00.

6   Price, of course, is a critical factor behind the paper explosion. Thus a department store features simple A-line dresses made of what it calls "devil-may-care cellulose fiber and nylon." At $1.29 each, it is almost cheaper for the consumer to buy and discard a new one than to send an ordinary dress to the cleaners. Soon it will be.

But more than economics is involved, for the extension of the throw-away culture has important psychological consequences.

7   We develop a throw-away mentality to match our throw-away products. This mentality produces, among other things, a set of radically altered values with respect to property. But the spread of disposability through the society also implies decreased durations in man-thing relationships. Instead of being linked with a single object over a relatively long span of time, we are linked for brief periods with the succession of objects that supplant it.

Vocabulary

ruthlessly   inextricably   boutiques
benignly

Topics for Discussion

1. Do you think that the "spread of disposability" has extended itself beyond "man-thing" relationships—to human relationships as well? What is there in your personal experience to confirm your answer?

2. What are some of the ecological problems generated by the increased availability of disposable products? Are these problems serious? How might some of them be solved without serious inconvenience to people?

3. What changes would take place in your own life if most throwaway products (ball-point pens, paper napkins, aluminum foil) were replaced by reusable products?

4. Name some products likely to be found in disposable varieties in the future. What of the possibility of disposable rooms for houses, of disposable body features?

5. If body parts might some day become disposable, what then of disposable memories? If traumatic experiences and withered friendships could be totally erased from the mind, what would replace these memories? Would the world be changed for better or worse?

Rhetorical Considerations

1. What is the organizational strategy of this essay? In what sense is paragraph 7 the most important part of the essay? How do the

first six paragraphs prepare the reader for the central idea of paragraph 7? What is that central idea?

    2. How does paragraph 7 work with paragraph 1 to provide unity in the essay?

    3. Is the first sentence of the essay too stilted?

    4. How do the examples for comparison in paragraphs 2 and 3 contribute to the essay?

    5. Why is the example of the disposable wedding gown the most powerful example in the essay?

Cities Need Old Buildings

Jane Jacobs

Jane Jacobs (b. 1916) is a writer who has been concerned with the study of cities and urbanism. Her books include The Death and Life of Great American Cities *and* The Economy of Cities.

1   Cities need old buildings so badly it is probably impossible for vigorous streets and districts to grow without them. By old buildings I mean not museum-piece old buildings, not old buildings in an excellent and expensive state of rehabilitation—although these make fine ingredients—but also a good lot of plain, ordinary, low-value old buildings, including some rundown old buildings.

2   If a city area has only new buildings, the enterprises that can exist there are automatically limited to those that can support the high costs of new construction. These high costs of occupying new buildings may be levied in the form of rent, or they may be levied in the form of an owner's interest and amortization payments on the capital costs of the construction. However the costs are paid off, they have to be paid off. And for this reason, enterprises that support the cost of new construction must be capable of paying a relatively high overhead—high in comparison to that necessarily required by old buildings. To support such high overheads, the enterprises must be either *(a)* high profit or *(b)* well subsidized.

3   If you look about, you will see that only operations that are well established, high-turnover, standardized or heavily subsidized can afford, commonly, to carry the costs of new construction. Chain

stores, chain restaurants and banks go into new construction. But neighborhood bars, foreign restaurants and pawn shops go into older buildings. Supermarkets and shoe stores often go into new buildings; good bookstores and antique dealers seldom do. Well-subsidized opera and art museums often go into new buildings. But the unformalized feeders of the arts—studios, galleries, stores for musical instruments and art supplies, backrooms where the low earning power of a seat and a table can absorb uneconomic discussions—these go into old buildings. Perhaps more significant, hundreds of ordinary enterprises, necessary to the safety and public life of streets and neighborhoods, and appreciated for their convenience and personal quality, can make out successfully in old buildings, but are inexorably slain by the high overhead of new construction.

4   As for really new ideas of any kind—no matter how ultimately profitable or otherwise successful some of them might prove to be—there is no leeway for such chancy trial, error and experimentation in the high-overhead economy of new construction. Old ideas can sometimes use new buildings. New ideas must use old buildings.

5   Even the enterprises that can support new construction in cities need old construction in their immediate vicinity. Otherwise they are part of a total attraction and total environment that is economically too limited—and therefore functionally too limited to be lively, interesting and convenient. Flourishing diversity anywhere in a city means the mingling of high-yield, middling-yield, low-yield and no-yield enterprises.

Vocabulary

gregarious   archaic   syndrome
epoch

Topics for Discussion

1. What kind of old buildings do cities need?

2. What kind of neighborhood were you raised in? Did it have old buildings? Did you ever have any childhood adventures in an old building?

3. What does Jacobs mean when she says, "New ideas must use old buildings"?

4. In view of what Jacobs says in this essay, what do you think of government programs to tear down old buildings and build new ones?

5. What assumptions does Jacobs make at the beginning of the second and third paragraphs?

Rhetorical Considerations

1. Where is the thesis of this essay stated?

2. Paragraphs 2 and 3 both begin with "If." Is this a good paragraph opening?

3. How has Jacobs organized her argument? What details does she offer to support her thesis?

4. Throughout this essay Jacobs begins many of her sentences with dependent clauses. What are some of the functions these clauses serve?

The Full Circle:
In Praise of the Bicycle

Stefan Kanfer

Stefan Kanfer is a staff writer for Time *magazine.*

1   Everyone knows that Leonardo da Vinci invented the armored car and the alarm clock. Now historians have unearthed his most remarkable achievement. There in the musty libraries of Madrid lay the neglected sketch of a bicycle. How logical that the Renaissance man should have invented the Renaissance machine.

2   Even the most dedicated jogger must admit that his sport is purely hygienic. The bouncing exercise never allows the eyes to rest; the country seems to jiggle by on springs. The motorist glides on air and shock absorbers, but his speed undoes him. The scenery is a blur, the highlights only a few seconds in duration. And his

exhaust clouds the air he travels through. The cyclist pedals between his two contemporaries. Neither pedestrian nor driver, he is a happy anomaly, a 20th century centaur. Away from trucks and taxis, he has no competition; all turf is his. The novice and the regular both know the cyclist's high. It derives, in part, from the knowledge that the energy comes from a live body, not from fossil fuels. The legs pump, the heart answers. After a few trips, the rider feels the course of his own blood and knows the truth of Dr. Paul Dudley White's promise: the bicycle is an aid to longevity. (White took his own advice and pedaled into his late 80s.)

3   It is this freedom, from gas and even from roads, that has brought the American bicycle to its new prominence. For the first time since World War I, cycles are outselling cars. Moreover, the machines are no longer a juvenile item. As recently as 1969, only about 12% of bicycles sold in the U.S. were adult in design. This year the lightweight, diamond-framed "mature" model will account for 65% of the market.

4   In fact the contraption was never meant to be a child's device. *Pace* Leonardo, some researchers have perceived the outlines of bicycles in the frescoes of Pompeii and the tombs of Egypt. In any case, it was not until 1816 that the German baron, Karl von Drais, devised a recognizable model of the contemporary machine. That bike had everything a rider would want—except pedals. The cyclist walked perched on a saddle and propelled himself by running and gliding. In the mid-19th century rubber tires replaced the old boneshaking metal rims and high-wheelers elevated the rider far above the crowd—making crashes all the more resounding.

5   In a series of premonitory events, John D. Rockefeller gave presents of expensive bicycles to close associates, and lady cyclists abandoned their acres of crinoline for "rational clothing." H. G. Wells and George Bernard Shaw could be seen atop their new machines, and *Scientific American* soberly announced that "as a social revolutionizer [the bike] has never had an equal. It has put the human race on wheels, and has thus changed many of the most ordinary processes and methods of social life."

6   Alas, a greater revolutionizer was on its way. As the century changed, so did inventions, mores and wheels. The automobile ruthlessly honked the bike from the road. In the field of romance, it displaced its predecessor; enclosed in steel and glass, the young couple enjoyed a privacy that was denied them even in the parlor. The bicycle abruptly became an exiled device, to be used somewhere between kindergarten and acne.

7   It might have remained a thing of beauty and a toy forever. But

the agent of its obscurity was also the cause of its revival. For too long, the combustion engine befouled the atmosphere and lulled Americans into a dangerous sloth. But today, the new conservation and the high incidence of circulatory and cardiac diseases have caused the natural life to be reappraised. The bicycle no longer seems juvenile: indeed, it offers the country transportation, romance and exercise at a fee that advertisers like to summarize as "pennies per day."

8   Or dollars, if the rider is so inclined. The renewed fascination with bicycles has brought with it a new fashion, as capricious—and expensive—as *haute couture*. Now discriminating enthusiasts can buy a futuristic ten-speed British Hetchins for $900, or the Italian Colnago for $1,200. Such merchandise features an airiness that makes spider webs appear cumbersome, and offers gears so refined that they ought to be able to do logarithms. Yet the superbikes' forward motion does not differ substantially from that of the cheaper models. Non-*aficionados* often wonder whether it might be cheaper to buy ten $100 models, replacing each one as it gets worn out. Or, more likely, stolen; bicycle theft has become America's fastest-growing crime.

9   Even more unfortunate than the new bike rip-offs is the old anarchy. Any visitor to Europe has wondered at the rapid transit of pedaling citizens in Dublin and London, Paris and Berlin. In America, pandemonium reigns supreme. Some riders go with traffic; others against it. Some obey vehicular signs; others move with the pedestrian tide. The result: an estimated 456,000 emergency-room visitors in 1974. And more are expected this year.

10   Still, given the risks of robbery and the hazards of traffic, the true believers will not forsake their mounts for something better. In fact, there is nothing better. The bike rider may not get there as fast as in the cab or the family car. But along the way he is creating conditions of health, enjoying the weather and collecting some valuable human truths: every forward motion costs effort; balance means a total involvement in the task; energy has its limits; to stop precipitately is to court disaster; and, of course, a skill once learned is never quite forgotten.

11   As the air carries the perennial message of spring, millions of cyclists will be reiterating those precepts, echoing the only literary work in which they shine. In *A Connecticut Yankee in King Arthur's Court,* Mark Twain recalls the anachronistic day on which King Arthur was saved from his enemies: "By George! here they came, atilting—five hundred mailed and belted knights on bicycles!

The grandest sight that ever was seen! Lord, how the plumes streamed, how the sun flamed and flashed from the endless procession of webby wheels!"

12   For Arthur, read humanity; for knights, read riders. The sun still flames and the webby wheels still flash; the procession grows longer every day. For an increasing number of Americans, the bicycle has become the Great Rescuer—and the only first-class transportation left to humanity.

Vocabulary

hygienic	duration	anomaly
centaur	longevity	frescoe
premonitory	crinoline	capricious
haute couture	*aficionado*	pandemonium
vehicular	precipitately	perennial
reiterating	precept	anachronistic

Topics for Discussion

1. Why does Kanfer call the bicycle "the Great Rescuer"? What does he mean by this term?

2. Name at least two of the advantages of using a bicycle according to Kanfer. Do you agree that these are advantages? Could you also argue that these are disadvantages?

3. Is Kanfer being serious when he claims that pictures of bicycles have been found in the frescoes of Pompeii and the tombs of ancient Egypt? Why would he make such a claim?

4. Using a bicycle depends upon where you live. How would geographical location influence your attitude toward the usefulness of the bicycle?

5. What does Kanfer mean when he calls the cyclist "a 20th century centaur"?

6. Do you think the bicycle could become a major form of transportation? Consider, for example, what the effects would be if only bicycles were allowed in New York, Chicago, Philadelphia, or Los Angeles.

7. In what way is the bicycle the "Renaissance machine"?

Rhetorical Considerations

1. Kanfer is doing more than praising the bicycle in this essay; he is really arguing for greater use of the bicycle. What are the kinds of evidence he presents to support his case? Compare, for example, the reasons he advances in paragraph 2 with the reasons in paragraph 10.

2. Kanfer concedes that there are disadvantages to owning and using a bicycle. How does he acknowledge these disadvantages without weakening his argument? See particularly paragraph 10.

3. Paragraph 8 seems to violate two rules of grammar: it begins with a coordinating conjunction, and it is a sentence fragment. How does this sentence function rhetorically in the essay? Is the sentence effective as the first sentence of the paragraph and as a transition between paragraphs?

4. Examine the first sentence of each paragraph after the introductory paragraph and list all the transitional devices used to tie the paragraphs together. What kinds of transitional devices are used? How well do they succeed in unifying the essay?

5. This essay is relaxed and informal. What are some of the devices Kanfer uses to achieve his tone? Look particularly at paragraphs 2, 6, and 8. What is Kanfer's attitude toward his reader?

Man's Fourth Adjustment

Harlow Shapley

Harlow Shapley (1885–1972) was an astronomer, educator, editor, and author of numerous books and articles on science.

1   The scattering of galaxies, the habits of macromolecules, and the astounding abundance of stars are forcing those who ponder such matters to a further adjustment of their concept of the place and functioning of man in the material universe.

2   In the history of the evolving human mind, with its increasing knowledge of the surrounding world, there must have been a time when the philosophers of the early tribes began to realize that the world was not simply anthropocentric—centered on man himself.

The geocentric concept became common doctrine. It accepted a universe centered on the earth. This first adjustment was only mildly deflationary to the human ego, for man appeared to surpass all other living forms.

3   The second adjustment in the relation of man to the physical universe, that is, the abandonment of the earth-center theory, was not generally acceptable until the sixteenth-century Copernican revolution soundly established the heliocentric concept—the theory of a universe centered on the sun. Man is a stubborn adherent to official dogma. Eventually, however, he accepted the sun as the center not only of the local family of planets, but also of the total sidereal assemblage, and long held that view.

4   He had slowly given up the earth-center. But why, in spite of increasing evidence, did he then hold so persistently to the heliocentric view? Was it only because of vanity—his feeling, nourished by the unscientific dogmatists, that he is of paramount significance in the world? There were several better reasons for his second delusion. For example, the Milky Way is a great circle, a band of starlight that divides the sky into two nearly equal parts. It is of about the same brightness in all its parts. By implication, therefore, the sun and earth are centrally located. Also, the numbers of stars seemed to the early census-takers to fall off with distance from the sun as though it were central, and such a position for his star among the stellar millions brought to man a dignity of position not at all disagreeable.

5   The shift from the geocentric to the heliocentric concept doubtless had some philosophical impact in the sixteenth century, but not much. After all, the hot, turbulent, gaseous sun is no place for the delicate biology in which man finds himself at or near the top. Earth-center or sun-center seemed to make little difference to cosmic thinking during the past four centuries. But then, less than forty years ago, came the inescapable need for a third adjustment—one that should have deeply affected and to some extent has disturbed man's thoughts about his place, his career and his cosmic importance.

6   This shift has dug deeply into man's pride and self-assurance, for it has carried with it the knowledge of the appalling number of galaxies. He could accept rather cheerfully the Darwinian evidence of his animal origin, for that still left him at the summit of all terrestrial organisms. But the abandonment of the heliocentric universe on the authority of the astronomical evidence was certainly deflationary, from the standpoint of man's position in the material world, however flattering it was to the human mind.

7   The "galactocentric universe" suddenly puts the earth and its life near the edge of one great galaxy in a universe of millions of galaxies. Man becomes peripheral among the billions of stars of his own Milky Way; and according to the revelations of paleontology and geochemistry, he is recent and apparently ephemeral in the unrolling of cosmic time. And here is a somber or happy thought, whichever mood you prefer. There is no retreat! The inquiring human has passed the point of no return. We cannot restore geocentrism or heliocentrism. The apes, eagles and honeybees may be wholly content to be peripheral ephemerals, and thus miss the great vision that opens before us. For them, egocentrism and lococentrism may suffice; for us, no! And since we cannot go back to the cramped but comfortable past (without sacrificing completely our cultures and civilizations), we go forward and find there is more to the story.

8   The downgrading of the earth and sun, and the elevation of the galaxies, is not the end of this progress of scientific pilgrims through philosophic fields. The need for a further jolting adjustment now appears—not wholly unexpected by workers in science, nor wholly the result of one or two scientific revelations.

9   Our new problem concerns the spread of life throughout the universe. As unsolicited spokesmen for all the earthly organisms of land, sea and air, we ask the piquant questions: Are we alone?

10   From among the many measures and thoughts that promote this fourth adjustment of *Homo sapiens sapiens* in the galaxy of galaxies (the metagalaxy), I select three phenomena as most demanding of our consideration. The first refers to the number of stars, the second to catastrophes of ancient days, and the third to the origin of self-duplicating molecules.

11   To the ancients, only a few thousand stars were known; to the early telescopes, however, it was a million; and that astounding number has increased spectacularly with every telescopic advance. Finally, with the discovery that the "extragalactic nebulae" are in reality galaxies, each with its hundreds or thousands of millions of stars, and with our inability to "touch metagalactic bottom" with the greatest telescopes, we are led to accept the existence of more than 10^{20} stars in our explorable universe, perhaps many more.

12   The significance of this discovery, or rather of this uncovering, is that we have at hand—that is, the universe contains—more than one hundred million million million sources of light and warmth for whatever planets accompany these radiant stars.

13   The second phenomenon, the expanding metagalaxy, bears on the questions: Do planets accompany at least some of the stars that

pour forth energy suitable for the complex biological acitvity that we call life?

14   We now accept the observational evidence for an expanding universe of galaxies. The rapid expansion of the measurable part of the metagalaxy implies an increasingly greater concentration of these cosmic units (galaxies) as we go back in time. A few thousand million years ago, the average density of matter in space was so great that collisions, near encounters, and gravitational disruptions were of necessity frequent. The crust of the earth, radioactively measured, is also a few thousand million years old, and therefore the earth and the other planets of our sun's system were "born" in those days of turbulence. At that time countless millions of other planetary systems must have developed, for our sun is of a very common stellar variety. (Miss Cannon's catalogue of spectra reports forty thousand sun-like stars in our immediate neighborhood.)

15   Other ways in which planets may form—other than this primitive process of the early days—are recognized. The contraction of protostars out of the hypothetical primeval gas, giving birth on the way to protoplanets, is an evolutionary process now widely favored. It would imply the existence of countless planets.

16   The head-on-collision theory of planetary origin has also been considered. But the stars are now so widely dispersed that collisions must be exceedingly rare—so very unlikely, in fact, that we might claim uniqueness for our planetary system and for ourselves if planet birth depended only on such procedure. The expanding universe discovery, however, has shown the crowded conditions when our earth was born.

17   Passing over details, we state the relevant conclusions: *Millions of planetary systems must exist.* Whatever the method of origin, planets may be the common heritage of all stars except those so situated that planetary materials would be swallowed or cast off through gravitational action. In passing we note that astrophysicists have shown that our kinds of chemistry and physics prevail throughout the explorable universe. There is nothing uncommon here or now.

18   Remembering our 10^{20} stars and the high probability of millions of planets with suitable chemistry, dimensions and distance from their nutrient stars, we are ready for the question: On some of these planets is there actually life; or is that biochemical operation strangely limited to our planet, No. 3 in the family of the sun, which is a run-of-the-mill star located in the outer part of a galaxy that contains a hundred thousand million other stars—and this galaxy but one of millions already on the records?

19   Is life thus restricted? Of course not. We are not alone. And we can accept life's wide dispersion still more confidently when our third argument is indicated.

20   To put it briefly: biochemistry and microbiology, with the assistance of geophysics, astronomy and other sciences, have gone so far in bridging the gap between the inanimate and the living that we can no longer doubt but that whenever the physics, chemistry and climates are right on a planet's surface, life will emerge and persist.

21   This consequence has long been suspected by scientists, but the many researches of the past few years in the field of macromolecules have made it unnecessary any longer to postulate miracles and the supernatural for the origin of life.

22   The astronomical demonstration of the great number of stars, and therefore the abundance of life opportunities, naturally leads to the belief that countless planets have had long and varied experience with biochemical evolution. Thousands of kinds of terrestrial animals are known to develop neurotic complexes, that is "intelligence." It comes naturally. No higher animal is without it in high degree. Could it be otherwise on another life-bearing planet?

23   And here we must end with the simple but weighty proposal: There is no reason in the world to believe that our own mental stature has not been excelled by that of sentient beings elsewhere. I am not suggesting, however, that *Homo* is repeated. There are a million variations on the animal theme.

24   In conclusion, I need not emphasize the possible relevance to philosophy and perhaps to religion of this fourth adjustment in man's view of himself in the material universe.

Vocabulary

galaxy	geocentric	heliocentric
cosmic	peripheral	ephemeral
egocentrism	logocentrism	*Homo sapiens*
metagalactic	biochemistry	microbiology

Topics for Discussion

1. Does the significance Shapley places on our discovery that we do not live at the center of the universe seem real or important to

you? Does it really matter to you one way or another that you live on a rather out-of-the-way planet orbiting a fifth magnitude star?

2. Why was the position of the earth so much more important to people of other eras than it is, perhaps, to us? Would it make you feel more comfortable to go back to one of the old theories? What does Shapley say about going back?

3. Do you think that life exists on other planets? If so, what might that life be like? What do you think would happen if human beings came into contact with that life?

4. This is for real: there is a political grouping in Latin America which advocates unconditional assistance to UFOs. What might be the basis for such a position?

5. Can you think of a fifth adjustment humanity might have to make?

Rhetorical Considerations

1. Is this essay basically inductive or deductive? Do you find it suspenseful? How does the title make for suspense?

2. The first paragraph contains only one sentence. How is that sentence structured? Does its structure reflect in any way the structure of the entire essay?

3. Does Shapley's discussion of the "collision theory" detract from the essay's unity or does it add something of interest?

4. Does Shapley really prove anything scientifically in his essay, or does he merely suggest some questions? What is the value in writing an essay which only suggests questions?

The Cosmic Prison

Loren Eisley

Loren Eisley is Benjamin Franklin Professor of Anthropology and the History of Science at the University of Pennsylvania.

1   "A name is a prison, God is free," once observed the Greek poet Nikos Kazantzakis. He meant, I think, that valuable though language is to man, it is by very necessity limiting, and creates for man an invisible prison. Language implies boundaries. A word spoken creates a dog, a rabbit, a man. It fixes their nature before our eyes; henceforth their shapes are, in a sense, our own creation. They are no longer part of the unnamed shifting architecture of the universe. They have been transfixed as if by sorcery, frozen into a concept, a word. Powerful though the spell of human language has proved itself to be, it has laid boundaries upon the cosmos.

2   No matter how far-ranging some of the mental probes that man has philosophically devised, by his own created nature he is forced to hold the specious and emerging present and transform it into words. The words are startling in their immediate effectiveness, but at the same time, they are always finally imprisoning because man has constituted himself a prison keeper. He does so out of no conscious intention, but because for immediate purposes he has created an unnatural world of his own, which he calls the cultural world, and in which he feels at home. It defines his needs and allows him to lay a small immobilizing spell upon the nearer portions of his universe. Nevertheless it transforms that universe into a cosmic prison house that is no sooner mapped out than man feels its inadequacy and his own.

3   Scarcely had the moon flight been achieved before one U.S. Senator boldly announced: "We are the masters of the universe. We can go anywhere we choose." This statement was widely and editorially acclaimed. It is a striking example of the comfort of words, also of the covert substitutions and mental projections to which they are subject. The cosmic prison is not made less so by a successful journey of some two hundred and forty thousand miles in a cramped and primitive vehicle.

4   To escape the cosmic prison man is poorly equipped. He has to drag portions of his environment with him, and his life span is that of a May fly in terms of the distances he seeks to penetrate. There is no

possible way to master such a universe by flight alone. Indeed, such a dream is a dangerous illusion.

5   This may seem a heretical statement, but its truth is self-evident if we seriously try to comprehend the nature of time and space, which I, as a child, had grasped by intuitive perception when held up to view Halley's comet, the fiery messenger that had flared across the zenith in the spring of 1910, startling viewers innocent of science. "Seventy-five years," my father had whispered in my ear, "seventy-five years and it will be racing homeward. Perhaps you will live to see it again. Try to remember."

6   And so I remembered. I had gained a faint glimpse of the size of our prison house. Somewhere out there beyond a billion miles in space an entity known as a comet had rounded on its track in the black darkness of the void. It was surging homeward toward the sun because it was an eccentric satellite of this solar system. If I lived to see it, it would be but barely, and with the dimmed eyes of age. Yet it, too, in its long traverse, was but a flitting May fly in terms of the universe the night sky revealed.

7   So relative is the universe we inhabit that as we gaze upon the outer galaxies available to the reach of our telescopes, we are placed in about the position of a single white blood cell in our bodies, if it were intelligently capable of seeking to understand the nature of its own universe, the body it inhabits.

8   The cell would encounter rivers ramifying into miles of distance seemingly leading nowhere. It would pass through gigantic structures whose meaning it could never grasp—the brain, for example. It could never know there was an outside, a vast being on a scale it could not conceive of and of which it formed an infinitesimal part. It would know only the pouring tumult of the creation it inhabited, but of the nature of that great beast, or even indeed that it was a beast, it could have no conception whatever. It might examine the liquid in which it floated and decide, as in the case of the fall of Lucretius's atoms, that the pouring of obscure torrents had created its world.

9   It might discover that creatures other than itself swam in the torrent. But that its universe was alive, had been born and was destined to perish, its own ephemeral existence would never allow it to perceive. It would never know the sun; it would explore only through dim tactile sensations and react to chemical stimuli that were borne to it along the mysterious conduits of the arteries and veins. Its universe would be centered upon a great arborescent tree of spouting blood. This, at best, generations of white cells, by enormous labor and continuity, might succeed in charting.

10   They could never, by any conceivable stretch of the imagination, be aware that their so-called universe was in actuality the
prowling body of a cat or the more time-enduring body of a
philosopher, himself engaged upon the same quest in a more gigantic
world and perhaps deceived proportionately by greater vistas. What
if, for example, the far galaxies that man observes make up, across
void spaces of which even we are atomically composed, some kind
of enormous creature or cosmic snowflake whose exterior we will
never see? We will know more than the phagocyte in our bodies, but
no more than that limited creature can we climb out of our universe,
or successfully enhance our size or longevity sufficiently to thrust
our heads through the confines of the universe that terminates our
vision.

11   Some further "outside" will hover elusively in our thought,
but upon its nature, or even its reality, we can do no more than
speculate. The phagocyte might observe the salty turbulence of an
eternal river system, Lucretius the fall of atoms creating momentary
living shapes. We suspiciously sense, in the concept of the expanding universe derived from the primordial atom, some kind of oscillat-
ing universal heart. At the instant of its contraction we will vanish.
It is not given us to know, nor can our science recapture, the state
beyond the monobloc, nor whether we exist in the diastole of some
inconceivable being. We know only a little more extended reality
than does the hypothetical creature below us. Above us may lie
realism it is beyond our power to grasp.

12   This, then, is the secret nature of the universe over which the
ebullient senator so recklessly proclaimed our absolute mastery.
Time in that universe is in excess of ten billion years. It recedes
backward into a narrowing funnel where, at some inconceivable
point of concentration, the monobloc, or "primeval atom," containing all the matter that composes the galaxies exploded in the one
gigantic instant of creation.

13   Along with that explosion, space itself is rushing outward.
Stars and the great island galaxies in which they cluster are more
numerous than the blades of grass upon a plain. To speak of man as
"mastering" such a cosmos is about the equivalent of installing a
grasshopper as Secretary General of the United Nations. Worse, in
fact, for no matter what system of propulsion man may invent in the
future, the galaxies on the outer rim of visibility are fleeing faster
than he can approach them. Moreover, the light he is receiving from
them left its source in the early history of the planet Earth. There is
no possible way of even establishing their present existence. As the
British astronomer Bernard Lovell has so appropriately remarked,

"At the limit of present-day observations our information is a few billion years out of date."

14   It has been estimated that the time required to reach the nearest star to our own, four light-years away, would be, at the present speed of our spaceships, the equivalent of more than the whole of written history; indeed one hundred thousand years would be a closer estimate—a time as long, perhaps, as the whole existence of Homo sapiens upon earth. And the return, needless to state, would consume just as long a period.

15   Even if our present rocket speeds were stepped up by a factor of a hundred, human generations would pass on the voyage. An unmanned probe into the nearer galactic realms would be gone so long that its intended mission, and the country that sent it forth, might both have vanished into the mists of history before its messages could begin to be received. All this, be it noted, does not begin to involve us in those intergalactic distances across which a radio message from a spaceship might take thousands of years to be received and a wait of more thousands before a reply would filter back.

16   Two years ago I chanced to wander with a group of visiting scholars into a small planetarium in a nearby city. In the dark in a remote back seat, I grew tired and fell asleep while a lecture was progressing. My eyes had closed upon a present-day starry night as represented in the northern latitudes. After what seemed in my uneasy slumber the passage of a long period of time, I started awake in the dark, my eyes fixed in amazement upon the star vault overhead. All was quiet in the neighboring high-backed seats. I could see no one. Suddenly I seemed adrift under a vast and unfamiliar sky. Constellations with which I was familiar had shifted, grown minute, or vanished. I rubbed my eyes. This was not the same universe in which I had fallen asleep. A queer sense of panic struck me; it was as though I had been transported out of time.

17   Only after some attempt to orient myself by a diminished polestar did the answer come to me by murmurs from without. I was not the last man on the planet, far in the dying future. My companions had arisen and left, while the lecturer had terminated his address by setting the planetarium lights forward to show the conformation of the heavens as they might exist in the remote future of the expanding universe. Distances had lengthened. All was poised, chill, and alone.

18   I sat for a moment, experiencing the sensation all the more intensely because of the slumber that had left me feeling as though ages had elapsed. The sky gave little sign of movement. It seemed to

be drifting in a slow, indeterminate swirl, as though the forces of expansion were equaled at last by some monstrous tug of gravity at the heart of things. In this remote night-sky of the far future I felt myself waiting for the inevitable, the great drama and surrender of the inward fall, the heart contraction of the cosmos.

19   I was still sitting when, like the slightest leaf movement on a flooding stream, I saw the first faint galaxy of a billion suns race like silverfish across the night and vanish. It was enough: the fall was equal to the flash of creation. I had sensed it waiting there under the star vault of the planetarium. Now it was cascading like a torrent through the ages in my head. I had experienced, by chance, the farthest reach of the star prison. I had also lived to see the beginning descent into the maelstrom.

20   There are other confinements, however, than that imposed by the enormous distances of the cosmos. One could almost list them. There is, for example, the prison of smells. I happen to know a big black hunting poodle named Beau. Beau loves to go for walks in the woods, and at such times as I visit his owners the task of seeing Beau safely through his morning adventures is happily turned over to me.

21   Beau has eyes, of course, and I do not doubt that he uses them when he greets his human friends by proffering a little gift such as his food dish. After this formality, which dates from his puppyhood, has been completed, Beau reverts to the world of snuffles. As a long-time and trusted friend, I have frequently tried to get Beau to thrust his head out of the world of smells and actually to see the universe. I have led him before the mirror in my bedroom and tried to persuade him to see himself, his own visible identity. The results, it turns out, are totally unsatisfactory, if not ludicrous. Beau peers out from his black ringlets as suspiciously as an ape hiding in a bush. He immediately drops his head and pretends to examine the floor. It is evident he detests this apparition and has no intention of being cajoled into some dangerous, undoggy wisdom by my voice.

22   He promptly brings his collar and makes appropriate throaty conversation. To appease his wounded feelings, I set out for a walk in the woods. It is necessary to do this with a long chain, and a very tight grasp upon it. Beau is a big, powerful animal, and ringlets or no, he has come from an active and carnivorous past. Once in the woods all this past suddenly emerges. One is dragged willy-nilly through leaf, thorn, and thicket on intangible trails that Beau's swinging muzzle senses upon the wind.

23   His deep, wet nose has entered a world denied to me—a mad world whose contours and direction change with every gust of air. I

leap and bound with a chafed wrist through a smell universe I cannot even sense. Occasionally something squawks or bounds from under our feet and I am flung against trees or wrapped around by a flying chain.

24   On one memorable occasion, after a rain, Beau paused, sniffing suspiciously between two rocks on a hillside. Another rabbit, I groaned mentally, taking a tighter hold on the chain. Beau then began some careful digging, curving and patting the soil aside in a way I had never before witnessed. A small basin shaped by Beau's forepaws presently appeared, and up from the bottom of it welled a spring-fed pool in which Beau promptly buried his snout and lapped long and lustily of water that I am sure carried the living tastes and delicate nuances of information disseminated from an unseen watershed.

25   Beau had had a proper drink of tap water before we started from home, but this drink was different. I could tell from the varied, eager slurping sounds that emanated from Beau. He was intoxicated by living water that dim primordial memories had instructed him how to secure. I looked on, interested and sympathetic, but aware that the big black animal lived in a smell prison as I, in my way, lived in a sight prison. Our universes intersected sufficiently for us to be aware, in a friendly fashion, of each other, but Beau would never admit the mirror image of himself into his mind, and try as I would, the passing breeze would never inform me of the shadowy creatures that passed unglimpsed in the forest.

26   There are, of course, still other prisons in the universe than those dominated by the senses of smell or sight or temperature. Some involve the length of a creature's lifetime, as in the case of five-year-old Beau, who gambols happily about his master, knowing him to be one of the everlasting immortals of his universe.

27   The dream that there are men elsewhere in the universe, alleviating the final prison of human loneliness, dies hard. Nevertheless, a wise remark Santayana made many years ago should discourage facile and optimistic thinking upon this very point. "An infinite number of solar systems," the philosopher meditated, "must have begun as ours began, but each of them must have deviated at one point from ours in its evolution, all the previous incidents being followed in each case by a different sequel." In voicing this view, Santayana betrays a clearer concept of the chance-filled course of genetics and its unreturning pathways than that of some astronomers. The Mendelian pathways are prisons of no return. Advances are made, but always a door swings shut behind the evolving organism. It can no longer mate with its one-time progenitors. It can

only press forward along roads that increasingly will fix its irrevocable destiny.

28   Ours is a man-centered age. Not many months ago I was perusing a work on space when I came across this statement by a professional astronomer: "Other stars, other planets, other life, and other races of men are evolving all along, so that the net effect is changeless." Implied in this remark was an utter confidence that the evolutionary process was everywhere the same, ran through the same succession of forms, and emerged always with men at the helm of life, men presumably so close to ourselves that they might interbreed—a supposition fostered by our comic strips.

29   In the light of this naive concept—for such it is—let us consider just two worlds we know about, not worlds in space, but continents on our own planet. These continents exist under the same sun and are surrounded by the same waters as our own; their life bears a distant relationship to ours but has long been isolated. Man never arose in the remote regions of South America and Australia. He only reached them by migration from outside. They are laboratories of age-long evolution that tell us much about the unique quality of the human experience.

30   The southern continents of our earth do not maintain the intimacy of faunal exchange that marks the Holarctic land masses encircling the basin of the polar sea. Instead, they are lost in the southern latitudes of the oceans, and for long intervals their faunas have evolved in isolation. These lands have been, in truth, "other worlds."

31   The most isolated of these worlds is Australia. With the insignificant exception of a few late drifters from outside, this marsupial world is not merely an ancient world. It is a world in which ground life, orginally represented by a few marsupial forms, has, since the Mesozoic era, evolved untroubled by invading placental mammals from without. Every possible ecological niche from forest tree to that of underground burrower has been occupied by the evolutionary radiation of a slower-brained mammal whose young are born in a far more embryonic condition that that of the true Placentalia.

32   This world remained unknown to Western science until the great exploratory voyages began. Somewhere in the past, life had taken another turn. Chance mutation, "total contingency" in the words of the American paleontologist William King Gregory, had led to another universe. The "world" of Australia contained no primates at all, nor any hint of their emergence. Upon that "planet" lost in the great waters they were one of an infinite number of random potentialities that had remained as unrealized as the whole

group of placental mammals, of which the Primate order is a minor part.

33   If we now turn to South America, we encounter still another isolated evolutionary center—but one not totally unrelated to that of Eurasia. Here, so the biogeographers inform us, an attenuated land bridge, at intervals completely severed, has both stimulated local evolutionary development and at times interrupted it by migrations from North America. Our concern is with just one group of animals, the South American monkeys. They are anatomically distinct from the catarrhine forms of the Old World, and constitute an apparent parallel emergence from the prosimians of the early Tertiary.

34   Once more, however, despite the fact that the same basic primate stock is involved, things have gone differently. There are no great apes in the New World, no evidence of ground-dwelling experiments of any kind. Though fewer carnivores are to be found on the South American grasslands than in Africa, the rain-forest monkeys, effectively equipped with prehensile tails, still cling to their archaic pathways. One can only observe that South America's vast rivers flow through frequently flooded lowlands, and that by contrast much of Africa is high, with open savanna and parkland. The South American primates appear to be confined to areas where descent to the ground proved less inviting. Here ended another experiment that did not lead to man, though it began within the same order from which he sprang. Another world had gone astray from the human direction.

35   If, some occasionally extrapolate, man was so ubiquitous, so easy to produce, why did two great continental laboratories, Australia and South America—"worlds," indeed—fail to reproduce him? They failed, we may assume, simply because the great movements of life are irreversible, the same mutations do not occur, circumstances differ in infinite particulars, opportunities fail to be grasped, and so, what once happened is no more. The random element is always present, but it is selected on the basis of what has preceded it.

36   There appears to be nothing foreordained about the human emergence, nor any trend demanding man's constant reappearance, either on what we have seen to be the separate "worlds" of this world or elsewhere. There can no more be a random duplication of man than there is a random duplication of such a complex genetic phenomenon as fingerprints. The situation is not one that is comparable to a single identical cast of dice, but rather it is an endless addition of new genes building on what has previously been incorporated into a living creature through long ages. Nature gambles, but

she gambles with constantly new and altering dice. It is this well-established fact that enables us to call long-range evolution irreversible.

37   Finally, there are even meteorological prisons. The constant circulation of moisture in our atmosphere actually played an important role in creating the first vertebrates and, indirectly, man. If early rivers had not poured from the continents into the sea, the first sea vertebrates to penetrate streams above sea level would not have evolved a rigid muscular support, the spine, to enable them to wriggle against down-rushing currents. And if man, in his early history, had not become a tree climber in tropical rain-forests, he would never have further tilted that same spine upright or replaced the smell prison of the horizontal mammal with the stereoscopic, far-ranging "eye-brain" of the higher primates. If space permitted, such final dice throws, in which leaf and grass, wave and water, are inextricably commingled with the chemistry of the body, could be multiplied. The cosmic prison is subdivided into an infinite number of unduplicable smaller prisons, the prisons of form.

38   We are now in a position to grasp, after an examination of the many prisons that encompass life, that the cosmic prison many men, in the excitement of the first moon landing, believed we had escaped, still extends immeasurably beyond us. The lack of any conceivable means of travel and the shortness of our individual lives both prevent the crossing of such distances. Even if we confined ourselves to unmanned space probes of far greater sophistication than those we now possess, their homing messages through the void could be expected to descend upon the ruined radio scanners of a civilization long vanished, or upon one whose aging scholars would have long since forgotten what naive dreams had been programmed into such instruments. We have detected that we exist in a prison of numbers, otherwise known as light-years. We are also locked in a body that responds to biological rather than sidereal time. That body, in turn, receives the universe through its own senses and through no others.

39   At every turn of thought a lock snaps shut upon us. As societal men we bow to a given frame of culture—a world view we have received from the past. Biologically each of us is unique, and the tight spiral of the DNA molecules conspires to doom us to mediocrity or grandeur. We dream vast dreams of utopias and live to learn the meaning of a Greek philosopher's judgment: "The flaw is in the vessel itself"—the flaw that defeats all governments.

40   By what means, then, can we seek escape from groveling in mean corners of despair? Not, certainly, by the rush to depart upon

the night's black pathways, nor by attention to the swerving wind vane of the senses. We are men, and despite all our follies there have been great ones among us who have counseled us in wisdom, men who have also sought keys to our prison. Strangely, these men have never spoken of space; they have spoken, instead, as though the farthest spaces lay within the mind itself—as though we still carried a memory of some light of long ago and the way we had come. Perhaps for this reason alone we have scanned the skies and the waters with what Henry Vaughan so well labeled the "Ecclips'd Eye," the eye incapable of quite assembling the true meaning of the universe but striving to do so "with Hyeroglyphicks quite dismembered."

41   These are the words of a seventeenth-century mystic who has mentally dispatched inward vision through all the creatures until coming to man, who "shines a little" and whose depths he finds it impossible to plumb. Thomas Traherne, another man of that century of the Ecclips'd Eye, when religion was groping amid the revelations of science, stated well the matter of the keys to the prison.

42   "Infinite love," he ventured, "cannot be expressed in finite room. Yet it must be infinitely expressed in the smallest moment . . . Only so is it in both ways infinite."

43   Can this insight be seen to justify itself in modern evolutionary terms? I think it can.

44   Close to a hundred years ago the great French medical scientist Claude Bernard observed that the stability of the inside environment of complex organisms must be maintained before an outer freedom can be achieved from their immediate surroundings. What Bernard meant was profound but is simple to illustrate.

45   He meant that for life to obtain relative security from its fickle and dangerous outside surroundings the animal must be able to sustain stable, unchanging conditions within the body. Warm-blooded mammals and birds can continue to move about in winter; insects cannot. Warm-blooded animals such as man, with his stable body temperature, can continue to think and reason in outside temperatures that would put a frog to sleep in a muddy pond or roll a snake into a ball in a crevice. In winter latitudes many of the lower creatures are forced to sleep part of their lives away.

46   It took many millions of years of evolutionary effort before life was successful in defending its internal world from the intrusion of the heat or cold of the outside world of nature. Yet only so can life avoid running down like a clock in winter or perishing from exposure to the midday sun. Even the desert rattlesnake is forced to coil

in the shade of a bush at midday. Of course our tolerance is limited to a few degrees of temperature when measured against the great thermometer of the stars, but this hard-won victory is what creates the ever active brain of the mammal against the retarded sluggishness of the reptile.

47   A steady metabolism has enabled the birds and mammals to experience life more fully and rapidly than cold-blooded creatures. One of the great feats of evolution, perhaps the greatest, has been this triumph of the interior environment over exterior nature. Inside, we might say, has fought invading outside, and inside, since the beginning of life, has by slow degrees won the battle of life. If it had not, man, frail man with his even more fragile brain, would not exist.

48   Unless fever or some other disorder disrupts this internal island of safety, we rarely think of it. Body controls are normally automatic, but let them once go wrong and outside destroys inside. This is the simplest expression of the war of nature—the endless conflict between the microcosm and macrocosm.

49   Since the first cell created a film about itself and elected to carry on the carefully insulated processes known as life, the creative spark has not been generalized. Whatever its principle may be, it hides magically within individual skins. To the day of our deaths we exist in an inner solitude that is linked to the nature of life itself. Even as we project love and affection upon others, we endure a loneliness that is the price of all individual consciousness: the price of living.

50   It is, though overlooked, the discontinuity beyond all others: the separation both of the living creature from the inanimate and of the individual from his kind. These are star distances. In man, moreover, consciousness looks out isolated from its own body. The body is the true cosmic prison, yet it contains, in the creative individual, a magnificent if sometimes helpless giant.

51   John Donne spoke for that giant in each of us. He said: "Our creatures are our thoughts, creatures that are borne Gyants . . . My thoughts reach all, comprehend all. Inexplicable mystery; I their Creator am in a close prison, in a sick bed, anywhere, and any one of my Creatures, my thoughts is with the Sunne and beyond the Sunne, overtakes the Sunne, and overgoes the Sunne in one pace, one steppe, everywhere."

52   This thought, expressed so poignantly by Donne, represents the final triumph of Claude Bernard's interior microcosm in its war with the macrocosm. Inside has conquered outside. The giant confined in the body's prison roams at will among the stars. More

rarely and more beautifully, perhaps, the profound mind in the close prison projects infinite love in a finite room. This is a crossing beside which light years are meaningless. It is the solitary key to the prison that is man.

Vocabulary

sorcery	cosmos	tactile
phagocyte	primordial	oscillating
diastole	maelstrom	catarrhine
prosimians	prehensile	

Topics for Discussion

1. How does language imprison us? Have you ever found yourself at a loss for words? What did you do in that situation?

2. Eisley speaks of "prisons of the universe." What does he mean?

3. Is Eisley's concept of the universe as a vast prison an optimistic or pessimistic view of man's relation to the universe?

4. Do you agree with Eisley that people can never master the universe?

5. What is the "endless conflict between the microcosm and macrocosm"? What does it have to do with the cosmic prison?

6. Do you agree that "ours is a man-centered age"? Are there any signs that there is a shift away from this view?

7. On what grounds does Eisley reject that idea that human beings may have emerged on other planets as well as earth?

8. What is "the solitary key to the prison that is man"?

Rhetorical Considerations

1. Where does Eisley state his thesis? Does his introduction lead logically to his thesis?

2. Throughout his essay, Eisley attempts to make large quantities comprehensible. How does he do this? What metaphors does he use?

3. Examine the first sentences in Eisley's paragraphs. How does he achieve variety in his opening sentences?

4. What effect does Eisley achieve with his account of the walk in the woods with Beau?

5. Does Eisley use any technical language that you cannot understand? How does he explain complex technical concepts? What kind of vocabulary does he use?

6. Read the rhetorical analysis at the end of this section.

The Moral Un-Neutrality of Science

C. P. Snow

Charles Percy Snow (b. 1905) is an English novelist, essayist, and writer on the arts, sciences, and government who has been Rector of the University of St. Andrews, Scotland, and Parliamentary Secretary of the Ministry of Technology.

1   Scientists are the most important occupational group in the world today. At this moment, what they do is of passionate concern to the whole of human society. At this moment, the scientists have little influence on the world effect of what they do. Yet, potentially, they can have great influence. The rest of the world is frightened both of what they do—that is, of the intellectual discoveries of science—and of its effect. The rest of the world, transferring its fears, is frightened of the scientists themselves and tends to think of them as radically different from other men.

2   As an ex-scientist, if I may call myself so, I know that is nonsense. I have even tried to express in fiction some kinds of scientific temperament and scientific experience. I know well enough that scientists are very much like other men. After all, we are all human, even if some of us don't give that appearance. I think I would be prepared to risk a generalization. The scientists I have known (and because of my official life I have known as many as anyone in the world) have been in certain respects just perceptibly more morally admirable than most other groups of intelligent men.

3   That is a sweeping statement, and I mean it only in a statistical sense. But I think there is just a little in it. The moral qualities I

admire in scientists are quite simple ones, but I am very suspicious of attempts to oversubtilize moral qualities. It is nearly always a sign, not of true sophistication, but of a specific kind of triviality. So I admire in scientists very simple virtues—like courage, truth-telling, kindness—in which, judged by the low standards which the rest of us manage to achieve, the scientists are not deficient. I think on the whole the scientists make slightly better husbands and fathers than most of us, and I admire them for it. I don't know the figures, and I should be curious to have them sorted out, but I am prepared to bet that the proportion of divorces among scientists is slightly but significantly less than that among other groups of similar education and income. I do not apologize for considering that a good thing.

4   A close friend of mine is a very distinguished scientist. He is also one of the few scientists I know who has lived what we used to call a Bohemian life. When we were both younger, he thought he would undertake historical research to see how many great scientists had been as fond of women as he was. I think he would have felt mildly supported if he could have found a precedent. I remember his reporting to me that his researchers hadn't had any luck. The really great scientists seemed to vary from a few neutral characters to a large number who were depressingly "normal." The only gleam of comfort was to be found in the life of Jerome Cardan; and Cardan wasn't anything like enough to outweigh all the others.

5   So scientists are not much different from other men. They are certainly no worse than other men. But they do differ from other men in one thing. That is the point I started with. Whether they like it or not, what they do is of critical importance for the human race. Intellectually, it has transformed the climate of our time. Socially, it will decide whether we live or die, and how we live or die. It holds decisive powers for good and evil. *That* is the situation in which the scientists find themselves. They may not have asked for it, or may only have asked for it in part, but they cannot escape it. They think, many of the most sensitive of them, that they don't deserve to have this weight of responsibility heaved upon them. All they want to do is to get on with their work. I sympathize. But the scientists can't escape the responsibility—any more than they, or the rest of us, can escape the gravity of the moment in which we stand.

Doctrine of Ethical Neutrality

6   There is of course one way to contract out. It has been a favorite way for intellectual persons caught in the midst of water too rough for them.

7   It consists of the invention of categories—or, if you like, of the division of moral labor. That is, the scientists who want to contract out say, *we* produce the tools. *We* stop there. It is for *you*—the rest of the world, the politicians—to say how the tools are used. The tools may be used for purposes which most of us would regard as bad. If so, we are sorry. But as scientists, that is no concern of ours.

8   This is the doctrine of the ethical neutrality of science. I can't accept it for an instant. I don't believe any scientist of serious feeling can accept it. It is hard, some think, to find the precise statements which will prove it wrong. Yet we nearly all feel intuitively that the invention of comfortable categories is a moral trap. It is one of the easier methods of letting the conscience rust. It is exactly what the early 19th century economists, such as Ricardo, did in the face of the facts of the first industrial revolution. We wonder now how men, intelligent men, can have been so morally blind. We realize how the exposure of that moral blindness gave Marxism its apocalyptic force. We are now, in the middle of the scientific or second industrial revolution, in something like the same position as Ricardo. Are we going to let our consciences rust? Can we ignore that intimation we nearly all have, that scientists have a unique responsibility? Can we believe it, that science is morally neutral?

9   To me—it would be dishonest to pretend otherwise—there is only one answer to those questions. Yet I have been brought up in the presence of the same intellectual categories as most western scientists. It would also be dishonest to pretend that I find it easy to construct a rationale which expresses what I now believe. The best I can hope for is to fire a few sighting shots. Perhaps someone who sees more clearly that I can will come along and make a real job of it.

The Beauty of Science

10   Let me begin with a remark which seems some way off the point. Anyone who has ever worked in any science knows how much esthetic joy he has obtained. That is, in the actual *activity* of science, in the process of making a discovery, however humble it is, one can't help feeling an awareness of beauty. The subjective experience, the esthetic satisfaction, seems exactly the same as the satisfaction one gets from writing a poem or a novel, or composing a piece of music. I don't think anyone has succeeded in distinguishing between them. The literature of scientific discovery is full of this esthetic joy. The very best communication of it that I know comes in G. H. Hardy's book, *A Mathematician's Apology*. Graham

Greene once said he thought that, along with Henry James's prefaces, this was the best account of the artistic experience ever written. But one meets the same thing throughout the history of science. Bolyai's great yell of triumph when he saw he could construct a self-consistent, non-Euclidean geometry; Rutherford's revelation to his colleagues that he knew what the atom was like; Darwin's slow, patient, timorous certainty that at last he had got there—all these are voices, different voices, of esthetic ecstasy.

11   That is not the end of it. The *result* of the activity of science, the actual finished piece of scientific work, has an esthetic value in itself. The judgments passed on it by other scientists will more often than not be expressed in esthetic terms: "That's beautiful!" or "That really is very pretty!" (as the understating English tend to say). The esthetics of scientific constructs, like the esthetics of works of art, are variegated. We think some of the great syntheses, like Newton's, beautiful because of their classical simplicity, but we see a different kind of beauty in the relativistic extension of the wave equation or the interpretation of the structure of deoxyribonucleic acid, perhaps because of the touch of unexpectedness. Scientists know their kinds of beauty when they see them. They are suspicious, and scientific history shows they have always been right to have been so, when a subject is in an "ugly" state. For example, more physicists feel in their bones that the present bizarre assembly of nuclear particles, as grotesque as a stamp collection, can't possibly be, in the long run, the last word.

12   We should not restrict the esthetic values to what we call "pure" science. Applied science has its beauties, which are, in my view, identical in nature. The magnetron has been a marvelously useful device, but it was a beautiful device, not exactly apart from its utility but because it did, with such supreme economy, precisely what it was designed to do. Right down in the field of development, the esthetic experience is as real to engineers. When they forget it, when they begin to design heavy-power equipment about twice as heavy as it needs to be, engineers are the first to know that they are lacking virtue.

13   There is no doubt, then, about the esthetic content of science, both in the activity and the result. But esthetics has no connection with morals, say the categorizers. I don't want to waste time on peripheral issues—but are you quite sure of that? Or is it possible that these categories are inventions to make us evade the human and social conditions in which we now exist? But let us move straight on to something else, which is right in the grain of the activity of science and which is at the same time quintessentially moral. I mean, the desire to find the truth.

The Search For Truth

14   By *truth,* I don't intend anything complicated, once again. I am using the word as a scientist uses it. We all know that the philosophical examination of the concept of empirical truth gets us into some curious complexities, but most scientists really don't care. They know that the truth, as they use the word and as the rest of us use it in the language of common speech, is what makes science work. That is good enough for them. On it rests the whole great edifice of modern science. They have a sneaking sympathy for Rutherford, who, when asked to examine the philosophical bases of science, was inclined to reply, as he did to the metaphysician Samuel Alexander: "Well, what have you been talking all your life, Alexander? Just hot air! Nothing but hot air!"

15   Anyway, truth in their own straightforward sense is what the scientists are trying to find. They want to find what is *there*. Without that desire, there is no science. It is the driving force of the whole activity. It compels the scientist to have an overriding respect for truth, every stretch of the way. That is, if you're going to find what is *there,* you mustn't deceive yourself or anyone else. You mustn't lie to yourself. At the crudest level, you mustn't fake your experiments.

16   Curiously enough, scientists do try to behave like that. A short time ago, I wrote a novel in which the story hinged on a case of scientific fraud. But I made one of my characters, who was himself a very good scientist, say that, considering the opportunities and temptations, it is astonishing how few such cases there are. We have all heard of perhaps half a dozen open and notorious ones, which are on the record for anyone to read—ranging from the "discovery" of the L radiation to the singular episode of the Piltdown man.

17   We have all, if we have lived any time in the scientific world, heard private talk of something like another dozen cases which for various reasons are not yet public property. In some cases, we know the motives for the cheating—sometimes, but not always, sheer personal advantage, such as getting money or a job. But not always. A special kind of vanity has led more than one man into scientific faking. At a lower level of research, there are presumably some more cases. There must have been occasional Ph.D. students who scraped by with the help of a bit of fraud.

18   But the total number of all these men is vanishingly small by the side of the total number of scientists. Incidentally, the effect on science of such frauds is also vanishingly small. Science is a self-correcting system. That is, no fraud (or honest mistake) is going to

stay undetected for long. There is no need for an extrinsic scientific criticism, because criticism is inherent in the process itself. So that all that a fraud can do is waste the time of the scientists who have to clear it up.

19   The remarkable thing is not the handful of scientists who deviate from the search for truth but the overwhelming numbers who keep to it. That is a demonstration, absolutely clear for anyone to see, of moral behavior on a very large scale.

20   We take it for granted. Yet it is very important. It differentiates science in its widest sense (which includes scholarship) from all other intellectual activities. There is a built-in moral component right in the core of the scientific activity itself. The desire to find the truth is itself a moral impulse, or at least contains a moral impulse. The way in which a scientist tries to find the truth imposes on him a constant moral discipline. We say a scientific conclusion—such as the contradiction of parity by Lee and Yang—is "true" in the limited sense of scientific truth, just as we say that it is "beautiful" according to the criteria of scientific esthetics. We also know that to reach this conclusion took a set of actions which would have been useless without the moral nature. That is, all through the marvelous experiments of Wu and her colleagues, there was the constant moral exercise of seeking and telling the truth. To scientists, who are brought up in this climate, this seems as natural as breathing. Yet it is a wonderful thing. Even if the scientific activity contained only this one moral component, that alone would be enough to let us say that it was morally un-neutral.

21   But is this the only moral component? All scientists would agree about the beauty and the truth. In the western world, they wouldn't agree on much more. Some will feel with me in what I am going to say. Some will not. That doesn't affect me much, except that I am worried by the growth of an attitude I think very dangerous, a kind of technological conformity disguised as cynicism. I shall say a little more about that later. As for disagreement, G. H. Hardy used to comment that a serious man ought not to waste his time stating a majority opinion—there are plenty of others to do that. That was the voice of classical scientific nonconformity. I wish that we heard it more often.

Science in the Twenties

22   Let me cite some grounds for hope. Any of us who were working in science before 1933 can remember what the atmosphere

was like. It is a terrible bore when aging men in their fifties speak about the charms of their youth. Yet I am going to irritate you—just as Talleyrand irritated his juniors—by saying that unless one was on the scene before 1933, one hasn't known the sweetness of the scientific life. The scientific world of the twenties was as near to being a full-fledged international community as we are likely to get. Don't think I'm saying that the men involved were superhuman or free from the ordinary frailties. That wouldn't come well from me, who have spent a fraction of my writing life pointing out that scientists are, first and foremost, men. But the atmosphere of the twenties in science was filled with an air of benevolence and magnanimity which transcended the people who lived in it.

23   Anyone who ever spent a week in Cambridge or Göttingen or Copenhagen felt it all round him. Rutherford had very human faults, but he was a great man with abounding human generosity. For him the world of science was a world that lived on a plane above the nation-state, and lived there with joy. That was at least as true of those two other great men, Niels Bohr and Franck, and some of that spirit rubbed off on the pupils around them. The same was true of the Roman school of physics.

24   The personal links within this international world were very close. It is worth remembering that Peter Kapitza, who was a loyal Soviet citizen, honored my country by working in Rutherford's laboratory for many years. He became a fellow of the Royal Society, a fellow of Trinity College, Cambridge, and the founder and kingpin of the best physics club Cambridge has known. He never gave up his Soviet citizenship and is now director of the Institute of Physical Problems in Moscow. Through him a generation of English scientists came to have personal knowledge of their Russian colleagues. These exchanges were then, and have remained, more valuable than all the diplomatic exchanges ever invented.

25   The Kapitza phenomenon couldn't take place now. I hope to live to see the day when a young Kapitza can once more work for 16 years in Berkeley or Cambridge and then go back to an eminent place in his own country. When that can happen, we are all right. But after the idyllic years of world science, we passed into a tempest of history, and, by an unfortuante coincidence, we passed into a technological tempest too.

26   The discovery of atomic fission broke up the world of international physics. "This has killed a beautiful subject," said Mark Oliphant, the father figure of Australian physics, in 1945, after the bombs had dropped. In intellectual terms, he has not turned out to be right. In spiritual and moral terms, I sometimes think he has.

27   A good deal of the international community of science remains in other fields—in great areas of biology, for example. Many biologists are feeling the identical liberation, the identical joy at taking part in a magnanimous enterprise, that physicists felt in the twenties. It is more than likely that the moral and intellectual leadership of science will pass to biologists, and it is among them that we shall find the Rutherfords, Bohrs, and Francks of the next generation.

The Physicist, a Military Resource

28   Physicists have had a bitterer task. With the discovery of fission, and with some technical breakthroughs in electronics, physicists became, almost overnight, the most important military resource a nation-state could call on. A large number of physicists became soldiers not in uniform. So they have remained, in the advanced societies, ever since.

29   It is very difficult to see what else they could have done. All this began in the Hitler war. Most scientists thought then that Nazism was as near absolute evil as a human society can manage. I myself thought so. I still think so, without qualification. That being so, Nazism had to be fought, and since the Nazis might make fission bombs—which we thought possible until 1944, and which was a continual nightmare if one was remotely in the know—well, then, we had to make them too. Unless one was an unlimited pacifist, there was nothing else to do. And unlimited pacifism is a position which most of us cannot sustain.

30   Therefore I respect, and to a large extent share, the moral attitudes of those scientists who devoted themselves to making the bomb. But the trouble is, when you get onto any kind of moral escalator, to know whether you're ever going to be able to get off. When scientists became soldiers they gave up something, so imperceptibly that they didn't realize it, of the full scientific life. Not intellectually. I see no evidence that scientific work on weapons of maximum destruction has been different from other scientific work. But there is a moral difference.

31   It may be—scientists who are better men than I am often take this attitude, and I have tried to represent it faithfully in one of my books—that this is a moral price which, in certain circumstances, has to be paid. Nevertheless, it is no good pretending that there is not a moral price. Soldiers have to obey. That is the foundation of their morality. It is not the foundation of the scientific morality.

Scientists have to question and if necessary rebel. I don't want to be misunderstood. I am no anarchist. I am not suggesting that loyalty is not a prime virtue. I am not saying that all rebellion is good. But I am saying that loyalty can easily turn into conformity, and that conformity can often be a cloak for the timid and self-seeking. So can obedience, carried to the limit. When you think of the long and gloomy history of man, you will find that far more, and far more hideous, crimes have been committed in the name of obedience than have ever been committed in the name of rebellion. If you doubt that, read William Shirer's *Rise and Fall of the Third Reich*. The German officer corps were brought up in the most rigorous code of obedience. To them, no more honorable and God-fearing body of men could conceivably exist. Yet in the name of obedience, they were party to, and assisted in, the most wicked large-scale actions in the history of the world.

32   Scientists must not go that way. Yet the duty to question is not much of a support when you are living in the middle of an organized society. I speak with feeling here. I was an official for 20 years. I went into official life at the beginning of the war, for the reasons that prompted my scientific friends to begin to make weapons. I stayed in that life until a year ago, for the same reason that made my scientific friends turn into civilian soldiers. The official's life in England is not quite so disciplined as a soldier's, but it is very nearly so. I think I know the virtues, which are very great, of the men who live that disciplined life. I also know what for me was the moral trap. I, too, had got onto an escalator. I can put the result in a sentence: I was coming to hide behind the institution; I was losing the power to say no.

A Spur to Moral Action

33   Only a very bold man, when he is a member of an organized society, can keep the power to say no. I tell you that, not being a very bold man, or one who finds it congenial to stand alone, away from his colleagues. We can't expect many scientists to do it. Is there any tougher ground for them to stand on? I suggest to you that there is. I believe that there is a spring of moral action in the scientific activity which is at least as strong as the search for truth. The name of the spring is *knowledge*. Scientists *know* certain things in a fashion more immediate and more certain than those who don't comprehend what science is. Unless we are abnormally weak or abnormally wicked men, this knowledge is bound to shape our

actions. Most of us are timid, but to an extent, knowledge gives us guts. Perhaps it can give us guts strong enough for the jobs in hand.

34   I had better take the most obvious example. All physical scientists *know* that it is relatively easy to make plutonium. We know this, not as a journalistic fact at second hand, but as a fact in our own experience. We can work out the number of scientific and engineering personnel needed for a nation-state to equip itself with fission and fusion bombs. We *know* that, for a dozen or more states, it will only take perhaps six years, perhaps less. Even the best informed of us always exaggerate these periods.

35   This we know, with the certainty of—what shall I call it?— engineering truth. We also—most of us—are familiar with statistics and the nature of odds. We know, with the certainty of statistical truth, that if enough of these weapons are made, by enough different states, some of them are going to blow up, through accident, or folly, or madness—the motives don't matter. What does matter is the nature of the statistical fact.

36   All this we *know*. We know it in a more direct sense than any politician because it comes from our direct experience. It is part of our minds. Are we going to let it happen?

37   All this we *know*. It throws upon scientists a direct and personal responsibility. It is not enough to say that scientists have a responsibility as citizens. They have a much greater one that that, and one different in kind. For scientists have a moral imperative to say what they know. It is going to make them unpopular in their own nation-states. It may do worse than make them unpopular. That doesn't matter. Or at least, it does matter to you and me, but it must not count in the face of the risks.

Alternatives

38   For we genuinely know the risks. We are faced with an either-or, and we haven't much time. The *either* is acceptance of a restriction of nuclear armaments. This is going to begin, just as a token, with an agreement on the stopping of nuclear tests. The United States is not going to get the 99.9 percent "security" that it has been asking for. This is unobtainable, though there are other bargains that the United States could probably secure. I am not going to conceal from you that this course involves certain risks. They are quite obvious, and no honest man is going to blink them. That is the *either*. The *or* is not a risk but a certainty. It is this. There is no agreement on tests. The nuclear arms race between the

United States and U.S.S.R. not only continues but accelerates. Other countries join in. Within, at the most, six years, China and several other states have a stock of nuclear bombs. Within, at the most, ten years, some of those bombs are going off. I am saying this as responsibly as I can. *That* is the certainty. On the one side, therefore, we have a finite risk. On the other side we have a certainty of disaster. Between a risk and a certainty, a sane man does not hesitate.

39   It is the plain duty of scientists to explain this either-or. It is a duty which seems to me to come from the moral nature of the scientific activity itself.

40   The same duty, though in a much more pleasant form, arises with respect to the benevolent powers of science. For scientists know, and again with the certainty of scientific knowledge, that we possess every scientific fact we need to transform the physical life of half the world. And transform it within the span of people now living. I mean, we have all the resources to help half the world live as long as we do and eat enough. All that is missing is the will. We *know* that. Just as we know that you in the United States, and to a slightly lesser extent we in the United Kingdom, have been almost unimaginably lucky. We are sitting like people in a smart and cozy restaurant and we are eating comfortably, looking out of the window into the streets. Down on the pavement are people who are looking up at us, people who by chance have different colored skins from ours, and are rather hungry. Do you wonder that they don't like us all that much? Do you wonder that we sometimes feel ashamed of ourselves, as we look out through that plate glass?

41   Well, it is within our power to get started on that problem. We are morally impelled to. We all know that, if the human species does solve that one, there will be consequences which are themselves problems. For instance, the population of the world will become embarrassingly large. But that is another challenge. There are going to be challenges to our intelligence and to our moral nature as long as man remains man. After all, a challenge is not, as the word is coming to be used, an excuse for slinking off and doing nothing. A challenge is something to be picked up.

42   For all these reasons, I believe the world community of scientists has a final responsibility upon it—a greater responsibility than is pressing on any other body of men. I do not pretend to know how they will bear this responsibility. These may be famous last words, but I have an inextinguishable hope. For, as I have said, there is no doubt that the scientific activity is both beautiful and truthful. I cannot prove it, but I believe that, simply because scientists cannot

escape their own knowledge, they also won't be able to avoid showing themselves disposed to good.

Vocabulary

apocalyptic	bizarre	quintessentially
empirical	deviate	

Topics for Discussion

1. Do you agree that "scientists are the most important occupational group in the world"? Can you think of any other occupational group that might be more important?

2. What does Snow mean by moral qualities?

3. What is the doctrine of ethical neutrality of science? What do you think of this doctrine? What does Snow think of it?

4. Snow speaks of the esthetic satisfaction of science. What does he mean? What does he compare this experience with?

5. In what way is science a self-correcting system?

6. "Scientists have to question and if necessary to rebel." What are some of the implications of this statement?

7. Snow says that "the world community of scientists has a final responsibility upon it." What is this responsibility? Why do scientists have it?

Rhetorical Considerations

1. This is an essay by a scientist who is also a novelist. What is the style of the prose? Is it what you would expect of a scientist?

2. Upon what premise does Snow base his thesis? Where is that premise stated?

3. What is Snow's thesis? Does he state it anywhere in the essay?

4. What use does Snow make of specific examples?

5. How clearly does Snow define such terms as *ethical neutrality* and *truth*? Examine two or three of his definitions and determine whether they are specific and understandable.

The Great Whale's Mistake

Russell Baker

Russell Baker is a syndicated columnist appearing in the New York Times.

1   A mother whale and a father whale were swimming along the coast with their adolescent son whale when the mother sighted a school of people on the beach.

2   "Thar they boil," she sang out in her eerie whale voice.

3   "What's that?" asked the son whale, who had never seen a school of people before, or even a stray person.

4   "That's people, son," said the father whale. "You see them all up and down this coast at this time of year. They cover themselves with oil and lie up there on the sand and boil themselves until they sizzle."

5   "But they're such little things," said the son whale. "I'll bet I could swallow one whole and have him live in my stomach."

6   His mother said she would not want her stomach filled with anything that had been boiled in oil and had sand all over it. Moreover, she said, it would be very unhealthy because people were filled with smoke and hot dogs.

7   "What do people do?" asked the young whale.

8   "They sit on the beach and stare at the ocean," the father whale said. "And they eat hot dogs."

9   The mother whale said they also walked into the ocean now and then and flopped around in the water for brief periods and made such clumsy splashes that the fish had to get out of their way.

10   "They seem to be useless," said the son whale. "Why did the Great Whale make people anyhow?"

11   "Son," said the father whale, "no creature in the Great Whale's universe exists without a purpose. If the Great Whale made people it was for a good reason."

12   "Maybe people are the Great Whale's way of keeping down the hot-dog population," the young whale suggested.

13   "There are some things," said the mother whale, "that even whales can't understand. We must accept the world as it is and live in harmony with it."

14   The father whale called their attention to a small group of people who had detached themselves from the school and were

getting into a metal box mounted on wheels. When they were all inside, the metal box moved along the beach throwing up a great cloud of sand and destroying vegetation and birds' nests.

15   "What are they doing now?" asked the son whale.

16   "Making garbage," said the father whale. "People make almost all the garbage in the world, and they use those little moving boxes to do the job."

17   He showed his son the dark gases which spewed out of the box and pointed out the efficiency with which the beach grasses and the birds' eggs were quickly converted into garbage.

18   "And inside the box," the said, "they are also preparing more garbage."

19   At that moment six beer cans came flying out of the box, followed by a bag containing a half-eaten hot dog, a mustard jar, some banana peels and an empty plastic body-oil container.

20   "Maybe that's the reason the Great Whale made people," said the young whale. "To make garbage."

21   "The world doesn't need garbage," growled the father whale.

22   "Now, now," said the mother whale, who was always uneasy in the presence of religious speculation, "we must accept the world as it is and learn to live in harmony with it."

23   "Sometimes," said the father whale, "I think the Great Whale doesn't know what he's doing."

24   "Your father has been very sensitive about garbage," the mother whale explained. "ever since he dived into 800 tons of fresh sludge that had just been dumped off the New Jersey coast. He smelled like a sewer for weeks."

25   "Eight hundred tons of sludge!" cried the young whale. "Wow! That's what I call garbage production!"

26   The young whale was so excited that he spouted, and the people on shore saw it and cried, "Whales!" and somebody threw a beer bottle at them. The whales made for deep distant water and later that night as they drifted off the Gulf Stream admiring the stars a large ship passed by and spilled oil over them, but they remained in harmony with the world as it was, and afterwards dreamed of the unfortunate people far behind them making garbage through the sweet summer night.

Topics for Discussion

1. What is the point of this story? Can you state in one sentence what Baker is saying in his story?

2. Who or what is the Great Whale?

3. Why does someone throw a beer bottle at the whales at the end of the story?

4. Why do the whales say that people are useless? Are the whales logical in their criticisms of people? Do you agree with the whales? If people are not useless, what are they good for?

5. Defend the actions of the people in the story. Answer each charge made by the whales.

6. Do you sympathize with the whales? Why? Have you ever done any of the things the people in the story do that the whales find incomprehensible?

Rhetorical Considerations

1. What is the point of view of the story? How does this point of view contribute to the effectiveness of the story?

2. Why does the son whale ask so many questions? How do these questions contribute to the structure of the story?

3. What do the short paragraphs contribute to the story?

4. Each whale exhibits a different attitude. What does each attitude contribute to the organization and development of the story?

The Future of Man

Pierre Bertaux

Pierre Bertaux (b. 1907) has served the French government in a variety of offices ranging from Undersecretary for Foreign Affairs (1936–1937) to Director General of National Security (1949–1951) and has held professorial posts at the University of Rennes, Toulouse, Lille, and Paris.

1   We all say that we must plan for man; we repeat that *man* is—or has to be—our point of reference.

2   But what is man and who is man? Whom and what do we mean, exactly, when we say that word? In this context, we mean

normally "the Western white civilized male adult"—who is in fact only a very small percentage of the human race, even if we consider, perhaps rightly, that this sort of human being outweighs in importance the rest of humanity. But if we take another index, for instance, a statistical one, we would mean and consider as typical for mankind the largest race, age, and sex group. That is young Chinese females.

3   Second: we assumed until recently, without even discussing the matter, that mankind is a stabilized species; that man has not changed since the beginning of history and will remain what he is now. We believed that biological evolution is a very long-range affair that takes millions of years for every step. Consequently, as we are concerned with the near future, and especially with the next fifty years, biological evolution should be irrelevant for the definition of man.

4   As a humanist I believed for a long time that man was, is, and will be very much the same. But ten years ago I began to reflect on the possibility, then new to me and perhaps now new to you, that the evolution of man (biologically and genetically speaking) has not yet come to an end, that there is no reason why it should not go on; that it *is* indeed going on and that the next phase already has begun, that it goes on very quickly, and that fifty years, two generations, may be a significant period.

5   Paradoxically, Marxists do not accept the idea of a further evolution of mankind, because Karl Marx, a contemporary of Darwin, meant that since the beginning of history, man evolves only within the framework of social organization. In the backlog of the Old Testament and the philosophy of Hegel, Marxists are the last fixists in the world. They say: "man has no biology any more, just history."

6   I do not pretend to know more than anyone else about what future man will be. I just have the feeling that this is a problem with which we are directly concerned and which requires some attention.

7   Although we do not know what future man will be, nevertheless we are shaping him, and I would like to quote Nietzsche: "Man shapes his own future, and that, as well by what he does as by what he fails to do."

8   If we admit that mutation may be an adaptative reaction to environment, then those who are shaping the environment of man are in a way shaping man himself.

9   Are there any means to make a sensible guess about the next step in the evolution of mankind? It seems to me that three different approaches may be helpful.

10   The first one is to study the preceding steps in the biological evolution and to try to find out if there is a general trend. Those last steps are not so far in the past that we are unable to recollect them. Indeed the last one was taken at the beginning of history. We have an extraordinarily accurate statement of a mutation in the Old Testament: that is the story of Esau and Jacob; Esau belongs to the archaic hunter-type, Jacob is the new sort of man.

11   The trend of evolution seems to be determined by the increasing density of population and the still rapidly increasing density of contact and information, which has certainly a physiological and probably a genetic effect. As long as the evolution of the environment toward more density will be going on, one may assume that the trend of genetic mutation will follow a parallel line; so that some extrapolation from evolution in the past to evolution in the future is admissible.

12   There is a second approach: some analogy exists between what is now happening to mankind and what has happened and happens to animals. This analogy holds especially in two cases: first, when the density of an animal population exceeds certain limits; and second when animals are domesticated. Konrad Lorenz, the famous observer of animals, thinks that many features characteristic of modern humanity are closely connected to those observed when animals are domesticated. Even if some scientists do not accept yet the idea of genetic mutation caused by environment, they must admit domestication as hard fact. A tame goose does not breed wild geese: there seems to be no turning back from domestication. The retreat is cut off and man seems to be beyond the point of no return. Perhaps mankind is now making the step which some bees—not all of them—made about fifty million years ago when they invented the hive and social organization, without which their descendants cannot survive.

13   A third approach is to observe what is now happening with mankind, in order to test the assumption that man is evolving. There seems to be some evidence that a new type of man is appearing. Its original characteristics are purely psychological; new instincts, new inclinations, and a new behavior. They are a degree more gregarious—or, as David Bazelon says, more groupish—than the typical man described by humanists, from Plato to Hemingway. These new people cannot stand isolation; they need contact; they want to be together. Their normal way of life is to be inside a group.

14   This evolution has already gone so far that, if one of the archaic solitary type desires to retire in privacy and to be left alone, he is sent to the psychiatrist for treatment of what the new people

call an antisocial syndrome. By the way, I would assert that most intellectuals, most artists, most inventors, most creative individuals—if not all of them—are just that sort of archaic, solitary man.

15   If we can find a trend in evolution of man, how can we define its characteristics? The first one I have already mentioned: future man is a gregarious being, much more that the *homo sapiens* of old. A French entomologist, Rémy Chauvin, observed that bees of the social species are unable to make the simplest decision if they are not in a group of at least ten or twelve—about as many as the optimum board of directors. And they are not able to survive if there are not at least two hundred of them to share in the division of labor. The isolated bees are not able to survive.

16   The second characteristic of the trend is the changing relationship between man and woman and their respective roles in human society. Our historical societies are male societies, in contrast to animal societies which are essentially female. This shift of sex values since the beginning of human historical society is by no means normal or natural, and it could be very temporary. It may have lasted as long as the historical period, which may be now nearing its end: no more than a transition period of a few thousand years. The predominance of the male element entails the explosive character of historical societies since the beginning of history. I mean by "explosive" the instability which expresses itself as well in wars as in rapid technological change. War and technology both are male concerns.

17   The predominance of the male element in our culture is evident in the language we use. When we mention animals, we refer to "the dog," not "the bitch," to "the horse," not "the mare," to "the lion," not "the lioness"—whereas the lioness is the active supporting element of the family, hunting for all of them including the male.

18   When we refer to mankind, meaning both men and women, we say "man." And history as it is told is the history of men, not of women.

19   Even God is male, at least in modern Western religions. It is quite possible that in prehistorical times the Supreme Beings were female, as cave-paintings and twenty thousand-year-old sculptures suggest.

20   During the past fifty years our male societies founded on some sort of enslavement of women are returning to—biologically speaking—a more natural situation, where the more stable female element progressively asserts itself, until it perhaps predominates.

21   If we believe—as we all probably do—that the most formidable challenge to humanity *today* is the population explosion, then we

must conclude that only the female part of society is able to meet the challenge and control demography. Modern contraceptives are largely, if not exclusively, female contraceptives. They mean a much more decisive turning-point in the history of mankind than atom-energy and space-research taken together.

22   But then no one can foretell the consequences of the generalization of contraception for the new status of women, who have been regarded till now as the conservative element in society—indeed, as the keeper of its values. I confess that, as a man, I would not venture a guess at what their new pattern of values will be. Just one thing seems to appear: in our male cultures, when we said "sex" we meant the woman. Once the women are freed from their sexual and reproductive enslavement and the tables are turned, not the female, but the male will be sexually attractive, as it mostly is with animals. There are some signs that this change is already taking place.

23   I have discussed first the possibility of extrapolation from the past to the future, then the changing relation of sexes. A third characteristic of the trend concerns the future of intelligence. The intellectual activity has until now been an individual and organic matter: an activity of the individual brain. This is now changing too. Which way is it taking? It is not an unprecedented evolution. Already the history of technology and industrialization reveals a model of evolution from individual organic activity to a new form of mechanized collective organization of labor and production. The tool replaced the hand, the machine replaced the muscle-power, industry replaced handicrafts. But this process had not until the last decade really affected intellectual activities. Now we have come so far that thinking is no longer an essentially individual and organic activity, but something new, what some of us call "organized," others "artificial," intelligence as opposed to organic intelligence.

24   What is decisive now is not the IQ of individuals, but the IQ of groups associated with computers—the IQ of corporations, or "social systems," as Bertrand Gross calls them, including in the term associated nonhuman resources and technology.

25   But then, what is the future of individual organic intelligence—of brain activity? We have to refer once more to the precedent of industry. The essence of modern industrial organization is the production of more and more complicated goods by less and less skilled workers. The skill is not any more expected from the worker, but from the machine. It is very likely that the same sort of evolution will affect the substitution of artificial to organic intelligence. That is, less and less intellectually skilled people will be able to make increasingly more complicated and increasingly better calculations.

26　　If you ask me, I should say that this probably means a further decline of human organic individual intelligence; a decline which has possibly been going on for many thousands of years. It is not a gloomy, pessimistic view of things. As individual intelligence declines, collective intelligence increases. And individual intelligence is by far not required to enjoy life. Perhaps the contrary is true, especially in the way the "new people" conceive being happy as the goal of their life.

27　　If all of this—or at least some of this—is valid, what is then the measure of our responsibility? This measure is already given by the fact that most of our environment now is man-made.

28　　Let me quote Theodosius Dobzhansky, who says in his book, *Man Evolving*: "By changing what he knows about the world, man changes the world he knows; and by changing the world in which he lives, man changes himself."

29　　In our context I would say: now that so much of the environment of man is man-made, by reshaping his environment, man is now—consciously or not—shaping the man of the future.

30　　I said, consciously or not. Our second responsibility is to be conscious of it, to cultivate some image of the future.

31　　We have—I mean modern Western man has—a useful image of space. I would like to stress that this three-dimensional image of space is by no means natural, but a very good working *invention* of the Italian Renaissance.

32　　Our image of time is by far not so precise and not so clearly outlined as our image of space, but it exists nevertheless.

33　　Everyone, in every circumstance of life, refers—mostly without knowing it—to some image of the future he has in mind. A girl who gets married has some idea, however fantastic, of what her married life will be, or ought to be; she has an image of her married future. This image of the future varies considerably from one person to another. Some have a rudimentary, poor and shortsighted, others a detailed, rich and far-reaching image. In a way, man's worth is equal only to his expectations for his future.

34　　The most important changes in a personality are closely related to some change in its image of the future; the adult has a different time-perspective from the child's, and in old age again the time-perspective becomes quite different. There is hardly a deeper change in a personality than an alteration in its image of the future. The first step in brainwashing consists of destroying this perspective.

35　　Not only individuals but groups are attached to an image of the future, the importance of which cannot be overestimated. Politics, for instance, especially at election time, consists mainly in selling to the voters appealing images of the future. So does the advertising business: buy our new car, smoke our cigarettes, drink our whiskey—and *then* you will be happy.

36   It is not my aim today to examine how far certain images of the future are adequate, that is, whether or not they have any chance of being fulfilled. At present I am concerned only with the image of the future as a psychological phenomenon—and an essential one whose importance is just being discovered.

37   A few years ago the Dutch sociologist, Dr. Frederick L. Polak, studied the images of the future underlying the major civilizations: the ancient Greeks and their idea of fate, the old Jewish tradition and its prophets, Christianity and its vision of eternal life, the Renaissance and its utopia, the Age of Enlightenment and its idea of progress, Marxism and its ideology, the American society and American way of life—and he found that every one of them had developed a characteristic and original image of the future. Each culture seem to have its own unique image of the future.

38   These images may take many forms: aspirations, hopes, fears, expectations, ideals: they may be part of a religious, ethical, philosophic, or political creed—in any case, they are a major and decisive characteristic of any civilization. Polak goes so far as to say: the history of culture is the history of its image of the future. Such images are not only characteristic of the originality of a civilization, more than that, they are a good indicator if its vitality, of its dynamism. A people with a dynamic image of the future is like a car with a powerful engine. A weak or poor image of the future does not furnish the driving force necessary to propel a people through the challenge of history.

39   "Thinking about the future," says Polak, "is not only the mightiest lever of progress but also the condition of survival."

40   Positive images of the future can be regarded as a primary causal factor in cultural change. And every culture has just the future that is contained in the dynamic force of its images of the future. The future of a culture can be predicted by the power of its thinking about the future. No culture can maintain itself for long without a positive and generally accepted image of the future. A culture which shuts itself up in the present or, what amounts to the same thing, in a shortsighted perspective of the future, has no future.

41   To use Polak's own words: "through his images of the future we come to know man, who he is and how he wishes to be, what his thoughts are, what he values most highly, what he thinks is worth striving for, and whether he thinks it is attainable. . . . Certain types

of men hold certain types of visions, subject to their temper and spirit; tell me what your vision of the future is, and I will tell you what you are.''

42   In the context of this new view of human society and culture as well as of individual existence, we see that we are not only *pushed* by the past—as the historian is accustomed to demonstrate—but we are also strongly *pulled* toward the future. The actual achievement of the goals we had set is irrelevant; what is important is that the dynamic force of a strong and rich and powerful image of the future has exerted its action on us.

43   We can do very little about the fact that we are mostly determined by our past and by our environment—that is, by the forces which push us from behind. But our image of the future is subject to our own decision. Here we have a choice, here we are free, here we are responsible. It is correct to say that we ourselves are our own fate, inasmuch as we are free to choose our image of the future.

44   Our epoch has seen the triumph of science. And there is no science without a fundamental belief in determination. But on the other hand we need to believe in human freedom and responsibility. We should not accept fatalism. Scientists are—in one way or another—personally confronted with the problem of contrast between our belief in determinism and our belief in the freedom and dignity of man. Everyone has his own way of solving the problem and the way he does it is his own intimate and personal affair.

45   Perhaps we have here one possible model of a solution which it would be worthwhile to explore, a solution which could be especially valuable to the social scientist. I will try to express it in few words.

46   The future—in the form of the psychological fact of the image of the future—is capable of becoming an element of determination in the causal chain. Through an image of the future, the time-to-come is already affecting the present.

47   Man seems to be perfectly situated to create his own images of the future, not only according to his temperament, spirit, and experience, but also according to his ideas about his own responsibility and capabilities as well as their relationship to natural and historical forces.

48   If we admit that the image of the future can be effectively introduced as an efficient—and a most efficient—element in the chain of causality; if we further admit that our image of the future is in some way and to some extent our own choice and responsibility; then we have here not only a way of reconciling our belief in determinism and our belief in freedom, but also a direct challenge.

49   A century and a half ago, at the Congress of Vienna in 1815,

the French statesman Talleyrand said: We have to be future-minded. ("Il faut avoir de l'avenir dans l'esprit.") It was true at that time, when after the Napoleonic War Europe had to be rebuilt for the first time; but it is now truer and more urgent than ever, now that the whole world of man ("la Terre des Hommes"), as Saint-Exupéry said, has to be rebuilt.

50   As I said at the beginning, I do not pretend to know anything about the future man. But there is little doubt that what he will be depends in a way on our present thought about the future of man, however awkward and tentative this thinking may be.

Vocabulary

gregarious   archaic   syndrome
epoch

Topics for Discussion

1. Do you agree with Bertaux that human evolution is still taking place? If so, do you think human beings will ever achieve qualitative change again, i.e., that people will someday become suprahuman? What do modern philosophers and contemporary art say to this point? Have you read Teilhard de Chardin or seen the movie *2001*?

2. Do you agree with Bertaux that modern people are becoming more groupish? Are people who like to be alone really looked upon as oddballs in our society?

3. What changes in relationships between men and women do you envision for the future of "man"? Do you agree that *men* have been responsible for war and the negative use of technology throughout history? Do you think things would have been different had women been in charge?

4. Do you agree with Bertaux that language is unfair to women? Consider the title of this essay. To what extent can language be changed by fiat?

5. Do you believe that the population explosion constitutes "the most formidable challenge to humanity today"?

6. Do you have an eschatological view of history? That is, do you think human evolution is moving toward some ultimate goal, a goal either already decided by God, fate, or whatever, or in the process of being outlined and projected by humanity itself?

Rhetorical Considerations

1. Often, interesting speeches and essays begin by catching the attention of the listener or reader with some startling or surprising fact. Read Bertaux's second paragraph. Do you understand how he implements this rhetorical principle? Could he have exploited this comment at other places in the essay?

2. Can you determine the organizational basis of this essay? What implications do the opening paragraphs have for the remainder of the essay?

3. Bertaux's scattered one-sentence paragraphs are more effective for speech making than for essay writing. How would you combine these short paragraphs without eliminating the ideas contained in them? See especially paragraphs 27-32.

4. Is Bertaux's tone tentative or assertive, or does he modulate between the two?

The Jigsaw Man

Larry Niven

Larry Niven (b. 1938) is the pen name of Lawrence Van Cott, a science fiction writer whose works include World of Ptavvs, Gift From Earth, *and* The Shape of Space.

1   In A.D. 1900 Karl Landsteiner classified human blood into four types: A, B, AB, and O, according to incompatibilities. For the first time it became possible to give a shock patient a transfusion with some hope that it wouldn't kill him.

2   The movement to abolish the death penalty was barely getting started, and already it was doomed.

3   Vh83uOAGn7 was his telephone number and his driving license number and his social security number and the number of his draft card and his medical record. Two of these had been revoked, and the others had ceased to matter, except for his medical record. His name was Warren Lewis Knowles. He was going to die.

4   The trial was a day away, but the verdict was no less certain

for that. Lew was guilty. If anyone had doubted it, the persecution had ironclad proof. By eighteen tomorrow Lew would be condemned to death. Broxton would appeal the case on some grounds or other. The appeal would be denied.

5   His cell was comfortable, small, and padded. This was no slur on the prisoner's sanity, though insanity was no longer an excuse for breaking the law. Three of the walls were mere bars. The fourth wall, the outside wall, was cement painted a restful shade of green. But the bars which separated him from the corridor, and from the morose old man on his left, and from the big, moronic-looking teenager on his right—the bars were four inches thick and eight inches apart, padded in silicone plastic. For the fourth time that day Lew took a clenched fistful of the plastic and tried to rip it away. It felt like a sponge rubber pillow, with a rigid core the thickness of a pencil, and it wouldn't rip. When he let go it snapped back to a perfect cylinder.

6   "It's not fair," he said.

7   The teenager didn't move. For all of the ten hours Lew had been in his cell, the kid had been sitting on the edge of his bunk with his lank black hair falling in his eyes and his five o'clock shadow getting gradually darker. He moved his long, hairy arms only at mealtimes, and the rest of him not at all.

8   The old man looked up at the sound of Lew's voice. He spoke with bitter sarcasm. "You framed?"

9   "No, I—"

10   "At least you're honest. What'd you do?"

11   Lew told him. He couldn't keep the hurt innocence out of his voice. The old man smiled derisively, nodding as if he'd expected just that.

12   "Stupidity. Stupidity's always been a capital crime. If you *had* to get yourself executed, why not for something important? See the kid on the other side of you?"

13   "Sure." Lew said without looking.

14   "He's an organlegger."

15   Lew felt shock freezing in his face. He braced himself for another look into the next cell—and every nerve in his body jumped. The kid was looking at him. With his dull dark eyes barely visible under his mop of hair, he regarded Lew as a butcher might consider a badly aged side of beef.

16   Lew edged closer to the bars between his cell and the old man's. His voice was a hoarse whisper. "How many did he kill?"

17   "None."

18   "?"

19   "He was the snatch man. He'd find someone out alone at night, drug the prospect and take him home to the doc that ran the ring. It was the doc that did all the killing. If Bernie'd brought home a dead prospect, the doc would have skinned *him* down."

20   The old man sat with Lew almost directly behind him. He had twisted himself around to talk to Lew, but now he seemed to be losing interest. His hands, hidden from Lew by his bony back, were in constant nervous motion.

21   "How many did he snatch?"

22   "Four. Then he got caught. He's not very bright, Bernie."

23   "What did you do to get put here?"

24   The old man didn't answer. He ignored Lew completely, his shoulders twitching as he moved his hands. Lew shrugged and dropped back on his bunk.

25   It was nineteen o'clock of a Thursday night.

26   The ring had included three snatch men. Bernie had not yet been tried. Another was dead; he had escaped over the edge of a pedwalk when he felt the mercy bullet enter his arm. The third was being wheeled into the hospital next door to the courthouse.

27   Officially he was still alive. He had been sentenced; his appeal had been denied; but he was still alive as they moved him, drugged, into the operating room.

28   The interns lifted him from the table and inserted a mouthpiece so he could breathe when they dropped him into freezing liquid. They lowered him without a splash, and as his body temperature went down they dribbled something else into his veins. About half a pint of it. His temperature dropped toward freezing, his heartbeats were further and further apart. Finally his heart stopped. But it could have been started again. Men had been reprieved at this point. Officially the organlegger was still alive.

29   The doctor was a line of machines with a conveyor belt running through them. When the organlegger's body temperature reached a certain point, the belt started. The first machine made a series of incisions in his chest. Skillfully and mechanically, the doctor performed a cardiectomy.

30   The organlegger was officially dead. His heart went into storage immediately. His skin followed, most of it in one piece, all of it still living. The doctor took him apart with exquisite care, like disassembling a flexible, fragile, tremendously complex jigsaw puzzle. The brain was flashburned and the ashes saved for urn burial; but all the rest of the body, in slabs and small blobs and parchment-thin layers and lengths of tubing, went into storage in the hospital's

organ banks. Any one of these units could be packed in a travel case at a moment's notice and flown to anywhere in the world in not much more than an hour. If the odds broke right, if the right people came down with the right diseases at the right time, the organlegger might save more lives than he had taken.

31   Which was the whole point.

32   Lying on his back, staring up at the ceiling television set, Lew suddenly began to shiver. He had not had the energy to put the sound plug in his ear, and the silent motion of the cartoon figures had suddenly become horrid. He turned the set off, and that didn't help either.

33   Bit by bit they would take him apart and store him away. He'd never seen an organ storage bank, but his uncle had owned a butchershop. . . .

34   "Hey!" he yelled.

35   The kid's eyes came up, the only living part of him. The old man twisted round to look over his shoulder. At the end of the hall the guard looked up once, then went back to reading.

36   The fear was in Lew's belly; it pounded in his throat. "How can you stand it?"

37   The kid's eyes dropped to the floor. The old man said, "Stand what?"

38   "Don't you know what they're going to *do* to us?"

39   "Not to me. They won't take me apart like a hog."

40   Instantly Lew was at the bars. "Why not?"

41   The old man's voice had become very low. "Because there's a bomb where my right thighbone used to be. I'm gonna blow myself up. What they find, they'll never use."

42   The hope the old man had raised washed away, leaving bitterness. "Nuts. How could you put a bomb in your leg?"

43   "Take the bone out, bore a hole in it, build the bomb in the hole, get all the organic material out of the bone so it won't rot, put the bone back in. 'Course your red corpuscle count goes down afterward. What I wanted to ask you. You want to join me?"

44   "Join you?"

45   "Hunch up against the bars. This thing'll take care of both of us."

46   Lew found himself backing away. "No. No, thanks."

47   "Your choice," said the old man. "I never told you what I was here for, did I? I was the doc. Bernie made his snatches for me."

48   Lew had backed up against the opposite set of bars. He felt them touch his shoulders and turned to find the kid looking dully into his eyes from two feet away. Organleggers! He was surrounded by professional killers!

49   "I know what it's like," the old man continued. "They won't do that to me. Well. If you're sure you don't want a clean death, go lie down behind your bunk. It's thick enough."

50   The bunk was a mattress and a set of springs mounted into a cement block which was an integral part of the cement floor. Lew curled himself into fetal position with his hands over his eyes.

51   He was sure he didn't want to die *now*.

52   Nothing happened.

53   After a while he opened his eyes, took his hands away and looked around.

54   The kid was looking at him. For the first time there was a sour grin plastered on his face. In the corridor the guard, who was always in a chair by the exit, was standing outside the bars looking down at him. He seemed concerned.

55   Lew felt the flush rising in his neck and nose and ears. The old man had been playing with him. He moved to get up . . .

56   And a hammer came down on the world.

57   The guard lay broken against the bars of the cell across the corridor. The lank-haired youngster was picking himself up from behind his bunk, shaking his head. Somebody groaned; and the groan rose to a scream. The air was full of cement dust.

58   Lew got up.

59   Blood lay like red oil on every surface that faced the explosion. Try as he might, and he didn't try very hard, Lew could find no other trace of the old man.

60   Except for the hole in the wall.

61   He must have been standing . . . right . . . there.

62   The hole would be big enough to crawl through, if Lew could reach it. But it was in the old man's cell. The silicone plastic sheathing on the bars between the cells had been ripped away, leaving only pencil-thick lengths of metal.

63   Lew tried to squeeze through.

64   The bars were humming, vibrating, though there was no sound. As Lew noticed the vibration he also found that he was becoming sleepy. He jammed his body between the bars, caught in a war between his rising panic and the sonic stunners which must have gone on automatically.

65   The bars wouldn't give. But his body did; and the bars were slippery with . . . He was through. He poked his head through the hole in the wall and looked down.

66   Way down. Far enough to make him dizzy.

67   The Topeka County courthouse was a small skycraper, and Lew's cell must have been near the top. He looked down a smooth

concrete slab studded with windows set flush with the sides. There would be no way to reach those windows, no way to open them, no way to break them.

68   The stunner was sapping his will. He would have been unconscious by now if his head had been in the cell with the rest of him. He had to force himself to turn and look up.

69   He was *at* the top. The edge of the roof was only a few feet above his eyes. He couldn't reach that far, not without . . .

70   He began to crawl out of the hole.

71   Win or lose, they wouldn't get him for the organ banks. The vehicular traffic level would smash every useful part of him. He sat on the lip of the hole, with his legs straight out inside the cell for balance, pushing his chest flat against the wall. When he had his balance he stretched his arms toward the roof. No good.

72   So he got one leg under him, keeping the other stiffly out, and *lunged.*

73   His hands closed over the edge as he started to fall back. He yelped with surprise, but it was too late. The top of the courthouse was moving! It had dragged him out of the hole before he could let go. He hung on, swinging slowly back and forth over empty space as the motion carried him away.

74   The top of the courthouse was a pedwalk.

75   He couldn't climb up, not without purchase for his feet. He didn't have the strength. The pedwalk was moving toward another building, about the same height. He could reach it if he only hung on.

76   And the windows in that building were different. They weren't made to open, not in these days of smog and air conditioning, but there were ledges. Perhaps the glass would break.

77   Perhaps it wouldn't.

78   The pull on his arms was agony. It would be so easy to let go. . . . No. He had committed no crime worth dying for. He refused to die.

79   Over the decades of the twentieth century the movement continued to gain momentum. Loosely organized, international in scope, its members had only one goal: to replace execution with imprisonment and rehabilitation in every state and nation they could reach. They argued that killing a man for his crime teaches him nothing; that it serves as no deterrent to others who might commit the same crime; the death is irreversible, whereas an innocent man might be released from prison once his innocence is belatedly proven. Killing a man serves no good purpose, they said, unless for

society's vengeance. Vengeance, they said, is unworthy of an enlightened society.

80   Perhaps they were right.

81   In 1940 Karl Landsteiner and Alexander S. Wiener made public their report on the Rh factor in human blood.

82   By mid-century most convicted killers were getting life imprisonment or less. Many were later returned to society, some "rehabilitated," others not. The death penalty had been passed for kidnaping in some states, but it was hard to persuade a jury to enforce it. Similarly with murder charges. A man wanted for burglary in Canada and murder in California fought extradition to Canada; he had less chance of being convicted in California. Many states had abolished the death penalty. France had none.

83   Rehabilitation of criminals was a major goal of the science/art of psychology.

84   But—

85   Blood banks were world wide.

86   Already men and women with kidney diseases had been saved by a kidney transplanted from an identical twin. Not all kidney victims had identical twins. A doctor in Paris used transplants from close relatives, classifying up to a hundred points of incompatibility to judge in advance how successful the transplant would be.

87   Eye transplants were common. An eye donor could wait until he died before he saved another man's sight.

88   Human bone could *always* be transplanted, provided the bone was first cleaned of organic matter.

89   So matters stood at mid-century.

90   By 1990 it was possible to store any living human organ for any reasonable length of time. Transplants had become routine, helped along by the "scalpel of infinite thinness," the laser. The dying regularly willed their remains to the organ banks. The mortuary lobbies couldn't stop it. But such gifts from the dead were not always useful.

91   In 1993 Vermont passed the first of the organ bank laws. Vermont had always had the death penalty. Now a condemed man could know that his death would save lives. It was no longer true that an execution served no good purpose. Not in Vermont.

92   Nor, later, in California. Or Washington. Georgia, Pakistan, England, Switzerland, France, Rhodesia . . .

93   The pedwalk was moving at ten miles per hour. Below, unnoticed by pedestrians who had quit work late and night owls who were just beginning their rounds, Lewis Knowles hung from the

moving strip and watched the ledge go by beneath his dangling feet. The ledge was no more than two feet wide, a good four feet beneath his stretching toes.

94   He dropped.

95   As his feet struck he caught the edge of a window casement. Momentum jerked at him, but he didn't fall. After a long moment he breathed again.

96   He couldn't know what building this was, but it was not deserted. At twenty-one hundred at night, all the windows were ablaze. He tried to stay back out of the light as he peered in.

97   This window was an office. Empty.

98   He'd need something to wrap around his hand to break that window. But all he was wearing was a pair of shoesocks and a prison jumper. Well, he couldn't be more conspicuous than he was now. He took off the jumper, wrapped part of it around his hand, and struck.

99   He almost broke his hand.

100   Well . . . they'd let him keep his jewelry, his wristwatch and diamond ring. He drew a circle on the glass with the ring, pushing down hard, and struck again with the other hand. It *had* to be glass; if it was plastic he was doomed. The glass popped out in a near-perfect circle.

101   He had to do it six times before the hole was big enough for him.

102   He smiled as he stepped inside, still holding his jumper. Now all he needed was an elevator. The cops would have picked him up in an instant if they'd caught him on the street in a prison jumper, but if he hid the jumper here he'd be safe. Who would suspect a licensed nudist?

103   Except that he didn't have a license. Or a nudist's shoulder pouch to put it in.

104   Or a shave.

105   That was very bad. Never had there been a nudist as hairy as this. Not just a five o'clock shadow, but a full beard all over, so to speak. Where could he get a razor?

106   He tried the desk drawers. Many businessmen kept spare razors. He stopped when he was halfway through. Not because he'd found a razor, but because he now knew where he was. The papers on his desk made it all too obvious.

107   A hospital.

108   He was still clutching the jumper. He dropped it in the wastebasket, covered it tidily with papers, and more or less collapsed into the chair behind the desk.

109   A hospital. He *would* pick a hospital. And *this* hospital, the one which had been built right next to the Topeka County courthouse, for good and sufficient reason.

110   But he hadn't picked it, not really. It had picked him. Had he ever in his life made a decision except on the prompting of others? No. Friends had borrowed his money for keeps, men had stolen his girls, he had avoided promotion by his knack for being ignored. Shirley had bullied him into marrying her, then left him four years later for a friend who wouldn't be bullied.

111   Even now, at the possible end of his life, it was the same. An aging body snatcher had given him his escape. An engineer had built the cell bars wide enough apart to let a small man squeeze between them. Another had put a pedwalk along two convenient roofs. And here he was.

112   The worst of it was that here he had no chance of masquerading as a nudist. Hospital gowns and masks would be the minimum. Even nudists had to wear clothing sometime.

113   The closet?

114   There was nothing in the closet but a spiffy green hat and a perfectly transparent rain poncho.

115   He could run for it. If he could find a razor he'd be safe once he reached the street. He bit at a knuckle, wishing he knew where the elevator was. Have to trust to luck. He began searching the drawers again.

116   He had his hand on a black leather razor case when the door opened. A beefy man in a hospital gown breezed in. The intern (there were no human doctors in hospitals) was halfway to the desk before he noticed Lew crouching over an open drawer. He stopped walking. His mouth fell open.

117   Lew closed it with the fist which still gripped the razor case. The man's teeth came together with a sharp click. His knees were buckling as Lew brushed past him and out the door.

118   The elevator was just down the hall, with the doors standing open. And nobody coming. Lew stepped in and punched O. He shaved as the elevator dropped. The razor cut fast and close, if a trifle noisily. He was working on his chest as the door opened.

119   A skinny technician stood directly in front of him, her mouth and eyes set in the utterly blank expression of those who wait for elevators. She brushed past him with a muttered apology, hardly noticing him. Lew stepped out fast. The doors were closing before he realized that he was on the wrong floor.

120   That damned tech! She'd stopped the elevator before it reached bottom.

121   He turned and stabbed the Down button. Then what he'd seen in that one cursory glance came back to him, and his head whipped around for another look.

122   The whole vast room was filled with glass tanks, ceiling height, arranged in a labyrinth like the bookcases in a library. In the tanks was a display more lewd than anything in Belsen. Why, those things had been *men*! and *women*! No, he wouldn't look. He refused to look at anything but the elevator door. *What was taking that elevator so long?*

123   He heard a siren.

124   The hard tile floor began to vibrate against his bare feet. He felt a numbness in his muscles, a lethargy in his soul.

125   The elevator arrived . . . too late. He blocked the doors open with a chair. Most buildings didn't have stairs; only alternate elevators. They'd have to use the alternate elevator to reach him now. Well, where was it? . . . He wouldn't have time to find it. He was beginning to feel really sleepy. They must have several sonic projectors focused on this one room. Where one beam passed the interns would feel mildly relaxed, a little clumsy. But where the beams intersected, *here,* there would be unconsciousness. But not yet.

126   He had something to do first.

127   By the time they broke in they'd have something to kill him for.

128   The tanks were faced in plastic, not glass: a very special kind of plastic. To avoid provoking defense reactions in all the myriads of body parts which might be stored touching it, the plastic had to have unique characteristics. No engineer could have been expected to make it shatterproof too!

129   It shattered very satisfactorily.

130   Later, Lew wondered how he managed to stay up as long as he did. The soothing hypersonic murmur of the stun beams kept pulling at him, pulling him down to a floor which seemed softer every moment. The chair he wielded became heavier and heavier. But as long as he could lift it, he smashed. He was knee deep in nutritive storage fluid, and there were dying things brushing against his ankles with every move; but his work was barely a third done when the silent siren song became too much for him.

131   He fell.

132   And after all that they never even mentioned the smashed organ banks!

133   Sitting in the courtroom, listening to the drone of courtroom ritual, Lew sought Mr. Broxton's ear to ask the question. Mr.

Broxton smiled at him. "Why should they want to bring that up? They think they've got enough on you as it is. If you beat *this* rap, then they'll persecute you for wanton destruction of valuable medical sources. But they're sure you won't."

134   "And you?"

135   "I'm afraid they're right. But we'll try. Now, Hennessey's about to read the charges. Can you manage to look hurt and indignant?"

136   "Sure."

137   "Good."

138   The persecution read the charges, his voice sounding like the voice of doom coming from under a thin blond mustache. Warren Lewis Knowles looked hurt and indignant. But he no longer felt that way. He had done something worth dying for.

139   The cause of it all was the organ banks. With good doctors and a sufficient flow of material in the organ banks, any taxpayer could hope to live indefinitely. What voter would vote against eternal life? The death penalty was his immortality, and he would vote the death penalty for any crime at all.

140   Lewis Knowles had struck back.

141   "The state will prove that the said Warren Lewis Knowles did, in the space of two years, willfully drive through a total of six red traffic lights. During that same period the same Warren Knowles exceeded local speed limits no less than ten times, once by as much as fifteen miles per hour. His record has never been good. We will produce records of his arrest in 2082 on a charge of drunk driving, a charge of which he was acquitted only through—"

142   "Objection!"

143   "Sustained. If he was acquitted, Counselor, the Court must assume him not guilty."

Vocabulary

silicone   hypersonic

Topics for Discussion

1. Do you agree with Niven that "human technology can change human morals"? To what extent do you think technological advances have influenced morality during your lifetime? Which changes have been for the better, do you think, which for the worse?

2. One question already raised by organ transplants is how to determine the precise moment when death occurs. Do you think it right to take organs from someone injured beyond help in an auto accident but who might not die for a few days?

3. Would you accept an organ transplanted from someone who had been killed in an accident?

4. Can you imagine other reasons arising in the future for reinstatement of the death penalty? Another science fiction writer tells the story of a future earth turned radioactive wasteland where everyone must submit to death at age sixty so that the population can eat. Evaluate this situation.

5. If organs could be transplanted indefinitely, then people could probably live for a thousand years. Perhaps they might live indefinitely. How would this near absence of death change the way people live? Would there be a tendency for people to choose several lives, perhaps starting over every fifty years?

Rhetorical Considerations

1. What kind of sentence structure does Niven mainly rely on? Does his use of short, pointed sentences have anything to do with the theme of the story?

2. How would you characterize the tone of this story? Do you think Niven's air of impersonality lends it a frightening effect?

3. What do you imagine the urban landscape in the story looks like? Do you find it quite similar to that of the 1970s? Why has Niven pictured it this way?

4. What is the irony in the last sentence of the story?

Rhetorical Analysis

Loren Eisley: The Cosmic Prison

Loren Eisley deals with the vastness of the universe and humanity's place in it. The cosmos of which human beings are such a small part is so vast as to be beyond measure, and yet we have measured it. This last statement is a *paradox*—a seemingly contradictory statement that nevertheless contains some truth. How is the cosmos both measureless to man and yet measured? Scientists tell us that for a number of reasons we cannot really measure the universe. First, we simply do not have the instruments to do the job. Second, the universe is constantly expanding and thus any measurement would be valid only for one point in time.

Our galaxy, the Milky Way, has a diameter of some one hundred thousand light years, and the number of detectable galaxies is between one hundred billion and one trillion. And yet human beings do measure the universe every time they use language. The very fact that we can name something in a sense measures it, imposes limits on it. Thus, we measure the universe with our greatest invention, language.

Throughout his essay, Eisley uses paradox to illustrate his description of our place in the universe. The very title of the essay is a paradox. How can anything as large as the cosmos be a prison? A prison may be a single room or a large building, but whatever it may be, its function is to confine. The cosmos is a prison, Eisley says, because it does precisely that—it confines us, it imposes limits on us. We are prisoners of our cosmos.

But the concept of a cosmic prison is difficult to comprehend, so Eisley attempts to make his paradox more understandable by breaking up the cosmic prison into a series of smaller prisons. Eisley cites the example of the dog named Beau who lives in a world of smells that human beings cannot perceive. Beau can enter a world denied to us, a world "whose contours and direction change with every gust of air." But Beau is a prisoner of his world of smell just as we are prisoners of our world of sight. We are also prisoners of temperature, confined to the limited areas of the universe where the temperature can sustain us. We are also prisoners of our very form, our bodies. The nature of our bodies limits us. And we are prisoners of time. Our bodies respond to biological, not sidereal, time, and we live so briefly compared to the seemingly timeless universe. All of these smaller prisons and more Eisley describes in an attempt to explain and make more concrete his basic paradox of the cosmic prison.

Eisley also uses personal incidents three times to further illustrate his paradox and make it more concrete, more comprehensible. First he recounts the time his father pointed out Halley's comet to him. It was then, Eisley says, that he had some comprehension of time and space. The second personal incident Eisley uses for illustration is the time he fell asleep in the planetarium and woke up by himself surrounded by silence and the stars. It was then, Eisley tells his reader, that he sensed what the universe would be like at the end of time. He had experienced "the farthest reach of the star prison." The walk in the woods with his friend's dog Beau is the third personal incident Eisley recounts. As discussed before, Beau reveals to Eisley the prison of smell. All of these personal incidents help to illustrate vividly and concretely what the reader may otherwise find too abstract and intangible to completely grasp.

One other illustration used by Eisley is not personal, but serves the same purpose as the other three. Eisley attempts to give his reader some understanding of the size of the universe and humanity's relation to it with the example of a single blood cell. Just as this cell would encounter a vast world which it could not really comprehend, so is a human being a small particle in the universe. The cell could never understand the full complexity of the living body of which it is a part. And certainly the cell could never know of the world outside the body which contains it. So too it is with us. We cannot even see all the galaxies in the universe. We do not know if our universe is part of anything larger, just as the cell does not know if its world is a part of anything larger. This illustration is really an *analogy* in which something unfamiliar is compared with something familiar. It is easier for the reader to understand the relationship of the cell to the body than to understand the relationship of human beings to the universe. Eisley makes a rough comparison, saying that our relation to the universe is something like the relation of the cell to the body.

The cosmic prison is like all other prisons—lonely. People cannot hope that they are not alone. It is a dream that there are others elsewhere in the universe, vast though it is. Using the history of humanity's evolution on earth, Eisley again makes a comparison. Just as our development on earth was not inevitable and is really the product of a series of chances and gambles on the part of nature, so the same conditions exist throughout the universe. The possibility of a random duplication of humanity in another galaxy is as possible as the random duplication of fingerprints.

How else to describe the cosmic prison? Eisley points out that a trip to our nearest neighboring star would take four light years. But since the concept of a light year is so abstract, he makes it more concrete by pointing out that a spaceship traveling at speeds science is now capable of generating would take over one hundred thousand years to reach the star. And if the number one-hundred-thousand is a little abstract, Eisley mentions that this is a time longer than the existence of human beings on earth.

To speak, then, of mastering the universe is the height of stupidity and ignorance. Eisley compares it to making a grasshopper secretary general of the United Nations. By its very nature humanity cannot conquer its cosmic prison, for we are prisoners within various prisons—time, temperature, body, and many others.

But there is a key to the cosmic prison, and that key is another paradox. People can escape their prison not by turning outward to the stars but by turning inward to themselves. "The body is the true cosmic prison," for it contains the consciousness of the creative individual. It is the body that makes a human being "a magnificent if sometimes helpless giant." The mind is what frees a person from his prison, for the mind is free to roam at will among the stars and to encompass within it all of the universe. Eisley's conclusion is, like his beginning, a paradox, a seeming contradiction. We conquer without by turning within. Although trapped by the prison of the body, we are free to roam the universe. The paradox of the cosmic prison is solved by the paradox of infinite love in a finite room.

Eisley discusses the contradiction of what he calls the cosmic prison, and he not only discusses but concludes his essay with more paradoxes. In the course of his discussion, he uses illustration to clarify not only his contradictions but his explanations of them. There are, of course, other rhetorical devices in this essay, and you might want to reread the essay, locate some of them, and examine how they work to clarify the basic paradox of the essay.